Books by William Prochnau

A Certain Democrat (coauthor)

Trinity's Child, a novel

Once Upon a Distant War:
David Halberstam, Neil Sheehan, Peter Arnett—Young War
Correspondents and Their Early Vietnam Battles

William Prochnau

ONCE UPON A DISTANT WAR

William Prochnau is a former national correspondent for *The Washington Post* and author of *Trinity's Child*, an international bestselling novel. He has also written for *Vanity Fair, Life, Vogue, The New York Times Magazine*, and the *Times of London Magazine*. He made two reporting tours of the Vietnam War. A native of Seattle, Prochnau lives in Washington, D. C.

ONCE UPON
A DISTANT WAR

ONCE UPON
A DISTANT WAR

David Halberstam, Neil Sheehan,

Peter Arnett—Young War Correspondents

and Their Early Vietnam Battles

WILLIAM PROCHNAU

VINTAGE BOOKS

A Division of Random House, Inc.

New York

For my mother, Florence, and for Laura

FIRST VINTAGE BOOKS EDITION, SEPTEMBER 1996

Copyright © 1995 by William Prochnau

An excerpt from this book appeared in *Vanity Fair*. Portions
of earlier drafts also appeared in *The New York Times Magazine*,
The Washington Post Magazine, the *APF Reporter* of the
Alicia Patterson Foundation, and the *Gannett Center Journal*.

Due to limitations of space, permissions acknowledgments
can be found on page 549.

The Library of Congress has cataloged
the Times Books edition as follows:
Prochnau, William W.
Once upon a distant war / William Prochnau.
p. cm.
Includes index.
ISBN 0-8129-2633-1
1. Vietnamese Conflict, 1961–1975—United States.
2. Vietnamese Conflict, 1961–1975—Press coverage.
3. Sheehan, Neil. 4. Halberstam, David. 5. Browne, Malcolm W.
6. Vietnamese Conflict, 1961–1975—Journalists. I. Title.
DS558.P75 1995
959.704'3373—dc20
95-7327
Vintage ISBN: 0-679-77265-0

Author photograph © Laura Parker

Random House Web address: http://www.randomhouse.com/

Printed in the United States of America
10 9 8 7 6 5 4 3 2 1

Vietnam is a graveyard of lost hopes, destroyed vanity, glib promises, and good intentions.

—The lead sentence filed by *Time* magazine correspondent Charles Mohr for an August 9, 1963, cover story. The sentence was not published.

Contents

Once Upon
a Distant War

1

A NICE LITTLE WAR
IN A LAND OF TIGERS AND
ELEPHANTS

Malcolm Browne, a tall and gawky thirty-year-old former chemist whose red hair would soon turn sandy, stepped down in a sweat from Flight One, Pan American's new around-the-world jet service.

Saigon's heat, humid and oppressive at 96 degrees, hit the new man from the Associated Press like a wave. Just out of Baltimore, where winter had arrived in a sudden early surge, Browne wore the only suit he owned, a wool one. Over one shoulder he lugged a useless topcoat; over the other a battered $25 Japanese camera he had picked up secondhand.

On the hot tarmac at Tan Son Nhut Airport two photographers took his picture, one for South Vietnam's secret police, the other for a small English-language newspaper called the *Times of Vietnam*. It would not take Browne long to realize that there was little difference between the two. Otherwise, the arrival did not seem auspicious. No military man met him with a jeep and driver as a correspondent from America's premier news-gathering agency might have been welcomed to a war zone in another time and place. Those at the American Embassy, soon to be bogged down with an onslaught of arrivals of a different sort, noted the date—November 11, 1961, a Saturday—with only passing interest. Beneath lazily turning fans inside the low, open-air terminal building, South Vietnamese customs officials languidly riffled through his single suitcase, glanced without interest at the wry smile on Browne's passport photo, and waved him through.

———

In the beginning it was such a nice little war.

"A dapper, debonair little war in a land of tigers and elephants," enthused the CIA man in one of the dark novels written later by Ward Just, a distinguished correspondent whose life after Vietnam was consumed by bleak, Conrad-like trips deep into the American soul.

In 1961 the United States stood at the height of its power, primed by a national "can-do" attitude that anything lay within its reach and sustained by a near-religious certainty about the rightness of its goals. During this first of the few, but hyperkinetic, Kennedy years, "saving" South Vietnam became one of those goals. The trickle of Americans passing through Saigon during the fifties turned abruptly into a relentless stream.

The newcomers had little historical reference to the place. Vietnam, clinging to a tropical peninsula south of China, was not a prominent Second World War battleground still tugging at American memories. Nor had the French in their final colonial struggle in Asia just a few years earlier left Americans with more than scratchy, newsreel-vague recollections of a strange war in an unknown place called Indochina. The American government had spent $2 billion supporting that lost cause and another billion after the French departed in 1954. But, to workaday Americans, Vietnam remained as distant and obscure as any place in the world. Official Washington did not know it much better. Two examples make the point:

George Reedy, an aide to Lyndon B. Johnson, accompanied the Vice President on a visit early in 1961. Reedy, an intelligent man, realized soon after he landed that he didn't have the foggiest notion where he was. He found a map, searched for Saigon, and positioned it in relation to more familiar landmarks to give himself that sense of place that comforts seasoned travelers.

General Maxwell Taylor, a prince in Kennedy's Camelot and his special assistant for military affairs, made a fateful fact-finding trip in October, only weeks before Mal Browne's arrival. A newspaper reporter following Taylor observed that, throughout his inspection tour, the general continually referred to the object of his attention as South Korea.

Both Johnson and Taylor returned to Washington and recommended major increases in military aid for the little Asian trouble spot, seeing it as a strategically crucial Cold War prize.

Vietnam, a place so foreign to their experience that it often took on a storybook surreality, captivated Americans. It became a fairy kingdom, a toy country as alien and enticing as the Siam of *The King and I*, as remote and mystically alluring as Shangri-la. Vietnam was not simply exotic. It was erotic. And narcotic.

In the cities women of exceptional Asian beauty—tiny, porcelain, ephemeral images of perfect grace—wafted past. They did not walk, they glided, oblivious to the Western faces swiveling to follow the silken trail of their raven hair and flowing white *ao dais,* the uniquely Vietnamese pants-gown that so remarkably enhanced their femininity. Or they flowed by in serene waves on fleets of Saigon bicycles, their conical sun hats tilted back neatly on proud shoulders.

Buddhist monks, with heads shaved and lithe bodies cloaked in saffron robes, moved silently through a babble of Hindu money changers. Down narrow Asian alleyways expatriate Chinese with three-strand beards and opaque eyes introduced visitors to the ancient pleasures of the poppy—one pipe, two pipes, three pipes, four; the brown gum bubbling into amber, the rock-hard smoker's couch softening to velvet at the first inhalation, the stranger drifting blissfully to a still more exotic land.

Outside the cities, the countryside turned to a poet's panorama unchanged for centuries. To the south of Saigon, in the broad delta of the Mekong River, ageless peasants toiled in endless green seas of rice. To the north, sinewy Montagnard tribesmen still carried spears as they had in the Stone Age, the men clad in loincloths, the women bare-breasted.

Strange religious sects abounded. One, the Cao Dais, kept a pink-and-blue cathedral. A single huge Masonic eye hovered over the church's entrance. Inside, the Cao Dais worshiped icons of their saints—Buddha, Joan of Arc, Jesus Christ, and Victor Hugo—with equal passion. Vietnam's Buddhists, who would soon move to the forefront of Mal Browne's story, were almost inexplicable in Western terms, mixing ancestor and animal worship into their mystic journey along their religion's Eightfold Noble Path.

The little war flared intermittently in brutal attacks. Wispy figures appeared suddenly in the black-pajama garb of peasants, did their violence, and then, just as suddenly, melded back into the shadows of triple-canopy jungle. A faceless youngster emerged briefly from a sidewalk crowd and rolled a sapper's grenade into a Saigon bistro, then disappeared into the natural cover of teeming Asian streets.

The American-supported Saigon government called the guerrillas the Viet Cong, a derogatory term for Vietnamese Communists. The Americans would bastardize the name further, abbreviating it to VC, codifying it in radio lingo as Victor Charlie, shortening it again to Charlie, and, in the end, when the going got very rough, restoring a begrudging measure of respect. "Mister Charles," the Americans would finally call the enemy when the war turned big, mean, and impossible.

But, in the beginning, even the war was an enticement. It gave the outsider, as Graham Greene had described it while the French still fought there, "that feeling of exhilaration which a measure of danger brings to the visitor with a return ticket."

A few of the early arrivals found the country dark and ominous, and could not wait to leave. "It was a sinister place," said Homer Bigart, a renowned *New York Times* war correspondent who arrived six weeks after Browne. "There was a feeling in the air. The place was unlucky, and you could watch it corrupt the Americans." He hated it.

But Bigart was an exception, and even he did not foresee how much the place would corrupt or how much the visitors would corrupt the place. In 1961 there was no sense of impending disaster, no sense of an *Apocalypse Now* future. Vietnam remained a place where adventurers could roam, and unwary nations as well as unwary men fell hopelessly and dangerously in love, captivated, sucked up, as Michael Herr would put it much later and long after it was too late, by some sort of irresistible Venus's-flytrap.

Halfway around the world at the White House on November 11, 1961, the day Mal Browne arrived in Saigon, the National Security Council met in an unusual Saturday session.

The Kennedy administration, after weeks of debate following General Maxwell Taylor's October inspection trip, approved a plan to step up its military commitment to South Vietnam. Since 1954 the United States had maintained a nominal force of 685 military advisers in the country, the number allowed by the Geneva Accords that had ended the French colonial war and split the country into halves. Earlier in the year the Americans had secretly begun to violate the Accords, sending in additional advisers to help the beleaguered South Vietnamese government. Now Washington would commit much more—thousands of military advisers, squadrons of helicopters, detachments of armored personnel carriers, more dive-bombers, assault weapons, antipersonnel mines. This, too, the government would foolishly try to do secretly. The plan was called Project Beef-Up.

The Vietnam that became burned into the American psyche, a Vietnam with *whump-whump-whumping* Hueys and Cobras and Chinooks blackening the skies, with half a million American soldiers bogged down hopelessly in the jungles . . . that Vietnam remained years away.

But this was the beginning.

———

As Mal Browne moved past the somnolent Vietnamese functionaries at Tan Son Nhut Airport, neither he nor his distant bosses at Associated Press had any special insight into the luck of his timing. To his editors in New York the arrival marked only a routine transfer of bodies at one of their backwater, if exotic, Asian outposts. To Browne, disengaging from his second failed marriage, the adventure, the romance, and the splendid isolation of the place were lure enough. He stood eleven time zones, almost a half-spin of the globe, away from his old world. But the coincidence was remarkable, marking Browne forever as the first of a new and contentious breed of American war correspondent. No more unlikely character could have been cast in the role.

A loner in a boisterous crowd, Browne was a man of quirks and eccentricities. He even looked improbable, cutting the figure of an Ichabod Crane, not a Hemingway, his six-foot frame carrying a bare-sustenance 145 pounds, his Adam's apple ever pumping, his eyes ever savoring one of life's hidden jokes. His redhead's skin was almost translucent, so fair it lobstered up in minutes in Vietnam's hot sun.

Outside the airport he lighted up a cigarette, one from the four packs a day he chain-smoked. He held it between long spidery fingers, one of which sported a ring mounted with a golden death-head's skull. In the heat his wool suit sagged into a wet wilt, causing him to hike up the trousers and reveal the bright red socks he wore everywhere. During an army tour in the fifties he had found red socks on sale at the PX and bought them all. He had worn them ever since, and the spot of red would be there ever after, peeking out of the bottom of combat fatigues, business suits, and occasional tuxedos. Mal Browne was a character. He cultivated his idiosyncratic image; he liked to provoke.

Born in New York's Greenwich Village at the height of the Great Depression, Browne came by his quirks honestly. The pubs and coffeehouses of the Village had also given birth to the storied Bohemian Brigade, a rabble-rousing tribe of nineteenth-century war correspondents who delivered more terror to generals than truth to the public during the American Civil War. But the youthful Browne showed no early sign of following in those footsteps. The son of an architect father forced by the hard times to design wooden squirrels for Central Park, and a Quaker mother deeply devoted to pacifism, Browne turned his sense of adventure inward to science. He studied chemistry and, for five years after graduating from Pennsylvania's genteel Swarthmore College, he probed for his truths in a laboratory. Only a late army draft call would pull him away from his test tubes. Sent to Korea with the postwar border forces, Browne first drove a tank, then landed a job on the soldiers' newspaper, *Stars and Stripes.* He began mixing new sets of chemicals, heating photo-developer fluid over bonfires in the harsh Korean winter. He learned to type with his gloves on, two-fingered hunt-and-peck style at 10 below zero, and never returned to his test tubes again.

Vietnam hooked him quickly. Inside the toy country Browne found a toy war.

To the south in the Mekong Delta, young Vietnamese troops

in baggy American-surplus uniforms marched off to battle with oversized M-1 rifles slung over their shoulders and live ducks hanging, heads down and squawking, from their gun belts. Aging Second World War fighter planes lumbered home from unexplained sorties with arrows jutting out of their metallic hides. The first of the crew-cut and leathery American "counterinsurgency experts," those Green Berets trained at distant Fort Bragg to survive alone in the jungle on a diet of palm tree rats and tropical beetles, told tales of shadowy hit-and-run ambushes by guerrillas who fought with coconut hand grenades and bamboo land mines, or sudden assaults by nomadic tribesmen still armed with shields and spears.

Inside that disarming time warp the newly arriving men from the high-tech other side of the world peered through their cultural filter at a nice little war and came away with a fascinated, sanitized illusion of immunity for both themselves and their mighty country. There were many illusions in Vietnam.

If the countryside and its little war were captivating, Saigon was addictive. The Europeans still called it the Paris of Southeast Asia, a city of broad avenues lined by tamarind trees, pastel French villas hidden by walls splashed with flowering mimosa and brilliant bougainvillea, and bustling open markets where wrinkled peasants hawked black thousand-year eggs, fresh tiger lily buds, and the everyday fare of fresh bok choy. Airline pilots approaching the city looked out over a sea of low-slung, red tile roofs and radioed for landing instructions from Paris Control, their code for the tower at Tan Son Nhut.

But Saigon was also a place of endless Oriental intrigue, a bottomless pit of plots and cabals and schemes. The Asians gave it a different nickname: "the forest of tigers."

Browne moved into a tiny office at 158 Rue Pasteur, kitty-corner from the alternate palace of South Vietnam's puzzling leader, Ngo Dinh Diem—he could literally stare across the palace grounds, over the balustrade, and into the windows. Also across the street sat the police station, a happenstance that at first seemed more convenient than ominous.

The office was a rudimentary workplace. Hungry dogs wandered in off the busy street, as did prying plainclothes cops. Even without the visitors, the place was cramped—a clutter of banged-up file cabinets, rickety desks, and two battered old Remington upright typewriters. The single green plastic phone had been broken so many times it was patched together by dirty-white adhesive tape. In the back the bathroom doubled as a darkroom, with three Chinese stoneware jars of developer fluid perched precariously on the commode. Horst Faas, the German-born photographer who arrived six months later, recalled that the enlarger sat on top of the toilet seat. On busy days, which were coming, no one in the office of America's leading news service took a pee.

The American media had not been particularly alert to the slowly accelerating developments in Southeast Asia in 1961. The year had been full of diversions, a time of great change and plentiful news elsewhere, not the least of which had been the coming of John F. Kennedy.

Kennedy had descended on Washington and the world's most powerful nation like a young king—dynamic, charming, vigorous, the first president born in the twentieth century, the first born in The American Century. Coming after the lulling years of Dwight Eisenhower, Kennedy promised verve and action. The media thrived on verve and action, these being basics, along with disaster and pathos, of an elemental definition of news.

Kennedy was also crisis prone. He had come into office sounding dire warnings about a nonexistent missile gap with the Soviet Union. But if the gap didn't exist, other problems did. Less than three months after his inauguration, a boyishly smiling Russian named Yuri Gagarin became the first man to orbit the earth in space. "I am eagle!" the cosmonaut exulted, and it seemed as if the Soviets not only had usurped America's new frontier but its historic emblem as well. Five days later American prestige took another beating with the grotesquely failed Bay of Pigs invasion of Cuba. In June the new President met in Vienna for a testing of wills with the Soviet premier, Nikita Khrushchev. Kennedy fared badly, although the media image of the handsome American royal coming up against the squat Russian peasant briefly disguised the failure. Kennedy would be that good at media images, the first to manipulate them. But suddenly there were crises breaking out in Berlin, Cuba, the Congo, as well as the home-grown wrenching of racial turmoil in the South. None of these had an easy answer. And, after Vienna, the shell-shocked young President needed a place to prove his moxie, especially to the Russian who had pushed him around with such ease. "We have to confront them," Kennedy privately told James Reston, the chief of the *New York Times* Washington bureau. "The only place we can do that is in Vietnam. We have to send more people over there."

Rumblings of trouble had emerged from Southeast Asia throughout the year. But in late 1961 Vietnam remained so low on the radar screen of the distracted American press that Browne found Saigon manned by a small and motley crew: a handful of underpaid wire-service reporters, struggling freelancers, and journalistic adventurers. The corps was bolstered by the wistful French and the ubiquitous Brits, who kept a man or two on hand in memory of empires lost.

By far the most memorable of the lot was a devilishly suave thirty-three-year-old Frenchman named François Sully, a part-time stringer for the American newsmagazine *Newsweek*.[1] Sully loved camaraderie, combat, adventure, women, and luxury, and spent most of his life making all those loves compatible.

A teenage Resistance fighter against the Nazis, he arrived in Vietnam in 1947 as a French paratrooper. He never went home, steering an expatriate course from failed tea planter to rogue war correspondent. No one fully trusted his news; it came spiced with a good French bias. But he was such a dazzling character, filled with such wonderful joie de vivre, that he was beloved nevertheless by all but the governments who endlessly mucked around in Vietnam. The stories about him were legion.

Trapped behind enemy lines during the French war, he bluffed his way out by pretending he was a Russian and shouting "*Heong ho!*"—a triumphant "Hurrah!" for the revolution—each time he ran into a guerrilla roadblock. During the war's last days he wangled his way inside the doomed garrison at Dien Bien Phu. A fastidious dresser, he arrived at the besieged outpost in perfectly pressed fatigues, which he shed at the end of the day for a pair of

---

1. The full list of resident correspondents included John Griffin, whom Browne replaced at AP; Mert Perry of UPI; Peter Smark of Reuters; Jerry Rose, a stringer for *Time* magazine; David Hudson, a freelancer; François Nivolon of *Le Figaro*; Pierre Chauvet of Agence France-Presse; John Stirling of *The Times* of London, and Sully.

navy-blue silk pajamas with white piping. Crawling into his sleeping bag, he toasted his grimy colleagues from a silver hip flask of Courvoisier. "Good for the morale," he said with a grin, and dropped off to sleep amid the pounding of the incoming artillery.

In 1961 Sully was a handy person to know. The war was still so small—little more than hit-and-run skirmishes—it was often hard to find. The correspondents got little help from either the Vietnamese or American governments. The Vietnamese found the tradition of an unfettered press both alien and absurd. Why confide in foreign reporters about a war they were losing, sometimes embarrassingly? To the Americans the correspondents presented a less cultural but nevertheless highly political problem.

This was not like past wars. Because Project Beef-Up directly and openly violated an international treaty, Washington unrealistically wanted to fight on the sly.[2] And it wanted the reporters to go along with the fiction, to play the ostrich. The emperor was naked, but it would become unpatriotic to say he was wearing no clothes. When the policy didn't work, American officials clammed up, covered up, and lied—not only to the public and the press but eventually to themselves.

So the reporters had to find the war on their own. Information, good and bad, acquired by almost any means, became everything, and it came from strange places. The reporters frequented a collection of cafés and bistros, making their rounds just as a reporter back home might do his daily check of the offices at city hall. It was a romantic beat:

Brodard's, a sassy little French bistro famed for its ice cream and hot rumors; Givral's, the brassy, noisy café across Saigon's famed Rue Catinat[3] from the Continental Palace Hotel; and the place the correspondents called Cheap Charlie's, a hole-in-the-wall, neon-lit Chinese restaurant where lunch went for twenty cents and information was often passed for less.

2. The North Vietnamese had been violating the agreement from the beginning, infiltrating both men and supplies into the South. But the United States played on a larger, grander stage, and presumably was tied to a stricter standard of international law.
3. By 1961 Rue Catinat had been renamed Tu Do Street, the name by which it would be known to a generation of American GIs. But in these early years almost everyone stuck with the more romantic French name.

As Browne quickly discovered, getting the story in Saigon required what he later called "methods uncomfortably close to those used by professional intelligence units."

Over the next two years the rumor mill became such a Saigon fixture that the correspondents gave it a name: Radio Catinat. Picking up word, maybe a few whispers from a wizened waiter at Cheap Charlie's, the correspondents would bolt into the street, hail one of those beat-up little Renault taxis, and race to a nearby jungle battlefield. That was the way it worked: a tip, a dash, and take a cab to war.

Nobody was better at the game than François Sully. After fourteen years, he had sources planted in every office and smoke-filled hangout in town. He knew where to find the girls and where to find the spies and, because the two seemed to go together, mixing business with pleasure seemed the essence of Gallic good sense. And he *understood* things. He knew that, after a century of colonialism, the best eateries in town were French and Chinese. But he also knew that if you wanted to get in on the nightly gripe sessions of the Vietnamese military you went to one of downtown Saigon's two Vietnamese restaurants. Dong Khanh's was the favorite, and there, over lemongrass soup and Ba Moui Ba rice beer, you could get plugged into news of the latest plot to overthrow Diem or today's battle disaster in the south.

Sully and Browne made an unlikely pair. Browne would forever be the quirky loner, the skinny guy with red socks who went home to his tiny apartment every night to listen to booming Wagnerian operas instead of joining his buddies out on the town. A friend once asked what he did each night at home and he replied, "Make paper airplanes." The telling thing about Mal Browne is that the friend believed him, envisioning an intent man laboring over a fleet of intricately designed foolscap flying machines. Sully was so different—outgoing and carefree, a man who would talk his way through the girls, the spies, and the bullets until his luck finally ran out a decade later in a burning helicopter. Even then he would make one last valiant attempt to live, leaping from the plummeting machine and dying hours afterward from his 75-foot fall rather than the flaming crash.

But in the beginning it was all so heady and exotic that, if the Frenchman mentioned that the target of the night was La Cigalle, a garish nightclub in the teeming Chinese district of Cholon, Browne, like the others, canceled everything else.

At La Cigalle, run by a tough Corsican, the information flowed with the best French wines. Saigon bankers drank next to Viet Cong spies and, as Sully pointed out, the bankers often had reason for inscrutability. Sometimes *they* were the Viet Cong spies and the Viet Cong spies doubled for the government's secret police. Nothing was as it seemed. Agents from half a dozen countries and as many mysterious Vietnamese political factions mixed easily with American colonels who drank too much and diplomats who chased too hard. All too obvious CIA men eyed lingering French operatives from the Deuxième Bureau as if they were the real enemy. Then, as a winsome Vietnamese singer warbled a sad ballad of love in singsong French soon to follow the demand curve to canary-soprano English, someone whispered the tip: a hit-and-run ambush in the south—and the good guys got stomped, so don't expect to hear it from the embassy.

Early the next morning Browne jumped into a Renault cab and bumped south down Highway 4 into the delta. By evening he was back in the little office on the Rue Pasteur, Saigon's timid lizards skittering across the sick-green ceiling as he batted out his 500-word report, punishing the old Remington with the same hunt-and-peck assault he had learned in Korea. Browne was not a poetic writer, and the Associated Press of the day demanded a straightforward, nuts-and-bolts approach. But the quiet ex-chemist had trouble keeping the exuberance out of those first stories. A wire man ends his stories "30." But Browne so loved this place that he took a few liberties. The name of the popular local rice beer meant "thirty-three" in Vietnamese. So he ended his early cables:

BA MOUI BA
BROWNE.

Then he headed for the radio-telegraph office, the PTT, striding out into a warm evening filled with strange sights and wondrous smells, past darkened pagodas and tiny shops with joss sticks burning in the windows and shelves cluttered with healthy brain pills and the ancient Chinese aphrodisiacs of powdered rhinoceros horn.

No aphrodisiac was needed. Browne had few illusions about

Vietnam's harsher realities. But like so many who came before and after, he was quickly seduced. Mal Browne fell instantly and madly in love—"the greatest love I've ever had," he said, "and the greatest I ever will."

———

One of the harshest realities about South Vietnam in late 1961 was its ruling family. In a time when despotic leaders were as much the rule as the exception throughout the world, the South Vietnamese government was not the cruelest—nor even the cruelest supported by the United States. But it may have been the most bizarre. Charles Mohr, whose bosses at *Time* magazine supported the family even more passionately than the U.S. government and thus opened their correspondent to unusual access to the palace, summed up his impressions succinctly: "They were the most neurotic family I've ever known about, *even in history*. They simply were a bunch of dingbats."

Vietnam had been divided north and south in 1954, with the North going to the Communists who had ejected the French and the South going to the non-Communists. Ho Chi Minh, a national hero who had led the anticolonialist revolution, took over North Vietnam. The South had more trouble finding a natural leader. But by late 1954 Ngo Dinh Diem, an obscure and often-puzzling ascetic who had gone into exile in Paris and the United States during the war, took control in Saigon. Diem was staunchly anti-Communist and the United States bought in quickly. The new leader became known as America's Mandarin, her Puppet Without Strings.

A round little man with a soft, baby face, Diem could be spartan and monastic in his religious devotions, ruthless in his rule. Early in his regime he purged and killed thousands of political, religious, and other opponents as he consolidated power in his factionalized and artificial nation. But recently he had become detached and inward, mystifying visitors with long, soporific monologues followed by longer retreats into deep meditations. In a land of many unusual religions Diem practiced a stern form of Roman Catholicism inherited from proselytizing French priests. As his troubles grew, Diem withdrew further, meditating more, communicating less, and handing off many duties to his brother. It was a fateful hand-off.

If Diem became more bewildering than despotic, his brother, Ngo Dinh Nhu, looked and often acted the embodiment of evil. His sharp-edged hawk face split by an unnerving smile, Nhu[4] was rigid, scheming, double-dealing, highly intelligent, and hopelessly neurotic. He had also begun the steep slide into the erratic behavior of a heroin addict. Brother Nhu, as the American correspondents called him, ran the secret police, was the second most powerful man in the country and, at times over the next two years, appeared more in control of the family enterprise—which was South Vietnam—than did Diem.

The sense of wickedness was enhanced by Nhu's wife, who acted as First Lady for the unmarried Diem. Madame Nhu's capacity for intrigue was boundless. A fiery and starkly beautiful woman given to lacquered hairdos, scalpel-like scarlet fingernails, and wild tantrums, Madame Nhu looked and acted like the diabolical femme fatale in the popular comic strip of the day, *Terry and the Pirates.* Americans gave her the comic-strip character's name: the Dragon Lady.

Two other brothers, Thuc and Can, extended Diem's hold. They ran South Vietnam's second-largest city, the old imperial capital of Hue 400 miles north of Saigon. The city was also the family home, and the two brothers controlled it and the country's northern reaches with an iron hand that sometimes exceeded Diem's grip on the national government.

Ngo Dinh Thuc was an ostentatious Roman Catholic archbishop, an ambitious cleric who believed in the richest mix of church and state. Thuc also held a devout faith in power, money, and taking his pleasures on earth as well as in heaven. Can handled the secular side as an old-fashioned Oriental warlord. He used a band of toughs, his own secret police, and an army that usually fought the Viet Cong more effectively than Diem's government troops.

Madame Nhu's family was also brought into the act. Her father, Tran Van Chuong, served as ambassador to the United States, her mother as informal ambassador to the United Nations. They were quite a pair. He had become rich collaborating with both the French

---

4. The Vietnamese placed their family name before given names, which technically made the brothers the Ngo brothers. The formality was rarely followed. Even in Vietnam they were called Diem and Nhu.

and the Japanese, who occupied Vietnam during the Second World War. She, a great beauty as was her daughter, occupied herself with extravagant parties and an entourage of lovers while her husband made the money.

The two sides of the family would soon have a great falling out. "They are very much like medieval inquisitors who were so convinced of their righteousness that they would burn people for their own sake," Tran Van Chuong said of Diem and Nhu as he resigned his post in Washington in mid-1963.

Nhu responded in kind. Let his father-in-law return to Saigon, he said, and he would string him up in the central square, with Madame Nhu tightening the knot around his neck. The feud came to a dark and unsettling end almost twenty-five years later, long after the end of the Vietnam War, when the parents were found murdered in their Washington home. Madame Nhu's brother was charged with the crime, but his trial was interrupted and he was committed to a mental institution when he was found too delusional to continue.

Reaction to the American press followed the family's personality patterns. Diem could never understand why the Americans could not control their reporters the same way he controlled his. But he was philosophical about it. "If you bring in the American dog," he said, "you also must accept the American fleas."

Brother Nhu was inclined toward more activist measures, using his secret police to harass, beat, and arrest reporters. The government's most extraordinary figure, Madame Nhu, eventually came up with the most straightforward suggestion. Burn them alive, she said, "and I'll provide the match."

Nor did the family bow quietly toward its benefactors in Washington. As the Kennedy administration edged in deeper, it also sought to quiet criticisms at home by forcing the regime to make political changes—allow greater individual freedoms, crack down on corruption, and implement land reforms in the countryside where the Communist guerrillas drew their greatest support and where the government, if it were ever to succeed, would need to gain the confidence of the people.

It was to this unlikely family that the United States had sent $1 billion since 1954 and the Kennedy administration had now decided to chase with still more wealth and blood. Diem liked the billions. He did not like the advice. In late 1961, as Browne settled in, the Diem-controlled Saigon newspapers were filled with harsh attacks on the United States and "the velvet-covered iron hands of the colonialist imperialists" attempting to "strangle" Vietnam by placing conditions on its aid.

The Kennedy people were devout Cold Warriors, convinced that the United States, as the activist young President had put it in his inaugural address, was engaged in "a long twilight struggle" against the forces of Communism. They were also convinced that they could beat the Communists at their own game. In 1961 that meant meeting insurgency with counterinsurgency, combating black-pajama guerrillas with Green Beret special forces who lived just as comfortably in the night. Counterinsurgency became a Washington buzz word, the capital's new game.

Now, with Project Beef-Up, Vietnam would become counterinsurgency's first test, a handy tropical practice field for the war of the future. A basic ingredient of this new kind of war was stealth —and secrecy, a degree of secrecy unusual in an open Western society. This would be a problem, a serious one. Again, the government expected the press to ignore the self-evident. Not even the Vietnamese went along.

As Project Beef-Up got underway, the Vietnamese-language press in Saigon was anything but quiet about the "velvet-covered iron hands" reaching out from Washington. Nor did silence reign in the English-language press in the United States. Three days after Mal Browne's arrival, *The New York Times* published a story headed:

U.S. OFFICERS CROWD SAIGON ON
"ROUTINE MISSIONS"

Stealthy the beginning was not.

———

The muddy Saigon River winds lazily through the capital city, providing a natural harbor that, in 1961, was populated by a picturesque collection of junks, sampans, a few small military patrol boats, and the usual waterfront assemblage of oceangoing ships of call. A few miles to the south the Saigon empties into the broader

Dong Nai and begins thirty miles of meandering through some of the world's densest jungles and mangrove swamps before emptying into the South China Sea. Within weeks the Americans would begin to dump toxic defoliants on the impenetrable tangle along the riverbanks. But the effort would never succeed in rooting out the guerrilla fighters entrenched in this jungle stronghold. The little men in the black pajamas watched everything that moved up Saigon's waterway supply line; always did, always would.

On December 11, a month after Browne arrived, Stanley Karnow of *Time* magazine made one of his periodic visits to Saigon. Leisurely drinking a Ba Moui Ba with an American military information officer at the riverside Majestic Hotel, Karnow's eyes bulged as the American aircraft carrier *Core* suddenly loomed around a bend and cautiously maneuvered through the junks and sampans. Lashed to the deck of the *Core*, in open view, sat the first fleet of forty American helicopters.

"My God," said Karnow, "look at that carrier!"

"I don't see nothing," the officer replied.

Karnow walked away thinking that the little war would not remain little much longer. Knowing how many eyes had watched the carrier steam up the river, he also concluded that his government's efforts at secrecy were aimed more at fooling the American public than fooling the Viet Cong guerrillas. So did a visiting correspondent from *The New York Times*, who reported in a December 12 dispatch from Saigon:

South Vietnamese and United States official circles kept the entire operation under strict security wraps despite the fact that the *Core*, towering high above the surrounding rice paddies and with her unmistakable deck cargo visible for miles, had to travel upstream for about 45 [sic] miles through a countryside said to be alive with communist agents and sympathizers.

Even without an announcement of the vessel's arrival, thousands of persons lined both banks of the narrow, muddy Saigon River to watch the former World War II auxiliary carrier tie up at a pier in front of the Majestic Hotel [with] hundreds of grinning, waving [American] servicemen [on deck].

Well before the carrier's arrival the attempts at secrecy had taken on an almost comic tone. *Stars and Stripes* had announced the ship's departure from San Francisco fifteen days earlier, even identifying the helicopter companies and their home bases. The eyes along the river provided more information, as did prying eyes in the welcoming crowd. Saigon was a city of spies. Within days North Vietnam's Radio Hanoi broadcast not only the number and type of choppers but their serial numbers as well. So much for secrecy. But not for foolishness. The Defense Department, in a cable to Saigon, asked for an investigation to "track the source of the leak."

The fiction that the growing American force was advisory and noncombatant also quickly took on darkly ludicrous overtones. By the end of the year the American military force had grown to 3,200 and was climbing rapidly at the rate of 1,500 a month. Just before Christmas the first of the new American "advisers" was killed in a jungle ambush. But wounded American soldiers were denied the Purple Heart because their government denied they were at war. Not long after Browne's arrival, *Life* magazine, the premier publication of middle America, published a full-color photograph of a U.S. napalm strike. Despite the obvious, Washington insisted until 1964 that it was not using the flaming jelly in Vietnam.

The charade began an escalating friction between the correspondents and the American officials in Saigon, who received daily "rockets"—critical cables from their bosses in Washington—demanding that they keep the lid on what not only the reporters but the guerrillas and their legions of spies could see with their own eyes. It was a hopeless job and a preposterous one as well, one that would taint the relationship between the government and the media from day one in Vietnam.

But from the beginning the instructions from Washington to Saigon had been as clear as they had been foolish and unrealistic.

On November 28, 1961, Secretary of State Dean Rusk had tersely cabled the American Embassy:

DO NOT GIVE OTHER THAN ROUTINE COOPERATION TO CORRE-
SPONDENTS ON COVERAGE CURRENT MILITARY ACTIVITIES IN
VIETNAM.

On December 7, four days before the *Core* steamed into Saigon with an open deck laden with violations of the Geneva Accords, Rusk sent a further awkward order to lie about the obvious:

NO ADMISSION SHOULD BE MADE THAT ACCORDS ARE NOT BEING OBSERVED.

Looking back on it much later, some American officials could see the absurdity of their position, and the inevitably doomed outcome. "We were making clear violations of the Geneva understanding and we were determined not to convict ourselves out of our own mouth," William Trueheart, the U.S. deputy ambassador to South Vietnam, said. "This was not a very realistic position. It was at the root of the really bad problems we had with the press, this no-comment kind of position on things that were self-evident to anyone on the ground." Trueheart remained convinced that the policy was one of "foolishness, not duplicity." In either case, it was made for disaster.

Conflict between the press and the government is so deeply rooted in the American experiment in democratic government that it has become part of the country's central nervous system. In the years following the Second World War, some of the natural antagonism between the press and the government muted itself, particularly on foreign affairs. America suddenly saw itself in a life-and-death showdown with Soviet and Chinese Communism. The world was being divided up, and the division solidified by burgeoning arsenals of city-killing nuclear weapons. American correspondents newly arriving in a foreign country routinely checked in first with the ambassador, then with the CIA's head of station, and often worked out a mutually beneficial arrangement for sharing information. Including secrets. Which were kept. The State Department often considered correspondents, even—perhaps even more so—from the prestigious *New York Times,* as useful extensions of foreign policy. Many correspondents, looking at a changed world in which they, too, were part of superpower hardball, viewed themselves the same way.

Vietnam immediately became sharply different. The very nature of the war was new to America, and neither officialdom nor media had worked out rules for untidy covert conflicts that were not so covert. The mutual confidentiality disappeared in the government's paranoia over its own actions. In Saigon, American officials refused to confirm, on or off the record, the most obvious facts. The reporters, quite naturally, scrambled for secondary and sometimes less-reliable sources (although, as time wore on, the information from those sources often proved to be more accurate than the highly politicized official reports going to Washington). It was an extraordinarily self-destructive policy, one that began with lies to the public and press and soon led to the government lying to itself.

Even the most sensitive secret of the heavily censored Second World War, a secret so closely held it was kept from Vice President Harry Truman, was shared with a newspaper reporter. William Laurence of *The New York Times* not only was made privy to the super-secret of the atomic bomb but he was also taken to Alamogordo to view its first test. But, in Vietnam, aircraft carriers in the Saigon River became official mirages, like UFOs.

Nor was the situation helped by the nature of the American officials dispatched to Vietnam. In Washington, President Kennedy actually *liked* reporters. He confided in them, dazzled them, and often, with his charm, controlled them.

Not so the President's representatives in Saigon. They had neither the intellectual flexibility to work out new rules as they went nor the political sophistication to deal with men they clearly considered their inferiors. Homer Bigart would later describe the conditions as worse than those he found working behind the Iron Curtain. "You couldn't believe anybody," he said. "Half the time the Americans didn't even know where they were, let alone know what to tell you, and the South Vietnamese government made the Kremlin look like an open society."

Ambassador Frederick (Fritz) Nolting, an aristocratic Virginian, viewed the tiny and relatively inexperienced press corps as a bumptious rabble and, at times, retreated from the correspondents behind weeks of silence. Part of his problem came from Washington's firm and unrealistic orders. He took the orders for secrecy literally. And under no circumstances would his primary instructions to hold things together with the difficult Diem regime have been easy.

But, in the attempt, Nolting often looked foolish. He argued with reporters that Diem truly was a popular leader "because his picture is everywhere," and then grew distressed when newsmen scoffed at such unusual logic in a dictatorial society. He became so politically cautious that, before one television interview, he replaced an embassy painting of Thomas Jefferson with one of George Washington because he thought Washington was less controversial.

General Paul Harkins, the American military commander who arrived in February 1962, seemed at his best parading in tropical dress whites bedecked with his Second World War battle ribbons. Harkins was a handsome former polo player and onetime aide to General George Patton. But, unlike Patton and most other Second World War generals, Harkins refused to tell correspondents about armed engagements until days after the battles were over.

Even some who worked with Harkins wondered what Patton would have thought of his protégé. John Mecklin, a former *Time* correspondent soon to arrive as the chief American press officer, was forever puzzled by the general's intransigence. Mecklin had been among the war correspondents covering the Normandy invasion when the legendary Patton briefed the press on a top-secret breakout operation known as Operation Cobra. Several correspondents passed the information on to reporting colleagues in other commands, and Patton erupted. The general accused the correspondents of "blabbing" and "risking the lives of tens of thousands of American soldiers." At the end of an unforgettable tirade, Patton added: "It is not my intention, however, to change my policy of telling you everything I know." Patton kept briefing; the reporters stopped blabbing.

In the end Harkins was best remembered for his order forbidding American soldiers from kissing their Vietnamese girlfriends good-bye at the airport lest such displays offend President Diem's monastic sensibilities.

In this zoolike setting the little band of correspondents opted for gathering their leads from Radio Catinat and, broadening their base of sources with American field advisers, who were growing increasingly frustrated that their pessimistic reports were being ignored first in Saigon and then in Washington. The situation produced an inevitable mix of insightfully accurate and flamboyantly inaccurate stories. Both kinds infuriated the Saigon authorities, and their angry retreats into deeper isolation and stricter secrecy drove the correspondents still further from official sources.

———

Meanwhile, Mal Browne wandered farther afield from the Rue Pasteur. He soon began to see the dangers and began communicating them home.

On his first trip outside Saigon, Browne traveled fifteen miles northeast to a small airstrip outside the little town of Bien Hoa. Project Beef-Up had already moved into full swing, with sunburned Texas construction crews laying the thick strips of steel mesh that would quickly turn raw, red land into new runways. Browne was astounded. Old propeller-driven T-28 trainers jockeyed for takeoff positions with vintage SC-47s, and he immediately began snapping photographs with the battered Ricoh reflex camera he had brought from Baltimore. As he turned to leave, a crisp American MP stopped him and stripped the exposed film from his camera.

Riding back to Saigon, Browne mused that the problem was not that his photographs showed American warplanes. The problem was that they showed "blond, Western faces in the pilot's seat"— evidence that, in these first days, contradicted the American cover story that the new "advisers" were noncombatants.

To the American pilots the fiction that the Vietnamese were flying the combat missions while they advised from the backseat quickly became a joke. They took to calling their Vietnamese trainees "the sandbags." To avoid more confrontations like the one with Mal Browne, American correspondents were barred from the burgeoning air base at Bien Hoa for the next two years. By then, dozens of American flyers were dead in combat, and Washington's admission of the obvious came only after the angry widow of a downed American pilot gave *U.S. News & World Report* her dead husband's last, bitter letter complaining that his buddies were not getting credit for their work.

Browne also moved out on forays with the Army of the Republic of Vietnam, commonly known as the ARVN and nicknamed Arvin. In the field it became Arvin versus Charlie, and Arvin rarely got the best of it. Not only did the young South Vietnamese troops have trouble finding their enemy, but their heavily politicized and often corrupt commanders usually ducked serious battles.

Browne quickly saw the problem. Diem feared his best French-trained commanders and reduced them to desk jobs in Saigon, where they had fancy titles but no troops. Let them fill the cafés with their talk of coups, which they did. But how would they mount one, commanding only desks? Meanwhile, the field commands were given to preening palace favorites, paid in privilege, money, women, and rapid promotions. The war had moved very near Saigon, battles often fought only twenty or thirty miles away. The field commanders understood their unspoken priority well: They and their troops were coup protection, ready to retreat quickly to save their patron from his own people in the streets of Saigon. Meanwhile, to fight and be defeated by the Viet Cong meant losing face and favor. The better course was to avoid showdowns or fight charade battles. They were good at both. Being men who came by privilege so easily, they also were good at tromping on the people they were in the field to protect, the peasants.

In late December Browne went on his first full mission with the ARVN—a 300-man amphibious assault near a complex of hamlets crisscrossed by muddy Mekong Delta canals. As the troops came ashore at dawn, their landing boats crashed into sampans, catapulting families into the water.

The day became a long, muddy slog without action. In mid-afternoon the unit entered a village and spooked a man—farmer? guerrilla?—into a frightened sprint into his paddy. A thunderous volley of automatic weapons fire brought him down. He died minutes later in the arms of his wife. It was an introduction to the war that Browne never forgot. For a terrible moment the woman's eyes rested on him, the huge Western interloper, her gaze haunting him so much that he wrote of it often over the years to come: "Her face showed neither grief nor fury; it was unfathomably blank." Shortly afterward, the Vietnamese commander called off the mission. "It's not a good idea to be moving around out here when the sun goes down," he said.

Over the next months Browne went on several such missions, and they were all lessons in how difficult it would be for the Vietnamese government to win this war in its own countryside. All the missions failed. After one disaster, an American adviser shook his head in dismay. He had planned the attack intricately, and the ARVN had surrounded a group of guerrillas. Then their commander refused to move in. "Old Buddhist custom," the adviser said ruefully. "Always allow defeated enemy honorable path of escape. I didn't know I had so damned many Buddhists in this battalion." Later, Saigon reported a "body count" of fifty. Not a body had been found. But Browne had found an angry new American military source in the field, an American who would talk.

At times the can-do young Americans made comically ingenious attempts to overcome the frustrations. Browne watched one adviser capture bedbugs and rig a box to electronically amplify the sounds they made when they sensed people. He tried to use it to smell out Charlie even if Arvin would not. Like a thousand more sophisticated American devices to follow—from the swooping helicopters that would deprive Charlie of his mobility to the infrared beams and phosphorous flares that would light the night in which he hid —the bedbug machine didn't work.

Browne also discovered that the war was anything but dapper and debonair. In isolated villages he saw the bodies of hamlet leaders beheaded by the Viet Cong. Soon he found that the brutality became horribly infectious. "There were no good guys in Vietnam," he said later. And in 1965 he wrote *The New Face of War*, a book describing his early years in Vietnam. The cover photograph showed a bright-eyed American GI thrusting forward the decapitated head of a Viet Cong guerrilla.

Browne's daily reports began to take on a bite. American newspaper editors published more Associated Press dispatches about America's new little war. The Vietnamese authorities hauled Browne in for a weekly dressing-down about his increasingly gloomy reporting. The American Embassy, catching more incoming rocket fire from Washington, complained that Browne was too young and inexperienced for a complicated job in a newly complicated world.

As 1961 neared its end, and Browne watched the American commitment expand, he began working on a memorandum for the correspondents he now knew would follow him. Future correspondents, he wrote, would find the people of Vietnam "pleasant and agreeable." They would find Saigon enticing and the nightly embassy parties a seductive lure. News, however, would come the hard way, and the newcomers "should expect very little help from most official sources." Among the American officials, Browne advised, the higher the rank, the less help a correspondent would get. As to Vietnamese officials, the correspondents would be regarded "as 'scabby sheep' and treated accordingly."

Mal Browne never lost his entrancement with Vietnam. He would marry a Vietnamese of high station, a vivacious woman named Huynh thi Le Lieu. When they met during his first weeks in Saigon, Le Lieu worked as the Diem government's deputy director of information, and it was she who called him in for weekly lectures about his "malicious" reporting. Their early dates were marked by loud arguments growing out of crossed loyalties. Less than two years later, at the height of the 1963 crisis, Browne would find it necessary to jam a loaded Schmeisser submachine gun into the chest of a Diem agent who came in the middle of the night determined to collect Le Lieu as a traitor bound for an uncertain fate.

Nor, even with that, did Browne ever lose his certainty that the country was worth saving. Fourteen years later, in 1975, he would be in Saigon at the end. Friends remember him that last day, sitting on a battered combat helmet, head in hands, weeping, waiting for the last helicopters to lift away from a wrecked country and a wrecked dream. By then, his deepest personal ties were in Vietnam. He and Le Lieu had been married for a decade, and he spent most of the last weeks trying to get his extended family—personal and professional—out of the collapsing country. But he had not been able to convince Le Lieu's mother to make the trip to America with them. The old woman distrusted the ways of the Americans even more than the French, surely more than the northerners at the edge of the city. She stayed, and died two years later in what became Ho Chi Minh City.

"Vietnam is dangerous, confusing and frustrating," he wrote in another warning to unsuspecting newcomers at the end of 1961. "There is a sinister fascination about the country into the grip of which most foreigners fall. . . . I am no exception."

After less than two months in the country, the atmosphere in Browne's cluttered little office on the Rue Pasteur had also changed. Above his battered Remington the new man from the Associated Press hung a trophy brought in from the jungle. Visitors were shocked. But to Browne it served as a reminder that beyond La Cigalle and the narcotic lure of the Rue Catinat, far from the glittering embassy parties and easy talk of Saigon, something altogether different was happening in the charming land of tigers and elephants. Above his typewriter the introspective son of a Quaker mother had hung a severed and withering human hand.

2

THE CHANGING OF
THE GUARD

Back home, television had lent itself to the creation of the first media president and had changed American politics forever. Soon the strange new hypnotic power of the tube would deliver up another phenomenon: the living-room war, spilling blood on the rug in millions of suddenly not-so-comfortable American homes. Eventually, shrewd generals, like shrewd politicians, would learn to manipulate television's images to their advantage. The result, three decades later, became the controlled, false-sterile Orwellian visions projected from the Persian Gulf.

But in 1961, on the battlefield, television was too young.

In the field, an early television crew was a sight to behold, three men bound together by snaking cables, prisoners of their revolutionary but awkward technology, lugging old Auricon or Filmo or Bolex cameras that weighed thirty-five to fifty pounds, packing another hundred pounds of gear needed for their trade or simply to stay alive in the jungle—sound equipment, film packs, batteries, tool kits; food, water, rain ponchos, spare clothing, sometimes weapons. They were the future. But they lumbered through the brush like caravans of old pack elephants linked trunk to tail.

Occasionally a crew would stumble into action—the bang-bang that New York later demanded as the staple of television war.

Charles Kuralt, then a young CBS correspondent, walked into it during a brief visit shortly before Browne's arrival. With him were his cameraman, carrying a Filmo, and a soundman with a tape recorder unsynchronized to the film. The action, an ambush just outside Saigon, was sudden, brief, and extremely violent. The correspondent and his crew hurled themselves to the ground, the careening Filmo and sound recorder running open to catch what they could. Half the patrol, nineteen men including the Vietnamese lieutenant who had been talking to Kuralt, died almost instantly. In moments it was over, typical of the hit-and-run war. By sheer luck none of the TV crew was hit.

Back in Saigon, Kuralt pieced together his new kind of story. The Filmo had captured a swirl of indistinct black-and-white chaos, with not an enemy shown. The sound man recorded the random, disconnected *pop-a-pop-a-poppa* of gunfire and an occasional human shriek—"wild sound," they called the unsynchronized noise. Kuralt's crew wove the two together, then patched the correspondent's studio-recorded voice over the top.

Technologically, Kuralt's piece was not much advanced over the newsreels of the Second World War. The earlier newsreels had been composed in much the same way: a narrator dramatizing events on silent film, the thunder of the big guns drummed up literally—*Tha-WHUMP! Tha-WHUMP!*—by a sound-effects technician in the studio. But Kuralt's film was magically different. It could be transmitted directly into American homes. Even after a two-day trip to New York by airplane, the ethereal television image had stunning immediacy.

The clip caused a flurry of we-have-seen-the-future excitement at CBS and, within a very short time, television would pass the newspapers once and for all as Americans' primary source of news. But not quite yet.

Television remained an *enfant trouvé*, a journalistic foundling that still yielded status, wisdom, and influence to the written press. So little did the print media think of this childlike intruder in 1961 that the White House Correspondents Association denied membership to television reporters, arguing that they were not true journalists. TV was radio with pictures, no personality of its own, living in a black-and-white world without uplinks or downlinks from satellites that weren't there, without videotape or Minicams or million-dollar salaries. CNN's global village was not yet a dream, it was a fantasy. The showcase evening-news programs, the front pages of the three commercial networks, were only fifteen minutes long and the "anchors"—the term was not yet part of the language —relied largely on what the trade called "rip and reads." Instead of anchoring reports from an array of far-flung correspondents, Walter Cronkite ripped the story off a wire-service ticker and read it into the camera. Television news was still in the process of inventing itself. It would be four years after Kuralt's pioneering story before CBS sent a full-time correspondent to Vietnam.

That left a handful of print correspondents—Browne, Neil Sheehan, David Halberstam, Charley Mohr, Peter Arnett, the German photojournalist Horst Faas, and a few others—with unusual influence over the emerging Vietnam story. For the next two years they would dominate both the words *and* the images sent home from the war.

In this brief but crucial period they would also establish the skeptical standards for a new generation of war correspondents— and television as well. These were provocative, new, adversarial standards that broke from the old and would be used to chronicle America's disaster in Vietnam and events long after. In so doing, this small group of young men would bring down upon themselves the wrath of every power structure they confronted—the White House, the Pentagon, the South Vietnamese government, the old guard of the press itself, even their own bosses. It would be the last time such a small group of journalists would wield such influence. Their extraordinary adventure would mark the beginning of the era of the modern media, and, ironically, the beginning of the end of the golden age of print.

———

The American press had no shortage of seasoned war correspondents in 1961. Only sixteen years had passed since the end of the Second World War, less than a decade since Korea. Many of the Second World War veterans—Walter Cronkite, Edward R. Murrow, Wes Gallagher, Drew Middleton, Eric Sevareid—were perched at or near the pinnacle of their profession in Washington and New York. A few, such as Homer Bigart, whom many considered the greatest war correspondent of the era, had practiced their trade nonstop for two decades, there being no rationing of violent conflict since the end of the big war.

The press establishment also had a powerful contingent of old

Asia hands who had cut their teeth on the Pacific wars. They were often dashing figures: Keyes Beech, a bantam rooster of a man but a true mid-century American tough guy who showed up everywhere bullets started flying; Jim Lucas, who bedded down in the muck with the grunts and glorified GI Joe; Richard Tregaskis, who boosted home-front morale after Pearl Harbor with heroic stories of marines inching their way back across the Pacific islands toward the homeland of the enemy; Peter Kalischer, who stuck with his boys on one of the Korean War's deadliest winter retreats; Marguerite Higgins, the now-aging "girl" correspondent immortalized for her Korean exploits in the kind of *Life* magazine picture spread usually reserved for movie starlets.

Having won their spurs and their Pulitzers at Asian battle-grounds with names like Guadalcanal, Tarawa, Iwo Jima, Pork Chop Hill, and Inchon, this old guard held a proprietary interest in the region. With a few notable exceptions, they also had a profound intolerance for the newcomers about to intrude upon their turf.

None had a greater proprietary interest, nor greater intolerance, than the prominent Washington columnist Joseph Alsop. He was a man obsessed by his Second World War experiences in China, and few newsmen of the era could claim his influence or his powerful biases. John Kennedy made the last social visit of his inaugural night at Joe Alsop's Georgetown home, where the President and the columnist talked over turtle soup until well after midnight.

Alsop's dinner table became the salon of power during the Vietnam years. All the President's men gathered there, nudged by evening with good wines and erudite conversation and stung by morning with blistering columns that moved them deeper and deeper into Alsop's hawkish take on the world. Alsop's game became one of those inexplicable Washington perversions: Joe was so charming, his foie gras the best; Mac and Bob and Dean all came, chuckling about what he had done to them in the morning, a ritual in their lives as Romans.

The columnist had wasted no time in getting started on Vietnam, flying to Saigon with Max Taylor as the plan for Project Beef-Up was formulated in October 1961. Max, Kennedy's "good" general, would always be at Alsop's table, but the columns immediately put the heat on. Taylor seemed "bewildered" by guerrilla warfare and the new answer: counterinsurgency. The columnist worried in print about a "pseudo-Taylor" report. "The danger here will only be increased," he wrote ominously from Saigon, "if indecisive half measures are the only result of the Taylor mission." Taylor took the prod and continued as a favorite guest. For the next two years Alsop used the opinion page of *The Washington Post* and his influential column, "Matter of Fact," to goad Kennedy forever deeper into Vietnam.

But Alsop did not play his dinner-table game when he began his assault on the young Saigon correspondents. They were dangerous, and he turned merciless. These young men, with their "egregious crusades," could lose Vietnam as surely as misty thinking had lost China, then Cuba.

So the Young Turks hardly had the war to themselves. The old guard kept their credentials current by swooping in and out of Vietnam using the new modern convenience of the jet airplane. But, in a war that would be so unlike previous wars, there was no substitute for being stationed on the ground.

The adaptation to Vietnam would be difficult for the old guard. Their lives had been marked indelibly by wars with clear-cut front lines and clear-cut objectives, "good wars" like the big one in which ground gained meant ground kept, liberated towns stayed liberated—and the townspeople greeted the good-guy Yanks with cheers and waving American flags. Korea had hinted at something different. But even Korea had the simplicity of clear-cut aggression, of traditional invasions by uniformed troops, of front lines, of yardage gained and yardage lost that the correspondents, like sports writers, could measure in terms of fumbles and touchdowns—and victories and defeats.

The little war in Vietnam was, and would be, radically different. The touchdowns were invariably called back, the points returned. The "liberated" villagers all too often greeted the "good guys" with homemade grenades instead of flags. Most of the old-timers had trouble adapting their experiences to the new vagueness.

The most notable exception was that remarkable warhorse, Homer Bigart.

———

Homer Bigart had been shot at in anger in some part of the world during each of the past twenty years. At fifty-four, he had followed war from the hills of Italy to the islands of the Pacific to the mountains of Korea, and countless other places already becoming asterisks in the history books.

Over the years the myth grew, enhanced by the so-called generation gap that tore at society later in the sixties, that America's Vietnam policy was ruined by young, inexperienced correspondents unblooded in earlier wars.

But now came Bigart, a most unlikely candidate for generational rebellion. He arrived as the contemporary of the generals, and in fact he had seen more combat than any of them. He also had become that rarest of birds—a prominent establishment journalist who did not buy into all the catechisms of the Cold War. A paradoxical man both shy and almost foolishly brave, he was anything but political. A doubter, a skeptic, an iconoclast who rejected the jingoistic simplicities of the day with their Red Menaces and Yellow Hordes, he also rejected the notion that the United States had to back every tinhorn dictator who rationalized his excesses by opposing the Communists.

Bigart was suspicious of the establishment in any form, including that rock of the establishment, his own newspaper, *The New York Times*. Having begun his career on the highly regarded but less lofty *New York Herald Tribune*, he acted almost apologetic about his midlife desertion from the failing newspaper to the great gray monument of *The Times*. His distrust of authority figures was total. His disregard for generals, ranging from MacArthur to Patton, had been epic, surpassed only by his disdain for editors. Damned clerks, he dismissed the pencil-pushers in his life, and grew so contemptuous of them that he refused to read his own stories after the prose had been despoiled by their touch.

So perhaps Bigart's age disqualified him from generational revolt. But he was the perfect prototype for the defiant generation to come. By the time he arrived in Vietnam shortly after New Year's in 1962, Bigart's exploits had made him an ageless rebel himself. The young correspondents hero-worshipped him.

Neil Sheehan arrived in Vietnam a few months later, and followed Bigart around like a puppy dog. David Halberstam, who would succeed him as the *Times* man in Vietnam, eventually to surpass him in celebrity but never in legend, was equally awe-struck. "We were his linear descendants," Halberstam said. "I never wrote a story in Vietnam without thinking that Homer was going to read it." Mal Browne worried at first about getting "big-timed," never quite accepted him as a Vietnam regular—residents, they called themselves—but loved him nevertheless: "a prince, who saw through it all from the beginning."

Vietnam would, by choice, be Bigart's last war. He had made his first visit to Saigon in 1945 when the Americans, heady from their Second World War victories, made the ill-fated decision to help the French reclaim their lost colony. He returned again in 1951 and 1953, writing increasingly gloomy reports about the French failures. By 1962 his gloom was pervasive, but this time the failures were American.

To Browne, Vietnam was exotica, to Bigart a curse. He found Saigon's bottomless intrigues sinister and corrupting. "The place made my skin crawl," he said. He made no secret of his feelings, in and out of print. Fritz Nolting lived the rest of his life unforgiving of him. He was convinced that Bigart had come to Vietnam with a hopeless prejudice and, of course, he was right. Within weeks, Bigart had become the scourge of the brass once again. General Harkins complained about him endlessly. Nolting openly despaired. Diem wouldn't even honor *The Times* with one of his soporific monologues.

If Browne had already begun tweaking the authorities and their "secret" war, Bigart now cannonaded them. He brought with him one of the world's great reservoirs of knowledge about the folly of war and the foibles of the men who planned them. Few wars or their makers could have withstood his scrutiny. The Vietnam War, flawed from the outset in concept, theory, and execution, was not one of them.

During the past twenty years Homer Bigart had spent the majority of his time on the ground with the grunts. But two aerial combat missions during the Second World War had done the most to form the man and frame his views.

In February 1943, having arrived in London only weeks earlier on his first war assignment, Bigart joined a group of correspondents on a bombing raid against heavily defended German submarine pens. Among the others was Walter Cronkite, then a young wire-service correspondent for United Press. But by far the most famous was Robert Post, a correspondent from *The New York Times*.

It was a terrifying assignment, the casualty rates still running as high as 25 percent on raids into Germany, and the reporters were spread out among the fleet of B-17s, Bigart in the lead plane. Over the English Channel swarms of German Messerschmitts came up to challenge them. Bigart, like his colleagues, joined the U.S. airmen in firing the bombers' .50 caliber guns, a violation of the Geneva Convention on warfare but a routine one in the Second World War, as it has been in most others.

The German fighters dogged the B-17s all the way to their target at Wilhelmshaven and all the way back. At the end, simply surviving made for both exhilaration and an extraordinary story. The reporters were exultant, high on their own adrenaline, as they pounded out their stories. Then they were abruptly brought back down to the real world. One of their group had not made it. Post's plane had been shot down, and probably by friendly fire from the B-17s. There was never any indication that a correspondent had fired the errant shots. But the haunt remained forever, still showing in an interview just before Bigart's death at eighty-three:

Q: One of your first missions was a flying mission and that was the one in which Post was shot down.

A: Post. Post of *The New York Times*. Yes.

Q: Yes. And some of the reporters were actually firing the weapons on the flight, weren't they?

A: Yes. Including me. I grabbed a machine-gun. I heard the skipper say, "Who fired that burst?!" Absolute silence on my part. But I don't think I shot one of ours down.

Q: Were the guns available because the crewmen were wounded or because there were extra guns?

A: We were taught to use them. The dummies.

Bigart would risk his life a hundred times, some thought in foolhardy fashion, in the years that followed. He would migrate from battle to battle, war to war. But after Wilhelmshaven he would never find war dapper or debonair. Nor, no matter how often he put himself in harm's way, would he ever fire another weapon in anger.

A flight at the end of the war influenced him almost as much and led to the first of two Pulitzer prizes. In August 1945 he found himself inside a B-29 bomber chronicling the mood of a crew flying toward Japan on a bombing mission at the moment the war ended. Inside the droning Superfortress he captured a wrenching Catch-22 scene: Halfway out, the crew monitored President Truman's announcement of the Japanese surrender as well as a radio report about dancing in the streets of San Francisco. "I hope all you boys out there are as happy as we are," the radio crackled to the fighting men in the Pacific. They weren't. A short-wave radio report was not enough; the crew needed a mission-abort order from their headquarters. Bigart watched the high and bleak drama as the crew, wanting neither to kill nor be killed in a war already over, droned on toward Japan. It was as if the plane were lost in a bureaucratic time warp. The order didn't come.

Bigart never learned how many Japanese died in the small target city of Kumagaya. But the experience taught him a more important lesson: wartime logic, with all its wonderful numerical certainty so favored in far-off war rooms, was, as he put it, bullshit.

The assignment of Homer Bigart to Vietnam had far-reaching consequences. Almost two decades after Wilhelmshaven and Kumagaya, he was not just Bigart the famed war correspondent. He was Bigart of *The Times*, a newspaper whose influence dwarfed all others.

Bigart's appearance became the first sign that Vietnam would become a *New York Times* war, a distinction that lasted not just through the little war and its coming showdown in 1963, but also throughout the long and tortured entanglement. That distinction did not always rest easy at a newspaper as steeped in the establishment as it was in its own sense of greatness. It was anything but eager at that moment for a brawl with the U.S. government. But, despite occasional skittishness inside the bastion at Broadway and 43rd, skittishness that would reach its peak in 1963, *The Times* kept sending in its best and backing them publicly. That was far more than most did. No other American newspaper assigned a full-time correspondent to the war during these crucial early years, a terrible indictment of the media of the day.

Bigart cleared the way later that year for David Halberstam, whose pointed, angry reporting would leave the first great scars on America's Vietnam policy and make him the single most controversial correspondent of the war. Years later, after the war became big and brutal, *The Times* would still lead the way. Its Vietnam bureau would invariably be larger than the others and overflowing with talent. By the mid-sixties Sheehan had gone over, as had Mal Browne and Charley Mohr. At one point the newspaper's Vietnam team consisted of Mohr, Sheehan, and R. W. (Johnny) Apple, Jr., a superstar grouping no one could touch. In the early seventies Sheehan unleashed the Pentagon Papers. Sydney Schanberg, another great rebel who thrived at least briefly in the ranks of the establishment *Times*, peeled the veneer off later lies as the war spread into Cambodia.

Bigart was a big, slow-moving, crusty man with an acute eye for detail. But he was easy to underestimate. He had become overweight, terse, and grumpy, and couldn't see beyond his reach without his eyeglasses. In the heat of the day he strolled down the Rue Catinat in a dark American business suit that gave him more the look of a lost Midwestern banker than a rogue war correspondent. At the wrong times, usually when he was angry, his speech broke into an unlikely stutter. In contrast to the sophisticated Ivy Leaguers favored by *The Times* for overseas assignments, he read little history, spoke no foreign languages—and suffered no one's pomposity. Shortly after arriving, a solicitous Vietnamese official addressed him in French, offering him an expensive Parisian cigarette. "*Je ne* smoke *pas*," he replied, and that was the last time anyone heard Homer Bigart communicate in anything other than straightforward, albeit occasionally stuttering, English.

Still, to underestimate Bigart was a fatal mistake. "All Homer has is a form of portable ignorance," a friend said at the time. "He shows up knowing little and then finds out everything." Unlike many big-name reporters, whose egos sometimes blind them to the obvious, Bigart had a deceptively helpless manner. He operated as if he knew absolutely nothing about anything. He was the kind of reporter, a colleague once said, who would show up at the scene of a murder, see the knife sticking out of the victim's back, and ask, "Cause of death?" His questions were so elemental, simple, and persistent they became known in the trade as "Homer's All-American Dummy Act."

The Vietnam of early 1962 gave him a natural target. Within weeks he was casting the secrecy as silly, support for Diem as foolish, and the strategic importance of this distant and backward place as dubious.

He did it in the pure Bigart style that had made him a cult hero at journalism schools and city rooms everywhere. Almost immediately he discovered a battle in which backwoods Katu tribesmen—"hostile aborigines," he called them—attacked a Vietnamese patrol and their American advisers with poisoned spikes and Stone Age arrows. He wrote:

> Although the Vietnamese maintain that the Katu are heavily infiltrated with Viet Cong Communists, it is extremely doubtful that they have ever heard about Marx or Lenin.

By early 1962 the Americans were moving their technology—helicopters and fertilizers, armored personnel carriers and 2,4,5-T herbicides—into Vietnam by the shipload. Bigart's instincts told him that technology, power, and even ingenuity, those hallmarks of the American way that had turned the tide in the Second World War, were more likely to sink into the muck of this swampy outpost.

After the Katus, he devoted an article to cats, and like Browne's piece on technological improvisation with bedbug boxes, its opening paragraph became a perfect parable about bureaucratic absurdity in the Vietnam era before most Americans knew there would be a Vietnam era:

> SAIGON, VIET NAM, Feb. 4—American antimalarial spray killed the cats that ate the rats that devoured the crops that were the main props against agitation in the central lowlands of South Viet Nam. The result: a hungry, embittered rural population tending to support the Viet Cong insurgents.

Indeed, American technology so wrecked the rich Mekong Delta rice fields, which led Asia in exports, that by 1965 South Vietnam was importing her staple food from Louisiana.

But after the cats, Bigart found the dogs. The American military, upset with South Vietnamese soldiers who would rather visit their families than stand duty at night, brought in German shepherds as sentries. Checking out one unit, Bigart found four of the five dogs, as well as their trainer, ill from jungle ailments:

They needed three months to adjust to the tropics. Mean-while the [Americans] discovered that each dog required $1.20 worth of frozen horsemeat a day; a Vietnamese soldier gets by on 19 cents of rice. Gadgets will not win this war, and neither will dogs.

Bigart was driving them nuts, but it didn't slow them down.

———

Within a three-day period in January, Ambassador Nolting intentionally misled an executive committee of Congress, and President Kennedy told his first overt lie about Vietnam to the American public. Both were covering up a new escalation known as FARM-GATE, which placed Americans directly into combat with only the faintest pretense of an advisory role.

The air force mission was made to order for the kind of war the United States wanted to test in Vietnam. FARMGATE used volunteers from a secret outfit known as Jungle Jim, the air force's little-known counterinsurgency rival of the army's Green Berets. Jungle Jims were put through rigorous covert-warfare training, then asked a series of ten questions about their willingness to perform unusual missions. The last two were: "Would you wear civilian clothes?" and "Would you go knowing that if you were captured your government would disclaim any knowledge of you?" Only bachelors were taken and, when accepted, they were told only that they were going to "Country 77."

Jungle Jims had been in Vietnam and in combat for months, training South Vietnamese airmen to fly close support for ground troops. But now the missions changed dramatically. By putting a single Vietnamese aboard, the Americans were given the green light to fly "any missions they wished." The new orders meant that the Vietnamese were relegated to no role at all. The Jungle Jims flew old planes manned by as many as a half-dozen crew members. All but one would now be an American. With the new orders, the crews sometimes took up a single Vietnamese desk sergeant.

On January 13 the Jungle Jims flew their first mission mere hours after Nolting had assured a closed session of the Senate Foreign Relations Committee that "as of now" no Americans were engaged in combat. Two days after the missions began, the question was put flatly to President Kennedy in a televised press conference: "Mr. President, are American troops in combat in Vietnam?" Kennedy gave a one-word answer: "No." By the end of the month the Jungle Jims had flown 229 combat sorties.

In March, Jerry Rose, a stringer for *Time,* and David Hudson, a stringer for NBC, confronted Nolting with the full story. They even knew the code name: FARMGATE. Nolting lied his way out of it but cabled Washington that "we should give further thought to the adequacy of our present line." Washington disagreed. A year later, with FARMGATE sorties exceeding 1,000 a month, casualties mounting, and news stories becoming routine, Nolting tried again. Secretary of State Dean Rusk wired back, almost panicky: To change the story now "would put the lie to all high officials" who had stuck by it all along. With FARMGATE, the attempts at secrecy in early 1962 took on an Alice in Wonderland quality.

Back home, the White House press corps was taken on guided tours of the Fort Bragg training ground for the Green Berets, men with charcoal-blackened faces, jaunty berets, and exotic jet-assisted backpacks with which they leaped broad rivers and came down fighting,[1] knives in hand. The Green Berets made great Sunday supplement reading. But the government insisted that the counter-insurgency forces were not fighting in the only counterinsurgency war the United States had going. They were.

High American officials paraded through Saigon, adding to the charade. The President's brother, Attorney General Robert F. Kennedy, stopped off for two hours in February and held a press conference at the heavily guarded airport. Against a backdrop of teeming American military activity, Kennedy took it upon himself to argue that the United States was involved in a struggle, not a war. The incredulous reporters pushed on:

Q: What is the semantics of war and struggle?
A: It is a legal difference. Perhaps it adds up to the same thing. It is a struggle short of war.

1. Like most of the other gadgets, the Buck Rogers jet packs didn't work and never made it into combat.

The semantics suffered further as Americans began to die more regularly. In mid-February 1962 eight were killed when their plane went down during a psychological-warfare mission. On successive days *The New York Times* trumpeted the unspeakable.

In Washington, James Reston, to whom Kennedy had confided his need for Vietnam months earlier, began his column in unusually blunt fashion:

> WASHINGTON, Feb. 13—The United States is now involved in an undeclared war in South Vietnam. This is well known to the Russians, the Chinese Communists, and everyone else concerned except the American people.

The next day, from Saigon, Bigart wrote that the crash exposed "the fiction that United States servicemen are keeping discreetly in the background. . . ." He also added a bizarre new reason for the secrecy: American officials were being less than candid, they told Bigart, because they were afraid of "hurting Vietnamese feelings."

The one-two punch from *The Times* rattled windows at the White House. At a news conference, the President reacted defensively, denying that he was being unduly secretive and insisting, now in somewhat vaguer language, that the United States had no combat troops, "in the generally accepted sense of that word," fighting in Vietnam.

Bigart continued to cause trouble simply by nosing around. Washington imposed a news blackout on the wounding of an American sergeant because of its sensitivity to the policy of refusing the Purple Heart to "noncombatants." Bigart visited the sergeant's unit and found bullet holes in eight of the company's twenty helicopters. "The crews cannot follow the subtlety of Washington thinking," he wrote. The policy was reversed the next day. But relations with the press got worse, as Deputy Ambassador William Trueheart acknowledged in a wry cable to Nolting, still in Washington for meetings:

> FOREIGN CORRESPONDENTS MORE THAN CASUALLY RESTIVE OVER ALLEGED "CLOSE-MOUTHED" ATTITUDE OF U.S. OFFICIALS HERE.

By the time of Kennedy's press conference in February, just ninety days after the beginning of Project Beef-Up, his administration clearly had a severe press problem. But governments suffer from an often fatal inability to recognize that severe press problems usually come from severe policy problems. Kennedy didn't see it either. The result was an elaborate set of care and feeding instructions that came to be known as Cable 1006.

State Department Cable 1006 was the brainchild of Carl Rowan, a former newsman who, like many others, had been drawn into the government by the first media president. As assistant secretary of state for public affairs, Rowan was a natural bureaucratic choice to polish up press policy. He also had some drawbacks. After joining the government, he regularly displayed a need to show his independence from his old craft. "This so-called concern about the public's right to know," Rowan said early on, "is really concern about the fourth estate's right to make a buck." This had not endeared him to his old colleagues.

Rowan began with good intentions. He warned that the policy of secrecy not only would cause "a major domestic furor" but would provoke "a completely hostile press and insure that the newsmen will write just the things we hope to prevent." He was right. But his guidelines only made it worse. Later, Cable 1006 would become the target of 1963 congressional hearings, and Rowan would scream foul about taking the blame for a problem he had tried to cure. But by the time his instructions made it to Saigon, it was difficult to see how they could have cured anything.

"Correspondents should not be taken on missions whose nature [is] such that undesirable dispatches would be highly probable," said one. Another suggested that newsmen be told that "frivolous, thoughtless criticism" of President Diem was counter to the national interest and "only makes our task more difficult."

The results were predictable. Harkins banned the correspondents from the new helicopters, although reporters had ridden all manner of military vehicle to battle in every previous American war. Nolting, after trying to explain to Homer Bigart that he should avoid "frivolous, thoughtless criticism" of Ngo Dinh Diem, retreated farther behind the safety of George Washington.

43

Rowan's memo turned the "press problem" into what would be known for the next two years as the "press mess."[2]

———

For a time in early 1962 the helicopters seemed to turn the military tide, sweeping in low over the wilderness to catch the Viet Cong in lairs they had once found safe.

In March, Admiral Harry D. Felt, the Honolulu-based commander in chief of American forces in the Pacific, announced that the South Vietnamese had finally "gone on the offensive" in fleets of the old banana-shaped, troop-carrying H-21s. Thanks to Cable 1006, however, the correspondents were stranded on the ground, and ferried in *after* selected battles. "Body count runs," Bigart sarcastically called the flights, and a grim new term was added to the lexicon of the war.

Nothing outraged Bigart more than banning him from the helicopters. He had logged hundreds of hours in combat aircraft, and now these new political generals, pipsqueaks when he had won his spurs, were going to ban him from the primary military vehicle in their little "nonwar"? His outrage turned to fury when the military blinked at their own rule and allowed their favorite, Joe Alsop, aboard a flight. The fury grew so great that he started stuttering. Someone usually fared badly when Homer Bigart started his stammer.

As haughty at war as he could be charming at his dinner parties, and somewhat of a dandy, Alsop showed up in war zones sporting a stylish swagger stick, a Panama hat, and a half-dozen leather suitcases to which he steered the nearest general's aide. Years earlier in Korea Bigart had watched Alsop at the Yalu River border with China, waving his swagger stick like a saber and ordering generals about with outrageously dangerous and unwanted advice. "Cross the river!" he berated them. "Confront the Chinese!"

2. Rowan later returned to journalism as a Washington columnist. He has screamed foul, ever since, about the uniformly harsh interpretations of his role in Cable 1006. But he saw the cable as it went out. Its results, as Pierre Salinger conceded later, "were to repress rather than give out information."

Now Bigart saw Alsop as a strutting outsider making an invasion of a different kind: onto his turf. He was not one to suffer slights silently. He immediately gave up on the generals at hand and shifted the pressure to those other scorned authority figures back home. He fired a cable to Emanuel R. Freedman, *The Times*'s foreign editor.

FREEDMAN, IF YOU CANNOT PROTECT ME FROM THIS PETTY PENTAGON FAVORITISM YOU WILL HAVE MY RESIGNATION FORTHWITH.

Bigart made it onto a flight two days later.

The assault, against a Viet Cong–held village called Cai Ngai in the dense jungle at Vietnam's southernmost tip, began before sunup. In the darkness just before sunrise, the chopper's blue cabin lights cast eerie shadows off the two hulking American gunners as they hand-hauled tiny Vietnamese troopers up through the doors. Helicopter warfare was relatively experimental. But the Korean-era H-21 Shawnees were neither new nor comfortable, nor were they very safe. Nicknamed the Flying Bananas by their crews, they were ungainly craft with two large rotors and they landed like big, awkward birds, rump down. The Viet Cong soon began calling them "the Angle Worms."

Lightly armored and used only for rapid troop movement, the craft had no seats and Bigart jammed himself in among the dozen nervous Vietnamese troopers. Someone shouted: "Pull pitch!" The rhythmic thumping of the blades intensified, the chopper lifted off and, accompanied by a fleet of others, beat its way south at eighty miles an hour.

Less than an hour later the helicopters roared in low and abruptly on Cai Ngai, the big Americans manning the .30 caliber machine guns. Below, in the morning light, Bigart could see black-pajama-clad men fleeing into the woods from a cluster of thatch huts. By the time the H-21s had landed and Bigart and the ARVN troops had disembarked, the guerrillas were gone, leaving behind three dead. The shoot-out was over.

Bigart pronounced the raid a success, with the Viet Cong so surprised that they left their morning meal untouched as they fled. But, even so, his account did not mesh well with Admiral Felt's optimistic words about a tide-turning offensive. Even surprised, the guerrillas fought back before retreating. Five choppers were struck by Viet Cong fire and one was shot down. Still more telling, the young South Vietnamese soldiers' lack of enthusiasm for a fight remained unchanged by their new mobility.

After taking Cai Ngai without a casualty, the ARVN troops dawdled under coconut trees as an exasperated American adviser attempted to prod them into the chase. "Let's get this thing moving," the American pleaded. "Boom, boom, left, right, left, right." A Vietnamese officer complained that the guerrillas were too far away. "How far is too far?" the American demanded, pointing out that the range of an M-1 rifle was 500 meters. My troops are hungry, the Vietnamese officer replied. "They can eat tonight," the American said. But they ate in the village—raiding the henhouse, the Americans called it—and the adviser gave up.[3]

The Vietnamese commander reported a "body count" of twenty-eight dead, although only the bodies of the three killed in the landing assault were counted. The others, reported killed as they attempted to flee, were never found. That would have required chasing the guerrillas into the surrounding jungle, far more adventure than the ARVN commander wanted. Bigart concluded his story: "As usual, the main enemy force got away."

Despite the Pentagon's mistrust of the correspondents, Bigart imposed a crucial bit of voluntary censorship on himself after the mission. At the request of the American command he did *not* report that American gunners fired the shots that presumably killed the three Viet Cong. Long after he left Vietnam, he responded much like his young successors when asked about the criticism heaped on them for their aggressive reporting. "Aggressive?" he harrumphed. "I was far too inhibited."

Nor did withholding the news of active American involvement in the combat at Cai Ngai do anything to improve relations with Harkins or the increasingly strident Saigon government. Over the next months other reporters were occasionally allowed to accom-

3. Oddly, after all of the hullabaloo, much of this account did not make it into *The Times*, the clerks having cut it, which might help explain why Bigart never read his stories after publication.

pany missions. But, otherwise, Harkins continued to keep the lid screwed on tightly. The tiny American press corps chipped away steadily at the total secrecy, which had become an impossible policy to sustain. But the correspondents simmered as the little war widened and they were boxed farther away from the action. Bigart complained that he had never felt so isolated by American officials.

———

Barely three months into Project Beef-Up, shortly after dawn on February 27, 1962, two American-built AD-6 Skyraider fighter-bombers took off from one of the new American-built runways at Bien Hoa, briefly flew east toward the nearby South China Sea, and then turned back toward Saigon. On this morning there were no "blond Western faces" in the cockpits. Instead the planes were piloted by South Vietnamese Air Force officers. For almost an hour they dove at the presidential palace in downtown Saigon, strafing, bombing, and napalming in an attempt to assassinate President Ngo Dinh Diem.

The attack nearly destroyed the palace and injured Diem's sister-in-law, Madame Nhu, who fell through a bomb hole two floors from her bedroom to the basement. Diem was unhurt, and the plot, unsophisticated by the byzantine standards of Saigon, fizzled. But it served as a reminder of how precariously America's Mandarin held the reins of power in South Vietnam. It also fanned the ruling family's paranoia, which needed little encouragement. No event would do more to hobble the ARVN and frustrate the gung ho Americans trying to get the Vietnamese to carry their war against Communism. Diem's commanders would fight the strangest of wars. They risked few casualties, fearing the wrath of the palace, and they fought always with an eye on the back door and a quick retreat to Saigon to protect their jobs.

Plots against Diem had begun almost from the day he had taken power in 1954, and continued nonstop thereafter. He survived a shelling attack on the palace by the national police in 1955 and another serious assassination attempt in 1957. In November 1960, just days after Kennedy's election, the Vietnamese military's so-called "paratroopers' coup" came within a hair of succeeding, with five battalions of paratroopers controlling large parts of Saigon for two days before Diem and Nhu maneuvered their way out of trouble.

The family had survived for almost eight years for two reasons: American support and an almost total lack of credible alternative leadership in a country created by outside powers after the French defeat. Diem could be such a troublesome client, however, that the American support was not always so unstinting—and Saigon's plotters knew it. Ambassador Nolting later wrote in his memoirs that scarcely a week went by during his two and a half years in Saigon that someone didn't approach the American Embassy with a plan to get rid of Diem.

The Americans' ambivalence, and their willingness to listen to all the intrigues, did little to calm the Vietnamese leader's fears or make him more pliable. President Eisenhower had virtually given up on him by the end of his presidency. In August 1960 the CIA secretly warned Eisenhower that "adverse trends" would "almost surely in time cause the collapse of the Diem regime." Three months later the Americans were tipped off in advance to the para-troopers' coup. They didn't bother to warn Diem—and he knew it.

Still, if Diem had all but worn out his welcome with the Eisen-hower people, the Kennedy administration publicly re-upped with vigor. Nolting was sent to Saigon with explicit orders to stroke him into compliance. During Vice President Johnson's visit, the exuberant Texan had taken to the streets of Saigon and "pressed the flesh" in the style of an American political campaign, then had astounded the American correspondents traveling with him by calling Diem "the Winston Churchill of Asia."

If the attack on the palace started Diem's paranoia running again, it sent the volatile Madame Nhu running wild. She began ranting about the "pseudo liberals" and "capitalist colonialists" in Washington, and rarely let up over the next eighteen months. But, for once, the embassy knew nothing about the plot. The Americans were tied in too tight. Bigart, who thought the whole family was both evil and crazy, composed a jingle that he tried out in a letter to his *Times* colleague and friend, Betsy Wade.

"It's a queer set-up, but our leader in Washington has decided we must live with it," Bigart wrote. "I am composing a song, to be sung to the tune of 'I'm an Old Cowhand,' that runs:

We must sink or swim
With Ngo Dinh Diem.
We will hear no phoo
About Madame Nhu.
Yippee—i—aye, i—aye, etc.

The jingle seemed to have little market—not much of one, that is, until the old rebel slipped the key phrase under the green eyeshades of *The Times* copy editors and on to the front page a week later.

From that moment on, the policy of the U.S. government became "Sink or swim with Ngo Dinh Diem."

———

Halfway through Bigart's six-month tour, the old war correspondent's reporting had disrobed the secrecy and infuriated just about every official in Saigon. Harkins, who complained that Malcolm Browne was too young and François Sully too French to cover the war fairly, told Washington that Bigart was too old, too grouchy, and too cynical. Nolting's early dislike for him turned nasty, so much so that the two barely conversed and, when they did, the ambassador completely misunderstood Bigart's acerbic wit. President Diem chafed at the "sink or swim" jingles, grumbled about this most irritating of the American fleas, and finally decided to kick Bigart out of the country.

Expelling *The New York Times* from a country into which the United States was now pouring both blood and wealth was no trivial matter. But like many of the crises early in the dark American experience in Vietnam, this one had a comic, Keystone Kops air about it.

Late on a Friday afternoon Bigart was summoned abruptly to the South Vietnamese Department of Information—the Office of Truth, he called it—and told to be on the next plane out of the country.

Why? he asked.

For spreading "false and tendentious" information about the people and government of South Vietnam, responded his accuser.

Bigart shrugged. He had been kicked out of better places and assumed he had been done in by the sink or swim line. At the embassy, however, he learned that Diem was also expelling Sully, the aggravating French "spy" for *Newsweek*.

The twin expulsions left Nolting in an unhappy pickle. The American ambassador would have been as pleased as Diem to see both men gone. Only a few days earlier he had had a memorable exchange with Sully, one the Saigon correspondents delighted in retelling. At a reception Nolting had challenged the Frenchman for his downbeat reporting about the progress of the war.

"Why, *Monsieur* Sully, do you always see the hole in the doughnut?" the ambassador asked.

"Because, *Monsieur l'Ambassadeur*," Sully responded, "there is a hole in the doughnut."

But Nolting, under instructions from the State Department, pleaded with Diem that expelling the journalists would be a "disaster." Diem filibustered but backed down.

Only then did Bigart learn the real reason for his near miss. With one brief exception a year later, there never was direct censorship in Vietnam. But, in these early days, each dispatch was translated for the palace before it was released to the cable office. Bigart's offending article, a friendly Vietnamese information officer told him, was a "Talk of Saigon" column, a lighthearted collection of items known in *Times* parlance as a "talker."

It was basic Bigart, *The Times* adding a perfect irony by not bothering to print it. The story's only audience was the Diem truth squad. In the lead item Bigart wrote about the first USO show in this war Americans weren't fighting:

> "Laugh With the Girls," as the show is called, is the ultimate manifestation of the American presence here. It played to capacity houses in downtown Saigon and at nearby Tan Son Nhut Airport. Some observers said the total attendance may even have exceeded the limit of 685 men set by the Geneva cease-fire agreement for foreign military personnel in South Vietnam. . . .
>
> Bored with their supporting and advisory roles in an apparently endless tragedy that few of them understand, the Americans responded to the 90-minute revue of songs, jokes

and the inevitable striptease with whistles, yells and cheers. . . .

But it wasn't the USO item that got Bigart in trouble. It was a trailer at the bottom of the column:

> Besides amusement, Saigon offers instructive glimpses into the workings of the authoritarian Vietnamese regime. Pictures of Ngo Dinh Diem are plastered everywhere. But Americans rarely see him in person for he is very aloof. Americans are more likely to encounter South Vietnam's indomitable Mme. Ngo Dinh Nhu, palace hostess for the bachelor President and First Lady of Vietnam. . . .
>
> Mme. Ngo Dinh Nhu will be going abroad soon. However, reports that she will be absent for several months have been discounted as wishful thinking by Government sources. . . .

Anything in the article might have set off the palace. But, according to Bigart's source, the problem was all a mistake. In translation, the words about the "aloof" president and the "indomitable" First Lady had been twisted to leave "salacious" implications about their relationship.

Bigart was not altogether happy about his reprieve. In the sometimes convoluted values of journalism's world, expulsion made for a mixed bouquet. The downside was that it gave the correspondent a one-way ticket away from his story. But it also had an upside. It pinned a badge of courage on a correspondent; he had to be doing something right to make a government so angry. Bigart had been expelled twice before from Communist East European countries. Getting bounced from Saigon, a place he didn't like anyway, would not have been all bad news.

The next day Bigart talked to Nolting, and the ambassador naively expected a thank-you or "possibly even a change of attitude," as he wrote later. Instead, Bigart chewed him out, partly a reflection of a real desire to go home, partly a gruff expression of his newsman's black humor that most would have laughed off. The Virginia gentleman ambassador didn't understand, never would, and never forgave him, although he did get off a good parting line. Well then, Nolting said dryly, he supposed Bigart would have to "sink or swim with Diem" a while longer.

Writing about the slapstick episode in the in-house publication *Times Talk,* Bigart acknowledged his mixed feelings:

> This has not been a happy assignment.
>
> Saigon is a nice place to spend a few days in. The food and wine are good, the city is attractive, most hotels and restaurants are air conditioned. But to work here is peculiarly depressing.
>
> Too often correspondents seem to be regarded by the American mission as tools of our foreign policy. Those who balk are apt to find it a bit lonely, for they are likely to be distrusted and shunned by American and Vietnamese officials.
>
> I am sick of it. Each morning I take a pen and blot off another day on the Saigon calendar. At this writing, I have 83 days to go.

———

All the fuss simply made Bigart more of a hero to the young correspondents, especially Cornelius Mahoney Sheehan. Just twenty-five years old and as green as Irish grass, Sheehan arrived in April. A Harvard honors graduate, he had just finished an unhappy army tour of Korea and Japan. United Press International, the underdog news agency and legendary for being miserly, picked up Sheehan for $75 a week and soon sent him to Asia's new hot spot. The job kept Sheehan just the way UPI wanted him, forever running and forever broke, his checks bouncing so regularly his buddies joked that he had them printed at the nearby Michelin rubber plantation.

Over the next year, in the secret government cables complaining about young and inexperienced correspondents, no name would show up more often than Neil Sheehan's. He arrived the rawest of rookies and made all the raw-rookie mistakes. He also became one of the best correspondents ever to set foot in Vietnam, becoming a legendary figure himself.

Most of Sheehan's lessons came the hard way, the first after only two weeks on the job. On a Saturday night he got a spectacular tip from a senior American military man in the officers' club bar. Two hundred Viet Cong had been killed in one of the largest battles of the war forty miles south of Saigon near My Tho, the American whispered to him. Sheehan competed head to head with Mal Browne in a bare-knuckles wire-service rivalry in which minutes often separated success from failure. Now he barely had time to confirm that the battle had been fought and then struggle with the archaic communications system to make the Sunday papers. He ran with it, and Sheehan's scoop shoved every Sunday-morning Vietnam story, including Bigart's, off the front pages.

Sheehan went to bed giddy with his first success. The phone rang after he had been asleep only two hours.

"Sh-sh-sheehan," the angry voice stuttered. "Get dressed. We are going to My Tho. There better be two hundred b-b-bodies down there, k-k-kid."

There were fifteen bodies at My Tho. Sheehan's source had been too far into officers' club martinis. The young newcomer filed what is known in the trade as a rollback. "And it was a helluva rollback, from two hundred bodies back to fifteen. I was lower than a snake's belly, certain I would be canned."

Bigart just laughed. "Don't feel so bad about it, kid," the *Times* man said, the stutter gone now. "Just don't do it again while I'm here." Sheehan didn't. But he learned a quick, hard lesson about Vietnam body counts.

Sheehan learned one other crucial lesson from Bigart, and it may have been the most important lesson of the war. Just before Bigart left for home, the newcomer followed him on a final ARVN mission in the delta. For two days they slogged through the muck. Not a shot was fired; not a guerrilla spotted despite adamant promises that their South Vietnamese battalion had a major Viet Cong force trapped. After the washout, as the other correspondents headed back to Saigon, nothing more to gain from this one, Bigart stayed on and deluged the debriefing officers with his usual endless, simplistic questions. Sheehan was getting a lesson in Homer's All-American Dummy Act. He finally showed his impatience.

"For God's sake, let's go home," he complained. "We've been out for two days, we're exhausted, nothing happened. There's no story."

"No story, kid?" Bigart leveled the young newcomer with a withering stare.

"No. Nothing happened. Let's get out of here."

"It doesn't work," Bigart growled. "That's the story, k-k-kid. It doesn't *work*."

3

WHAT FOOLS WE
MORTALS

John Mecklin drew a deep breath, sucking in the hot, heavy air. The rainy season was near, and fond memories flooded back. Most outsiders dreaded the monsoons. Not Mecklin. The first torrential rains brought out the crickets, millions of them, and the crickets brought out the kids, it seemed like millions of them, too, chasing after the crazily leaping insects. Vietnamese mothers extracted the essence of some exotic sauce from the catch, an Oriental culinary treat Mecklin hoped he had missed. But the chase was delightful, the streets filling with a terrific din—the racket of crickets, kids, and cyclos—as the Vespas and Lambrettas careened away from the little boys as they careened after the bugs as they careened away from the little boys. The ritual often continued till one o'clock in the morning. Mecklin had loved it, loved all the sights and smells of the old Saigon he remembered.

Now, in May 1962, the new government press attaché, the man sent in to solve the escalating press problem, shook his head in disbelief. What god-awful thing had happened to the charming, enticing Paris of Southeast Asia he had known?

Only days earlier he had sat through the last of all the tidy Washington briefings with their multilayered flip charts and plastic overlays, their color-coded graphs with lines moving with bureaucratic certainty in all the right directions, their statistics adding up to all the proper preordained pluses.

But no briefing could have prepared him for this.

In six short months American bureaucracy had run amok and the city buckled visibly under the foreign weight. Mecklin knew the ways of Washington well, how detached from reality the capital could get, especially in the rambunctious early days of a new administration. He understood what had happened: Vietnam had become a fad, a bureaucrat's hula hoop, and everyone wanted a spin. The American bureaucracy had spread like crabgrass, choking everything from Saigon's economy to its very soul.

Inflation had become grotesque, with housing prices alone increasing more than tenfold. The man from USAID outbid the man from HEDSUPPACT who outbid the man from MAC-V in an orgy of American dollars that benefited only Saigon's corrupt landlords. Americans with new ideas came and went so fast the embassy's telephone book was out of date before it was published. The downtown American PX, already feeding the invidious Saigon black market with underarm sprays and Revlon lipsticks, was stuck with thousands of dollars in bad checks from in-and-outers long gone and untraceable.

Along the captivating Rue Catinat glitzy, neon-lit, go-go joints with names like The Florida Club, Uncle Sam's, and Honeymoon Lane sprang up overnight. Young GIs competed with burly American construction workers who elbowed aside State Department functionaries, all vying for the attention of miniskirted Vietnamese bar girls drinking "Saigon tea." The girls earned more in one evening than their brothers earned in a year toting American-made rifles.

This was the way Washington wanted to run its covert war? This was what they had sent him over here to help keep secret?

An intuitive man now entering his forties, Mecklin had developed a deep sense of the absurd from seeing too many wars and too many human plans gone awry. Another of the newsies drawn to Kennedy's Camelot, he was a former *Time* war correspondent who had watched the French fail here. Now he shuddered at the thought that history was repeating itself, that his country might make a still *worse* mess of it. This was no way to defeat the tenacious guerrillas who had humbled the proud French.

Six months into Kennedy's new policy and his instincts told him what Homer Bigart almost simultaneously told young Neil Sheehan: *It doesn't work.*

Mecklin's new job was to convince Bigart, Sheehan, and their colleagues to the contrary. It would be a hard sell. As the new Saigon head of the United States Information Agency, a job that also made him the chief civilian press officer for the American Mission,[1] he had been given clear marching orders: Clean up what Washington now openly and irritably called the "press mess."

But did Washington know what it really wanted? The words of Assistant Secretary of State Robert Manning, also a former newsman, echoed in his mind as he surveyed the results of the massive American buildup. Manning had described the quandary plainly. Washington wanted the American involvement "minimized, even represented as something less in reality than it is."

Something less in reality than it is?

The American military, fascinated by its new ball game, had grown so top-heavy that the United States often had more generals in Vietnam than the South Vietnamese army. The social demands became so great that the American Women's Association began a cocktail-glass rental business. At the officers' clubs martinis went for thirty-five cents and steak barbecues became a Sunday staple. The newcomers were not exactly melding quietly into their new environment.

But Vietnam had also become a political fad, and the social technicians had arrived in force as well. Some of the programs were simply zany. Understanding neither the language nor the culture, one study group spent weeks composing a propaganda slogan for matchbook covers. The group finally came up with the wording. In the countryside, however, the peasants had no idea what to do with the new curiosity. They had never seen paper matches before. Another proposal, mercifully discarded early, called for airdropping Sears catalogs into the jungle to show the Viet Cong what they were missing by not rushing to The American Way.

Mecklin thought about the painful laughs he once got out of Graham Greene's novel *The Quiet American,* which captured the naiveté and egocentric certainty of the American tinkerers playing around the edges of the French mess years earlier. In one of his

---

1. The term American Mission can be confusing. Because of the peculiar American situation in South Vietnam, the upper levels of the embassy and the military were combined into one management group, the Mission. Technically, the ambassador was in charge.

favorite passages, a British friend tries to explain the title character to a mystified Vietnamese woman:

> "He belongs to the American Economic Mission. You know the kind of thing—electrical sewing machines to starving seamstresses."
> "Are there any?"
> "I don't know."
> "But they don't have sewing machines. There wouldn't be any electricity where they live."

Was real life now outstripping fiction? The morale of the Americans trying to do good deteriorated so rapidly that three or four a day were being shipped to Manila for psychiatric care. A government psychiatrist, brought in to help, was sent back in three months. With emotional problems.

Make America's involvement *something less in reality than it is?* The place had become an American circus.

Still, shock over the Americanization of Saigon was one thing. The depth to which the other war had so quickly rooted between Saigon's tiny press corps and his new government employers stunned him. His marching orders should have been clear from the instructions in Carl Rowan's Cable 1006. But he didn't take the orders literally and didn't think anyone else would either. He was wrong.

Already one embassy official had directed him to tell the correspondents how to write a story. That will backfire, Mecklin had replied: "It's like trying to tell a New York taxi driver how to shift gears." The official was unyielding: "Then the correspondents not only are bastards, they're un-American bastards."

Mecklin was prepared for trouble but not for the bitterness. How could everybody possibly be so angry already? This thing is still only six months old, for God's sake. Top American officials routinely transposed the "a" and "r" in Bigart's name—making it Big Rat[2]—and made unseemly jokes about the correspondents' near

---

2. Transpositions are a daily fact of life in newspapers, even in star bylines. Ironically, a typo like that in Bigart's byline in the old days at the *Herald Tribune* had caused the copy boys to give him the same nickname: Big Rat. But at the *Herald Trib* it was delivered with fondness.

misses in combat. Mecklin had lost friends in these same jungles. He had been only yards away from Robert Capa when the famed photographer was killed in the last days of the French war. The sick jokes were not funny.

The new government man also found the attacks on the reporters' trustworthiness, and even their patriotism, foolish and self-defeating. Mal Browne of AP had stopped checking with the embassy, a practice the embassy found irresponsible. Mecklin thought so too. Then he discovered that for months embassy officials had refused to confirm anything Browne asked them. Hundreds of government man-hours were wasted in paranoid investigations of leaks whose source often proved to be the correspondents' own eyes. "A man from Mars admitted to official inner circles in both Vietnam and Washington," Mecklin later wrote, "could have been excused if he got the impression that the newsmen, as well as the Viet Cong, were the enemy."

Mecklin, a solid man of solid credentials, seemed the ideal choice to nip the press mess in the bud, saving the U.S. government years of grief. He knew the players and, like most, he believed in the essential rightness of trying to "save" countries like Vietnam from the Communists. That is why he had been sent. But, arriving, he found a hopeless deadlock between, as he put it, "the newsmen who said two plus two equals three and the officials who said two plus two equals five." He never would make the twain meet. The battle only became more heated, and soon the newsmen were openly shaking their fists and shouting "Liar!" as U.S. officials stridently responded "Traitor!"

Meanwhile, Mecklin had some more immediate work to do. In his first week on the job his old employer, *Time* magazine, was due in town, looking for a cover story. That would be easy. Far more daunting was the arrival the following week of Defense Secretary Robert S. McNamara, making his first visit to Vietnam. McNamara's visit would make the press mess worse. Mecklin could sense it.

——

In 1962 *Time* magazine reigned as America's most successful journalistic aberration. Unlike the grime-gray and often tedious newspapers of the day, *Time* was colorful, slick, packaged, and cutely well written, bothering with only a perfunctory pass at objectivity. The magazine was, in fact, an unabashed propaganda organ for The American Way or, at least, the view of it as seen by its messianic founder and publisher, Henry Luce. Together with its sister publication, *Life*, the weekly newsmagazine was immensely influential. *Time* and *Life* wielded their power in places that the other great media institution of the day, *The New York Times*, did not bother to go. *The Times* could take the intelligentsia, and did. But *Life* sat on the coffee table of every middle-class home in America; *Time* became the intellectual bible of the Elks' Club in Peoria, the Rotarians in Walla Walla, the housewife in Flint. The Sulzbergers and *The Times* pitched straight at the ruling elite and became part of it. Henry ("call me Harry") Luce took middle America, and from there reached back up into the political power structure of the country.

Luce's power, like that of his magazines, crested after the Second World War, when American dominion spread easily through a worn-out world. He traveled easily with it, empire-building. No less a Cold Warrior than Winston Churchill called the publisher one of America's most powerful men, and his flagship newsmagazine sailed the world's waters with an imperial Churchillian sense of mission.

Born in China, the son of American missionaries, Luce had a vision to sell and he sold it with a missionary's zeal. On the eve of the Second World War more than twenty years earlier, as the United States wrestled with less certainty about its world role, Luce brushed aside all doubts. He declared the dawning of "The American Century" in terms that made earlier journalistic cries of Manifest Destiny tame by comparison. If Manifest Destiny planted a divine imprimatur on the "right" to push ever-westward across the continent, clearing American consciences for the dirtier parts of the task, the declaration of The American Century extended the blessing beyond the horizon to the rest of the world. Luce's vision was blunt, righteously self-certain, and remarkably arrogant. Americans, he pronounced months before Pearl Harbor, should "exert upon the world the full power of our influence for such purposes as we see fit and by such means as we see fit."

In the waning days of American isolationism, the proclamation from the publisher of those flossy, glossy, propagandistic magazines met largely with intellectual sneers. But two decades later, Luce was living out his messianic dream. The tenets of his foreign policy had become the tenets of his country's foreign policy. The American Century lived, with Harry Luce determined to perpetuate the very American rightness of it all.

Nowhere did he want it to work so much as in Asia. To Luce, the greatest failure of mid-century American foreign policy had been the "loss" of China to Mao Zedong and the Communists. Now only Ngo Dinh Diem, the "tough miracle man" of South Vietnam, and a few American soldiers stood between hope and the loss of all Asia. Vietnam had become a cause, a *Time* cause.

During John Mecklin's first week on the job his old boss decided it was time to forget the secrecy nonsense and pump up the American public about what was at stake. A *Time*-hype cover story on General Paul Harkins—the new American commander had been an understudy of George Patton, no less!—would do nicely. To do the job, Luce sent in one of his best, Charley Mohr.

At thirty-four, Mohr ran on equal parts of raw energy, raw danger, and raw Chivas Regal. He could spin great, well-embellished barroom tales till early in the morning and, just a few hours later, completely charm a president, a general, an ambassador—even, as it soon would turn out, a Madame Nhu. A Nebraskan, with fine cornsilk hair and a softly rounded face that created a perfect newsman's disguise, Mohr carried with him a Midwesterner's ingrown wariness of political extremes. Some said Charley agonized too much, that he carried too many devils within him. But he was shrewd, tough, and almost universally admired. Mohr was a comer and Luce gave him the ultimate Lucian accolade: "A reporter, and how!"

Eight years earlier Luce had lured Mohr away from an apprenticeship at United Press. When Luce offered a job, he offered the world—and limitless supplies of money to go with it. Mohr looked at empire, looked at a salary that would double, triple, quadruple, looked at an expense account that would fly him first class anywhere in the world, allow him to rent everything from elephants to airplanes and buy all the Chivas Regal he could drink. Charley Mohr didn't think twice.

Mohr moved into *Time*'s Washington bureau, and he moved fast. Soon he was covering the Eisenhower White House as he would cover everything else, with youthful brashness and uncanny access to the right people. When Vice President Nixon prepared for his famous kitchen-debate trip to the Soviet Union in 1959, Mohr got a private briefing. When Nixon made his first bid for the Presidency, Mohr brassily asked Ike to list the Vice President's ideas that had become part of his administration's policy. Eisenhower's groping answer became a political classic: "If you give me a week, I might think of one."

But Charley Mohr, the landlocked Nebraskan, eyed more distant horizons. To be part of an empire, you marched through its outposts. Europe . . . India . . . Africa . . . the far reaches of a new American world. Luce kept pushing his favorite toward Asia. Mohr ducked and dodged. Asia was booby-trapped ground at *Time*.

When you signed on for the first-class trip with Luce, you signed on with your eyes open. It was an unusual journalistic journey. Each week hundreds of first-rate correspondents filed stories from all over the globe. In New York, high-paid editors and writers honed, rewrote, packaged, added Lucian perspective. It was a package that, with American daily journalism still stuck in its who-what-where-when blandness, with opinion, point of view, advocacy the worst of sins, became enormously successful. No bylines appeared in *Time*. Group journalism, they called it. In reality, the magazine produced unabashed personal journalism and the one, ever-looming if unwritten byline was that of Henry Robinson Luce.[3] Other views were ridiculed, other facts ignored. Mohr accepted the pact. He was a man of the Cold War. He bought the American view of the world, bought The American Century.

But Asia? Mohr was also a realist. Better *Time* men than he—Theodore H. White, John Hersey—had come a cropper trying to mesh reality with their boss's single-minded, blinders-on view of

3. *Time* was rife with stylistic fluff. It coined the word "tycoon" to glamorize American capitalists, and once ran five straight tycoons on its cover. It diminished politicians it didn't like, invariably Democrats, with derisive *Time*-slang, once writing off a big-spending senator as Cadillackadaisical. Among its quirks was an insistence on using the middle name of those so honored to make its cover. In its early days one cover-bound tycoon (middle name: Percy) rebelled, telling Luce to back off or lose a rich advertising account. Young Luce backed off. He rarely did again. Soon Henry Robinson Luce was a more powerful tycoon than any candidate for his cover.

China. White, one of the great journalists of the era, had covered the upheaval in China with passion and distinction. For his reward he had been called a pinko in his own magazine, had languished in near exile during the McCarthy Red-hunting years, and had only recently made it back with his best-selling *The Making of the President 1960*.

When Luce pushed, and pushed hard after the 1960 elections, to get Charley out where it *counted*, Mohr bobbed, weaved, and compromised, choosing New Delhi. Luce groaned but reluctantly sent his ace White House correspondent off to the bowels of India. Mohr thrived, and when Luce visited, Mohr organized the trip like a potentate's tour. He even rented the elephants, several of them, to take Luce and Ambassador John Kenneth Galbraith to Jaipur and the Amber Palace. In an empire you traveled like an emperor.

In the spring of 1962 it was time to move again. This time Mohr wanted a lifelong dream: Nairobi. Luce moaned at Mohr's lack of regal vision: Good grief, Charley, we don't even *have* a bureau in Nairobi. Mohr insisted. Luce opened a Nairobi bureau.

Mohr's bags were packed for Africa when Stanley Karnow abandoned the Hong Kong bureau. Luce was desperate. In all his far-flung holdings no posting was more important. Hong Kong was Luce's window on China, a coastal outcropping of British rock where Luce could peer over the border at Shum Chun into the forbidden playground of his youth. Not even Luce, with all his power and money, could buy a ticket through the gate. But he could buy a perch on the rock, put his best talent there, chip away at the edges, watch. Now Hong Kong had also become Luce's elbow in Vietnam, a two-and-a-half-hour commute to Saigon. He wanted Charley Mohr for it. Nairobi could wait for six months. Mohr knew it was time to pay the piper. He shrugged at the inevitability of it all, and strode into the minefield.[4]

Now, on his first trip to Vietnam, Mohr's mind flashed back to conversations with Galbraith in Delhi. The ambassador was a distant dove in the Kennedy administration, warning JFK repeatedly that he was walking into quicksand. He spoke to Mohr about his

---

4. Karnow retained his interest and influence in Asia, but never returned to the bureau. Eventually he wrote one of the major works about the war, *Vietnam: A History*.

concerns, too, but found no interest. "It's an inconsequential event," Mohr had rebuffed Galbraith, "in an inconsequential place."

In Saigon the consequence seemed more substantial. Mohr, like Mecklin, marveled at the signs of the city's new war footing—an American war footing. The U.S. military contingent had grown to almost 7,000, only God seemed to know how many civilians inflated the number, and kept on climbing.

Mohr arrived on a Monday, knowing, by his own admission, absolutely nothing. He took a suite of rooms at the Caravelle Hotel, Saigon's finest, where he was joined by two stringers, Jerry Rose and Mert Perry, and set out to work fast. The magazine would "close" on Saturday with all the reporting, writing, editing, politicizing, and conversion to *Time*-speak locked up in five pages of type behind a heroic cover photo of General Paul Donal Harkins. But Mohr's specialty was crash covers. Given a week, he had been known to churn out prodigious files of 20,000, even 30,000, words that New York then trimmed and groomed into final form.

Mohr also knew that, despite the press mess, doors would open for him. Diem might brush away the other troublesome fleas, but he had Mohr to the palace.[5] Nolting might stiff others for weeks, but he saw *Time* immediately. Charley Mohr was briefed high and low. "Progress briefings," they were called, for the can-do Americans had no room for anything less.

Harkins, for whom a *Time* cover would be a career pinnacle, rolled out the red carpet: breakfast with his wife, Elizabeth, at their white stucco villa; one-on-one talks in his flag-bedecked office near the colorful Central Market; and the ultimate public-relations ploy, a flying tour of the "front" in his private plane. During the tour the general and the correspondent paused to inspect an elite Vietnamese Rangers' training camp where Americans were teaching the tiny soldiers to plummet from trees down eighty-foot wires, screaming, "Rangers kill! Rangers kill!"

---

5. The bombing put the presidential palace out of commission for the rest of Diem's days. He and his entourage moved just two city blocks from the old parklike compound to the more urban fortress named for a famed Vietnamese emperor, Gia Long. It stood diagonally across a street corner and vast lawn from Mal Browne's office on Pasteur.

By week's end, Mohr was back at the Caravelle churning out the copy. Rose and Perry were in awe of Mohr, an in-house legend they quickly concluded was anything but overrated. Very cautiously, they tried to coach him, warn him that the government briefings were loaded, that he had picked up only part of the Vietnam story.

Mohr took an instant liking to Perry. A six-footer who ran well over 250 pounds, Perry was so fat he sometimes had trouble negotiating the small footbridges in the delta. The Vietnamese called him "the Water Buffalo," and they endangered their position by breaking into gales of laughter every time the American teetered on the narrow bamboo treads and then crashed over the side with a tremendous splash. His girth was exceeded only by his good humor, his good humor only by his inability to take any guff from anyone. He had been *Time*'s stringer only briefly, the weeks that had elapsed since he quit UPI, opening that spot for Neil Sheehan.

One of the few married correspondents, Perry and his wife, Darlene, had lived in penury on UPI's wages. During the bombing of the palace he had scored a tremendous scoop, getting the only telephone call out of the country before the government shut down the communications system. He beat Mal Browne's AP story by hours. There could be no greater triumph for a wire-service man. Homer Bigart's story never did get home, one of the great humiliations of the old pro's career.

Perry figured the time was right to wheedle "a little more noodle money" out of UPI. To do that he had to deal with another legendary character, the Tokyo bureau chief, Asia Earnie Hoberecht.

At a time when the typical UPI office looked as if a typhoon had just swept through a very small pack rat's nest, Asia Earnie wore a homburg to work and negotiated his way through the rubble with a malacca cane. Hoberecht, who spoke and wrote Japanese, had discovered a sure-fire road to riches in postwar Japan: romance novels. His first book was technical—about the American art of kissing. The market for vicarious pleasure proved insatiable. He churned out two a month. James Michener once visited Japan to talk about American authors. But whenever he mentioned Ernest Hemingway, he was corrected: You mean Ho-Ba-LECHT.

Michener made a point of meeting the famous author after that and found Hoberecht in the UPI warren on the top floor of the

Mainichi Shimbun Building. It was 1957; Hoberecht was a tall, good-looking man in his early thirties, his hair a sandy red and his moustache pencil-thin. He wore "a flashy tie, his trademark, a pin-stripe suit with wide lapels, and highly polished tan shoes." He was a dude. The malacca cane and a ten-gallon Texas hat added character. Ignore that hat, he told Michener: "It's my latest affectation. A man in my position has to be talked about or he's forgotten." Usually he wore the homburg.

Some thought Earnie's net worth exceeded that of UPI. Others thought that wasn't saying much. But he protected the struggling news agency's money as if it were his own. A UPI man visiting Tokyo in the mid-sixties, Leon Daniel, recalled Earnie's complaint: "Do you have any idea how much the war in Vietnam is costing me?"

Hoberecht was not the man to ask for more noodle money. Young men seeking to live in exotic places and get their names in the paper doing it were a dime a dozen. And that's about what he planned to pay them. Richard Clurman, then chief of correspondents for *Time*, found UPI's salary practices fascinating because they were the exact opposite of his magazine's. He once asked Hoberecht what he paid Neil Sheehan when Sheehan did a brief moonlighting stint for the UPI night desk while still in the army. "Oh, I didn't pay him anything," Hoberecht replied. Clurman laughed and thought that must mean very little indeed. He was wrong. It meant nothing. So Hoberecht's response to Perry's request was terse, followed by an expression of surprise about the young man's avarice. Perry's return cable was even more terse: two words that told Hoberecht he could do to himself what he had been describing in his Japanese romance novels all these years.

The story delighted Mohr, and he also laughed when Perry, a *Time* veteran of mere weeks, described Vietnam as "Henry Luce's Disneyland." But he didn't heed Perry's cautions, or Rose's either.

The *Time* cover story of May 11, 1962, had some prescient observations. The United States was into Vietnam, Mohr wrote, for the duration "even if it takes a decade—as well it may." For the first time he used the phrase that would mark and damn the war, the need "to win the hearts and minds of the people." In New York, his editors did not see the irony in accompanying that observation with a photo of a Viet Cong prisoner carried away hog-tied to a bamboo pole. On the cover Harkins stared out, steely-eyed with certainty, under the headline: "What It Takes to Win." The general became another Patton, "the same, certainly, in their drive to win." Nolting became a "big, rugged handsome Virginian" born to his task. Defense Secretary Robert S. McNamara, arriving that week for his own tour, would find "a remarkable U.S. military effort, mounted in [a] few short months. . . ." It was a Lucian call to arms.

As early as the next week Charley Mohr started having some regrets. By the end of the year he would look back on his maiden effort with embarrassment. "Stenography," he derisively called it.

———

It was the beginning of the computer age, the coming of a new binary religion with machines producing The Answers by reducing the questions to their ultimate simplicity—zero-one, plus-minus, yes-no, black-white, win-lose, good-bad. There would be no maybes, no grays, no doubts, no hey-wait-a-minutes. Can't argue with the numbers. Can do.

No one bought into the religion more than Robert S. McNamara. He was a total believer, driven by a passion for the rational. A micromanager with a photographic memory, a business prodigy with a zest to "do good," McNamara was the toast of Kennedy's Camelot, a new Washington hero. With his numbers, this brilliant secretary of defense would remake a Pentagon bloated by the Big War and the Cold War. With his numbers he would build better high-tech weapons for less money, get more bang for the buck rationally.

And with his numbers he would win the troublesome little war. He would put a slide rule to Vietnam and forever see light at the end of the tunnel. In the computer of his mind he would run all the zero-ones until they came out his way.

This self-certain, super-rational, penultimate mid-century American man—this man of instant don't-look-back decisions—would quantify Vietnam in so many different ways that they inevitably began calling it "McNamara's War." In Vietnam they said the schoolchildren were taught reading and writing and McNamara so, when they grew up to be good little guerrillas, they could counter each whiz-kid ploy with a simple ploy of their own. Which they did. They learned to use their captured American weapons to lead McNamara's helicopters like ducks, and bring them crashing down into the marshes the same way. They collected GI garbage and made grenades out of beer cans. They learned to make explosives out of the fertilizer the Americans gave the farmers and from the plastic boot soles McNamara gave the ARVN. They hid so well, lived so many different lives, crossed and crisscrossed so many vague jungle borders that McNamara's numbers not only failed him, they misled him. His zeros were wrong, his ones off-kilter, his answers kitty-wumpis.

McNamara's War became a war that would suck the soul out of a generation and break the best of men, none more totally than Robert Strange McNamara himself.

The young Saigon correspondents saw his folly sooner than most. It was not because they were particularly insightful or wise. Largely it was because they were there, in Saigon—or, more important, because they were not *there*, on the Potomac where the glitter and the glamour of the Kennedys could overwhelm good sense, where the McNamara aura could subdue intuitive reason.

"I would not believe Bob McNamara lied," said Joe Alsop, "unless he came to me personally and told me he had lied."

What proof for the Young Turks! Washington became not only distant but dangerous. "We were all young," David Halberstam said. "We had no ties to Washington. We didn't want to go to Bobby's parties at Hickory Hill. What the Kennedys thought of our work didn't mean shit."

No one but the man himself tied the curse of Vietnam more closely to McNamara than Halberstam. In his tone-setting book with the ruefully damning title, *The Best and the Brightest*, which he published in 1969, Halberstam widely assigned the blame, but no one received more than McNamara. He had been the best, the brightest; he had been "everything but wise." McNamara lost himself in his numbers, failed to smell the stink in the air. "He did not serve the country well," Halberstam concluded; "he was, there is no kinder word for it, a fool."

Later Halberstam would be angrier and blunter, for he became a very angry man. "Of all the players," he said, "McNamara was the most despicable. He was the biggest liar of the war."

To Neil Sheehan, McNamara "personified the hubris" of the

Americans, and "hubris," a word out of Greek tragedy, became the favored word to describe the architects of the great American delusion in Vietnam, to describe America's comeuppance in the sixties.

You can't argue with the numbers. McNamara added them, subtracted them, caressed them, worshiped them, demanded them. *"Ah, les statistiques!"* a South Vietnamese general told Roger Hilsman in 1963. "Your secretary of defense loves statistics. We Vietnamese can give him all he wants. If you want them to go up, they will go up. If you want them to go down, they will go down." And they did. Vietnam became a game of numbers, none of which meant anything.

Body counts became the favorite. Vietnam became a war of "attrition." We would "attrit" the enemy, kill him, and kill him again, until he was gone. Then the numbers would add up and it would be over. Colonel Barrie Williams, an army intelligence officer who also served as an ARVN infantry adviser, recalled the problem: "A field commander's success was determined by body counts. We used to count blood stains, and, you know, one man can bleed over six acres of area." In the Pentagon it became downright silly. "We were trying to quantify everything," Williams said. "It all was an outgrowth of McNamara's mentality. There was a category 'killed by artillery,' one for 'killed by air,' and I can't remember the exact words for the acronym now, but we started a category called KA-BOOM-TA. When we couldn't determine who had killed this individual, he was placed in a category for killed by more than one weapons system. KABOOM-TA."

George Allen, a CIA analyst who often went out with the ARVN, remembered: "Infants were counted as enemy dead. Any dead object on a battlefield, even cows and chickens, were included." This caused awkward problems. "Eventually," Allen said, "you had killed more people than you had acknowledged were there."

Halberstam saw the result: "There were 30,000 Viet Cong when I arrived," he said. "There were 30,000 killed while I was there and there were 30,000 Viet Cong when I left."

Numbers are basic, and twisted, in any war. The press is hardly above the numbers game. In Korea, briefers were prodded for persisting in being vague about "Chinese hordes" pouring over the borders. "Will you tell us," dead-panned Michael Davidson of the *London Observer*, "how many Chinese battalions go to a horde, or vice versa?"

In Vietnam simple unqualified numbers were sought for headlines, for summaries, for television's brevity, for determining who "won." The media had a voracious appetite for digits, good or bad. Chet Huntley, an NBC anchor, routinely referred to the body counts as "the total score." Michael J. Arlen of *The New Yorker* found the press as guilty as the government, providing an endless market for statistics and ways to "measure progress numerically— so many yards gained rushing, so many villages pacified, earnings per share up, body counts down, carloadings steady."

McNamara remained a Washington hero, of the liberals, oddly, and was made so largely by the Washington press, until the end of his seven-year tenure. By that time 500,000 American troops were in Vietnam, attriting an ever-larger enemy in ever-larger numbers. All manner of American ingenuity and technology, in which McNamara believed as fervently as his numbers, had been applied to the problem. In a war for "the hearts and minds" of the people, McNamara had approved the poisoning of the forests and fields with defoliants, and the creation of "free-fire zones" where anything that moved would be shot. Finally, McNamara floated his ultimate plan—construction of an electronic barrier to stop the infiltration of new guerrillas so bedeviling his attrition theory. Someone else did the numbers. An electric fence? The country was almost as large as California, its land border longer than the Western Front in the First World War. McNamara's last plan died quietly.

Still, to the end, the man with the austere, rimless glasses and straight, slicked-back hair mesmerized Congress with his numbers.

Part of Colonel Williams's job entailed updating and revising the numbers for McNamara's "black book," which was carried to congressional hearings by another colonel, known as McNamara's "elbow man." Rarely was the elbow man at a loss for a statistic. "We used to joke that he could pull out the number of linear feet of foreskin circumcised off the Viet Cong for the past year," Williams said.

The absurdities multiplied as time went on. In 1967 a dozen top intelligence officers, including George Allen, were dispatched to a secret CIA retreat where they were to combine all the numbers into one huge index. They called it the Vietnam War Dow Jones Index. For three days the analysts up-weighted defections, down-weighted body counts, cranked in bomb tonnage and battalion days by the ARVN.

"The trouble was, the index didn't show you anything," Allen, by then a ranking CIA analyst, said. "It was crazy, just crazy." The group threw it all in and got drunk for the rest of the week.

Not long after that, McNamara quit. He did not willingly speak about Vietnam again for almost three decades.

Once, he was compelled to talk, in General William C. Westmoreland's 1984 libel trial against CBS, a trial about numbers. Wistfully, almost spookily, he spoke repeatedly of the "black-pajama people" who had defeated his logic and technology. He was like a man who had lost a religion. He had grown disdainful of the liturgy, the numbers, never had believed them; they could be off by a "factor of two, three, ten," and "the whole damn thing [was] much ado about nothing because nobody in their right mind would think that there were 297,000—zero, zero, zero—enemy in South Vietnam." Robert McNamara wore a haunt about him, and the mea culpa he wrote in 1995 intensified the sense of it.

In May 1962, however, as he landed in Saigon for the first of nine inspection tours of the war, McNamara stood at the height of his power, his optimism undimmed, his self-confidence uncontained, his arrogance total. He was the best of the best, the brightest of the brightest. The correspondents, with one exception, were immensely curious.

———

Homer Bigart was unusually grouchy. In the past week, while *Time* magazine was getting the red-carpet treatment, Harkins had vetoed new requests for combat rides on the helicopters. The Vietnamese were harassing him by delaying his twenty-three-cents-a-word rush cablegrams till deadlines were missed, and both governments had been caught in flat-footed, obvious, and silly lies in a press conference. "Anti-Press Campaign Seen" grumped a Bigart story's headline on the eve of McNamara's forty-eight-hour visit.

Now the government seemed up to more of the same, claiming a shortage of helicopters made it impossible to provide transportation for correspondents on McNamara's tour of the countryside.

McNamara's itinerary included visits to two new "strategic hamlets," the brainchild of Brother Nhu but a program McNamara himself had approved. The goal of the Strategic Hamlets program was to deprive the Viet Cong of support in the countryside. To do that, the government forcibly moved the country's peasants from their traditional villages and into fortified government hamlets—in effect, bamboo stockades. The old villages were burned, and, with them, the ancient burial grounds of the ancestor-worshipping peasants.

François Sully once again infuriated President Diem with this *Newsweek* description of the operation known as Operation Sunrise:

> Swooping down on villages in territory controlled by the Viet Cong, Vietnamese soldiers ordered 205 bewildered farm families to pack up their belongings. Then, the soldiers burned the villagers' huts and marched the families off to a government "strategic hamlet" in the nearby valley of Ben Tuong. Some of the peasants went voluntarily, attracted by a government payment of $20, but many had to be forced. Others fled into the jungle to join the Viet Cong.

So much for hearts and minds. Bigart watched the same scene and expressed shock that Americans had lent themselves to a program so cruel, inhumane, and smacking of a concentration-camp mentality. McNamara's approval of the program, he wrote, had given the United States "moral responsibility" for what surely would become "charges of American complicity in allegedly cruel acts. . . ." Bigart could not find a single happy face among the peasants as he watched a large group of American colonels and civilian observers "inspect the stockade where the first group of families uprooted by Operation Sunrise were sitting dejectedly." His analysis was tart:

> Only a few months ago, Administration officials in Washington were denying press reports of the ever-deepening involvement of the United States in this war. Now the

Americans were taking on a drastic program that was certain
... to be bitterly resented by the peasantry....

In Washington, Secretary of State Rusk responded with an almost hysterical cable to Nolting. "Why do large groups of Americans inspect anything?" he demanded. "Why do operations have
such American-sounding names as Sunrise and FARMGATE?"
American visibility in South Vietnam gave Bigart the opening to
assign " 'moral responsibilities' and other similar concepts" to the
United States, the cable said, ending:

... GET COOPERATION OF ALL CONCERNED TO DEVISE MEANS OF
MINIMIZING U.S. PRESENCE AND REDUCING PUBLIC IMPRESSION
U.S. GOING BEYOND ANNOUNCED OBJECTIVES.

Rusk was living in a rarefied world. New American military
personnel were now arriving at a rate of 1,500 a month. American
civilians were poking into all elements of Vietnamese life. And his
fellow Cabinet officer was about to become a presence quite difficult to minimize.

After the expulsion attempt, Bigart assumed that banning Saigon's tiny press corps from the McNamara tour was merely a cover
for another swipe at Sully and him. He would have none of it. His
famously angry stutter hit John Mecklin like a jackhammer. The
new press aide quickly found helicopter space for a two-man
"pool" to represent all. The pool members: Bigart and Charley
Mohr.

It became a pivotal moment. The Strategic Hamlets program
represented the heart of the Diem regime's attempt to win over its
own people. But it was a fool's contraption, doomed by all the laws
of human nature. Over the next forty-eight hours the reporters
would see this clearly. They would also see that McNamara did
not.

Robert Strange McNamara bounded off his plane exuding certainty. Following him down the ramp at Tan Son Nhut on May 9,
1962, were the medal-bedecked chairman of the Joint Chiefs of
Staff, General Lyman L. Lemnitzer, and the commander of United
States forces in the Pacific, Admiral Harry Felt. On the ground he
was greeted by General Harkins and Ambassador Nolting. They

looked, Bigart thought, like a veritable flying wedge of American power.

The group was soon aloft in a fleet of H-21s heading toward the new showcase hamlet at Ben Tuong, forty miles northwest, the strategic hamlet that had grown in the past few weeks out of the scene Bigart and Sully had witnessed. In the open doors of the Shawnees sunburned American gunners stood at their weapons like an airborne praetorian guard, squinting over the .30 calibers for glints of trouble in the dense green forest below.

The press chopper landed first and Mohr, barely in the country a week, was disturbed by the look of the place. Ben Tuong was without trees, grass, or vegetation of any kind, a field of dust surrounded by a dry moat. Sharpened bamboo stakes jutted out from the moat's far side. Limp barbed wire ran along its dry bottom. Long, straight rows of identical huts baked in the hot clearing. Damn, Mohr thought, it *is* a concentration camp. He tried to envision what the burned villages must have looked like—an Asian chaos of kids, fluttering ducks and chickens, wonderful cooking smells, chattering people. There was no chatter, no chaos, here, even after the chopper blades had shut down.

McNamara emerged down-dressed for the sullen heat—Sears suntans, hiking boots ("his Matterhorn boots," Mohr called them), an open-mesh, baseball-style farmer's hat on his head. The secretary moved quickly, one of the world's most powerful men, a man accustomed to action and decisions. He strode purposefully to one hut and peered in. A terrified woman, clutching a child, peered back. He found a toothless old man, talked to him through an interpreter, jotting left-handed notes in the notebook he carried everywhere.

For an hour Bigart watched wryly. He prodded Mohr: See any able-bodied men? Except for Diem's soldiers, only a handful, Mohr realized. The fighting-age men were still in the woods with the Viet Cong, where they had escaped the roundup a month before.

As McNamara prepared to leave, his eye caught something he had not seen on the way in, a cluster of concrete pillboxes surrounded by heavy entanglements of concertina wire.

"What are those?" he asked an American colonel.

"Pillboxes, Mr. Secretary."

McNamara scowled and protested: "But they aren't big enough to hold all the people."

"They aren't for the people," the colonel replied. "They are for the hamlet officials in case the hamlet is overrun."

"But what about the people?" McNamara demanded, his concern clearly real. The American colonel, who served in the field, not in politicized Saigon, tried to give this powerful American leader an honest answer *and* a lesson in Vietnam: "The Viet Cong don't want to hurt the people, Mr. Secretary. They're all related to them. The last thing most of the people would want to do would be to get in those pillboxes."

Dead silence followed. Mohr noticed General Harkins staring furiously at the back of the offending colonel's neck. McNamara seemed deep in thought. Mohr concluded that McNamara was far too bright to not get the message. He also concluded, however, that the message was unacceptable. McNamara had already moved too far into the mire psychologically. The silence continued, awkwardly. Finally, a Vietnamese officer broke the impasse: "Mr. Secretary, it would be too expensive to build pillboxes for all the people. However, we can instruct them to built slit trenches in front of their houses."

Harkins broke into a smile. McNamara seemed relieved.

"Slit trenches," Bigart groaned audibly. "Jesus Christ!"

But McNamara had already left-handed two words in his notebook and, surrounded by his flying wedge, had begun double-timing toward the H-21s, problem solved.

The next day the entourage visited another hamlet. This one had been attacked recently. McNamara was surprised to find that the hamlet had no radio and help was four hours away by runner.

"Get these people a radio," he ordered rationally. But nothing was going to make sense in Vietnam. Bigart had already figured that out. In reporting the episode the next day he observed that the Viet Cong had attacked a nearby hamlet *because* it had a radio. The Viet Cong wanted it and they took it.

The radio episode didn't end there. Later that day McNamara ordered communications for all the hamlets. Several months and $52 million later, 2,200 hamlets had radios. Only then did the problem become evident. No one answered the hamlets' distress calls.

No helicopters swooped in to help; no cavalry rode to the rescue. Diem's troops had no intention of riding to anyone's rescue in the middle of the night in Vietnam.

Within little more than a year, the Strategic Hamlets program failed catastrophically. Estimates of the number of peasants moved forcibly into the encampments ran into the millions. But by the end of the next year, most of the people had faded back into the forests and paddies, stronger allies of the Viet Cong than ever. The radios left with them, the nucleus of a newly sophisticated Viet Cong communications system. The broken hamlets cooked in the sun, home to only a few peasants too old to go back and rebuild. Ben Tuong, showplace of showplaces, was overrun in August 1963.

Years later, ironies abounded. After the war Ngo Dinh Nhu's top aide for the doomed program, who toured with McNamara, revealed himself as a lifelong Viet Cong agent. Ben Tuong also turned out to be something of a showcase area for the guerrillas. It was built in the heart of the Cu Chi tunnel region, virtually on top of the secret underground maze in which the guerrillas lived, worked, retreated, hid, and ran their command posts throughout the long war. Long afterward, older and presumably wiser Americans revisited the valley of Ben Tuong, not to see the long-gone edifices they had built above the ground but the lasting monuments the guerrillas had built beneath it. The tunnels have become premier tourist attractions.

Just before leaving, McNamara met with the unhappy press corps. The scene was the living room of Nolting's ambassadorial residence, an inner sanctum to which the scruffy little band had rarely been admitted before. The secretary burst into the room on the run, always in a hurry, so many decisions waiting, unshaven from his two days in the field and still dressed in his dusty Sears suntans and Matterhorn boots.

Bigart could be a spectacle at a press conference. With his stutter, he would try to ask a question only to have a colleague roll over him. Each time his halting attempt was overwhelmed, he grew angrier. Finally, red-faced with frustration, he would lumber to his feet, throw his hands up in front of everyone, and bring the proceeding to a temporary halt by shouting, "N---n---now, j---j---just wait a s---s---second . . . !"

But, among this group, he was so senior as to be venerated. He was also ready.

McNamara made the mistake of asking the disgruntled correspondents if they had any complaints.

"Mr. Secretary," Bigart answered abruptly, "we're not getting enough news."

McNamara, who had been reading far more news from Vietnam than he wanted, laughed. "Well, Mr. Bigart, that's not my impression. My impression in Washington every morning is that you're getting a great deal of news—a very great deal."

Bigart grumped. "Yes," he said stonily. "But I'm having to work too hard for it."

Bigart went on to complain about Harkins holding back both access and information. McNamara didn't budge in his support of the general, although privately he was anything but overwhelmed by Harkins's sagacity.[6] He lectured the correspondents, a trifle presumptuously, that secrets had to be kept for "security reasons." He also accused the reporters of "blowing up" problems and causing their country "grave problems" at home.

Bigart grumped again, and the questions moved uneasily into other areas.

What did McNamara think of the situation after forty-eight hours in the country?

"I am tremendously encouraged by what I saw."

Might he feel differently if he stayed longer?

"Absolutely not," he said, and the reporters shot surprised glances at each other.

Someone asked, off the record, what he thought of Diem.

"One of the advantages of my job is that it has given me the privilege of meeting some of the great men of the world," McNamara said. "And I want to tell you that President Diem will rank with the two or three greatest I have been privileged to meet."

Bigart rolled his eyes. In his article that day, May 11, 1962, he

6. McNamara once asked Harkins, "How long will it be, Paul, before we can turn all this back to the Vietnamese?" Harkins stumbled, "Huh?" McNamara then reminded the general that his primary mission was to train the Vietnamese to fight their own war.

used the unusual word "cheerful" to describe McNamara's assessment of the war. He also wrote:

> His visit left Americans and South Vietnamese with these impressions:
>
> First, the Kennedy Administration still is rigidly following its "sink or swim with Diem" line.
>
> Second, the Administration regards President Ngo Dinh Diem as a remarkable national leader. . . .
>
> Third, the Administration believes the American correspondents here are giving a distorted picture to Congress of American involvement in the shooting war. The Administration feels the reporters are magnifying the incidents where American service men find themselves in combat situations and are writing too much about American casualties.

It is unclear whether McNamara was aware of how much he was asking of the correspondents, who were already suppressing many military details and reluctantly playing along with some of what the government told them were the "political sensitivities."

At the time of McNamara's visit, only about twenty Americans had been killed in action, most in plane crashes. But the number of casualties was growing, and the number of specific combat clashes between the Americans and the Viet Cong was growing even faster.

Coincidentally, the day after McNamara departed, Viet Cong ground fire riddled the helicopter of Colonel Frank Clay, one of the top U.S. advisers in the delta. A week later Colonel Clay, his pilot, and copilot, as well as a visiting colonel—four Americans, in all—were wounded in a similar attack. Bigart was aboard the second flight, which was in hot pursuit of a uniformed VC platoon, Americans at the guns. As before, Bigart wrote about the assault and the woundings but withheld the details that Americans led the attack and fired the gunship's weapons.

It was a kind of self-censorship McNamara seemed not to perceive and exactly the kind of event the American government was vigorously denying to the American public. Bigart may have been getting under the government's skin with his pessimistic reporting, but, in this case, he gave far greater detail in a letter to his sister than he did to the public:

We jumped in the lead helicopter and in a few minutes we made a pass at low level directly in front of the Communists. I watched from a window while the machine gunner sprayed the field and another American soldier popped with a carbine from the rear window. I could see they were Viet Cong regulars, in green uniforms and carrying packs, and they were beautifully disciplined. They returned fire, and we caught two .30 caliber bullets in the nose of the helicopter.

The American public would not read that kind of detail about American involvement in the far-off war for some time to come. But the government's assaults on the correspondents continued, escalated, in fact, to indictments of their truthfulness, fairness, even their manhood and their very loyalty to their country.

4

OLD MAN, YOUNG MAN

Homer Bigart left Vietnam a month later, glad to be gone and two governments glad to be rid of him.

It would be the old warhorse's last battle. He returned to Vietnam once, on a political campaign trip, of sorts, in the bedeviled year of 1968. Standing in the barricaded and battered streets of Saigon, the utter foolishness of the escalations astonished him. The eight thousand "advisers" he left behind had swollen to a combat force of more than half a million. American combat deaths ran more than two hundred a week, ten times the total for the entirety of his six-month stay. The war still went badly. He had returned with Curtis E. Le May, the retired air force general who was running for vice president on the ticket of the segregationist George Wallace. Le May's innovative solution was to bomb North Vietnam "back into the Stone Ages." Bigart did not think it was a very good idea.

On leaving the little war in 1962, he had considered the remote possibility of placing American combat troops in Vietnam, of fighting the land war in Asia that even General Douglas MacArthur had warned against. It had seemed imprudent beyond any of the follies he had seen during his unpleasant months in the land of Diem. So harebrained did he find the prospect that he waited until the last paragraph of his last story to deal with it. As usual, his commentary was insightful:

No one who has seen conditions of combat in South Vietnam would expect conventionally trained United States forces to fight any better against Communist guerrillas than did the French in their seven years of costly and futile warfare. . . . Americans may simply lack the endurance—and the motivation—to meet the unbelievably tough demands of jungle fighting.

Bigart left with other warnings, that the war would not be won with the "gadgets" that so entranced his rationalist countrymen, that Americans were being drawn into a moral quagmire of "senseless brutality" in which prisoners were summarily executed and worse, in which American advisers were becoming benumbed by the "charred bodies of women and children in villages destroyed by napalm bombs." The United States still officially denied using napalm.

But it was the commitment to the little Mandarin, Ngo Dinh Diem, which Bigart found the most ill-fated.

In these first months of American involvement, Bigart wrote, Diem had turned more "secretive, suspicious, dictatorial"—to the point where he seemed "incapable of winning the loyalty of his people." Tying American hopes to a man who preferred to use his troops to discourage coups rather than fight the enemy was "doomed in the long run" and, Bigart wrote presciently, could leave Washington with the unpleasant option "of ditching Ngo Dinh Diem for a military junta. . . ."

Bigart could not restrain himself from taking a few parting shots at Ambassador Nolting and his secretive embassy, both in print and in the long sessions he so loved over adequate and aged scotch in the Caravelle Hotel's tenth-floor bar, his favorite watering hole.

In his last days he got into his cups with William Pfaff, a columnist for *Commonweal* researching a book on emerging Asian nationalism. Bigart complained that Saigon had the worst American Embassy and the sorriest excuse for an ambassador he had seen in twenty years of overseas reporting. Pfaff considered Bigart "one of the great shit detectors" in American journalism. He passed the gist of the conversation along to a colleague, who passed it to the White House with strong urgings to take Bigart's views seriously. The reporter, Pfaff wrote, "regards the Embassy, obscenely and accurately, as 'clerks, clerks, clerks.' " Clerk, of course, was Bigart's ultimate insult, usually reserved for his editors: "Those pallid clerks who control my destiny." Enriched by whiskey, delivered with a bite, the word invariably became embellished with one of Homer's few affectations, a slightly British pronunciation that turned "clerks" into "clarks." Pfaff loved it.

In 1951 Kennedy had visited Indochina as a thirty-four-year-old congressman, receiving all the upbeat briefings from the French that his own men now provided to visiting VIPs. Before leaving, however, a talk with a small group of correspondents gave him a broader view. He went home saying that the French could never win their colonial battle. Three years later, with Dien Bien Phu falling and Kennedy a U.S. senator, he sounded a most pessimistic note about moving in Americans to replace the French: "I am frankly of the belief that no amount of American military assistance in Indochina can conquer an enemy which is everywhere and at the same time nowhere, 'an enemy of the people' which has the sympathy and covert support of the people." Of the correspondents he had spoken to in 1951, Kennedy was impressed most by Homer Bigart. He wrote him a thank-you letter. Ironically, in 1962, Pfaff's letter ended up buried in the National Security Council's do-nothing files. No one in the Kennedy administration ever spoke to Bigart about Vietnam.

Most of the American public still ignored the war. But Bigart's cautions did not go completely unnoticed. The magazine *The Nation* noted his final article, with its troublesome warnings taking most of a full page of *The Times,* and observed that "if he is unheeded at least we shall have the small consolation of knowing we deserve what we got."

By the time he reached Vietnam Bigart was cranky and out of sorts, hating the place the moment he got there and hating it every day he stayed. He didn't like the climate. He despised the secrecy. His letters home were a litany of complaints, albeit often offset by his humor: "I've applied to be shot at," he wrote in an early letter, "but getting the necessary security clearance from U.S. and Vietnamese propaganda engineers takes time."

He found almost no one he liked or trusted, American or Vietnamese, except for a few of the reporters. In a letter to his successor,

David Halberstam, a comment about General Harkins's chief military public-information officer was typical: "Worse than useless."

"The city is full of American spooks trying to silence the few Americans who will level with correspondents," he continued, then added a stern warning: "Never reveal your sources." Of the reporters, he predicted that Halberstam would like François Sully of *Newsweek*, "although you may find him a little hard to take at first. He is inclined to be mischievous with the Ambassador and generals, but he is so good-natured and hard-working that you have to forgive him his bias—he doesn't think we are any better than the French." Malcolm Browne was a "hell of a nice guy and able," but, oddly, of Neil Sheehan, who bird-dogged him so closely during his last two months, he had not a word to say.

Through it all, he fought regularly with his editors, who often made clear their dismay with the dreaded point of view that found its way into his articles. But Bigart thrived on his in-house rebellion, playing it like a good chess game, devising a new maneuver each day against the unseen opponent in New York. He wrote with such care, such art, that he often succeeded where others had failed. His offending line would be so groomed it would slip through unseen or, spotted, would be built into the story so integrally, supported by so much linguistic brick and mortar, that to take it out would be a deadline disaster, causing the whole story to collapse. This he did day after day, never bothering to look to see if he had won the game. Once, just before his death at eighty-three, he was read one article from Vietnam. He laughed uproariously. "Did that get in *The Times*? They must have been asleep."

The Times mounted serious attempts to rein him in. But he was incorrigible. Midway through his Vietnam tour Freedman chastised him for his "polemical" reporting and added insult to injury by asking the old pro for an outline of his next Sunday article. Bigart described his response to the foreign editor in a letter to Betsy Wade:

It was two days before I could trust myself to reply. Cold, correct, Presbyterian, I drew about myself the pristine mantle of the Fourth Estate, unleashed the sword of the FREE PRESS, and smote the clerk with THE WORD: "I know *The*

New York Times has a high regard for the personal dignity and intellectual honesty of its correspondents and that you would never ask me to present a false picture of the situation here. As ever, etc."

At the same time Halberstam waged a similar war with his editors during his tour of duty in the Congo.[1] In Vietnam Halberstam's battles would take on epic proportions—everything about Halberstam tending to become epic—and the cannon fire back and forth between the New York office and Saigon roared almost daily.

In the end the memory of Bigart in Vietnam would fade in the white heat of the supernova of the man who followed him. But he had established skepticism as the rule of thumb. He had made it *pro forma* once again to challenge authority, a lesson that had been lost on many of the reporters of his generation in the heat and planetary danger of the Cold War. The old man's parting shots became marching orders for the new group of young correspondents about to take over.

As Bigart packed, David Halberstam still trudged through the Congo, where tribal warfare marked emerging African independence from European colonialism. The Congo often seemed more significant than the Kennedy administration's buttoned-up war in Vietnam, and Halberstam regularly pushed Bigart off the front page. It would be two months before Halberstam broke free, the last, and most flamboyant, to join the group.

The two men could not have been more unlike, Bigart of the old school, a college dropout, not quite over the hill but near the beginning of the roll, tiring, but always a craftsman who sculpted each story agonizingly slowly into a virtual work of art; Halberstam of the new school, a Harvard man of the generation that would begin to retool the old hard-drinking *Front Page* image of the press, not quite a rookie but pink-cheeked enough to aggravate generals, absolutely tireless, a reporter who collected so much information under pressure that he sometimes wrote stories so fast and so long and with such unbridled enthusiasm that they bordered on incomprehensible. But Halberstam idolized Bigart, and both were rebels on a grand scale.

1. Now the country of Zaire.

Mal Browne kept more to himself. But in the coming crisis no one would follow the Bigart standard more closely, showing more scornful skepticism toward the dissemblers. And, if Bigart forgot Neil Sheehan in his letter to Halberstam, Sheehan would never forget Bigart. He sucked up every lesson, forever called Bigart "the professor," and counted himself blessed as a graduate of a very special advanced school of journalism. He was still learning his lessons as Bigart struck a red line through the last day on his calendar—June 30, 1962—and headed for Tan Son Nhut Airport and home.

Sheehan saw him off. Several VIPs were aboard, the Saigon-Washington commute now routine. When the two had finished their good-byes, each turned away, Sheehan heading for the exit. Bigart did an abrupt about-face and growled one last lesson:

"Never leave the airport until you can see the plane in the air," he said. "It could crash."

———

Neil Sheehan felt both the monsoons and Mal Browne closing in on him.

Browne was in an expansive mode, getting ready to add two newcomers to the AP bureau on the Rue Pasteur, the New Zealander Peter Arnett and the German photographer Horst Faas. Both were already next door, whiling away their time in what they were calling the "phony war" in neighboring Laos. But they were due in Saigon at any moment and Sheehan already felt overwhelmed.

Sheehan would be forever outgunned and outspent by his wire-service rival. He had trouble getting his expense checks, let alone more help, out of Asia Earnie Hoberecht's tight-fisted operation in Tokyo. So Browne's new team would become the Goliath of the tiny world of the Vietnam press corps. Sheehan was afraid it would keep him pinned down in the city, the worst of all fates. The war wasn't being fought in Saigon, and the young UPI man wanted to get out to see and feel the action.

The monsoons would soon be working against him too. South of the city the first rains had brought tender shoots bursting through the soil, greening up the boundless riches of the rice fields. Soon the deluges would come, and, by late summer, the water would wash over the tops of the dikes, flood the paddies, and the bounty would multiply with fish swimming among the rice, all part of an ancient natural cycle.

The word was that the fighting stopped then, nature's cease-fire. The word was a myth. Diem's armies, their officers urban and gentrified, their equipment unable and their leaders unwilling to slog through the mud, stopped fighting. Not so the Viet Cong. It became the time of the guerrillas' greatest gains, as if they were part of the natural cycle too. The Americans were too new to know that. Some things they would never know. But, in early summer, Sheehan broke loose to go down to the Mekong Delta as often as he could before the floods came.

One of the great rivers of Asia, the Mekong was known in time-less legend as the sacred serpent. Drawing its headwaters from high in the Tibetan Himalayas, it winds 2,600 miles through China, Burma, Laos, Thailand, and Cambodia before forming a vast allu-vial plain in southern Vietnam and then emptying into the South China Sea. In that fertile delta the river created one of the richest rice-producing regions in the world and almost half of South Viet-nam's sixteen million people lived there. The river also created a remarkable place to fight and hide—a 75,000-square-mile lowland lattice of marshes, paddies, swamps, and forest groves. Villages dotted the landscape, many connected only by a network of tribu-taries and canals so small and numerous that they defied mapping. It was natural guerrilla turf and the guerrillas controlled most of it. By 1962 the delta had become the war's primary battleground.

Two surprises lay in store for Americans arriving in 1962. First, South Vietnam was far larger than most thought, pinched narrow like a fishhook but stretching 700 miles from the artificial northern border with Ho Chi Minh's North Vietnam at the 17th Parallel to a swampy peninsula jutting south into the Gulf of Siam. The second surprise was, given all this roaming room, how close the wispy war encroached on Saigon.

It remained a hail-a-cab war and to get into the middle of it Sheehan needed only to motor down old Highway 4 into the delta.

Like everything, the drive itself became a lesson in the war. Out the window of his Renault Sheehan could see expanses of young sugarcane that soon, like Iowa corn, would be tall and leafy enough to hide a battalion. He thought of an old television documentary he had seen, scratchy black-and-white footage from the guerrillas' earlier war . . . a bridge in the jungle, an old French bomber circling slowly above in search of targets, the bomber finally lumbering away, the bridge quickly becoming a mass of movement as the camouflaged men hugging its floorboards rose and marched on.

Along the highway Sheehan saw reminders everywhere of the French failure—sentry-manned watchtowers every few miles, mud forts built to give the Tricolor a presence in the field, the forts and towers still used by Diem's forces. Useless static artifacts in a war of movement, the Viet Cong overran the little outposts almost at will. Even as a raw rookie, Sheehan knew one thing: This flat, straight, macadam road might be owned, tenuously, by the government during the day. But it was taken back by the Viet Cong at night. Every night.

Just outside My Tho, Highway 4 abruptly became a spectacular crimson archway. Flamboyante trees, their boughs aflame with red blossoms, lined both sides of the road, the brilliant color closing in over him. Then Sheehan's car turned off the main road, passed a banana grove, stopped briefly at a guarded wrought-iron gate, and pulled into a dirt courtyard outside a two-story stucco building of vaguely French architecture. Each time he arrived, Sheehan smiled at the look of this place of war. Two large white crosses still pointed forlornly upward from the red tile roof, reaching in vain toward a heaven forgotten. Once a school for Catholic priests, it had been appropriated as the headquarters of the U.S. Army's advisory detachment to the 7th ARVN Division. The Americans called it the Seminary and had strung a volleyball net across the courtyard.

In mid-1962 half a dozen dusty American outposts like this, and many, many smaller ones, were strung the length of South Vietnam. The advisers who occupied them were professional soldiers all, the country's best, no draftees in Vietnam. In the larger outposts the leathery Americans, usually commanded by an officer of colonel's rank, advised the pivotal fighting units of the South Vietnamese Army. At the moment no ARVN division was more pivotal than the 7th, no advisory command more crucial than the one at the Seminary.

Sheehan had first come here with Bigart. The 7th Division operated in the northern delta, crucial ground that pressed hard against Saigon's underbelly. It was the most visible of Diem's fighting divisions and the most politicized. It naturally drew the reporters. The place made news and could be reached easily. From here the correspondents could also most easily hook on to a helicopter mission. Bigart had flown out of here to Cai Ngai and then later with Frank Clay, the commander of the advisers at the Seminary when the colonel had been shot up chasing Viet Cong. By now, however, Clay had rotated home and been replaced by Lieutenant Colonel John Paul Vann, a tough little bulldog of a man with a perennial sunburn and a rasping Southern accent that twanged hill-country but was really poor-boy, lower-middle-class Norfolk.

Sheehan and Vann had a rare appointment with fate. But their first meeting left the newsman notably unimpressed.

Vann set him up on his first chopper mission and, at a preflight briefing the night before, Sheehan thought the colonel overdid the rah-rah. "All right now," he began in a voice that ground like river gravel, "when you go out tomorrow, remember that these people need help and you oughta write positively about what you see." The pep talk went on and on: *Get on the team . . . be one of the boys . . . you-all help out.* Sheehan thought Vann sounded like a backwoods Harkins.

In fact, John Paul Vann gave every evidence of being a rising star among the army's field advisers in Vietnam. Enlisting at eighteen, he had moved steadily through the ranks—first as a grunt, then a B-29 navigator, then, in Korea, as the commander of the first airborne Ranger company to use guerrilla tactics behind enemy lines. Now thirty-seven years old and a light colonel, the army had run him through most of its top staff schools and he had come out a slightly more polished version of what he had been when he went in—a rough-hewn, dedicated soldier who was militarily creative, politically conservative, and spoke his mind. Word had it that Vann was destined for a quick rise to full colonel and then to his first general's star. Even the voice, with its scratchy accent (a Southern accent never being a drawback in the American military), added to the sense of the right man being at the right place at the right time. Vann was so highly regarded that Harkins enthusiastically directed correspondents down to the Seminary to get Vann's go-go message from the field.

But Sheehan's first instincts about the man were dead wrong.

John Paul Vann was anything but a Harkins. Within months he would be one of the correspondents' best—and most controversial —sources. Vann played it smart. He actually *admitted* screw-ups, *conceded* losses, because they were part of the game, part of any game. The admissions, of course, made him more believable. Harkins was disbelieved on *everything* because he would never admit that *anything* went wrong. Vann, with the dogged drive of a born door-to-door salesman, accepted the losses, then pitched the little victories, taking the reporters into his confidence to explain unconventional strategies and tell them how to win this new kind of war.

Vann was also a born manipulator, a user primed by a natural instinct for the con. Within a very few months he would be fed up with the war's progress, furious at Diem's nervous and political reluctance to commit his troops to battle. He grew even more disenchanted with Harkins's failure to deal with reality. The general began to override Vann's views and stifle his reports while continuing to exude optimism in the face of obvious, sometimes disastrous, setbacks. Vann decided to take a more direct route to Washington. The powers that be—the President, the Joint Chiefs of Staff, McNamara—could read it in the newspapers over breakfast.

Vann was hardly the first operator to learn this basic technique in intragovernmental communication, American-style. But his timing was ideal. By then the reporters had given up on official sources and were actively cultivating the men in the field. Other American officers began talking, too, but Vann would be the fountain. He cultivated reporters, taught them about tactics, coached them on strategy—and slipped in his message. The reporters knew the nature of the game and had few qualms. If he was using them to advance his own cause, well, they were using him too. Their craft was a never-ending series of trades. That was the system, the thin bedrock of all journalism: Be used and use, and maybe a little truth will come out. If it is just one person's truth, well, the other side has access to the same system, often more access. It was a barter made every day in the smallest city hall, every day in the Oval Office. And it was made in Vietnam. In Vietnam, however, the men with more natural access —Harkins, Nolting, visiting firemen like McNamara—were either so inept or so unwilling to lower themselves to dealing with the young and often unruly correspondents that they simply lost their access to them. The reporters went elsewhere.

In the great dispute between the government and the press that built to an explosion in 1963, then festered throughout the war and long afterward, none of the young resident correspondents challenged U.S. involvement in Vietnam or the war itself. "I thought war was a glorious adventure," Sheehan said. "We all believed in the cause. We believed totally in the American cause." The correspondents thought the war was *right*. It was the strategy that was wrong, Diem that was wrong. They believed the colonels in the field, disbelieved the generals in Saigon. In effect, the first coup d'état in Vietnam was the coup of the American colonels over the American generals. And, in the beginning, the colonel of colonels was John Paul Vann.

As the summer wound on, Sheehan developed a better sense of Vann, although he would never show himself completely. Vann was a believer. He believed in the war, believed it could be won, believed it would be won by capturing hearts and minds. He scoffed at Washington's charade of talking about counterinsurgency while sending in more artillery, more fighter planes, more napalm. This was a war requiring discriminate killing, a war of knife thrusts, not bombardment. Artillery was for fearful troops who wanted to kill from a convenient distance. But artillery didn't discriminate. Children died with infantrymen, closing hearts and minds.

Word also began filtering back to Saigon about the man's aura. He thrived on two hours sleep, went everywhere, took remarkable risks to prove his point. Each week he drove where no American drove, using the delta's perilous back roads to visit all his province chiefs. At night, he took his jeep out alone, grenades rattling loose around his feet, challenging the Viet Cong, playing his own high-stakes poker with them. The travels into the darkness were no more than showings of the flag, bluffs. But Vann was saying: *You do not control the night.* The talk about him became almost mystical. John Paul Vann was quickly becoming a legend.

Cornelius Mahoney Sheehan was about to become a young man trapped. Vietnam would weigh on him as it did none of the others. Of the early group he would become the bedeviled one—the poet, a man of haunts and torments. Even at twenty-five, when his mood swings allowed him to be carefree, happy-go-lucky, puckish at times, he seemed to have been created with ghosts and goblins in his genes, demons that had to be fought into submission, beaten back in bloody hand-to-hand emotional combat.

Maybe it was the Irish in him, for the brogue still rolled nicely off his tongue. But even at the beginning he was a difficult man to peg. With some he seemed rigidly intense for a man so young; with others, a cut-up and hilariously funny mimic. He could be painfully quiet. He could be as ferociously impassioned as an inquisitor. People saw what they wanted to see. The man who became his best friend, David Halberstam, saw him as ebullient, reveling in every moment of their grand adventure. The description flabbergasted the woman who later became his wife, the writer, Susan Black Sheehan: *Neil? Ebullient? You're kidding!*

He was a handsome man, even Hollywood handsome. Charley Mohr's wife, Norma, thought him the image of Robert Taylor, one of the day's heartthrobs. Standing almost six foot two, slender but not skinny, he carried himself pine-tree straight, his skin soft white, the slightly rounded edges of an outlasted baby face toughening up just right, adding command to his hazel eyes. His hair was dark and wavy, parted on the left and combed upward so that the waves crested in a style that had been modified only somewhat from what, in his teen days, was called a pompadour, not very stylish in a jungle where only crew cuts grew. Sheehan remained oblivious to all that, both the style clashes and the allure. But he quickly struck up a romance with a young and beautiful Vietnamese woman with the exotic nickname Blue Lotus, an upper-class *Saigonnaise* but a fast mover who dressed for moving fast. For two years her constant complaint was that Neil always worked, never played.

Blue Lotus was right about that. If Sheehan was anything, it was driven. He was also the most studious of the group, the most curious about the war's antecedents, not just about the French but back through centuries of Vietnamese history. If the Cold Warriors tried to pitch the war to him as an extension of Chinese Communism, one of their themes, he would argue that they were just plain wrong. In Asia, Communism had been around for only a few ticks of the clock. The Vietnamese had been fighting the expansive Chinese for a millennium. If need be, Sheehan said, they'd fight the

Chinese again with the same tenacity that they had fought the French.[2]

The probative part of Sheehan was an unexpected trait in a young hireling for a rambunctious wire service. To UPI, history was everything that had happened more than one twelve-hour news cycle ago, and of absolutely no worth. More in tune with his bosses' value system was the trait that irritated Blue Lotus: He worked endlessly.

He assaulted stories, often until he drove himself into a frenzy. Life became a series of fourteen-, fifteen-, sixteen-hour days, mixed not with an occasional day off but an occasional all-nighter. His temper would flare, his nerves fray. The constant sleep deprivation turned into sleeplessness and eventually into lifelong insomnia. He would suffer from compulsions, guilts, doubts, depressions, fears.

At the beginning, like all the young newcomers, he suffered from the Hemingway disease. War was great; war was grand. Get shot at; prove you're a man. The day after that first rousing briefing from Vann, Sheehan plodded through the mud of the delta with troops from the ARVN's 7th. He caught a rarity: a real dustup. Bullets flew and people, good guys and bad, fell. A deep, almost sensual thrill ran through him. "Some people got killed around me," he said. "Not too many dead. Small arms fire. The ARVN got scared. I looked at them and said to myself, 'Look how fearful they are.' I wasn't afraid."

Six months later the Hemingway disease disappeared abruptly and forever on a different battlefield. War lost all its glory for Sheehan then, just as it had for Homer Bigart twenty years earlier over Wilhelmshaven. In its place came the fear. Mildly at first and then awfully, a cloying, creepy fear of death, his death, that seemed to lurk in every jungle shadow. It was hardly unnatural to be afraid in war, but for Sheehan it became so powerful it would have become debilitating had he not possessed such extraordinary discipline. He had to beat it back every day, go through a ritual stiffening of himself every morning, or it would overwhelm and

2. Sheehan was proved right. After the American war, when the Chinese marched across their contested border into a presumably weakened Vietnam, the Vietnamese not only repulsed the invasion but humiliated the Communist giant by doing so with such ease.

paralyze him. The inner battles took a terrible toll. But he won them, even if, at times, the cost became enormous.

By fall Vann would be courting David Halberstam, making the cold but correct calculation that bartering with *The New York Times* offered greater rewards than trading with lowly UPI. Vann not only would get his message delivered with the morning papers, he would get it delivered in the newspaper of clout. Halberstam was a calculator, too, and with Vann's help he would ride the war to immediate fame.

Still, during the hot, wet summer before Halberstam's arrival, Sheehan was drawn repeatedly down Highway 4. He and Vann talked long and late, two men who did not need the night for sleep, Sheehan having no inkling how one day far in the future Vann would draw him in and suck up much of the rest of his life.

Long afterward, men still had trouble detaching from Vietnam, a war that not only took a nation's youth but its youthfulness too.

Battle-fatigued young soldiers marched into middle age in fraying jungle fatigues trimmed with both battle ribbons and peace symbols. . . .

Old generals, their once-chiseled and jut-jawed visages fading on yellowing *Time* magazine covers, battled to the grave for reputations gone in the only war America ever lost. . . .

Ghostly McNamaras, wraiths of men long detached from their power, wandered Washington's streets almost unnoticed. . . .

Journalists were no exception—shell shock, battle fatigue, delayed stress syndrome, call it what you like. The ailment is as common to war correspondents as soldiers. William Howard Russell, whom the British like to call the first war correspondent, came home from the Crimean War in 1856 flushed with fame, riches, and horrible nightmares. He terrified his wife by bolting out of bed in the middle of the night, crying: "Tumble out! Tumble out! There's a sortie!" As to being first, he dismissed himself as "the miserable parent of a luckless tribe." Ernie Pyle, who became famous as the Second World War's voice of the dogface soldier, hovered near a nervous breakdown before he was killed by a Japanese sniper. Vietnam's list would be long and littered with pain. But none would have more trouble freeing himself of the war than Sheehan. He would finally break out, long after many had given up on him, having forgotten about the determination.

The grit was there from the beginning. He may have arrived the youngest and least experienced, but he did not arrive a blank slate. He had grown from hard-scrabble soil, and already had fought battles against tough odds—including one with a ruthless opponent that took down the most formidable of fighters and almost took him down too. Angst-ridden poet he was, but his edges were chipped from flint. Sheehan had broken out of prisons before.

———

Holyoke, Massachusetts, was a working-class town, past its prime before it had one, ninety miles and a world west of Boston, a light year or two farther if you were a kid with a name like Cornelius Mahoney Sheehan. It was a place, like the Pennsylvania coal-mine towns in the John O'Hara novels of the day, that an ethnic kid got out of quick or got stuck in for good.

"I was talking to Stash Malek tonight," Sheehan's younger brother, Patrick, wrote him in Vietnam. "It was the first time I've seen him in about two years. He lives above Joe Chesty's. He has two kids now. He is working for O'Connell's oiling cranes. He wishes he had gone to school."

School was the ticket, all right, but it was a ticket not easy to come by.

The first of the American Sheehans, Neil's paternal grandfather, Patrick Joseph, arrived in Holyoke in 1901. He was a latecomer in the great Irish migration. Across town the refugees of the potato famine of the 1850s were a good two generations up on him, and, even on the home turf of the Daughters of the American Revolution, they seemed upscale indeed. Proper Bostonians called the rambunctiously successful early arrivals the Lace Curtain Irish, rarely in flattery. But to Patrick Joseph Sheehan the Holyoke bunch were the Whiskey Irish and he strove to catch up with them. A farmer, he brought to America part of the old sod and part of his homeland's soul too. Home had been Ireland's hard west coast where icy Atlantic winds whistled up Dingle Bay into County Kerry and through the starkness of his tiny village, Killorglin. It took all hands to eke out a living, and no nonsense would be tolerated about family responsibilities. Girls could tinker with frills like education, perhaps even go on to normal school and become teachers. Boys went to work. Early.

Old Man Sheehan scraped together enough to buy a small dairy farm on the outskirts of Holyoke, and, as his sons grew strong, he pulled them out of school to work the farm. Not one graduated from high school and Neil's father got the yank from ninth grade, where he had been the brightest boy in his class.

Neil, born during the depression, a kid during the Second World War, could see the same thing coming for him. It might have been so had he lacked the spunk that manifested itself so many times later in his life—and a strong-willed Irish mother who had no intention of keeping her boys down on the farm.

Neil's father had married a girl just off the boat, an O'Shea from Stradbally, also in County Kerry. Mary O'Shea would never forget that trip in steerage, the humiliation of it at age seventeen, and the vow she had made then that no children of hers would suffer such degradations. Her first view of America was not the immigrant's dream. She arrived on a Friday after Ellis Island had closed. The ship's owners found a way for the other passengers to leave the ship. But not those in steerage. They stayed aboard till the island reopened on Monday morning. It was a cruel deed keeping them down in that hole, Mary O'Shea told her eldest son, and he should be prepared for cruelties in life. But not the cruelties of the farm. Mary O'Shea hated it, hated the smell of the cow dung, the endless work seven days a week, 365 days a year, the money that never quite paid the bills. She gritted her teeth and swallowed her County Kerry pride every time she had to leave a wedding party early so Patrick could do the four o'clock milking. Don't be a farmer, she told her son; don't be a farmer like your father.

It was not easy to duck. At age eleven Neil was put to work on the farm at $1 a day, three hours after school and Saturday and Sunday as well. By the time he was thirteen he was running the dairy at $3 a day. It was good money for a kid, part of the bait, the same lure that kept the coal miner's son in the mines, the millwork-er's boy in the mill.

As a youngster Sheehan quickly learned that lifelong art of pry-ing extra hours out of his day. Even with his time squeezed to the hilt, he became something of a very young man about town. At age twelve he bought a set of drums and soon caught on with a band that played Polish polkas on Saturday nights in Holyoke's work-ing-man's bars. The job delivered up an occasional free beer to the underage drummer and brought in another $5 too. Already good-looking, he began wearing those high, black waves and speaking in a kind of Holyoke jive talk. You got the stack, Jack. It wings, it swings, it sings, Jack. To his younger brothers it was the height of sophistication. They still imitated him ten years later.

Meanwhile, at the farm, Neil took out some career insurance. He never learned how to milk a cow. It was a difficult avoidance handled artfully and deliberately. "I knew that if I learned how to milk the cows I was going to be a farmer like my father," he said later. "So I shoveled a lot of cow manure, but I carefully avoided learning how to milk."

The showdown came one year into high school, when he was fifteen. He wouldn't make it to college without a scholarship, but his grades were suffering. He looked around at the town's old-line WASP families sending their teenagers off to prep schools. Even the Whiskey Irish were doing it. He hunkered down and won a scholarship to a prep school, Mount Hermon, near the New Hampshire line. The Sheehan house was the scene that night of a good, old-fashioned Irish family donnybrook. It was a terrible fight. His father was furious. How could his son do such a damn-fool, blockheaded thing? But Mary O'Shea Sheehan stood by him resolutely. "The boy is going," she said. He went. At Mount Hermon the grades turned up and, after two years, so did his ticket to anywhere —a scholarship to Harvard, which made his hardworking father as proud as he had been angry.

Suddenly, the Irish dairy farmer's son was surrounded by wealth, privilege, and the sons of the ruling class being groomed to take over the job themselves. The Aga Khan was there. So was Jay Rockefeller. But, even at seventeen, he had a sense of himself and a lack of awe or envy. The *Advocate*, Harvard's literary magazine, drew a rich crowd—Whitney Ellsworth, who became publisher of *The New York Review of Books*, a Long Island Bingham, others. It also drew the Irish poet in Neil Sheehan, and the flush crowd at the *Advocate* became his best Harvard friends.

Once, long afterward, Sheehan took Susan to Holyoke and showed her the not-so-scenic sights. He pointed to a highway cloverleaf and said, "See, I worked on that." She asked if it bothered him that he had to work summer construction jobs while his pals did the casinos in Cuba, galavanted at Europe's chic hideaways, or partied the months away at beachside family mansions. Sheehan looked at her as if the thought had never occurred to him. "Whitney was Whitney Ellsworth and I was Neil Sheehan," he said.

They partied heavily at Harvard too. With a couple of drinks the young Irishman from the sticks became a riot, his brogue growing so thick it seemed he had emerged in their midst straight from the rutted roads of Killorglin. With a few more, he became an Irish terror. His friends took to calling him Gogarty Sheehan after Oliver St. John Gogarty, an Irish poet he loved. Gogarty was also the model James Joyce used for the hard-drinking, carousing medical student in *Ulysses*. The new Gogarty's antics became part of Harvard lore.

One night his pals put him to bed of great necessity only to have him leap up moments later, throw on a raincoat and tennis shoes —but nothing else—and race out for a hamburger.

Another episode became more notorious. After an unusually wet celebration by the *Advocate* staff, young Neil stretched out for the night on the second-floor boardroom table, only to be awakened by the sound of students protesting a local election in the street below. He ran to the window in his underwear to root them on, then threw a typewriter through the glass with a thunderous roar of support. He woke on the table the next morning threatened with dismissal for inciting a riot he couldn't remember. The campus incident became the buzz of Boston and even made *Time* magazine, which intoned about the dangers of student unrest. The year was 1956, almost a decade before Vietnam made the campus escapades of the fifties look like fraternity follies. But it was a close call for Sheehan. He survived, and went on to graduate *cum laude* two years later. But he also took with him out of Harvard the makings of a curse.

Sheehan had no idea what to do with his life. Newspapers didn't interest him—"those scribblers," as he and his collegiate literati at the *Advocate* had put down the fire-engine chasers at the college newspaper, *The Crimson*. He joined the army, stunning the Harvard crowd, and took a full three-year hitch. In return, the army promised to teach him Arabic and assigned him to the U.S. Army Security Agency, an electronic eavesdropping outfit requiring top-secret clearance. With the Harvard episodes and an overnight stay in a Boston jail on his record, he barely cleared. Then, at the army language school in Monterey, California, he was arrested for public drunkenness. The city fined him $25. The army dealt with him more harshly. His clearance was pulled, his Arabic program scuttled. The *cum laude* Harvard man was recycled as a lowly pay clerk and banished to the cold, desolate hills up against the demilitarized zone between North and South Korea. It was an awful job in a dreadful place, like doing an unhappy God's penance for leaving the farm. He had almost three years to go.

Sheehan soon ditched the clerk's job and cast his lot with the scribblers, anything looking better than a pay clerk's dreary toiling. He joined the division newspaper, the *Bayonet*. It proved to be Neil Sheehan's second luckiest move. But nothing seemed able to dig him all the way out. He was miserable.

A kid from the Bronx named Bernie Weinraub became a buddy. He found Sheehan the most witty, intellectually challenging, wonderfully argumentative, full-of-life-Irish, perplexing, and troubled guy he had met in the army. It dumbfounded Weinraub,[3] who went to City College of New York, that a Harvard honors graduate had joined the army for three years and ended up in the same godforsaken place as he. But whenever he probed the sore spot, Sheehan stiffed him. The army had screwed him, he replied, and would say no more, as if to elaborate would be to admit that he had screwed himself worse.

Weinraub knew Korea was hell for Sheehan. But during the day there was no moping. They worked zestfully, filling the voids with thrusts of good-humored political give and take.

"You're a classic New York Jewish lib," Sheehan put down Weinraub's arguments, adding a jab about the "hypocrisy of the liberals."

"And you're a classic, mackerel-snapping Irish right-winger," Weinraub fired back.

So he seemed to be, Sheehan's early politics landing somewhere near the old-line Republican conservatism of Robert Taft.

But Weinraub could never be quite sure. Sheehan delivered his arguments with a reflectiveness unusual in the conservatives he

3. Weinraub went on to join *The New York Times* and build his own solid career.

had known. He also delivered them with a grin and a wink, like a good Irish pol covering his flank.

It was the nights that turned awful. Night after freezing night Sheehan walked to the enlisted men's club and drank relentlessly until closing time. At 1 A.M. he weaved back into the ice-cold barracks, always with the same loud and mournful, wake-the-dead moan: "Mother of God, Mother of God."

It was clear to Weinraub and clear to others, too, that Sheehan, at age twenty-three, had a dangerously serious drinking problem. The unit's top sergeant, the first of two wise sergeants who interceded in Sheehan's life, thought a transfer to Tokyo might help. Weinraub visited him a few months later and he was a changed man—dry, happy, working for *Stars and Stripes*, wearing civilian clothes. He had become a carefree man-about-town, discovering all the best hideaways and meeting all the right people.

He came down to his last months in the army before he slipped again, this time worse than ever. The drinking had escalated in college, then again in Korea. Now it came in wild, blackout binges. Ray Herndon, a young Texan, came to *Stars and Stripes* about that time. He drew the barracks room next to Sheehan and they became friends. He sometimes became his keeper. On his binges Sheehan had taken to drinking saki from massive, two-and-a-half liter bottles. He'd disappear with the stuff and Herndon would go out on rescue missions down tiny back streets, into strange Tokyo neighborhoods, eventually finding him sprawled, out cold, the empty bottle nearby. Herndon hauled him home to sober him up for the day's work. He didn't always succeed.

One bad morning Sheehan came in and a sergeant, who was a typesetter, said: "You're drunk again. The colonel's going to fire you. He's going to ship your ass back to Korea."

"I can't help it," Sheehan blurted out. "I'm an alcoholic."

Thirty years later Sheehan has no idea why he said it. He had never said it before, not even to himself. It wasn't in his lexicon. This was long before the day of celebrity tell-alls. Alcoholism was the rare word, drunk the common one. He had some vague family history with the problem, a drunk uncle, a lost brother of his grandfather. He had watched a friend of his father's die a horrible jaundiced death from cirrhosis of the liver. But in Holyoke there were no alcoholics. There were drunks, suffering from the Irish curse. And they were old drunks, not vital, virile young men. Young men were impervious, immortal. In Holyoke the survivors wept and made bad Irish jokes. Why did God invent booze? So the Irish wouldn't rule the earth.

"Do you want to do something about it?" the sergeant asked.

"Yes," he replied.

"Then go home and sleep. Don't have another drink. I'll fix it with the colonel and I'll be by to pick you up tonight."

That night he stood in front of a group of strangers, who included the sergeant, a general's wife, and a senior American diplomat passing through from Washington. "I'm Neil," he said. "I'm an alcoholic."

Sheehan never touched a drop of alcohol again. "You see a bottle of Dewar's scotch," he says. "I see a bottle with a skull and crossbones on it."

He stayed in the Alcoholics Anonymous group until UPI shipped him to Saigon, which had the need but not the group. So he continued to practice the rituals on his own, including the prayer each night asking for one more day. But Sheehan, who would now go on to conquer so much more in life, took no risks with this one. In the French restaurants that all the young correspondents loved, he had his buddies taste-check the soups and sauces for wines before he would indulge.

———

As Sheehan arrived on the scene in 1962, his colleagues did not see him as a man of terrible battles already won, terrible battles yet to fight. He was the kid, so young, so fresh, so brash, so Irish.

Charley Mohr remembered a scene, and always loved it. At the press conference for McNamara during his first visit to Vietnam, Sheehan had been in the country only three weeks. He had sat quietly while old Homer Bigart dominated the questioning and McNamara had started down his fatal road of endless optimism.

Sheehan had been awestruck by the man but astonished by his words. How could McNamara express such confidence when he had been in Vietnam only two days? How could he say it when the Americans had been there only six months?

When McNamara started to leave, Sheehan could control himself no longer. He bolted out the door behind him, catching him as he was entering his waiting car. Quickly, and wonderfully naively, he promised the powerful cabinet officer the protection of speaking off the record.

"Mr. Secretary, how can you be so optimistic when you've been here such a short time?"

McNamara's eyes, gleaming like lasers through those tight, rimless lenses, locked on the intrusive young reporter.

"Every quantitative measure we have shows that we're winning this war," he said.

Then McNamara settled back into his seat, a marine guard slammed the car door, and the secretary of defense raced away, past the little shops with joss sticks in the windows, past the low bougainvillea-draped villas of the bourgeoisie, past the endless slums of shanty hooches on stilts, off toward the airport and the comfort of home, half a world away.

The next time McNamara came to Saigon, Cornelius Mahoney Sheehan stood among a knot of correspondents on the tarmac. When McNamara burst out of the plane brimming with all that boundless certainty, Sheehan turned to his buddies and said in a perfect stage-whisper mimic of Charlie Chan:

"Ahh, so, another foolish Westerner come to lose reputation to Ho Chi Minh."

5

WE BAND OF BROTHERS

Until Project Beef-Up, most of the news from Southeast Asia had come out of neighboring Laos, a little landlocked kingdom in which warring princes jousted for control of a people who liked to fight but not kill. This was a concept puzzling to the world powers jockeying for control of the region and frustrating to correspondents whose editors had sent them in to find the bang-bang.

Kennedy's Cold War strategists shook their heads despairingly when the warring factions halted one battle to attend a water festival together. Ray Herndon, who, like Sheehan, joined UPI in early 1962, found himself running the bureau in Vientiane a week after he signed on in Tokyo. Rascally and rambunctious, he had the time of his life. But he doubted that any reporter sent there for the "crisis" that spring saw a battle outside a bar, despite occasional colorful accounts to the contrary. Still, the story moved briefly from Vietnam across the ill-defined border to Laos, and an odd interlude it became.

Like Vietnam, Laos had been governed by France until 1954. But where the French exploited Vietnam commercially and trained a Vietnamese bourgeoisie to run the exploitation for them, they treated Laos with languid neglect. In 1962 it remained an extraordinarily isolated and backward land of deep forests and forbidding mountains, a place locked in by its neighbors—China, Burma, Thailand, Cambodia, and the two Vietnams—like a tiny piece of a jigsaw puzzle. The Land of the Million Elephants, Laos was called,

102

and, if so, that gave it one elephant for every two people. The Westerners drawn there gave it still other names, invariably taken from the fantasylands of their youth. Never-Never Land, they called it, and The Land of Oz.

The local cast of characters fit the fantasyland names. First came the warring princes, who appeared in public beneath white parasols and dressed in pantaloons of golden silk bolts that wound around and between their legs, then were tucked in at the waist to give them the slightly bowlegged look of tiny men wearing expensive diapers. Souvanna Phouma led the centrist faction, making him anticolonialist and vaguely anti-American, which left him with no Cold War base. Souvanna's half-brother, Souphanouvong, headed the leftist Pathet Lao, making him known as the Red Prince and giving him the Soviets, Chinese, and North Vietnamese, which kept him forever looking over his shoulder. The third prince, Buon Oum, loved pleasure to a degree impressive even by Laotian standards and delegated his authority to Phoumi Nosavan, an evil-looking general who led the rightists, making him pro-American and heavy into opium. Filling out the picture were various other princelings of obscure lineage, mountain warlords who vied to corner the opium trade, and a changing lineup of rebel military officers like the five-foot-one-inch paratrooper captain, Kong Le, a favorite of some Americans until he began shifting his forces from faction to faction with all the speed to be expected of an officer in the airborne.

It is safe to say that never was the Cold War waged in a more unlikely setting. That, of course, deterred the Cold Warriors not one whit.

In the dusty streets of the capital, Vientiane, lanky pilots from Air America, outfitted in the barely clandestine CIA airline's gray uniforms and swashbuckling Australian bush hats, brushed shoulders with beefy KGB operatives improbably posed as cultural attachés. Mao Zedong's agents took in the wash along with other chits behind the sun-bleached wooden storefronts of Chinese laundries baking under hot tin roofs. Tough little spooks from Ho Chi Minh's North Vietnam eyed their old colonialist bosses in Charles de Gaulle's Deuxième Bureau with a wonderfully irritating air of new-found superiority. The Brits and the Poles offered other outlets, and swarthy Corsicans stayed on to grow rich as the middlemen for all the needs of this brief Laotian moment in the Cold War sun —the girls, the boys, the connections, the information, the greased route to a bureaucrat who required a bribe. And, of course, the opium. The country's only cash crop littered the streets in bales large enough to sit on, brought in from the mountainous Laotian corner of the Golden Triangle by those jaunty men from Air America. "Just hauling rice," the pilots drawled. But everyone except the far-off American public knew that the fruit of the poppy was CIA wampum, used to buy guns for the right warlords or the right warlords for the guns.

The dusty main drag of Vientiane could have been Main Street in old Dodge City had it not been for the Harleys and the rickshaws parked where the horses would have been tethered. Or the single traffic light, installed earlier that year. Herndon had gone to the ceremony—progress comes to Laos. The honorary first driver became so entranced by the technology that he ran down a pedestrian. For months Laotians came from miles around to see the new attraction, stopping for several light changes and then moving on through, usually on red. The government finally brought in a policeman to direct traffic beneath it.

It was in this place that the crème de la crème of America's Asian press corps converged briefly in late spring for one last diversion —the Laotian crisis of 1962—before returning once and for all to the more serious business of Vietnam.

In 1961, before Project Beef-Up, Laos occupied most of America's concern in Southeast Asia. Dwight Eisenhower had warned his successor that the trouble would come from there, not Vietnam, and Kennedy had continued the warnings to the American public.

At the time, the so-called domino theory commanded the operative wisdom about the region's fate. Conceived by Eisenhower, the theory gained its catchy name, and, with it, inviolate force, from Joseph Alsop. The idea was simple if not simplistic: Let one of the little Southeast Asian countries fall to Communism and the others would topple next, one after the other, like a string of dominoes. Kennedy believed it, and said so. But Laos frightened him. How could modern armies maneuver in those rugged mountains? How could supply lines be secured with no coastal ports? When he chose to stop the tumbling dominoes in neighboring South Vietnam instead, he also tried to establish a neutral Laos.

In the spring of 1962, when the warring princes agreed to a coalition government, he seemed about to pull it off. Then, in a series of last-minute attacks, the Red Prince and his Pathet Lao nearly unhinged everything. In May, Kennedy moved boldly, flying 3,000 marines to Thailand's northern outpost of Udorn, just thirty-five miles from Vientiane.

With combat-ready U.S. troops on the doorstep, the press stormed the dusty capital with the kind of force yet to be seen in Vietnam. All the big names arrived at once—Beech and Kalischer from Tokyo, Alsop for the usual saber-rattling from Washington, an entourage from Hong Kong that included Charley Mohr, the only one who would find more than he expected in the Land of the Million Elephants. Suddenly, Vientiane swarmed with a motley crew of solid pros, eager new itinerants like AP's Peter Arnett and Horst Faas, ordered to pause there en route to Vietnam, and the usual group of wandering hopefuls and adventure-seekers who trekked endlessly through Southeast Asia.

Pamela Sanders, a young and lost soul in search of excitement and the press credentials to deliver it, vagabonded into town in the middle of the crisis. A strikingly beautiful but bored daughter of expatriate privilege in Manila, Sanders quickly found the hotel favored by the correspondents—four shabby stories of cracking stucco called the Constellation and run by a man everyone needed to know, Maurice Cavellerie. Comfortably astride two worlds—his father was Corsican, his mother Tibetan—Cavellerie had his hand in every deal in town. More important, he gave virtually unlimited credit to any news hack who entered his run-down hostelry, a business disaster but a public-relations success. Sanders walked into an open-air lobby where two British correspondents sat at a rickety table decorated with a beer-bottle centerpiece flying a flag of sticky flypaper black with dead prisoners. A barefoot waiter served them whiskys with soda. On an otherwise stark wall, curious brown lizards peek-a-booed out of the jammed hotel's mail slots, which carried labels:

New York Times, Asahi Shimbun, Time-Life, Daily Express, Tass, Stars and Stripes, Hsin Hua, Associated Press, Agence France-Presse, Tanjug, Christian Science Monitor, La Stampa, Komsomolskaya Pravda, U.S. News & World Report, Daily Worker . . .

Sanders was enthralled. She was also somewhat overwhelmed:

How could a place as obscure and forlorn as this draw such an elaborate and exotic cross section of the world's press?

Peter Arnett was a man born to action, on duty or off, and now he was out of sorts.

Arnett's experience in Laos in May and June 1962 reinforced an old journalistic saw: His business thrived on crashes, not safe landings. The problem with John Kennedy's ploy with the marines was that it had worked. The Pathet Lao had temporarily stopped their nibbling. That made for good diplomacy but humdrum journalism, reducing Arnett's life to regular runs across the muddy Mekong to the makeshift marine base at Udorn. From there, AP expected a steady feed of hometowners, those yawners in which Lance Corporal Fenwick assured Mr. and Mrs. Fenwick and all the folks back home that the chow was fine and the flag worth defending, even in Udorn. It was a weak follow-up to his first visit to Laos when, during an uprising that closed down his communications, young Arnett clamped his story between his teeth, dived into the Mekong, and swam his scoop across the river.

No one showed more talent for filling downtime than Peter Arnett. He lived, as Faas put it, "a life full of salsa," thriving on adventure, good whisky, Asian art, and the world's women, not necessarily in that order.

But the Laotian story had quickly turned into a dull dud. He had grown weary of the princes and their shadow battles. He had frittered away enough time at the local dice game, Cameroon, and put in enough all-nighters at the Green Latrine, the dive given its garish name for reasons apparent to anyone who passed through its doors. Arnett had even begun to develop a deaf ear to the rustle of Laotian sarongs. For him, that was *true* boredom. He was that eager to get on with it in Vietnam.

By the time he reached Vientiane, Arnett was twenty-seven years old and had ten years of itinerant newspapering behind him. But he still seemed the rookie, still seemed what he always would be: a dukes-up kid from the wrong side of the tracks on the wrong side of the world who would take on anybody and challenge anything, including the odds. Born in a tiny whaling station on the southernmost point of New Zealand, Arnett began life with nothing below him but Antarctica, descended through several generations from one of the first English whalers and a native Maori princess. He grew up restless, joined the New Zealand army at seventeen, just missing Korea, and then broke his mother's heart by skipping university to enter the wasteland of his local newspaper's city room. But to young Arnett it was a wasteland with a passport.

A natural vagabond, he shipped out on a tramp steamer to Sydney before he turned twenty. Two years later he landed in Bangkok at a time when Southeast Asia coursed with opium smugglers, pirates, revolutionaries, and obscure little wars. It was everything he had dreamed. "I was the wide-eyed innocent," he said. "I was Kipling's Kim, watching out on the world." When he ran out of money, which was soon, he walked into the *Bangkok World* and asked for a job. "Can you type?" inquired a tired American. When he said he could, the man's face brightened. "Good," he said. "You can have mine."

In 1959 Arnett first ventured to Vientiane, where he scruffed a few bucks as a wire-service stringer and edited a small newspaper fated for neither greatness nor longevity. In fact, the paper didn't survive its first government upheaval, the new regime closing it down and sending its editor packing not long after his swimming episode. But the expulsion launched Arnett, gaining him his first journalistic badge and a job with Associated Press, which sent him to Indonesia. In the spring of 1962, he got tossed out of there, too, freeing him for Laos and then Vietnam, his résumé embellished by expulsions from two countries.

Legends glued themselves early to Arnett. Some swear his escapades inspired *The Year of Living Dangerously*, the Australian adventure film about a daredevil correspondent in revolution-torn Indonesia. One early story about Arnett, both true and cherished by his colleagues, comes from his first brief Laotian tour. Arnett had spent a long, hard night at the Green Latrine with Cavellerie and woke the next day to discover that he had slept through the best story of the year, an escape by the Red Prince from the government pokey. He also discovered a bit of luck: Vientiane had been so quiet that he was the only reporter left in town.

Arnett blithely telegraphed stories to all three competing wire services. Because he wanted a job with AP, he filed with them first, sending off a very late but top priority "Bulletin" paragraph. Next he sent two paragraphs to Reuters with the lesser priority, "Urgent." Then he sent off a regular dispatch to UPI, and headed back to the Green Latrine. Two days later the congratulatory messages returned:

From AP:

THANKS STOP YOU 15 MINUTES AHEAD ON SOUPY ESCAPE

From Reuters:

LAGGED ON INITIAL BREAK BUT AMPLY MADE UP IN DETAIL

From UPI:

THANKS FOR HELP IN CRISIS

Checks from each followed.

Arnett stretched just past five foot six with a lift from his combat boots, weighed 140 soaking wet from a monsoon rain. But his face wore the roguish look of a pug. A high, battering-ram forehead loomed over a nose permanently relocated in a teenage boxing match. A broad chin, set in a permanent jut, anchored the image in bedrock. He looked like "an Anglo-Saxon Belmondo," one of his buddies said, likening him to the rugged French movie hero of the time.

Loud, boisterous, and always laughing—sometimes at inappropriate moments—his pals loved him. He was also as tough as he looked. In the real year of living dangerously just ahead no one would fall into more street brawls with Brother Nhu's secret police. He also showed no qualms about taking his short fuse into more distinguished quarters. A group of astonished diplomats once had to pull him off Joe Alsop at an embassy dinner after Arnett took the columnist's prattlings personally.

In Vietnam the Arnett legends mounted. He stayed longer, took more chances, and wrote more words read by more people than any war correspondent in any war in history. He drove governments to more than their normal quota of irrationalities. Diem's people beat him. Lyndon Johnson tried to have him removed as a "dangerous foreigner" and "Communist sympathizer." He was not one to cover real battles out of a Saigon bar. He went looking and became one of the war's great combat correspondents, strapping a Mauser submachine pistol to his side as he forged deep into the wilds to battles the generals would never see. Over the years, in his hyperactive wire-service rush to judgment, he made mistakes. Once he caused a terrific flap with a flash story about a possible violation of the international ban on gas warfare, only to gradually tap the story back over the next hours to a nonstory about tear gas. But he also ground out the daily report of a war that ran forever in circles, occasionally writing the piece that captured the very essence of its pathos and pointlessness. It was Arnett who quoted a U.S. Army major uttering one of the war's most memorable lines: "It was necessary to destroy the village in order to save it." As the war wound on and on, hundreds of American reporters paraded through, a mandatory step on a career path that eventually led them back home to become their generation's anchors and commentators, editors and columnists. Ticket punching, the Vietnam year came to be called. But Arnett stayed on and on. "I had no ticket to punch," he said. And perhaps he didn't. He seemed perfectly cast for a war without heroes. "If you had to invent a reporter for the Vietnam War," David Halberstam said, "you would have invented Peter."

He stayed even beyond the end in 1975, rejecting the last helicopters off the roof of the American Embassy, taking his chances with the approaching North Vietnamese so that he could finish what had become his story. When an AP editor in New York ordered him to leave, he told the editor to go screw himself. A few hours later, when the first North Vietnamese regulars marched into the AP office, he offered them warm Cokes and cookies, then went on punching out the story on his battered old portable.

Arnett's last dispatch that day captured the wreckage of lives and fool's-gold policies inside the ransacked embassy. Almost thirteen years had passed since he had first come to Vietnam and the battered building struck him as a symbol of power's frail underpinnings. A bronze plaque honoring five U.S. Marines who had died defending the building during the Tet Offensive in 1968 lay, names down, amid the rubble. Safes were broken open. Overturned file cabinets spilled documents marked in red: SECRET. Rolls of now-worthless Bank of America payroll checks were scattered about, unraveled like toilet tissue by the looters.

On the roof, about fifty desperate South Vietnamese, having tied their fates to the Americans for a generation, still huddled around the helicopter pad, waiting for choppers that would never come. Arnett tried to reach them. But tear gas flooded the building, driving him back down the stairs. It was there that his story abruptly ended. Someone had finally pulled the plug.

———

Horst Faas hoisted himself back aboard the Air America Beechcraft on a hot day in June, taking the seat next to the pilot after yielding the backseats to two young agents. It had not taken Faas long to see through Air America's Laotian cover story. Hauling rice indeed.

The pilot, more at home in the CIA airline's stripped-down C-123 cargo planes, revved the engine and swung the four-seater around, pointing it down a short, dirt runway. In his forties, and already heavily weathered, he ignored Faas.

In the back the two youthful spooks, brown and lean, their hair close-cropped, their attitudes full of the bushy-tailed eagerness that seemed to infect all young Americans during the Kennedy years, had suppressed grins as they watched the photographer climb aboard. Faas was a sight—a big man, 220 pounds, with arms like German sausages and a gut that bulged proudly from good living. He wore two 35-millimeter German Leicas around his neck. A third, with a barrel lens, hung from his left shoulder like a machine gun. Film packets bulged from his clothes wherever he didn't. Just turned twenty-nine, Faas still wore his poundage like baby fat, giving him the look of a young German burgher. The agents, a year or two younger, kept in sinewy trim with marine-style, hand-clap push-ups. Faas looked as if he trained by arm-wrestling pâté. He lived for the next meal, a gourmand who somehow found Beaujolais in cans to take on his forays deep into the jungle. But, aboard the CIA plane, the smiles *were* suppressed. Faas had pulled himself aboard with light-footed ease. And, in the field in this remote part of Laos, he had outwalked them all.

Once again, however, he had found nothing. This was not good for a combat photographer. He had arrived from Algeria, where the bodies were strewn in the streets. A few months earlier it had been the Congo. Not hard to find action there. But in this place, Faas, like other newsmen sent in during the lull, could find nothing. Five weeks in Laos and he had not taken a combat photo, not even found a sign of war's destruction.

Today had been typical. Washington had announced, and the stateside newspapers had dutifully reported, a skirmish at a "strategic stronghold" up the Mekong. Faas and the agents had gone searching and found a sleepy trading post run by an old Chinese, some fully intact mud huts, a few dozen Lao farmers and their oxen working flooded fields. If there had been a battle, it had been the most polite one Faas had ever seen. The German photographer could be a literalist and he wondered: Who reported these ghostly events? Not the CIA. Laos crawled with American agents. The spooks were as mystified as the correspondents.

The plane bumped down the primitive strip, and climbed away from the mud huts and the river, turning back toward Vientiane. The pilot, also a CIA employee, continued to stare ahead stonily. The younger men spoke freely, joking, asking Faas about Algeria and the Congo, exchanging bits of information. But the pilot's silence bordered on hostility.

Faas understood. Almost two decades had passed since the Second World War, but the bitterness had not. Like Faas, the men in back had been kids and had memories. The pilot had been a young man, almost surely a soldier. He had hatreds. The bad blood from the big war lingered long, flashing periodically. With his guttural accent, his name and looks, his attraction to combat, and the natural bullying ways of a photographer, Faas became easily typecast, sometimes unfairly. He spent most of his life after Vietnam denying that he had ever uttered the words that followed him everywhere, making such good copy: "Vot I like iss boom-boom. Oh, yes."

Still, being proud, stubborn, Germanic to the core, Faas did little else to disabuse anyone of the stereotype. If anything, he stuck his chin out: "I was very grown up in 1945 and ended in the Hitler Youth, a junior military man, *ja?*" He rarely added that he was eleven years old at the war's end and had been bombed out of every childhood home, including one in Poland just twenty-five miles from Auschwitz. Only through luck did he avoid being thrown into Berlin's final defense when the mad Führer sent children into the line against hardened Allied troops. In the turmoil of postwar Europe he scrambled to find work as a freelance photographer, caught on with AP in Bonn when he was twenty-three, and left for the Congo five years later.

Like most war photographers, he shot everything he saw, including scenes far too awful for the sensitivities of American newspaper readers. As he became Vietnam's premier combat photographer, pushing deeper and deeper into the jungles, closer and perilously closer to the war's dark heart, the collection of unprintables became more ghoulish. The most memorable showed a famous American general's son, also an officer, playing "soccer" with the severed heads of Viet Cong prisoners. The army turned itself inside out, sending generals to plead with him to suppress the photos. Their efforts were pointless. The Associated Press never had any intention of printing them.

His buddies bought none of the war-lover imagery. Early on, they learned that Faas fanatically minimized risks. He gave combat units closer inspections than most commanding officers and, if he didn't like what he saw, he didn't go out with them. His stock in trade was trouble. But when it arrived, he wanted to be surrounded by the best. He had no interest in dying.

One day a few months hence Faas would baffle Halberstam by refusing to leave Saigon. Halberstam thought Faas fearless and he chided him until the German finally wagged a disapproving finger and said: "Ach, Dave! I don't get myself killed on a day when I can't get my pictures in the paper." Then Halberstam understood: The outside world was consumed that week with the Cuban missile crisis, making any risk in Vietnam pointless. They drank beer.

Faas inevitably found his share of trouble anyway. In December of 1967, Faas would be seriously wounded, the barrel telescopic lens of his Leica deflecting a shrapnel burst from his vitals, his *very* vitals: "I looked down and a big gush of blood was coming out of that area and I thought, 'Oh, my God, the jewels are gone.' " Instead, the lens had deflected the shrapnel into his leg. He almost lost it, and almost lost his life when the doctors went along with his pleadings not to amputate. But his closest call had already come in the Congo, where Katanganese rebels captured him. Hearing his accent, the Katanganese thought he was a Belgian from whose colonial rule they had just broken away. Faas talked his way out of a slow and painful death but not till after the Katanganese forced him to endure many indignities, one of the lesser being to eat his press pass.

In Vietnam Faas and Halberstam would become Saigon's odd couple, continually perplexing some of the old guard—the German and the Jew, living together in a grand villa only a *New York Times* expense account could afford, Faas, oblivious to politics, hating the intrigues of Saigon, plunging deeper and deeper into the jungles toward the war's core; Halberstam, as political as they come, ambitious, too, a man with his own agenda who always played to the footlights. . . .

Now, the little Beechcraft descended toward Vientiane. The pretentious old French villas looked enduring from his perch in the clouds. But on the ground they were crumbling, powerful jungle vines strangling them as the tropical forests methodically took back what had always been theirs. This place was history, not news, and no one knew the difference better than a good combat photographer.

—

The strange little interlude in Laos ended without incident on July 23, 1962, two months after it started, when the two princes and the general sat in the cross-legged lotus style beneath a huge statue of Buddha, shaved-head bonzes chanting in the background as the leaders made promises they had no intention of keeping. But for most of the press it had ended long before, the big names, the Beeches and the Alsops, moving on early to find more rewarding Asian datelines. Diplomatic safe landings were *not* their stock in trade. Even the journeymen, Arnett and Faas, headed for Vietnam a month before the ceremony.

The departure of the heavy hitters produced a bonanza for Pam Sanders. In an era when journalism's male caste system reigned virtually supreme, especially in the macho world of foreign correspondence, Sanders had arrived, hitchhiking, flat broke, and carrying less than commanding credentials—a letter from a Manila newspaper for whom she had written occasional columns. But, with the pros gone, she quickly lined up stringing jobs with *The*

113

New York Times, London's *Daily Express,* and, the most lucrative catch of all, Time-Life.

Given her gender and her looks, the winks and jokes about war and its camp followers flowed freely. But vagabonds, adventurers, wanderers, and drifters of all sorts found quick, if not enriching, piecework in the backwaters of Southeast Asia.

As the war grew in Vietnam, the opportunities would mount and, later, in the sixties, the odd mix of top-of-the-line correspondents and unknown, often eccentric floaters added to the craziness of the war and the controversy about the press. Youngsters showed up with credentials from their school newspapers and quickly found themselves hedge-hopping around the country in military aircraft courtesy of the U.S. government. Everyone seemed to have a favorite, top-this-one tale: the French correspondent, dressed in business suit, tie, and expensive dress shoes, who stepped off a helicopter into the middle of a blazing firefight; the Brit who showed up among camouflaged troopers carrying a plaid suitcase and bowler.

Some of the drifters went on to celebrity of sorts, the sixties counterculture finding antiheroes among a group of literally high-flying photographers who saw and painted the war through a psychedelic haze of mind-bending drugs. They often showed up simply to "make the scene," barely knowing how to point a camera. Tim Page, a young Brit who became a legend for his hallucinogenic trips and foolhardy daring as well as his superb photographs, arrived in Saigon after walking across Asia. The news agency that gave him his first job needed to show him how to load a camera before sending him out. UPI displayed the wisdom of handing Dana Stone a loaded 35-millimeter before his first assignment. But, in combat, Stone needed a colleague to show him how to unload it. Stone's buddy, Sean Flynn, spent most of his time playing out in real life the Hollywood derring-do of his swashbuckling father, Errol Flynn. Flynn had death wish written all over him and, in that, he finally succeeded. He and Stone disappeared without a trace in the chaos of the foolhardy 1970 invasion of neighboring Cambodia.

This all came much later and Sanders at least had some credentials, better than those of many men who got the jobs. But she quickly fueled the murmurings. Along with Time-Life, she also landed Charley Mohr.

Marriages can become the second casualty of war, succumbing almost as quickly as the truth. Sustained relationships and journalism are a contrary mix. Reporters covering wars, political campaigns, even baseball, disappear for months into intense and surreal worlds virtually impenetrable to outsiders, then emerge unable to adjust to the quieter pleasures of normal life.

Even so, l'affaire Vientiane blossomed with such sudden and half-comic flamboyance it seemed possible only in the Laotian land of make-believe. Amid the barefoot waiters and flypaper flags of the romantically ramshackle Hotel Constellation, Time's sophisticated ace correspondent fell, moonstruck, smitten totally like a bedazzled teenager.

Trained in the grand tradition of Henry Luce, Charley Mohr did nothing in a small way. Not only did he immediately declare his undying love but also his plans to marry. Not only did he announce this to Sanders, but also to his wife, whom he had just ensconced with their two children in a borrowed house in Hong Kong, and to his employers in New York. As if to stress how serious he was, he asked Time to move him, along with Sanders, off to that other love, Nairobi, a request that sped the titillating news throughout the Lucian empire. Then he moved out of the borrowed Hong Kong house and into the crown colony's legendary Foreign Correspondents' Club, further telegraphing the gossip throughout the Far East.

It was difficult to say who was more surprised, Sanders or Norma Mohr. In the wonderful romantic rush of it all, and as proof of its nobility, Charley had yet to consummate the love. The affair was real enough, but it floated on gossamer—all hand-holding, surreptitious smooches, and fairy-tale adventures in a land of little princes in silk pantaloons.

The gossip spread so far and wide that almost everyone in the tight little community of Asia-watching assumed that the romance continued through the coming year of living dangerously, with Charley side-slipping regularly to Vientiane and Pam stealing into Saigon. The trips were made, but the romance didn't travel. Norma Mohr was a shrewd woman, full of hard-headed determination. Her response was ingenious. If you're going to destroy our marriage, she told Mohr, for God's sake go back to Laos and sleep with the girl first. Which Charley did. The gossamer turned brittle, the fairy tales freighted up with guilt. It was back to the real world.[1]

For Sanders, still working for *Time,* the affair continued to cause fluttery moments. Not long after it ended, the newsmagazine's powerful chief of correspondents, Richard Clurman, visited Vientiane on a tour of his far-flung outposts. Like all of *Time's* top executives, Clurman traveled like a potentate. Some thought he set standards for extravagance topped only by Luce himself. Clurman jetted about his domain, which was the world, with two first-class seats—one for himself and one for his briefcase. The briefcase story would seem almost certainly apocryphal until Clurman is asked about it. He flew with two seats, one bought by Luce, one gladly donated by the airline. He also had a rueful sense of the extraordinary amount of money *Time* lavished on its enterprise. Once, chewing out an incompetent correspondent he couldn't bring himself to fire, he got off a classic line about *Time's* affluence. "You," he said, "are the kind of luxury only *Time* magazine can afford."

Clurman was a worldly man and one of inherently good intentions.[2] Pam Sanders had nothing to worry about from him. Still, she flitted nervously all over Vientiane setting up meetings, including a sitting with one of the princes. When a royal aide inquired just how important this man was, she replied in French, "He is a very important man indeed. He is the chief of the correspondents of all the world." When Clurman arrived, a formal invitation to the sitting awaited him. It was addressed, in French, to the chief of the correspondents of all the world. Clurman thought that was just fine. The issue of *l'affaire Vientiane* never came up.

Sanders continued to work for *Time* in Laos for two years. But the story had long since moved. The Sanders-Mohr escapade marked the ending, a fitting one, perhaps, of the brief diversion into the land of the little princes before the story shifted back

1. The Mohrs remained married the rest of Charley's life. But, despite her toughness, the dalliance that gave others so much gossipy diversion came at great cost to Norma Mohr. She later described that first year in Hong Kong as one of the worst of her life, full of sickness and woe.
2. He was also smart, and unafraid of giving his opinionated boss news others would consider dangerous heresy. As early as February 2, 1962, six weeks after the buildup began, he told Luce in a memo: "We cannot make it in Vietnam with Diem."

once and for all to the deadly serious drama unfolding in Vietnam.[3]

———

In Saigon, Mal Browne's romance had reached a crisis point of its own.

Huynh thi Le Lieu was an unusually bright, serious, and handsome young woman and, by the summer of 1962, Browne was very much in love. Le Lieu was also a complicated person living in a society far more complex than most Americans, whose way was to reduce everything to the simplicity of good guys and bad guys, would ever understand. The story of her life was not unusual in Vietnam, and it could have stood as a red warning flag to outsiders mucking around so blithely in a country at war with others and itself for so long.

Le Lieu's family came from the bureaucratic gentry trained by the French. Her mother was a schoolteacher, her father had been an assistant province chief in the strategic Mekong Delta province of Kien Hoa. The Viet Minh, predecessors to the Viet Cong, assassinated him a decade before she and Browne met.

After her father's death, young Le Lieu was sent to Paris to complete her education. By the time she returned in 1959, her country had been divided north and south, and both Hanoi and Saigon were vying to convince educated expatriates to join their cause. Le Lieu chose Saigon. It seemed a simple choice to ally herself with the government now opposing the forces that had killed her father, and for Le Lieu it was. For others, even within her family, the choice was not so simple.

The Americans insisted throughout that this was not a civil war. But Vietnamese families put the lie to that. Virtually all had relatives on both sides, brother pitted against brother, father against son in the searing family cleavages common in a country divided

3. It was not that trees stopped falling in Laos, just that no one stayed around to hear them. The Pathet Lao pulled out of the coalition in 1964 and resumed fighting, American aircraft pounded the mountains for years in a fruitless effort to stop North Vietnamese infiltration into South Vietnam on Laotian legs of the Ho Chi Minh trail, and, in 1975, the same year Saigon fell, the Pathet Lao took Vientiane. By that time the Laotians had learned to kill with much more relish.

against itself. Even the Huynh family, with its powerful emotional draw to Saigon, split into two wings and remarkable interrelationships. In one of the most remarkable, Le Lieu's brother had married the daughter of the man who ordered the killing of her father. These were complex people.

By the summer of 1962, Le Lieu had moved into Browne's tiny studio apartment above his office, a move that did not put her in good stead with the paranoid regime. But Le Lieu had also lost confidence in the regime.

One of the peculiarities of the Diem government was that it had been organized almost as a shadow image of the hated Communist government to the north. Le Lieu began to find it oppressively regimented. On Thursdays she was required to attend self-criticism sessions. At least once a week she had to wear the blue uniform of solidarity. Where the North used Communist ideology to place a straitjacket on open thinking, the Diem family employed an opaque doctrine called "personalism" to accomplish the same end. Madame Nhu organized youngsters into youth groups paralleling Young Communist leagues, her favorite being a paramilitary group of teenage girls. Le Lieu began looking for a way out.

Splitting was not easy. To minimize the risk, she took a four-month job in Sydney setting up a Vietnamese language service for Radio Australia. Suddenly Browne, the loner, was more alone than ever, going home each night to an empty apartment and his booming Wagnerian operas.

Meanwhile, he had grown almost as fed up with the Americans in Vietnam as Le Lieu had with her government, having entirely written off Ambassador Nolting and the embassy. As for the military, little had improved since Bigart's battle over the helicopter missions months earlier. General Harkins seemed constitutionally unable to deal with the press, even after proddings from Washington. Finally, in exasperation, Browne sent the general a formal protest, complaining that the U.S. military had tightened up so much that "even trivial details" were withheld, that reporters did not have access to "field maps or briefings," that it was almost impossible to get a helicopter ride and "photographs of 'touchy' subjects usually are prohibited." These included "battle casualties, Americans flying Vietnamese planes, prisoners . . ."

Browne continued:

None of us expects the government of Vietnam to pay much attention to the press, except as a potential propaganda organ. But we are not gathering news for Vietnam. Our primary concern is for Americans.

Then he added:

Like soldiers, we, too, have our traditions, in the light of which this is a strange war. The AP has been covering wars for 100 years, and has had its share of battle casualties. An AP correspondent died with Custer at the Little Big Horn (an ambush remarkably similar to some of the fights here) and there have been many others since. Somehow or other, we have managed to keep the people accurately informed. And we are proud of this tradition.

The letter went unanswered.

———

Arnett walked into the office on the Rue Pasteur for the first time on June 26, 1962. He took one look at the severed hand Browne had hung in the corner and almost walked straight back out. Other gruesome souvenirs littered the office—bloodstained canteens and punji sticks, grotesque photos of bodies, primitive Viet Cong weapons. Browne himself was a sight. The red socks glared at Arnett. So did the golden death's-head ring his new chief wore prominently on his right hand. It took Arnett some time to conclude that Browne's eccentricities were those of a war hater not a war lover.

Faas came in from the dry hole of Laos the same day, oblivious to Browne's trinkets. He had seen worse, collected worse, too, in both the Congo and Algeria, where basic barbarism had guided the wars. Now he had only one interest: laying claim to the office's tiny bathroom for his darkroom equipment.

The arrival of the newcomers gave the Associated Press by far the largest press operation in Vietnam and marked milestones in two of the most extraordinary careers in the history of war journalism. But Arnett was not yet the scourge of generals and politicians. Browne ran the AP office in Saigon like no news organization Arnett had ever known. In his native New Zealand the press had been meek and unthreatening. The little newspapers in Bangkok and Vientiane had their moments but clearly existed at the pleasure of fickle governments, as the sudden demise of the *Vientiane World* had proved. Young and eager, a foreigner wanting to make it in a new world, Arnett was a sponge soaking up fresh ways. Working for AP in Indonesia and Laos, he had buddied up to the CIA station chief and worked closely with the American ambassador. It seemed clear to him that American correspondents, even the men of the vaunted *New York Times*, essentially represented the foreign-policy interests of their country. And so they had.

But in Vietnam all this was turned topsy-turvy. When Arnett made a routine call on John Mecklin, the press attaché snapped that Browne had not talked to the embassy for three months. Browne just shrugged. Don't waste your time with them, he said, and handed Arnett his now-famous twenty-page memorandum. "Don't believe any official statement," Arnett read. "Write only what you see." Browne may have been private, reserved, and a trifle strange. But he was the most confrontational journalist Arnett had ever met.

It took the newcomer some time to realize that he had landed in the middle of a vast sea change in American journalism. In two months he would meet a young journalist even more abrasive and confrontational than Browne, the last man in the band of brothers present at the beginning, David Halberstam of *The Times*.[4]

Meanwhile, Arnett began absorbing his lessons. On an introductory assignment, Browne sent his new assistant out on a story that by now was a sitting duck—the Strategic Hamlets program. Arnett came back with a piece about rural woe, farmers separated from their families, ancestor worshippers separated from their ancestral burial grounds, seas of sad faces penned up in treeless camps surrounded by bamboo fences and polluted moats. Browne liked it.

Arnett also quickly began building his new legend. He simply

4. Another young New Zealander who arrived in 1962, Nick Turner of Reuters, found the Americans' confrontational ways less appealing. He stuck with the old school, patiently reporting the government's pitch and following the bad news too. Turner, however, came to the same conclusion as the others. As he put it later, American officials peddled him "a load of codswallop."

had the flair. Not long after arriving, he bought a white Kharman Ghia and deprived the entrepreneurs in the Renaults of substantial business. What had been a taxicab war became, to Arnett, a white Ghia war. If the military refused to take him to battle, Arnett countered by following their helicopters.

"It wasn't as if they were going far," he said. "It was a little war. So you just watched them take off and followed them. There were roads most everywhere, no land mines in those days, and we were young and stupid, so you know, we could do it, and you could live forever."

He started a trend. Soon others bought cars, and the Vietnamese scrambled to stay in the lucrative business. By the time John Sharkey, a radio-television stringer, arrived a few months later, Saigon had two sidewalk vendors renting huge American cars—"It was a sight, those great big boats with white upholstery and radios and air-conditioning in a town of putt-putt French taxis."

———

In August Madame Nhu took off on another of her toots.

Earlier in the year she had criticized the small corps of American reporters as "pseudo liberals" who didn't understand that they were supposed to be on her side. But now her assault turned bizarre. Amid outlandish charges that the The New York Times had taken a $40,000 bribe to print an interview with a Viet Cong leader, Vietnam's First Lady ranted that the paper was "part of an international Communist conspiracy" intentionally sandbagging her country.

As the hubbub grew, she granted a rare interview to Neil Sheehan. In Gia Long Palace she sat in a high brocade chair, stiff-backed and strikingly beautiful in a flowing pink ao dai, servants hovering around her obsequiously. But her obsidian eyes were impenetrable and hard, Sheehan thought as he began questioning her. Has the American press been infiltrated by the Communists? "That is for sure," she answered, and pointed to The Times. The Communists, she said, "always choose the most famous or the most serious institutions such as Harvard University and The New York Times." Sheehan stifled a chuckle, which would have been the worst palace form. But, being a Harvard man, he could feel those long, rapier fingernails scratching at him too.

By 1962 Madame Nhu had become one of the most powerful figures in South Vietnam, occasionally rivaling her husband and, some thought, even her increasingly withdrawn brother-in-law, President Ngo Dinh Diem. She had also become one of the most strident, neurotic, and feared. *Time* magazine usually flattered her. But even *Time* observed that the dainty tap of her ivory fan resounded through the country "like the roll of kettledrums."

Vietnam's history is filled with strong women playing heroic roles in times of national crisis. Almost 2,000 years before the Americans arrived, the celebrated Trung sisters organized a rebellion that drove out the Chinese. Legend has it that one of their commanders gave birth on the battlefield, strapped the newborn to her back, and then rallied her troops to victory. Two hundred years later a twenty-three-year-old woman in golden armor led another rebellion, riding an elephant into triumphant battle against the ubiquitous Chinese.

Powerful and often greatly feared women were also a phenomenon in modern Asia. In China, Jiang Qing sometimes struck more terror into the hearts of enemies of the revolution than her ruthless husband, Mao Zedong. In Taiwan, the island redoubt to which the Chinese losers had retreated, Madame Chiang Kai-shek, the agelessly beautiful wife of the nationalist leader, often overshadowed her husband. Stanley Karnow observed that these strong Oriental women became even more imperious and conniving as their husbands declined. Madame Chiang overtly interfered in the politics of her American benefactors, even attempting to sway elections. As Mao grew senile, Jiang Qing usurped and used his power so malevolently that she barely escaped execution after his death.

In Vietnam, Madame Nhu seemed determined to play out both the ancient and modern roles.

The First Lady had been born Tran Le Xuan (Beautiful Spring) thirty-eight years earlier to a family of immense wealth. She grew up pampered with excess in a great Hanoi house that employed twenty servants, including a liveried coolie who toted her to and from school in a rickshaw. Still, from an early age, she also found herself in a terrible rivalry with her mother, a Buddhist aristocrat and ravishing beauty who moved through Hanoi's salon society with the regal air of an empress. Wealthy Vietnamese women were known for doling out money to their husbands for opium and women to keep them docile and controllable. Tran Le Xuan's mother went along with part of the tradition. But she took her own lovers. One, apparently, was a self-proclaimed intellectual and political activist named Ngo Dinh Nhu. When Nhu first came on the scene he was twice Xuan's age and called her "little niece." But, even in her teens, Tran Le Xuan exhibited the strong will that later caused others to tremble. As her mother presented a string of young men suitable for marriage, she rebelled, insisting on Nhu. They were married in 1943, a fateful alliance.

From the moment her brother-in-law, Diem, shakily took power in 1954, Madame Nhu became an opinionated and outspoken force. Saigon soon learned that those Dragon Lady fingernails could be as sharp as scalpels. At first Diem's control was so tenuous that most of the country seemed to be openly plotting against him. One general regularly boasted that he would overthrow Diem but keep Madame Nhu as a concubine. Furious, she confronted the offender at a Saigon party, denounced him as too gutless to pull off a coup, and added that he would never have her anyway "because I will claw your throat out first."

Even in a family once described as part Bourbon, part Borgia, she quickly became embarrassingly disruptive, calling her husband a coward and criticizing Diem as too cautious in putting down his rivals. The brothers grew so irritated they briefly sent her to a convent in Hong Kong. But nothing silenced her.

She viewed herself as a feminist. By 1962 she had used a seat in the National Assembly, where few had the temerity to oppose her, to foist on the country ultra-moralistic legislation to "protect Vietnamese womanhood." Gossipy Vietnamese society loved to tell outrageously salacious, and probably untrue, tales about her sexual antics. But while she flouted a kind of Oriental black-widow sexuality—reminding Halberstam of the "diabolic antigoddess" characters in James Bond novels—her public agenda was pure bluenose. Madame Nhu's bills outlawed divorce, contraceptives, abortion, prostitution, dancing, beauty contests, even songs about love.

But, in the grand tradition of the Trung sisters, the First Lady's greatest public love was her women's paramilitary militia, whom she dressed up like Girl Scouts and personally gave pistol-shooting practice. "My little darlings" she called her young weekend warriors.

On August 20, 1962, *Newsweek* magazine called them something else. Beneath a photo accompanying a dispatch from François Sully, a New York editor wrote this caption: "Female militia in Saigon: The enemy has more drive and enthusiasm."

All hell broke loose.

———

Sully was in deep trouble. He had neither selected the photograph nor written its caption. But that did not make it past the cultural disconnect. He became a target of opportunity and, for Madame Nhu, an irresistible one. Her campaign against *The Times* quickly deflated in favor of painting Sully as the new Western devil—a "coward" who had been "bought" by the Viet Cong to insult all Vietnamese womanhood. Her husband put secret-police agents on his tail, three men "disguised" in black leather coats following him everywhere. Saigon's government-controlled newspapers had a field day. Orchestrated by the First Lady, sensational front-page articles accused him of crimes ranging from spying to opium smuggling to engaging in sex orgies. One story reported that "the colonial journalist" had been seen "eating Vietnamese rice," a new form of Western exploitation.

Sully was one of a few French reporters lingering in Vietnam, most clinging woefully to lost dreams. But there was nothing woeful about Sully. He was all exuberance. He had also tied in with the new centurions, although the Americans would never fully trust him. Their wariness toward the French bordered on paranoia. But the very force of his personality made him a bridge.

It was Sully who would regale the newcomers about the glory days they had missed. Having put behind the bleak memories of the Second World War—memories of collaboration at home and humiliated armies in the field—the French returned to Indochina determined to reassert themselves with a new imperial extravagance. Still more wealth was exploited from the rubber plantations, the bounty lavished on extravagant dinners with the best wines, the best caviar, served beneath glittering chandeliers in expansive governors' houses. The parties served up the best women, too, a point the irrepressible Sully always mentioned—Asian, Eurasian, French women as beautiful as any in Paris and wearing the same Paris fashions, driving the same expensive Citroëns.

And the army he had arrived with! How he loved to talk about it. If the French army had been humbled in Europe, it came back to Asia with the toughest Legionnaires and the best officers their national military academy, St. Cyr, could produce.[5] They lived graciously in the field. A meal in the officers' mess began with an aperitif, perhaps a vin blanc cassis. Silver and crystal adorned a white-clothed table. Lunch would arrive in courses announced by an officer's aide as if the streets of Paris awaited outside the doors —soup, then fish, then steak, then salad. All for the glory of France! Sully would laugh and laugh. But he still packed his silver flask of cognac, his silk pajamas too.

As an expatriate, Sully had failed at almost everything. But he had a way about him. He held on to the glories without illusions. He remained a habitué of the Cercle Sportif, Saigon's grand relic of the French years. The sports club, guarded by regal tamarinds, sat just across the street from the palace grounds. It boasted twelve tennis courts, an Olympic-size pool surrounded by bikinis from the Riviera, stylish restaurants, darkened bars, mahogany-paneled reading rooms. Native waiters in starched white jackets moved through the rooms tinkling little bells as they delivered messages to members. Only the most beautiful, upper-class Vietnamese women—the *Saigonnaisses*—filled the bikinis at poolside. Outside, on the groomed grounds, old generals from a different war played *boules,* the French game of lawn bowling.

With great self-certainty the Americans played their own game of moral superiority over the French (the French fought for a rightfully discredited system of European exploitation and were doomed to lose, the Americans for freedom and democracy for the people and were foreordained to win). Over the years the Cercle Sportif stood as an ironic reality check on self-deception, providing a plush window through which those who cared to see could take a wry look into the way the fly trap sucked everyone in. In 1968, the worst year of the American war, the club remained the center

5. By 1954, French officers were being killed faster in Indochina than St. Cyr could graduate new ones.

of Saigon society, its colonial trappings unchanged. General William C. Westmoreland, the American commander, played tennis there virtually every day of his four-year tour. As he prepared to return home, defeated, the general gathered together his Vietnamese ball boys. "You have served me well," the general said. "You have been faithful. I would like to reward you." The kids looked up with the hungry anticipation of the children of war. "Here is your reward. You may have all my tennis balls." Then he left.

Sully lived in a small bungalow not far from the sports club, a perfect bachelor's place with a courtyard slung with tropical coral vines. Seeming to know every available beautiful woman in town, he gave parties only fools would miss. Sheehan had been around only three months and Sully had already put him together with Blue Lotus. Arnett had been in town a month when he got the call and then fended off everyone at the party to walk away with a stunning young woman, Nguyen Thu Nga, or Nina, whom he married two years later.

But now all that was threatened. For two weeks Madame Nhu kept Sully twisting in the wind. In the columns of the *Times of Vietnam*, a shrill English-language newspaper run by an American couple with business ties to the regime, she kept up a daily drumbeat: August 22—"The Decline and Fall of *Newsweek*"; August 27 —"Editors Continue to Decry *Newsweek* Article"; August 31— "Continue Attack on *Newsweek* and Sully." The Vietnamese-language newspapers condemned his "poisonous pen" and cursed him for "deflowering" Vietnamese womanhood.

The First Lady toyed with Sully like a tigress with wounded prey. The Vietnam Women's Solidarity Movement demanded that the government expel the offensive *Newsweek* man. But the group *belonged* to Madame Nhu and Madame Nhu *was* the government.

For the regime it all seemed a godsend. Six months earlier Diem had reluctantly backed down from expelling the two correspondents it wanted rid of most: Homer Bigart and François Sully. Now Bigart had left and Sully, without the protective blanket of U.S. concern for *The Times*, stood as naked as a jaybird.

It quickly became clear that the American government would do little to shield him. He was French. The deputy ambassador, William Trueheart, wrote him off as a *pied noir*, a derogatory term used at the time mostly to describe lower-class French who had gone native and lost their roots in Algeria.[6] Benjamin C. Bradlee, then the Washington bureau chief for *Newsweek* and a buddy of the Kennedys, rummaged around Washington power circles and concluded that no help was coming. Roger Hilsman, the assistant secretary of state for Far Eastern affairs, told Bradlee that Sully had been in Vietnam fifteen years and two years in "that place" were enough for anybody. At the White House he found rumblings that the Kennedy people thought Sully "had another agenda, that he was a French spy, I guess."

In early September Diem expelled him.

Sully's colleagues made a futile, sometimes comically sophomoric, attempt to save him. Mal Browne was the angriest, fed up with being treated like a "scabby sheep." Earlier, the newsmen had formed the Vietnam Foreign Correspondents Association and elected Browne president. Now he called a meeting to formulate a protest to Presidents Diem and Kennedy.

Even among the correspondents, whose ranks were swollen by obscure freelancers including a Catholic priest and a man who later blew his cover and came out as a CIA agent, the prevailing Francophobia made for a cantankerous meeting. Sheehan took up the solidarity front but thought Sully a "little far out." Only later did he conclude that the jaunty Frenchman had been the best of them all on the central issue—whether the Americans had any business being in Vietnam at all—and the others, including himself, were too self-certain, too wrapped up in their certainty about the American mission and power and moral right.

The session, held in Browne's office, ended in disagreement and a rump group adjourned to a room in the Caravelle Hotel. The meeting continued boisterously till early in the morning, the drinks flowing freely. Drunken shouts of "Coward!" resounded through the halls. Jacques Nevard, a visiting *New York Times* correspondent, walked methodically around the room shouting into the air-

---

6. Trueheart, who sooner than most began to see the dimension of the problems being created by the embassy's approach, later said he had misunderstood the term's derogatory nature, thinking it was simply a slang phrase for expatriate.

conditioning vents where the correspondents assumed the bugs had been planted. "Fuck you!" he yelled and then moved on to the next vent: "Fuck you!" Finally, in what was not their finest hour, they called in Sully and asked him if he had ever been a Communist or a French spy. No, he said to both questions. Only David Hudson, an NBC stringer who later went to work for the legendary CIA man, Edward Lansdale,[7] voted against protesting to the two governments.

The next day the correspondents sent off the protests. It was like spitting into the wind. Diem replied that he would not bow to the "iniquitous blackmail" of the American fleas. The White House promised to "continue to assist you in any way feasible." Even John Mecklin thought that a classic brush-off. Saving Sully wasn't feasible.

Meanwhile, the happy-go-lucky Frenchman began planning his own farewell party at the bungalow near the Cercle Sportif. He also found that becoming a *cause célèbre* had its moments. Young Vietnamese girls stopped him on the street and asked for his autograph. When he tried to pay his final taxes, a sum of several hundred dollars, the tax official refused the money, shaking his hand instead and praising him as a friend of Vietnam.

Everyone showed up at the party, including the latest and last arrival, who had stepped off the plane that very day.

The next morning the group drove out to Tan Son Nhut to see Sully off. Horst Faas photographed the scene. Sully is standing in the middle, grinning from ear to ear, holding a last protest banner printed in Vietnamese. Browne is off to one side, Sheehan to the other, Arnett reaching up to drape an arm around Sully's shoulders. Standing in the background is the new arrival from *The New York Times*.

The background was not a normal place for David Halberstam and he would not remain there long.

---

7. Lansdale had already become the prototype for the main character in the two best-read novels about early Vietnam, *The Quiet American* and *The Ugly American*.

6

HALBERSTAM'S WAR

He arrived on a very hot day. The monsoons had a month to run and the heavy air off the South China Sea collected a gray fullness as it passed over the flooded delta each morning before settling over the city. But a quick, venting downpour had turned the September evening soft with tropical balm, ideal for an outdoor party.

John Mecklin had met him earlier at the airport, a rare hint of embassy recognition that a twenty-eight-year-old sent to Saigon by *The New York Times* might have an impact on American policy. But now David Halberstam looked around at the party-goers clustered in the tropical courtyard, moving in and out of the stucco bunga-low, and saw no sign of the press attaché. In fact, he saw no one from the embassy, no one in American uniform, no one at all with the clipped, self-certain, early sixties look of official Washington.

So that's the way it will be, he mused. Just like the South.

Ambition loomed large in the New Yorker and not only in the usual ways. It drove him to live the history of his time, up close, positioning himself at its turning points and watching, sometimes even tinkering, to mold it to his own view.

Nothing but journalism could offer such wide-ranging entrée to all he wanted. So, seven years earlier, in 1955, Halberstam had grabbed its free ticket and started the ride. It took him straight out of Harvard into the Deep South, long before most of his peers and only a year after the Supreme Court's historic 1954 civil-rights decision, so early in the gestation of his generation's seminal story that he wasn't sure whether a young, white, Jewish kid from the North should be afraid asking questions in rural Mississippi.

Now he was in Vietnam, early again.

For the moment, however, looking around at the farewell party for François Sully, he nursed the feeling of déjà vu: So it will be "us" versus "them" here too. Mississippi all over again. But here it would be the vaunted Kennedy liberals who were reluctant to be caught socializing with the "outside agitators," not the redneck pols in the small towns of the South.

About that, he was right. Not once during his fifteen-month tour would the correspondent from America's leading newspaper be invited into the home of the American ambassador, Frederick Nolting. The Kennedys of Camelot would attack his patriotism, his bravery, his youth. They would shun him. They would try to have him removed. Their client would go farther, following him through the streets, assaulting him, threatening him with mob hits by Saigon gangsters. Those, of course, were all merit badges of his trade. Add the lying, the stonewalling, and the plain foolishness of powerful men, and Halberstam was positioned to become more identified with an ill-starred war than any correspondent since William Howard Russell brought down a British government with his stories from the Russian Crimea. The mix needed still more, of course: It needed the very distinctive characteristics of David Halberstam himself. But those were there too.

For now, the new man leaned against a wall next to his buddy from the Congo, Horst Faas, examining the other party-goers almost as if he were casing them. Peter Arnett emerged through an archway splashed with the pink of cascading coral vine, wearing a pretty young Vietnamese woman on his arm and a crooked grin on his bulldog face. Halberstam liked him immediately. Neil Sheehan came up, Harvard to Harvard, and said hello. Groomed on a UPI budget, he looked downright seedy in scuffed shoes, crumpled black trousers, a $1.98 short-sleeved white shirt. But he also wore exotica on his arm—a stunning *Saigonnaise* whose every curve seemed to have been sewn tightly into an expensive Parisian party dress.

As the couple left, Halberstam whistled softly under his breath. Faas let out a rumbling laugh. Never wears the same dress twice, he said of Blue Lotus, adding in that thick German accent, "You vill love zis place, David. It iss VUN-derful!" Faas had shared the African life of the past year, a good story but a mean time. In the chaos of the Congo, they had lived almost like monks. They would not in this new place.

At Sully's party Halberstam felt dog-tired after too little vacation and a flight from Leopoldville[1] to Paris to Hong Kong to Saigon. But he couldn't disguise his exuberance over simply being there. Halberstam would forever display a redeeming boyish enthusiasm that would soothe some of the scratches from sandpaper traits that made him too quick to lash out in anger, too slow to forget a slight. Now he felt as if he had been elevated to a cloud just shy of heaven. "This has everything," he told himself, in awe of his good fortune. "A war, a highly dramatic and emotional story, great food, a beautiful setting, and lovely women." Where else could he romance a woman with the best French cuisine and wines in the evening, shower in luxurious hot water at a modern hotel the next morning, take an early cab to the airport, eat a tense breakfast with helicopter pilots, and then fly off into that special high of combat in California technology that gave off the illusion of being forever above, beyond, and immune to harm? And fight the good fight against a dissembling government? It was a young reporter's dream.

At the bungalow he followed the flow of the crowd, the usual motley mix of French expatriate pals of Sully's, a few Vietnamese bold enough to risk offending the regime, and the other reporters —a couple of French, a couple of Brits, the stringers dreaming their own dreams, and the cock of the walk in Saigon, Malcolm Browne. The AP man had been in town almost a year now, building himself an imposing bureau and reputation. With Homer Bigart gone, he had clearly become the story's driving force.

Early on, Browne came up to say hello, the only one without a good-looking woman hanging on his arm, Le Lieu having retreated to her Australian exile. The conversation had been intelligent, open, friendly—and brief. Browne did not stay long at the party, wouldn't have come at all if he hadn't been the leader in trying to save Sully from expulsion. He was an odd-looking duck, Halberstam thought—that bobbing Adam's apple, the red socks, the ring,

1. Now Kinshasa.

131

a solid gold bracelet on his left wrist. Mal's insurance policy, Faas explained the bracelet, worn as barter for his life if he is ever captured. The theory did not inspire confidence in the German. Halberstam shrugged. Idiosyncrasies didn't bother him. He was most interested in Mal Browne. Just hours off the plane, Halberstam had already begun recruiting.

While Halberstam scrutinized, the others took their measure of him. Within the Saigon press corps, a twenty-eight-year-old foreign correspondent from *The New York Times* cast an imposing shadow. Unlike the authorities, they did not see him as wet behind the ears. He had seven years of impressive work behind him and reporting, like baseball, is a young man's game. Too soon the legs go, the drive diminishes, and you learn to nick the corners with a change-up instead of loosing that once-blazing fastball that had been even better when it was a little wild. Or you drop out. At twenty-eight, Halberstam stood near the peak of his journalistic powers. His reputation had preceded him. Halberstam's rookie foreign work in the Congo had received wide acclaim. *The Times*'s foreign desk might nitpick him, but the newspaper nominated him for a Pulitzer Prize and he won the American Newspaper Guild's Page One Award. But just the fact that *The Times* had sent him would have established his bona fides.

Watching him, the others saw a big man—six foot three and 185 pounds, with close-cropped black hair, utilitarian plastic glasses, and long arms that flew as he talked, swooped as he made a point. He had many points to make. He was gregarious, full of opinions, full of himself. He was bright and talked bright. His face, youthfully clear and earnest, stopped just short of handsome. The eyes behind the horn-rims told everything—clamping on you in the first burst of anger, flashing the first sign that he had discarded you as a fool or accepted you as a worthy, twinkling with mirth before the laughter began rumbling up out of his chest. The need for camaraderie, the single-mindedness, the anger, the humor, the super ego, the generosity, all the forever conflicting parts of David Halberstam spilled first out of the dark pools of those eyes that hid nothing.

If you looked hard at the rest of the face, you also saw that it would grow more imposing with age. If you knew him very well, you understood why: David Halberstam was a man so driven he could create legends and myths, even create himself.

François Sully would leave the next day. As his party neared its end, the Frenchman revisited the newcomer whose life he now would pass like a ship in the night. A huge Gallic grin split his face as he told the man from *The New York Times* that he was entrusting him with a most important duty.

Halberstam looked at him in anticipation.

Sully then said that he was counting on the new man to see to it that *monsieur l'ambassadeur*, Mr. Nolting, continued to be reminded of the hole in the doughnut.

The mirth started behind the eyeglasses, then rumbled slowly up out of the gut into a roar of laughter. Halberstam had heard about the now-famous doughnut exchange and assured Sully that he would take on the obligation as a matter of honor. Of that, no one need have worried. Within months Ambassador Nolting would be asking Halberstam why he persisted in seeing the hole in the doughnut. And Halberstam would be replying: Because, Mr. Ambassador, there *is* a hole in the doughnut.

———

The next day, his second in Vietnam, Halberstam wondered briefly if his us versus them judgment had been made too hastily. Nevard took him to lunch with the CIA's Saigon station chief, John Richardson. Richardson gave him an unexpectedly good lead.

Afterward, Halberstam asked his colleague what was up. Did this happen often?

Nevard smiled. "No," he said, "it's the first time he's told me anything. They're making a play for you. They're very, very glad that Homer's gone."

The American hierarchy misread that one badly. What Bigart had reported with almost melancholic disdain, Halberstam now would report with youthfully energetic outrage. But the story would remain the same: a disaster in the making.

———

Several months later Bigart wrote a second letter half-apologizing for not warning Halberstam about "a place I almost went nuts in."

No apology, of course, had been needed. Halberstam was ecstatic about his assignment. For Bigart, it had been different. "When I escaped last summer," he wrote, "I felt wormy and run down. *The Times* gave me a very thorough checkup, but couldn't find anything wrong. I guess it was mental." He had been thoroughly, perhaps medically, depressed. Whatever, Bigart's reporting had left a warning with such authoritative command that ignoring it, *The Nation* had added in that farewell appraisal, would lead the United States down "a road as broad and well-paved as the one which leads to hell."

Now, inadvertently, *The Times* had escalated. The newspaper was hardly itching for a brawl with the government, particularly over issues as tendentious as the Cold War and Communism. The newspaper considered itself the best in the country, perhaps the world, and few quarreled with the presumption. It had fifty foreign correspondents spread around the globe when the overwhelming majority had none, a handful had one to a few, *The Washington Post* just two. It also considered itself liberal, in the classic sense of the word, and others usually granted it that, as well—liberal, Cold Warrior, and anti-Communist not being a contrary mix at the time.

Still, *The Times* had not weathered Joe McCarthy's blighted march through American life well. Hysterical charges had flown only a few years earlier, including one that the paper harbored as many as 126 card-carrying Communists on its staff. Eventually, one was found and fired, but the experience so rattled the paper that it briefly took the distinctly illiberal position that it would also fire anyone who exercised Fifth Amendment rights against self-incrimination. Three former party members were fired, one by telegram before he got off the witness stand. The right wing pounced on this as evidence of Moscow's infiltration into the great institution; the left scorned the lack of moral backbone. But it was Cuba over which *The Times* had taken its most recent cuffing.

In the fifties Fidel Castro had become a folk hero to millions of American romantics as he and his bearded revolutionaries fought through Cuba's mountains to bring down the right-wing dictator, Fulgencio Batista. No American correspondent became so identified with the cause as Herbert Matthews of *The Times*. When Batista reported Castro dead in 1957, Matthews smuggled himself into the rugged Sierra Maestra and proved otherwise. His interviews and stories at Castro's hideout heightened the myth and sped the march that ended New Year's Day 1959 with Batista fleeing the country. Matthews captured the triumphant scene in Havana with un-*Times*-like jubilance:

> The hunted young man who for three hours whispered his passionate hopes and ideals into my ear in the gloomy jungle depths on February 17, 1957, is now the chief power in Cuba. . . . , the greatest hero their history has ever known.

Legitimate doubt existed, perhaps even in Castro's mind, as to whether he was a Communist. The American right wing was certain he was, the rightists seeing all revolutionaries marching to one distant drummer. The American government wasn't sure but saw Reds everywhere. Castro said he wasn't. Matthews returned in mid-1959 and concluded: "Castro is not only not Communist but decidedly anticommunist." In 1960 Castro publicly reversed himself. Some thought the spooked American government had pushed him into it. But virtual reality became reality in the sixties too. Matthews became the bogeyman—the man who lost Cuba—and *The Times* never allowed him to write about the subject in its news columns again. Instead, isolated in his small, tenth-floor office, he wrote unsigned editorials.

The newspaper took a terrible beating on the subject. *Time* magazine attacked. Joseph Alsop, who had a peculiar passion for reporters who misplaced countries, wrote that Matthews did more to lose Cuba than politicians ever could. As Halberstam arrived in Vietnam, almost four years after Castro had taken power, pickets still marched around his home office, waving their stern placards: DOWN WITH MATTHEWS AND ALL COMMUNISTS OF THE NEW YORK TIMES. One sign showed Castro sitting happily on a small palm-treed island waving a stogie and a rifle. I GOT MY JOB THROUGH THE NEW YORK TIMES, he announced in a takeoff on the paper's classified advertising slogan. The humor was not infectious inside the executive offices of the newspaper. The issue would not go away. While Homer Bigart and David Halberstam wrote from Vietnam, the U.S. Senate held ten hearings on Cuba's turn to Communism—with Matthews and *The Times* coming up in each one.

So the newspaper was hardly spoiling for another fight that

might lead to more charges that it was soft on America's implacable enemy. In Vietnam the newspaper would be more aggressive than any other, cover the war more thoroughly and cover it better. But the keepers of the flame at Broadway and 43rd did not have to feel *comfortable* about it, and they would come to feel most uncomfortable indeed. But that only made the paper's choice of its first two Vietnam correspondents all the more remarkable.

Bigart and Halberstam were both powder kegs, fiercely independent, strongly opinionated, fearless of powerful forces, including their own newspaper. Bigart ranked on any list of the best reporters in the history of *The Times*. Halberstam was clawing his way onto the lists and would be on most by the time he left Vietnam. With the Kennedy administration still harboring pipe dreams of a war fought quietly, and no other American newspaper taking it seriously enough to station *any* correspondent in Vietnam, the reporting of these two men started reverberations that would quake long after the last American finally left.

Bigart seemed devoid of ambition that would carry him beyond the confines of an eight-column page. He never added to his own legend by telling war stories, never wrote a book. When a colleague once asked why, he said simply: "I like it over at the end of the day." Halberstam's ambition and ego towered over everything. An overwhelming need to leave his mark drove him, and his favorite expression best described the drive: fire in the belly, a man had to have fire in the belly. Throughout his life he would make enemies and lose friends over the power of that need. Sheehan once asked him about a ruthless college-days battle with a friend over the managing editorship of the Harvard *Crimson*. How did he let it get so out of hand? "I guess I'm a killer," he replied.

But Bigart and Halberstam also had strong common threads that made their appointments still more exceptional. They pulled at shackles like wild beasts. Neither ever fully became a man of *The Times*. Bigart's soul was forever ensconced at the paper of his youth, the old *New York Herald Tribune,* a free-wheeling reporter's paper that bled to death slowly and died not long after he returned to New York. *The Times* was simply too stodgy for him. For Halberstam, the world's most powerful newspaper, which fed the ambitions of so many, seemed to stand in the way of his. He felt closed in by its warring principalities and fiefdoms, its overweening sense of obligation, its rigid formulary. Less than four years after leaving Vietnam, he quit the newspaper to go it on his own.

Nor were Bigart and Halberstam ideal *Times* men in the eyes of the regimented newspaper. Great institutions go through periods of calcification and revival, and *The New York Times* of 1962 was just beginning to emerge from a period in which it had become unusually hidebound, almost like the medieval church. *The Times* had rules to follow and these men didn't follow them, *refused* to follow them. They fought relentlessly, and not always respectfully, with the high priests, the editors. At a time when objectivity was a tenet of the journalistic religion, fairness its highest canon, these reporters actually had their own opinions, God and *The Times* forbid.

Bigart played his daily chess game. Halberstam simply overwhelmed the paper, sending volumes, then volumes to back up the volumes, then curt cables. He was such an indefatigable, unrelenting, dauntless, self-certain, take-no-guff collector of informational bits and pieces that his opinion would seem to become fact. He was a maker of what would later be called conventional wisdom. Conventional wisdom can be more conventional than wise. But Halberstam was so good at it that he built the conventional wisdom for an entire generation, and much of it lasted.

———

François Sully wasted no time evening matters with the palace. En route to the United States, where a prestigious Nieman fellowship had been arranged for him at Harvard, Sully stopped only two and a half hours out of Saigon and, from Hong Kong, wrote the most blistering account to date about Vietnam's ruling family.

Reporting from an unfriendly foreign posting is a never-ending balancing act. How much of the story does a correspondent tell without going over that invisible line beyond which the unfriendlies will kick him out of their country? How much does one hold back before reaching the point at which the stories become valueless? Foreign correspondents have a derogatory name for work that is too defensive. They call it "visa reporting."

Even the best correspondents are somewhat defensive, practicing occasional visa reporting if only subconsciously. To do otherwise is suicidal. The best correspondents protect their flanks as a story builds and then escalate the risk-taking as the story peaks or they are about to leave.

Neil Sheehan, who learned by following Bigart, remembered how "the professor" had escalated. "Homer used his ammunition very carefully," Sheehan said. "He raised the temperature very slowly. As he reached the end, his stories got rougher and rougher. He was counting the days. So we learned to calculate how far we could go without being thrown out. It was always a trade-off."

François Sully was not a visa reporter by anyone's measure. If anything, he was too rambunctious, too much the wild hare. Kicked out on a fluke, his blunt reporting had nevertheless earned adequate black marks at the palace. In Hong Kong he had no visa concerns left at all, and his report showed it. Billed in the September 24, 1962, *Newsweek* as a look at a "crisis in leadership now confronting South Vietnam," it could never have been written in Saigon. In Sully's article Diem become "reddish and bloated . . . a virtual prisoner in his own quiet palace." He described the victors in the family coup torridly, Nhu as "a vicious political infighter with an unquenchable thirst for power." But Sully saved his fiercest shots for Madame Nhu. She had become "the most detested personality in South Vietnam." He concluded: "A beautiful, gifted, and charming woman, she is also grasping, conceited and obsessed with a drive for power that far surpasses that of even her husband."

Even some in the American Embassy, while wincing at the provocative, even-the-score language and the trouble it was certain to cause, thought the charges closer to true than false. Diem had begun a troubling retreat from the everyday world. Madame Nhu and her husband eagerly filled the void.

At the palace, however, Diem blew so sky-high that for once the First Lady felt no need to speak. He banned *Newsweek* from South Vietnam indefinitely and warned that other publications "peddling propaganda harmful of the national cause" would be banned in the future. He also promised to place stricter controls on individual correspondents.

Sully's buddies gave him a silent round of applause. But they also winced. They had a good idea what "stricter controls" meant and they began looking over their shoulders more often. They knew who would be behind them: the Mat Vu, Brother Nhu's ever-present secret police.

———

Despite almost a year of aggressive reporting by Bigart, Mal Browne, and others, David Halberstam arrived in a Vietnam that remained obscure and of little interest to most Americans.

The military commitment had quietly crept to 10,000 men. Officially, the American death toll stood at 25, but Washington fudged shamelessly on early casualty figures. Men shot down while defoliating forests or ferrying troops or flying FARMGATE flights were often listed as noncombat deaths or missing in unexplained plane crashes. Even so, the toll was small and these were professional soldiers at the height of the Cold War, not the kid next door drafted for a war he didn't understand.

The civilian contingent had also grown substantially, with American bureaucrats advising on everything from rice production to land reform. They were involved at almost every level of Diem's government (a major irritant, emphasizing, as it did, the incompetence of his own people). Saigon seemed overrun by Yanks, with more arriving every day.

Still, the Kennedy administration's policy of minimizing its involvement, of representing it as "something less in reality than it is," enjoyed a measure of success that would be unimaginable in a later world. Never again would it be possible to conduct an enterprise of such magnitude over such a length of time beneath the consciousness of the American people. Project Beef-Up was now ten months old.

The suspicious reporters in Saigon irritated the White House, but the fact was that they weren't registering with the public. So what if there were half a dozen angry young men out there trying to mess up the works? Who listened to them? Kennedy, with his charm, kept the far more powerful Washington press corps eating out of his hand. The old Asia hands came and went, generally supporting Washington. Reporters from lesser American newspapers visited occasionally, often flown over at government expense. But they invariably covered the war in Hemingwayesque I-was-there style or gave it the rah-rah treatment of a sports event. The resident correspondents wrote them off as "the feather merchants."

But the polls showed that most Americans still didn't know where Vietnam was—and didn't care. In fact, most pollsters didn't even bother to ask.[2]

But the messiness of Kennedy's crisis-prone presidency had at least as much to do with keeping Vietnam out of the news as his silent-war policy. Vietnam rarely bulled its way above the page-one fold into the banner-line columns where readers found the racial turmoil in the South, debate over the nuclear test-ban treaty, negotiations with Khrushchev, the Berlin crisis, the Cuban crisis—or even the crisis in the Congo.

On the day in 1961 that Kennedy made his muted announcement about moving men and supplies into Vietnam—the beginning of the war—*The Times* played the story at the bottom of page one. The lead story came out of the Congo, with the byline: By David Halberstam. It would be months before Halberstam would move back onto the front page with the regularity he had gained in Africa. Still, from the moment he landed, he knew his timing was perfect. He had youth, *The Times*, and the story. Nothing like this would happen to him again, and he decided to go for it all.

Like Malcolm Browne before him, Halberstam immediately became entranced by Vietnam, caught up in the fly trap. Also like Browne and the other resident correspondents, he found nothing untoward about his country's commitment to this far-off land.

Born into a first-generation family's straightforward patriotism, reared during the easy certainties of the Second World War, coming of age during the Cold War, Halberstam saw his country not only as America the Great but America the Good. Like his country, he had a strong moralistic bent—too much the self-certain sermonizer, his critics would say. But if Vietnam couldn't defend itself against the advance of the Communists, then his powerful country not only should help but had a *moral* duty to do so. Ngo Dinh Diem and the family triumvirate in Saigon troubled him. But America

2. The Gallup organization apparently asked its first Vietnam question in May of 1964. Halberstam had come and gone by then, Kennedy and Diem were both dead, and the U.S. military had been involved 30 months. The poll showed that 63 percent of the American public paid "little or no attention" to the war.

supported many dictators, some of them far less attractive than Diem. And if Diem didn't come around, he had a simple answer: Dump him, just as they ought to dump most of the damn-fool Americans running the show in Saigon. So it wasn't the wisdom of America's presence in Vietnam that he began to question: "I thought Vietnam was worth saving. I thought that long after I left." And some of his early dispatches had a decidedly gung-ho ring.

Watching the American military men in action, Halberstam wrote in an early piece, "is as impressive as watching Alan Shepard or one of the other astronauts for the first time on TV." America had its "varsity" playing in "just another extension of the Cold War," and the varsity was lean, mean, and tough. "There is a swagger to the American walk which is considerably accentuated in American military men . . . and they don't seem to doubt that they ought to be here."

Nor did Halberstam foresee the agony ahead. He confidently wrote that America's experience in Vietnam "will almost certainly never reach the harsh sense of alienation that came to haunt both the French Army and the French people. . . ."

Two years later he would chronicle these early days in a book called *The Making of a Quagmire* and still later enhance his fame with a devastating analysis of American leadership, and hubris reached, in his best-seller *The Best and the Brightest*.

Halberstam would parlay those books into legendary status as the point man in a new era of deep hostility between the press and the government that would last long after the war ended. After he left Saigon, and the war began to rip at the very fabric of America later in the bedeviled sixties, some enshrined him as the first journalistic laureate of the antiestablishment rebels who stormed the streets, filled the air with taunting obscenities, and spelled their country's name with a Germanic "k." But not once, during his Vietnam years or well afterward, did he question America's right, even her need, to be there. His criticisms were of methods and foolishness, lying and self-delusion, of a failure to set a policy that could win. He was not part of those sixties excesses, nor of the firebrand journalistic excesses that sometimes accompanied them. Nor did he see them coming, although he clearly helped lay their foundation.

Halberstam fell under Vietnam's spell and watched the GIs fall too. His kicker, the final sum-it-all-up paragraph in that early article, described a scene in one of the Rue Catinat's new "Honeymoon Lane" dives as an enrapt American soldier watched a lovely Vietnamese singer purr "Lonesome Me" in newly acquired English. The Yank suddenly thumped the bar and exclaimed, "My God! We *can't* let this go over to the Communists." The reader could be excused if he heard Halberstam in the exclamation too.

So Halberstam was not of the sixties generation. He was not *of* any generation, but a man out of the ambivalence of the fifties whose peers struggled for generational identity of *any* kind. They had one foot balanced in the righteous self-certainties of the era of Pax Americana following the Second World War, the other sliding into the righteous self-certainties of the bitterness ahead. Such slippery generational footing can provide the best ground for looking in both directions and sometimes the best for truly lasting disillusionment. As time wore on, Halberstam would draw on both vantage points to become not the laureate of an America turned evil, the sixties notion, but the biographer of his own biting and sermonistic vision of an America failed. Long before others began preaching that gospel, Halberstam became the evangelist of decline. He chronicled the failed dream in Vietnam. A generation later he would still be chronicling the lost dream with the fall of Detroit to other relentless Asians.

It was this book, *The Reckoning*, the third of a set, his trilogy, that seemed to complete a life's work about Halberstam's America. They were BIG books, literally, a total of 2,211 pages; with BIG-book titles about BIG issues painted on a BIG canvas. Everything about Halberstam had to be outsized. His nature demanded it as self-validation. So he painted his heroes and villains as Prince Valiants in white, Prince Valiants in black; large, so they would rise farther and fall harder, making larger dents in the sprawling landscapes of his works. John Kenneth Galbraith took him mildly to task about his super-hero style in a larger-than-life profile of CBS founder William S. Paley in the second of the three books, *The Powers That Be:*

> . . . Do watch your mood. It is much too heroic for the subject. After all, Paley is a mildly comic figure and most of his

lieutenants much more so. So, you will say, were Westy and William Bundy, but they were getting people killed.

P.S.—*TIME*, in my day, was also very funny.

Of course, by that time Halberstam had already created West-moreland and Bundy as larger than life. And if the iconoclastic Galbraith found *Time* funny, Halberstam saw the magazine and Henry Luce as the looming forces behind The American Century that led to the hubris that led to the fall. Halberstam took it on himself to countermand Luce. Ironically, the two men were remark-ably alike, mission-oriented, self-certain, evangelic, creators of al-most Homeric myths. Neil Sheehan described his young buddy in Vietnam as a "messianic innocent," a description that flawlessly fit Luce as well.

The Powers That Be became a landmark, a study of the media before it became a fashionable topic. As the media grew more influential in American life, it became common among journalists, still is among some, to disingenuously diminish themselves—we have no power, we send out no armies, we raise no taxes; we only carry messages. Halberstam had no tolerance for such humbug-gery. The press had power, the power to create images and myths, to tilt history, drive large forces—Manifest Destiny, The American Century, the Decline of America. It was BIG. If not, from whence did he draw his own power? Which he needed. And which he would use in Vietnam.

He wrote other books, two youthful novels as well as books about rowing, basketball, and baseball. He wrote a best-seller about the fifties, the decade out of which he had emerged. But it was a curiously undone book. The little books were about his loves, and usually made charmed reads. The big books were about his needs, and often grew lumbering. But his needs were to make his mark, to create himself as he created his characters, BIG, a Prince Valiant among the observers of his time. He would do that.

The real puzzle in David Halberstam, who became such a burr in the side of the establishment, was that he seemed *so* predestined, *so* obligated, to become part of that establishment—and that he felt so driven to succeed and fulfill the obligation. He seemed carved out of the dream he would later see as failed.

The personal story of the Halberstam family read like a multigenerational Ellis Island melodrama. Both sets of his grandparents had been Jewish immigrants, one escaping religious and political persecutions in Poland, the other in Lithuania. Both had large families and, in classic immigrant fashion, sacrificed to thrust their children closer to their new country's promise. Blanche Levy was the first member of the Lithuanian family's American generation to attend college. She became a teacher. The poorer Polish family, forced to make choices, singled out Charles Halberstam as its chosen one. He became a doctor, although his timing would never be as good as that of the two sons he and Blanche begat. Two great wars and the depression deprived Charles of reaping the full promise of the land of milk and honey to which his parents had been drawn. Filled with the pride and patriotism of an immigrant's son, he interrupted college to become a medic in the First World War, struggled as a young doctor during the economic collapse, then returned to Europe at age forty-four as a combat surgeon in the next war. He died prematurely in 1950, leaving a family lifted to the lower middle class economically but taken far beyond in drive and spirit.

The two sons were born in New York City at the height of the depression—Michael in 1932, David in 1934. Unlike most Jewish youngsters of their era, they led rootless lives, following their father's medical and military careers through town after new town —El Paso, Austin, Rochester, Minnesota, the Connecticut hamlet of Winsted they loved to call home. After their father returned from Europe, the family moved to Westchester County—the "outer edge of Bronxville," David called it—and the brothers graduated from Yonkers High School. So they grew up city boys, an appellation David never did like. He preferred small-town virtues, the virtues of his father. They became his vision of what America should be. Make-up ball games. Walking to school. Norman Rockwell.

In Winsted one of the other boys in town was a Syrian kid named Ralph Nader and the Halberstam boys were taken aside early and told that there would be no nonsense about the Arab boy, because this was America and the hatreds had been left behind in the old world. The young Halberstams found out the hard way that not all children were given that message. After each move they heard the taunts and earned their spurs all over again. They grew up brash and independent, and, invariably, they fought only once in each new neighborhood. The boys were neither tough nor big— David would not sprout to his full imposing height till his college days. But they were tenacious. They held ground taken, a quality instilled by their father. People could push you around in the old country, Charles Halberstam told his sons; they could push you around here, too, but in America you could push back.[3] Blanche, who filled in the family's often meager income with part-time teaching jobs, taught them that education enabled them not only to fight back but to join. The boys were bright, and they brought home the good grades their mother demanded. But, on their own, they also learned a few lessons in mid-century Americana: Good grades, for boys, demanded social atonement. They immersed themselves in the solid American sports, football, basketball, and baseball, at which neither was particularly talented. But they kept at them. No one would ever catch a young Halberstam with a sissified tennis racket in his hand, ruining everything.

At the time of their father's death, David was sixteen, his older brother eighteen, and the family finances marginal. But Blanche Halberstam had no doubts about what lay ahead for her two sons, and neither did they. She sacrificed again, and Michael went on to Harvard. David followed two years later. In just two generations the Lithuanian and Polish émigrés had thrust their progeny to the highest handhold on the climb to the American establishment.

Harvard cost a then-staggering $1,700 a year, $800 of which Blanche eked out of her husband's life insurance, with the rest earned by the boys during the summers. Michael chose medicine as had his father. David chose more unconventionally—journalism, an intellectually dubious craft that did not yet fit into Harvard's elitist vision of its duty to prepare the next generation's leaders. Being Jewish, and with neither American lineage nor money, he saw himself as an outsider and felt that the Harvard of the fifties "had accepted us academically but was not yet ready to accept us socially." He chose an outsider's route.

The young man's timing, as usual, was perfect. The two great

3. Michael died in 1980 in a tragic extension of that quality, shot dead after he surprised and chased an armed burglar out of his suburban Washington home.

wars that had interrupted his father's life—and the dramatic social changes forged out of the agonies of the depression—now placed the son at a unique time in history. The wrenchings of the twentieth century had moved the United States into unprecedented affluence and power. Both its dollar and its industrial/military might dominated the world, pushing America finally and irretrievably out of its traditional isolationism and suddenly into empire. Others of Halberstam's Harvard generation would make safer moves toward the establishment through economics, international relations, government, or the law. Halberstam was no less determined. But he was drawn to a more electric profession, one "covered with no boredom," as he put it. Luck was on his side. But so was instinct. He sensed that the changed world would soon propel the news of events to a level of importance rivaling the events themselves. And he was right.

Young Halberstam gravitated quickly into the Plympton Street sanctum of the *Crimson* building, often spending fifty or sixty hours a week at the college newspaper. He wore a trench coat and drooped a cigarette out of the side of his mouth, not in the fashion of Harvard men but in the fashion of the old hard-drinking, underpaid, socially marginal news reporters of the past. But these young *Crimson* aces would not be formed in the *Front Page* mold. Anthony Lukas, who went on to win a Pulitzer Prize, spurned the dreariness of collegiate news and covered the rampages of Joe McCarthy instead, earning the envy and razzing of his collegiate buddies when the Red-baiting senator cheerily began calling him Tony. Halberstam's best friend, Jack Langguth, eventually replaced him in Saigon. John Updike wandered around the fringes, writing satire for the *Harvard Lampoon* and starring for the Poon softball team in the literary squad's annual embarrassment with the newsprint boys. One year Updike played eight of the Poon's nine positions to no avail, the Crimsons winning twenty-three to two. Years later Halberstam and two other former *Crimson* hands, Stanley Karnow and Burt Glinn of *The Saturday Evening Post*, sent a postcard from Saigon to a pal from Plympton Street, Anthony Lewis. It said: Viet Cong 23, ARVN 2, and Lewis understood. In the past *The Crimson* had produced its share of remarkable men. Franklin Delano Roosevelt had been its editor. Another former editor, John Fitzgerald Kennedy, would soon move into the White House. But Halberstam and most of his young colleagues had no intention of using *The Crimson*'s pulpit and Harvard's ticket into traditionally heady realms. Their headiness lay in deadlines; their dreams focused on *The Times*.

Graduating in 1955, Halberstam surprised his *Crimson* friends, most of whom were using the ticket to lock up jobs with the country's most prestigious news organizations. Brasher than ever, eager to make his mark on the world, he wrote off the newspaper of his collegiate dreams because he didn't want to get lost in "the Number Thirty-five slot in *The Times* Washington Bureau." Instead, he took a $46 a week reporting job on Mississippi's smallest daily newspaper, the West Point *Daily Times Leader*, certain that he could plunge headlong and influentially into the South's racial problems.

After seven months in the small and unflinchingly segregationist Mississippi town, and more intolerable compromises than David Halberstam would endure at any other time in his life, the job ended abruptly when the town leaders began organizing a local chapter of the supremacist White Citizens' Council. He watched the subtle change in the townspeople he knew and saw it for what it was—dark and ominous, vigilantism. He wrote the story. The *Times Leader*'s editor rejected it. Halberstam tried to stick by his guns. The editor shook his head, then stared at him silently for a moment. "David," he finally said, "you're free, white and twenty-one, and can do anything you want." Halberstam accurately took that to mean in some place other than Mississippi. The story was killed. He left two days later.

But he stayed in the South, moving to the respected *Nashville Tennessean*, and also hoping to write, as he put it, "for a larger, intangible, invisible journalistic jury, which somehow would know what I was doing and would reward me." For the next four years he covered humdrum along with civil rights and politics, writing occasional articles for the small national journal, *The Reporter*. It reached that "invisible journalistic jury." James (Scotty) Reston, the chief of *The Times* Washington Bureau, called.

At *The Times* Reston ran the ultimate principality. He managed the Washington bureau like an independent nation only loosely aligned with the superpower in New York. A highly conventional man himself, he had an eye for talent and didn't mind boat-rockers.

Among his hirelings were Tom Wicker, Max Frankel, and the puckish Russell Baker, and one day he would add Sheehan and Mohr
(Browne would be hired by New York). He gave his men—they
invariably were men[4]—rare running room. Working for Reston
became the envy of all those lost in the maw of the New York
newsroom where, as Gay Talese put it, hordes sat "waiting for
another *Titanic* to sink." And being a Reston man, as Halberstam
would learn, could pay dividends long after a recruit had crossed
the moat into one of the paper's less hospitable duchies.

Even so, Halberstam had a rocky start. Wallace Carroll, the bureau's news editor, became the first *Times* editor to discover that
Halberstam's writing did not always match his trenchant reporting.
Carroll made the new recruit rewrite his first story five times. But
that wasn't the real problem. He arrived in 1961, the week of John
F. Kennedy's inauguration. He also landed in the pickle he had
feared: the Number Thirty-five slot in a Washington bureau of
thirty-five reporters. He hated it and, the short time he was there,
picked up an everlasting skepticism, a downright distrust of, the
Washington press corps. They were a kept group in a company
town, he decided, and the arrival of the glamorous Kennedys only
made the arrangement more onerous. "Suddenly, you're being
courted in a way that does neither side any good," he said. "The
Gridiron dinner was almost like a Marxist caricature of the American press. You stay around long enough and you get into the club
and your publisher can fly in with his four richest friends and you
get the assistant secretary of defense and some top guy from the
White House as your guests—it is an enormous corruption." He
saw the Kennedys as infiltrators: "It was as if they had a plant in
every bureau, an agent in every office." And often, he thought, the
agent was the guy sitting next to him in the sanctum of *The New
York Times* Washington bureau.

His brief experience in Washington built him a sturdy set of
armor for the assaults to come in Vietnam, both from the press and
the government. But for the first time in his life he did poorly. Even
as the capital began to throb with change, Reston watched his

---

4. Mary McGrory, whose writing helped define Washington for the next
thirty years, applied for a job in Reston's bureau. He offered to hire her if
she would also work the switchboard. She passed.

bright, twenty-six-year-old recruit founder. Finally, Reston pulled him aside and softened the news with a characteristic *Times* side-slip. "Dave, maybe you need a hotter climate and darker people," he said, making it sound as if he were sending Rudyard Kipling off to see the other empire. Halberstam leaped at the offer and found himself en route to equatorial Africa.

Halberstam landed in the Congo with his trench coat, a stylish collection of Abercrombie & Fitch bush clothes, and a variety of anti-dysentery potions whose vastness was exceeded only by his enthusiasm. Henry Tanner, the exhausted *Times* resident corre-spondent, had been covering the newly independent country's cha-otic tribal war for most of a year. He took one weary look at his eager young replacement and wished the new man luck with his useless array of medicines. Then he dryly observed, one *Times* man to another, that the trench coat would surely keep Halberstam warm, and bush clothes by Abercrombie & Fitch were an inge-niously daring idea in a country where European mercenaries were favored targets. Halberstam changed outfits, and thrived.

The Congo was a tough rookie's war, with barely disciplined United Nations multinational troops attempting to quell a rebellion by undisciplined tribal warriors from the southern region of Ka-tanga. The Katanganese thought the white correspondents were UN troops, the UN troops thought they were mercenaries, and some of the worst dustups came in the bloody confusion of street fighting. The old-timers delighted in spooking the newcomer. They showed him the press car, a beat-up little Volkswagen bug air-conditioned by a dozen bullet holes in each side. The holes on this side came from the Katanganese, they told him; on that side from the UN. He laughed—until the fighting suddenly flared up and they piled in, roaring off down the street in a careening zigzag.

He wrote youthfully zestful letters home, one of which described an Indian general with a death wish who invited him along on all his dangerous missions. The general called him "Garrison," and his gut wrenched every time he heard the words "Come along, Garrison." Once, facedown in a wet ditch with a Katanganese mor-tar pounding at them, he asked, "Why me?" The general thought that was very funny. "I like you, Garrison," he replied. "You're the only one I've met who's not afraid to admit he's a coward."

Some of that vividness crept into his stories, which was difficult in those days at the gray old *Times,* and his reputation was quickly made in New York. So was his reputation with his desk editors, who fought to save the gray. Emanuel Freedman, the foreign editor, chastised him: His stories were too long, pontificating, and opinionated. It was the beginning of a long, escalating, and eventually bitter battle with the pallid clerks. But Halberstam's buddies wrote, too, praising him, urging him to fight the good fight and, as Russell Baker put it, don't cave in and "start writing Nyktimes style."

Over the next twelve months the front page opened up, the first awards rolled in. Halberstam was on his way, although he yielded few hints that he was on his way to a rebelliousness that would spawn a deeply questioning journalistic style that yielded to no icons, surely not government icons, except the First Amendment.

In the Congo Halberstam played mostly by the old rules. He checked in regularly with the CIA men, and, in the accepted fashion of the day, thought nothing of doing a little routine information trading. He became a close friend of the American ambassador, Edmund Gullion, and found no reason to distrust him, just as Gullion found no reason not to confide in Halberstam. He was one of the boys. It would take, he said later, "the mendacity" he found in Vietnam to change that.

——

A shoot-out between Malcolm Browne and David Halberstam became inevitable the moment the new man stepped down into Vietnam's high-noon heat. The conflict had all the trappings of the Old West: The town simply wasn't big enough for the two of them.

It would be difficult to find two men much more different in temperament, style, life goals. But the conflict had little to do with any of that. It had to do with control. On that, the men were remarkably the same. They both wanted it.

Browne, in his loner's introspective way, intuitively had a better fix on their problem. Years later, he laughed and said: "When I'm in a group I like to either control or maintain my autonomy." Throughout his life, Mal Browne would maintain a lot of autonomy. But, for him, withdrawing had a certain beauty that Halberstam would never see. Within his autonomy Browne could create his own control. To the outside world, Bigart had totally dominated the story during his six months in the country. But not to Browne. In his mind, Bigart, whom he admired greatly, was an in-and-outer who never became part of the game. He built his own unusual rationale: "Homer stayed at the Caravelle. He didn't live off the economy. I didn't consider him a resident correspondent." And, with that, Bigart was banished from Mal Browne's world.

Still, by the time Halberstam arrived, Bigart was indeed gone and Browne clearly controlled the story. Sheehan's drive and quick learning were making him a force to reckon with. But Browne had such a head start. He had the best Vietnamese sources and good connections to the French. He wrote off virtually all the Americans except those in the field, and he had built the largest and most powerful bureau in town.

Halberstam, in his youthful enthusiasm, couldn't understand why Browne wouldn't want to share that. He genuinely wanted to work with him, as he had worked with wire-service correspondents in the Congo.

The practice was fairly standard, the two work operations being so different. The wire-service man was bound to breaking news and deadlines, with minutes, sometimes seconds, meaning the difference between success and failure. The tabulations would come back from the home office weekly, sometimes daily: LED WITH BOMBING ALL CYCLES CHEERS CHEERS MORE CHEERS or 12 MINUTES LATE ON CHOPPERS LOST EAST COAST AYEMS 3–14 CRANK IT. The pressure became so intense that the overworked wiries had a special phrase for the tics and twitches that came from the never-ending terror of getting beat. Wire-service angst, they called it. The "specials," as they called the Halberstams and correspondents from other dailies who popped in and out of town, rarely competed on deadline reporting. That left them with the freedom to go into the field more often, delve deeper, and accumulate more insights and sources. Ideally, the wiries would backstop the specials in exchange for which the specials would share sources, insights, the broader view, and some of the workload.

Halberstam was an immensely social being. He feared loneliness and treasured the group. No one thrived more, nor had more fun, in the we-band-of-brothers life. Always, after the Vietnam year, he would speak of it as a time of "we," a beautiful, wonderful time when "we" fought the bastards down, "we" broke through the bullshit, "we" did it *together*, as a group. David Halberstam could also be exceptionally generous, giving as much as he took. But he could not give up control, and in the charmingly naive part of him, the big overgrown boy part, he didn't seem to understand that. It was a time of "we," but he would be the leader of us.

So Horst Faas's big and gregarious friend from the Congo simply began to show up at the office at 158 Pasteur, grazing the wire stories, bumming a typewriter or a phone, or just schmoozing from his long sprawl on the torn, plastic couch.

Peter Arnett watched in awe. Halberstam represented everything Arnett wanted but thought out of his reach. He played on the world stage, a rising star for the best team in the game, a man Arnett's age who could, he presumed, not entirely correctly, walk up to a Walter Lippmann and say, "Howsitgoin, Walt." The two of them developed a friendship that continued all their lives. But the touch of awe remained. As controversial as Halberstam became later, and at times so abrasive he would drive away his best friends, no one ever said a crosswise word about him to Arnett. Over the rapidly nearing mean season, the little street fighter would get into brawl after brawl with the Mat Vu. But whenever he got in too deep, Halberstam magically appeared, clenching his big fists and stretching menacingly to his full height, which was a foot taller than most of the police agents. Many years later, stationed in Moscow, Arnett got banged up good in a tussle with the KGB. He remembers two things about the fight: the other Western reporters running away as he looked up from the pavement, and thinking: "Dave would never have let this happen to me."

Browne held him in no such wonderment. AP had several Vietnamese on the payroll. With the arrival of Arnett and Faas—Faas had even taken over the bathroom!—the little office with the sick-green walls grew hopelessly crowded. Desk space was limited, typewriters were at a premium, and the single plastic phone, battered and taped up like a crash victim in desperate need of the last rites, was worth fighting over. Browne found Halberstam a nuisance, and a threat too.

The routine continued precariously through the fall with Halberstam accompanying Arnett and Faas into the field on stories. Then, according to Browne, Halberstam popped the question. He asked for a permanent spot and suggested they work collaboratively.

Browne answered with a quick and flat no. According to Halberstam, there was no request. He saw it wasn't working—"You just couldn't reach Mal"—and drifted away.

From that point forward stories involving Browne and Halberstam would have two versions, their recollections of each other sometimes veering far from anyone's reality. Thirty years later Browne would recall, in a variation of the theme on Bigart, that Halberstam had arrived in Vietnam almost a year later than he actually did, at a date well after most of the work was done. Halberstam would remember that Browne had been more office manager than reporter, rarely muddying his boots in the field.

Ironically, in 1963 they would share the Pulitzer Prize for their work. They had different views of that too. Halberstam, ungenerously, would say that the conventional wisdom was that Browne hadn't deserved it, that Sheehan had done better work. Browne would express his own typically iconoclastic view: Life wasn't about prizes, he didn't much like the impact the Pulitzer had on him and, for all the trouble it could be, almost wished he had never won it. Worst of all, the attention intruded upon his privacy. Nothing could be worse than that.

Browne seemed to forget the rift, as if nothing had happened, and in a sense not much had: Someone had asked him for office space and he had said no. To Halberstam, however, as thin-skinned as he could be generous, it became a slight, unforgettable and unforgivable. Faas, who did not get off to the fastest start with his bureau chief and later shared housing with Halberstam, looked back on the rift and the sometimes childlike high jinks of the young correspondents and concluded that Mal Browne was the only adult in the group.

Browne would go on to his career at *The Times*, continue with distinguished reporting from Vietnam, other wars, and Eastern Europe. Eventually, he would become a first-rate science reporter, the chemist returning halfway to his first love. Always a private man, he spent little time embossing his Vietnam legend, none enhancing his image. Halberstam, as was his way, started in on that job immediately and, thirty years later, it was almost as if Browne hadn't been there.

Halberstam was left needing a wire-service workmate and a place to work. He had two choices. One was Nick Turner, a young

New Zealander who had arrived a few months earlier to run the British news agency Reuters. Halberstam had worked with the Reuters man in Africa and it had gone well. Turner also had a Vietnamese aide whom everyone, including Bigart, thought was the best in town—Pham Xuan An, a wiry little man in his mid-thirties who could cut red tape, roust out information, and talk poetry and philosophy as well as run a story to ground on deadline. Having a good Vietnamese aide was crucial, and An was the best, even when he disappeared for a few days, obvious to all that he had a secret love stashed somewhere. But Turner had one serious problem: His quarters were in the offices of the Vietnam Press, the South Vietnamese wire service. Halberstam thought VP was an outright propaganda voice for the Diem regime, and it was.[5] So he gravitated more and more toward his fellow Harvard man, Neil Sheehan. He liked the kid. He had balls, and Halberstam had never seen anyone work so hard. UPI pushed him grotesquely. But Sheehan pushed himself just as hard, often past the point of exhaustion. After one all-nighter too many, Sheehan, to Halberstam's great amusement, fell sound asleep while taking a story over the telephone. Halberstam found him with his head on the kitchen table they shared as a desk, the phone still cradled to his ear, a voice screaming at him from the other end. Sheehan was out cold.

Meanwhile, Halberstam set about doing what Browne figured he would do all along: He took control of the story.

Over the next ten years, as the little war grew larger and uglier, America's self-destructive obsession in Vietnam would come to be known by many possessive nicknames:

McNamara's War, for the ultimate rationalist who deluded himself into believing that passions in the jungles could be overcome by machines, exotic electronic barriers, and elaborately contrived numeric equations;

Johnson's War, for the haunted man who dreamed of fighting a different war on poverty at home but allowed his inner devils to drive him to "nail the coonskin to the wall";

Nixon's War, for the man who vowed "peace with honor" but took longer finding peace than his country did fighting the Second

5. Turner moved out of the offices in 1963 as the going got rougher with the Vietnamese.

World War and looked for honor in the destruction of the little neighboring kingdom of Cambodia;

And, eventually, Television's War, for the new technological marvel that would grow to unprecedented influence as it brought the agony home in a way undreamed by earlier generations.

But all that came later. Over the next year, during the first great Vietnam crisis, the one that led the United States into the muck for a decade, the war would not even become known as Kennedy's War. It would take on a different nickname, a pejorative one that came out of the White House and the Pentagon.

They called it Halberstam's War.

7

THE MAKING OF AN
ANGRY MAN

David Halberstam spent most of his first month immersing himself in the byzantine ways of Saigon, attempting to break through to American officials who gave him nothing of value after Richardson's tip, and, as had the others in their first days, soaking up the enchantment of the city.

The Rue Catinat ran roughly parallel to Pasteur, just two blocks east of Browne's office, and Halberstam quickly learned his Radio Catinat rounds, bounding with unabashed enthusiasm and those long, aggressive strides from Givral's to Cheap Charlies to Brodard's. He listened to the grumbling of the French as the street adapted to new times coming—hamburgers and banana splits replacing *fromage* on a *baguette*, Yankee French fries ousting *pomme frites*, at least in name; bar girls greeting passersby in the fractured English of "Hi, Yank" or "You, Joe" instead of the jangling *"Bonjour, Pierre"* that had assured them for so long that the girls were theirs. The American horde had even begun calling the grand avenue by its new and dreadfully utilitarian name, Tu Do. But to the correspondents it remained Catinat, the soul of Saigon, a street of beautiful women, pickpockets, whores, money changers, and dentists who pulled teeth on the spot for ten cents.

Halberstam loved it, and his colleagues soon found that a stop at Brodard's meant more to him than an information hustle. It took fuel to drive all that energy. Halberstam ate prodigious amounts— soup, shrimp, a steak, French fries, two pieces of pie with ice cream, two milks and an iced coffee, then another steak because the hungering always lingered. This for lunch. He attacked food with the same mix of boyish enthusiasm and aggression with which he attacked everything.

The Catinat was also home to Saigon's three major hotels. At its foot the old Majestic looked out over the Saigon River where the ghost ship, the carrier *Core,* had arrived nine months earlier. Farther up, on opposite sides of bustling Lam Son Square, stood the contrasting hostelries that became the symbolic centers of the two wars in Vietnam.

Elegantly low-slung and European, the aging Continental faded with the French now. The ceiling fans in its spacious rooms revolved above old mosquito netting collapsing around beds that sagged too much even for the most nostalgic. It was a romantic wreck with red damask decor, swaying chandeliers, threadbare rugs, cold and cold running water, and a rate of $10 a night, with breakfast. It was the ideal UPI hotel and Neil Sheehan stayed there before burrowing into the still more economical windowless back room of his office.

Halberstam moved temporarily into the new ten-story Caravelle across the square. Saigon's skyscraper, the Caravelle heralded the future. It had smaller rooms, firmer beds, a garish French moderne motif, and a telephone in every room, making it the favorite of the technocratic Americans. But the Caravelle became the hotel of the American war because of its roof. A few years later American VIPs —junketing congressmen, Pentagon generals, big-byline Washington journalists—would gather there for a nightly ritual. They ordered their martinis in the tenth-floor restaurant, then carried them outside to the roof to watch the fire and light show of their big new war tightening around Saigon. The rooftop was so wonderfully *above* it all, safe and untouchable like the American airplanes that pounded the jungles against a foe who had no airplanes.

He was of the Sinatra generation, Halberstam liked to say, and so were most of the older, professional soldiers sent in during these early "advisory" times. Elvis swiveled elsewhere. The song that played longest in the newfangled jukeboxes invading Vietnam was Tony Bennett's "I Left My Heart in San Francisco." Except in Halberstam's room. He had taken to country music in Nashville, picking up spare change writing album liner notes for Chet Atkins. Now he and Charley Mohr, as unlikely a pair of country boys as Saigon would see, stayed up late into the night, sending the mournful twangs of lost loves flooding into the hallways. Then, finally, they would put on Marty Robbins's "Gunfighter Ballad" and argue raucously about how many KIA, WIA, and MIA—how many killed, wounded, and missing in action—Robbins had in the lyrics. They'd add a Vietnamese body count, quadrupling all the numbers, and laugh and laugh.

But Saigon was not the place to cover the story and Halberstam itched to get out. He quickly saw what others in the group already knew: Most Vietnamese officials were either hopelessly corrupt or terrified of the ruling family, so they lied or said nothing. Sheehan pointed out one sinister character in the palace circle who strutted around town in an expensive white linen suit and Panama hat swinging a swagger stick with a dagger concealed inside.

The Americans were of no more help. Harkins made Halberstam yearn for his Indian general in the Congo. Nolting would be no Edmund Gullion. The blind optimism, the can-do clichés, the total faith in Diem that seemed so mindless: Diem's picture was in every window in town, therefore he must be popular? Had Nolting ever been outside Virginia? The American Mission had a surreality about it, an air of hocus-pocus.

Still, in his first venture out of town, north to the coastal town of Da Nang, Halberstam's reporting was almost sunny, as the headlines reflected:

September 19, 1962:
SOUTH VIETNAMESE INFLICT A MAJOR DEFEAT ON REDS

September 21, 1962:
PEASANTS WORK AS TROOPS HOLD OFF GUERRILLAS

September 24, 1962:
VIETNAM STRIKES AT REDS' BASTIONS

While in Da Nang, Halberstam learned of plans to introduce HU-1As, the soon-to-be-famed Hueys, a greatly advanced turbojet helicopter gunship that would ride shotgun for the old flying bananas the *Core* had brought in. In 1962 the United States stood at the height of its empire, the greatest military empire in the history of the world. Its men and riches and technology were holding off the new Gauls in every corner of the globe—almost a million men stationed in more than 100 countries. But it was the technology that instilled such cockiness in the Americans—the deadly Minuteman missiles just now being planted in the fields of Montana to let Khrushchev know we could reach across the top of the world to punish him ("My ace in the hole," Kennedy called the city-killers); the new silent submarines, so much more fearsome than Hitler's archaic U-boats that had terrorized the seas two decades earlier; the supersonic airplanes, like McNamara's pet F-111 (then still on the drawing boards and known as the TFX for tactical-fighter, experimental), which, using terrain-tracking radar, would slip down into the weeds, 300, 200 feet off the ground, and dash 1,500 miles an hour toward its target. Indeed, the F-111 eventually provided a classic object lesson in the empire's—and its Augustans'—blind faith in technology. It was a McNamara numbers extravaganza gone berserk. The plane was born into never-ending controversy, including a bitter year-long Senate investigation over whether politics had motivated the choice of contractors and, then, whether the plane as conceived by McNamara would work at all. Eighteen days after McNamara finally left the Pentagon in 1968, the air force rushed the first six planes to Vietnam during the Tet Offensive. On their third day the first crashed mysteriously. Two days later a second crashed, apparently due to a failure of the terrain-tracking device, and the rest were grounded. A month later they returned to service and a third crashed on the first day's mission. They were quietly recalled. Four years later, as the last Americans were being withdrawn, the F-111s returned. On the first flight, one crashed. Three weeks later another crashed and they were grounded. There were debates about America's power. But, in 1962, there was no thought of a reckoning, not even by David Halberstam.

In Vietnam the helicopters emerged, almost otherworldly in their technological superiority to a foe who just months earlier had used coconut grenades. Through much of 1962 almost everyone—even the doubting reporters—agreed that the helicopters had, at the least, staved off collapse. How could little men in black pajamas possibly hold up against the big iron birds? Halberstam, reporting the imminent arrival of the Hueys, offered one cautionary note, writing that some advisers were afraid the ARVN was becoming too "dependent" on the choppers. But the news of the new helicopters glowed in *The Times*, and Halberstam did not ask a pivotal question: If the first helicopters had been so successful, why was it now necessary to bring in armed gunships to protect them?

Back in Saigon, Sheehan pestered Halberstam to go south for the real action, and in early October they planned the trip. The day before leaving Sheehan broke his arm at the shoulder in a Saigon traffic accident, reducing him to one-handed typing and taking him out of combat for six weeks. The accident was quintessential Sheehan. Saigon's chaotic traffic moved in endless, noisy waves of bicycles, cyclos, motorcycles, pedicabs, half-demolished French taxis, and now American jeeps and Detroit behemoths. Pedestrians quickly learned the Saigon Weave to survive a street crossing. Not Sheehan. Impatient, preoccupied, always running behind, he plunged in headlong. He was taken out by a motorcycle.

So, exactly a month after he arrived, Halberstam found himself motoring down Highway 4 alone, past the useless concrete block-houses he remembered from *The Quiet American;* through the rich, flat lands now turning golden for harvest, remembering how Faas had marveled over it: "So beautiful it is like a page out of the Bible." It also was the place where, with the rainy season now ending, everyone expected a new Viet Cong offensive. He drove beneath the flamboyante trees and made the left turn to the guarded grillwork gate of the Seminary.

Inside he was greeted by a muscular American officer whose half-smile cut through a raw-boned face burned beet red by the delta sun. If there was a reluctance to help reporters in Saigon, there seemed none here. Halberstam had heard all the legends about this man and the answer to his first question fit those tales: A combat patrol? John Paul Vann repeated. Hell, yes, you can go out first thing in the morning. Then the half-smile turned wry. "Well, Halberstam," he added, "the first thing you'll learn is that these people may be the world's greatest lovers, but they're not the world's greatest fighters."

Halberstam left before dawn, landing with a company of Vietnamese troops in the muck of waist-high marshland grass outside the targeted village. The men moved through the grass in a "slow, tiring crawl," firing almost no shots, and by the time they entered the village, the peasant huts contained only frightened women and children. Halberstam did make one mental note about Nolting's line regarding Diem's popularity. There were no pictures of Diem here. Outside the village, sometimes walking waist-deep in water, he passed Viet Cong flags painted on trees and antigovernment slogans posted everywhere. Meanwhile, Company C ended the day with a body count of one dead peasant of uncertain politics and a school of catfish floating belly-up after a mortar round landed in a muddy canal.

But there had been action. In the afternoon, with Company C deployed along a canal, the racket of a major battle ricocheted through a line of trees a few hundred yards away. The trees obscured the ground action, but Halberstam had watched the helicopters come in and, moments later, heard the first staccato bursts of the firefight. A second group of choppers swooped in with reinforcements, this time only to be met immediately by furious light-arms fire. Then came the fighters with rocketing, strafing, napalming.

That evening, back at the Seminary, Halberstam was exhausted from his first mission. His neck had turned as burned red as Vann's face, his soaked feet shriveled to wrinkled white. He had never before felt such a rookie. But his host wanted to talk.

Vann wore a small bandage. He ignored the wound but made no attempt to diminish what had happened on the other side of the tree line. The first helicopters had landed unmolested, a platoon of ARVN Rangers then moving cautiously toward a village not unlike the one Halberstam had entered. The Viet Cong waited until the Rangers were almost on top of them, then cut them down, killing or wounding thirty-four of the forty men. Vann dispatched reinforcements and, typically, rode one of the helicopters in himself. Two were shot down, including Vann's. The American gunner riding next to him had been killed outright and most of the dozen ARVN troopers aboard were killed or wounded. Thirty-nine bullet holes were found in Vann's helicopter. His only wound was a nick by a piece of flying metal, another episode in the legend.

But the colonel quickly moved the talk off that. Instead, finding a tired but receptive listener, he began one of his manic all-nighters. "These are good people," he said with empathy but frustration. "They can win this war if someone will show them how." *Who do*

you think beat their pants off today? Those were their brothers out there.
With a professional soldier's respect, he described what his enemy
had done this day. First, they surprised the surprisers. Then, they
did not break and run when the heavy stuff came in. They dug in,
took it, and when they finally left, they carried away their dead
and wounded, both out of respect and, Vann assumed, to deprive
the ARVN of any sense of achievement. Vann shook his head. They
had even carried out the brass casings of their spent cartridges to
refill them and use again.

Vann talked more than usual. *The Times* had been on his turf on
a pivotal day. And he wanted *The Times.* This was the opening
ploy in the use-and-be-used game and both men were world-class
players, each of them far better than the other understood that
night.

So, Vann told Halberstam, the Viet Cong have lost their fear of
the helicopters. They have learned how to take them out of the sky,
wait them out, ambush them at their most vulnerable as they land.
Thirty-nine bullet holes. He whistled. Just a few months ago they
ran. Do you know what this means for the Viet Cong? More confidence, more boldness. Do you know what it means for us? More
technology, more firepower, more heavy-duty conventional war
equipment.

Halberstam examined this unusual professional soldier intently.
Vann kicked at the floor in disgust, his gravelly poor-boy voice
rasping like sandpaper now. Washington paid lip service to counterinsurgency tactics, but it was a parlor game to the President and
his men. The old guard in Saigon went for the same constipated,
conventional methods the French had used and lost. *You're a smart
guy, Halberstam. What do you hear up there? World War II!* Vann
sarcastically repeated a line he had heard too often in too many
American officers' clubs: Grab 'em by the balls and their hearts and
minds will follow.

"This is a political war and it calls for the utmost discrimination
in killing," he continued, sounding a theme he told all the reporters. "The best weapon for killing is a knife, but I'm afraid we can't
do it that way. The next best is a rifle. The worst is an airplane, and
after that the worst is artillery. You have to know who you are
killing."

Halberstam watched the cocky little soldier's ruddy fingers jab the air for emphasis. This guy is a real red ass, he thought, a Halberstam vote of approval. He was perfect, and Halberstam knew what to do with a perfect source. You listen, you learn, you write. But you're careful. You do not use everything. You store like a squirrel. You do not use his name unless the politics of it, the politics he needs to live by in his life and career, are as safe as a full house and he gives you the nod. You protect him at all costs. But you make sure his story gets told. That's what he wants, whatever his reasons. You don't care about his reasons. You shrug at the unspoken trade. That is the game. It is age-old and time-honored, Halberstam thought, to the degree that he thought about it at all. It was ingrained in him.

In the dim night light of the Seminary, Vann continued: Did you notice the topography out there? Halberstam felt as if he had been looking up at mud all day. But he remembered Sheehan's vivid description, and now he understood it. From the air, Sheehan had told him, the delta is a flat, endless sea of green, crisscrossed with canals, and your first overwhelming surprise will be how much it teems with life—farmers, water buffaloes, villages, whole cities on stilts. Then, on the ground, you can't see anything. It swallows you up, hides everything, as if you are totally alone.

Vann gave a more military description. The paddies seem to stretch forever, he said, but each village is bordered by a tree line. The Normandy hedgerows of the Mekong Delta, he called them. Charlie uses the village, but under attack he moves into the cover of the trees and, in trouble, slips out through the canals. Artillery commanders and pilots prefer the easier targets of the villages, where they can see people moving. It's not as if the Viet Cong are *never* there. But the peasants take the brunt of the heavy stuff, always will. Hearts and minds. Talk to the air force.

The new hardware created another darkly ironic problem. Not long ago the guerrillas fought with makeshift weapons, some left from the French war, others taken in simpler battles, some honed out of whatever was at hand—bamboo, glass, and metal salvaged from American garbage. Now they fought with automatic rifles and American-made land mines. They armed themselves with the very stuff the United States was sending over to defeat them, much of it taken in the field, some surreptitiously funneled to them by agents and corrupt black marketeers straight off the docks of Saigon, the shipping crates unopened. It was Darwinian, Vann said. Using the world around them, the Viet Cong evolved into whatever they needed to be.[1]

At the first light of dawn, Vann was still talking: stories of palace corruption that filtered down to field commanders; political cronyism that produced inept officers who ducked battles; good Vietnamese officers who were recalled and never seen again after suffering casualties displeasing to Diem.

Halberstam's exhaustion had left him. Such a find he had made. He chuckled at the paradox: How could one state, Virginia, send two such starkly different men to this place—this tough little redneck, John Paul Vann, and the aloof aristocratic know-nothing, Fritz Nolting?

After that long night in October, Halberstam's stories swiftly turned in another direction. Again, the first headlines reflected the change:

October 9, 1962:

VIETNAM WAR A FRUSTRATING HUNT FOR AN ELUSIVE FOE

October 11, 1962:

VIET CONG MAINTAINING STRENGTH DESPITE SET-BACKS

Before leaving the delta, Halberstam also wrote what newspapers called a "soft feature." But this one had a bite:

MY THO, VIETNAM, Oct. 10—The Communist guerrillas threw
a party for the peasants at a village near here a few days ago.
It was a propaganda party and the Communists served food,
tea and weapons.

The weapons were captured recently from Government
forces. The peasants were regaled with stories of how the

---

1. At about the same time the French historian and journalist Bernard Fall visited Hanoi and heard a remarkably similar assessment from North Vietnam's prime minister, Pham Van Dong. Dong seemed to relish the idea of increased American military aid. The more the Americans send, Dong said, the worse it will become for them. It sounds as if the South Vietnamese are caught in a vicious circle, Fall suggested. The northerner smiled. "Not a vicious circle," he said, "but a downward spiral."

Communists, or Viet Cong, had taken the weapons, which
had been paid for by the Americans.

In his first Sunday "blockbuster" from his new posting, Halberstam abbreviated the lesson from his new mentor. But the lesson
was clear: "It should be reported," he wrote October 21, "that there
is considerably less optimism out in the field than in Washington
or in Saigon and that the closer one gets to the actual contact level
of this war, the farther one gets from official optimism."

On the drive back up Highway 4, through the new enticement
of the delta, Halberstam marveled at his good luck. Back at the
Seminary, John Paul Vann did too. They were made for each other.

———

In Saigon, the wooing of David Halberstam did not last long.

Only days after his arrival, General Maxwell Taylor whisked
through on one of those in-and-out inspection skims the correspondents had begun to ridicule. But it was new to Halberstam and he
followed Taylor on the whirlwind visit to strategic hamlets and
showplace battlegrounds. In a heavily guarded village in the highlands north of Saigon, while bare-chested Montagnard tribesmen
sat on their haunches silently watching, the twenty-eight-year-old
correspondent walked up to the four-star general.

"General Taylor," he said, offering his hand. "David Halberstam
of *The New York Times*."

Without a word, Taylor spun on his heel and walked away.

Taylor could have been deep in thought, distracted, even hard
of hearing. But the young correspondent was cut out to judge the
general's rejection in only one way—as a personal slight of, like
everything in his life, epic proportions. *Boy, oh boy*, he thought,
staring at the retreating general's back, *why didn't you just slap my
face?* For once, Halberstam was too dumbstruck to say anything.
But it became an unpardonable snub that spanned a lifetime. Three
decades later he still bristled: "Taylor is the most overrated public
figure in the last thirty years. Everybody thought he was a Ridgway
and he turned out to be Max Taylor. You can quote me on that. He
lacked the fiber of a Ridgway."

Other reporters noticed quirks in Taylor. Jerrold Schecter of *Time*
heard Taylor repeatedly refer to South Vietnam as South Korea, a

habit he had apparently been unable to break since his first visit. Taylor returned from the trip and reported that the Saigon press corps "remains uninformed and often belligerently adverse." He suggested that it was time for Kennedy to start talking to publishers to get some "responsible reporting" in Vietnam. It was a suggestion that Kennedy rejected for the time being but, as it turned out, not long enough.

When John F. Kennedy looked around for a military leader for Project Beef-Up in late 1961, most of his aides, caught up in their romance with an unconventional counterinsurgency war, urged him to pick a younger commander, even leap-frogging the right man up through the ranks. Instead, Taylor presented him with his protégé, a fifty-seven-year-old product of the army's horse-cavalry era, Paul Harkins. The choice could not have been more conventional—nor more fateful.[2] Roger Hilsman, a pivotal Kennedy man who had led commandos into unconventional warfare in Burma during the Second World War, later called the appointment Kennedy's worst mistake in Vietnam. By the time the general left Vietnam two years later, screwing up in the army was known as "pulling a Harkins."

On his arrival in February 1962 Harkins sounded the battle cry of those can-do times: "I am an optimist, and I am not going to allow my staff to be pessimistic." He immediately labeled his status reports to Washington "Headway Reports" and produced figures to match the upbeat format even when it meant ignoring the accounts of his men in the field. Nothing was allowed to disturb his eternal optimism. Told by the CIA's George Allen that the agency had discovered six additional Viet Cong battalions—about 1,500 men—operating in the delta, he responded, "What? We've killed more than that in the last six months. I can't send that to Washington." He didn't, and seemed to believe his own con.

During McNamara's May 1962 visit Harkins told the defense secretary the war "will be over by Christmas." That and "light at the end of the tunnel," a French line that nevertheless became a McNamara favorite, became the keynote phrases of false optimism in Vietnam. A quickly buried one was the "Explosion Plan." For

2. General Westmoreland, who replaced Harkins, was also a Taylor protégé—and also a most conventional man.

most of his first year it was the hallmark of Harkins's secret strategy for ending the war. The general sprang it directly on President Diem on September 7, 1962. For once, Diem listened to someone else for hours instead of vice versa. Harkins wanted him to gather together every soldier, sailor, airman, civil guard, village self-defenseman, Montagnard scout, and paramilitary woman in Madame Nhu's troupe—some 450,000 fighters, he estimated. This force would be "exploded" simultaneously on the unsuspecting and outnumbered Viet Cong. William Trueheart, the deputy ambassador who accompanied Harkins to the meeting, sighed many years later: "I don't think he had a new idea since the Second World War."

Others were less kind. "Is there a plan? The answer is no," Roger Hilsman reported after a quick trip to Saigon. Instead there was "great confusion," he reported, adding that Harkins's new tune was a "nationwide intensification" of ARVN offensives. "This is his word now for the so-called explosion." The Explosion Plan so embarrassed the administration that it was kept a tighter secret than FARMGATE, and died a much more rapid death.

In early 1964, when Westmoreland came to replace the first of America's defeated Vietnam generals, he found Harkins languishing at a tropical pace, regularly repeating a refrain from Kipling:

> *The end of the fight is a tombstone white*
> *With the name of the late deceased,*
> *And the epitaph drear: A Fool lies here*
> *Who tried to hustle the East.*

Then he would nod and smile, the man who thought it would be over by Christmas in no hurry now to do anything.

Harkins's trouble with the press became immediate, total, and deadly. How could this man, bred on old army graces and handed an impossibly "secret" war, confide in the young and rambunctious Saigon press corps? In any case, having no problems—except, as he told McNamara, the press itself—he had nothing to confide. When Faas asked Harkins for a chance to photograph him in field dress outside Saigon, he replied tersely, "Forget that kind of a picture. I'm not that kind of general." That could have been the poorly worded but calculated response of a general in a war that was not supposed to be a war. But it reinforced the newsmen's image of Harkins as a former polo-playing dandy who preferred tropical whites and the old colonial splendor of the Cercle Sportif to problems he did not want to see because he did not plan to report them.

Eventually it would be the lying—"the great Saigon lying machine," as Halberstam called Harkins and team—that drew the wrath of the reporters. But in 1962 nothing caused greater friction than his refusal to allow them to join major combat operations or even inform them that such missions had begun. He openly let the reporters know he viewed them as a channel to the Viet Cong, and therefore as security risks. The idea was not only silly and insulting, it was self-destructive.

After Halberstam's first visit with Vann, clashes between the correspondent and the general became inevitable. Cocky and short-fused, Halberstam ignited easily. Angered, he responded unforgettably. A huge clenched fist would slam into a table, an explosive and profane curse silence a party. And all would be registered in that elephantine memory that *never* forgot.

"A man of compelling mediocrity," Halberstam once wrote of Harkins, the kindest description of the man ever to emerge from his pen. In a very short time, the words would escalate. "That's where the lying sonofabitch lives!" he startled one visitor as they drove down a pleasant Saigon street, Halberstam suddenly shaking his fist at a shaded villa near the tennis club. Still later, he brought a Saigon restaurant to dead silence with a crashing fist and a loud pronouncement. Harkins, he exclaimed, should be court-martialed and shot.

Harkins did not fail because of poor press relations. Nor did the United States's policy in these first two tentative years in Vietnam. But rarely has a team of American officials with such a uniform blind spot been gathered together for such an important task. And rarely have the ramifications been so long-lasting and negative. America's Saigon team had scarcely more sophistication about the press than Diem and the Nhus.

Their actions often seemed downright bizarre even by the strange norms of Cold War paranoia. In November 1962 Hawaii-based Admiral Harry Felt, commander of all U.S. forces in the

Pacific (CINCPAC) and Harkins's direct superior,[3] sent the Pentagon a long and complaining cable about the Saigon press corps. The negative reporting appeared to stem, Felt wrote, from "a well-planned anti-Diem whispering campaign going on in Saigon" and produced with "all the earmarks of a top public relations agency, U.S. or European, financed by someone in either South Vietnam or North Vietnam." Felt asked the Pentagon to get to the bottom of it and, if true, the information "should assist in convincing the correspondents" to scrutinize their stories more closely. The only public relations firm that turned up was a Madison Avenue agency that Diem paid through 1961 to make him look good in the United States.

Meanwhile, back from the delta, Halberstam arranged for another lunch and a long off-the-record briefing from the man who had helped him on his second day in town. This time Halberstam came away convinced that John Richardson had intentionally done more to confuse than to edify him. By now his CIA contacts from the Congo had begun to flock to the hot new action in Southeast Asia like bees to honey. Vietnam was a spook's dream, and the agency forever had a better fix on Vietnamese reality than the American military. The wars between the two became brutal. Of the Saigon Station Chief, however, Halberstam's friends chuckled. In private, they said, Richardson confessed to a secret envy of the Communists: They not only controlled their reporters, they ran them.

The saddest figure among the top hands was Nolting. A man of small-town nobility, his background read Faulknerian: at times a peanut farmer, at times a teacher of philosophy, and then an investment banker whose family, in the Southern manner, ran the little Virginia tobacco-country town of Chester. His country had made Nolting a man of Europe—giving him a broadsheet of continental postings from NATO to Paris. Not once had he set foot in Asia

3. Throughout the long war the military chain of command required the American commander in Vietnam to report through CINCPAC in Hawaii, causing some unusual situations. Not once in their four years of mutual agony in Vietnam did Harkins's successor, General William C. Westmoreland, pick up the telephone and call his commander in chief, President Lyndon B. Johnson. Westmoreland did not have the authority, he told me. Nor did the President call him. Even Johnson felt it necessary to go through channels.

until he came over to hold the hand of America's Mandarin. And that was his job. "Get along" was the way his deputy and hometown friend, William Trueheart, described the orders. His country disserved him in the assignment and made it impossible for him to serve it.

The commitment to Diem was far from universal. The political counselor in Nolting's embassy, Joseph A. Mendenhall, left the job three weeks before Halberstam arrived with blunt, unconditional, cabled advice for Washington:

RECOMMENDATION: GET RID OF DIEM, MR. AND MRS. NHU AND THE REST OF THE NGO FAMILY.

Even during the planning for Project Beef-Up, a few saw the dangers. Undersecretary of State George W. Ball warned Kennedy that he did not have control of all events. Presidential decisions can take on a life of their own, he said, and this one could draw as many as 300,000 American troops into a war on the Asian mainland. Kennedy laughed. Events would not control him; he would control events. "George, you're supposed to be one of the smartest guys in town," the President said. "But you're crazier than hell. That will never happen."

Kennedy had made his choice and given Nolting his marching orders. Nolting followed them—eventually right over the side of the ship. Before departing for Saigon, a friend warned him that Vietnam "puts a blight on everyone who touches it," an ailment the French called the yellow sickness. After he left, Nolting felt the blight for the rest of his life. He wore his sadness and bitterness too. In Saigon he often looked the fool when the fault was not his. But he also looked the fool when that indeed is what he was. How else to put it about a public official who couldn't understand, and let it anger him, when the press persisted in using its own word, "war," over the government-preferred choice, "pacification"? To Nolting such behavior became a sure sign of ingrained hostility, and no one seemed more hostile than David Halberstam.

Richard Clurman recalls a conversation with Nolting as the crisis intensified in 1963: "He finally got around to press coverage— everybody got around to press coverage—and he said, 'I won't even talk to David Halberstam. He's printing lies, so I won't talk to him.' I said, 'Mr. Ambassador, you're aware that President Kennedy reads his stories before he even sees your dispatches.' And he said, 'It doesn't matter. I won't talk to him.' " According to his very angry memoirs, Nolting briefly entertained hope for Halberstam but changed his mind within weeks. Halberstam's articles began "like drops of acid," he wrote, turning public opinion against his man, Diem.

Not long after returning from his trip down Highway 4, the new man from *The New York Times* arranged his first full-fledged interview with the ambassador. The first formal meeting between the foreign correspondent from America's premier newspaper and the nation's highest-ranking overseas official normally would be a serenely civilized engagement, analogous in a rough and considerably lesser sense to an ambassador's presentation of his credentials to a foreign head of state. Normally.

In 1962, the embassy looked like anything but an outpost of empire. It was located in a six-story, falling-down mess, an old office building located on a shabby street corner near the river and not far from Sheehan's office. Next door was an even more ramshackle apartment house, and out the dirty window of the ambassador's sixth-floor office he had a view of the back terrace of a family's Buddhist shrine piled high with junk and burned-out joss sticks. It was not a place that fit his white tropical suits. The meeting soon didn't fit him either.

After a quick exchange of pleasantries, Halberstam began by asking if the problems in the Mekong Delta were as troubling to the ambassador as they seemed to him.

Nolting interrupted to ask if *The Times* planned to cover the press conference of a Viet Cong defector scheduled that afternoon.

Halberstam replied that he had heard about the defector, thought the story could be left to the wire services; as you know, Mr. Ambassador, that's what the wire services are for . . . and how was that again about the delta?

The interview quickly became anything but analogous to the presentation of credentials.

"Why don't you people do any of the regular things?" Nolting asked, his voice suddenly rising.

Before Halberstam could reply, the patrician ambassador turned florid and bolted to his feet.

"Why are you in here wasting my time?!" he demanded.

Then, abruptly, Nolting took Halberstam by the arm and escorted him straight to the door.

Later in the day John Mecklin, the press attaché, asked Trueheart how the meeting had gone.

"Oh, okay," Trueheart replied. "Except the ambassador threw Halberstam out of his office."

———

Rarely again would David Halberstam go so quietly from a room.

The lines had been tautly drawn between the Saigon press corps and the government well before his arrival. Now they would snap. Relations would disintegrate into a mutual standoff of cold fury and hot shouts—Liar! Traitor! Scoundrel! Fool!—with an American foreign policy teetering precariously in the void between. John Mecklin had arrived as the government fixer months earlier, joking that the book he would write afterward would be called *My Life in a Squirrel Cage.* When he finally went home, broken and defeated like the others, the title had changed. *Mission in Torment,* he called his two-year experience.

Many forces played a role in the breakdown, the primary one being ill-conceived and poorly executed government policies. But when admirers and critics alike sought to personify the great Vietnam crisis of 1963, a crisis that left the United States with both feet teetering at the edge of the dismal swamp, they zeroed in on one man: David Halberstam.

It was Halberstam whom Madame Nhu said she'd barbecue. It was Halberstam who kept American generals at work, dismantling his stories word by word in their effort to discredit him. It was Halberstam about whom President Kennedy ranted, finally asking *The Times* to remove him from the country.

Halberstam was such an explosive character, and became even more so later in life as he became mythologized and mythologized himself, it became easy to paint him as one-dimensional cardboard, a good guy, a bad guy, follow your own politics or your own sense of decorum, and take your choice. But the twenty-eight-year-old who showed up in Vietnam, destined to become such a catalytic force, was no simple cardboard character. He was a camouflaged man, deeply complex and conflicted—his insecurities erupting as

fire-breathing self-certainties, his doubts and losses raging as mon-
umental ego, his other inner mysteries surfacing in great generosi-
ties, sharing, and kindnesses.

Halberstam became a leader not because he was born to it but
because he needed it so. He took over without plotting or guile but
by sheer force of will. When the total social animal ran into rebuff
from the total lone wolf, he abandoned Mal Browne for the duration and longer, using his magnetic pull to draw Mal's men, Arnett
and Faas, to the edge of his orbit. The thought of loneliness consumed him. It was so *lonely* in Mississippi, he confessed, so *lonely*
in Washington and the Congo. He would dodge the loneliness in
Vietnam, by creating the group, his band of brothers, his buddies.
It would be them against the world, them against the corruption
and lying of Saigon, them against the haughtiness and compromise
of Washington, them against the restrictions and the small-
mindedness of New York and Tokyo. The tighter the world closed
in, the heavier the incoming fire, the more he thrived. He exulted
in it. "Oh what a bunch of shit!" he would thunder. "Isn't this
wonderful?!"

So now this big, loud, loose cannon, with all the firepower of *The
New York Times* in his armory, suddenly began careening through
Kennedy's nonwar. He was relentless, single-minded, obsessive;
defensive, thin-skinned, quick to take offense; highly intelligent,
impatient with fools, judgmental; obnoxiously self-certain, naively
moralistic. *My God, they* lied *to me.* He was also boyish, exuberant,
bursting with eagerness. He reveled in the very fun of it all, talking
wondrously of it: "We were the center of our own universe. Nothing else mattered. We didn't worry about shoes for the kids, or
wives, or the insurance man. We didn't worry about Kennedy.
What happened in America wasn't real. When I heard John Kennedy was trying to get rid of me, my response was: 'Well, fuck
him.' What did John Kennedy know about this world, our universe? Nothing in America had any reality for us. It was just something that happened in The Land of the Big PX."

Boundless energy drew all these conflicting traits into one, and
made the one work. Some days he would spin out his thousands
of words, working so late, wearing even at his bottomless reserves,
that the natural paranoia of all isolated foreign correspondents
would overtake him. The story from his universe would become so

173

important, and so threatened by the whims, that he would cable the same words off in three or four different directions—via Paris, via Tokyo, via Singapore—to assure the treasure's arrival in New York. *The Times*'s foreign desk suddenly found itself buried under a mound of inexplicably duplicated, triplicated, quadruplicated twenty-three-cents-a-word Halberstam epic. The editors seethed and fired back: Slow down, knock it off, STOP!

But they were just clerks back in The Land of the Big PX.

Halberstam would forever provoke strong passions in others, forever be volcanic himself. Some of his less likable traits dug deeper into his being as he grew older.

Clurman remembers a time in the eighties when Halberstam drove Barbara Walters, crying, from a Manhattan table, so brutally did he assault her opinions at a dinner party.

"David, you have everything going for you," Clurman lectured him the next day. "Why do you do things like that?"

"Well, you just can't let people get away with that sort of thing," Halberstam replied.

Push the wrong button and you could measure the explosive force in kilotonnage. Push the right one and he purred, the most helpful friend you ever had. Both friends and enemies took on Homeric proportions, just like the larger-than-life characters yet to make their appearances in his books. But get crosswise with him and the friend of a lifetime could end up in a feud for a decade. He and Gay Talese, who together dreamed the great dreams of the young before both became famous writers, had a falling-out so spectacular it was like going to the mattresses in Mafia warfare in Manhattan.

In the end it was the anger that seemed to drive everything in David Halberstam.

Clurman, a friend, looks back and says that, as chief of correspondents at *Time* magazine, all that visible and vocal anger would have made him nervous about someone on his staff. Clearly, the trait, being so *un*-Times-like, troubled his own editors far more than the large cable bills and the over-long stories they received from their difficult young star.

But Clurman also wonders. "It's an interesting hypothetical question. If David had gone off to that war without all that anger, would things have been different?"

From the moment he landed overseas Halberstam scrapped with New York over everything—editing, opinion, story concepts; salary, vacation, expenses, and more. He became, almost immediately, the newspaper's enfant terrible, its brilliant brat. But it was his battle with the foreign desk that became a *Times* epic.

In the superstructure of a large newspaper there are two kinds of editors—editors who manage and editors who edit. It was the latter group, the copy editors, that had driven Bigart into a life of not reading his own stories in print. They tinkered with reporters' dispatches and queried them about obscure detail. Bigart would not distinguish them with the name editor at all but gave them the diminished title copy readers. Once, in a fit of pique while covering the Israeli trial of Nazi mass murderer Adolf Eichmann, he inserted a description of the defendant in his story: "Eichmann reminded some of malignant little copy editors." The line did not travel well.

Now Halberstam picked up the cudgel. But he did it with more verbal violence and, of course, the unforgivable sin of youth. The editors back home on the foreign desk were old school. They did not ask, "Will you?" They said, "You will," and they didn't waste cable charges on softeners. The approach was not reserved for Halberstam, but few responded to it as combatively. The exchanges between the new boy wonder and the desk, as the battery of editors was called, rattled back and forth like machine-gun fire across a no-man's land.

In 1962, power in the news department of *The New York Times* was distributed among three powerful and autonomous principalities—the daily operation, the Sunday department (which included all the weekend sections except the regular news sections), and the liberated New World of Reston's Washington bureau. It was cumbersome, odd, and made for Borgia-like fights for both turf and the news. A dozen years earlier all three had sent competing reporters to Korea. They fought their own war within the war. According to Gay Talese in *The Kingdom and the Power*, the internecine battle became so bitter a Washington man tried to have a New York man thrown out by the army, claiming he was a psychotic. The dispute went all the way to Douglas MacArthur, who ruled for New York.

Within the principalities power broke down into fiefdoms. But at times it floated for years before settling into place. Such was the case with the foreign desk. Emanuel Freedman had the title as foreign editor long before he had the authority. For a correspondent gone from the office for years, the subtle shifts in command could be as mysterious as the inner workings of the Vatican. One day in Tokyo Greg MacGregor, a veteran Far East correspondent, received a cable:

WHY YOU CONTINUALLY BYPASSING THIS DESK STOP PLEASE EXPLAIN STOP FREEDMAN.

Confused, he showed the cable to Keyes Beech of the Chicago *Daily News* and asked if Beech knew anyone named Freedman.

"He's your boss, you goddamned fool," Beech replied.

That made it a tough cable to answer. Freedman had been foreign editor for six years.

Freedman clearly was a quiet man and, by most accounts, a decent one too. His night assistant made up for it. Nathaniel M. Gerstenzang stood five foot one inch tall. "Everything about him was small except his brain, which was narrow," said one of his underlings. He was a compulsive nitpicker, a man who had spent too long in the almanac. In *The Whole Truth*, a comic novel, Robert Daley veiled him thinly as an obsessive editor named Bangelhorster who endlessly badgered the paper's correspondent in Algiers. Was the Algerian rebel leader named Ahmed Ben Bella or just Ben Bella? Some swear Daley used the actual cables, and who knows? The incident was thinly veiled indeed. When Bernard Kalb was stationed in Djakarta, where the nagging cables awoke him in the middle of the night, Gerstenzang went on a spree. Why did Kalb persist in omitting the Indonesian president's first name from his stories? Because he has no first name, Kalb replied. It was to no effect. Gerstenzang's pestering continued for weeks until Kalb yielded in desperation. ACHMED, he cabled. And for a few days *The Times* had a scoop: Achmed Sukarno it was, and for months to come the imaginary name would reemerge periodically from clippings in the newspaper's library, catch an uninitiated editor unawares, and make still another appearance in the newspaper of record.

Gerstenzang was responsible for the daily messages to Freedman's stable of correspondents, and terse and niggling cables they were. Paranoia grows exponentially with distance. "Foreign correspondents are the most insecure human beings on earth," said Betsy Wade, who broke the copy desk's gender barrier (they banished spittoons her first day on the job). "Even a message saying the sun came up this morning brings back a reply: 'What do you mean by that?' " But no one had a greater talent for aggravating the trait than Gerstenzang. He could not convey the simplest message without antagonizing. Others in the office watched Freedman take him to the corner for lectures on good manners in cable-ese. It was all to no avail. He was the man at the other end of the correspondents' only tether to the real world. But his missives arrived at distant *Times* outposts amid wars and insurrections, scraping like fingernails across a blackboard. "The dialogue of the deaf," Ted Shabad called communications between the foreign desk and the field, and he had worked both ends.

Still, the copy editors below Freedman and Gerstenzang wrenched some pretty awful writing into passable prose, and often the remakes came on the wordy pieces from Halberstam. There was nothing about a vaunted *Times* byline that guaranteed lucid communication. Historically, the paper had minimized writing, especially from the foreign staff. "The theory was, get the stuff in here and we'll fix it up," said Cleve Mathews, who worked the desk.

Getting it in there was not easy in the early sixties, a time when revolutionary strides in communications loomed just over the horizon but reality remained stuck in the nineteenth century. In his rookie year in the Congo, Halberstam's admirers on the foreign desk, and he had them, marveled over his youthful ingenuity at finding ways to get stories out of the jungles and into the office. The chaotic condition of the Congo and its communications meant that his stories often arrived in a dozen pieces, out of order, yesterday's lead mixed into today's body, some parts missing and presumed dead on a spike in an African cable station. The arrival was both a mess and a miracle. The writing was usually only the former. From the beginning Halberstam's prose was ponderous, difficult, convoluted—and always long. "He was a wonderful reporter," said Mathews, "but his writing just slogged on and on. Even today, every time I read one of his books, I want to copyedit it."

The newsroom also lagged at the end of a fast-fading era. Soon there would be computers and photocopiers, lasers for photos, earth satellites relaying the news, cold type replacing the grandeur of hot lead. The third floor gave no hint of that. On the 43rd Street side sat the fiefdom of Freedman and Gerstenzang, an arc of old desks stacked with paper mounded like sandbags against the flood. In the cramped work openings sat the technology of the day: a canister of pencils finely sharpened, a pair of scissors, a paste pot.

The cables landed on the desks each afternoon after one machine had triple-spaced them (the assumption being that they needed lots of space for editing) and a pre-Xerox contraption had dealt them out in vaguely damp copies for everyone from the managing editor down to the pencil editor. The triple-spacing and the wet copying meant that the stories landed in wads, often twenty pages or more. The work began: Cut it, paste it, rearrange it; down-style it, up-style it, spell it, clarify it, transpose it, all this done in the special hiero-glyphics and curlicues of the copyediting trade. Then, with the tough stories, came the real job: recompose it in a fine, neat hand, filling up the triple spaces, careful not to break down paste-weakened paper fiber. It could be an arduous job, physically drain-ing. "A tough one came in thick and went out crumbly," said Wade.

David Halberstam's reporting came in thickest and went out crumbliest. On the desk, catching him was like pulling the short straw. Once, at the height of the Congo story, Harold Gal edited him for forty-three nights in a row. Later, his colleagues threw a party for him in the back room of a Times Square restaurant called the Blue Ribbon, where the owners added an extra finger of whis-key for the late crew. They presented Gal with an enormous ribbon lettered in French: FIRST-CLASS COPY EDITOR WITH PALMS.

Not long after Halberstam's arrival in the Congo, Gerstenzang fired the first salvo. He advised the new man of "flaws" in his work, including "fuzzy writing" and "free-wheeling conduct of which you have given evidence." He added: "I have no fears you will take these comments amiss."

Gerstenzang clearly did not know David Halberstam. Back from Leopoldville with deadline speed came a three-page, single-spaced letter challenging each point, yielding on none. (Unlike his editors, Halberstam would never use a hundred words when a thousand would do.) The rookie correspondent concluded the missive un-abashed: "I would like . . . to say we understand each other, but I am afraid the problem is more serious than that."

It remained so even after higher-ups intervened. "It must be clearly understood that this paper is edited in New York," Clifton Daniel rebuked Halberstam in June 1962. Daniel would soon be-come managing editor of *The Times* and carry with him an abiding aversion to super-ego reporters whose independent stardom chal-lenged the editors' control. Knock it off, he ordered, before the back and forth "aggravate[s] a situation that has already been aggra-vated too much."

Halberstam was undeterred. The running battle escalated throughout his stay in Vietnam. In Saigon "to Gerst" would be-come a new verb form. First Neil Sheehan, then Charley Mohr, then other buddies sounded the same complaint when they had trouble with their desks. They had been Gersted.

———

In late October the correspondents got another reminder from the palace about just how tenuous their presence in Saigon had be-come.

Two months after the Sully expulsion the Diem government abruptly kicked out another reporter, James Robinson, a visiting Hong Kong–based correspondent for NBC television. Robinson's expulsion came amid almost as many absurdities as the Sully ejec-tion. A regular visitor, Robinson had been in the country only two weeks and had not yet filed a story. Technically, he was ejected for a minor visa violation. In reality, he had committed a far more dastardly deed. After a typically rambling, three-hour interview with President Diem, Robinson made the mistake of telling his interpreter the talk had been "a waste of time."

NBC, like all of infant television, remained a trifle wet behind the ears journalistically. The network did not distinguish itself with a cloying plea to Diem to save Robinson because of the work it had done showing "your valiant efforts to stop the spread of Commu-nism in Southeast Asia."

The Saigon correspondents made what was now becoming a boilerplate protest to the Diem government: The expulsion was "an unjustifiable infringement of traditional principles of freedom of the press." The correspondents' protest was as hopelessly naive as the NBC attempt was groveling. Traditional principles of freedom? There were none in Vietnam, of course, neither for the press nor the people. For either the American government or the press to think it could implant such alien beliefs in a 2,000-year-old culture, developed in isolation even from its own Asian neighbors, illustrated part of the problem with the United States being there in the first place.

But the correspondents went through their motions. And the palace, tiring of receiving telegrams of complaint from the unwelcome little band causing such trouble, responded predictably. "We in Vietnam have had enough of the calumnies and insults that the unscrupulous and unreliable heap upon our Chief of State. . . . ," the reply began. As usual, Madame Nhu responded even more vigorously. Vietnam, she angrily told the reporters, had no use for "your crazy freedoms."

Robinson's expulsion came in the midst of the Cuban missile crisis and quickly faded from view. But not before a flurry of talk among the reporters about whether a brief stint of visa reporting might not be the best strategic move at the moment. They couldn't bring themselves to do it.

———

The now-familiar sound of the helicopters awakened Mert Perry grumpily and far too early on November 22, 1962, Thanksgiving Day morning. The staccato roar of the old wooden-rotor H-21 Shawnees had become routine background noise since the arrival of the carrier *Core* almost a year ago. But this sounded like an armada. Perry rolled heavily out of bed.

Next to him, the noise also awakened Darlene Perry. She bolted upright, as if coming out of a very bad dream. The Perrys were the only married couple among the small group living in Saigon. That probably would have made Darlene the Earth Mother even if she hadn't had a lovable, down-home Midwestern sense of hearth about her. She had become news central, social coordinator, magical producer of apple pie. Everybody loved Mert, their big, fat, take-no-shit buddy. And everybody loved Darlene. But the ancient H-21 helicopters terrified her, made her a nervous wreck every time Mert went near one. The old buckets of bolts had been going down right and left lately. She knew the guys were afraid of them, too, or they wouldn't make macho jokes about flying the Boneyard Specials. A few weeks earlier Mert had been heading out the door when Darlene suddenly burst into tears. "I know where you're going," she accused. "You're going out in those old helicopters that are held together with Elmer's Glue!"

On Thanksgiving morning, however, Darlene Perry sank back into her pillow with a sigh of relief. Mert wasn't going anywhere. The men had been furious for the past two weeks because the South Vietnamese government, upset again, had banned them from all helicopter flights. Darlene was secretly delighted.

The Perrys had a downtown apartment near the river and above Neil Sheehan's UPI office and his claustrophobic back bedroom. From the window they had a pleasant view. From the roof the view became panoramic. Perry stuck his head out the window, then quickly lumbered up to the roof. Against the pewter-gray dawn sky, the choppers swarmed like noisy locusts as they fanned out toward the north, then banked northeast. Perry methodically began counting.

In a few years the rhythmic *whumping* of chopper blades would orchestrate the deadly theme music of the big war. But Americans had made little combat use of helicopters in their last war in Korea, and, by late 1962, the new airborne tactics were still evolving. The prevailing view on tactics held that the new air mobility would enable friendly troops to leapfrog quickly over rough and un-friendly territory, overwhelming an enemy with surprise. Some of the flaws in this idea, as applied in Vietnam, were becoming clear, and the tactic had its detractors within the American military. One of them was Colonel Wilbur "Coal Bin Willie" Wilson, coinciden-tally the senior American adviser aboard the H-21s that Mert Perry, now fully awake, carefully counted. Coal Bin Willie was known in the army as a taskmaster who, like John Paul Vann, spoke his mind. He had picked up his nickname stateside when he punished a lazy recruit by ordering him to empty a coal bin, clean it, whitewash it, and fill it again with the same coal. Wilson thought the helicopters provided another excuse for laziness among the ARVN troops. All the choppers were good for, he complained, was "rattle-assing around the country," irritating the Viet Cong with mosquito bites that did no lasting damage.

At this moment, however, Coal Bin Willie Wilson was making military history, and Mert Perry, perched on his rooftop, sensed it. His eyes bulged as the count of fading choppers reached almost fifty. Perry toted up what this told him. Each H-21 carried an American crew of four—two pilots and two gunners—who ferried twelve Vietnamese soldiers and their U.S. advisers to battle. That meant the operation involved more than 200 Americans and about 600 ARVN troopers, maybe more. Coal Bin Willie was rattle-assing off on the largest assault in the history of helicopter warfare.

Perry hot-footed it down the stairs and hammered on the street-level door until the insomniacal UPI correspondent emerged, bleary-eyed.

Filled in, Sheehan became furious. Just cleared of a medical grounding for his broken arm, he had run head-on into the new palace edict. He had not been out on a mission for almost two months. But this was outrageous. American officials could blame the Vietnamese for the latest ban, but he blamed Harkins. These were American helicopters with American crews, and the operation Perry had just spotted put more Americans at risk than any combat mission since Korea. Not only were there no correspondents along, but, as usual, General Harkins had not bothered to warn them, once again ignoring a courtesy between military and press that dated back a century.

The two reporters immediately set to work, Sheehan sending up a near-toxic cloud from the Salem menthols he chain-smoked to subdue the usual wire-service angst of his deadline, Perry helping because of the luxurious weekly pace afforded him as a *Time* stringer. It was not a difficult story to check out. The reporters did not need sources to run risks or betray orders. As with most reporting, they merely needed bits and pieces and the knowledge to add them up. Half a dozen phone calls confirmed what they already knew: Virtually every working H-21 in the Saigon area was in the air. Simple deduction also told them where they were headed. Perry had seen that: into the great forest redoubt known as War Zone D.

The special zone began only thirty-five miles northwest of Saigon and spread to the Cambodian border. But it would harbor the

Viet Cong and frustrate the Americans throughout most of the war. Almost impenetrable jungle deterred overland assaults. Dense, triple-canopy forests hid the ground from prying aircraft. Even with chemical defoliation already under way, the riverbanks inside Zone D provided such natural ambush cover that the life expectancy of men on riverine patrols was measured in months or weeks. So secure did the guerrillas feel inside their redoubt that they had built entire villages, rest facilities, even a road capable of handling heavy tanks.

One day earlier the ARVN, aided by their American advisers, had begun their first major attack on War Zone D, combining infantry with paratroop and river assaults. Harkins's people still refused comment on the operation, and now stonewalled on the helicopters. But Sheehan had the story aced and took some pride in it. It was no investigative masterpiece, just good, smart, professional work. Not bad for a guy only seven months on a killer job. Still, he lived with the terror-stricken memory of that big rollback with Homer Bigart during his first rookie weeks. He made a few more calls, using a tested routine for tying the last knot: *Don't tell me anything. Just warn me if I'm wrong.* He wasn't.

Harkins blew a fuse. He launched a full-fledged investigation to discover who had "leaked" about the helicopters, having no idea that Perry had simply counted most of them. The investigation sent plain-clothes counterintelligence officers squirreling around Sheehan and his known sources as if someone had given away the Manhattan Project. To everyone but Harkins the scene came straight out of *M*A*S*H* and consumed more military man-hours chasing ghosts, as John Mecklin described it later, than counting casualties in War Zone D, which soon proved to be few.

Reports began to filter back that the massive assault had drawn a blank, producing almost no casualties. Still, Harkins's information officers stonewalled on all detail. The South Vietnamese, eager to even up with their American pests, reinforced the wall of silence. Mecklin, whose chore was to solve the press mess, sat in his office at the embassy, trying to calm his former news colleagues while confiding to some of his new ones in the government that he couldn't believe how matters could get so screwed up. On the third day Harkins finally learned that the "leak" had come off Perry's roof. Reluctantly, he lifted some of the secrecy.

At the military press briefing that afternoon, Sheehan asked one of the first questions. What was General Harkins's reaction to the outcome of the operation?

"Uncle Paul," the public-information officer replied in a good-old-boy tone, "doesn't want his name used."

Sheehan's Irish flared.

"You tell *Uncle Paul*," he shot back in a brogue with a burr that burned, "that he is the American commander here, that he releases the American helicopters and American men, and he puts their lives at risk, and that *Uncle Paul's* name goes in my stories."

A few hours later Mecklin also had a hostile visitor. David Halberstam charged through Mecklin's door in his usual aggressive gait, slapped a letter to Ambassador Nolting onto his desk, and sat down, waiting, in a rage.

The letter angrily charged that Harkins had unnecessarily denied information to the American public when two hundred of their young men had risked their lives. Then it continued:

> The reason given is security. This is, of course, stupid, naive and indeed insulting to the patriotism and intelligence of every American newspaperman and every American newspaper represented here. Let me point out that we, as our predecessors in times of conflict have been, are fully prepared to observe the problems of security [and] to withhold printing classified information. . . .
>
> Let me also point out that from the moment that fifty helicopters landed at a given point in Zone D, certain aspects of the operation lost all classified status. You can bet the VC knew what was happening; you can bet Hanoi knew what was happening. Only American reporters and American readers were kept ignorant. . . .

Mecklin winced as he read on. Halberstam wrote that the incident had changed him from "a neutral bystander into an angry man." Mecklin tried briefly to convince the man from America's most powerful newspaper that he was overreacting. Halberstam demanded to know if he would pass the letter on. Mecklin promised that he would give it to the ambassador, who, the last time he had dealt with Halberstam, had kicked the *New York Times* correspondent out of his office. Mecklin thought the situation couldn't get much worse. He was wrong.

8

REBELS IN THE FIELD:
THE COLONELS

John Mecklin's experiences the previous time around had been tragic, symbolic, and filled with foreboding. He had literally watched the lights blink out on the French.

With *Life* photographer Howard Sochurek, Mecklin rode the tin-can seats of an old C-47 on one last night-flight attempt to land at the doomed garrison at Dien Bien Phu. The pilot circled and circled, then refused to go down through the guerrillas' intense ground fire. Supplies were kicked out by parachute instead, Mecklin watching them disappear into the ink and then reappear briefly in the "slow-motion blossoms of garish red flames from the Viet Minh mortars." Most landed outside the French perimeter. Finally, a fatalistic voice crackled up from the ground: *rien à signaler*, nothing to report. The French did not try again. It was over.

But a walk with another photographer along a valley road only weeks earlier had left the indelible mark.

In 1954 Robert Capa was easily the world's best-known war photographer. He had come quickly to fame with an unforgettable Spanish Civil War photo catching a soldier at his "Moment of Death"—stopped in mid-stride by an enemy bullet, head thrown back, arms outstretched, rifle falling away. Later, a darkroom error added an ethereal blur to his pictures of the D-Day landing at Normandy, turning merely very good photographs into the stuff of art. He became a celebrity of both salon and battlefield.

One hot night in late March, bivouacked with French troops in a small Vietnamese town, Mecklin and Capa sat up late working on the photographer's bottomless supply of cognac. The talk turned to the usual complaints, Mecklin bitching heartily about French secrecy. Capa waved him off. "The trouble with all you guys who complain so much about French public relations is that you don't appreciate this is a reporter's war," he said. "Nobody knows anything and nobody tells you anything, and that means a good reporter is free to go out and get a beat every day." The next day Capa died in Mecklin's arms.

On that sullen afternoon Capa moved ahead of the troop column to set up a shot. Moments later a French officer stunned Mecklin: *Le photographe est mort.* Impossible, Mecklin stammered, the photographer can't be dead. But seventy-five yards up the road, he found him. Capa had stepped on a mine, one leg blown completely away, a terrible, sucking wound torn in his chest. Mecklin tried to speak to his friend. Capa made one last motion and stopped. Later, at a field hospital, a doctor looked up from a pointless examination and asked, "Is this the first American correspondent killed in Indochina?" Mecklin nodded. The doctor shook his head. "It is a harsh way for America to learn."

Now, eight years later, Mecklin was not a happy man. His new boss, Secretary of State Dean Rusk, complained openly that he was too close to the press. The press saw him as a turncoat peddling disinformation. He took to drinking too much, a man torn between the responsibilities of a difficult new marriage and the memory of a first love. That last conversation with Capa, one he would have long forgotten but for the awful day after, haunted him. He had become the French. And if the French had made Indochina "a reporter's war," the Americans were doing it in spades.

Mecklin saw precisely what was happening. He was no great admirer of the Saigon correspondents. He considered them green and prone to error, especially in perception. They were, he thought, "unbending puritans" who walked around "with basketball-sized chips on their shoulders." Halberstam's performance in his office had done nothing to change his view. But he also saw Harkins and Nolting planting the seeds of their own destruction. Being bull-headed with the resident correspondents would not cause the pages of *The New York Times* to run blank or the tickers of the wire services to clack emptily. On the contrary, it would drive the reporters, as Mecklin knew it would have driven him, to find a new network of sources. In 1962, a rich harvest was to be had.

The military force now growing methodically in Vietnam was unlike any in American history. Historically, the isolationist United States had relied on citizen armies, farm boys and street kids, teachers and merchants, drawn up suddenly and thrown into the breach when peril threatened. Rarely was an American army ready, and the early carnage in the country's wars was often terrible. But this force was different. It was professional, elite, ambitious, and self-certain, the advance guard of a new empire born out of The Bomb and the wreckage of two world wars in thirty years. Of the 11,200 American military men in Vietnam by the end of the year, not one was a draftee, few if any doubted their right or need to be there, and most saw their tour not as dirty duty but as a desirable career opportunity. Vietnam became a handy tropical practice field—"the greatest continuing war games we've come up with," an officer told Halberstam.

The Vietnam of 1962 drew the best the United States had to offer —sons of its most famed Second World War generals, top-echelon graduates of West Point, bright men from nowhere who had risen through one of America's greatest mid-century strengths, its openness to merit. Its warriors had attended the best staff schools, studied for advanced degrees in philosophy as well as military science. These were men on the rise, men who intended to get ahead in their profession, and Vietnam was the place to be. "The word is out," the officer continued. "If you want to stay on the ball team, you go to Vietnam."

In the roughhouse of career advancement, the military takes a backseat to no institution—not to the brutal dueling of corporate life, not to the deadly character assassination of politics, not to the ruthless candlelit conniving of the church. So the corps of young officers on the move included all the usual players—the innovators, the strategists, the heroes and the do-gooders, the cynics and the hustlers, the sycophants, the men who would dig their boots into the ribs of their best friend to reach a higher handhold on the climb. Out of this group would come the military's next generation of leadership.

Halberstam delighted in watching the infighting, learned from it too. In Vietnam, there were two generals named Stilwell, each a brigadier, a general with one star. One was Joe Stilwell, Jr., son of the legendary "Vinegar Joe" Stilwell who had taken no guff from his superiors or the Japanese and became one of America's great no-nonsense, frontline generals. His son was cut from the same rough cloth, opting for the combat of the battlefield over the combat of the cocktail party. The other was Richard Giles Stilwell, a brilliant if pretentious man whose tack was more political. He glued himself to Harkins, the way Harkins had to Patton, and became his chief of operations, backing his boss unflaggingly in the ruinous optimism passed on to Washington and the deadly undercutting of those who didn't.

Once, when all were in the same room, Joe Stilwell took Halberstam aside and said, "I'm Joe Stilwell. I'm only gonna get one star. He's Dick Stilwell. He's gonna get four. I'm a good guy. He's a prick." From that moment on, to the correspondents, the two generals became known as Stilwell the Good and Stilwell the Bad. Four years later Joe Stilwell disappeared in a plane crossing the Pacific, carrying with him just one star. Dick Stilwell advanced to three.

Still, the personal rivalries paled alongside the bruising turf battles between the service branches. If the Pentagon used Vietnam as a practice field to develop the playbook for future wars, the services tangled to see who would carry the ball. In 1962 no two branches clashed more openly than the army, which had moved into the air with their helicopters, and the air force, which didn't like the intrusion.

Pamela Sanders, who wandered in occasionally from Laos, usually got a more macho treatment than the male correspondents. She was taken on almost every wild combat ride the little war had to offer. The action sometimes made her wonder if war made men out of boys or boys out of men. But she also concluded that "the war between the army and the air force could get meaner than the war with the Viet Cong."[1]

1. Later, the rivalries shifted. Westmoreland once threatened to quit his ill-fated command. But he was not driven to the brink by the bugaboos now entrenched in popular thought: that civilian interference and political limitations hobbled his efforts, that an irresponsible media deprived him of public support by insisting he was losing when he was certain he was winning. Westmoreland, an army man, threatened to resign over a spat with the marines.

The animus became supercharged. Neil Sheehan watched the village-bombing dispute reach prodigious proportions. The air force had almost 2,000 men in Vietnam by late 1962, one for every two South Vietnamese airmen. Despite Washington's mirrors game about their role, through FARMGATE Americans had virtually taken over the South Vietnamese Air Force, flying most of its missions. John Paul Vann complained regularly to Saigon that the bombing was killing "many, many more civilians than it ever does VC" and that the slaughter was defeating efforts to win over the peasants.

At his best, a reporter skims the surface of a story, writing, as is often said, the first rough draft of history. Years later Sheehan fleshed out the full story of the great bombing battle. In Saigon, Vann's immediate superior, Colonel Daniel Boone Porter, a scholarly looking but flinty officer, pushed the complaint to the hilt. His adversary was a tall, good-looking brigadier general named Rollen (Buck) Anthis, the air force commander under Harkins's overall command. A colonel taking on a general, Porter nevertheless became a festering thorn. Again and again, he hammered at Anthis: *Your attacks are killing the people we are here to help. They have no place in this kind of war.* Anthis grew hostile and his arguments circular: *You're exaggerating; the strikes are made at the legal request of the South Vietnamese; war is hell.* Porter became blunter: *Come on down and see the stretched-out corpses of the women and children and old people.* Anthis continued to duck and dodge. For Anthis it was necessary to assume the villages were Viet Cong bastions. What else could the air force bomb in this will-o'-the-wisp war? In wars of shadows, wars without set-piece targets, would the air force have any role? Anthis never did look. He knew better, knew the moral predicament it could place him in. Angry as they were, Porter and Vann found it difficult to blame him. Like a lawyer, Anthis was doing his job. They blamed Harkins, whose job it was to sort out such disputes. Harkins was the Supreme Court. The court demurred; the bombing continued. Later, Harkins found a rationale: Orientals respect power, he said, and the bombing made the peasants afraid.

Americans marveled at the dark plots and scheming of the Vietnamese. But in the realm of intrigue, the American military held its Occidental own. Reporters love intrigues and rivalries. They open mouths. They breed stories. In the field the reporters also found another asset: They could develop a high degree of camaraderie with the new American fighting man.

The reporters who, in years to come, followed this first cadre of correspondents into Vietnam would be greeted by military public-affairs officers imploring: *Don't be a Halberstam, don't be a Sheehan.* But the idea that this early group carried with them an antimilitary bent, polluting a generation of reporters, is one of the enduring myths of the war. Sparks flew between the correspondents and the whitewashers in Saigon—and crackled halfway around the world from those two power centers in The Land of the Big PX, the White House and the Pentagon. In Saigon, the correspondents became unwanted intruders; in Washington, pariahs. But in the field? As schoolchildren, the correspondents, even Peter Arnett in New Zealand, had watched all those heroic Hollywood movies of good-guy Americans, triumphant GIs showered with flowers as they rode into liberated villages, smiling GIs showering urchins with the American benevolence of Wrigleys and Hersheys. Americans came to do good—it was liturgy—and in Vietnam Americans had also come to do good.

So, in the field, the correspondents were among good guys. To be initiated into the fraternity it took just one tree-skimming landing under fire in a Shawnee, one slogging patrol through the mud and leeches of the delta, one surrounded overnighter with a handful of Green Berets and Montagnard tribesmen in the mountains. In the field, they became buddies.

In Saigon the rap was that they were too young and green. This complaint became perhaps the greatest canard. War is for the young. So is journalism—no part of it more so than war journalism. Most of the old-guard correspondents, about to become harshly critical, had covered their first wars at even younger ages—Marguerite Higgins a mere twenty-four years old in Second World War Germany, Richard Tregaskis twenty-six and Keyes Beech twenty-eight as they began following the marines across the Pacific. Even the harshest of them all, Joseph Alsop, had yet to turn thirty when he joined forces with the Flying Tigers, not as a correspondent but a high-level aide, in his beloved China. The military detractors were equally hypocritical. Westmoreland, who arrived after Halberstam left, mentioned him as the spoiler three times in his book, *A Soldier Reports*, each time adding the appellation "young." At

Halberstam's age Westmoreland had already made lieutenant colonel and led his artillery battalion across North Africa against Rommel and back into Europe through Sicily.

In the field they were the same age as the advisers doing the toughest and most demanding work—captains who advised at the crucial battalion level, the best of the new majors just kicked up a notch precisely because they were so good. The major who commanded the new Huey helicopters—so crucial to the army's war with the air force and the Viet Cong—was a year younger than Mal Browne and only two years older than Halberstam.

Slogging through the mud, the correspondents and the soldiers became friends, not adversaries. They'd send off appropriate congratulations:

> MAJOR PAUL RAISIG
> US MAAG COMPOUND
> BAC LIEU, VIETNAM
> SIR. WHATEVER HAPPENED TO CAPTAIN RAISIG? CONGRATULA-
> TIONS. HALBERSTAM PERRY SHEEHAN

When a buddy shipped out for home, they'd tender small gifts, maybe a cigarette lighter engraved with all their names and, as one was, a raw, men-among-men greeting: IVAN: NUMBER-FUCKING-ONE!

They'd show up for the other departures, too, the quiet little ceremonies on the blazing tarmac at Tan Son Nhut when friends began going home KIA. In his recollections—an unfinished diary of sorts—that Sheehan began writing in 1967, he described the difference between those later heart of darkness days and the innocence of 1962. By 1967 "death overwhelmed us." It had become impersonal. But, in the beginning, there were no mass ceremonies, no endless rows of body bags. "Death was almost romantic then because it came in small doses." At the funeral ceremonies "everyone knew the man who had died, everyone believed in the cause and there was hope that the deaths were meaningful." Each man got his own words, his own eulogies, occasionally from a correspondent. At the end, when the honor guard played taps, all the buddies saluted.

In the beginning, the reporters often carried weapons and took on mildly participatory combat roles. In late 1962 Mal Browne made an official request on behalf of the correspondents for training on the U.S. military firing range, although not all his colleagues thought it a good idea. John Stirling, a stringer for various London newspapers, was one of Saigon's more colorful characters. Half Asian and half English, Stirling was a slight man with an incongruous foghorn voice. For days, he stomped angrily in and out of the AP office asserting his disapproval in a voice that rattled glass like a sapper's grenade: "What are you trying to do, Browne? Get us in a war?!"

If anything, the correspondents became too close to, not too distant from, the military. Sheehan, the Irish brooder, later felt great pangs of guilt about spotting for a helicopter crew strafing fleeing men shortly after he arrived.

Most of the correspondents also asked themselves later if the closeness had helped them miss the biggest story of all—that all these well-meaning, we've-got-the-answer, do-good Americans had no business being in Vietnam at all, that the entire enterprise was an invitation to disaster. But that was an impossible story in 1962. Everything militated against it. The times the reporters lived in. The constricted nature of the institution they represented. Their own Cold-War-with-Mom's-apple-pie backgrounds. And the absolute incredibility of the thought that their government might be stumbling into committing ground troops, divisions, to this place. Even Maxwell Taylor was a member of the Never Again Club, a loose-knit group of Washington strategists dedicated to the idea that, after Korea, the United States could never again allow itself to bog down in an Asian land war. The best journalism can only deal with what is there, what's in the arena. In 1962 Vietnam was right.

Many years later, when questioning America's involvement became as natural a part of the times as it was unnatural in 1962, Ward Just asked Halberstam what would have happened if he had focused, not just on the lying and whether the war was being won or lost, but on the Cold War mentality that drew the United States into Vietnam in the first place. "Oh," he pondered briefly, "that would have made me almost unemployable in a situation like that, I think."

In any case, Halberstam was a believer, as were the others, Cold Warriors all. He wrote home to James Reston: "I am impressed by what a bold and difficult thing we have undertaken here. . . . we are going up against the best revolutionaries of our time on their home ground in a type of war which they have almost invented." It was Washington's "sugar coat," he added, that "artificial optimism hardly justified by conditions" that boded ill.

Meanwhile, the optimism continued boundlessly. On November, 15, 1962, Ambassador Nolting declared: "The most determined pessimist must now concede that the tide is turning against the Communists." Some of the top field advisers were not so sanguine.

The enemy learned fast. Captured documents showed just how shrewdly the Viet Cong, terrified of the helicopters at first, had learned to fight back. The guerrillas studied the old H-21 Shawnees. They noted that the choppers had only one troop-exit door, on the left, and the pilots invariably favored that side, to protect the landing ARVN troopers. So the guerrillas adapted, setting up ambushes to blindside the predictable attack patterns.

The ARVN did not learn fast. ARVN patrols continued to demand three-hour midday breaks for lunch and siestas, usually after stealing food from the villagers they were supposed to win over. They headed home at the first sign of darkness. Their commanders, fearing the wrath of Diem, avoided casualties and rarely pursued the guerrillas on the ground. Coal Bin Willie had been right: The helicopters spoiled them. After the rainy season ended in October, the Americans expected the Viet Cong to open a major offensive and had tried to preempt it with two large ARVN assaults—Operation Morning Star, using 6,000 troops in mid-October, and the War Zone D operation. The Viet Cong cockily waited them out and then began their own far more successful attacks.

The endless stream of positive reports, often directly contradicting the view from the field, began to seriously trouble some of the senior advisers. Vann was not alone. Lieutenant Colonel Jonathan (Fred) Ladd, the son of an army general and the top adviser in the entrenched Viet Cong bastion of Camau at the southern tip of Vietnam, was a less manipulative man. But he left no doubt about his concern. He once lined up Halberstam and two other reporters in the familiar three-monkey pose: hear no evil, see no evil, speak no evil. He took their photograph and roared with laughter.

The concern was infectious. Griping is a given among the dog soldiers, the grunts, in any war. Not so with gung-ho, ambitious young officers. On one of his forays Halberstam found the young officer-advisers totally confident "that they belong to the very best military force in the world." He also found them singing this ditty to the tune of "Twinkle, Twinkle Little Star":

We are winning, this we know.
   General Harkins tells us so.
In the delta, things are rough,
   In the mountains, mighty tough.

But we're winning, this we know.
   General Harkins tells us so.
If you doubt that this is true,
   McNamara says so too.

It was into this combustible mix of ambitious young officers, dueling military services, and worried advisers—plus the narcotic of raw adventure—that Harkins and Nolting, through their stubbornness, had banished the resident correspondents. It was like banishing a reporter to heaven. The middle-rank advisers and the correspondents bonded across their natural barriers. The longer the correspondents spent outside Saigon, the less they needed the stonewalling of Harkins and the no comments of his public-information officers. Until they didn't need them at all.

"We couldn't get anything out of the official sources," Sheehan told researcher Deborah Kalb, "and therefore they lost control of us. Entirely. It was a very good thing for us. Each reporter had to go out and build his own intelligence system."

Sometimes the system worked ingeniously. Sheehan developed one source, an American captain, who never told him a thing. He called and said, "Get cracking." Signaled, Sheehan would race to the captain's office at Camp Le Van Duyet, an old French cavalry post on the boulevard to Cholon, and ask a friendly Vietnamese colonel for the reports. The reports would appear, often marked TOP SECRET. The colonel would walk away while Sheehan read them. Eventually, the Vietnamese colonel would become the real source, one of the best of the war, and Camp Le Van Duyet the center of Saigon's ultimate intrigue.

Another was a mysterious "colonel" first introduced to him by Homer Bigart. He operated in the ramshackle outskirts of Saigon from a strange office with an encoded buzzer that opened the door. It was a place "full of oddball radios and Danish Madsen submachine guns and Schmeissers and Swedish K's stacked in the corner and these guys coming in and out in what we called tiger suits, those spotted camouflage uniforms." Sheehan was so agog it took him three visits to figure out that the place was CIA using Special Forces on loan. But he had found a first-class source, a teacher. The colonel issued warnings, guidances. When Harkins announced that the ARVN had killed 21,000 Viet Cong in 1962, Sheehan got a cautionary: The numbers are nonsense, the logic worse. If you are killing more people, there are more people to kill. That means guerrilla strength is growing. Become optimistic, the colonel instructed, when body counts go down.

Sheehan saw the "colonel" often, never dismissed a get cracking call, talked with the men in the field—and ignored Harkins. Vietnam became, once again, "a reporter's war."

Mecklin saw all this coming, saw it coming special delivery. Within months the handful of reporters often knew more about what was going on than the government itself. They had better sources than Harkins and Nolting—or, at least, better sources than the general and the ambassador would listen to.

At Brodard's one day late in the year Radio Catinat flashed the gossip that Joe Alsop, never one to use a simple line if a pompous one would do, had been heard boasting that he never talked to anyone below the rank of colonel. That gave the group a good laugh. With a few exceptions, such as Stilwell the Good, the Young Turks weren't talking to anybody *above* the rank of colonel.

At the White House, President Kennedy began getting his news from *The New York Times* before it arrived in his intelligence reports. John Kennedy would never be an admirer of the Saigon reporters, certainly not of David Halberstam. But aides remember the President slapping *The Times* down on his Oval Office desk one day and barking in exasperation: "Why can I get this stuff from Halberstam when I can't get it from my own people?" The White House, like the bumbling Harkins, began to demand sweeping, but equally ineffective, security investigations to plug the leaks.

The little band of correspondents, Mecklin later wrote, stood on the verge of achieving "an influence in the making of U.S. foreign policy that had been equaled in modern times only by the role of the New York newspapers in precipitating the Spanish-American War. . . ." That was not much of a compliment, but it amounted to enormous influence.

———

The outside world, with all its normal workaday cares and problems, intruded into all this headiness only occasionally. It bulled its way in for Halberstam, suddenly and rudely, in two most threatening ways near the end of 1962.

The first bolt struck shortly after his angry Thanksgiving tangle with Harkins. Forwarded from ancient address to ancient address in the methodically persistent manner of the old U.S. postal system, a letter arrived from an outfit accustomed to different relations between young men and generals. It came from his draft board.

The draft was not yet an explosive political issue and Halberstam had not thought of it in years, having served six months of active duty in the army in 1957. He had joined under the Reserve Forces Act, a program designed to draw down the size of the active military while keeping a large ready reserve available for rapid mobilization during the edgy Cold War peace after Korea. The RFA quickly became a favorite of athletes and other fast-trackers. It offered that short career interruption of six months—a draftee like Browne went in for two years, a regular volunteer like Sheehan for three—in exchange for a commitment of eight years in the ready reserve. The first year, Halberstam did his weekend warrior duty and attended the required summer camp. The next year he asked for and received an exemption from those duties because of his erratic hours at the *Tennessean*. Such dispensations—the eight-year commitment remained intact—were not unusual. Halberstam never looked back, charging headlong into the rest of his life.

Now, two problems threatened to trip him up. During that career trek from Nashville to New York to Washington to Leopoldville to Saigon, Halberstam had neglected to keep in touch with his reserve unit. Meanwhile, the crisis-prone Kennedy administration kept slipping into those international showdowns for which the reserves had been designed. Only weeks after Halberstam's arrival in the Congo in 1961, Kennedy mobilized 300,000 men to rattle sabers over the construction of the Berlin Wall. A month after Halberstam arrived in Vietnam a year later, the entire American military establishment slept with its boots on during the high tension of the Cuban missile crisis. It is unclear whether his unit was ever activated. But during all the hubbub no one could find Private Halberstam.

So along came the letter from Local Board Number 20 in Torrington, Connecticut, near the little town he always called home, Winsted. Because his reserve unit had not heard from him for four years, it said, the board was about to change his draft classification from Standby Reserve to 1-A.

Halberstam flinched, and with good reason. In 1962, with a classification of 1-A at age twenty-eight, he could be marching before he knew it. The situation contained a touch of the absurd. In the past fifteen months, Halberstam had seen more combat than any draftee in the U.S. Army. Back in the old days his predecessor, Homer Bigart, had gone to Europe to *avoid* the draft, which was standard and acceptable procedure for a correspondent during the Second World War. But Halberstam's dealings with the reserve had been haphazard at best. He had screwed up royally and now saw everything drifting away in the most ironic fashion imaginable. Drafted!? They couldn't do it. They wouldn't do it. All he had to do was explain. He replied confidently: *He had not been dodging; he had been standing on the hottest front lines of the Cold War.*

That should take care of that, he thought. He was wrong. Before Halberstam's trouble with his draft board could be resolved, he would quietly call on *The Times* itself for help, an awkward embarrassment. But that would be months later, after the war and the story had heated up still further.

Meanwhile, the second intrusion posed a more immediate problem. On December 8, 1962, striking printers closed down *The Times* and a citywide newspaper strike followed in New York. Halberstam found himself in the middle of the biggest story of his life without a newspaper to print it.

The newspaper strikes of the era could be long, bitter, and often violent. A deadly combination of forces—economic, technological, American lifestyle changes—had begun to crimp the country's romantic, free-wheeling newspaper culture and would soon change it forever. That colorless, boxed-in newcomer, television, still peddled its news in fifteen-minute evening packages with most of the details cadged from the newspapers and the wires. But in scarcely more than a year, according to a Roper poll taken at the end of 1963, more Americans would get their news from the tube than the sheet. Cities that once lit up with the rowdy, rambunctious Extra-Extra-Read-All-About-It competition of ten, twelve, fourteen daily papers would soon be down to one fat, rich survivor whose only extra came in the advertising rates. No one felt more threatened than the printers, and their fears were justified. The ink-stained crew in the back shop had became an anachronism. Reporters and editors soon would set their own stories in type and correct them, too, on that mechanical bugbear of the printers, the computer. The bruising strike lasted 114 days, one fourth of the total time David Halberstam was in Vietnam.

For a foreign correspondent at *The New York Times* a strike was not as devastating as it would be at a lesser newspaper. *The Times*'s overseas reporters were union-exempt, which also exempted them from the sometimes touchy decision about whether to honor the printers' picket lines as did most, but not all, of the unionized reporters in New York. The foreign staff continued to work and get paid. *The Times* also had outlets other newspapers didn't, and these were not shut down. Two months earlier it had begun a Western edition with a small circulation, mostly in California. It also published an international edition and circulated a news service subscribed to by seventy-two out-of-town newspapers.[2] Halberstam wrote almost as much and almost as often during the strike as he did afterward. But not for New York. In Washington the White House and the political/military establishment got bootleg copies of the Western edition or read him through the news service, and with increasing irritation. But it was still a time of serious diminishment, not something Halberstam took to easily. Writing for *The Times* without New York was like performing in *The Sound of Music* without Broadway. After a month of it he added a plaintive footnote to a letter to Reston: "Please end the strike. It is no fun riding

2. The Western edition, an attempt to move toward a national newspaper, was ahead of its time and folded a year later, as did the international edition a year after that. In 1980 *The Times* successfully launched a national edition.

helicopters here anyway and even less when you don't have a paper."

His friends back home understood. The letters from his pals, the young journalistic literati still reaching for recognition beyond eight rigid columns of type, became more regular.

Gay Talese wrote minor classics, filled with irreverent humor about the newspaper he so desperately wanted to escape for bigger and better things and filled with bawdy references to Halberstam's old girlfriends. In February, with the strike entering its third month, he wrote that, while he knew David didn't feel the same way, he enjoyed the change because it gave him the chance "to get away from the big mother tit that is *The Times.*" He wrote:

> ... There was always the daily disturbance of *The Times*, there was always the sweeping merry-go-round of events each day to take me out of reality, to place me, instead, in someone else's *reality*, and thus afford me an escape. This is what newspaper writers really are, you know: full-time unionized escapists: they are also peeping toms and record-ers: they peep into the lives of other people, however briefly, then skim off the top and record it in the great vault of microfilm. When we die, we will have left to posterity sev-eral rolls of microfilm each. . . .

Halberstam, Talese thought, was cut from somewhat different cloth, destined, he had written in an earlier letter, to become foreign editor or even editor of the newspaper. Now he added:

> Instead of where you are, getting buzzed by crazy helicopter jockeys, you could at this very moment be in the sack with old M———, doing the *London Times* crossword on her belly. But you are an adventurist, you are under the influence of Hemingway. Someday you will make the Vietnamese battles sound like the Spanish Civil War, and you will make helicop-ter pilots as glamorous as Hem made ambulance drivers, *non?*
>
> Well, David, you are continuing to do brilliant work, but your talent is being appreciated by approximately eighty-nine businessmen in California and about fourteen in Paris.

But fear not: you're on microfilm. I am sure this does not humor you; forgive. I am confident the strike will be over before March, before the Easter advertising thickens the newspaper. Then you will be back on Page One for all New York to see, and I, for one, will be happy for you. . . .

The strike did end in March, at about the time Halberstam would return to dealing with his unexpectedly starchy draft board.

———

Meanwhile, Madame Nhu made another of her flamboyant returns to the headlines, accusing the Americans of dancing.

Earlier, this strange and complex woman, a convert at the time of her marriage from Buddhism to a dour kind of Roman Catholicism, had forced her "morality bill" through the assembly over Diem's wishes. In banning dancing, her target appeared to be the new Western sensation, the twist, which most of the Sinatra-generation advisers thought took the sex *out* of dancing. But, for consistency, Madame Nhu banned the ballet too.

In a rambling radio interview she also took her usual shots at the press. Self-control was not one of Madame Nhu's strengths, as the coming year would show vividly. She volunteered that the American correspondents in Vietnam were not Communists. They were worse than Communists: "They are intoxicated by Communism. They believe whatever the Communists say and they speak for them, but in a Western tone. That is why they are worse."

The Taft Republican Neil Sheehan shook his head in wonderment. How she hates us, he thought.

The American Embassy admitted that dancing had taken place at one of its parties. It promised a full investigation.

———

As 1962 neared an end, Halberstam and Sheehan had military sources dug in from one end of the country to the other. Browne had established his own network, sometimes overlapping but spread thinner but more evenly across the story's landscape.

Halberstam dwelled on the soldiers. He went most happily where Harkins had driven him, taking with him one large advantage over the wire men: the luxury of time. During December alone he spent nineteen days in the field. With his gregariousness, his enthusiasm, and his deep need to draw people into his orbit, he rarely returned to Saigon without new taproots into the story. He became a collector.

What Sheehan lacked in time, he made up by adding hours to the day like a scared kid on the run. But, of them all, he was the most introspective. In his diary he wrote about how he loved to sit beneath the sullen fans in the Continental's open-air veranda bar —the Continental Shelf, the old-timers called it. He would sip *citron pressé*, the tart French soft drink, and "watch the girls walk by after siesta, just enough bars on the street then to give it a colorful and corrupt air but not a tawdry one."

At first he did not see "the enormous injustice hidden in the slums behind the large brick buildings, and the corruption in the faces of the upper-class Vietnamese men and women walking on the Rue Catinat, the discontent in the bland faces of the *cyclo pousses*." In the beginning "to a young man, with his adrenaline up, it was a marvelous, pungent atmosphere" and he reveled in it. Only gradually did he begin to see Saigon as "a world made possible by the unjust society the French had built from a plantation society imposed on the peasantry, an economy the upper-class Vietnamese *entier* and *fonctionaries* class was now trying to inherit. It was a world that the peasants had long ago considered to be totally alien." It bothered him later that in his early days he felt only the slightest nagging, hardly a conscious thought at all, that this "was a world the peasants could not help but want to destroy."

Sheehan and Halberstam had not quite teamed up, but the two Harvard men had begun to feel the strong orbital pull. They were a natural team, both driven but so different.

Just before Christmas Halberstam ventured out again, this time as far afield as he could go. The remote camp called Dak Pek could have inspired a John Wayne movie. There, six miles from the Laotian border, sixty miles from the nearest government stronghold, tucked into the rugged Annamite Mountains near a major outlet of what would soon be known as the Ho Chi Minh Trail, a handful of Special Forces men trained Montagnard tribesmen in the black art of counterinsurgency warfare. The place was spectacularly beautiful, spectacularly isolated, and spectacularly vulnerable. The Montagnards called it "the land of one more mountain." The

Americans called it "Little Dien Bien Phu" and took pleasure in warning the visitor that if the VC didn't get him, the tigers would.

At Dak Pek Halberstam met a tough marine veteran of the bloody beach landings at Okinawa and Iwo Jima and later a winner of the Silver Star in Korea. George (Speedy) Gaspard became an instant legend, a man who could lead his charcoal-smudged Green Beret A Team into the night to slit throats or spring them for off-duty carousing in Da Nang or Saigon where they'd inflict more damage than a half-dozen VC sapper squads.

Speedy Gaspard went quickly into the source book, the buddy book too. When he rotated back home the following summer, a letter he wrote Halberstam wryly articulated, in rough-hewn humor and irony, the bonanza the reporters found as they moved farther away from Harkins and his contemptuously unhelpful headquarters:

Dear David:

Dave, Neil, Mert and the rest of you fourth estate fellers, through a stroke of Army orders you have become my implacable enemy. You are now a group of insidious sob sisters, preying on the emotions and passion of the American Taxpayer and his apple-pie cooking Mother. In other words I have been ordered to . . . THE U.S. ARMY INFORMATION SCHOOL!

There was not much doubt about where Speedy Gaspard came down in the scrap between the brass and the newsies. But, as if to authenticate the message, he added a ribald postscript reminding Halberstam of that first trip to Dak Pek: "P.S. Do you know what a tiger is? A 700-pound pussy that eats you!" Halberstam became so enamored of the Special Forces operative that he later made Gaspard the transparent model for his lead character in a war novel, *One Hot Day*.

But, of all the finds in those first Vietnam months, none could match the impact of the dashing young major with the unlikely Cold War name. Ivan Slavich changed everything. He gave them the skies.

A taut former marine who had gone army, Slavich looked every inch the professional soldier, clean-cut, well-scrubbed, his blond hair clipped in a spiky crew cut, his khakis pressed to such a fine razor's edge the reporters joked that you could get a Purple Heart, if they gave them in this war, just by brushing up against him. A onetime paratrooper, he did everything with verve and élan. And he loved trouble, simply couldn't stay out of it.

Slavich came in with the Huey helicopters and, inside a month, he commanded them all. The HU-1As seemed a godsend—faster, more powerful and maneuverable, far better armed than the dilapidated old H-21s that drove Darlene Perry to tears. The new ships were called Iroquois. But everyone took the technical designation, HU-1A, and verbalized it as Huey, a name that stuck to modification after modification throughout the long war. These original Hueys carried four 7.62-millimeter machine guns and two rocket pods, each with eight rockets, all mounted outside the helicopter just above its skids. It was an awesome array of firepower, more than that carried by Second World War fighter planes, and the rockets screamed low with a terrifying roar before exploding in a cascade of orange flame. The Huey's primary problem was its size —it could carry no more than six or seven troopers, half that of the old H-21. So the first Hueys came in as what they were—gunships —and flew cover for the increasingly vulnerable flying-banana troop carriers. The Hueys ratcheted up the war between the army and the air force one more notch and would soon escalate it further. The army had co-opted an air force mission as surely as if it had brought in its own fighter escorts for troop carriers. Soon the Hueys would be roaming on their own and eventually they would fly shotgun for other Hueys, which would carry the troops. The air force had fits. Slavich loved it. It was his job to give the air force fits.

Halberstam got an early dose of Slavich. He hopped a ride on one of the major's first ventures to the Camau Peninsula, a Viet Cong haven of nearly impenetrable lowland swamps into which government troops set foot only in terror-stricken steps. Except for one invaluable asset, the peninsula had little strategic value. Camau was a Cambodian name meaning ''black water,'' and the peninsula held most of South Vietnam's reserves of charcoal. Cut off the charcoal supply and the Viet Cong deprived Saigon of the fuel to cook its meals, boil its tea. It caused not only hardship but severe political unrest too. Air attacks were given virtually free rein in

Camau, so much so that the air force liaison man, a major named Bill Burgin, took a sort of Wild West pride in calling himself "the only law south of the Mekong." The Hueys' Camau incursion was unusually successful. Ten guerrillas were captured. Slavich was exultant. "Halberstam, you sumbitch!" he exhorted the hitchhiking reporter. "You go back and ask your friend Burgin if he's got a T-28 that can land in these paddies, capture him some Communists, and take off again!"

If John Paul Vann had his agenda hidden in a honeycomb, Ivan Slavich's trade was out in the open, his deal there for anyone to see. He took the reporters everywhere. His job was to sell the army and the Hueys—to fend off those bastards in the air force—and what better sales force than the press? For the correspondents, the problem of access was suddenly over. If they didn't fly out with Slavich, they could drive to his little makeshift headquarters at nearby Tan Son Nhut and interview the pilots coming back in.

Slavich had some protection from above for a style that kept him in hot water with almost everyone. His superior and guardian angel was Stilwell the Good, and even Harkins took a schizo-phrenic approach to his free-wheeling young major. The army man in the commanding general privately approved of his triumphs over the air force. But the new open flow of information to the press gave him ulcers. Slavich got more visits from the heat than a safecracker on parole. One evening Sheehan stopped by his head-quarters, a rudimentary camp of wall tents set on low platforms, just as a counterintelligence officer drove up to investigate new reports of leaks to the press.

"Oh, Jesus Christ, the CID's here," Slavich groaned. "Get the hell in there and hide." He pointed to his tent.

Sheehan ducked inside and under the major's bed, taking a snarled web of mosquito netting with him. From the hideaway he listened to an unforgettable performance, half soft talk and half bluster, ending on the latter. "Get the fuck off me," Slavich ordered the CID man, "and get the fuck off my base."

All the correspondents had mixed feelings about the helicopters. Even with the new Hueys, safety was a relative term. The first ones came with armor that provided some protection from ground fire. But the heavy plating slowed them down, making them easier to hit. Eventually the armor, except around the cockpit, was stripped off to gain speed and maneuverability. Riders were never so sure about the trade-off. From that point on, and throughout the war, correspondents and soldiers alike took off their flak jackets and sat on them. Protecting the vitals, they called it. Helicopters were inherently unsafe vehicles. Browne had already been shot down once, a harrowing ordeal in Camau, and would be shot down twice more. Sheehan wrote in his diary about getting ready for a mission: "Remember the getting up in the morning, the nervousness and the gagging and how one could not sleep the night before. Remember the itchiness of the scalp and nauseous Army breakfast of cold eggs and weak coffee. . . ."

But Vietnam had already become a helicopter war. By giving the reporters the helicopters, Slavich gave them the war. "After Ivan came in, you just couldn't bullshit us anymore," Halberstam said. "We could find out anything."

Slavich also had verve, that very special exuberance that made him one of the boys. The lost breakfasts, the danger, all faded from thought on the flights home as Slavich tuned in the music and asked: How about dinner? Then, still skimming the treetops, he would get on the radio and tell the military operator to get him Saigon 22–412. "Sir!" he snapped when Mert Perry answered in his apartment. "The U.S. Army wishes to invite Mr. and Mrs. Perry to join Major Slavich and Mr. Halberstam for dinner." And they would be off to watch the spooks ply their trade at La Cigalle or eat cracked crab at the Diamond.

Slavich sneaked Pam Sanders aboard one mission, two choppers out scouting or perhaps just goofing off, she never was quite sure. Sanders had a way of simply stopping the action. She was not merely pretty, she was a bombshell, a long-legged, stunning blond who would have turned heads in New York. In the paddies, in the jungles—and she made a point of going to the deepest, darkest outposts—jaws dropped when she emerged in combat gear that suddenly seemed designed for an entirely different purpose. Shortly after Westmoreland arrived in Vietnam a year later, he inspected a Special Forces camp near the Laotian border in one of the most isolated parts of his command. As he stepped down from his helicopter, Sanders appeared out of the woods in clinging fatigues. A courtly Southerner, Westmoreland was aghast. He returned to Saigon and immediately banned all women correspondents from overnight trips in the field. It caused a terrible row among the handful of women correspondents, and the general quickly reversed himself. But Sanders had that kind of effect. She was a one-woman Christmas show. Slavich quickly grew bored with the mission he had laid on for her. "Oh, fuck it," he said suddenly. "Let's go to the beach." Both helicopters banked east across the great mangrove forests toward the old French holiday spa of Cap St. Jacques and the breathtaking beauty of the white sand beaches of the South China Sea. They landed in time for lunch in the picture-book village of Vung Tau. There they sat, whiling away the afternoon drinking Ba Moui Ba beer in a seaside café, a breathtaking blond in jungle fatigues and a dashing major in parade-ground khakis surrounded by the open-faced young Americans from the helicopter crews. One of the pilots played the guitar and sang, his favorite being "Scarlet Ribbons." It was a most unusual war, Sanders thought.

———

Late in the year Halberstam and Horst Faas moved out of the Caravelle, tired of feeling like transients, tired of phone calls clickety-clicking with the heavy-handed taps by Brother Nhu's security men. Faas found the new place, a large villa vacated by a German diplomat on a quiet, tree-lined street a fifteen-minute walk from downtown.

The house at 104 Phan Dinh Phung was almost embarrassingly colonialist, a huge place, with a head man who had been the major-domo for a French general, a cook, and a squad of servants inherited from the departing German. The head man, who always wore a tie, was less than impressed with the social status of the new occupants, who never wore ties. But the cook, known as the Bep, which is Vietnamese for kitchen, took to the hearty and hungry journalists as if given a new lease on life. Early each morning the Bep sought approval of the dinner menu, then headed happily to market. He usually returned while Halberstam and Faas lingered at breakfast. Weighted down with fresh food, but proudest of his main course, he would display a large paper bag for both to see, then upend it on the floor, sending half a dozen live crabs skittering sideways underfoot. Twelve hours later dinner was served in the candlelit dining room, each new course summoned by the tinkle of a bell.

In creature comforts the villa lacked only two things—a telephone, which meant that Halberstam now had to deal quickly with the problem caused by Mal Browne's rebuff, and hot water. The latter was resolved one morning with the arrival of a jeep bearing two soldiers and a military-issue hot-water heater. "Sir!" one of the men said, snapping off a salute. "Major Slavich considers it uncivilized to live without hot water. Sir!" The men quickly installed their contraband.

If the villa on Phan Dinh Phung stood as a symbol of the old colonial opulence and excess, the activities inside often bore a closer resemblance to a rebel camp. Visiting newsmen were invited over for the Bep's elaborate dinners and Halberstam's relentless proselytizing, a sales pitch that grew less successful as the criticism from Washington grew meaner and the original group pulled in tighter on itself. The villa also became bunk and breakfast for the men in the field, who often had no place to stay when they came to Saigon. The results were occasionally spectacular.

Down from the mountains came Speedy Gaspard and his entire A Team, a Green Beret complement of a dozen men that ran the gamut from scouts to radio operator. They ran the gamut in other ways, too. At three o'clock in the morning the outraged head man woke Halberstam and took him downstairs to the enormous living room. There, one of Speedy's men and a sinewy pedicab driver were chasing each other over the furniture and around the immense room, a pretty Saigon bar girl having retreated, wide-eyed, into a corner. Halberstam settled the argument. But the next morning the head man, determined to make his point about the new occupants' lack of social graces, took Faas outside and triumphantly pointed to the shrubbery. The frolicsome Green Beret was sound asleep in the rose bushes.

———

The American Mission's dog and pony show for visiting VIPs had become predictably routine: optimistic briefings by Nolting and Harkins, a quick trip to a "successful" strategic hamlet, and off for home after a tough-job-but-we-can-do-it speech at the airport.

Senate Majority Leader Mike Mansfield's visit in December rocked everybody back on their heels. Among other deviations, the majority leader asked for a private briefing from the rebellious reporters.

Mansfield was an unusual American politician. A pipe-smoking Montanan who came as close to scholarly as the system allowed, he had risen to his powerful post less than two years earlier when Lyndon Johnson vacated it to become Vice President. The Senate's passage from the arm-twisting Texan to the mannerly Montanan had been bumpy. How could that home to a hundred contrary egos be controlled by reason rather than fear? After LBJ, Mansfield seemed a Milquetoast, a patsy. He wasn't.

Mansfield, who later distinguished himself as ambassador to Japan, also had an abiding interest in the Far East. He had first met Diem in Saigon in 1955 and had been impressed with the new leader, whom *Time* had begun hailing as "the miracle man" of Southeast Asia. But, seven years later, Mansfield had grown deeply concerned. He thought Diem had deteriorated and was alarmed by the emerging power of the Nhus. As for the correspondents, he had no illusions that they had a stranglehold on the truth in Saigon. But neither was he foolish enough to believe that their reporting could be all smoke and no fire.

His meeting with Nolting went poorly. A fellow senator asked an innocent what-if question: How would Diem do if an election were held today? Nolting inexplicably passed the question to his aide, William Trueheart, who, respecting Mansfield's intelligence, answered candidly. The question did not go to the point, he said; half the peasants in the countryside didn't know who Diem was. Mansfield frowned. Trueheart winced, sure the majority leader thought he was trying to be cute. He wasn't. Elections weren't the issue. Clearly, *more* than half the peasants didn't know who Diem was. Nolting, still making the simplistic his-picture-is-everywhere argument, was furious.

The next day Mansfield met with four of the reporters—Halberstam, Sheehan, Browne, and Peter Arnett. Halberstam did most of the talking: The ARVN was losing ground, not gaining; Diem was disrupting the war effort, not leading it; Nolting and Harkins were lost in their own hopeless optimism and misleading if not lying to Washington. Mansfield listened for four hours. At the embassy, Nolting stewed. He couldn't believe the majority leader of the

United States Senate would dignify these troublemakers. He became so angry he later accused Mansfield of driving "the first nails into Diem's coffin." But the meeting left the correspondents ecstatic. After months of attacks, someone in Washington had finally listened to them.

The glow would not last. But the next day, as Mansfield left, the dog and pony show took another unscripted turn. At the airport Mansfield set aside the embassy's prepared speech and gave one that pointedly refused to express optimism. Afterward, he spotted Trueheart. "I think you were right," he told the deputy ambassador, who winced again.

In Washington John Kennedy fumed. When Project Beef-Up began, Kennedy had one rationale for secrecy. A year later he had other reasons. But he still wanted the story minimized. His administration had been drained dry by foreign crises. He simply didn't need his own Senate leader publicly drawing attention to yet another foreign-policy problem.

Even with 12,000 men now at risk and the small Saigon press contingent picking away, the President had been remarkably successful in keeping Vietnam on a back burner. If Kennedy's shrewdness and charm had tamed much of the powerful Washington press corps, some of the glitter was beginning to fade, with complaints about White House "managed news" during the missile crisis and the first soundings about the government's "right to lie" in an all-or-nothing nuclear world. Still, Kennedy was perfectly suited for lion taming. The times were right for it too: the dying moments of America's age of innocence, the false dawn of the age of the media. Pierre Salinger, Kennedy's press secretary, looked back from a far different world thirty years later and told an interviewer how he contained unwanted stories: "I'd simply tell a joke. Everybody would laugh and that would be the end of the story."

The White House couldn't contain the reporters in Saigon, and this irritated Kennedy. But who were they? A handful of young second- and third-stringers who couldn't call their publishers by their first names. A few far-off so-whats, the only one with any clout at all stranded now with his newspaper closed by an interminable strike. Hell, the newspapers in Washington, where the decisions were made, hadn't even bothered to station anyone in Saigon.

Where were *The Post, The Evening Star, The Daily News?*[3] Where were the powerful regional newspapers in Philadelphia and Chicago and Boston and Los Angeles?[4] Where was television? No one knew the power of television better than Kennedy. The networks had no correspondents based in Saigon. They had just begun to send in full-time stringers who were lucky to get on the brief nightly news a few times a month. Walter Cronkite, whose father-figure image became more trusted than any American politician during the Vietnam era, tried to explain television's early absence. "For one thing," he said, "we weren't interested in endangering our correspondents to do that sort of thing." Risky it was, and even more so packing an old television camera. But Cronkite's comment was disingenuous. The risks would be taken later. Television simply had not grown up. The delinquency of the great American newspapers was another matter. There was only one word for that: irresponsible.

Back home, Mansfield sent Kennedy a private report stronger than anything he had said publicly: "Seven years and $2 billion of United States aid later (after his first meeting with Diem), South Vietnam appears less not more stable than it was at the outset." Kennedy called the majority leader down to the Palm Beach White House the day after Christmas, took him out on his yacht, the *Honey Fitz*, and chewed him out.

Still, Vietnam was beginning to nag at Kennedy. Later he told his friend and aide, Kenny O'Donnell: "I got angry with Mike for disagreeing with our policy so completely, and I got angry with

3. *The Post* had just begun its move toward dominance and eventually a virtual newspaper monopoly in the nation's capital, then a three-newspaper town. Eager to build, eager to expand its influence within the city's power structure, the newspaper suffered from an awkward schizophrenia as a historically liberal voice among liberals fighting a war. It did not assign a correspondent until 1965. Its editorial policy wobbled, mostly in support of the war, until 1968. *The Post*'s failure to react in the city of the policy makers remains an embarrassment at 15th and L streets.
4. A few regional newspapers acted with distinction. The *St. Louis Post-Dispatch* regularly sent in its Washington correspondent, Richard Dudman, who saw through the futility and the inhumanity of the Strategic Hamlets program.

myself because I found myself agreeing with him." But he remained more inclined to lash out than reexamine.

As 1962 drifted toward 1963, Kennedy saw no reason that he couldn't keep the lid screwed on if he could just get his friends to keep their mouths shut.

———

At the Seminary, two days after Mike Mansfield's dressing-down in Florida, John Paul Vann received orders from Harkins's headquarters to take out a Viet Cong radio transmitter.

Of all the American gadgetry, the radio-intercept equipment was among the most productive. Not only could the Americans cross-vector the guerrillas' transmissions, but they could often identify the units they located. The Viet Cong usually communicated by old-fashioned Morse key, a telegraph tap sent by aging Second World War radios. They were very careful, sending in short, coded bursts the French had not been able to capture. The technological Americans could. The Americans also knew that the finger tap of a Morse operator is highly distinctive, almost as identifiable as a fingerprint. After months of intercepts, matched with after-battle reports and intelligence collections, the Americans could follow the movement of major Viet Cong units fairly reliably by following their radio operators. Tracking units from battle to battle, they could also estimate their size and capabilities: Were they at full strength? Under strength? The only thing they couldn't do was get the ARVN to fight them.

Vann had become deeply frustrated. He had been in Vietnam for eight months of a one-year tour. He had spent much of that time trying to motivate his Vietnamese counterpart into becoming an aggressive field commander. As shrewd as Vann could be, he had no idea what he was up against.

Colonel Huynh Van Cao provided a classic study in the problems the Americans faced. At thirty-four, he was a man on the move. He had been chief of Diem's palace military staff before turning thirty and figured on making general before turning thirty-five. He loved to play at war, carrying a swagger stick to match his swagger and working in an office designed as a replica of Napoleon's war room. He had written an autobiographical novel, *He Grows Under Fire*. But Cao had not grown under fire. During one battle he ran from his command tent and vomited, then returned and shut down the action. Cao grew through politics. He knew his 7th ARVN Division was the pivotal fighting force in the war's most crucial arena. He was also deeply sensitive to Diem's dislike of casualties. It was far easier to fake a victory than cover up losses. Most of all, he understood his primary duty: keep the 7th ready to race back up Highway 4 to Saigon.

But Vann needed a fighting commander and he had made Cao his challenge, praising him unstintingly to the Vietnamese and American press alike, hoping the clippings would become his opiate. Minor skirmishes became great victories. Vann's battle plans became Cao's battle plans. Body counts were inflated, not to make Vann look good but to build Cao's resolve, to make him the hero of the delta. Not once did Vann hint to outsiders, especially the correspondents, that the con was on. The correspondents became unwitting participants. They had to believe so Cao would believe.

For a while in the summer, when the first helicopters surprised the Viet Cong, the game looked as if it might work. Cao remained resolutely cautious, but the 7th did have victories. In July Diem gave him a huge hero's welcome and parade in Saigon. Ironically, it came after one of Cao's most flawed performances, filled with battlefield mistakes and missed opportunities. Privately, Vann was furious. Publicly, he inflated the body count and played out his game. He had created the hero of the delta.

Early in October the con collapsed, coincidentally on the day David Halberstam made his first trip to the delta. In the battle beyond the tree line, so many were killed and wounded that Diem called Cao to the palace for a humiliating rebuke. He came back a far more determined man but not in the way Vann had been shaping him. In fourteen actions over the next two and a half months the 7th Division lost a mere four men. Many of the battles were total shams. Not long before Vann received his order to take out the radio transmitter, Diem rewarded Cao's rediscovered wisdom. He made him a general, one of only eight in all of Diem's fighting forces. Cao was not quite thirty-five years old.

Vann nevertheless looked forward to the battle. Although Cao now had overall command of the region, Vann would have a new ARVN field commander. A success was crucial to the American, and he began to lay out a plan to trap the Viet Cong.

After a year of growing frustration, the American advisers had taken to sounding a common theme about the elusive guerrillas and their hit-and-run tactics: Make them stand and fight like *real* soldiers. The ARVN didn't help with their stand-back tactics, their preference for artillery and air strikes, their persistence in leaving a back door open to avoid a final, bloody showdown. But the Americans believed: *Make them stand and fight.* Then the firepower and the numbers would prevail.

The radio intercepts had pinpointed the Viet Cong force near two hamlets on the edge of the marshy no-man's land known as the Plain of Reeds, just fifteen miles from Vann. One was called Ap Bac. The American intelligence system, which projected norms as did most technology-based systems, told Vann to expect the usual 120-man reinforced radio company. The Viet Cong intelligence system had given its commander even better information: He knew he would be fighting the charmed American with his helicopters. Viet Cong spies in My Tho had monitored the preparations. The double agents, moles, and informers riddling Vietnamese society had also discovered who Vann was going after—and when. There would be no surprise for the Viet Cong commander in this attack.

If Vann had his political problems, the VC commander also had his. Documents captured some time later showed that the Viet Cong high command was concerned that the fearsomeness of the helicopters still undermined the psychological support among the power base the guerrillas needed so badly, the peasants. It was time to make a new show of force. It was time to stand and fight. The Viet Cong commander dug in outside Ap Bac and waited.

Unknown to Vann, the routine battle to take out a radio transmitter had assumed far greater dimensions, exactly the kind he sought. It was one of those rare moments when the needs of both combatants are the same. Wars turn on such moments.

Vann scheduled the attack on January 1, 1963. Cao, exercising his new authority, made one change. He delayed the attack by one day so American helicopter pilots would not have to fly with hangovers after their New Year's Eve revelries. The Viet Cong commander learned of the change almost as soon as John Paul Vann.

9

TURNING POINT

On the last day of 1962 General Paul Harkins called in the correspondents of the three leading American news organizations for a round of peace feelers. So hostile had the relationship become that the general's public-information officer, Air Force Colonel James G. Smith, had taken to sarcastically calling the reporters "the friendlies."

All four men smoked, Harkins from an ivory cigarette holder, Neil Sheehan and David Halberstam in the newsman's hard-bitten, droop-it-from-the-side-of-the-mouth fashion of the day, and Mal Browne in his usual unbroken chain. The general's spartan office quickly filled with the layered blue haze of the battlefield, with Saigon's nearby Central Market adding the appropriate background clamor. In a normal situation the gathering might have taken on the feel of a poker game—adversarial but tempered by year's-end bonhomie.

Sheehan was the angriest. Throughout December the general's counterintelligence operatives had continued hectoring his sources about leaks on the "secret" Thanksgiving Day assault Mert Perry had spotted from his apartment-house roof. To Sheehan the investigation was a heavy-handed effort to make everybody clam up on him. He demanded to know why Harkins was wasting the army's time and the taxpayers' money.

The fifty-eight-year-old four-star general peered down his hawk nose and over his cigarette extender at his twenty-six-year-old antagonist. "I don't know anything about that," he said.

Sheehan bristled. The investigation had such high visibility that John Mecklin openly joked about it. (Later, Mecklin wrote that the general's investigators left "gumshoe" prints all over town.) Sheehan asked again.

"I'll look into it." The answer came back with a brittle edge this time.

The other two reporters sat quietly. Browne had been through this dance before. Halberstam had said what he had to say in a withering article. The operation, he noted sarcastically, had netted three Viet Cong and seventeen dead water buffalo. "A Vietnamese statement . . . said that the 'enemy opposed a weak resistance to our move,' " Halberstam wrote. "In guerrilla warfare, this means the enemy got away."

But Sheehan still seethed. He tried still again, and this time Harkins erupted. Investigation or no investigation, he snapped, Sheehan's story had made him damned mad. "That's sort of giving information to the enemy," he said testily, "and that's something I don't think you ought to do. A lot of intelligence went out and it made me mad. The VC read *Stars and Stripes* too."

Stars and Stripes? Was the general serious?

So ended the old year. As usual, Harkins did not tip the correspondents to a major operation, Burning Arrow, scheduled in forty-eight hours. Nor did he advise them of the unnamed endeavor he had given to John Paul Vann the same day.

———

The day broke badly. At first light ground fog clung low to the delta, draping itself over the tree-line hideaways, obscuring thatch roofs and canals, hugging the marshes and paddies like a great, fluffed comforter. John Paul Vann also had other problems on January 2, 1963. A year into the war many of the tired, old H-21 Shawnees were out for repairs, and Burning Arrow had taken most of the rest. Vann needed thirty troop carriers to move an airborne battalion and retain any element of surprise. He got ten, meaning that he had to shuttle into position in three trips, one company at a time. Finally, his intelligence was wrong. Instead of a reinforced radio company of 120 men, a main force battalion of 340 guerrillas awaited him, dug into holes and trenches deep enough to stand in, hidden by natural cover so good they would remain invisible even after the fog burned off.

Still, Vann had the Viet Cong outnumbered more than four to one. He had them greatly outgunned, not only with superior arms but also with the usual terror weapons he so often censured— napalm, artillery, iron bombs, and a new entry: a virtually indestructible ten-ton armored personnel carrier, the M-113. On its first outings the APC had struck such terror into the Viet Cong they had come to call it the "green dragon."

On the other hand, courtesy of the United States and the Diem government, the Viet Cong no longer armed themselves primitively. Diem might not fight, but he insisted on flying his flag over those hopelessly indefensible mud forts left by the French. He manned them with a handful of men and the latest American weapons, which the defenders wisely dropped as they fled at the first approach of the guerrillas. A few days later the defenders would return, rearmed. The field advisers took to calling the forts "Viet Cong PXs," because the guerrillas could pick up what they needed almost as easily as a colonel's wife at the Saigon post exchange. The unit waiting for Vann, the 261st Viet Cong Battalion, had mortars, .30 caliber machine guns, Browning Automatic Rifles, semiautomatic M-1 rifles, and an assortment of other light weapons. Still, they had no mechanical weapon that could stop the armored M-113s. Nor did they have any weapon that, in logic, could turn back the superior manpower.

After eight months, Vann and his team had grown artful in the tactics of the delta. He might have trouble convincing the politicized ARVN commanders to fight, but he could lay on a plan that gave them everything but the will.

The target this day was a tiny hamlet called Tan Thoi. But the action quickly shifted to nearby Ap Bac, the equally obscure hamlet fifteen very tough miles from the Seminary and thirty miles southwest of Saigon. Vann had a special interest in the place. The October ambush, the firefight in which he had been shot down and the casualties had turned Cao once and for all to the sham-battle tactics that made him a general, had occurred only a few miles away. He wanted this one. Badly.

The delta terrain provided the hamlets with natural defensive positions that Vann and most infantry advisers now understood, but that others, most notably the air force, persisted in misunderstanding or ignoring. The tree lines grew like typhoon windbreaks in the flat, exposed expanse of the river's plain. A mix of banana trees, coconut palms, thick bamboo, and assorted tropical hardwoods made sightings from the air all but impossible and a barricade of lush, verdant undergrowth reduced ground-level visibility to a matter of feet—or inches. A lattice of canals and creeks, their banks often so overgrown they could hide scouts and runners, provided passageways to and from the thickets.

At Ap Bac the tree line curved to the west in a crescent around muddy rice paddies looking, from the air, like a gray lagoon. The northern rim of the crescent ran just behind Tan Thoi, which was further protected by another tree line to its north. The thin, southern line ran well out into the paddies. Ap Bac sat in the center of the crescent, further protected from an approach through the paddies by a man-made dike sprouting heavy tree cover. The dike provided the only "high ground"—a scant few feet but invaluable in such flat terrain. To the east, behind the crescent, lay a back door to open rice lands that gave way to swamps and eventually to the bleak and featureless Viet Cong hideaway, the Plain of Reeds, a virtually unlivable place with its soil poisoned by alum.

Vann's plan of attack was straightforward and, like most before men move and bullets fly, picture-perfect. During the night two battalions of civil guards, six hundred provincial troops, marched up from the south and approached the southern tree line. From the west, facing the muddy paddies inside the crescent, a company of thirteen M-113s with about two hundred men stood off about a mile. Expecting the guerrillas to be at Tan Thoi, Vann would begin the attack from the north with the battalion of heliborne ARVN regulars sent in swiftly shortly after dawn. He held two companies of airborne in reserve. The back door to the east was left open. If the Viet Cong could be driven into the flat rice lands in daylight, artillery and air strikes would destroy them. Otherwise, they would be surrounded and forced to stand and fight.

Like all Vann's operations, this one began from a little dirt airstrip at Tan Hiep six miles up the highway from the Seminary. There, his plan began unraveling immediately.

The morning fog broke just long enough to make the first lift at 7:00 A.M. Then it rolled back in, leaving the first company dug in and waiting at the north end of the battlefield. The fog held for two and a half hours, the delay causing one of the civil guard battalions, the least trained of the government troops, to make first contact. At 7:45 a patrol approaching the southern tree line was caught in a brutal cross fire. For the next two hours the battalion, inexplicably failing to radio the other forces deployed around Ap Bac, toyed with an assault on the lightly held line. At 10:00, with eight dead, most from the ambush of the first patrol, the civil guard commander did, as Neil Sheehan put it, "what was normal for a Saigon commander: he asked someone else to fight the war." He asked for the reserves, requesting a landing in the paddies inside the muddy crescent on the other side of the southern tree line. It was a recipe for disaster.

In Saigon, on that Wednesday morning, the correspondents went about their business unawares. None was at either of the day's major battles as a Homer Bigart, a Walter Cronkite, or an Ernie Pyle would have been twenty years earlier in the Second World War. Or as correspondents would have been in that first hot war of the Cold War, Korea. They were shut out. In the lingering lull of the holiday most were catching up on "kitchen" work, a correspondent's life not being all glamour and glory.

David Halberstam spent part of the morning fighting one of his never-ending private wars with New York. This one was over money. *The Times* charged its fully expense-accounted overseas correspondents a $12-a-day reverse living allowance to make up for room and board they no longer had to pay at home. Halberstam saw this as a bureaucrat's grotesquerie, which it was. Worse, it had not been charged to war correspondents in the past. In Halberstam's mind it became not only a slight but also the newspaper's equivalent of the government's absurd attempts to make Vietnam a nonwar. It also cost him money—potentially more than a third of his salary. Halberstam earned more than other reporters in Saigon, but by *Times* standards his pay remained relatively modest at $195 a week.

So, on the quiet morning of January 2, Saigon's angry young man prepared his customary thousand words of protest. The recipient of the letter was Richard D. Burritt, special assistant to Managing Editor Turner Catledge for hiring and personnel matters. Around the office, Burritt was known as The Shrink for answering questions with questions, then sitting back while his uncomfortable interviewees revealed far more about themselves than they ever intended to do. Matched against another Halberstam idiosyncrasy —never fire one clean shot when a nuke will do—Burritt's technique also seemed to work over the miles.

"I am first and foremost a war correspondent," Halberstam wrote, "covering a singularly nasty, difficult, demanding and frustrating war." He then warmed to the subject:

> ... This is a dirty and rugged war (note the quote in *Newsweek* from Ken Crawford, their senior editor who came out here for three weeks. Crawford, who is a veteran of World War Two coverage, called this "the dirtiest war I've ever seen.") He is dead right, and if it is dirty for the soldiers, then it is equally dirty for us. There are no briefings to attend, no easy way of coverage. The only way to get a story here is to walk through the swamps and climb the mountains and ride the helicopters into battle. I have been shot at innumerable times (more so, I am assured, than the average correspondent in World War Two). For one recent story I had to spend four days in a mountainous jungle-swamp area getting up each morning at four ayem and then crawling and climbing about seven miles a day until it was ten pm and sleeping on a wet blanket until the next morning. It is a rugged life; and intestinal sickness is a very basic part of the war. Believe me. In addition, I take the ultimate risk every time I go out ...

The Shrink's analysis went unrecorded. But newspapers have always been contradictory organisms. They attract bright young men and women too quickly too full of themselves. Prima donnas and troublemakers are a dime a dozen. Halberstam would rank at the top in all categories and, before his tumultuous tour of Vietnam was over, the newspaper would seriously consider recalling him. Also while he was in Vietnam *The Times* protected their man against a direct Presidential assault and raised his salary twice, first to $225 a week and then to $275.[1]

Neil Sheehan fought different wars at UPI and spent this morning in his endlessly hopeless struggle to keep up. As a bureau chief, even in a one-man bureau, he had managerial tasks and he hated them. Expense accounts. Shipping schedules. Running freelancers. Keeping books. Finding film crews for the insatiable needs of Fox Movietone News, the old UPI newsreel subsidiary fading rapidly into a bygone era. The more Movietone slipped, the more film UPI wanted. None of it fit Sheehan's romantic image of a war correspondent.

UPI forever hovered near the brink of financial ruin. Working for the woebegone wire service fit few normal images. For young reporters, the beauty of the place was simple: It provided a front-line training ground that opened up years before anyone else would hazard a chance on them. UPI sent Sheehan to Saigon two weeks after giving him his first full-time job, Herndon to Vientiane before he could change his clothes. The downside was also simple: It paid the young hirelings next to nothing and worked them to death. In between the upside and downside were so many peculiarities that all the experience in the world couldn't have prepared a reporter for them, and the jobs probably were best left to those who didn't know any better.

UPI's Asian headquarters in Tokyo left Sheehan outnumbered by his arch-rival, three reporter/photographers to one. But not only did Asia Earnie Hoberecht, UPI's hyperactive chief of Far Eastern operations, expect him to beat Mal Browne's team on news, he expected his man in Saigon to . . . SELL! and COLLECT!

It was a system described in no books on how to be a reporter, included in no curricula at any journalism school. The financial well-being of their employers may provide the lifeline for all re-

---

1. Trying to put 1963 salaries in perspective can be as misleading as leading. Salaries on larger newspapers were entering a major escalation— reflecting an influx of better-educated young reporters, a last burst of effective unionism, the media's growing influence, and general prosperity. At $275 a week Halberstam was well-paid.

porters. But separating reporting from revenues is a cornerstone of the American journalistic ethos. The alternative is rife with compromising conflicts. Asia Earnie didn't see it that way. He bombarded Sheehan with beseechments to sell the news service to the American Embassy, out of whom he couldn't get a straight news story, to local newspapers that branded him a Communist, even to Vietnam Press, Diem's own government-controlled and wildly propagandistic news agency. Hoberecht was a comic-opera character and his endless stream of memos had a comic-opera air about them. "Dear Neil," he wrote in a typical pitch:

> Somebody once said that war appeals to men because it is the greatest sport in the world, man hunting man with a gun.
> It also is said that big game hunting appeals to men because it is about the nearest thing to war—man with a gun versus a man-eating tiger.
> Other people believe that one of the greatest sports and greatest challenges in the world is *selling,* man taking money from man. . . .
> I'm counting on you to add a lot of new revenue in your area right away. So please launch a "selling" campaign and start ringing the bell.

Between bombardments on selling came fusillades on collecting. UPI seemed to have more deadbeats than a used-car dealer:

December 5, 1962:
Sheehan. You and your crew must go all out this month to get in every cent still owed UPI.

December 6:
The Flash Results from New York came in yesterday afternoon. They were so bad I couldn't get out this Memo yesterday. I was sad, sick and at a loss for what to say.

December 17:
(Attention all UPI Bureau Managers in Asia)
Tokyo, Dec. 17120 (UPI)—Hoberecht told all UPI Bureau

Managers in Asia that there are only fourteen days left in the year.

When Sheehan first arrived, he found the accounts in terrible disarray and, being eager, he took them seriously. The first address of a nonpaying client turned out to be a laundry in Cholon, Saigon's Chinatown. The proprietor eyed him suspiciously. Then a spark of recognition lighted up his face. "Oh," he said, "you the man who send me all the pretty pictures." The next half-dozen "clients" turned out to be opium dens, grocery stores, and herbal-remedy emporiums. The turnover in UPI's Asia bureaus was very rapid and Sheehan quickly sized up the situation with his long list of exotic nonpaying "clients." Some long-forgotten predecessor, well before Mert Perry left in his two-word huff, had found a different way to say fuck you to Asia Earnie before moving on.

On January 2 his biggest business headache was collecting from Saigon's pro-Diem English-language newspaper, the *Times of Vietnam*. The *Times*, run by an expatriate American couple of checkered background, was stiffing UPI on a long list of back bills. The most aggravating to Earnie Hoberecht was the tab for two of his favorite comic strips, *Peanuts* and *Bugs Bunny*.

Collect for *Bugs Bunny?!* It drove Sheehan nuts. But if Tokyo drove him nuts, he replied in kind and found himself forever in hot water. Headquarters had trouble getting as much as an expense account out of its harried bureau chief. Most of the time he stiffed Hoberecht as surely as did the *Times of Vietnam*. He simply ignored him.

It was a new year, however, and on this day he was trying to do some catch-up, head off a few rockets from up north. As usual, he wouldn't finish the job. The events under way thirty miles south in the Mekong Delta would irretrievably change Neil Sheehan's life.

————

Vann, flying in a small L-19 army spotter plane, first learned of the skirmishing to the south and the request for the reserves while watching the last of his heliborne companies maneuver into position on the northern line. It was 10:00, more than two hours after the opening clash. General Cao's successor radioed and asked him to scout a landing site for the reserve unit.

Whether Vann would have chosen to bring in the reserves at this point, and in this place, is moot. He was an adviser. A cunning, coercive, manipulative, perhaps brilliant one. But an adviser nevertheless, in command of almost no one. The war belonged to the Vietnamese, and, after a year of growing tensions between the uneasy allies, the hosts were increasingly eager to impress this on the guests. As this day wore on, ARVN officers who had been trained at Fort Benning, Georgia, and spoke English without difficulty, suddenly became unilingual. They isolated their American counterparts by politely but firmly denying them use of their radios, "keeping frequencies open" for orders they knew would never come if they didn't ask. The Americans were not immune to the epidemic of foolishness. Pride, ego, personality, and rivalries turned petty conflicts into calamities. It was a day that began with ground fog and ended in what battle analysts call the fog of war. The fog of war, as usual, proved far more dangerous.

Vann banked his spotter south over Ap Bac and quickly sensed that he had cornered a far larger force than his intelligence sources had predicted. He looked hard at the long, curving tree line. He had expected to find the guerrillas in the north, and some were there. He knew guerrillas were also in the distant southern tree line. Would the guerrillas deploy at the extremities without completing the crescent with a strong force along the high ground of the dike facing the muddy paddies? Not likely.

For fifteen minutes he flew low over Ap Bac and the dike. He *knew* they were there. He skimmed the treetops, probing, provoking, this charmed man who could be dead in seconds if the guerrillas wanted him. He saw not a gun-barrel glint, not a nervous man's twitch. They didn't want him. The Viet Cong wanted the helicopters.

By now the reserve unit had left Tan Hiep and approached in ten Shawnees, with five of the new, invulnerable Hueys flying shotgun. Vann radioed them a landing site 300 yards from both the center and southern tree lines, the distance being the point at which the effectiveness of the Viet Cong's light weaponry fell off. In the little, experimental nonwar of 1962 and 1963 the American command structure was vague and muddled. The lead pilot was responsible for his craft and didn't like being told how to do his job.

He did not have to take orders from John Paul Vann, and so he didn't.

The helicopters gave the southern line a wide berth but swept low into the paddies toward a landing 200 yards from the center line. The deadly dike exploded with gunfire. Fourteen of the fifteen helicopters were struck, many of them riddled with bullets. Within minutes four were downed, including one of the untouchable Hueys knocked down trying to run a rescue.[2] Three Americans were dead or dying and the reserves lay trapped inside the crescent.

In those minutes the small war changed. Ap Bac instantly became a turning point, not simply symbolic but the biggest setback since the carrier *Core* steamed up the Saigon River with the first Shawnees and their invisible crews a year earlier. It also marked, as Sheehan later wrote, "the end of the short era of innocence when the war was still an adventure."

Vann, watching helplessly from the spotter, understood the scope of the failure. Frantically, he moved on his first priority— getting the survivors out of harm's way. He called the armored personnel carriers. But he also knew it was still only 10:30 in the morning, a matter much on the mind of the Viet Cong commander as well. The commander's psychological victory was in the bag. Never again would the swooping menace of the helicopters induce such awe and fear in his men. But the ARVN still had him surrounded. The only way out lay in the killing field to the east. With more than eight hours till dark, he was trapped. If the ARVN could finally be convinced to fight, a disaster could still be turned into a costly but psychologically crucial victory for the government troops. Above, Vann tried to rally the troops. Below, the Viet Cong commander issued orders to his: Don't tarnish your victory; stand and fight to the last man.

2. Years later Sheehan discovered that the Viet Cong, whom Defense Secretary Robert S. McNamara disparaged as "little men in black pajamas," had been practicing. In the nearby Plain of Reeds they conducted silent target practice without ammunition, using cardboard models of both Shawnees and Hueys attached to bamboo poles and moved to emulate the helicopters' flight characteristics.

A mile from the trapped reserves, the APCs refused to budge. "I don't take orders from Americans," the commander said. And he didn't. Like General Cao, the subplot in his life was coup control. If he had the ideal tool for a rescue, he also had the ideal weapon for putting down a rebellion in Saigon. Diem kept the M-113s on a short leash. On this day, as all days, their commander was under orders to radio his position to Saigon once an hour. He was not about to risk Diem's anger without a command from someone with far more sway over his future than John Paul Vann.

So the day went.

In the mud near the broken helicopters a surviving American urged the reserves to fight their way out. Instead, they burrowed face down into the featureless mud, and, with the men on the dike shooting down on them, began dying with bullet wounds in their backs and rumps. When artillery support fell short of the dike, the trapped unit's forward observer refused to raise his head to adjust the fire. Nor would he let the American use the radio to do it, fearing the radio would bring orders to move. Skyraiders thundered in with a scorching napalm attack—on the empty thatched huts of the hamlet instead of the tree line. Vann flew over the civil guards and saw them lolling on their backs behind a low dike 500 yards from the desperate reserves they had called in to do their work. All firing had stopped. The guard commander, whose battalion's strength equaled that of all the Viet Cong deployed at Ap Bac, rejected urgings to move. His was a "blocking position," he insisted. Ironically, the guerrillas in the southern tree line felt trapped between the battalion and the reserves. They pulled out, but the guards were not engaging them actively enough to know it. Desperately, Vann planned another helicopter rescue to extract his wounded. Again the dike exploded in withering fire and the rescue ship was crippled, limping away to a forced landing nearby, a fifth helicopter down.

And so the day continued.

Four long and bloody hours passed before the first of the M-113s finally reached the reserve unit. Of the 102 men in the paddy, half were now dead or wounded.

More than political problems had delayed the M-113s. Marrying Yankee technology to Vietnamese reality always seemed to fall one turn of the screw short. The tracked APCs looked to be the ideal machine for a paddy war—until they reached a canal. The mini-tanks bogged down trying to climb the far bank, their tracks digging uselessly into the mud. Crews clambered out and fed brush to the tracks to gain traction. With the lead APC finally over the top, it began tow-pulling the others, not quite a blitzkrieg operation. Another flaw was discovered this day, and it was a fatal one. The M-113's firepower consisted of a squad of riflemen it disgorged and a powerful .50 caliber machine gun mounted on top. The gunner stood in the open hatch unprotected by armor, the gun thought to be so potent, three times as powerful as a .30 caliber, that the enemy would be dead or pinned down before he could fire back effectively. But what if the gunner couldn't see his enemy? What if his enemy was slightly above where he should be, dug into a dike hidden by greenery so thick it wouldn't even reveal a muzzle flash? What if his enemy didn't panic?

As the once-terrifying M-113s approached the trees, the guerrillas concentrated their fire on the gunners. Some went down dead. Others just went down, disappearing into the hatch. The first M-113s turned. Then one wavering assault of eight drew within fifteen yards of the dike. Suddenly men leaped out of the foliage, crazily bombarding the fearsome dragons with grenades that exploded harmlessly against the armor, spattering them with gunfire that ricocheted away. It was the first and the last time the Viet Cong were seen that day. But this time the machines ran.

General Cao added the last bizarre footnote to the battle of Ap Bac, calling for a late-day paratroop drop into the western paddies. Vann, beside himself, cursed and begged him to make the drop to the east, where, with flares, the paratroops might be able to keep the Viet Cong penned up till morning. The new general would have none of it. He wanted the Viet Cong gone, not trapped.[3]

The paratroops missed their mark, coming in at dusk so close to

3. Some lessons the Americans needed to learn over and over again. A year later, when Westmoreland arrived to replace Harkins, Cao greeted him on behalf of the South Vietnamese government. Westmoreland had to learn the hard way, as he wrote afterward, that Cao "excelled at reporting good news and at avoiding battle."

the tree line that the guerrillas picked them off in the air, so out of position on the ground that they skirmished with their own troops. Nineteen were killed, thirty-three wounded.

At 10:00 that night the Viet Cong commander marched his battalion out the back door. He had his men home in the Plain of Reeds before sun-up. Saigon would play wild games with the numbers. But he had lost eighteen dead, the government forces more than eighty. Three Americans had died.

The war turned that day. The war with the press would turn the next.

———

Sheehan got the first tip.

UPI's ground-level office at 19 Ngo Duc Ke was a testament to downhold. Two blocks from the waterfront and just around the corner from the Rue Catinat, the converted apartment's glass door and full glass window wall faced directly into Saigon's teeming street life, just as Saigon's teeming street life with its silent sappers and secret-police thugs faced directly in on the office. With open-air cafés now routinely wire-meshing their fronts against hit-and-run terrorists, Sheehan's exposure even made Hoberecht nervous. On a visit to Saigon in October Hoberecht, ever tight-fisted, had rejected Sheehan's plea for more help, assuring his young correspondent that Vietnam would quiet down soon. Returning to the airport, a sapper's grenade exploded uncomfortably close to his car. Soon afterward, Sheehan received a letter: "If I were you," Hoberecht wrote, "I would take that glass out of the front of your house and put up boards. At about three inches in front of that I would put some chicken wire so that when they throw the grenades it will make them bounce back." Sheehan never got around to it.

Inside, the living room became the office, its walls covered with charts, clipboards, and a six-by-eight-foot plastic-overlay map of Indochina on which Sheehan tracked battles in grease pencil. A kitchen table, buried under a mountain of paper, doubled as his desk, a foothill of dead cigarettes rising alongside from an old stand-up ashtray. Sheehan's Vietnamese aide, Nguyen Ngoc Rao, sat at a second desk, with a plastic-covered sofa and two shiny chairs completing the decor. Like Horst Faas, Sheehan used the bathroom as a photo lab. But, compared to UPI, the AP office six blocks uptown bordered on opulence. Browne and his team could go home at night. Sheehan *was* home. He slept in back in a dark, windowless bedroom, pushing through a cobweb of drying negatives to his morning shower. The rent was $144 a month, which he split with Tokyo.

No one in Saigon gave up a telephone. So Mert Perry, who lived directly above, kept UPI's old line, rigging a bootleg extension for Sheehan. A caller to Saigon 22–412 might get UPI, *Time,* or both. Interoffice communications were solved with a bang on the stove and a shout up the kitchen vent.

The call came in mid-afternoon, about the time the M-113s turned tail.

He dug for the phone, answering: "Sheehan."

"Get cracking," came the coded tip.

Few calls drew quicker responses than the terse messages from the American captain at Camp Le Van Duyet. But Sheehan made one hurried backup call. Gerry Zornow, a young navy lieutenant commander and a rare friend inside Harkins's public-information operation, also spoke in code. "Total blackout," he answered, the signal for a big one. Their arrangement was simple: Zornow wouldn't lie. He would confirm details or knock down bad leads. But Sheehan had to get his information elsewhere.

The adrenaline surge and that old blessing/curse, wire-service angst, jolted him into action. In the battle between the wires, Sheehan knew that falling behind by mere minutes meant that his story would languish on editors' desks while typesetters pounded Browne's into permanence. Sheehan kicked the stove hard— "Cover me, Perry!" he shouted upward—and shot out the door.

Two miles away, in a building with tall louvered windows opening out over the pounded red earth of an old cavalry parade ground, Sheehan's cryptic source was, as usual, nowhere to be seen. But the Vietnamese colonel had his reports waiting. Colonel Pham Van Dong[4] was a catch. A Vietnamese officer so competent he had risen to lieutenant colonel in the French army, his career had stalled under Diem. Sheehan cultivated him as closely as the American, and Dong would deliver some of the biggest stories of

4. Dong had the same name as, but bore no relationship to, North Vietnam's prime minister.

the war. Now, however, leafing through the battle reports, the young correspondent couldn't imagine anything bigger. The Viet Cong standing and fighting. Helicopters down. Americans dead. He whistled softly under his breath.

Back at his office Sheehan pounded Zornow with details and Zornow stood by his bargain. But Radio Catinat ran full tilt now with coffeehouse rumors and AP also moved quickly. The bulletins began flying in that strange language of the wires:

> URGENT PRESS
> UNIPRESS TOKYO
> 02154 VIETCONG GUNNERS DOWNSHOT FIVE RPT FIVE
> UNISTATES ARMY HELICOPTERS WOUNDING FOUR RPT FOUR
> AMERICAN CREWMEMBERS. . . . MORE SHEEHAN

Like a confident general, Browne deployed his troops—his "human wave," Sheehan complained to Tokyo. Faas was far gone somewhere in the jungle, an investment that would pay off on some later day. But Browne jockeyed Vietnamese stringers and aides into pivotal positions around town and dispatched Peter Arnett to the airport to interview Ivan Slavich's Huey crews as they returned from the scene. Halberstam also went to Tan Son Nhut. Despite the falling out with Browne, he worked easily with Arnett —another edge for ROX, UPI's cable code for its giant rival.

By sundown, with reports filtering back about the paratroop drop, AP's manpower began to show and Browne's forces pulled ahead. Overnight, UPI would tabulate the results—who used AP? who used UPI?—and rocket Sheehan with the box scores in the other big battle of the day: ROX versus UNIPRESS. Sheehan knew he was losing, and he could feel the assault coming . . . ROX 32, UNIPRESS 11 . . . ROX 14, UNIPRESS 3. . . .

But Ap Bac was destined to belong to Sheehan and the box scores could not change that. Shortly after dark he took the first risky step, gathering up his Vietnamese aide and interpreter, Rao, and recruiting the Reuters man, Nick Turner, to drive them on a perilous night run down Highway 4.

It was a spooky drive, one few reporters had taken. As they raced through the night, the moon glinted off the paddies, causing eerie shadows to dance among the banana fronds in the dense cover along the roadside. Every few miles they passed an old guard tower manned by a few edgy loyalists. But the lonely and indefensible towers only emphasized the reality of the delta: What the government controlled nominally by day, including the highway, slipped easily back to the rebels at night. After dark, people disappeared at roadblocks, snipers operated more boldly, crudely efficient land mines blew up reckless intruders.

Some of Sheehan's buddies thought the youngest of their lot knew too much for his own good about the ways of the Viet Cong. But the mines frightened him, and now he craned his neck, searching for flickers of candlelight in the roadside murk flying past them. The VC had no pressure mines. All were hand-detonated. Their specialists worked in teams, using primitively successful techniques:

"They put up Number Ten cans—old tomato cans, bean cans thrown away by the army—and they put them on the other side of the road with candles in them. You couldn't see them when you drove down the road, but they would clock your car as you went by the candles. And then the mine guy, the specialist, would get the interval and detonate the mine as you went over it." Sheehan paused in his recollection. "They were very good."

So the three of them drove recklessly fast, pushing the green, English-built Hilman Minx up to seventy miles an hour, dropping back briefly to fifty to throw off the candle timings, then accelerating again through darkened villages. Years later Sheehan thought the greatest danger of all might have been their speed on the dark, two-lane highway.

It was almost ten o'clock when they lurched into a hard right turn and up the narrow dirt road to Tan Hiep.

In the dark Sheehan knew the place well. He had come to the dusty outpost often just before daybreak, groggy and queasy after breakfast at the Seminary but ready for another of Vann's helicopter assaults. Outside the command tent, in the dim yellow glow of weak light spilling from within, he first saw Cao. If he had needed further confirmation, one look at the Vietnamese general would have given it to him. He found him in "a kind of nervous crisis," pacing up and down, speaking incoherently, compulsively running both hands through his hair over and over again.

Vann drew the reporters into the darkness near the landing strip.

There, where the Vietnamese couldn't see him, he filled them in—not fully, not entirely truthfully, for in Vietnam even Vann used the truth sparingly and only to his own advantage. To Sheehan, the adviser also seemed somewhat shell-shocked. He was not as forthcoming as usual, and Sheehan could sense explosive forces tugging inside the man. Vann had wanted so badly to have his enemy stand and fight. Now they had, and they had beaten him. "They were brave men," he finally said of his adversaries. "They gave a good account of themselves today."

As he spoke, the Viet Cong guerrillas were silently withdrawing under cover of night and General Cao's foolishness, carrying their dead and their expended shell casings with them.

Sheehan would make two more nerve-racking runs on Highway 4 that night, back to his office to write the story only he had now, then back again to Tan Hiep to take the first helicopter out at dawn to the battle scene. His story became a Vietnam classic, the most complete battle account from the early years of the debonair little war in the land of tigers and elephants. Even with Vann's reticence Sheehan's story contained more detail, better description, and far better analysis than any of the stories filed that day. It also went virtually unseen by the American public. Journalism's deadlines are unyielding. First will always prevail, and Browne swept the January 2, 1963, battle of ROX versus UNIPRESS.

That didn't mean Sheehan's story went unread. On the contrary, it had a small and passionate audience. It was torn off the clacking old wire tickers and given exclusive readings at the White House, the Pentagon, and, of course, General Harkins's headquarters in Saigon. By a quirk of the time zones the *Honolulu Star-Bulletin* was one of the few newspapers to run the story. That meant Harkins's Honolulu-based boss, Admiral Harry D. Felt, read Sheehan's account the way it was meant to be read: under a headline.

Admiral Felt did not like the story. Neither did the others who got exclusive reads at their desks on January 3. They didn't like it at all.

———

Sheehan and Turner arrived back at Tan Hiep without sleep just after sunrise on January 3.

Both Cao and Vann seemed new men. Spit-polish slick after a night at his luxurious home in nearby My Tho, Cao arrived moments after the correspondents, smartly snapping his swagger stick at the white-helmeted honor guard lining the way to his command tent. Although his enemy had slipped away in the night virtually with his connivance, he seemed a man with a plan. It was a plan in which Sheehan would soon find himself all too intimately enmeshed.

Vann watched the morning show with a thin smile. In fact, he was steaming, and Sheehan's instincts told him to grab that moment to talk to him. But Vann directed them toward two H-21 Shawnees, their blades already rotating. The reporters lifted off abruptly for a body-collection run to the battlefield.

Minutes later they passed over the shattered hamlet of Ap Bac, still smoldering from the massive air and artillery pounding of the day before. Sheehan shook his head. The hamlet, he was sure, had been empty—at least of combatants, who would have fought from the cover of the trees.

The choppers put down a half mile to the west, and the two passengers set off across the paddies, passing the bodies of the ARVN dead as they went. Most had been dead almost twenty-four hours now, little men rolled over but not otherwise moved, their booted toes pointing up, their bodies ripening and beginning to bloat in the morning sun, ants and insects invading them, flies assaulting them. Sheehan's stomach wrenched violently.

Near one cluster of bodies the correspondents met three M-113s carrying an American adviser and a group of benumbed Vietnamese troopers. Suddenly, the scene turned bizarre: The spooked ARVN soldiers refused to help gather up the bodies. The American exploded, screaming at them, shoving them off the machines, pushing and jerking them through the mud toward the bodies. During their first year in Vietnam, American advisers had been scrupulously polite to the Vietnamese foot soldiers—too paternalistic, perhaps, at times unconsciously edging into the colonialist ways that had driven this country into revolt in the first place. But the rule had been clear: kid gloves and soft words. Now the veneer was stripped away. The American loosed his fury; the Vietnamese stood by sullenly. To Sheehan this scene alone certified what he had already written. Ap Bac was a turning point, the battle the Americans had always wanted becoming a calamity instead. Nothing would be the same after this.

After a few moments watching the confrontation, Sheehan became angry, too: *These men would not help take their buddies home for burial.* He pitched in, grabbing twisted boots and tiny arms to hoist the bodies aboard the APCs. Then the anguished young man from Holyoke just one generation removed from County Kerry crossed himself, turned, and vomited into the delta mud.

Meanwhile, the other correspondents began heading in. David Halberstam and Peter Arnett had left Saigon at dawn on a changed Highway 4. The early-morning traffic of old Asia suddenly clogged the narrow road. Water buffalo pulled wooden-wheeled carts to market. Stooped old men trotted slowly in front of the impatient Americans, bamboo-pole carriers bending under the weight over bowed shoulders.

The highway had changed in other ways as well. If the Viet Cong might set up a night roadblock, the ARVN stopped traffic during the day. The ARVN could be almost as difficult to get past, their high command not wanting pesky American journalists in the area after a disaster. Halberstam and Arnett tried a ruse. They commandeered a car kept in Saigon by *Stars and Stripes.* They also commandeered a young marine combat correspondent, a sergeant named Steve Stibbens. It made for a journey with all the look of don't-touch priority. The car was a 1961 black Falcon with the logo of the newspaper, two crossed flags, on its doors. Stibbens, in full uniform, drove. Halberstam and Arnett rode in the back.

For Stibbens it was the beginning of a new life. A few days later he joined Horst Faas on a deep-jungle mission. "Dis iss your camera," Faas growled, peeling one of the Leicas off his barrel chest. "You never risk your life without your camera." The young marine had never taken a photograph before. But he became so enamored of Faas that he followed him everywhere. By 1963 Stibbens was named military photographer of the year.

The drive to the command post at Tan Hiep was uneventful. Halberstam and Arnett found Vann pacing the grounds. As Sheehan had sensed, this was the time to talk to him. The pensiveness was gone, replaced by anger.

"What the hell happened?" Halberstam asked.

"A miserable damn performance, just like always," Vann snorted, kicking a high-laced boot into dry red clay.

It was a remarkably candid statement and, while the newsmen would not use his name, Harkins would not need one of his Keystone Kops investigations to identify the source.

Meanwhile, a flurry of activity had begun around Cao's tent, with bold talk about a counterattack. Confused, Halberstam asked Vann where they thought the Viet Cong were. The colonel rolled his eyes. Everyone in the camp knew they had left in the night, *especially that damned fool Cao.* Cao was covering his ass.

Vann shuffled Halberstam and Arnett off on a surveillance flight over the battlefield. They would look but not land.

The AP and *New York Times* stories of the day before, while less detailed than Sheehan's account, had swept the play back home and captured the highlights of the defeat. They had also shaken the White House. Even strike-bound, *The Times* was President Kennedy's newspaper of record. He had grown up with it, teethed on it in his political family, read it religiously every day. He read it that day, too, even if he had to settle for a bootlegged and anemic Western edition. The headlines over Halberstam's account were blunt, a direct challenge to Harkins's ever-glowing optimism and to Washington's upbeat soundings, too:

VIETCONG DOWNS
FIVE U.S. COPTERS,
HITS NINE OTHERS

DEFEAT WORST SINCE BUILD-UP
BEGAN—THREE AMERICANS
ARE KILLED IN VIETNAM

Now, flying over the silent battlefield, Halberstam thought the scene below told the story more powerfully than he ever could. The carcasses of the helicopters lay broken where they had fallen. Bodies, some still tangled in the white parachute shrouds of the last botched drop, remained sprawled in the mud. The day-old tracks of the M-113s cut a kitty-wumpis pattern in the paddy muck, seeming to move in every direction, he thought, except toward the tree line. It was a diagram of failure.

It was only later that Halberstam learned that Sheehan was on the ground as he flew over. Returning to the base camp, the first person he and Arnett saw was Harkins, dressed, like Cao, in his parade-ground finest. Neither he nor Cao had been to the battlefield. Neither would ever go to the battlefield. He was not that kind of general, Harkins had told Horst Faas.

What did he think of the battle? Halberstam asked.

It was going well, Harkins replied. General Cao's forces now had the enemy surrounded. "We've got them in a trap," he said, "and we're going to spring it in half an hour."

Surrounded? A trap? Flabbergasted, the correspondents were at a loss for further questions. Common sense and a single flight over the battlefield told them that the ARVN had had their tails whipped and the Viet Cong were long gone. Did Harkins believe the things he said or did he believe he had to say them? The question had begun to perplex many, from Robert McNamara on down through some of the general's own staff officers. Most came to the same and most damning conclusion. Harkins believed.

Meanwhile, on the battlefield, Sheehan and Turner had walked to the hamlet and explored the now-deserted foxholes along the tree line and dike from which the Viet Cong had done so much damage. They found three bodies, the only bodies left behind. The reporters had picked up an unexpected escort, Brigadier General Robert York. Vietnam had become a favored Pentagon spectator sport. York was one of twelve American generals in Vietnam at the time, four more than in all of Diem's active forces. But the forty-nine-year-old Southerner was special. Not only had he been a tough combat commander in Europe during the Second World War, he had rare credits for this war, having been the official U.S. Army observer to the British when they had successfully quelled a Communist guerrilla war in nearby Malaya. The experience had not given him heart about Vietnam. The British had outnumbered the insurgents in greater numbers than ever seemed possible in South Vietnam and the job had still taken twelve years. But York was special in other ways too. He was relentlessly inquisitive, sticking his nose into everything. He asked questions. He even asked questions of correspondents because he knew they went places and talked to men his hidebound colleagues never saw. He went often into the field and got his uniform dirty when he went. Of the twelve generals, York was the only one to ever visit Ap Bac.

As the group walked out of the Viet Cong's vacated battlements and into the hamlet, Sheehan asked York one of those simple questions to which he knew the answer but that the rules of his game required someone else to say.

What happened here?

"What the hell's it look like?" York snapped impatiently. "They got away. That's what happened."

By now Sheehan and Turner were eager to return to Tan Hiep, question Vann, and make another run up the highway to dispatch what once again were extraordinary stories. York offered them a ride on his helicopter. Walking out along a dike, they watched a fresh battalion from Cao's 7th Division march back in. Suddenly, a howitzer thundered once from the south, then twice more, the shells whistling in among the nearby troops. Several were hit by shrapnel and fell screaming into the paddies. The rest dove in.

"Hey, that was pretty damned close!" the general's aide exclaimed.

Another boom sounded, followed by the horrible whining rush of the incoming shell. The explosion sent a mud gusher up from the paddies just thirty yards away. Then the explosions began marching quickly down the dike toward them.

"Let's get the hell out of here!" York yelled. But they made it only a few yards before an explosion rocked them. "Get down!" the general shouted, and they plunged into the mud.

Gone instantly was that feeling of the immortality of youth, of the special virtue of the manly test of battle, of his own remarkable immunity to fear and death, of his superiority to the soldiers who had shown their demeaning fright . . . all the exhilaration of that first firefight just months earlier left Sheehan instantly. Now he dug frantically into the mud, terror-stricken, on the incoming end of the technology, a little desperate man like the little desperate men he had watched from high above, zigzagging in fear across the paddies, throwing their arms up in hope before the gunners in the Hueys cut them down. He was going to die. He knew it. Dimly, he realized that this was friendly fire. Later he would discover it was

Cao's "counterattack," another of the general's sham battles designed to regain face in the palace. But that was another matter now. He was going to die.

During a brief lull, the men dashed a few more yards down the narrow dike. "Run for your life, boy!" the general's aide prodded. York heard the whistle—"Here comes another!"—and they dove again. Sheehan skidded off the dike into the dark gray mud of the paddy below. Clambering back up he found a softball-sized chunk of shrapnel dug in a few feet from Turner's head and a crater where they had burrowed in the first time. Sheehan wormed in deeper, barely able to breathe. The men in the foxholes had taken 600 rounds of this yesterday. He was certain it would have driven him screaming mad. An overwhelming rush of fear flooded through him. He began praying aloud and then cursed himself for showing his weakness to the others.

Suddenly, the shelling stopped and an eerie silence spread across the battleground, bloodied anew. Four ARVN soldiers were dead, twelve wounded. Then, once again, Sheehan was loading the dead, crossing himself, and fighting his tortured stomach.

Nothing was the same for Sheehan after that day. The next time he flew a helicopter assault he saw a different vision beneath him, "the man running for his life with the bullets and the rockets kicking up behind him," he confided to his log later, "and how awful it must have been for him, how the fear must have dissolved his bones as my bones had been dissolved in fear at Ap Bac and what an awful thing it is to torture a man this way before killing him." His belief in the American goal held fast. But not in the heroics. "I never saw glory in war again," he said later, "and I never again went into battle unafraid."

Back at Tan Hiep, Sheehan spoke briefly with Vann, now driven far beyond caution. Then the young correspondent looked across the grounds and spotted Harkins. A short time earlier the general had dumbfounded Halberstam and Arnett. Now the "trap" had been sprung and Harkins stood unflustered in his spotless uniform, his parade hat heavy with gold braid, his collar tabs glinting with four silver stars, his pants perfectly pressed, his street shoes polished to a high-buff black. One hand held a swagger stick tucked under his arm. The other held the long, white cigarette holder he had flourished four days earlier as he had tried to get the new year off on a different footing with the "gentlemen of the press." Shee-han looked down at himself. He was covered with mud and slime. Gray gunk seemed to ooze from every pore. Suddenly, he felt violently angry, a catharsis from the fear. Harkins had not gone to the battlefield to see where, or learn why, his own men had died. He would never would go to the battlefield even when it became, as it soon did, the scene of the greatest controversy of the little war. Sheehan took a deep breath and turned away. Exhausted, he found the next filthiest man around, Nick Turner, and headed back up Highway 4 to write.

———

In Saigon, at Gia Long Palace, the day had passed differently. The high and the mighty arrived in a steady stream, paying their respects. So did the flatterers, sycophants, and court hustlers. The occasion was Ngo Dinh Diem's sixty-second birthday, and he received his well-wishers in long, silken mandarin robes, a rare departure from the white sharkskin suits of his daily presidency.

The toasts ran long and flowery. "Born to be a leader," said one. A man "whose genius is outweighed only by his virtue," hailed another.

The bloody doings in the delta did not penetrate the walled palace on the president's special day. They would soon enough.

———

A week after the battle, Admiral Felt flew in from Hawaii for two days of meetings. Felt was short and slight of build (Harkins towered over him), but the admiral ruled his vast command like a Caesar.

The size of the press corps had temporarily quadrupled with outsiders—the smoke jumpers—descending on Saigon to get a piece of the biggest story of the little war before editors and public grew bored once again. Most of them showed up at Tan Son Nhut for the admiral's arrival. But only one question was asked.

Sheehan elbowed his way to the front of the pack, pressing for Felt's assessment of the battle.

"I'd like to say that I don't believe what I've been reading in the papers," the admiral replied. "As I understand it, it was a Vietnamese victory—not a defeat, as the papers say."

Felt turned to Harkins expectantly. The general took his cue quickly. "Yes, that's right," he said. "It was a Vietnamese victory. It certainly was."

With that, the officers turned abruptly to leave. As they started to walk away from the shouted questions, Harkins leaned over and told his boss who the questioner had been. Felt spun on his heel. Most of America may have missed Sheehan's stories on Ap Bac. Not Admiral Felt. In Honolulu he got them all—the headlines trumpeting "Viet Troops Fail Big Test," the stories calling it "one of the most humiliating defeats of the war."

"So you're Sheehan," he said, gravel grinding in his voice. "You ought to talk to some of the people who've got the facts."

Far less than that could trigger the Irish in Sheehan. He looked at these two spit-and-polish general officers, as permanently pressed as Harkins had been at Tan Hiep, and the same anger that had boiled inside him a week earlier flared again.

"That's right, Admiral," he shot back. "That's why I went down there every day." Then he added, eyeing Harkins, "You might try sending your own people down."

The reporters pounced on the fiasco to show that they had been right all along. No one could pounce like Halberstam.

"What made this defeat particularly galling to the Americans and the Vietnamese alike," he wrote, "was that this was a battle initiated by government forces in a place of their choice, with superior forces and with troops of the 7th Vietnamese Division, which is generally considered an outstanding one in the country. Today the government troops got the sort of battle they wanted and they lost."

Later he added a more personal view: "We had been writing about these problems all along and accused of exaggerating. But Ap Bac is where it happened. In spades. Exhibit A. It was the ultimate confirmation of everything we'd been writing. As a journalist, it's not a fear of being out there alone. It's a fear of not being right. This put the steel in us. It was the confirmation we were not crazy."

The story remained front-page news for days and not only *The Times* made noise. The Detroit *Free Press* ridiculed Harkins's mindless optimism as "thin and unconvincing whitewash."

John Paul Vann's not-too-anonymous words—"a miserable

damned performance"—were printed in virtually every newspaper in the country, so angering Harkins he decided to fire his free-wheeling colonel on the spot. He was talked down only when at least one other top officer threatened to quit if Vann went. But, with the army, Vann was finished.

The secret cables that washed back and forth among Saigon, Honolulu, and Washington often bordered on the bizarre.

Two days after the battle the army's Pacific watch report acknowledged the obvious: The battle "will provide the enemy with [a] morale-building victory." That same day, January 4, Harkins sent his own report to the Pentagon. It contained some remarkable observations. "The statement that it was a miserable damned performance can be taken either way," Harkins wrote, then failed to provide the other way. At times he seemed almost incoherent: ". . . [T]he VC equal the Germans and Japanese—the VC are a pretty tough lot and particularly the hard core. We found that out in Korea."

Harkins also set the Viet Cong casualty figures at 101 dead, a number even more detached from reality than the usual body-count fictions. Only three bodies were ever found, those discovered by York, Sheehan, and Turner. Clearly, the Viet Cong had carried off others. But York, an expert, looked at the evidence left behind and told Sheehan (and surely told Harkins) that perhaps a dozen other guerrillas had been killed. When the Viet Cong commander's elaborate after-battle report was captured much later, the number of dead was placed at eighteen, including the three left behind.[5]

The cables and messages repeatedly blamed the correspondents. The Joint Chiefs of Staff quickly shot a memo over to an unhappy

5. Body-count stories would become legend in Vietnam. Four years later a young captain named Bill Carpenter, who came to fame as the All-American "Lonesome End" on Army's football team, called napalm in on his own position when he found his unit hopelessly surrounded. He survived and, when headquarters called, he was asked for a body count. Still surrounded, many of his own men killed, he wasn't about to count bodies. Minutes later he got another call and was given a number that seemed plucked from thin air like one of those long passes from the past. It was. It was the number of his football jersey at West Point. By that time an acronym had been created for body counts too: WAGs, for Wild Ass Guesses.

President, assuring him that "initial press reports have distorted both the importance of the action and the damage suffered by the US/GVN forces." In fact, even as it greatly inflated enemy casualties, the military also understated ARVN casualties.

Admiral Felt cabled Washington that exaggeration by the wire services was commonplace:

I THINK IT IMPORTANT TO REALIZE THAT BAD NEWS ABOUT AMERICAN CASUALTIES FILED IMMEDIATELY BY THE YOUNG REPORTERS REPRESENTING THE WIRE SERVICES WITHOUT CAREFUL CHECKING OF THE FACTS [SIC].

He zeroed in again on Sheehan, reaching back to the rookie mistake over Viet Cong casualties that so raised Homer Bigart's hackles:

THE STORY BY SHEEHAN ON OPERATION MY THO IS A CASE IN POINT.

That incident was then seven months old.

The early stories were not error-free. Mal Browne briefly reported eight helicopters down instead of five. Sheehan passed on faulty information on how one of the Americans died. The errors were quickly corrected and the AP error didn't make it into the main edition of any major newspaper.

But as the battle became a cause, the government seized on the mistakes. At the White House President Kennedy's press secretary, Pierre Salinger, raised his eyebrows, shrugged his shoulders, and asked newsmen: "How can you believe those guys? They're too green. Look at the mistakes they make." The U.S. government became quite at ease using non sequiturs to turn black into white.

Still, John Kennedy's nervousness grew. Mansfield had told him only a week earlier that things were not what they seemed in Vietnam. Meanwhile, Kennedy had dispatched Roger Hilsman, about to become assistant secretary of state for Far Eastern affairs, to Saigon. A bulldog of a man, Hilsman sat down with the correspondents and chewed them out for being "too naive," later reporting to the President that the reporters were so "bitter" they "will seize on anything that goes wrong and blow it up as much as possible." But Hilsman minced no words with the President, either. He called Ap Bac "a stunning defeat" that reinforced the correspondents' judgment about the "inefficiency, bad leadership, and lack of aggressiveness" of Diem's troops.

More than one official with a vested interest to protect spoke out of both sides of his mouth. Felt kept up the victory talk in public and in reports that would reach political Washington. But officials who sat in on meetings between the admiral and Harkins told Nick Turner that Felt saw the battle as "a complete debacle." He would never show that in public, or, apparently, to his civilian superiors.

The reaction of the Diem government was flustered and typically bizarre. Madame Nhu blamed Vann for "confusing" the ARVN officers. Diem's official news agency, Vietnam Press, repeatedly referred to the government forces as "outnumbered," a peculiar claim for a force that also had the enemy "surrounded." The *Times of Vietnam* said in a January 9 editorial that it was the "humanity" of the regime that allowed the Viet Cong to escape. According to the *Times*, the guerrillas wore the black-pajama garb of the peasants and slipped out with the villagers of Ap Bac. The government forces let them go, the newspaper asserted, because they didn't want to harm innocent villagers.

Meanwhile, with Admiral Felt still in town, the commander of the VC battalion flamboyantly returned to Ap Bac and hoisted the Viet Cong flag over the hamlet, challenging General Cao to come and try again. Cao didn't budge.

When Felt left Saigon on January 11, the press conference at the airport was more formal. He was asked if he still thought of Ap Bac as a success. Yes, he did, and once again he turned to Harkins for affirmation. The general had been doodling on a pad and seemed preoccupied. But, as before, he quickly took his cue. "Yes, I consider it a victory," he said. "We took the objective."

Took the objective? It was a Second World War answer to a guerrilla-war question. The objective in an antiguerrilla war is to take the guerrillas, not the territory. Suddenly Felt and Harkins were bombarded by a dozen simultaneous questions about this new theory in counterinsurgency warfare.

Mal Browne broke through first, directing the question to Felt. The battle-starred admiral paused for a moment, as if wondering why all these newcomers seemed so unlike the fine fellows who had packed pen and paper alongside American troops in the glory days of the Second World War. Then Felt's eyes turned flinty and he growled his answer:

"Why don't you get on the team?"

10

WARNING SHOTS

Get on the team? Admiral Felt had challenged the sacraments, invited apostasy. The press, adversary of all, plays on no one's team—surely not the government's, with whom it feels ordained to live out a watchdog's role, the last check and balance in a wise system of checks and balances. The words went down like battery acid.

Yet, as impolitic as the admiral had been, his angry question was more basic than the reporters wanted to admit. Contrary to journalism's self-image? Sure. But reality? Like all large institutions, the press is heavy into sinning all week and purifying on Sunday. In time of war it had played a lot of team ball.

The first American war correspondent, George Wilkins Kendall of the *New Orleans Picayune,* had been the ultimate team player. First he stampeded his government into an unpopular war with Mexico in 1846. Then he fought alongside the invaders, glorifying them in heroic accounts that sent his penny paper's circulation soaring. Wearing the uniform of their country, Second World War correspondents took the rank of major, carried and fired weapons, even took prisoners and captured towns. Ernest Hemingway may have been a unique case, but he did nothing without becoming a participant. Usually accompanied by his own group of *partisans,* he wandered far afield from the troops he was covering and entered Paris as much a combatant as a correspondent a full day before the Allies arrived. Accounts of other correspondents taking prisoners were commonplace. According to Phillip Knightley in *The First Casualty*, a woman, British correspondent Evelyn Irons, and three other reporters held the occupants of a Bavarian town at gunpoint and accepted its surrender when they arrived ahead of advancing troops.

So, while Felt jarred the sensitivities of the young correspondents, the words came easily to his tongue. The press had *always* been on the admiral's team. And that, as the young Saigon regulars would soon discover, included more than a few of the senior correspondents now beginning to take an interest in Vietnam.

Vietnam pushed more diplomatic and politically adept men than Felt to rash bursts of anger. Secretary of State Dean Rusk, a rigidly self-controlled man, later erupted with a virtually identical challenge to reporters. The Kennedy administration endeavored to get the press on the team any way it could. JFK might woo reporters with the instant stardom of the small screen, but he also could be coercive. His attempt at "news management"—orchestrating the flow of the news to suit his purposes—and the claim of a government's "right to lie" to preserve itself provoked major public controversies.

Kennedy asked newspaper publishers to exercise "self-censorship" during the Cold War with Communism. "Every newspaper now asks itself, with respect to every story: 'Is it news?' All that I ask is that you add the question: 'Is it in the national interest?' " The proposal went over with the dullest of thuds. But, once the furor passed, the American press joined the team for the duration of the long Cold War, rarely prying into the secret society the government built to fight it, rarely examining some of the horrendously dangerous decisions made by the nuclear high priests.

These highly visible attempts to control the press at home diverted attention from the problems of a handful of reporters half a world away. But the endless turmoil of the Kennedy years did the most to divert the public's attention from Vietnam—and the President's too. At the beginning of 1963 there was no sense in the country or the White House that Washington was stumbling into a conflict that would become the most divisive since the Civil War. "Vietnam was on no one's radar screen," said Ben Bradlee, then Washington bureau chief of *Newsweek* as well as a Kennedy confidant. No one in the administration *or* the Washington media.

But, to the correspondents in Saigon, Vietnam was the world. Felt's challenge helped them draw the battle lines clearly, as only the young can. Get on the team? Felt and Harkins wouldn't even let them on the helicopters.

There would be two major turning points in 1963, one military and one political. The military turn had come at Ap Bac. The fatal political turn—Buddhist monks burning themselves to death in protest suicides, riots in the streets of Saigon, police invasions of the pagodas and brutal repressions by the regime—would arrive with the long, hot summer. The young correspondents would not join any team now. If they had been adversarial before, they would only become more adversarial. The correspondents, riding high off Ap Bac, would use both events like battering rams to prove that America's nice little war wasn't working.

Not long after the battle a British correspondent took John Sharkey, a new NBC stringer, to a seductively debauched Saigon party. Sharkey, another of Southeast Asia's youthfully wandering souls, had arrived a few months earlier from Peter Arnett's old paper, the *Bangkok World*.

The party, given by a ranking CIA agent, was a young vagabond's dream. In the darkened house fans lazily sifted clouds of smoke into hypnotic shadows. All movement seemed slow and desultory. Remarkably beautiful Vietnamese girls slinked past spies who mingled with the lowlifes they hired for odd jobs. People lay on couches, barely moving, taking the opium pipe.

"My God," Sharkey thought, "this is straight out of Evelyn Waugh." A few months earlier he would have been in seventh heaven. The party meant stories, sources, fun. Now it worried him. "I don't belong at an opium party given by a CIA official," he thought.

Opium scared off few of the reporters. Most tried it, and some used it regularly. Pam Sanders wrote Halberstam half-humorously, complaining about the visiting *Time* correspondents she regularly escorted through the opium dens of Vientiane, all claiming they were researching a story. "At night we have to go and smoke opium, which makes me violently ill," she wrote. "I wish they'd either do the damn story or drop it. All this nausea is doing terrible things to my digestive system."

But it wasn't the opium that bothered Sharkey. It was the CIA and the concern that he might compromise himself in, as he put it, "my position in the adversarial role with the government." So, with the purity of youth, he left.

Not all picked up the new banner. Joining the government's team seemed to come more easily with age and what Halberstam called "the deadly need to become an insider." Theodore H. White, the great rebel of China reporting a generation earlier, now thought nothing of proffering strong and private advice. "This South Vietnam thing is a real bastard to solve," White wrote Kennedy after a 1961 visit. "Either we have to let the younger military officers knock off Diem in a coup and take our chances on a military regime . . . or else we have to give it up."

Life's premier Vietnam photographer, Larry Burrows,[1] splashed napalm all over the pages of America's favorite photo magazine more than a year before the government admitted to its use. But he could also be a solid team player. *"Important,"* he flagged a photo for his editors in January 1963, immediately after Ap Bac. "The pilot in this picture, the man who actually fired the rockets, is an American pilot. But since, politically at least, Americans are only here as advisers it would probably do considerable harm if we print that fact . . . It is probably better to refer to the man as a Vietnamese pilot. . . ." The caption writer went along, adding some further cosmetics as well: "Object [of the napalm attack] is to sear the foliage and flush the enemy into the open."

The two young New Zealanders, Nick Turner and Peter Arnett, showed just how divided the reporters could become.

Turner ran with the firebrands, Halberstam and Sheehan, and loved the camaraderie of it, the sense of being part of a group of buddies against the world. But his experience in New Zealand and with the straight-as-a-string wire-service reporting expected

---

1. Burrows was such a perfectionist he might shoot six rolls to get one photo just right, carrying so much film into the field the canisters bulged out of the top of his socks. He had nine Vietnam covers to his credit before he was killed in 1971.

by Reuters left him uncomfortable with the new combativeness. "I didn't expect everyone to tell me the truth," he said later. "It was wartime. I didn't carry with me that thought carried by so many American correspondents that I had a God-given right to be informed about everything." Sometimes his new buddies made him uneasy. "Neil was a very volatile sort of character, very amusing, sometimes a bit over the top for me, but I liked his company." He also liked Halberstam. But Halberstam made him more uncomfortable. "I could understand Dave being angry and wanting to use his position to change many of the things that were wrong," Turner said. "But it often carried over into personal vendettas and often he saw things in clear-cut ideas that were not always clear-cut. I rather liked the thought that if you weren't confused, you were badly informed."

Arnett instinctively moved the other way. Being an adversary suited him far better than the style he had left behind at home, where the press had no quasi-constitutional role and no strong keep-the-government-honest tradition.

Being the AP newcomer, Arnett was sent to the afternoon military briefings, which everyone tried to avoid because they were so devoid of information.[2] Arnett loved them. Within months the feisty New Zealander became the champion of American journalistic rights, challenging the military spokesmen on constitutional points and the public's right to know. Sharkey walked in on one of Arnett's Kiwi-twang performances a few days after he arrived. Afterward, Arnett approached him sheepishly. Sharkey, he knew, had just received a Columbia University graduate degree heavy in First Amendment issues.

"Gosh, Jack," Arnett said, "don't you think you should take over?"

"No, no, not at all, Peter," Sharkey answered. He had been fascinated by this abrasive rough cut from the bottom of the world challenging the American military on constitutional grounds. "You're doing just fine. I couldn't do better."

Arnett kept it up for the next thirty years, all the way through Vietnam, more than twenty other wars, and behind enemy lines in

---

2. Later in the war, the briefings became known as the Five O'Clock Follies.

Baghdad. There, pursuing his adopted convictions under the most adverse conditions, he once again was accused by politicians, brutally and unfairly, of disloyalty.

———

Publicly, the unbounded optimism continued. Ten days after Ap Bac, in his State of the Union address, the President said: "The spearhead of aggression has been blunted in Vietnam." A Pentagon spokesman added: "We have turned the corner in Vietnam." Secretary of State Rusk said that the war effort was "producing excellent results." Harkins predicted that the war could be won "within a year." Everyone turned the screws on the correspondents.

In mid-January Army Chief of Staff General Earle G. Wheeler arrived in Saigon. He found the Vietnamese press on the warpath. In its pages Vietnam's lacquered lady, Madame Nhu, accused Vann —"the foreign militarist"—of causing the battlefield deaths of Vietnamese troops. Diem demanded removal of the "traitorous American colonel."

The palace attacks on the correspondents became absurd, railing at their failure to see that brave and outnumbered ARVN troops had surrounded and defeated the Viet Cong. Some of the assaults in the Diem-controlled press were simply mystifying. Wheeler picked up a local newspaper one day and found Cornelius Mahoney Sheehan staring up at him from the front page. Above the photograph ran a headline that read: THE AMERICAN ADVISER SHEEHAN; WHAT DOES HE REALLY WANT? No answer accompanied the headline. Nor did any story.

By now the correspondents had acculturated themselves to zany attacks in the Saigon newspapers. Sheehan's buddies found the photograph hilarious and began greeting him: "Okay, Sheehan, what *do* you really want?"

Wheeler returned to Washington to tell President Kennedy that the press situation was "terrible." But the war was being won.

In the administration's highest reaches Ap Bac caused a new round of scrutiny. But much of it was as detached from reality as the rantings in the Saigon propaganda sheets. The secret communications, many not made public till thirty years later, provide an extraordinary look at a government with blinders on.

Almost to a man the notables bought into Harkins's victory

claim, a deadly mistake that colored all attempts to deal with real problems. Rather than seek a fix that would avoid similar battle outcomes, they sought a fix to avoid similar stories.

Secretary of State Rusk cabled Nolting for another assessment of the "long-vexed question" of press coverage, seeking "suggestions as to how we may assist or encourage [the correspondents] to do [a] better job. . . ." He focused on one main point:

> REALIZE WIRE SERVICE CORRESPONDENTS HAVE DIFFICULTY IN LEAVING SAIGON . . . TO GO INTO COUNTRY.
>
> IF CORRESPONDENT HAS TIME, HOW DIFFICULT IS IT FOR HIM TO GET TRANSPORTATION A) TO COVER MILITARY OPERATIONS, B) TO GO INTO COUNTRYSIDE TO COVER STRATEGIC HAMLETS AND OTHER RURAL ACTIVITIES?

Get out of Saigon? The nighttime drives down Highway 4 by two wire-service correspondents, Sheehan and Turner, propelled Ap Bac from a major story to a symbol of failure. Arnett's trip with Halberstam the next day gave Harkins the opportunity to complete the destruction of his credibility. The idea that the correspondents sat around Saigon bars cooking up stories to aggravate the government became a Washington fixation. The problem was quite the opposite. The government couldn't keep the correspondents *in* Saigon because they didn't believe anything they heard there.

W. Averell Harriman, assistant secretary of state for Far Eastern affairs and as shrewd an infighter as ever maneuvered in Washington corridors, wrote Nolting a "Dear Fritz" letter noting that Harkins gave "excellent guidance" on press relations and Nolting also did "this kind of thing very well." Harriman was known among Washington's infighters as the Crocodile. He was not above subtle sarcasm or false flattery, and he was about to get into some covert rough stuff with the ineffective Saigon team. So the boilerplate language can be read either way. He also got down to specifics.

"I think the most damaging aspect of our press problem is alleged quotes of American military advisers criticizing their Vietnamese comrades in arms," he wrote, pointing to the "miserable damn performance" quote at Ap Bac. His solution: ". . . All American correspondents while on operations with United States forces might well be clearly identified by a name tag or by other means."

Did he think the reporters were eavesdropping? Averell Harriman, meet John Paul Vann, who also played by rules that would make Machiavelli blush.[3]

On February 5, 1963, Nolting cabled the requested assessment to Rusk. It began:

QUALITY OF REPORTING BY US NEWSMEN HERE IS PROBABLY AS GOOD AS AVERAGE REPORTING OF STATESIDE STORY LIKE EARTHQUAKE OR HOLLYWOOD DIVORCE.

Nolting also wrote that "major US news organizations like UPI, AP, and *NYTimes* use men (average age 27) with approximately same experience to cover Vietnam as they do routine stateside police beat," adding that "these particular American newsmen and this particular regime dislike each other to degree that verges on neurotic."

Fortunately for the government, Nolting's report never leaked. Unfortunately, the next one did.

Nolting asked John Mecklin for his own assessment. Forever whipsawed between old allegiances and new, Mecklin criticized the government some, the press some, and called for a new olive-branch approach. Nolting would have none of that. Mecklin revised the report, later calling it "the stupidest thing I ever did," and discovered that the embassy had begun to leak like a sinking ship. Long before Washington saw it, parts of his report resided in David Halberstam's hands. The correspondents, Mecklin wrote, were immature, malicious, and intellectually ill-equipped for the Vietnam story. "The American commitment to Vietnam," the report concluded, "has been badly hampered by irresponsible, astigmatic, and sensationalized reporting." Mecklin made equally strong criticisms of the government. But leaks are not leaked in the interest of fairness. The correspondents never saw those sections. They fumed.

After that, the war between the two governments and the newsmen seemed to outpace the stalled war in the field. Mecklin de-

---

3. The reporters already wore clearly defined name tags and usually a second tag that said "Bao Chi," Vietnamese for journalist—if for no reason other than insurance against being summarily shot if captured by the Viet Cong.

spaired and took to heavier drinking. An Australian reporter and old friend from the French war, Denis Warner, talked to the disconsolate press aide one evening.

"The place has the smell of Dien Bien Phu, doesn't it?" Warner volunteered.

Mecklin agreed, but he couldn't admit it. If it does, he replied, it has some of the smartest men in America fooled.

Warner looked at him in kindly disbelief and said quietly, "The French thought they were winning too. Remember?"

Mecklin said nothing, then asked if Warner wanted to go for a drink.

Mecklin was actually very ill. Shortly afterward, he flew to Clark Field in the Philippines for minor surgery. The doctors found cancer and shipped him to Bethesda Naval Hospital outside Washington. He returned in May to play out the rest of the nice-little-war phase of the long Vietnam drama, suffer through the surreality of the Buddhist crisis, then be recalled with almost everyone else of importance after the lid blew in November. The cancer killed him eight years later.

One State Department official, William Jorden, who once had been the *New York Times* Moscow correspondent, visited Saigon and had the cheek to report back that the emperor indeed wore no clothes.

"There is, I think, a serious misunderstanding of what has come to be called the 'press problem in Vietnam,'" Jorden began his March 21, 1963, report. He continued:

To ignore the many negative features in Vietnam is to dangerously delude ourselves. There is a vast multitude of problems and only by recognizing them can we hope to do something about them. A reporter who exposes such a problem may well be opening the door to its solution.

The quality of reporting by American newsmen from Vietnam is, in my opinion, exceedingly good. They are young (and) still learning their trade. But they are doing so with energy and seriousness of purpose. They spend a considerable amount of time in the provinces and the villages and with the military forces in the field. They have both better information and a better feel for the situation than many military officers in Saigon.

His report sank like a torpedoed tugboat.

After weeks of rat-a-tat assaults in both countries, Senator Mansfield came forward to say in the Senate what Jorden had said to no avail in private. "Reporters [in Vietnam] have been criticized for being young and hence immature, and on occasion for being too old and hence cantankerous. But whether too young or too old, the gist of the criticism is that the reporters do not know what they are talking about." Mansfield took a direct slap at the gossipy White House, asking what "qualifies any executive branch employee to judge the maturity or immaturity of the press?" He had talked to the correspondents at length, the majority leader said, and had found them to have the "same objectivity and alertness and appropriate skepticism" as reporters anywhere.

The beleaguered Saigon regulars were so delighted they cabled Mansfield that they were all thinking of moving to Montana so they could vote for him.

———

The American helicopter pilots had no doubt about whom to believe. Soon after Ap Bac they could be heard singing a song, written by one of their own. It was called "Ap Bac" and sung to the tune of "On Top of Old Smoky":

We were supporting the ARVNs
    A group without guts,
Attacking a village
    of straw-covered huts.

Four pilots are wounded,
    Two crewmen are dead.
When it's all over
    A good day for the Red.

An armored battalion
    Just stayed in a trance.
One captain died trying
    To make them advance.

254

The paratroops landed,
   A magnificent sight
There was hand-to-hand combat,
   But no VCs in sight.

When the news was reported,
   The ARVNs had won.
The VCs are laughing
   Over their captured guns.

The song went on for fifteen verses.

———

Meanwhile, General Harkins continued his campaign. In an interview with the *Times of Vietnam*, he stubbornly stuck by his fictions: "The government forces had an objective, they took that objective, the VC left, and their casualties were greater than those of the government forces—what more do you want?"

The *Times of Vietnam* didn't want anything more. It headlined the interview: AP BAC WAS A VICTORY—HARKINS REBUFFS REPORTS. The general played perfectly into the *Times*'s agenda. Earlier stories had been headed: NO APOLOGIA FOR VICTORY . . . BLAST AT FOREIGN PRESS . . . AP BAC VICTORY.

The *Times of Vietnam* was an odd place for Harkins to go for support. It lashed out at the American government as wickedly as it did the American press. Most wrote the paper off as a joke. But the joke could wear thin. It was a strange little sheet—at first glance so all-American, with wire reports on the new astronaut-heroes, color comics, up-to-date stateside sports scores, stock-market quotes, an Art Buchwald column. But a second glance revealed more—large headlines for full texts of Madame Nhu's fiery speeches, daily stories about brilliant ARVN triumphs in the field, editorials that, as did one after Ap Bac, accused the correspondents of responsibility for the deaths of ARVN and American soldiers.

Most of the major cities of Asia had similar newspapers, catering to colonies of expatriate Americans in the days of empire, catering to local strongman leaders too. Catering to the strongmen usually proved more lucrative.

In Saigon the paper was a mom-and-pop operation, run by a couple named Gene and Ann Gregory. Ann, blond and almost as high-strung as Madame Nhu, coincidentally was one of the First Lady's best friends. She spent her time translating Madame Nhu's speeches from the French,[4] showing movies to the Nhus' children, and keeping the newspaper's day-by-day operations going.

Gene Gregory was more the mystery. A man all soft corners and sleepy eyes, he worked briefly as a press officer for the United States Information Service in Saigon in the early fifties. By 1963 he rode around town in a chauffeured black Peugeot and had lingered on Saigon's murky edges so long that *Newsweek* reported gossip that he was "some sort of super-intelligence agent, a flabby James Bond." He was also close to the Nhus, making retreats with Brother Nhu to the family hunting lodge in the mountain resort of Dalat.

While Ann ran the paper, Gene Gregory concentrated on other business interests, which were varied and ran conveniently without competition. He wasn't riding in a Peugeot off profits from the newspaper. He reportedly had a contract to redecorate the bombed-out presidential palace. He also owned a factory that made batteries, for which he had a national monopoly. The *Times* ran advertisements in its front-page "ears," the boxes flanking the logo atop the front page. One often read: VANGUARD BATTERIES. THEY'RE GUARANTEED FACTORY FRESH. For the other, Gregory would try to find a paying customer: MEN! TAKE NOTE OF THIS HISTORIC OCCASION. THE OPENING OF MIMI'S FLAMBOYANT BAR.

Meshing the interests of their newspaper's two constituencies became increasingly difficult for the Gregorys in 1963. They made the businessman's choice.

The newspaper's outrageousness occasionally made news. But the correspondents, the target of much of it, treated the *Times of Vietnam* and its owners with abject contempt. When David Halberstam's editors requested a story about the paper, he cabled back:

---

4. Born into a high-society family, Madame Nhu could barely read or write her native language. She conducted her affairs in the language of the *haut monde*, French.

TO DO ANYTHING AT ALL ACCURATE ABOUT THOSE PEOPLE
WOULD BE LIBELOUS AND TO DO ANYTHING NON-LIBELOUS
WOULD BE TOO CHARITABLE.

But Sheehan, as usual, had the most difficult road. He not only suffered the insults, but also had to deal financially with the owners. After months of frustration he concluded that Ann Gregory was "hysterical" and Gene "a sleazy bastard." But he accomplished his first and last business coup just days after Ap Bac, signing Gene to a new contract on the *Bugs Bunny* and *Peanuts* comic strips so dear to Asia Earnie's heart and, in the doing, finagling $600 out of Gregory for his huge back bills. It was the last money UPI would get out of the couple. Instead, Sheehan came under siege. UPI LIES, LIES, LIES, one front-page *Times of Vietnam* headline thundered. Asia Earnie kept his young bureau chief's fingers to the fire on the Gregory account. But even the UPI accountants knew that the task was hopeless, as an internal memo acknowledged:

> There is something about our good friends [the Gregorys] that makes me feel this thing will never be what you might call regularized. It will all be up to Neil to put on his red suit and carry his bass drum, with the motto "deadbeat" across the face, and parade frequently in front of the *Times* office crying for a showerdown of money.

The *Times of Vietnam* lasted exactly as long as Ngo Dinh Diem. It published its last edition the morning of November 1, 1963, the day Diem fell, and was never heard from again.

—

Charley Mohr, his life chaotic enough, had used the New Year's holiday to shore up his shaky homefront in Hong Kong. That left it to Mert Perry to file the blunt and pessimistic report about Ap Bac to the magazine that didn't want to hear it. Many more "ominous" defeats like this one, Perry wrote, and America's little war "could escalate quickly into something almost as nasty as the French agony from 1950 to 1954." *Time*'s New York rewrite men blue-

penciled the stringer's emotional warning. But they finally ig-
nored Harkins too. Even *Time* called Ap Bac a defeat, heading
Perry's watered-down report: THE HELICOPTER WAR RUNS INTO
TROUBLE.

Mohr flew in the next day in time to take the lead in the
correspondents' meeting with Roger Hilsman, a hardball player
with a saw-toothed edge to his talk. He had trouble forgetting
his own deeds of daring as a jungle fighter in Burma, and
sometimes thought he could use the same rules in the jungle of
the government's bureaucratic warfare. Later he wrote that his
instincts had been with the correspondents and his only disagreement came when Mohr told him that the Diem government hated
the correspondents and hated the United States too. According to
his recollection he replied that "it was not our objective to be
liked, but to get a job done." The reporters heard something
considerably more blistering: they were too naive, not tough
enough for the dirty jobs that needed doing in the dangerous
new world America was preordained to run. It was not a
successful meeting.

Hilsman had played tough guy with the wrong man. The look
of Charley Mohr could be deceptive, corn-silk eyebrows softening
an average, Midwestern face. But that was the only part of Mohr
that was soft, the only part that was average. Five years later, in a
war none of them could yet imagine, Mohr would find himself
pinned down with a company of marines during the bloody Tet
Offensive. The outfit had taken a terrible mauling during a week of
door-to-door fighting in the beautiful old city of Hue. Casualties
had run high, even the chaplain killed, and a marine lay twenty
feet away in the rubble, shot through the neck, moaning horribly
and badly exposed to enemy fire. It was the kind of setting an
enemy waits for, ready to take down half a dozen more as they try
to rescue their buddy. But Mohr leaped up, two other correspondents following, and zigzagged through an angry burst of shots to
pull the man back to safety. It was a remarkable act of courage. The
two others, David Greenway of *Time* and Al Webb of UPI, were
wounded by a mortar, Webb seriously. In 1980, twelve years later
and five years after the unhappy war ended, the marines awarded
the three correspondents the Bronze Star for bravery, the only

newsmen decorated in a war in which so many thought the media was the enemy.[5]

Still, as 1963 began, Mohr looked back with distaste on his maiden performance in Vietnam and that glowing cover story on Harkins the previous May. It was the worst kind of smoke-jumper reporting, he thought. He had leaped in, gone to all the government's dog and pony shows, and written. He had seen too much of that since from the big-byline reporters. "Stenography," he still growled in self-criticism. "It wasn't reporting. It was goddamned stenography." Slowly, he had become disenchanted with the endless optimism, the secrecy and the failures, the hopeless regime. Now he listened to Hilsman's heavy-handedness, flew over the scene at Ap Bac, talked to John Paul Vann, heard out the other reporters—and made the final turn. He cabled *Time*'s chief of correspondents, Richard Clurman: "In the briefest possible summary my opinion is: The situation stinks."

It is important to repeat what it meant to "turn" in 1963. Mohr would support the war for many years before concluding that it was wrongheaded. To turn in 1963 meant to go from optimist to pessimist about the conduct of the war, not the war itself. It embarrassed Mohr when the mythmaking took over later, making him one of the early antiwar heroes. He didn't like the myth at all. It wasn't true, and, unlike some of the others, he didn't want it to be true. "We were children of the Cold War," he said. "We believed." He went home briefly in 1964 and discovered that many Americans were not debating the narrower issues the reporters had debated—whether Diem was the right man, whether a certain policy or strategy was correct. In an unfinished private memoir he wrote: "They were debating a different question: Should we have ever gotten into the Vietnam War in the first place? I was genuinely surprised. For, on that score, I had never held any doubt." Charley

5. During Tet, Mohr carried and used at least two weapons, a customized Beretta handgun and a standard-issue M-16 rifle. He fired them offensively as well as defensively—to the stern disapproval of many of his colleagues. Johnny Apple thought Mohr's love of weapons dated back to his youth on the High Plains where guns were an inherent part of the culture. The first thing Mohr did when Apple arrived in 1965 was slap a Beretta in his hand.

Mohr, far more than the others, was a man of war. He loved the smell of cordite, perhaps too much.

Keyes Beech, the old Asia hand from the *Chicago Daily News*, complained half-seriously that he didn't like to go into the field with him. "You always look like the fucking company commander," he told him. To Beech, company commander meant target. "You always have your helmet on, your pack on, your forty-five caliber on. It must be the goddamn Prussian in you."

But they had too much respect for each other not to go out, and once, in the mountainous Central Highlands, they took a rash of incoming fire. Beech was insufferable afterward, bitching that it was Charley's fault, that goddamn pack, that goddamn helmet. Afterward, they stayed out the night. Highlands nights could become very cold and for a long while Mohr let Beech, who had not brought cold-weather gear, shiver.

"Well, smart-ass," he finally said, "you wanta share my poncho?"

Beech was sheepish. "Jesus, in the marine corps you could get twenty years for that," he muttered. Then he added, "Hell, yes."

To have Mohr with them was a terrific boost for the Young Turks. He was only a few years older, thirty-four at the time. But they were big years, *Time* years at the White House, years on the presidential campaign trails, years riding elephants, for God's sake, with publishers and ambassadors. And he was so good. He knew all the tricks: how to interrupt Diem's monologues by solicitously offering the chain-smoking president a light and slipping in his question during the ever-so-brief pause to accept the foreign journalist's proper show of homage; how to get a quote tuned when it wasn't quite right for his story. "I'm having trouble reading my notes, but I think this is what you said," he would tell his source. Then he would read it the way he wanted it. The subject would ponder briefly, think he sounded unusually wise, and reply, "Word for word, Mr. Mohr." The other correspondents idolized him. Halberstam called him "our generation's Homer Bigart."

He was also such fun to be around, an urbane and witty man, quick with the repartee of the barroom or the black gallows humor of the battlefield. In Saigon dives he sat around with the boys, Chivas in hand, and acted out all five parts in spontaneous playlets about their favorite comic troupe. First he would play Harkins,

Troop carriers in the nice little war in a land of tigers and elephants, 1962.
AP/WIDE WORLD PHOTOS.

Stone-age
Montagnard
tribesmen
in loincloths
"chat" with
David Halberstam.
DAVID HALBERSTAM
COLLECTION.

Mme Nhu inspects
spear-carrying troops.
AP/WIDE
WORLD PHOTOS.

Ambassador Nolting
and General Harkins
chat in tropical dress
whites at Saigon
lawn party.
FRANÇOIS SULLY/
BLACK STAR.

Diem, second from left, and extended family pose in classic mandarin dress.
AP/WIDE WORLD PHOTOS.

Brother Nhu.
AP/WIDE WORLD
PHOTOS.

Above: Young Peter Arnett began
a thirteen-year Vietnam odyssey.
AP/WIDE WORLD PHOTOS.
Left: So did Horst Faas, the
tough German photographer.
HORST FAAS PHOTO.

Right: The grand old man of
the early Vietnam correspondents,
Homer Bigart, shown at end of the Second
World War which made him famous.
AP/WIDE WORLD PHOTOS.

Peripatetic McNamara, on an early chopper tour, came often but saw little. AP/WIDE WORLD PHOTOS.

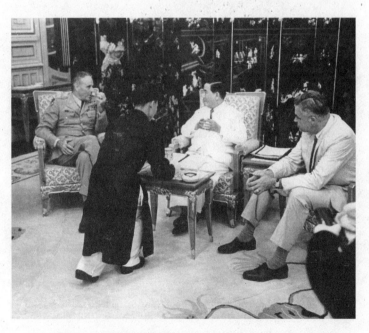

Maxwell Taylor and Nolting meet with Diem, who spoke in monologues often lasting hours. AP/WIDE WORLD PHOTOS.

Charley Mohr was the toughest of them all.
THE NEW YORK TIMES.

Vietnam would become the Living Room War, but in 1963 television had
a long way to go: Peter Kalischer with CBS cameraman
and soundman in what they called the monkey-grinder shot.
MRS. PETER KALISCHER COLLECTION.

The gang sees off legendary François Sully after he is expelled. Halberstam, who arrived the day before, is barely visible in uncharacteristic spot at back.

NICK TURNER COLLECTION.

Neil Sheehan speaks with a U.S. adviser after the battle of Ap Bac, which started him down his long, long road.

STEVE STIBBENS PHOTO.

The Dragon
Lady, Mme Nhu,
became a cartoon
favorite. She offered
Halberstam a match to
"barbecue" himself like
protesting Buddhists.
LePELLEY IN *THE CHRISTIAN
SCIENCE MONITOR* © 1963 TCSPS.

See no evil, speak no evil, hear no evil—Colonel Fred Ladd, a good
source, caught Mert Perry, Halberstam and Ray Herndon in a pose symbolizing what the government wanted from reporters.
FRED LADD/DAVID HALBERSTAM COLLECTION

Right: Mal Browne, Arnett, and Faas in the AP office on Rue Pasteur. Sheehan called them the "human wave." HORST FAAS PHOTO.
Below: Sheehan, at rear was alone at UPI until Halberstam moved in, helping even the odds. Herndon came later. The wires' war within the war became known as ROX vs. UNIPRESS. NEIL SHEEHAN COLLECTION.

Beverly Deepe, one of the first young vagabonds to land in the tiny Saigon press corps, was the girl next door, a symbol of the rapidly fading apple-pie fifties. BEVERLY DEEPE COLLECTION.

The war was not all muddy boots. AP's Browne
in a tuxedo at a Saigon party with General Harkins.
AP/WIDE WORLD PHOTOS.

Sheehan, Blue Lotus, Herndon and Halberstam at the Eskimo.
All the Young Turks had beautiful Vietnamese girl friends.
RAY HERNDON COLLECTION.

Pam Sanders, another vagabond, turned heads in Green Beret
outposts and the Saigon bistro, L'Amiral. The Perrys are at left.
PAMELA SANDERS COLLECTION.

Above left: Joseph Alsop used his column to castigate the "egregious
crusaders." AP/WIDE WORLD PHOTOS. *Right*: Keyes Beech, the classic old
Asia hand, took his days off in nearby Thailand.
MRS. KEYES BEECH COLLECTION.

Marguerite Higgins
fought it out with
Bigart in Korea,
then continued
the private war
with Halberstam
in Vietnam.
AP/WIDE WORLD PHOTOS.

The reporters came
in from the jungles for
new battles in the streets.
Browne sometimes
seemed as enigmatic as
the unworldly
Buddhists themselves.
AP/WIDE
WORLD PHOTOS.

Arnett, a dukes-up rookie, could find trouble anywhere.
Above: Led away by gun-toting Saigon police.
AP/WIDE WORLD PHOTOS.

Halberstam steps in to pull the cops off his bloodied pal.
MALCOLM W. BROWNE PHOTO/PETER ARNETT COLLECTION.

Front page of *Stars and Stripes* on November 1, 1963, the day of the successful coup against Diem. The page became a collector's item, symbolizing Harkins' eternal optimism.

Faas stands in front of the shot-up AP bureau
the morning after. The war had twelve years to go.

mimicking his mannerisms with the long ivory cigarette holder; then the aristocratic Nolting, then the mystical Diem, the conspiratorial Brother Nhu, and always ending on the Madame, flashing his fingernails like filleting knives and raging in the voice of an angry canary: "I'm not let little David Halberstam ruin my government!" In combat, when others were praying, Mohr would wisecrack. Once, when the bullets came far, far too close, he dug in deeper and said, "I'm beginning to feel like the actress who asked, 'Who do I have to screw to get *out* of this movie?' "

Having made his turn, Charley Mohr began fighting his own guerrilla war against the Time-Life fortress in far-off Rockefeller Center. He was good. He'd win one, lose a couple, then lose another and win another. He told his wife, Norma, he thought he might bring *Time* around. Norma thought Charley could do about anything. But she didn't have good feelings about this. She knew what had happened to others when they had gone up against Lucian doctrine. She also knew what Charley faced inside that forty-seven-story bastion in Manhattan.

Henry Luce had set up a management structure as peculiar as that of *The Times*. He had given Clurman, his chief of correspondents and a sophisticated liberal, total control of the hiring and firing of the best-of-breed, lavishly rewarded reporters. But Luce was not a simple man. He set up checks and balances, much as had the country's Founding Fathers. He gave Otto Fuerbringer, his managing editor and a Teutonic, rock-ribbed conservative, total control of the magazine's content. Clurman could hire Pulitzer Prize winners but not guarantee them a word in the magazine. Fuerbringer could fire no one but could freeze out the most golden of the golden until they gave up and quit. Clurman was a power. Fuerbringer was *the* power. The Iron Chancellor, they called him, a man who often hugged the Lucian line tighter than the boss did himself.

To Fuerbringer, who had covered the military for *Time* during the Second World War, the row of tilting dominoes in Southeast Asia quickly became a holy war. Stanley Karnow remembers a parting conversation as he prepared to leave the Hong Kong bureau, a move that made way for Mohr. It came in the spring of 1962, at the time of the flare-up in landlocked Laos that caused Kennedy to send the marines into nearby Thailand. Karnow, who had been in Southeast Asia for three years, warned that pushing in Laos might be dicey. It was not an easy place to fight a mechanized war. The Iron Chancellor scoffed: The Commies wouldn't *dare* escalate back, threatening real war. Karnow was taken aback. Why not? "Because we've got the Seventh Fleet off their shore and we'll blow the hell out of them," Fuerbringer replied. Good God, Karnow wondered, was he serious? Laos didn't have a shore. How did Fuerbringer plan to get the carriers through the Annamite Mountains?

The navy would indeed do immense damage in the coming big war in Vietnam. But control it? Stop it? Win it? Technology simply wasn't the answer—in Laos or Vietnam. These countries might have been technologically backward, lost on the other side of the world, mere warts on the map of the American mind. But Vietnam had a coastline longer than California's, and a population as large. Could anyone believe that a foreign fleet, any foreign fleet, could stop an insurrection in California? The vision of a muscle-bound Soviet navy trying to control guerrillas in the Sierra Nevada, the northern mountains and forests, the southern deserts; in the urban canyons, the barrio, the wastelands of Los Angeles; that vision quickly becomes ludicrous.

But Fuerbringer *was* serious, and Karnow had the sense not to push the point. To do so would run in the face of *Time* dogma, Luce dogma, Fuerbringer dogma—run in the face, for that matter, of mid-century American dogma about its own omnipotence.

So Norma Mohr listened to Charley and nodded her head. But she feared this would end badly.

———

John Paul Vann also played a very dicey game in the months after Ap Bac, adding another twist to the charmed-life legend. Time and again Harkins almost fired him, his fury boundless at his insubordinate subordinate. Vann ignored him. He seemed foolhardy, flaunting that old death wish almost as surely as he had when rumbling alone at night through Viet Cong territory, grenades rattling loose in his jeep.

One day John Sharkey walked in on Vann as he briefed officers from Harkins's office. Seeing him, Vann launched into a tirade: "Now you goddamn reporters, you watch what you say, hear?! I don't like you runnin' around down here pokin' around and criticizing everything." Sharkey flared briefly. Dammit, he thought, I'm getting morally mugged by this guy. Then he shrugged. Vann was doing some normal protection of his backside, a rare event. His leaks had become a flood. What really irritated Sharkey was that they weren't coming his way. They flowed in only one direction: toward David Halberstam and the power of *The New York Times*.

"Both were outsiders trying to be somebody," Neil Sheehan wrote later of the two men who seemed to have fashioned the perfect trade. "Through Halberstam, Vann was to achieve his greatest impact on events during the opening phase of the American war. What Halberstam learned from Vann was to help make him one of the most famous journalists of his time."

For Halberstam the first months of 1963 became a bonanza. He commuted to the Seminary, returning with a roar of delight: "Jesus Christ, have I got a helluva story!"

In one he reported that the ARVN's sham battles had become epidemic. General Cao had begun using American intelligence to avoid rather than make contact with Viet Cong units. He used it to find the "battlegrounds" he liked best—those where the enemy didn't exist. Halberstam gave dates and places of the phony firefights. The source was so thinly covered he could have disguised him just as well by using his initials: according to JPV.

Vann's brazenness began to worry Halberstam. He felt guilty about the degree to which he was putting the man at risk. Not only were the stories cutting off his path to general, they imperiled any kind of army future. Halberstam implored him to be more careful. Vann ignored him. He was a man with a mission larger than his career. He was more than an army officer, he told Halberstam. "I'm also an American citizen with a duty to my country."

To the twenty-eight-year-old reporter the words rang so romantic, so patriotic, they seemed braver than the jeep rides in the night. John Paul Vann would sacrifice himself to get the facts to the American people. He was a genuine hero, a legend in his time.

Vann was very good at adding that extra narcotic lure.

———

The old Asia hands began showing up with more regularity and less friendliness now. One was Richard Tregaskis, who had his reputation etched in newsprint long before he arrived in Vietnam.

A generation earlier Tregaskis hit the beach at Guadalcanal, the only war correspondent on hand as the marines took their first bloody step in the long haul back across the Pacific islands toward Tokyo. Newspaper extras began screaming heroic reports from the Japanese-held rock in the Coral Sea, giving the homefront its first sense that American boys would turn the tide. The Tregaskis stories so nurtured the nation's hopes that they became a best-selling book and then a hit movie, *Guadalcanal Diary*. They also helped set the standards for American war correspondence in that last "good war," making Richard Tregaskis famous in the doing. He was twenty-six years old at the time.

Skinny and gangling, towering over everyone at six foot seven, Tregaskis seemed more kid than man. Marine commanders worried how a man that big and that awkward could keep his head down under fire, the last thing they needed being a dead correspondent from the International News Service. But Tregaskis tromped everywhere with the troops and, when the action slowed, he bitched with them about the chow and asked about their girls and families back home. Tregaskis remained on Guadalcanal for seven weeks and left for other battles, so legend has it, only when his relentless slogging wore out the last pair of size fourteen boots on the island.

Twenty years later Tregaskis came to Saigon to write another book, *Vietnam Diary*. Approaching the city, he mused about the differences a generation can make. "It took weeks aboard transport ships to get our forces in position to attack the Japanese," he noted. "Heavy cruisers and destroyers provided a massive naval bombardment; an umbrella of dive-bombers and fighter planes from aircraft carriers covered our assault." Now, he wrote, he cruised comfortably into the war zone aboard a new 707 commercial jetliner. At Guadalcanal a landing meant a beachhead of bloody fighting and, if lucky, a night in a wet hole. In Vietnam he fought only Saigon's chaotic traffic to bivouac at the swank Caravelle Hotel.

There would be no wet foxholes for Tregaskis this time. Harkins and the brass gave him the VIP treatment with upbeat "headway" briefings followed by lunch amid the rich mahogany of the Cercle

Sportif. He was choppered to the action in the morning, choppered back to the Caravelle at night. For Harkins, dealing with men of his own generation came as a welcome relief from constant scrapping with the "kiddie corps." These men had been blooded in his era, saw the world through a Second World War prism. They also came and left quickly. That helped.

Tregaskis was no pushover. But Harkins was right about his perspective. He would write about American fighting men as he had a generation earlier—as tough, human, sometimes brave, and sometimes frightened men doing a mean job that had to be done. But he was also a believer. He would cover Vietnam as a man on the team, just as he and his colleagues had been on the team in the total war that formed them, a war of unquestioned evil, unquestioned good, and unquestioned need.

Not long after Ap Bac David Halberstam rented a car and invited his older colleague along for a day in the delta.

The two had much in common. Both had been thrust young and early into the epic story of their generation. Halberstam was only two years older than Tregaskis had been at Guadalcanal. Both had courage and luck—the luck of timing, their profession's most treasured talisman. Halberstam towered over others, as had Tregaskis. Even the boyishness seemed the same. While Tregaskis, Ernie Pyle, and a handful of others had set the tone for reporting the Second World War, Halberstam and a few of his buddies were setting the tone for a dozen years of war reporting from Vietnam. But if Tregaskis covered his era as the time of America's grand triumph, Halberstam would cover his as the time of his country's grand delusion.

Halberstam felt a touch of hero worship for this older man who had stormed ashore in the kind of war he would never cover. He was also a salesman, a proselytizer. He liked to bring others in around him, inoculate them against the government's propaganda. He looked forward to the day in the delta, followed back in Saigon by a premier-class French dinner and old war stories well told.

The trip would be a routine run, Halberstam said, like checking out City Hall on a slow day back home. No firefights had been reported, no troops on the move. But Tregaskis would get a different view because Halberstam planned to introduce him to his own sources—American advisers who saw the war before it passed through politicized Saigon's rosy filter. Tregaskis shrugged. Why not? He had heard the tales about the brash young newcomer from *The Times*. You couldn't get away from Harkins without having your ears bent on that subject. But, hell, he had been young and brash once too.

As promised, officer after officer told stories about ARVN commanders who wouldn't fight, about leadership so lacking that no ARVN officer above the rank of captain would venture into combat, about "ghost" battles that magically became victories in Saigon, about enemy body counts that tripled, quadrupled, increased tenfold as they moved up through the command levels.

In late afternoon Halberstam drove back up Highway 4. He felt good, mission accomplished and dinner at his favorite French restaurant, L'Amiral, only minutes away. Tregaskis had been unusually quiet on the ride back. Then the legendary Second World War correspondent turned toward the soon-to-be-legendary Vietnam correspondent. "If I were doing what you are doing," he said, "I'd be ashamed of myself."

———

It was a warning shot over the bow.

Nothing would heighten the sense of isolation as much as the attacks from their own kind. You could take away all the Americans at the embassy. You could take away the American military brass and their boot polishers. You could say by-my-leave to your main tie to home, your editors, with whom a state of war was eternal anyway. But Tregaskis stung. Many in the old guard had been the childhood heroes of the Saigon correspondents. Until now, they had also been a crucial lifeline to the world. But that lifeline was soon gone too. Other warning shots followed quickly, and then the warnings stopped and it became downright mean. "It got very lonely out there," Halberstam said.

Of all the troopers in the old guard, Keyes Beech was the favorite of the new generation. An ex-marine, Beech was a compact little man and, in 1963, a year shy of fifty. But he looked as if he had just arrived from Parris Island, where a few good men had reduced him, permanently, to muscle and steel.

A combat correspondent for the marines in the Second World War—a job with a life expectancy that was the envy of no one—

Beech boasted coral cuts on his fanny from every island and blood-ied atoll from the Solomons north to Tarawa and Iwo Jima. In Korea, he won his Pulitzer for the *Chicago Daily News*, combining extraordinary valor with dramatic flair as he covered the most painful event he could imagine: a marine retreat. His lead became a master work in the lore of both the marines and war correspon-dents:

YONPO AIRSTRIP, KOREA—"Remember," drawled Col. Lewis B. "Chesty" Puller, "whatever you write, that this was no retreat. All that happened was we found more Chinese be-hind us than in front of us. So we about-faced and attacked."

The story continued with stark detail of marines freezing to death and Chinese assaulting them as they picked their way back down through frozen mountain passes they had taken earlier. "Strange and terrible things" happened, the frozen bodies of Chi-nese and Americans alike stacked like cordwood to make protec-tive bunkers, water canteens bursting from the frozen water inside, weapons freezing during the twelve-day, forty-mile battle.

Beech became a local hero. His fame quickly spread far beyond, and any young reporter worth his salt fantasized about living such a life. But it was in Chicago, that very special town, where women were said to swoon when he strutted into the newsroom on home leave from his post in Tokyo. In Chicago newsboys screamed his name over the noisy hustle of State Street and the roar of the El. The *Daily News* plastered it across billboards and glued it to the sides of their trucks. A spunky, elbows-out sheet, the *Daily News* ran the stories from its legendary Pacific correspondent in three-inch high, double-decker, front-page headlines: BEECH TELLS SAI-GON TERROR; WE CLAWED FOR OUR LIVES! Keyes Beech's name ran in bigger, bolder type than David Halberstam's headlines.

In Vietnam he wore a faded marine fatigue cap so well-worn that Morley Safer, who came along later as a pioneer of the television revolution, said it must still have the sands of Iwo in it. Jokes about the cap were not considered funny. Keyes Beech was gung ho. Brave and tough, he spoke in a raspy growl that carried so much of the bite of Chicago in it that no one would guess that he was a Southerner who had adopted the town. Terse, tough-guy lines and blunt criticisms rolled out of him. But they arrived devoid of rancor. Halberstam liked him. Arnett adored him. They all wanted him as one of their own. He could not have been more different from them. They were Ivy Leaguers. He was a Tennessee farm boy who dropped out of school at fifteen and began beating his way around the newspaper minors, taking more than a decade, plus a war, to make the bigs. He believed that the United States had a special role to play in the world, and the press had a role in supporting it. They believed that the United States had a special role to play in the world, and the press had a role in watch-dogging it. They puzzled him.

But when he came down from Tokyo, which he did often, he hung out in Sheehan's office like one of the boys, which he was, telling old war stories and new girl stories. Once, on home leave later in the war, he visited his son at Berkeley, the heart of the student antiwar movement. The boy asked him to come speak to the students. "No thanks," he replied, "I just left one war." That's the way he was in Saigon. One war was enough.[6]

But after Ap Bac the relationship briefly became prickly.

Beech made it to the scene soon after the battle, one of the first outsiders to arrive. After spending time with Sheehan and Halberstam, he made the same immediate assessment: "A 'bad show' in which everything went wrong," he wrote. Then he went to Saigon and listened, as always, to the brass. He came all the way around and, in the doing, took a whack at his buddies. "If we are losing the war in South Vietnam, as has been recently suggested, nobody will be more surprised than the Viet Cong," he began a report a week later. He quoted those favorites of the military briefers for a decade to come: captured documents and body counts, the latter running five to one in favor of the government, he reported.

6. It was only later, when the war was over and the sour taste was all America had left, that Beech became angry and joined in the national search for scapegoats. Once, during a college seminar, he exploded at Safer, the correspondent in a famous televised incident in 1965 when marines were filmed torching a village with Zippo lighters. "You're one of that new breed of super-slick TV hit men," he lashed out. Safer, usually a gracious man, fired back that Beech was just "an old hack." Vietnam was a war that strained all grace.

The Young Turks bristled. Sheehan, in particular, was taking heavy fire. What the hell was Beech doing?

Halberstam, who enjoyed going into the field with him because he was brave but not foolhardy and always good company, was the first to shrug it off. Suddenly, he laughed uproariously and waved the irritation away with a giant sweeping motion of his arm. "You know what he's like," he said. "You go out and he shares all the same doubts with you. Then you get back to Saigon and there's Keyes, saluting the flag." The others laughed, too—to hell with it —and Beech went on hanging out at Sheehan's office, which is where they all wanted him.

The next incident was not so easy to laugh off.

The inauguration of John Kennedy had elevated Joseph Alsop to the heights at which he was certain he belonged. He reigned as a lordling of American journalism. If his Georgetown dinners had become command performances for the men of Camelot, they also drew the publishing giants who signed fledgling reporters' paychecks. A few years later Alsop hosted a special dinner party for the publisher of *The Washington Post*, Katharine Graham, and her heir obvious, Donald Graham. Don, just out of Harvard, had been drafted and was leaving for Vietnam, one of the few members of his social class to make the trip. But Alsop made certain that the young man who would one day sign the check for "Matter of Fact" received the right kind of send-off. He was served the best champagne and cognac. He was also served CIA Director Richard Helms, National Security Adviser McGeorge Bundy, and Secretary of Defense McNamara.[7]

Alsop's ties to Asia ran deep, though largely to an Asia gone. He had served as a military aide to General Claire Chennault, whose Flying Tigers helped China battle the invading Japanese in the late thirties. After the Japanese surrender, watching his beloved China turn Communist and most of a continent seem to slip away, his interest in the Far East became not simply proprietary but fanatical. The domino theory, which he had so faddishly named, drove American foreign policy with unthinking recklessness in Southeast Asia. He saw the theory in even bleaker terms than the policymak-

7. Katharine Graham was served half the bill for the party.

ers. If Vietnam fell, Indonesia would go under, Taiwan be "destroyed," Japan and the Philippines neutralized, and the United States "forced out of business as a Pacific power." Being a nominal Democrat gave him even more clout in the Kennedy years. Still, he remained so much the Cold Warrior that Henry Luce heaped praise on him. "The eloquent voice of Joe Alsop," *Time* wrote, "has dedicated itself to the cause of scaring tranquil humanity into its wits."

As the mandarin of journalistic mandarins, Alsop's visits to Vietnam became a sight to behold. "We received him like a visiting head of state," said Barry Zorthian, a later government press adviser. The columnist demanded, and received, his own aircraft and often traveled about the countryside in an executive military plane with two full colonels as escorts. Slight and balding, he was a pompous man and almost everyone had a story about the trait. Homer Bigart had known him since Alsop, an imperious young sprout out of the Eastern establishment, first went to work at the *New York Herald Tribune* as a reporter. Bigart, the progeny of less privileged folk, had been at the *Trib* five years and was still a copyboy. In those days newsrooms operated with a universal and time-tested way of hailing a copyboy, a method that has succumbed since to countless political corrections. On his first day at work the twenty-one-year-old newcomer used it on the twenty-four-year-old veteran. "Boy!!" he barked across the room. Some said Bigart's stutter started then and there. Several months later Bigart had occasion to look through Alsop's desk and found a drawer filled with uncashed $35-a-week paychecks. At the time Bigart was earning $15 and sending part home to his parents in Pennsylvania. But Bigart delighted in the find and told the story the rest of his life. "Joe was waiting till they a-m-m-mounted to something," he said, "so he wouldn't be embarrassed at the b-b-bank."

Not long after Ap Bac, Alsop staged a different kind of command performance for the young Saigon correspondents. "You'll be like those fools who lost their jobs in China," Alsop began his lecture. "I tried to help them. I tried to warn them. But they never listened." He paused for effect. "But I testified for them at their hearings, and, never fear," he intoned, "I shall testify for you as well."

If the correspondents snickered, they didn't laugh loudly. Most had been teenagers during the wrenching "who-lost-China" debate and the orgy of McCarthyism. But they were all too aware of the casualties, including some respected newsmen who had taken hold of the same kind of red-hot poker they now found in their hands.

———

Neil Sheehan took the next direct hit. Richard Tregaskis, in preparing his new book, bluntly accused Sheehan of fumbling the Ap Bac story and injuring his country by doing it. Tregaskis wrote:

> One of the younger and brasher correspondents wrote an excited, emotional story about the fact that . . . the ARVN artillery killed three of their own troops and wounded 11 by mistake. I talked to Galfund [an Army information officer] about it and reminded him of the old artilleryman's slogan: the V-sign, given with two fingers, to indicate that in an artillery barrage, 2 percent of our own troops will be hit by shorts. That doesn't mean artillery couldn't always be better, but people get hurt in a war, like it or not.
>
> I'm afraid the critical news dispatches about Ap Bac will do a lot of harm in the U.S.

It was a strange shot coming from a man who was precisely the same age as Sheehan, twenty-six, when he began reporting from Guadalcanal. Tregaskis also might have found it strange had he bothered to find out that the "shorts" fell miles from the nearest enemy troops. But he didn't.

11

BATTLE STATIONS

During all the hubbub David Halberstam moved into Neil Sheehan's office. It became an alliance that changed the landscape.

For Halberstam, a move had become a necessity. The villa improved all life's amenities except the one a reporter couldn't live without. It had no telephone, and, in 1963 Saigon, it wouldn't get one. But, mostly, Halberstam needed company. He was no loner. Watching Sheehan handle himself at Ap Bac and then flourish in the fuss afterward, he saw a kindred soul.

Sheehan leaped at the buddy arrangement, bulldozing the litter aside so Halberstam could wedge his Olivetti portable into a clear spot facing him across the kitchen table. The Olivetti was an avant-garde machine with a pale-blue carrying case, the kind a *Times* man would carry and soon would be *de rigueur* for all foreign correspondents. Halberstam had already pounded it half to pieces. Kindred souls perhaps. But they soon discovered that, on one side of the table, the deadline-a-minute wire man agonized over every word. On the other side, the special, with a schedule that seemed pure luxury, banged them out at .30 caliber speed. Sheehan could keep Halberstam waiting for dinner two, three hours on a story one fourth the length. It was the only grave sin in a relationship that flowered immediately. They liked each other, thrived on each other's verve, drew on each other's energy. Upstairs, Mert and Darlene Perry found themselves with another rambunctious communicant banging at the old stove and bellowing up the kitchen-vent intercom.

They were like two overgrown college boys, determined to use the school newspaper to do in the football coach and have fun in the process. His first day in the office Halberstam took the grease pencil to Sheehan's huge plastic-overlay map and flamboyantly drew in "Harkins's Trap"—a ridiculously large open-jaw contraption that looked like a bear trap. Beneath it he wrote: "To Be Sprung in a Week or Two. Semi-Automatic Gas-Operated." [1] It stayed there for the duration.

Blue Lotus fixed up Halberstam with a friend, a schoolteacher named Ricki. [2] Until then he had run through a string of brief romances, the most serious with a nightclub singer who sang melancholy Vietnamese love songs in a lonesome-dove voice that would send flickers through any red-blooded young man. But now Ricki, a beauty who ran in the same fast lane as Blue Lotus, replaced them all. Unfortunately, Ricki was Catholic and married, if separated. That created a heavy load of potential problems in Madame Nhu's fundamentalist land of Oriental blue laws. The romance was doomed from the outset. But it lasted through most of the year, coming to an abrupt end in a French farce of letters falling into the wrong hands, an irate gun-wielding husband, and an abiding fear of expulsion for the least heroic of reasons. Meanwhile, however, Neil and Blue Lotus and Dave and Ricki became a foursome whenever the women could shake the men loose from work. Neither was an easy shake. "David wasn't going to let any skirt get in the way of his story," said Pam Sanders, who liked Halberstam and sent him coquettish letters from Laos ("See you soon. Put some baby oil on your hands.").

For the two of them work always provided the best of times, and Sheehan needed the new arrangement as badly as Halberstam. His performance at Ap Bac had been a personal triumph, but Mal Browne had won the battle of the box scores. Even Sheehan's day didn't have enough hours to keep up with the overwhelming forces across town on the Rue Pasteur. He would continue pestering

1. The old M-1 rifle, about to depart the scene for the M-16, was semiautomatic gas-operated.
2. Ricki is a pseudonym. The person is real.

Tokyo for help Hoberecht didn't want to send. But no one in Saigon could help even the odds as much as David Halberstam.

They rarely ran together. To do so would be a waste of resources. Instead, they met each morning, usually with Perry and Rao, often with Charley Mohr now, mapping out their leads and listening to the latest assaults on them from two governments. "He said that?" Halberstam would say. "Well, piss on him." Then they would deploy in different directions, meeting again at the end of the day to compare notes.

If the Thanksgiving Day episode had inflamed them, the New Year's fiasco at Ap Bac and the raw lies afterward radicalized them. Halberstam and Sheehan became two angry young men determined to get the truth, right the wrongs, and nail the bad guys. That would become a large and controversial agenda. It would mean getting rid of a foreign government and changing an American foreign policy as well as sending an ambassador, a four-star general, and a CIA head of station home in disgrace.

Meanwhile, if the U.S. government stood firm and united in public as Project Beef-Up moved into its second year, quiet rifts began beneath the surface. Kennedy's early foreign-policy setbacks had been so devastating that he and his men had locked in hard on the crisis he considered least important, Vietnam. He could not lose another one, and he made that abundantly clear. "There are limits to the number of defeats I can defend in one twelve-month period," he confided in the privacy of the White House. So bleak did his advisers see the young President's beginning that they had talked of the need to "save" his presidency.

So the first year in Vietnam had a rally-around-the-presidential-seal quality to it. The Diem doubters within the administration, mostly in the State Department, obscured their sentiments in cabled euphemisms and "contingency planning": how to deal in a "post-Diem Vietnam" should he "pass from the scene." After Ap Bac, the words turned more active. After the next crisis—the bizarre Buddhist uprising that would soon blindside everyone, along with Diem's even more bizarre reaction to it—Kennedy's government would split wide open and the cable talk turn blunt: overthrow, coup, even the occasional use of the taboo word, assassination. The plots and intrigues inside the White House would rival those in Gia Long Palace.

Human nature is perverse. The closer the government's position edged toward the story the correspondents had been delivering all along, the harsher its attacks on them became. Wars were coming on many fronts.

The teaming of Halberstam and Sheehan also divided the small Saigon press corps into two competing camps, battle stations for the combat ahead. The Halberstam-Sheehan axis included Mohr, Perry, Nick Turner of Reuters, and eventually Ray Herndon, whom Hoberecht finally sprang from Laos to help Sheehan. Mal Browne was backed by his two stalwarts, Peter Arnett and Horst Faas (although Faas often talked to his roommate about his discoveries in Vietnam's outback), and bolstered later by additional AP hands sent from Tokyo during crises. Others who went with Browne included Sharkey; François Nivolon of *Le Figaro*, who became best man at Browne's wedding to Le Lieu in 1966; John Stirling; and Beverly Deepe, the *Newsweek* stringer.

Deepe, the only woman in the Saigon group, was another of the wanderlusters who freelanced her way around the world writing stories about headhunters in Sarawak and forbidden views of China out of the porthole of a Polish steamer docked in Shanghai. If Pam Sanders, blond, sexy, and uninhibited, gave off a preview of the wide-open sixties, Beverly Deepe, brunette, gentle, and unprepossessing, played with perfect comfort in the girl-next-door world of the fading fifties. A woman at war, she wrote, should be a "living symbol of mother, sweetheart, and the apple-pie world back home." Only twenty-five years old, she landed in Saigon in February 1962, the day after the bombing of the presidential palace, and stopped her wandering. She held on tenuously until the *Newsweek* job opened up with the ouster of François Sully. Her greatest joy became getting Halberstam rocketed with one of her stories.

Other correspondents, visiting more often now, usually settled on one office or the other. Keyes Beech thought that the teaming of Halberstam and Sheehan more than evened the odds between the two wires. The two of them were outgoing and open, Browne forever private and self-protective. When a special walked into 19 Ngo Duc Ke, Halberstam and Sheehan opened their files and their heads to them. The visitors naturally responded by sharing what they had: "Have you got this?" Beech marveled at the way it worked. "It was very shrewd. They had everybody working for them."

Browne acknowledged that he had a severe case of what he called "specials syndrome." To him, the special was the correspondent in Evelyn Waugh's satirical novel *Scoop*, "the fellow who comes in and extracts what he can from you and then tops it with some entertaining lead and sends it out under his byline." Browne got rocketed for those stories and he hated it. So he spurned collaborative journalism, arguing that it led to the creation of a single mindset, to running in a pack. These were all very real dangers. But the differences in the operating styles at the two command posts evolved mostly out of the differences in the personalities of the commanders. They saw the story alike, a disaster in the making. Browne simply kept to himself and kept his information there too. "I like to be a loner," he said.

Not that the competitiveness and differences diminished the besieged, us-against-the-world camaraderie: An outside attack on one became an attack on all. More than once Halberstam stepped in with all his hulk to pull Brother Nhu's goons off Arnett or Sharkey. More than once Browne defended Halberstam when the assaults turned mean.

Otherwise, they scrapped like reporters in an old cutthroat battle in a do-or-die, two-newspaper town back home. As much as Halberstam and Arnett liked each other, they never again went out on a story together. At the end of the year, as Halberstam headed home and Arnett settled in for the very long haul, the two men embraced at Tan Son Nhut Airport. "I wish it could have been different, Peter," the rising *Times* star said almost wistfully. Arnett shrugged. So it went. The tough little guy from the bottom of the world would come into his own after Halberstam left and the American combat troops arrived. In many ways he would personify the bigger war, a war of the dispossessed, not the Ivy Leaguers. More than twenty years later Halberstam, by then famous, helped Arnett, whose ticket still had not been punched, get his daughter accepted by Harvard. If a Jewish kid only one full generation removed from the fringes of Russia could do it in the fifties, why couldn't an immigrant kid, half Vietnamese and half New Zealander with a touch of Maori in the mix, do it in the eighties? Elsa Arnett graduated in 1989 and became a reporter, like her father.

Inevitably, as the Vietnam story escalated toward spectacular turmoil in 1963, the spotlight shown brightest on Halberstam. He had that lightning-rod quality about him—and he had the platform. This also made the Halberstam-Sheehan faction (especially with Charley Mohr on board) the focal point of the controversy.

Sheehan sometimes got lost in the glare. He was so young it became easy to underestimate him and, in the eyes of some, Halberstam's powerful personality dominated him. Halberstam scoffed at the thought. "The truth is it wasn't true," he said later. "My stories showed up in *The New York Times* and made my reputation bigger. His disappeared into the black hole of UPI. In the leg work, in the brain-trusting we did every day—where are we on this one? who should we see?—it was really fifty-fifty. He was way ahead of me on knowing that the French-Indochina war was at the core of why it wasn't working, that the legacy of the French was important. He had better CIA sources. I had better military because I could travel more. But we'd sit there every day as if we were putting a jigsaw puzzle together. He'd say what does this mean, connect this to this, something happened at Bien Hoa. I'd say, oh, yeah, that's interesting because I was over in Ben Tre and somebody said such and such . . . Sure, I had the better outlet, and I rocked the White House more than he did. So the government cables came back to Saigon: That fucking Halberstam. But actually and emotionally it was completely fifty-fifty."

Their similarities were compelling. Both were classic mid-century Americans driven by a heritage of immigrants' milk and honey dreams and bread and water sacrifices. Sheehan, like Halberstam, took his angers face-to-face with a Harkins, a Felt, a Nolting, a McNamara. Still, they were also such striking young men, each in his own right, friends had a tendency to remember them later only for their differences. In his memoirs, James Reston compared them this way:

> Halberstam was a human lie detector, with an explosive temper, a profane vocabulary, a talent for getting into brawls and the physique to muscle out of them. Sheehan was a gentler sort. His tours of the blasted villages . . . reduced him to tears.

They were, indeed, salt and pepper—or pepper and salt.

—

The 114-day New York newspaper strike ended on March 31, 1963, liberating Halberstam. Three days later, Vann left for home. The departure was bittersweet.

In his last months at the Seminary all his battles had been political and, excepting his forays with Halberstam, all had been lost. Those not-so-anonymous words—"a miserable damn performance"—had rattled back and forth in scores of angry cables between Washington and Saigon. Harkins, unable to fire him because of the uproar it would cause among other officers in the advisory group, fell back on a bureaucracy's favored alternative. He made Vann a nonperson. So did the rest of the army. This man who had seemed destined for a general's stars was going home to a dead end. He would quit the army, if not Vietnam, for good.

The spring of 1963 was a time of the first major turnover of U.S. personnel, the original corps of eager Yanks ending a year's tour somewhat less enchanted with the "can do" American magic that would rescue Vietnam from itself.[3] Vann's boss, the good soldier Daniel Boone Porter, had left six weeks earlier after submitting a highly pessimistic end-of-tour report. Harkins deep-sixed it. It was never seen again in Washington or anywhere else.

At the airport on April 3 a small group of soldiers and a few correspondents saw Vann off. On behalf of the newsmen Halberstam gave him a silver cigarette box engraved: "To Lt. Col. John Paul Vann, Good Soldier, Good Friend, From His Admirers in the American Press Corps." The names of all the members of that first platoon of Vietnam correspondents were also inscribed on the box. Afterward, Halberstam pulled Vann aside and once again expressed the fear that had been spooking him for months. "I was always scared that we were going to hurt you," he said. Vann looked at him with a soldier's sturdy half-smile. He made a telling reply: "You never hurt me more than I wanted to be hurt."

By coincidence, Neil Sheehan flew out on the same plane, his

3. The one-year tour of duty, designed as a morale builder, became an American curse throughout the long war. It deprived U.S. personnel of any sense of continuity, any institutional memory, and doomed them to make the same mistakes over and over again.

first trip home in three years. He sat next to Vann but learned little more about the core of the man. Those discoveries—the hidden truths about Vann's last army days and so much more—would come out much, much later when Sheehan had his own, different haunts to quell. The stories from the delta, the lessons Vann taught the reporters, were true enough, as true as one man's version could be, as true as Americans would ever see in Vietnam. But the lure, the con, that great magnetic pull—this man is risking *everything* to get the truth out—was only a sharper's game. Vann had no army future to lose, had none when he arrived in Vietnam. His future had been washed out by a fatal flaw, a compulsive sexual need for teenage girls, often several a day; a need that eventually compelled him to keep a wife and family at home, a wife and child in Vietnam, a full-time mistress to compete with the Vietnamese wife, and daily sexual touch-and-goes to compete with them all.

There was something about the war in Vietnam that made it more sexual than most. America seemed as compelled to make love as war in the toy country in which it played for so long. Generals, diplomats, journalists, grunts, virtually all established sexual liaisons and, so far from home and their own realities, flaunted them. But it was a stateside affair with a fifteen-year-old baby-sitter that brought Vann down. The army had charged him with statutory rape. He beat the charges. He was good at that too. After days of practice, he fooled a lie-detector test (he admitted the affair to his wife). But he would not reach the top after that. No matter how many generals promenaded through Saigon with beautiful young Vietnamese women on their arms, they would never take him in among them with the sniff of scandal on his khakis. He knew it. He had nothing to lose, neither general's stars nor army career. So he enhanced his legend with the martyr's lure, using the sham to polish his image for another day.

"He lied to Halberstam and manipulated him, doing so naturally with the same talent he sought to work on Cao," Sheehan concluded later. "He had deceived everyone in Vietnam."

Halberstam would have none of that thinking. What difference did it make—he snorted at the very naiveté of the thought—if Vann had embellished the transaction with a hustle? What difference did it make if, as a twenty-eight-year-old, he had become starry-eyed? The stories were true. A trade was a trade, and sometimes you did business with scalawags. "It's an age-old and time-honored tradition," he said. "It was about I can use you and you can use me."

The journalist in Sheehan agreed. He had played by the same rules. But something in Vietnam dug into Neil Sheehan like an angry wood tick, forcing him to purge himself of it and all the fears it produced by going beyond journalism's frontiers. So one day he would begin scraping away at all the layers of John Paul Vann, all the layers of his country's grand delusion, and for a long while he would seem as lost as they became. In the end he would find that even the good, even the truths and the verities of the beginning, were built on a bright shining lie.

———

In conversation late in his life James Reston would become still softer in his description of Neil Sheehan and Vietnam. "He literally cared so much about it," Reston said. "Halberstam was hard-nosed. Sheehan wasn't. Sheehan just became ashamed of what he saw happening." Then Reston's voice would drop off to a near whisper: "Sixteen years. . . . He spent sixteen years writing his book. . . ."

The lives of all these rambunctious young reporters would be changed by their early days in Vietnam. But none would find his destiny so entwined with the war as the youngest of them all. Vietnam entranced him. Vietnam terrified him. Vietnam held him. The story of Neil Sheehan and the war would begin to read like the epic tale of a lost sailor drawn forever toward a deadly siren. To land was fatal, to sail away worse.

Reston hired him in 1964, briefly taking him away from it. At the time, to the young reporter, it seemed nothing short of lifesaving. The country had fallen into near anarchy. All the charm and romance had turned ugly, Babylonian and deadly, the violence random and meaningless. The intensity of the way he worked had left him frazzled, morbid, certain he had pushed his luck to the limit, his Irish blackness looking into the murk and seeing menace everywhere. "I was scared," he said. "I was convinced I was going to get killed."

Like most newcomers Sheehan was brought home for a shakedown cruise before returning overseas. A. M. Rosenthal, the new metropolitan editor, wanted nothing to do with baby-sitting hot-shot short-timers. Rosenthal, who soon would become one of the most powerful editors in the newspaper's history, greeted Sheehan tersely: "I need you like a hole in the head." Then he gave him his first assignment: Go to the Times Square subway stop and ask New Yorkers for directions to Grant's Tomb. Sheehan could hear the far-off siren's call over the din. His days would not always be happy at *The Times*.

By early 1965 the paper shipped him back overseas to another Southeast Asian hot spot, Indonesia. He stopped briefly in Saigon, going out on one mission. Never had combat terrified him so. The place had his number. Of that he was sure.

But later that year, as Lyndon Johnson shipped in the first marines and the American combat troops began building toward the hundreds of thousands, he returned again. The little war he and Vann had talked about in the Seminary, a subtle war of knife thrusts in the night, had become a grotesque parody—the countryside pockmarked with craters carved out by B-52s, forests shattered by heavy artillery and denuded by chemicals, foreign ground troops sweeping through the countryside in a new strategy called search and destroy. A year of that drained him in all ways, physical and emotional, and the terrible look of him worried his friends. Not yet thirty years old, he was pale and edgy, down thirty pounds, "a mere wraith of myself," as he put it. In his mind, death shadowed him again: "I knew I was going to die if I stayed any longer. I knew."

Reston brought him to Washington and suddenly it seemed Neil Sheehan had everything. Susan was pregnant with the first of their two daughters and the first of her books too. They found a house surrounded by stately oaks in one of the town's most fashionable neighborhoods. They were young and exciting to the power circles in Washington and New York, too, a new kind of power couple, a media couple, Neil a near-legend, Susan about to become a star at *The New Yorker*. But the ebullience in him, always so fragile, was gone. His friends found him increasingly glum and cheerless.

In 1968, during the Viet Cong's Tet Offensive, he asked to go back. *The Times* turned him down. It was the most violent period of the war, two hundred American combat deaths a week, six correspondents killed in one two-month period. To go would have been hell. The only greater hell was to not to go.

Rejected, brooding, stuck on the wrong side of the world, he couldn't leave his war. All his work turned toward it. He stayed with it at the Pentagon, stayed with it at the White House during the last days of a war-ruined presidency. As the war dragged on, as Nixon took longer to withdraw than Lincoln did to fight the Civil War, Sheehan's politics took their final shift. The signs of change had begun to show in a 1966 article, "Not a Dove, But No Longer a Hawk." In the unpublished recollections he began to write soon afterward he lashed himself with self-criticisms: "I always wrote stories as if we were engaged in a heroic, patriotic venture. How wrong I was."

By 1971 the young Republican from Holyoke, the Catholic conservative so certain of America's vision in 1962, would come full circle. Even at that late date the passion of his conversion shook *The Times* and all its establishment. In a book review Sheehan asked the question his colleague, Harrison Salisbury, considered the ultimate: Should American presidents and generals be "placed in the dock and made to stand trial for their lives" for war crimes? Then he broke the biggest story of the war: The Pentagon Papers. Here was Sheehan, the young man who had poked around in the ancient history of Vietnam when his employer only wanted the last twelve hours, unveiling the government's own top-secret history of the war, an account rife with deceit and self-deception. As it would in the great Buddhist crisis, now just ahead in 1963, the government responded with vengeance. Sheehan's honesty and patriotism were questioned. The government accused him of theft.[4] A federal grand jury, looking for violations of the Espionage Act, targeted him.

4. Sheehan got the Papers "over the transom." He was handed them—although in elaborate cloak-and-dagger fashion—by Daniel Ellsberg, the onetime McNamara "whiz kid" who had turned passionately against the war. But Sheehan was the one who got them for a very good reason. Ellsberg studied his range of trading partners closely, just as John Paul Vann had studied his. Sheehan got the Papers because he was Neil Sheehan.

Federal officials subpoenaed his bank records and hounded his friends and neighbors. He faced, then avoided, jail.

In the world of power journalism the assaults became badges of honor, legend enhancers. But nothing cheered him. His friends' worries deepened. His old buddy, Halberstam, found him pessimistic and morose. Salisbury thought he had turned dour at the height of his success. His editors saw only the brooder in him. What was wrong with him?

Sheehan was still a sailor lost, and now even the siren's call began to fade. Nixon finally *was* bringing home the last of the troops, the story slipping from the front pages and from the American consciousness, too, a bad dream to be forgotten. But to Sheehan it had been a narcotic. It had given him his fix almost every day of his professional life. He couldn't take the withdrawal. His melancholy turned still blacker. "It ate at me," he said. "I had to get it out of my system."

In 1972 John Paul Vann was killed. This man who had defied the Viet Cong with his solo drives through the night a decade earlier. *Come get me if you can. You do not control the night.* This man who had gone to fight a knife fight in the night and then quit the army, seemingly in a dispute over principle that cast him even farther into the role of the hero. This man who couldn't stay away. Halberstam had provided the return visa in 1964—a worshipful article in *Esquire,* the last chit, the hook Vann had cast so carefully finally making its snare. The catch that came in with it was revival. Five months later Vann was back in Vietnam as a civilian, starting that rise back through rank, power, and legend that finally made him what he could not become in the army, the civilian equivalent of a general.

But John Paul Vann at his death was not the John Paul Vann Sheehan thought he knew in those days of youth and innocence in the delta. Like his country, Vann had been drawn in by the delusion. Like his country, he had escalated from the naiveté of the beginning to the insanity of the end, talking with the same fervor about the effectiveness of the B-52s that he had used to reject terror weapons earlier: "Any time the wind is blowing from the north where the B-52 strikes are turning the terrain into a moonscape," he said not long before his death, "you can tell from the battlefield stench that the bomb strikes are effective."[5] This mystically charmed man who had indeed become a Vietnam legend, who had defied death a thousand times in a thousand ways, and won each roll of the dice, John Paul Vann was dead in a senseless, random, freak accident in a helicopter that, flying too low at night, hit a tree. As senseless as the war. Everything about Vann seemed to parallel the war, America's grand delusion ending, Vann's ended, and Sheehan saw his way out.

Or back in. Deeper. When everyone else had started home.

He called the book *A Bright Shining Lie*.[6] The ordeal of it became a legend that surpassed the legend of John Paul Vann. Sheehan's curse, Sheehan's blessing. He found a man who personified the national trip into moral quicksand and, in the writing, Sheehan became the personification of the inability to get out. America fought in Vietnam three times as long as it fought the Second World War. Sheehan fought his book longer than America fought in both.

Sixteen years . . .

Such good years, prime years. His children grew up, tots when he started, adults gone when he finished. Susan wrote five books. The world went on—OPEC, Watergate, Iran, Reagan, Contras, new little wars with new young reporters. But Sheehan still had his own to fight, alone, so he disappeared, farther and farther, deeper and deeper into the maw, "laboring year after year like some medieval monk," Salisbury described it.

At the beginning Sheehan went back to Vietnam one more time to track down what he could on Vann before it was lost along with everything else. The place had a putrid smell to it, going fast, a war lost but not over and more terrifying than ever. He had never seen anything like it, all military discipline gone, a time of frags and flowers, with drifty American kids as willing to kill their own officers as take a chance with the other side. Vietnamese girlfriends came into the camp at night, unchecked by guards, and he thought, "My God, they could kill us in our sleep." And he remembered the

---

5. Vann made this statement to Larry Stern of *The Washington Post*, who also had known him early in the war. The words stunned Stern, as they did others who had known Vann from the beginning.

6. "We had also, to all the visitors who came over there, been one of the bright shining lies," Vann had told an army historian after leaving in 1963.

old days, what the civilians did before the Americans caught on (and apparently had forgotten again). They came in, little old men, gnarled old women, playful children, pretty girls, and they paced off the distance to the command tent for the VC mortar squads. Jesus.

But it was the search for Vann's death site that set the fear, and the haunt, raging again. Vann had died in the Central Highlands, home of the Montagnards, those Stone Age tribesmen who fought with spears and poison arrows when Sheehan first arrived. No one remembered precisely where Vann had gone down. No one cared. The enemy had heat-seeking missiles that could take out a helicopter at 7,000 feet. It was no joyride up there when you were doing war business, and the pilot made it clear that he was taking the writer in only under orders. No heroics, no favors. This place was godforsaken and gone now. People just wanted to get home alive.

The helicopter approached the site at 9,000 feet and then descended so fast it felt to Sheehan as if they dropped like a stone. It was only when he leaped out and the chopper was pulling rapidly away that Sheehan realized the pilot had missed the landing site. He knew it instantly. Running low, away from the blades, his boot caught on a trip flare. He froze. The pilot had dropped him in the middle of a minefield. To the side, fifty, sixty yards away, stood a raw-boned Montagnard, dressed now in the uniform of the ARVN. Slowly, and very carefully, the man walked out to him, a remarkable act of bravery. Equally slowly and carefully, Sheehan followed him back, stepping in his footprints. The next day the Montagnard silently took him to another site. Sheehan knew immediately that it was right. The copse of trees stood alone and isolated in the proper place, the wreckage was right—a Ranger, which Vann had been flying. Slowly, he realized something else. The lonely trees, all others cut down, stood over a Montagnard cemetery, shading the primitive graves from the hot sun. So impervious we all thought we were. John Paul Vann had been hill-hugging and hotshotting to the end—*you do not control the night*—and, in the night, he had hit the valley's only trees, there to guard the dead. Sheehan started shivering, couldn't stop, and went home.

Then the odyssey started, the obsession took over, Sheehan's magnificent obsession, they said at first; Sheehan's curse, it seemed almost from the start.

He was home from his second trip only months when the subject of an earlier book hit him with a harassment libel suit. The suit quickly became messy. Delay the Vann book, the lawyers instructed, and help with the defense. Sheehan dissected his book page by page, writing a defense memo longer than the original manuscript. It took almost a year. Exhausted, dispirited, but free again, he decided to take a few days off at his rustic family cabin in West Virginia. It was November 1974. In the early evening the first wet snow of the season was falling when headlights emerged out of the white directly in front of him, a twenty-year-old, backwoods youth playing chicken in the twilight. The local youth walked away from the head-on collision and paid a fifteen-dollar fine for driving on the wrong side of the road. Sheehan suffered eleven fractures, with bones broken in both arms, his right knee, and his chest. The next year became pure hell—repeated operations, two months of hospitalization, four months before he could type even belaboredly, six months before he could drive a car, twelve months before the physical therapy was down to less than three hours a day. By the time he was finished with all the surgeries, the six-foot-two-inch young man who had bounded off a plane in Saigon in 1962 stood just six one.

Saigon fell while he was bedridden, his war gone for good, his book drifting too. By the time he put his hurting arms back to the typewriter in 1975, nothing came. By 1977 he still floundered—he earned less than $1,000 that year—and the agonies became awful again.

His insomnia returned. In the hospital he had come to dread the nights. "That does seem to be the time when the devils come out," his doctor had told him. For Sheehan, it ever would be. He began to work nights, sleep days, even those time zones of the soul, his circadian rhythms, set by a clock on the other side of the world. Years earlier he had liked to end his days with strolls beneath Saigon's graceful tamarind trees. Now, neighbors on their way to the office caught glimpses of the man ending his day with morning marches under Washington's towering oaks. The writer, they called him. Then the recluse. Then the hermit. He seemed lost in time and space. Nothing told as much as his face. Even in the early light his eyes burned with that same fiery intensity of youth. The other features began to yield to middle age, the black hair graying, skin taking on the soft pallor of a man too long in captivity.

He withdrew from almost everyone. Charley Mohr, who knew how he loved the contemplative walks of bird-hunting in the nearby Maryland countryside, called often, even into the later years. *Come on, Neil. Saturday. You'll love it.* But Neil begged off. *Saturday's a work day, Charley. Maybe next time.* Not once did they go. Even his old buddy, Halberstam, couldn't budge him.

Others had unusual contact. Keyes Beech, the old guardsman who often argued with Sheehan during the early days, recalled: "I'd get these calls in the middle of the night. I don't know what time, three A.M., I guess, because I was sound asleep, and this voice would say, 'Keyes, do you remember what happened at such-and-such a place in Vietnam on such-and-such a day?' I'd grunt something, which I'm sure started with 'Jesus.' Then he'd say thanks and hang up. Never did say who it was. A couple years would pass and I'd get another call."

Susan tried for a while to keep a social life of sorts going, an occasional dinner party at home. But dinner interrupted the beginning of Neil's workday. He couldn't hide his discomfort. His stomach would begin to hurt. The parties, intolerable disruptions, made him physically sick.

The compulsion was there from the beginning, ingrained in his character. The pain, the anxiety, the fear—the same deadly fear he felt in combat—set in later, and tried to take over again. He had to beat it down. Beat it down every day. The insomnia left him exhausted. The battles within drained him. For sixteen years he did what he had learned to do in Vietnam: He fought his demons.

"I got this overwhelming anxiety, the anxiety would just be enormous," he said, and his arms would stretch out as if the pain were beyond breadth, "and it went on for years and years and I had to find a way to control it. It would exhaust me, and I'd be absolutely exhausted trying to figure out how am I going to get to the top of this mountain. I would get so overwrought I would get this god-awful insomnia, and you have to sleep to work, and I had to work. Sometimes I'd make a breakthrough walking around the neighborhood. I'd fight a problem all night long, be terrified with anxiety, and ba-baboom, I'd get it. I'd come back and scratch it down on a pad and then I could sleep. But when you can't sleep, you get frantic. My stomach gave out on me, just terrible pains, and I was trying to live on chicken soup and rice. I lost fifteen pounds and was doubled up in pain. And I went to the doctor and had all the tests, and he said, 'Neil, there is nothing wrong with your stomach. It is just your nerves. It is stress. You can drink coffee. You don't have to survive on chicken soup. You have to learn to control the stress. Take hot baths and long walks.'

"I got tics in my eye. It's like in combat. You stay in combat for a week and you start getting twitches in your face and pains in your side. There was this battle in Da Nang, a little civil war really, and after a week of it I was gagging every morning for about fifteen minutes. It's a helluva lot of tension when you are sitting there trying to write a story in a building with a tin roof and people are shooting 81-millimeter mortars at you. It was like that, and it went on year after year. The only way to control it is to get up and YOU MARCH. It may be raining, it may be snowing, the sun may be shining, but you get up and YOU MARCH. The army taught me some of that. Get up! The ten-minute break is over! Get up! March! And so I slapped myself in the face, threw water over my face, and went on.

———

Sheehan's month of home leave in the spring of 1963 was pure heaven. UPI pried some work out of him. But the chores were ego-inflating. AP also brought Mal Browne home, and the news agencies strutted their new super bylines through a round of speeches and appearances during National Press Week in New York. It was heady stuff, a first taste of fame. The two men were also remarkably foresighted. Speaking to newspaper editors, Browne warned that the war in Vietnam could last another ten years and Sheehan said the Viet Cong fully expected to win because "Americans don't like long and inconclusive wars."

Sheehan went home to Holyoke, saw his family, saw how far he had moved from the world of Stash Malek. He had every intention of going farther. In New York he had dinner with Homer Bigart who was, he wrote Halberstam, still "grousing like hell about your foreign editor." Then he made the rounds of *The Times* brass himself, including the foreign editor, Manny Freedman, with whom he "didn't seem to connect on anything." The connection came in Washington with Reston.

Washington produced some revelations for a young man isolated in the world of Harkins and Nolting. Making his rounds, he concluded that some of Washington's "rosy optimism" was fading. "Some people at the top at least," he told Halberstam, "are beginning to realize that we could get bogged down if we aren't careful and if Diem doesn't change his charming little ways." With simple gumshoe reporting Sheehan had stumbled upon early signs of what, within months, would become brutal, almost medieval, infighting among Kennedy's lieutenants.

Sheehan made another discovery in Washington that only registered later. *Newsweek*'s Ben Bradlee approached him and, in his no-nonsense way, asked Sheehan if the newsmagazine should fire its expelled correspondent, François Sully. Bradlee, soon to become editor of *The Washington Post*, where he would make it the newspaper it was not in 1963, was fast becoming a legend. He had the name of a romance novelist's aristocrat—Benjamin Crowninshield Bradlee—and the look of a nineteenth-century riverboat gambler, his black hair slicked back and parted in the middle, his eyes as riveting as a man betting a broken straight, cocksure you'll back down. He took no guff from anyone. Years later, just days after *The Post* returned a Pulitzer Prize because its story had been partly fictionalized, the lowest point of his news career, he spoke to a visiting editors' convention. Bradlee held most other editors in low regard, an opinion he disguised poorly. Now they would get their inning. For the convention he wore an old tropical suit so godawful it looked as if he'd gotten it in a trade down after a bad day with a Hialeah bookie. Its color could only be described as puke green. Walking out of the newsroom he caught a knot of reporters staring at him. "Wearin' my fuck-'em suit," he said, clenching his fist and clasping his biceps in the unmistakable Mediterranean manner of giving someone the bird.

Bradlee talked like a longshoreman and thought like a spook. Now he rasped at the UPI rookie: "Is Sully full of shit?"

"It was all that Deuxieme Bureau rubbish," Sheehan said later. "Sully was French, which meant he wanted us to lose because they lost, which meant he spied for the Deuxieme Bureau." The idea was nonsense, he told Bradlee. Then he put the incident out of his mind. *Newsweek* sent Sully back to Vietnam at the end of the year.

Sheehan liked Bradlee, and Bradlee liked Sheehan well enough to try to hire him before *The Times* snatched him away. But Bradlee was a total creature of Washington. Some thought he later made *The Post* into something the transient national capital had never had before, its permanent establishment.

Bradlee's question about Sully was a subconscious warning. But a warning it was. Sheehan and his pals still lived alone and vulnerable in their own little world.

———

Halberstam suddenly had his own serious problems with Local Board Number 20.

It had been no time for a young man to ignore his reserve obligations. Back from Torrington came the stern word that his draft board was playing by the rules and holding firm on his 1-A draft classification. Halberstam found himself one deep breath away from boot camp.

He had not gone unwarned. In 1961, shortly after his arrival in the Congo, the Washington bureau forwarded him a packet of mail including a notice from the army. The short cover note from the bureau began jokingly, "Dear Pfc," then, after the usual kudos, closed: "In the meantime, be sure to take care of the enclosed. We don't want army eyes looking over our shoulders."

A month later, when he was wounded slightly during an air attack, his brother, Michael, warned him more directly:[7]

> I hate to bring up unpleasant matters, but something has been nagging me since your departure, namely your selective service status. I realize the old board in Nashville didn't

———

[7]. In the same letter Michael also gave him an early lesson about myth-making. Halberstam was wounded by flying glass but press reports hyped it into shrapnel. "Please forget about this 'glass or shrapnel' bit," his brother wrote. "*The Washington Post* said you were injured by shrapnel and what's good enough for Al Friendly ought to be fine with you. Was Hemingway ever 'injured by glass?' Of course not."

call you or anything when you were supposed to report for training, but discreet inquiries locally lead me to believe that it is the trainee's responsibility to make sure the obligation is fulfilled. Reason for bringing this up is the mobilization of numerous national guard units in this country, including much of the ready reserve.

Find a lawyer, "mentioning no names, of course," Michael counseled, because "something like this can be a real problem when the Govt starts re-checking its files, which it does in its own good time."

But David had been moving too fast to look back—and now his single-mindedness had produced the makings of a mess, the kind that might even bring his skyrocketing career back to earth. What the government had done in its own good time turned out to be the worst possible time for Halberstam. With *The Times* publishing again, his star had turned white-hot. "He was one of those people destined to flare in the skies like a bright comet," Betsy Wade, Homer Bigart's friend, said a trifle wistfully, knowing that Homer played life just the other way. As Halberstam heard again from Local Board 20, Times Square had begun to buzz with talk of a Pulitzer Prize, Gay Talese dubbed 1963 "The Year of the Halberstam," and the first of a dozen book offers arrived. More important, in Saigon he had become the center of a once-in-a-generation story about to explode. *His* story. One can only grasp at faded shadows to imagine what might have been if the government's right hand had known what its left was doing, if Harkins or McNamara or the most powerful man in the world, Kennedy himself, had known about that window of opportunity, that extended moment when David Levy Halberstam was theirs for the snatching. But Local Draft Board 20 in little Torrington, Connecticut, was a bastion unto itself. No player in the Vietnam drama ever got a whiff of it.

Halberstam did his best to keep it that way. With embarrassment, he brought the forces of *The Times* to bear, making clear his need for secrecy. "For varying reasons I don't want this to go through the cables here," he wrote. With embarrassment, *The Times* took it on. It was not the kind of problem the great gray lady enjoyed having dropped in her lap.

Manny Freedman kicked it upstairs to the managing editor,

Turner Catledge, who slid it over to his personnel assistant, Rich-ard Burritt. The Shrink first did what came most naturally. He checked Halberstam's story against the records of his job interview. According to the file:

> Halberstam said that he had been excused from summer camp in 1958 "and had heard nothing further about the mat-ter"; that he had been excused from weekly drill as well. "I hope this is no reflection on my patriotism," he said, "but I've been busy."

It was a test passed. His concept may have been less than pleas-ing, but, enhanced by his usual aggressive defense, it was the same one he used now. "If there are any negotiations over the business, verbal, legal or otherwise," he wrote Burritt, "I think these are important points:"

> I have never disobeyed any order from my reserve group. In fact I have not heard from the Army reserve since late 1958 when I went into a control group (at which point I felt I was still on call). For two of those years I was at my same address in Tennessee; since then with the brief tenure in Washington, I have been overseas. Thus if there is any blame or uncer-tainty, then I think part of it lies on the other side.

Burritt didn't find the blame-sharing argument a particularly wise approach. "You should write promptly, fully, and with all due courtesy and respect both to your local draft board and to your Reserve outfit," he instructed, suggesting an emphasis on his time in the Congo and Vietnam. He hinted at the discomfort felt at *The Times*, which was still suffering the slings of the super-patriots. "It would be highly inadvisable," Burritt added, "for *The Times* to make the first move in this situation."

The Times, however, did not sit on its hands. A great newspaper and its resources can have the feel of a parallel government. Vet-eran police reporters often dress, talk, and think more like cops than the cops themselves; pinstripes seem inked to the delicate hides of diplomatic reporters whose old newsie banter of stream-ers, reefers, and slop banks quickly gives way to the murmured jargon of *agrément* and status quo ante. At *The Times* the overseas staff became known as the foreign service, and at home its array of experts formed a shadow cabinet, often with the same bitter rivalries as the real thing. In the early sixties the newspaper's secretary of defense was Hanson W. Baldwin, a gray eminence who had covered the military since 1937. He had become such a hawkish Cold Warrior that he chastised Gary Powers, the U-2 spy-plane pilot shot down over the Soviet Union in 1960, for not saving his government from embarrassment by taking his suicide pill. As Halberstam's problem made the rounds internally at *The Times,* Baldwin opined that the abandoned Reserve unit had probably jarred the draft board into action and "one helluva legal snarl might be involved."

If so, the snarl was avoided. Halberstam took Burritt's advice, responding with melodramatic flourishes.

"I hope you will find—and I believe the *Times* officials will substantiate—that if I have been remiss in my obligation it is certainly not an attempt to dodge responsibility to my country," he wrote, "but rather the result of a young man following reporting assignments to two of the major cold war conflicts in the world."

He also followed an earlier suggestion. "I spent thirteen months in the Congo under almost constant danger," he continued, ". . . [and] in September 1961 I was wounded in the left leg by bomb fragments during an air raid."[8] In Vietnam he "helped carry out Vietnamese wounded under fire" and "participated in enough helicopter missions to have earned an Air Medal. . . ."

He summed up: "If there is any negligence in my case it is not a lack of patriotism nor a lack of a sense of commitment to my country. . . . I believe very strongly in what the United States and its Vietnamese allies are trying to accomplish in Vietnam, and I want very badly to be able to continue covering this war effort."

Halberstam had long since lost the address of his Reserve unit and asked Burritt to do the legwork, a request he soon regretted. Relaying copies of the retyped letters to the authorities, and formal cover letters from Freedman, Burritt expressed the hope "we've

---

8. The next year, writing in *The Making of a Quagmire,* he cemented the Hemingwayesque touch and made the war correspondent's mandatory blooding official: "I was nicked by shrapnel. . . ."

laid the 1A ghost [sic]." But The Shrink couldn't pass up the chance to signal the discomfort of the brass. In a handwritten postscript he added:

> Dave—I think patriotism should not be asked to substitute for non-performance of one's simplest duties to his country. I think you never again should have to ask another for the address of your reserve unit.—R.B.

Halberstam was left stinging with that final shot. But his awkward brush with the draft was over. The uproar the army would have caused by drafting David Halberstam in 1963, tempting as some might have found it, would have been a sight to behold. Still, even resolved, the news of it would have been pure gold to his growing list of foes, to a Harkins or a Marguerite Higgins, the militant celebrity correspondent and aggressive gossip who would soon be attacking his patriotism and courage more harshly than his reporting.

Looking back from the safety of three decades, Halberstam assessed his problem with more aplomb than he displayed at the time: "Let's assume Maggie Higgins attacks me. She attacks me for draft-dodging because I've not been doing two weeks of summer duty in Fort Drum or some fucking place. But I'm voluntarily in Vietnam getting shot at. It would have made me look like a hero and her like a fool."

Higgins, of course, never found out. Nor did anyone else, not even his buddy across the kitchen table, Neil Sheehan.

Still, aspersions on Halberstam's patriotism were outrageous and preposterous, Sheehan thought, and they were. These young men were believers, Cold Warriors. They would assault their government on the lying, on the self-deception and false optimism, the poor choice of allies, the sheer foolishness of much of what was happening. But the war itself? That was liturgy. To question it would take deeper insights, arriving later. "David was a *very* intense guy and *very* patriotic," Sheehan said later. "That was what produced all that anger. You've got to understand"—his voice rose to simulate the passion they felt in 1963—"WE THOUGHT *THESE PEOPLE* WERE *LOSING* THE WAR!"

Sheehan remembers one time when Halberstam came back from

the Seminary wracked with guilt. Vann had told him about his visits to province chiefs and how they offered him women. He *always* turned them down, Vann said, because sleeping with their women lessens you in their eyes. It was bad for the American image, bad for the war effort. The lecture was blatantly hypocritical, although neither Halberstam nor Sheehan knew it at the time. But Halberstam came back to the office deeply bothered. What about Ricki and Blue Lotus? Had he and Sheehan been undermining the war effort?

Halberstam's sense of obligation ran deep. Even after he began creating his giants, those larger-than-life saints and sinners in his books, no man ever became larger on his canvas than his own father.... Charles Halberstam, the immigrant's son, volunteering for the First World War, then volunteering again in middle age for the Second, sacrificing his best years for his country, bringing his family into the sacrifice, and then dying prematurely not long afterward. The father had made the son part of the sacrifice, deprived him, left for good when he was sixteen. It was a deed that might have pushed the son to a different kind of anger. But to young Halberstam it was such a big and proud thing his father had done that Charles Halberstam would forever be the ultimate hero. And David Halberstam could not live thinking less of himself.

Halberstam didn't let his near miss slow him down. He had a saying for others who moved their careers and lives at warp speed: "He's one of those fellows who follows you into a revolving door and comes out ahead of you." He could have been describing himself. He ran so fast he outran bad luck.

The draft board backed off just before his twenty-ninth birthday. He still seethed at Burritt—*let him pull his shrink crap on some twenty-two-year-old kid*—but he quickly returned to his old exultant self. In April he traipsed far south to the edge of the almost impenetrable Camau Peninsula mangrove swamps, visiting a new American advisory outpost at a place called Baclieu. Even his headline writer seemed caught up by his exuberance. Amid the stultifying dryness of *Times*-style, the headline hinted at boyish adventure: "... SO THERE I WAS, BASED IN BACLIEU," and his lead paragraph rang with the old GI Joe flair of an earlier time. There was no hiding the American presence at this isolated new post, he wrote:

One can tell the moment one lands at the dusty airstrip and sees the sign: "Baclieu International Airport. Elevation: Dry season, two feet above water; wet season, two feet below. Check with customs."

On April 10, his birthday, he flew with Ivan Slavich deep into the VC redoubt on the first all-Huey helicopter assault, Slavich's final victory over the air force. The mission became an unusual success—"the most effective and efficient use of American helicopters in this war," Halberstam wrote. Many guerrillas were killed and even more captured, flushed out of the jungle and pinned down in the flattened grass by the whirling blades of the choppers hovering just feet above their heads. "It was a roundup, just like a rodeo," Halberstam quoted one of the pilots as saying.

Halberstam's stories rang with such enthusiasm that it was difficult to imagine him as the scourge of anyone's military.

This particular moment provided a rare insight into the subtle evolution of Halberstam's thinking. He wrote and talked about it several times. In October he described the same event in *Times Talk*, the newspaper's in-house publication:

> Going into combat in one [of the Hueys] is a bit like watching a football game from a good press box seat. The whole scene develops in front of you very slowly—the water buffalo scurrying, the farmers remaining fixed and frozen and, suddenly, the Viet Cong kneeling, picking up rifles, and firing at the helicopters. At the helicopters? Hell no, at me. . . . Our helicopters pursued [one guerrilla] relentlessly, machine after man—it was a little like one of my dreams and I might have felt some sympathy if I had not carried out the bodies of dead government defenders from an outpost earlier in the week.

A year later, writing about the same mission in *The Making of a Quagmire*, he sounded like a different man, a man who had bored deeper into his own soul. Here is the same chase scene in his book:

> We bore down on one Viet Cong. The paddy's surface was rough and his run was staggered, like that of a good but

drunken broken-field runner against imaginary tacklers. We came closer and closer; inside the helicopter I could almost hear him gasping for breath, and as we bore down I could see the heaving of his body. It was like watching a film of one of your nightmares, but in this case you were the pursuers rather than the pursued. The [American] copilot fired his machineguns but missed, and the man kept going. Then there was a flash of orange . . . and the helicopter heaved from the recoil of its rockets. When they exploded the man fell. He lay still as we went over him, but when we turned he scrambled to his feet, still making for the canal, now only about fifty yards away. While we circled and swept toward him again he was straining for the bank, like a runner nearing the finish line. We had one last shot at him. Our copilot fired one last burst . . . as the guerrilla made a desperate surge. The bullets cut him down as he reached the canal, and his body skidded on the hard bank as he collapsed.

In her novel, *Miranda*, Pamela Sanders so thinly fictionalized the events, matings, and conversations of these days it is as if she played a tape recorder unedited into her book. She gives this account of a remarkably similar scene in which Miranda (Sanders) complains to Zimmerman (Halberstam) that "one doesn't even shoot animals from a moving vehicle. That's what it was like . . . shooting game from a Land Rover." Zimmerman relates a recurring dream:

In this dream there is a paddy field, deserted. It is high noon, the sun beats down, nothing moves. From the tree line, a small figure in black appears, looks about and begins to run across the field. . . . Then a flight of armed helicopters zooms in over the trees. The gunships chase the man across the field, strafing and rocketing. At the last second, he disappears, vanishing into the ground. The choppers circle, return and strafe, circle, return, strafe. They exit right just as a tank company and artillery pieces appear on the left. They pound the shit out of the field and rumble off stage right. Then a squadron of old T-28s and B-26s enters on the left and dive-bombs the field. They are followed by fighter-bombers who napalm it. It's a terrific dustup; the earth quails, distant trees tremble, nothing can live. At last they too depart, leaving the field smoking and ruptured. The sun shines. Nothing moves. It is very quiet. A head sticks up. A small figure in black pops up out of a hole, looks about and continues across the field . . .

Then Zimmerman adds:

Don't feel sorry for Charlie, Miranda. He's winning.

Some of the gung ho "first draft" writing in *The Times* surely can be ascribed to the rush of daily journalism, some to the rush of Hemingwayesque adventure. Halberstam was not the first, and surely not the last, war correspondent to find a special high in battle only to come down to earth with a different sense of it all later. But he would never have the kind of epiphany Sheehan had at Ap Bac. Sheehan would see that it had been wrong from the beginning and have deep regrets. Halberstam would see that it had been wrong from the beginning and become angrier and angrier. And he would forever treasure the young joys.

On the way back to Saigon the Huey crews turned carefree and jaunty, the pilots bobbing and weaving their powerful machines through billowing clouds that slowly turned from cotton-candy pink to flame red in the setting sun. Slavich started the singing, and, thirty years later, Halberstam still remembered the lyrics, to which he joined in:

We wish that all women
  Were fish in the ocean;
If I was a shark,
  I would show them my motion.

Oh, roll your leg over,
  Oh, roll their leg over. . . .

Moments later they dropped down on to the strip at their tent city at Tan Son Nhut, had a thirty-five-cent drink at the tiny helicopter-company bar, The Augur Inn, and headed downtown for dinner. On April 30 the documents showed up from his old Reserve command. He had been granted not a reclassification but a full and honorable discharge from the Reserve, obligation fulfilled.

On May 9, with Sheehan and Browne back from their stateside holidays, Halberstam took some R&R of his own, a three-week vacation with Charley and Norma Mohr in Hong Kong. That morning, not long before his departure, he received a call from the South Vietnamese press office. A press conference would be held that afternoon concerning the Viet Cong killing of eight Buddhists in the old imperial capital of Hue. Halberstam immediately became suspicious. Relations between the American correspondents and the Diem government had grown so sour that the government almost never called press conferences. And why would the Viet Cong kill a group of marching Buddhists? It smelled. But Halberstam was tired. After eight months, he needed a break. He skipped the press conference, taking the plane as planned to Hong Kong.

And so began the Buddhist crisis of 1963. With it the war would march into the streets of Saigon, just as it would into the streets of America a few years later. With it would come the searing protests of ascetic priests and antigovernment rebellions by students and other dissidents. Also with it would come the most brutal assault on a small group of young reporters in memory. In the end the crisis would topple Diem and, some believe, lock the United States into ten more years of war. But this first great Vietnam crisis began like the tree that fell in the wilderness. No one heard a sound.

12

FIREFIGHT ON THE EIGHTFOLD NOBLE PATH

John Mecklin found himself with one of those rare luxuries in a crisis—time to think.

He had left a shambles behind in Saigon. The leak of his ill-considered memo had occurred just days before his abrupt departure and the correspondents had exploded. They called him "Meck the Knife." Childishly—skins were worn so paper thin—they threatened him with a lifetime boycott. Even good-natured Mert Perry, hearing his work called irresponsible and sensationalized, flared completely out of character. Knowing Mecklin was leaving for surgery, he blurted out: "I hope the son of a bitch dies!"

A fine job he had done cleaning up the press mess, Mecklin thought bleakly as he flew to the Philippines. When the air force doctors at Clark Field gave him the grim news—cancer—he had all but decided to quit, regardless of the medical outcome. On the long, uneasy flight onward toward the navy surgeons at Bethesda he tried to busy himself with a half-read novel, but the slogan on the bookmark caught his eye. *Illegitimi non carborundum*, it read, the old mock Latin phrase for "Don't let the bastards wear you down." Despite himself, Mecklin chuckled. He had *two* sets of bastards, his old colleagues and his new.

In March the navy doctors granted him a muted reprieve. Recuperating, he made a hospital-bed resolution. He'd go back, but not for more of the wishy-washy same. He had temporized, compromised, tried to play both sides, and served no one well. Neither of his groups of warring *illegitimi* left Mecklin spellbound by their wisdom. He saw the men he worked for as patriotic and well-meaning but fated to make disastrous mistakes because of "psychological blinders" that left them with an extraordinary inability to see life as it was. Toward the press, they acted with "a self-righteous witlessness" that forever puzzled him. The reporters he found to be royal pains in the ass—also so self-righteous that their "unceasing complaints, however justified, became boring." It was not from his school of journalism that a reporter came in, as Halberstam once did, and ordered changes within forty-eight hours "or we'll blast the shit out of you."

Still, there was one crucial difference which he saw and Washington could not and would not see. The correspondents whom the policymakers so despised were delivering a straighter account than the men they had sent to Vietnam. The never-ending war with the press, he concluded, was serving the American people very badly indeed.

Before returning, he made the usual rounds. But he turned the routine consultations into hardball lobbying sessions. It was time to squawk less and listen more, he said; time for a peace treaty. The official press policy hadn't changed since Carl Rowan's disastrous Cable 1006 more than a year earlier. It was time for a new policy.

Eventually his evangelism took him to the White House and a one-on-one session in the Oval Office. John Kennedy listened intently as Mecklin spoke the unspeakable: The correspondents were as good as any anywhere; they usually reported more accurately than the President's government sources; they were "bitterly frustrated and angry at both the U.S. Mission and the Diem regime," and, for the most part, the American government had brought that anger down on itself. Never had he seen a situation more polarized. The press doesn't talk to us; we don't talk to the press. The government had created in Vietnam one of those rare occasions when a press policy threatened the larger national policy. It was time for a change.

Mecklin thought he read misgivings on the President's face. But Kennedy nodded and asked him to continue.

Now Mecklin knew he was skating onto the thinnest bureaucratic ice. The President didn't worry him. But passions had begun to run hot. Powerful men, rough-and-tumble infighters all, had their judgments, even their reputations, on the line. Win or lose with the President, he knew that these next few minutes could finish him as a public servant. They did. His new enemies would include men who would make Vietnam policy for the next five years, doubling up bad bets like drunks at the racetrack. Mecklin would become, in their eyes, a turncoat, and they would never forgive him. His end with the U.S. government would be so total that his book, *Mission in Torment,* published two years later, would be banned in the USIA library in Saigon, now part of his domain.

Mecklin ran his fingers through black hair graying too fast, and continued. We have confided so little in the Saigon reporters, he began, that they think we doubt their very patriotism. You should, he said, "personally instruct Washington agencies and the Mission in Saigon to cease excessively optimistic public statements, to stop complaining about unfavorable stories . . . and most of all to take the newsmen into their confidence." This had to come from the President personally, he added, or nothing would happen.

Mecklin had been right about Kennedy's misgivings. The interests of the government and the press had become so "highly conflicting" in Vietnam that he doubted any press policy would work, the President told his press secretary, Pierre Salinger, afterward. But he also told Salinger to work up a new policy plan.

Mecklin had been gone from Saigon three months. It had been, unexpectedly, a mostly quiet spring. Also unexpectedly, a new press policy awaited him when he arrived back in late May. It canceled out Cable 1006 and called for "wherever possible taking American reporters in Saigon further into our confidence." It also cautioned against expressions of undue optimism about the war. The policy had arrived with the clear imprimatur of the President, which gave it the clout Mecklin had sought.

For the first time since his arrival a year earlier, the beleaguered press adviser felt a surge of hope. But even as he basked in his sense of accomplishment, the slow-moving sound waves from the tree fall in Hue began reaching Saigon. Mecklin quickly found himself submerged in the biggest mess of all, one, he wrote, that "could not have been solved if Kennedy himself had come out to buy the newsmen a round of beers at the Caravelle bar."

———

The sound reached Washington slowly, too, where, as usual, the din of another crisis drowned out its first rumbles. This time, however, the crises would have unnerving similarities, with echoes and mirror images bouncing back and forth across the world and demanding massive change.

On May 8, the day the eight Buddhist demonstrators were shot in Hue, Martin Luther King, Jr., and 2,000 Negro protesters, many of them children, filled Birmingham jails. The segregationist police commissioner, Eugene (Bull) Connor, having run out of jail space, began using police dogs and high-powered fire hoses to drive off marching youngsters. The showdown filled the newspapers and television screens with pictures of children blown head over heels down Birmingham streets, the police looking on with attack dogs stretched two-legged against their leashes. Soon those images would be matched by street protests in Vietnam where unworldly Buddhist monks with shaved heads and saffron robes marched against the fire hoses, grenade launchers, and armored personnel carriers of an unruly government to which America had given its wealth and grace. It was the beginning of a long, hot summer, one day a photo of the blood-stained driveway of Medgar Evers, the next a Buddhist monk aflame in a grotesque suicide; George Wallace standing in the schoolhouse door, Ngo Dinh Diem's American-trained special forces battering down pagoda doors.

Still, at the beginning, the death of eight Buddhists on the far side of the world lay lightly on the minds of news editors. Both *The Times* and *The Washington Post* relegated the story to a few paragraphs on inside pages. Handled wisely, the Buddhist dispute might have faded quickly into oblivion. The shootings almost surely were an accident set off by panic. But, in Vietnam, wisdom would always be in short supply.

The crisis began innocently with an early May trip to Hue by Diem. If Vietnamese Buddhism had a cultural and religious center, it lay in the beautiful old city on the banks of the Perfume River. Four hundred miles north of Saigon, Hue was also the family birthplace, and Diem's brothers controlled the town, Ngo Dinh Can as a tough Oriental boss, a cross between Chicago's Boss Richard Daley and a mafia don; Ngo Dinh Thuc as an avaricious Catholic archbishop who preferred earthly real estate to the uncertain wisps of heaven.

At sixty-six, Archbishop Thuc was the eldest and wealthiest of the surviving brothers. "His requests for donations read like tax notices," a weary merchant told Stanley Karnow. The proceeds bought everything from rubber plantations to apartment houses. Diem revered him—as did Madame Nhu, which always proved more troublesome. It was to celebrate the twenty-fifth anniversary of Thuc's elevation to the Catholic hierarchy that Diem made the trip. The occasion was festive, and the archbishop arranged for yellow-and-white Vatican flags to fly in the streets alongside the national flag, a minor but symbolic violation of the law in a country in which a Catholic minority ruled a Buddhist majority. Several days later, on the 2,587th anniversary of the Buddha's birthday, Hue's Buddhists were barred from flying their own five-color banner, a time-honored part of their celebration. Simmering antagonisms stirred the usually stoic Buddhists into a major street protest. Some dispute remains about what happened next. The Diem government insisted that Viet Cong agents threw grenades and explosives into the crowd to provoke a riot. Eyewitnesses said a few nervous government troops opened fire, apparently using rifle-launched grenades. One woman and seven children were killed.

In Hue the demonstrations quickly grew larger and more ominous. But they moved toward Saigon at a Buddhist's methodical pace. The brothers gave Diem contradictory advice. The man of god, Archbishop Thuc, said: Crush them the way the troublesome religious sects, the Cao Dai and Hoa Hao, had been crushed in the fifties. The man of the flesh, Ngo Dinh Can, urged Diem to strike a deal. The Buddhists were not a sect, the tough old ward boss warned. Diem was in trouble, the warlord brother told him pointedly: His popularity in Hue had sunk so low not even a cat would turn out to see him. Diem laughed, and told visitors his brother was growing soft.

Roughly 70 percent of South Vietnam's people were thought to be Buddhists or had Buddhist roots.[1] Still, their sudden emergence as a force bewildered the Americans. "Who are these people?" Kennedy, now eighteen months into his buildup, asked an aide. "Why didn't we know about them before?" The President did not

---

1. Vietnamese religions were so crossbred over the centuries that the numbers were always in dispute.

get much help from his people in Saigon. At the embassy a single Buddhist scholar lectured to tiny groups about the Eightfold Noble Path, Greater Vehicles, and Nirvana, mainline Buddhist precepts more applicable in other Asian countries. The bonzes, as the monks were called, were somewhat traditional, but most of the people followed an aberrational form of the religion influenced over the centuries by Confucianism, Taoism, animism, and other Asian religions remote to Western thinking. The Americans, government and press, understood none of it.

It soon became difficult to determine whether the protests were religious, political, or both. Few in the American Embassy even knew a Buddhist bonze. The mystical Buddhists offered little help. John Helble, the U.S. consul in Hue, began meeting with one of their younger leaders, Thich Tri Quang.[2] Tri Quang proved of little help. He listened intently to one of Helble's questions, then stared deep into the darkness of the pagoda and replied, "The sky is blue, but the clouds drift across it."

In the next three weeks, with David Halberstam in Hong Kong, *The Times* published four small stories on the dispute and few American newspapers ran more. By the time he returned on May 28, as Halberstam later wrote, "any normal government would have settled the Buddhist incident." But Halberstam's luck was too golden for that. Diem had only succeeded in making the problem worse.

That very afternoon four hundred bonzes eluded Brother Nhu's secret police, no mean feat in their colorful attire, to conduct the first open antigovernment protest in the city in years. For three hours they prayed silently in front of the National Assembly building, a protest particularly galling to Madame Nhu, who took pride in her membership in the assembly. In a private meeting with protest leaders afterward, Diem denounced them as "damn fools." A government communiqué followed up by *announcing* that he had called them damn fools. In rapid order the Buddhists went on a hunger strike, their demonstrations spread throughout the country, eight were arrested for unlawful assembly, and, on June 5, more than sixty people were hospitalized in Hue, where Diem's troops seemed especially trigger-happy.

2. Thich is a Buddhist honorific, akin to Reverend or Doctor.

Halberstam had a field day, quickly dominating the story and propelling it onto the front page, where it stayed for the rest of the summer. His first day back Halberstam described the crisis as the sign of "deep-rooted discontent among a religious group that constitutes about 70 percent of the country's population." Within a week he pushed it to maturity: "What started as a religious protest has become predominantly political . . . and the Buddhists are providing a spearhead for other discontented elements." Halberstam had found his political Ap Bac, and he would make the most of it.

State Department records show how thoroughly Halberstam, in the mind of the government, could take over a story. The department's official history of the early Vietnam era,[3] something of a little Pentagon Papers, contains the major contemporary documents—cables, action orders, minutes of meetings, and so forth. During the three weeks Halberstam was gone, seven of twenty-six documents dealt with the Buddhist crisis. In the week following his return, fifteen of sixteen were devoted to the Buddhists, including a cable the first day that began: "*New York Times* reports today Buddhists still very upset . . ."

Still, the one searing moment that emblazoned the Buddhist crisis in the American mind did not come from David Halberstam and his powerful newspaper. It took that man of totally different temperament to do that. It took Browne—and his camera.

Browne had been in Vietnam almost two years now, and the skinny redhead had watched more with curiosity than frustration as the electric young reporter from *The Times* had taken away his story. Browne moved to his own rhythms. Of them all, the Quaker's son came closest to having a touch of Zen in him. Halberstam? The sky is blue, but the clouds drift across it.

As self-contained and even reclusive as he might be, as idiosyncratic and full of red-socks quirks, Mal Browne was not a man to be underestimated. His life had become considerably more blissful in the past six months. Le Lieu was back from Australia and they were deeply in love, sharing Wagner's booming romanticism in the little apartment above the office on the Rue Pasteur. As the Buddhist crisis worsened, Brother Nhu and his secret police tightened the noose on "turncoat" Vietnamese and hinted that Le Lieu was

3. *Foreign Relations of the United States, 1961–1963: Vietnam. Volumes 1–4.*

on their list. Browne kept a loaded Schmeisser submachine gun at the ready in their apartment. No one doubted he would use it.

Browne was an endlessly curious, methodical, and persistent man, traits as handy in his first career as a chemist as they proved to be in his second. He had entered the laboratory hero-worshipping J. Robert Oppenheimer and dreaming a young man's dream of great new discoveries on the frontier of nuclear physics. Instead, he ran into the realities of commerce. In 1954 an anti-American Guatemalan dictator threatened the world supply of chicle, a disaster for the chewing-gum industry. Browne solved the problem by creating a substitute at just about the same time the CIA solved the problem by ousting the dictator. His ersatz chicle hit the market simultaneously with a worldwide chicle glut and enjoyed only a brief run as the key ingredient in a product known as Hollywood Gum. Next the lab put the young scientist on the frozen blintz problem. The blintz was notoriously unstable, cracking when frozen. Browne "rubberized" the shells, enough to make a hero of any New Yorker except an inward man who sought no laurels. This might have gone on forever had the laboratory not put him on the aftershave-lotion dilemma. A client wanted a better-smelling benzaldehyde for its men's toiletry line. Browne pursued the problem with his usual zeal. But his new benzaldehyde had a crucial flaw. It exploded. So did the laboratory. Now, in June 1963, Mal Browne's persistence was about to create a more earthshaking explosion.

———

Early on the muggy morning of June 11 Browne sat wedged against a gilded statue of a fat Buddha. Only he had responded to the telephone tip directing him to the small pagoda filled with stoic bonzes in saffron and solemn nuns in virginal white.

Incense filled the room, numbing the senses, as did the ancient prayer droning over and over from a lean and ascetic monk. Browne drifted easily into a far world as a second monk quietly drummed a gourd in rhythm with the prayer's lulling monotone: "Na . . . Mo . . . Ah . . . Di . . . Da . . . Phat . . . ." For an hour the hypnotic prayer continued, the eyes of faithful and outsider alike glazing as its tempo slowly rose. Then, at nine o'clock, the ritual abruptly stopped.

Browne shook his head to clear it. He checked the cheap Petri camera New York had finally sent him to replace the battered old Ricoh reflex he had carried off Pan Am One, which now seemed so long ago. Then he followed the Buddhists into the street.

The protesters marched in two phalanxes, unfurling signs condemning the Diem government in both Vietnamese and English, a sure signal that the event was orchestrated as much for Mal Browne as Ngo Dinh Diem. At the head of the procession four monks rode in a gray four-door sedan.

Suddenly, at a busy downtown intersection, the procession stopped. One monk opened the hood of the car and withdrew a plastic five-gallon container of pink gasoline. The others led the oldest monk, Thich Quang Duc, to the center of the intersection, where he seated himself on a small brown cushion, hands folded in prayer, legs crossed in the lotus position.

Browne focused the Petri from the edge of the crowd twenty feet away. It captured Quang Duc as the gasoline was poured over his shaved head. It clicked as the silent old monk calmly lighted a match and burst into flames. The curious downtown crowd gasped, moaned, and went silent. The only sounds came from a young monk repeating over and again in Vietnamese and English: "A Buddhist priest burns himself to death. A Buddhist priest becomes a martyr" . . . and from the clicking of Mal Browne's camera.

Through the flames and yellow smoke he could see the agony contorting the old monk's face. But Quang Duc sat, unmoving. Browne went numb at the ghastliness of it. The stench became overpowering, and nausea swept over him. He forced himself to silently repeat f-stops and shutter speeds as a distraction. The Petri seemed to perform automatically. But it was Mal Browne who was on automatic, clicking frame after frame, changing roll after roll, methodically recording the ritual suicide. Quang Duc burned for five minutes before the camera recorded his charred body toppling over. It also recorded the beginning of the toppling of the Diem regime.

——

"Jesus Christ!" the President exclaimed.

John Kennedy had the newspapers delivered to him in bed on this morning. It had promised to be a big day. George Wallace, the arch-segregationist governor of Alabama, had vowed to stand in the schoolhouse door to stop Negroes from entering. Kennedy had vowed to move Wallace out of the way. Attorney General Robert Kennedy telephoned him at 8:00 A.M. about the Alabama problem, but the President was still in bed staring at Mal Browne's photographs. *Jesus Christ.*

Around the world the response was similar. The photos appeared everywhere, and everywhere they seemed to symbolize what was wrong with American involvement, if not in Vietnam, at least with Ngo Dinh Diem. In Europe the photos were hawked on back streets along with pornographic postcards. American clergymen reprinted them in full-page advertisements proclaiming, "We, Too, Protest." China distributed millions of copies throughout Asia and Africa as evidence of "U.S. imperialism." So much did Mal Browne's photos jar history that more than three decades later one is still affixed to the old gray sedan, part of a tourist attraction in the place now called Ho Chi Minh City.

In Saigon the reactions ran true to form.

Diem accused Browne of bribing the seventy-three-year-old monk and the other Buddhist bonzes of drugging him before setting him afire.

Even before the self-immolation, Madame Nhu had headed off on another of her sprees. In April, through her Women's Solidarity Movement, she accused the Americans of using their foreign-aid money "to make lackeys of Vietnamese and to seduce Vietnamese women into decadent paths." She had a point there. But Nolting and Harkins finally took umbrage and retaliated by standing her up at the family hunting lodge. The day before the suicide she took off again after "the UPI correspondent Cornelius Sheehan" and his "tendentious reporting." In a letter to UPI she accused Sheehan of "inventing tales" about Ap Bac and "distorting facts" about the incident in Hue. The warning was clear: Sheehan might have trouble with his upcoming visa renewal. Her favored *Times of Vietnam* trumpeted the complaints on the front page.

The suicide sent her into a rage that left Sheehan's sins forgotten. The First Lady's continuing tirades even had Diem and her husband concerned. In the palace they toned down her opening salvo. "Communists and Communist dupes," she said of the bonzes, tame stuff from her. But the days were long gone when the men could ship her off to a convent. She soon found a British television crew and said it her own way: What was all the fuss about? she asked. All the Buddhists have done is "barbecue a bonze," unpatriotically using "imported gasoline" to do it.

Washington and the embassy were furious. One of the first cables spoke desperately of the need "to keep Madame Nhu quiet." Within days, in the White House, Kennedy's Vietnam team was searching for ways "to get rid of (both) the Nhus." Then came the inevitable question: Should the whole family be dumped? In Saigon the coffeehouse gossip produced so many plots that the correspondents began calling them the *coup du jour*. Diem pulled the reins still tighter on his combat forces, moving them in closer on Saigon, and surrounded Gia Long Palace with armed police constantly abuzz on radio phones. The war in the field virtually stopped.

Apologists for Madame Nhu blamed the language barrier. At first she tried some corrective surgery on her troublesome tongue. Her English was wretched, she said, and the awful word had come from the Americans themselves. Her teenage daughter had overheard soldiers talking about Buddhist barbecues at the PX.

John Mecklin groaned. Saigon seemed to unravel day by day, until it took on all the trappings, as he put it, of "a mental institution."

"Neither the Vietnamese nor the Americans understood what was happening nor what to do about it," Mecklin wrote. "There were Americans who made jokes about 'bonze fires' or 'hot cross bonzes' or 'Buddhist cookouts,' almost as an escape mechanism. There was also something hypnotic about the mood. One day the young son of an officer of the American Embassy poured gasoline on his clothes and struck a match. He was seriously burned before the fire was extinguished. His only explanation: 'I wanted to see what it was like.'" The infection spread. In Washington a youth burned himself to death on the steps of the Pentagon. In the next few months six more monks and nuns immolated themselves in Vietnam.

The American community, which had come to Saigon so full of good can-do intentions, quickly fell, rudderless, into disarray. Ambassador Nolting had left for Washington consultations and a month's vacation two weeks *after* the first shootings in Hue. The day after the suicide, Nolting asked to be relieved of his post, by that time saving Kennedy the trouble of asking. Nolting would remain as ambassador until mid-August. But he continued blithely on with his vacation plans—a month of sailing in the Aegean Sea. No one in Washington told anyone in Saigon of Nolting's plan to leave. Even the man now wading through the mess in his place, William Trueheart, was kept in the dark.

No further attempts at moderation came from Madame Nhu. She did have trouble with translations of her invective, even from her revered French, which was usually handled by Ann Gregory of the *Times of Vietnam*. As the Buddhist crisis continued, the paper became shriller and stranger. It also left some wondering if Mrs. Gregory had oversold her language credentials to the First Lady.

PLEASE DON'T USE WOMEN FOR SOMBER PURPOSES, read the head-line above one story, which gave no further hint about what Madame Nhu had in mind. But her favorite assault word was "intoxicated," as in "intoxicated with Communism."[4] *The New York Times* was intoxicated, Halberstam was intoxicated, Sheehan was intoxicated, everyone was intoxicated. The climax came when the Gregorys' paper trumpeted a story headed:

MADAME NGO DINH NHU CALLS FOR
"CAMPAIGN OF DISINTOXICATION"

The story began:

A campaign of "disintoxication" must be opened immediately to disintoxicate those who really want to be disintoxicated, Madame Ngo Dinh Nhu said yesterday in extemporaneous remarks. . . .

Madame Nhu had been born a Buddhist and converted to Catholicism when she married Ngo Dinh Nhu. Vietnam in 1963 was a place of tenuous religious conversions. "Rice-bowl Catholics," the Vietnamese called Buddhist bureaucrats and military officers

4. The French words *intoxiquer* and *intoxicated* mean poison and poisoned, as in a mind poisoned by Communism. The translations, however, were made so literally it often sounded as if everyone in Saigon was on a drinking binge.

who made career advances after suddenly seeing the light from Rome—or Gia Long Palace. In some places entire villages converted to Catholicism to gain favor with the government. But Madame Nhu became a fanatic. She pressed for rigid enforcement of her "morality" bills; she brooked no dissent.

The Buddhist crisis brought the Nhus front and center as no trouble had before. Nhu became markedly more erratic, giving rise to speculation that his drug use had lurched out of control. Stanley Karnow once described him as a self-proclaimed intellectual revolutionary who "spins out his abstruse theories with the intensity of a college sophomore." But he was a wily man and now he talked of deals with the North Vietnamese, assailed the Americans and the Buddhists alike, openly called his brother too weak, and talked with various plotters about joining a coup attempt.

But it was Madame Nhu's Dragon Lady antics that threw everything off-kilter, and, given her peculiar and powerful relationship with the increasingly withdrawn South Vietnamese president, contributed so heavily to the demise of the family. It was as if Beautiful Spring, the tough little rich girl who had married Nhu to escape her powerful Buddhist parents, had gained two husbands in the bargain. Upper-class Vietnamese women controlled their men shrewdly, and Madame Nhu was nothing if not shrewd. A CIA report on the relationship said she had achieved the status, in Diem's mind, of being his "wife." The report cited a Vietnamese general and longtime palace intimate, who later plotted against Diem, as saying Madame Nhu was there "to comfort him after a day's work." The CIA report continued: "She is charming, talks to him, relieves his tension, argues with him, needles him and, like a Vietnamese wife, she is dominant in the household." The report continued: "There are no sexual relationships between Diem and Madame Nhu. In [General Tran Van] Don's opinion, [the] President has never had sexual relations."

Even platonically, however, the relationship was more intense and complicated than many marriages. Days after the self-immolation of Quang Duc, Diem, under pressure from the Americans, agreed to a highly public compromise with the Buddhists. The First Lady read it at lunch in Gia Long Palace and flew into one of her rages. "You are weak as a jellyfish," she screamed at Diem, hurling a serving bowl of chicken soup across the table at him. During the coming weeks she and her "other" husband, Ngo Dinh Nhu, effectively undermined the compromise and Diem's government as well.

There is a footnote to the "barbecue" episode. When someone described the nuance of the English word to her, she smiled and said it wasn't such a bad word after all. "If I had it all to do over again," she said, "I would say the same thing." She liked the word's "shock value," she said.

During eighteen months of dangerous foreign adventure in Vietnam, John Kennedy had been almost impossible to keep focused on what he had begun, so demanding did his other crises seem to him. Now, all that changed. As his house historian, Arthur Schlesinger, wrote, the Buddhists "finally made Vietnam a matter of top priority, even in the months of Bull Connor and his police dogs in Birmingham."

———

Suddenly there was no time in the day for Ivan Slavich's helicopter runs, no time for blackened-face adventures with Speedy Gaspard along the mountainous Laotian frontier. For the correspondents the action shifted overnight from the Mekong Delta and the Seminary to the streets of Saigon and Xa Loi Pagoda.

The pagoda, its ornate pinnacles and arches splashed with exotic color, rose abruptly out of a nondescript street near the edge of downtown Saigon. It quickly became the Buddhists' command post. Next door an old building housed the offices of the American economic-aid program. Ambassador Nolting's villa sat just around the corner. General Harkins lived in colonial style two blocks away, David Halberstam and Horst Faas a few blocks farther. Not far beyond Xa Loi, however, the grand houses gave way to the chaos of old Asia, where stilted huts flew the drying laundry of a million souls like the battle flags of the dispossessed. It was a good strategic location.

Reporters visiting Xa Loi stepped into a world they had not seen in their single-minded focus on the war. Entry to the walled complex came through a gate with two large wooden doors that opened heavily into a courtyard where ascetic monks and austere nuns, saffron and alabaster, mixed with the faithful: beautiful young Vietnamese women in their *ao dais* shimmering past ancient beggars;

313

free-spirited children racing around wrinkled grandmothers squatting in baggy black pants and smiling through teeth blackened with the stain of the juice of betel nuts. From a labyrinth of inner rooms the sound of gongs, tinkling chimes, and rhythmic chants emerged to compete with the children's chatter. Those invited into the inner sanctum sat for hours trying to decode the elliptical bonzes, drinking what seemed like gallons of tea, served as badly overripe cabbage boiled nearby. For years afterward Halberstam could not drink tea without smelling rotting cabbage.

As effective as the Buddhists became at using the press, the beginnings were difficult. The correspondents were no more adept, and far less patient, than the government people at dealing with cosmic riddles. Few of the Buddhists spoke English. Those who did, usually in an off-key singsong style full of misused words and often hilarious malapropisms, automatically became the press spokesmen. The results were often zany. One bonze, who had studied briefly at Yale, approached the correspondents, giving off the full aura of Buddhist mysticism, and began his conversations, "Boola, boola."

The primary spokesman became a frail, twenty-four-year-old monk, Thich Duc Nghiep. His name was so beyond the tongue of most of the Americans that the growing band of freelance photographers took to calling him Tic Tac Toe. Duc Nghiep's quirks were not limited to his name. He looked even younger than his years and spoke with a comically jerky accent that often made him sound ridiculous. He was also incurably conspiratorial, blatantly misleading when it served his purpose, and full of false alarms delivered up with an ingratiating smile. "Meestair Hammolsan," he said the first time Halberstam came to Xa Loi, "we know you are a special agent for Meestair Averell Harriman and you have a very important mission here." Halberstam never could convince him that he was not a spy. But it made no difference. Duc Nghiep wanted his message delivered no matter which channel Halberstam used.

From the beginning Duc Nghiep told the reporters that the Buddhists would dramatize their cause with either a flaming suicide or a public disembowelment. Almost daily he called them with heavy, if enigmatic, hints that the event would occur at the next day's demonstration. But the demonstrations came and went without spectacle, each day falling farther down the newsmen's list of priorities.

Not long before June 11 all the correspondents were called to Xa Loi for a major event, only to have Duc Nghiep send them away: "There will be no human sacrifice today, gentlemen." After the correspondents left, the Buddhists marched to Nolting's house for a demonstration. The correspondents were furious. Why did you send us away? Duc Nghiep smiled. "Ah, because when you left, the secret police left," he replied logically, "and when they were gone we could leave the pagoda and demonstrate." The correspondents bristled at their new role as decoys.

So Mal Browne was not surprised when he found himself alone on the morning of June 11. "Duc Nghiep became sort of a laughing stock with some newsmen," Browne said. "He spoke in a peculiar accent and explained the most gruesome details in such matter-of-fact fashion. He went into great detail to explain that you can't just douse yourself in gasoline, that it took a lot of experiments before they hit upon a mixture of two-thirds eighty-six-octane gasoline and one-third jet fuel or kerosene. All of this was said with his odd smile. It was all very bizarre and he lost a lot of people."

But not the eccentric ex-chemist, Mal Browne. And his exclusive photos brought more rockets raining down on his colleagues than any news event of the war. Neil Sheehan was still catching hell months later. David Halberstam didn't carry a camera, *The Times* relying on the wire services for photos. But it was no feather in his cap when Browne followed up on a tip he had ignored. Still, no one suffered more grief than Ray Herndon, the young Texan who was in town from Laos on something of a fluke.

UPI had kept Herndon in Saigon after he pinch-hit for Sheehan during his April vacation. (He recalls UPI's transfer procedures: "There was a famous telegram they'd send: GO SAIGON, FILL SHEEHAN TWO WEEKS. That meant I would stay the next umpty-ump years." After one temporary setback, he did stay, giving Sheehan some badly needed help.)

To cut costs, Herndon had been bunking at the villa with Halberstam. On the morning of June 11 both men overslept, Herndon, forever a hell-raiser, having spent the night cavorting around town and arriving home only hours earlier with a guest with whom he cavorted still longer. About nine o'clock Halberstam got a frantic message. Grumbling about being awakened for "just another demonstration," he nevertheless thumped on Herndon's door, then hurriedly dressed. Herndon groggily pulled on his khakis and a pair of shoes, forgetting the socks, and the two of them ran toward the scene only a few blocks away. Halfway there, Herndon stopped in mid-stride. He had forgotten something else—his cameras. "Oh, God," he panicked, "do I go back?" He shook his head and raced on.

The scene at the street corner shocked Halberstam. In front of him "flames were coming from a human being; his body slowly withering and shriveling up, his head blackening and charring." He took no notes, asked no questions—except of himself. Was he a reporter or a human being? Should he interfere, put the fire out? It was too late for that. But the questions were ones all the reporters would soon be asking themselves. The questions were perhaps too easily answered. The suicides were news.

Herndon was downright sick. The scene sickened him. The indulgences of the previous night sickened him. But nothing sickened him as much as the vision of his two 35-millimeter Leicas sitting on a table a few blocks away. He looked across at Browne, who could be as inscrutable as any Buddhist bonze, and thought the AP man returned his look with the faintest smile. "Oh, shit," Herndon said to himself, "I just lost the Pulitzer."

He also lost skin, and plenty of it. "It seems to me completely incredible that Herndon did not take a camera with him when he went to cover the burning monk," the New York pictures editor, Frank Tremaine, wrote Hoberecht. "I hope he remembered to take his pencil. . . ." Within days Herndon was on his way to the penalty box in Laos.

For Sheehan the incident reverberated through the summer. With Herndon in town, he had taken advantage of the help to make an increasingly rare visit to the field. To make matters worse, the mission was such a washout it barely made a story.

For weeks Hoberecht was relentless. He not only sent news of every client cancellation—a newspaper in Sydney complained that it lost 5,000 street sales—but an endless stream of patronizing notes. "See what a beating we took in your area because the AP news man there kept his head, remained cool, took pictures and got them out," he wrote June 17, adding a list of "tips" to avoid future trouble:

—Remain calm and cool.
—Keep your wits. . . .
—Check and double check. Get names and ages correct. Don't fly off the handle. . . .
—Be a professional.

With a year's worth of accumulated gripes (Sheehan, too, could cable back a feisty retort), every editor in Tokyo seemed eager to pile on. One sent Sheehan a copy of a news story that he labeled "Factual content, salient reporting," adding: "Note the stuff circled in red. These are the things that bring a story to life." The story was bylined "By Malcolm W. Browne" and, ironically, reported that the Buddhists "seem to have lost their initiative." A Tokyo photo editor rocketed: "Why, in heaven's name, did you pay $50 for those riot pix for? [sic] Where were our own people this time?" The word "this" was underlined three times.

Sheehan, exhausted, suffered in silence for weeks. Then Hoberecht made the mistake of waking him early one morning with a phone call. Once again he brought up the photo. No one ever challenged Hoberecht. But Sheehan had gone over the edge.

"God damn it, Earnie!" he shouted into the phone. "It was just fucking bad luck and I'm not going to take any more shit about it! It was bad luck!"

"Now, okay, Sheehan," Hoberecht replied, startled. "Settle down, Sheehan." He never brought it up again.

But no one ignored Thich Duc Nghiep after that. Nor would Xa Loi ever be the same. Halberstam latched onto the monk the way he had to John Paul Vann, making the walk to the pagoda each morning before heading down to Sheehan's office near the river.

Now the first early-morning sight and sound at Xa Loi was a monk with a bullhorn exhorting passersby: "Buddhism forever! Down with Madame Nhu!" Two sinewy bonzes drew back the wooden doors onto a courtyard scene that had taken on a carnival air, the abrupt change jarring Halberstam. Bonzes intently reading mimeographed summaries of their overseas news reviews strolled through the chaos of a new mob scene like Wall Streeters glued to the *Journal*. A man operating a hastily built souvenir stand pinholed him immediately in French, thrusting his offering forward. Halberstam looked down at a set of Mal Browne's photographs selling for seventy piasters, about a dollar, destined for the coffers of the cause. Monks with more bullhorns worked the crowd from the inside. Signs in Vietnamese and English were plastered to the stucco walls: YOUTH OF VIETNAM BE READY TO SACRIFICE YOURSELF FOR BUDDHISM! Other banners made scatological attacks on Madame Nhu, a favored Saigon pastime invading the pagodas. The mob scene was provided by the press. Where the ranks of the small group that had covered the beginning grew by perhaps a dozen early in the crisis, now the number seemed to swell by a dozen a day. The newcomers were of all stripes, from the big bylines of the old Asia hands and the Washington press corps to newcomers so green one asked where he could get a visa to the country of Viet Cong. Most of the new arrivals seemed to be photographers and, if there is only one certainty about American journalism, it is that photographers will take a backseat to no one when it comes to indelicacy, not even a Madame Nhu. "Hey, Tic Tac Toe!" they shouted at the newly renowned Buddhist spokesman. "When's the next barbecue?!"

Halberstam and Duc Nghiep wasted no time in developing a special relationship, each being of use to the other. It was an odd alliance, a gregarious Jewish reporter built like a nearsighted lumberjack and an enigmatic Buddhist priest as inward and gaunt as a long-distance runner. Other correspondents watched the courtship with a combination of awe and amusement, Halberstam pushing through the courtyard crowd to Duc Nghiep, smothering the bonze in a giant hug, planting a smooch on his cheek. "It was no little buss," said Don Becker, who helped Sheehan briefly at UPI, "it was a big, full *abrazzo*." Then the unlikely pair retreated into the relative calm of Xa Loi's inner sanctuaries to smell the cabbage, drink the tea, and probe at bridging their enormous culture gap.

Many Buddhists wanted to burn themselves in protest, the monk volunteered one day. Why don't you burn yourself? Halberstam responded, teasingly but curious. Duc Nghiep answered the question earnestly and with the patience of a teacher with a slow student. "Every priest has his job to do," he said. "Some priests burn themselves; my job is to talk to you." At another point Halberstam questioned the off-color attacks on Madame Nhu, which seemed in conflict with Duc Nghiep's contemplative and philosophical religion. "She is the Vietnamese Lady Macbeth," he answered. "She and her husband want to kill the King of England." Halberstam instinctively began to correct the Buddhist's Shakespeare, then wisely pulled back. Duc Nghiep clearly knew far more about the bard than Halberstam did about anyone in the bonze's culture.

The day the First Lady angrily threw the chicken soup at Diem, Halberstam passed along the gossipy news. Duc Nghiep turned so solemn even the smile faded. "The priests will be very unhappy," he said. The reply confused the newsman until he realized that Duc Nghiep considered the chicken soup to be a frivolous issue. He was more concerned about the news that had sent Madame Nhu into her tantrum: the signing of a compromise between the Buddhist leadership and the president. It was Halberstam's first inkling of a development that would alter the course of events: a split between the older, traditional Buddhist leaders whose goal was religious freedom and a younger, angrier group in their thirties and forties, men who didn't want a compromise. They wanted Diem.

As this also became clear to others, Halberstam and the group came under withering attack for being "manipulated" by the Buddhists.

The bonzes, few of whom had any real sense of the complex earthly world beyond their pagodas, became uncommonly good at press relations. Their black-market mimeograph machines (it was illegal for anyone outside the Diem government to possess copying machines) churned out press releases in broken English. They printed their protest signs in English, a major innovation in overseas political movements in a day when television's reach was still short.

But John Mecklin thought the key to the Buddhists' success with the correspondents was even more elemental: They opened up to them, trusted them with their plans and hopes and secrets. When everyone else considered the reporters enemies, the Buddhists treated them "like heroes at pagodas all over the country." Suddenly the correspondents, accustomed to looking over their shoulders in the streets, found themselves cheered by the crowds. As hard-nosed as Halberstam could be—"You don't go into this business to make friends"—he was a man whose uneasy psyche shriveled without company. He often mentioned the loneliness. "We felt completely without friends," he said and, at the memory, he added for emphasis: "How *lonely* we felt."

The unsophisticated Buddhists—Mecklin marveled at the irony of it—used the press more adroitly in the showdown summer of 1963 than the hopeless Vietnamese government or the ox-stubborn Americans, whose government had more press-relations experts under its employ than soldiers at war.

Mecklin wasn't the only one who was convinced. Madame Nhu raged on and her press mouthpiece, the *Times of Vietnam*, grew hysterical. XA LOI POLITBURO MAKES NEW THREATS, it headlined one day, MONKS PLOT MURDER the next. The newspaper's attacks on the American correspondents ranged from blunt and outrageous to downright silly. One article questioned why "so many young girls are buzzing in and out of Xa Loi early (and sometimes late) . . . ," then answered its own question: The Buddhists brought in the girls to provide sexual favors for the reporters.

The correspondents ignored the *Times of Vietnam* and shrugged off the charges of manipulation.

Halberstam reacted tersely, as he had to the charges of working too closely with John Paul Vann: *You get, you give; you give, you get —it's Journalism 101.* Browne was less political in his trades but equally certain of himself. Manipulated? "Sure," he said of the photos that were heard around the world. "A photographer who sees an elephant being towed on water skis under the George Washington Bridge will take the picture." And newspapers will print it. That was the nature of the game.

Meanwhile, in Washington, it was as if the State Department, which had granted the Pentagon a clear, open-turf run at its "nice little war," abruptly awoke and found the nightmare worse with its eyes open. Suddenly the State Department was tugging in one direction, the Defense Department in the other, and Kennedy swiveling in between. Saigon was no longer the capital of palace intrigue.

Instructions to the embassy on dealing with Diem turned sterner and sterner. In May, a contingency plan for "eventual change of government in South Vietnam" went out, carefully coppered against leaks with instructions about what to do if Diem died of old age. On June 11, hours after the immolation, Secretary of State Rusk sent secret instructions to carry a bluntly personal message to Diem threatening to "reexamine our entire relationship with his regime" unless he came to terms with the Buddhists.[5]

Still wedded to the policy Homer Bigart had called "sink or swim with Ngo Dinh Diem," the Pentagon grew nervous. In June, military personnel in Vietnam received a directive ordering them to avoid "gratuitous criticism" of the Diem regime. "As songwriter Johnny Mercer put it," the directive instructed, "you've got to accentuate the positive and eliminate the negative." The orders immediately leaked to Halberstam, who published them three days after the first flaming suicide.

Meanwhile, Nolting sailed on in the Aegean Sea, out of sight and out of touch. The man who inherited the dirty work after two years of American fawning over Diem was Nolting's boyhood chum, William Trueheart. Even though they received their orders from the same place, Nolting never forgave him. When he returned to Saigon briefly in July, the ambassador was furious. "I think he felt when he was away that I was responsible to him," Trueheart said. "I thought I was responsible to Washington."

So Trueheart would also suffer from the blight, the yellow disease. Nolting returned to the State Department and gave Trueheart a scathingly negative proficiency report. When Trueheart returned he found his name "was mud with the military" and half of his bureaucratic department too. He got the job he had been promised —director of Southeast Asian Affairs. But it suddenly was missing a key parcel, Vietnam. It left him, as he put it, "with the dominoes —Laos, Cambodia, Thailand, and Burma." It was like promising him New York and holding back Manhattan. After that, Trueheart's promising career foundered for a decade in the Sargasso Sea of the State Department. He retired a year before Saigon fell, his last posting being Nigeria. The two old friends spoke only once or twice again, a few words at happenstance meetings on the streets

5. Kennedy was not told of Rusk's cable. He found out about it three days later through the CIA and angrily put out the word: no more threats without talking to him. It was the beginning of his fruitless attempts to hold his government together on the Diem question.

of the Virginia tobacco town Nolting's family ran like the small-town Southern aristocrats they were. By that time Trueheart knew what everyone knew: Vietnam was a sinkhole for dreams and careers.

John Mecklin watched the policy changes with his usual sense of irony. As Trueheart became tougher on Diem, Washington grew increasingly nervous that someone might find out. Embassy operatives found themselves under strict orders not to be seen with a Buddhist, lest Diem lose face and become more offended than he already was.

The orders left the American Mission in the worst of fixes. In the midst of the war's greatest political crisis, the Americans had no sources inside the Buddhist movement. The press had them all, and the reporters were not sharing. The turnabout might have been humorous had not so much been at stake. Nolting and Harkins had refused to confide in the correspondents, fearing leaks to the enemy. But the Buddhists talked freely, even though leaks could mean prison or, as it turned out, death at the hands of Brother Nhu's secret police. The reporters did not leak, especially to the embassy, which might leak to the palace, and the government was left out in the cold. "Now it was *we*," Mecklin wrote ruefully, "who had become the bad security risk."

Washington grew furious at the repeated intelligence failures, unable to see the problem it had created.

"There was an almost frantic frustration back there at picking up the paper every morning and reading information that they hadn't received from us," Trueheart said.

But the farther the Kennedy government edged away from its troublesome mandarin, the meaner it became toward the messengers who had been providing the bad news all along.

———

Under the circumstances, the American Embassy's annual Fourth of July party became less than a gala event. By tradition the national birthday celebration brings together foreign diplomats, officials of the host government, and all factions of an American overseas community—diplomats to building contractors, news correspondents to tourists. In Saigon during the summer of 1963 this was an electric mix.

Trueheart hosted the party at Nolting's residence, the ambassador's temporary return still a week away.

At the party the correspondents seemed even more the outsiders —so exuberantly young, so blithely unencumbered by the responsibilities of conventional power. By now, most had beautiful Vietnamese girlfriends; all had the run of an exotic city and a high ride on a story that fast was becoming everyone else's misery. In the sea of white suits and dress whites, gowns and an occasional *ao dai*—but no Buddhists' robes—animosity bubbled with the champagne, particularly among the military wives. Snug in their own caste system, the wives' social duties rarely brought them face-to-face with the bylined men causing their careerist husbands so much grief. Now they bristled as the reporters moved through the crowd with brash grins and zesty self-confidence.

Suddenly, Alice Stilwell, the color rising in her face, wheeled on one correspondent barely old enough to be a captain under her one-star husband, Brigadier General Richard Stilwell—Stilwell the Bad to the irreverent newsmen.

"You're not married, are you?" she abruptly demanded.

Surprised, David Halberstam shook his head.

"You don't have children, do you?"

Rarely at a loss for words, Halberstam shook his head again.

"If you did," the general's wife continued, bitterly biting off each word, "you'd look at this war quite differently."

It would be years before Halberstam would concede that Alice Stilwell had a point, although hardly the one she intended. He would be long gone from Vietnam before he would agree that, older and more mature, perhaps even as a father, he indeed might have looked at the war differently. He might have seen, as he did later, that America had no business in Vietnam *at all*. At the time, however, the twenty-nine-year-old *Times* man recovered with a quick cocktail party riposte:

"Mrs. Stilwell, your man, President Diem, does not have children. If he did, do you think we would have the benefit of an improvement in his view of the war?"

Alice Stilwell stalked away, furious. Her husband never forgot nor forgave, developing a near obsession about the rude young man from *The Times*.

The obsession was mutual. Richard Clurman made one of his

periodic visits a short time later and talked to Stilwell at a different party. Halberstam walked up, listened to the general for a moment, and erupted.

"Bullshit, General!" he thundered.

Clurman, who had the diplomacy of a man whose job was to hold together a stable of temperamental *Time* correspondents, was aghast.

But Halberstam pressed on: "Why are you standing here telling our friend Clurman this bullshit? You're standing here lying and feeding him full of bullshit!"

Stilwell spun on his heel and left.

Clurman looked at Halberstam, whom he admired and considered a natural leader, but one who would lead more persuasively without the locker-room explosiveness. "Gee," he said gently, "that's an odd way to conduct a conversation."

"Well, they're a bunch of fucking liars," Halberstam replied. "I can't stand the way they feed you guys this bullshit every time you come over here."[6]

At the Fourth of July party, however, the event that would stay riveted in the minds of more party-goers occurred a few minutes after Alice Stilwell walked away. Diem was not in attendance but his official representative was, as were many ranking members of his government. When the traditional toast was proffered to him as the host government's head of state, Halberstam stood tall, straight, and stern in the middle of the room.

He clutched his glass to his chest. "I'd never drink to that son of a bitch," he announced, and he did not announce it quietly.

A much more subdued mention of Diem also marked that night at the embassy. Off in a quieter corner, two old friends met to carry on a careful conversation. One was General Tran Van Don, a dark and unusually handsome man who remained the figurative head of South Vietnam's armed forces although Diem had emasculated him, placing him in charge of one of the desks. The other was a rogue elephant CIA officer named Lucien Conein.

Conein was one of those marvelously murky, spy-novel characters who occasionally operate almost unfettered in American crises.

---

6. Halberstam does not recall the second conversation. "Sounds generic to me," he said, but he acknowledges similar moments with Stilwell.

French-born but sent to Missouri as a child, he had kept both his French citizenship and his Missouri drawl.

At the outbreak of the Second World War young Conein joined the French army, then deserted and escaped back to the United States when France fell. Recruited by the Office of Special Services (predecessor to the CIA), he was sent back into France to work with the underground. With the defeat of the Nazis, the OSS parachuted him into southern China with French and Vietnamese guerrillas to cross into Vietnam and undermine the weakened Japanese occupying force. He moved quickly in a dark world. By the time the Japanese fell he was in Hanoi, to which he returned in 1954 to undermine Ho Chi Minh and his nationalist forces as the French withdrew. Among his endeavors, he staged phony funerals at Hanoi cemeteries, planting arms instead of bodies as caches for future resistance fighters.[7] His background was pure Cold War intrigue, filled with tales of spiriting agents into Eastern Europe and training operatives for the shah of Iran. He always stood at the edge of some intrigue. Much later he told Stanley Karnow he had been approached to do the Watergate burglary that, through its bungling, led to the fall of Richard M. Nixon. "If I'd been involved," he said, "we would have done it right."

It was almost as difficult to dislike Conein as it was to trust him. Now in his forties, he was a bear of a man with a V-wedge hairline aimed at bushy eyebrows arching over eyes that twinkled mischievously before turning to ball-bearing steel. He used the embassy and an assignment as American liaison to Diem's Interior Ministry, or federal police, as his cover. The cover was as thin as tissue. Everyone knew he was a spy. But so murky and multilayered were the levels at which Conein worked that it made no difference. Sometimes openness is the best cover.

By this time the correspondents figured, accurately, that every telephone call they made was tapped. So they created code names for everyone. Two fingers were missing from one of Conein's hands, so he became "Mordecai," named after the turn-of-the-century Chicago Cubs pitcher, Three-Fingered Mordecai Brown.

7. The North Vietnamese learned this trick well and used it more effectively. During the 1968 Tet Offensive they dug up "graves" all over Saigon to retrieve arms for the assault on the city.

Tran Van Don had also been born in France, and had met Conein twenty years earlier while both were French soldiers. They had become so friendly that the Vietnamese general had a still different name for the CIA spy. Don called him Lulu.

At the Fourth of July party they hoisted champagne and told old war stories. But it was clear that Don had more on his mind. The two men retreated to a noisy downtown bistro where the music plugged other ears. There, very carefully, Don told Conein that he and other generals were plotting the overthrow of Diem. Would the Americans go along, or at least stay out of the way?

Don kept his information vague, Conein his answers more so. Both were in sensitive spots. Intrigue overlapped intrigue in Saigon now. Even by confiding in the wrong American Conein could pull the trigger on his old friend.

Lulu Conein was intrigued. This was his kind of ball game.

———

Halberstam always thought the Congo a more dangerous place than Vietnam. The warfare had been tribal and brutal, with a take-no-prisoners finality. A press card offered no protection, as Horst Faas discovered when he was forced to eat his, certain he was choking down his last meal. In Vietnam the correspondents went out under the protection of an army that did not want to engage the enemy, and faced an enemy disciplined enough to find no advantage in killing the *bao chi*, as the journalists were called.

Getting killed was an accident. The time still lay ahead when Vietnam would become, for reporters, the most dangerous war in history. In the vast sweep of the Second World War thirty-seven American correspondents were killed. By the end of the Vietnam War well over fifty foreign newsmen, including at least thirty-two Americans, would be dead. Precise numbers would seem easy to come by. But they aren't. The war was ambiguous. What were the qualifications? Killed in combat but not in plane crashes that may or may not have been caused by gunfire? Certainty? At the end, twenty were still missing in action. None ever came back. Should that last man, killed by the side he thought friendly, be included? Neither the first American, Robert Capa, nor the last correspondent killed in the American war, Paul Leandri of Agence France-Presse, make many lists. Capa was too early; Leandri took a bullet from a South Vietnamese cop.

It was the police who began to make the correspondents edgy as the Buddhists escalated their demonstrations into July and August, hot and steamy monsoon months that under the best of circumstances brought tempers to a raw edge. As the Buddhist crisis became more threatening, Diem seemed to slip into a summer spell, retreating deeper and deeper into his special world of self-made isolations. Not Brother Nhu and his fiery wife. To them the Buddhists, and the Americans, seemed a greater threat than the enemy in the field. With the United States pushing the palace as it never had before, Nhu began hinting publicly that he might seek an arrangement with the North Vietnamese and the Viet Cong. Better to stay in power with them than out with the Americans.

Meanwhile, Nhu's secret police, the Mat Vu, grew bolder. Most of their activities amounted to little more than half-comical penny-ante shenanigans. They bribed a Catholic priest to use the confessional to gain information from one of the girlfriends. They caused stories to disappear at the PTT, and held others up till they were no longer news. The phones became overloaded with so many taps that conversations became difficult, the tails so overt they clearly were meant to intimidate as much as to follow. Through the glass wall at 19 Ngo Duc Ke, Sheehan and Halberstam watched the agents lurk among the street crowds outside the office. In the oppressive heat they all wore the "trench coat" of a Saigon operative, a black leather jacket.

At first the two buddies responded in joyously sophomoric ways, using every B-movie counterespionage trick they could remember. They developed their "second-cab technique," always taking the second cab in line, assuming that the first was driven by one of their stalkers. They honed their relay system, taking one taxi to the crowded Central Market and suddenly leaping out, diving into the Asian mob and racing past the crowded stalls to the other side, where they leaped into another taxi. They did it with gusto and laughter, and Sheehan, the mimic, would do his Bogart imitation as he gave instructions to a driver who couldn't understand him anyway.

But the demonstrations, growing larger, more aggressive, and now taking in students and other protesters, were like a knife in the side of the family. At an embassy dinner with top officials of both governments one night in July, Mecklin watched Nhu get drunker and drunker, then leave well after midnight with a slurred rejoinder he had adapted from his wife: "If the Buddhists want to have another barbecue, I will be happy to supply the gasoline and the match." There would be no compromise.

As the street action heated up, Halberstam and Sheehan entertained an unlikely visitor. Allen Ginsberg, the Beat Generation poet, wandered into Sheehan's office in June and stayed for four days. Ginsberg became the guru laureate to two lost generations, first the Beats, then the hippies. As the antiwar protests grew large and powerful, he appeared at almost all, blessing the crowds with his monotonal mantra: "Ohmmmmmmmmmmmmmmmmmmmm." The reporters took Ginsberg to Xa Loi, where Duc Nghiep declared him not just a spy like the rest but a top-level CIA spy, so impressed was the Buddhist with the poet's long-hair, scraggly-beard disguise.

Ginsberg wasn't convinced that Vietnam was such a safe place. From Sheehan's office he wrote home to his lover. The scene "scairt" him, he confided; it was "like living in a mescaline nightmare." Reporters' nerves began to fray too. The tensions of the Buddhist crisis drained them more than the tensions of the war. They were overworked, hot, tired, tailed, bugged, never at total ease.

Three days after the Fourth of July party, about twenty plainclothes police cornered Mal Browne, the great offender at the burning of the bonze, and a handful of others in a small alleyway leading away from a Buddhist street demonstration. In June several newsmen, including Browne and Sheehan, had been detained and questioned for hours, and the petty harassments continued endlessly. But, until now, there had been no outright violence against the reporters.

Nhu's men first grabbed the smallest, Browne's AP colleague, Arnett. Always the story-first newsman, Browne shimmied up a telephone pole and began photographing the police as they knocked Arnett to the ground and began kicking him painfully with the pointed-toe shoes then in fashion in France. It was a dedication to duty that Arnett had some trouble appreciating in his boss until later. Battered and bleeding, unable to fight back, he suddenly felt a large hand hoist him up and away from the punishing shoes. At that moment Browne took his last photograph before the police hauled him down and smashed his odious Petri. But the film survived, and the last frame showed Halberstam, a head taller than anyone else, standing like a Sequoia between a badly battered Arnett and the police, his arm outstretched as if to stiff-arm the attackers. Arnett remembered the sound effects even better. Halberstam was growling. "Okay, you little sonsabitches," he challenged, "now you come after me."

That ended the fight but not the incident. Later that day the police collected Browne and Arnett from the office on the Rue Pasteur and took them to a safe house. They were told they would be arrested, although the interrogators remained vague about the charges. One charge would be assaulting two police officers, but hints ran heavy about considerably more serious offenses—organizing an illegal demonstration, or worse. The grilling was in French and Arnett winced when he heard the word *espionnage*.

That evening, after the pair's temporary release, the entire platoon of outraged Saigon correspondents stormed the embassy in search of help. They found none. Trueheart, skittish after six weeks of pressuring Diem, had pushed enough; Nolting would be back in a few days, and he would not add another protest now. He rebuffed the reporters. They never knew how badly. Mecklin had told Trueheart earlier that even Diem's press officers doubted the police account. But Trueheart had different doubts. He cabled Washington with a recommendation against a formal protest:

GIVEN EXTREME EMOTIONAL INVOLVEMENT OF CORRESPONDENTS THESE DAYS—AMOUNTING TO INTENSE HATRED OF ALL THINGS GVN, IN CERTAIN CASES—I WOULD NOT FEEL SURE ABOUT REFUTING POLICE.[8]

---

8. Trueheart was tired. Over the past six weeks his superiors at State had pushed him so hard to pressure Diem into putting a lid on Nhu, Madame Nhu, or both, he had just two days earlier sent them a one-line cable: TO NHU OR NOT TO NHU IS UP TO YOU.

The newsmen once again angrily cabled President Kennedy directly, accusing the Diem government of physical intimidation and the President's men of refusing them protection. Like their protest to the President over François Sully's expulsion, the action got them little satisfaction from the White House and plenty of trouble from their bosses.

Tokyo slapped Sheehan's wrist for trying to "make Unipress policy" on his own when "Unipress must be neutral, neither pro-Diem, pro-Communist or pro-anybody else." It added the usual brink-of-bankruptcy footnote: "Just received granddaddy of all downhold messages from New York."

Freedman starchily censured Halberstam: "We still feel that our correspondents should not be firing off cables to the President of the United States without authorization."

Another message came from *The Times.* "Dear David," wrote his buddy, Tom Wicker, who had begun covering the Kennedy White House,

> Please stop irritating those Vietnamese police and sending nasty notes to the President. He has got enough to do without being reminded of that mess over there. This is because the war is getting closer to home. There's a rising in Cambridge, Md., where our local Buddhists (Negroes) think they have been shut out of the pool long enough.

The next day the police pulled in Browne and Arnett and grilled them for five hours. A British Embassy official, acting on behalf of the New Zealand government, accompanied Arnett. No one accompanied Browne.

Again the reporters stormed the embassy, this time with Mecklin the target, and the four-letter words exploded like mortar rounds. Two months earlier, in his meeting with Kennedy, Mecklin had warned that the anti-press crusade could lurch out of control and prove deadly to long-term American interests. Now the angry shouts ricocheted through his office: He was a "gutless bastard" in a "cowardly government." So loud did the shouting become that another embassy officer finally rushed in, fearing Mecklin might be in physical danger. He wasn't, but his advice to Kennedy had been right: Events had run out of the control even of people who knew better. Mecklin blew sky-high.

Eventually, Secretary of State Rusk stepped in, instructing Trueheart to protest to the palace once again. By this time, however, the conniving Nhus smelled opportunity. They waited for Nolting, milking the incident for a week before the threats finally sank beneath the next crisis.

For a brief time after arriving in Vietnam, most of the correspondents had carried weapons in the field. With a few exceptions—Arnett loved his Mauser machine-pistol—they had stopped. Their reasons were simple. Captured with a weapon, making the case for their status as noncombatants might be a hard sell indeed. Second, only in an ambush would a weapon significantly improve their chances of survival. But why carry one for that eventuality? So many men went down in the first seconds that, if they survived that long, their choice of weapons would rest at their fingertips. Now, however, they began buying weapons for the city, although most were of mixed minds about it. Mert Perry bought a .25 caliber Beretta, the sight of which caused Sheehan to start giggling. The gun was so small it all but disappeared in the meat of Perry's huge hand. "Jesus, Mert," he laughed, "that's the kind of gun an actress is supposed to kill her lover with." Sheehan went out and paid a helicopter pilot $100 for a fancy, nickel-plated .38. Afterward, he stopped kidding Perry. He wasn't sure what made him more nervous, Brother Nhu's cops or his own gun.

In Washington, Kennedy's frustrations escalated with the bad-news headlines. During a visit by Canadian Prime Minister Lester Pearson, the President made an offhand request for advice about Vietnam. Pearson's reply was direct and seemingly simple: "Get out." Kennedy's wit and charm disappeared in a flash. "That's a stupid answer," the President snapped. "Everybody knows that. The question is: How?"

With the hottest part of the summer approaching, Halberstam wrote in *The Times* that Kennedy's nice little war had become a "tragicomedy."

13

Maggie and the
Rover Boys

Suddenly, everyone wanted a look. The ranks of the hard-core half-dozen often swelled to 100 or more, all wanting to drink tea at Xa Loi, all wanting to chopper out to report from the "front," all jauntily instructing the overworked army information officers to get them shot at but not shot. None arrived with quite the same thunderclap as Marguerite Higgins.

Maggie Higgins was no longer the girl wonder in a man's world, the audacious young woman who had captured German soldiers in the big war, assaulted Korea with such derring-do she became the darling of both the GIs and picture spreads in *Life* magazine, becoming the biggest celebrity in the game. In the summer of 1963 she was forty-two years old, that uncomfortable age through which so many reporters pass from young to old without pause for the middle years. She had not made a good passage. Married to an air force general, the reporter in her had hardened into a Cold War ideologue—"a fire-eating quote Commie-hater close quote," said Keyes Beech with a fondness not all shared. Having soared to celebrity's heights before turning thirty, she had developed an intolerance of youth that had calcified into obsession. "The young Rover Boys," she disparagingly called the Saigon correspondents, and she had her sights targeted on one well before she arrived.

By midsummer so many correspondents were traipsing through town that the United States Information Service had taken to posting their stories for all to read. The gang gathered around with great curiosity after Higgins landed in late July. As her stories went up on the board, the curiosity quickly turned to anger. *Jee-zuz*, Sheehan bristled, she's kissing all this off as "the invention of Machiavellian monks and gullible reporters." Halberstam seethed: "Four days on the ground and she's feeding people the whole line of crap."

Few of the Young Turks met Higgins during her stay in Vietnam. It was just as well. Ray Herndon was introduced to her one night at the Caravelle. She stared at him with a look of such disdain it stayed with him forever—"that withering so-you're-one-of-those-astigmatic-young-reporters look," he called it. Then she turned away. Peter Arnett saw her around town but knew her only through Halberstam's eyes: "Her name was never mentioned without him uttering the most awful epithets. He hated her viscerally." The feeling was mutual. She had fought an epic battle with Homer Bigart in Korea, a bitter war within a war that almost got them both killed. Now she would continue the scrap with Bigart's successor in Vietnam.

Beverly Deepe came away from the USIS bulletin board not angry but disillusioned. The twenty-six-year-old *Newsweek* stringer would marry a marine officer and live a life of *semper fi*. But she was also true to her own code and she took one look at her hero's stories and concluded that Higgins had sold out, become a propagandist. Deepe saw the famous correspondent just once in Vietnam, and was taken aback then too. The vivacious young woman, that pert blond in rolled-up khakis and tennis shoes who had leaped out of *Life*'s pages at a starstruck thirteen-year-old in Nebraska, had turned older than her forty-two years. She had gained too much weight. Gone was the sparkle the teenager had seen in her eyes. But it was more than that, Deepe thought. She looked mean and she looked sick. Watching her hero, she felt very sad. She didn't bother to introduce herself.

But to underestimate Maggie Higgins could be disastrous. If, like an aging ballplayer, she had lost her reporter's legs, she had also found a new playing field. Her home turf was now Washington, that strange city where, knowing the right people and making the right changes in your game, a reporter can play on bad pins forever. In the nation's capital she remained what she had always been—a holy terror with the most outrageous tactics in the business. "The firebug," McGeorge Bundy, the President's special assistant for National Security Affairs, called her, and he meant that Higgins would burn down a town to get the four-alarm story. She was the particular nemesis of *The New York Times*, the arch-rival of the dying but pesky *Trib*, and that role pleased her no end. She caused so much grief that *The Times* Washington Bureau established a "Maggie Higgins Hour." It began each night at 9 P.M., when the first edition of the *Herald Tribune* hit the streets in New York and the frenzied phone calls began arriving with orders to start chasing her exclusive stories.

Even in 1963 there was no one in American journalism quite like Higgins—and she would prove it all over again in Vietnam.

———

Keyes Beech didn't plan much. He liked to say he went through life just letting things happen. "One of the things that happened to me," he wrote later, "was Marguerite Higgins." She happened to a lot of people.

The year was 1950, and it had been a quiet spring in Tokyo. Five years after the end of the war in the Pacific, Americans showed little interest in a defeated nation methodically rebuilding itself with cheap cameras and tinny little cars without fins. Beech and the handful of American correspondents lingering in the Japanese capital passed their time with stories on the cherry blossoms and hope for action elsewhere on their far-flung Asian beats. Higgins arrived in April, demoted from her job as Berlin bureau chief to a duller and presumably safer (for the *Herald Tribune*) place. Thundering behind her was the wrath of almost everyone she had worked with. "She was a dangerous, venomous bitch," growled *Tribune* European correspondent Stephen White, "and a bad reporter." Julia Edwards, who first met Higgins at Columbia University in 1941 and later wrote *Women of the World: The Great Foreign Correspondents*, summed her up this way: "Big blue eyes, a high-pitched little girl's voice, and sex appeal were part of her arsenal. As a last resort, she used her head."

But Higgins had a way of having the last laugh. She was about to become the most famous, if also the most outrageous, woman foreign correspondent in history. And, even with her tail between her legs, she set off her customary seismic shock waves as she

landed in Tokyo. She arrived simultaneously with the publication
of a colleague's sensational novel entitled *Shriek With Pleasure.*

The book, Beech recalled, was about "a man-eating woman correspondent who, according to the author, another woman correspondent, acquired most of her stories by happily combining
business with pleasure." He continued: "Since the locale of this
bitchy little story was postwar Berlin and Higgins had just come
from Berlin, since the heroine was Irish and Higgins was unmistak-
ably an Irish name, and since the story ended with the unrepentant
heroine aboard an airplane for Tokyo, it was natural that Higgins's
arrival aroused more than ordinary interest in the press corps."

Beech was thirty-seven, Higgins twenty-nine. She was also a
willowy five foot eight, not quite beautiful, but pixieish and attractive in a way Hollywood had long since proved more beguiling
than perfection. The gritty ex-marine combat correspondent
needed her like he needed ten years of peace on the Pacific Rim.
But he had shared his Tokyo office with her *Herald Tribune* predecessor so he shared it with her, confident he could withstand her
wiles. He was right. She drove him nuts.

The first month she moped around, writing almost nothing,
complaining endlessly to the other correspondents about Tokyo's
boredom after the glamour of postwar Berlin. It did not endear her
to them. The second month she went to work. She followed Beech
everywhere, soaking up his sources, soaking up his stories too. For
Beech, it was like *Shriek With Pleasure* without the pleasure. By
June, Higgins had almost as many enemies in Tokyo as she did
in Berlin, and Beech began looking for another office. Then came
Korea.

What followed had the feel of predestination. The story of Marguerite Higgins always steered back toward war, always back toward Asia. Her parents met in a Paris bomb shelter during a First
World War German cannon assault, her mother stunningly French,
her father an adventuresome Irish-American aviator with no desire
to ever go home. She was born three years later in Hong Kong. At
six months she contracted a serious case of malaria, and the doctor
ordered her taken to the mountain city of Dalat in French Indochina. For her mother, it was a terrifying moment. Thirty years
earlier her father, the baby's grandfather, had served as an officer
in the French colonial forces in this land that later became Vietnam.

He contracted a rare tropical fever and died before she knew him. It was the beginning of an awful family haunting, yet to be played out fully. But little Marguerite recovered, establishing a lifelong tie to the land known to so few Americans. Many years later she would return to Dalat as the guest of the Ngo Dinh Nhus, who kept a treasured hunting lodge in the mountains near the city.

But nothing about Marguerite Higgins's life was predestined. Everything came through that unrelenting drive, that ambition so raw and unfettered it frightened and angered others, often because it rolled right over them.

By the time she reached school age, the dreams of her incurably romantic parents had faded into the reality of an Oakland bunga-low and the approaching depression. Theirs was the strangest household in the middle-class neighborhood, her father a redhead so full of Irish boyishness that his gallery of roguish First World War photos seemed to age faster than he did, her mother an exotic figure who simmered richly aromatic sauces in a tiny kitchen to which she retreated reluctantly in high heels and hair so blond you could almost read the label on the bottled assist. As the dream faded further, however, the Irish boyishness turned to drunken rampages, the exotic French flair to wild Gallic temper tantrums and fainting spells. It was a tough household for an only child.

Young Maggie made early discoveries, largely about boys. She also learned the downside of playing her game so openly. When she entered the University of California, she was blackballed by the sorority of her choice. It was the beginning of a lifelong pattern of public rebuffs and to-hell-with-it reactions. She didn't give a damn what the sorority sisters thought, or at least she never gave them the pleasure of showing it. Like Ben Bradlee, she donned her fuck-'em suit, no pun intended, and she wore it for life.

In 1942, at age twenty-two, Higgins talked her way into a reporter's job on the highly regarded *New York Herald Tribune.* Two years later she was en route to Europe as a correspondent. Behind her she left a badly battered first marriage and a series of encounters with men whose importance seemed to escalate with her profes-sional needs. With her she took a reputation as a young phenom who couldn't write. —"Her only limitation was literacy," wrote Richard Kluger in *The Paper,* a history of the *Trib.* But she reported as if she had been born to it. She stopped at nothing and scooped up everything. The *Trib* found the combination a bargain, especially when she proved shrewd enough to take as early lovers helpful men like Robert Shaplen, whose polished prose about Vietnam later graced *The New Yorker*, and John Watson, a heavy-drinking rewrite man who could turn the telephone book into poetry and was delighted to provide the service for the new young reporter.

But it was her reputation for perseverance, then ruthlessness, that grew the fastest. Shipping out to war, according to her biographer, Antoinette May, Higgins literally missed the boat. As the ship reached the outer edge of New York harbor, the pilot let down a rope ladder. Moments later, an astonished collection of GIs and a few correspondents watched a tall and slender young woman in full army uniform crawl back up. Her infantryman's helmet had skidded and blond hair spilled out everywhere. Janet Flanner of *The New Yorker* had never met Higgins. She felt an immediate urge to protect the young woman clinging so precariously to the side of the ship. A few years later she told friends: "If I'd know then what I know now, I'd have thrown her overboard."

Marguerite Higgins was not the first or only woman war correspondent, although she often made it seem that way. But, when she landed in England in September 1944, she invaded what remained very much a male tribal group. The war in Europe had only eight months to go. For more than six of them the men kept her chasing rearguard stories in London and Paris, not because she was Higgins but because she was a woman. When she made her breakout six weeks before the war ended, she did it with all the hell-bent zeal of a Patton.

Higgins learned quickly that transportation makes or breaks a war correspondent. The stories became legion of the lissome blond nuzzling up to pilots to hitch rides while other correspondents, and sometimes even the wounded, remained grounded. Higgins *always* got to go where she wanted to go. Her first coup gave her a plane and a jeep into Buchenwald just hours after Allied troops rolled back the veil hiding the madness of the Holocaust. But the real show came at Dachau, Hitler's original concentration camp. There the world caught its first glimpse of the Maggie Higgins whose exploits it would soon come to know.

Higgins was six miles away when she heard that American

forces were poised to take the camp. She commandeered a jeep and headed out in a beeline, even though the six miles still belonged to the Germans. With a reporter from *Stars and Stripes* driving, Higgins disarmed and accepted the surrender of dozens of retreating soldiers, quitting only when the jeep would carry no more captured weapons.

Nearing the camp, two jeeps carrying the advance guard of the American troops fell in behind the reporters. At the gate the American soldiers waited for their troops. Higgins and her colleague did not. The smell was overwhelming, but Higgins spotted a little courtyard planted primly with rows of budding roses. As she turned in for a look, her colleague screamed frantically at her, and she looked up at a watchtower. It was jammed with SS men, all of their weapons trained on her. As she wrote later, she had "the instinctive feeling there was absolutely no point in running." Instead, she shouted up to them: *"Kommen Sie hier, bitte,"* and they came—twenty-two SS men surrendering to a twenty-four-year-old woman from Oakland. After Dachau, no one ever said Maggie Higgins didn't have the guts to go with her gall.

The *Herald Tribune* led its paper with two sensational stories the next day—one from Dachau and one from Berlin, where Adolf Hitler had committed suicide. For Marguerite Higgins the war had lasted just six weeks, but she had ended it with a flourish.

Higgins would stay on in Germany five more years, becoming Berlin bureau chief at age twenty-six and covering the first eyeball-to-eyeball confrontation of the Cold War, the Berlin blockade and airlift. But she needed a hot war. Her pettiness got worse, her other antics too. She'd cop a story from a *Herald Tribune* colleague as quickly as she would from an arch-foe at *The Times*. James P. O'Donnell of *Newsweek* once decided to teach her a lesson. He set up a flawless sting, leaving a copy of one of his stories where Higgins couldn't miss seeing it. That night, very close to her deadline, they met at a party. What have you been working on? Higgins asked coyly. One helluva story, O'Donnell replied. Then he shook his head. His sources had backed out and he had been forced to kill it. Higgins paled and bolted from the room, cabling New York an urgent message to kill her story. The press run had already begun, making it neither an easy nor inexpensive chore. Meanwhile, O'Donnell had given the story to *The New York Times*; Higgins's editors read it there later that night. ARE YOU DRINKING? they cabled her angrily. She almost got fired.

Meanwhile, her sexual adventures escalated. The ultimate conquest became Major General Wilson Hall, the army's chief of intelligence during the Soviet blockade. But this one had a twist. Hall and Higgins fell in love. It was messy. Hall had his life-or-death secrets to protect *and* a wife and four children in the States. Eventually, they would be married. But that would have to wait until Marguerite Higgins had become the most famous woman war correspondent in history.

From Tokyo, Higgins and Beech made it into Seoul on the first plane carrying correspondents and the last to land ahead of the invading North Koreans.

Stunned by the surprise attack, the city didn't last the night. Beech, along with two other correspondents, made it out in a jeep he had grabbed at the airport. Higgins went with an American colonel. Ahead of them the South Korean defenders ran at full stride, throwing away their weapons as they went. They also blew bridges, one of which exploded in Higgins's face and cut off her retreat. She tried to make it across the river in an overloaded boat, which sank in water roiling with the spatter of North Korean bullets. She swam the rest of the way, then walked fourteen miles to safety amid South Korean refugees staring curiously at a tall, blond woman wearing a navy blue skirt and flowered blouse she had worn to the office the previous morning in Tokyo.

When she found Beech, she was mad as hell. But she had a better story than he did, and the *Trib* screamed it across page one under the headline:

SEOUL'S FALL BY A REPORTER WHO ESCAPED

Also on the front page was a one-and-a-half column picture of a "girl correspondent" looking very blond, very young, and very vulnerable. Soon, the photos would be widened to two columns.

Still, Higgins rarely strayed far from Beech's jeep again. Beech never had any doubt about the value of his wheels. "I would have killed to keep that jeep," he said. She had no doubt about its value, either. He shared his jeep and she shared her sleeping bag. It was the kind of deal both understood. Neither had any illusions about their odd relationship. But the crusty ex-marine grew fond of the woman who had begun to drive him crazy in Tokyo. "She was the best combat buddy I ever had," he said years later, and he meant that Higgins would pull him out of a jam as well as any man. At one point the army tried to kick her out of the country. In the military mind of the fifties, a war was no place for a woman. "I couldn't agree more," Beech said. "But it's all right for Higgins."[1]

The army wasn't alone in trying to banish Higgins. A week into the war, Homer Bigart arrived. He was already the best in the business and the *Trib*'s certified superstar as well, not yet having gone over to *The Times*. Marguerite Higgins would make him even better, and he would never forgive her for it. She felt the same way about him. They drove each other to risks that should have gotten them both killed, as most of the correspondents in Korea thought would happen. "As soon as Homer kills off Maggie or Maggie kills off Homer," said Tom Lambert of AP, "the competition will wane and so will the coverage of the Korean War." The beneficiary was the *Trib*, whose war coverage outclassed all others. *The Times* launched a virtual armada to counteract the feuding team, but to no avail. "Why are Homer and Maggie beating our asses off?" Hanson Baldwin asked Beech in exasperation. "That's easy," Beech responded. "They hate each other."

The two spoke just twice through the duration of the war, the first time moments after Bigart arrived. Not known for his diplomatic touch, Bigart ordered her back to Tokyo forthwith. The dialogue came from a B-grade Western.

"This is a small place," Bigart said. "There is no room for both of us. I will handle it alone."

Higgins jabbed her chin at him in stubborn refusal.

"You will leave," Bigart said, "or you will be fired."

She did not and she was not. The *Herald Tribune* knew when it had a good thing going. In addition to the feud that drove them, the newspaper had two correspondents whose starkly different styles complemented each other ideally.

1. General MacArthur apparently agreed as well. He personally countermanded the order after an outraged howl from the *Herald Tribune* and a personal plea from Higgins, for whom the seventy-year-old general had taken a liking.

Bigart's writing flowed seamlessly and elegantly. He was literary on deadline. "The fatal element in our defeat was a ground fog that rose quickly at dawn," began one of his first stories. The risk-taking began with that story too. He covered it from a foxhole. Only two other correspondents observed the battle. Both were killed, the first to die in Korea. The brushes with death became almost mystical. Richard Tregaskis watched Bigart go alone over a front-line hill and wondered aloud how he could possibly hope to make it back. On one frigid night that winter Bigart slept with two GIs in a foxhole so far advanced that they could hear the chatter of the Chinese who, by then, had entered the war. At dawn Bigart crept out to look around. Moments later he returned and both his companions were dead, killed in their sleep by an incoming mortar.

Higgins could not approach Bigart's writing beauty. But she had a remarkable eye, a penchant for the sensational—"There was only the burbling of blood on the shredded lips as he gasped hard, his breath forming red bubbles"—and a tendency to inject herself into the story. Bigart found her ways objectionable. Readers loved it. The *Trib* exploited it. And in bravery—or, as some saw it in both of them, stubborn foolhardiness—she held her own with Bigart every perilous inch of the way through one of the most miserable and dangerous wars America ever fought.

In September 1950 MacArthur decided to gamble with gaining back all he had lost with a landing at a forbidding beach known as Inchon. The Inchon landing became the largest amphibious assault since Normandy, and Higgins outmaneuvered both the U.S. Navy and Bigart to place herself in the midst of the bloodiest fighting. The navy tried to keep her safely on a hospital ship. Instead, as the landing began, Bigart found himself trapped aboard one of the command ships, unable to go ashore. Higgins had wangled her way onto a troopship and went in with the fifth wave, the first one seriously opposed by the surprised enemy. She was immediately trapped with thirty marines behind a rocky seawall down which the North Koreans began rolling hand grenades. At high tide the beach was so narrow the platform door of a following landing craft landed on two of the marines, crushing their legs. She came out of it unhurt, with a story that drubbed Bigart. She did less well with the navy. When she returned to her ship to file her story, the brass was furious. They immediately banned all women, which meant

Higgins, from the ships between 9 P.M. and 9 A.M. That was the only time the correspondents wanted to be aboard—to file their stories and get a good night's sleep. For the remaining days at Inchon Higgins handed her copy to Keyes Beech each night, then slept on the cold dock while the men bedded down in a dry bunk and awoke to a hot breakfast the next morning.

Incidents like that, together with Bigart's refusal to acknowledge her existence, gained Higgins some sympathy for the first time in her professional life. Bigart took a terrible hazing. The other correspondents paid Korean children to stand outside his tent chanting, "Homer loves Maggie," and coined a jingle to the tune of "Lilli Marlene":

Marguerite Higgins
Telephones the news,
She gets exclusive
Front-line interviews
While Homer crawls
Through rice fields wet
To scrounge some stuff
That she can't get. . . .

All this drove Bigart ever harder. But Higgins had a way of quickly dissipating favor among her colleagues. The stories about bumping wounded GIs raged on, as did other offenses. In the made-for-Hollywood story of Marguerite Higgins, it became difficult to separate fact from fiction. But when *Time* magazine cabled its correspondent, asking for a story about "the woman correspondent with an innocent face," he wired back: INNOCENT AS A COBRA.

The second and last conversation between the two *Trib* aces took place on a dusty Korean road and also had the feel of a cheap Western. Beech refereed, asking Bigart if he would talk to Higgins about a minor problem. The old pro paused a moment, then replied, "I don't see why not." With that, the two approached each other like wary gunfighters, exchanged a few words, turned, and never spoke again. Several years later, when a friend told Bigart that Higgins had given birth to her first child, he replied: "That's wonderful. Who's the m-m-mother?"

Homer Bigart came out of the war almost unanimously acclaimed the greatest war correspondent of his time. But Marguerite Higgins came out famous. In Korea, bedraggled GIs waved and cheered as her jeep drove by. Correspondents riding with her occasionally waved back, then sheepishly realized what Jimmy Cannon of the *New York Post* had long since concluded: "Riding in a jeep with Maggie is like being a jockey on Lady Godiva's horse."

In October, four months after she arrived, *Life* hit the streets, the barbershops, the doctors' offices, and the living rooms of America with its reserved-for-starlets picture spread on the heroic "girl correspondent" who "still manages to look attractive" while she digs in with the boys. Movie offers and book deals poured in. To her credit, Higgins stuck out the bitter winter and the terrible frozen retreat back down the Korean peninsula. That year, a record six Pulitzer prizes were awarded for foreign correspondence. Among the winners were Bigart, Beech, and Higgins, the first woman to win as a war correspondent.

With Korea, Marguerite Higgins had become a full member of the tribe, and few men had earned their ribbons more courageously. But she would never be far from controversy. It was a rich and storied lot she had joined, its ranks over the years including propagandists, opportunists, rogues, and a few out-and-out scoundrels as well as a long list of folk heroes, from William Howard Russell to Ernest Hemingway and Richard Harding Davis to Edward R. Murrow. Some reveled in war, others wept at its tragic waste. Young Winston Churchill covered the Boer War as an aristocratic horseman carrying both pen and pistol, concluding of the experience: "Nothing in life is so exhilarating as to be shot at without result." Ernie Pyle moved in closer on the men forced to live each day on oblivion's edge and took a different view. "If I hear one more GI say, 'Fuck my shit,' I'll blow my brains out," Pyle said shortly before a Japanese sniper's bullet did it for him. "Fuck my shit. That's what war adds up to."

Perhaps because she felt she had to be more like the men than the men themselves, Maggie Higgins came out of Korea with more of Churchill's flourish than Ernie Pyle's pain. If she could find a man as exciting as war, she confided to a friend, she would marry him. In 1952 she married the general from the Berlin airlift, Bill Hall. The fifties were a jingoistic time. But few could surpass Higgins in super-patriot bombast. She unhesitatingly advocated

the use of the atomic bomb against China. Of Communism, she
wrote:

> There may be strategic halts in the Communist-armed expan-
> sion, halts of several years. The Third World War is on. It
> began in Korea, and I'm glad the first battles I covered were
> so far from San Francisco and New York.

In 1963 it was clear to her that Vietnam had become the next
battleground in the defense of San Francisco. She had chafed at the
smart-alecky Vietnam reporting of her old foe, Homer Bigart. Now
his young disciples, "you arrogant upstarts," she told Mal Browne,
were running out of control.

———

Fritz Nolting also returned to Vietnam in July, just in time to deal
with the impasse over the threatened arrest of the two AP men,
Mal Browne and Peter Arnett.

During his ill-timed six-week absence, the city had taken on the
feel of a fortress under siege. At Gia Long Palace concertina wire
twisted through the bougainvillea like a deadly parasite, forming a
barricade behind which Diem, Nhu, and Madame Nhu isolated
themselves. In their palace talks about the correspondents, Nolting
had more trouble than ever keeping Diem focused. But Nhu, as
secret-police chief, seemed more than happy to keep Nolting, the
American government, and the two reporters twisting slowly in
the wind. More than a week passed—two weeks since the event—
before the trumped-up charges were dropped.

Meanwhile, President Kennedy dispatched yet another expert to
look at the press problem: Robert J. Manning, a former newsman
who had joined the administration as assistant secretary of state for
public affairs. Manning, who stayed in Saigon for four days, got
the credit for ending the impasse, Nolting another humiliation.

During his lame-duck month, nothing went right for the hapless
ambassador. Three more Buddhists committed fiery suicides.
American newspapers began running photo montages, pairing images of burning monks against dying American soldiers. In *The
Times*, Halberstam quoted an American colonel telling a departing

captain: "You're going home just in time. This whole place is collapsing."

Diem insisted on naming an outlying hamlet after the ambassador as a farewell gesture. It was a genuinely bad idea, certain to target the villagers for attack. Even Nolting resisted. But, as he had throughout, the ambassador acquiesced rather than insult his government's tottering client. The result became grotesquely symbolic. On the eve of the ceremony, an American helicopter accidentally strafed the hamlet, wounding six peasants. The next day a truck in the caravan escorting Nolting to the event struck and injured a small boy. The AP team he had rescued on his return inadvertently added bizarre insult to unending injury. AP sent out a botched first report that Nolting's car had run down the youngster and killed him. The story was quickly corrected. But Nolting left further convinced of what he had been convinced all along: a small, unruly, and irresponsible press corps was wrecking U.S. policy. He also left reminded once more of the warning a friend had given him more than two years earlier: Vietnam was a benighted place that, as the French had learned, "puts a blight on everyone who touches it."

The blight stayed with Nolting for the rest of his life. He died a bitter man, bitter about his sense of his government's capriciousness, about what he unrealistically considered his friend Trueheart's disloyalty, bitter mostly about the press and Halberstam's "drops of acid" in *The Times*. But Nolting had been a man disserved at the beginning, disconnected at the end. Robert Shaplen of *The New Yorker* recalled a conversation in which the ambassador had wished aloud that the correspondents would not take the American tradition of a free press so literally. It made his job so difficult, he said.

Meanwhile, Manning's brief visit produced some other fireworks. Brother Nhu gave him a blunt assessment of the correspondents' goals:

"These young reporters want nothing less than to make a new government," he bitterly told the American. "This is an exalting ambition, a stimulating pastime for three or four of them to get together to overthrow a government and create another."

Manning rushed to assure Nhu that "the nature of the American commitment" would not be made by "journalists either in Vietnam or elsewhere." In his private report to Kennedy, however, Manning came close to agreeing about the correspondents' motivations:

> The correspondents reflect unanimous bitterness toward, and contempt for, the Diem government. They unanimously maintain that the Vietnamese program cannot succeed unless the Diem regime (cum family) is replaced; this conviction, though it does not always appear in their copy, underlies all the reports and analyses of the correspondents.

None of the correspondents would have taken offense at that. They had become total and unabashed advocates. "Halberstam and I and the other reporters had seized on the Buddhist crisis as we had on Ap Bac," Sheehan wrote later. "We had been holding it up as proof that the regime was as bankrupt politically as it was militarily."

Pierre Salinger, rarely known for his devotion to journalistic purity as Kennedy's press secretary, expressed outrage at the blatant activities of the reporters. "It is a deep question of reportorial ethics whether the destruction of a government is within the legitimate framework of journalistic enterprise," he wrote later.

But was it so far out of the realm of journalistic tradition? Or only recent tradition?

The great British war correspondent, William Howard Russell, had not only brought down a government, he had brought down his *own* government. He had come home a hero from the Crimea, where he had given British readers the fool's tragedy of the Charge of the Light Brigade, the enduring heroism of Florence Nightingale, the horror of unprepared soldiers freezing in the Russian winter. So he came home a hero to the people but not to the British commander who was sacked, not to Queen Victoria or Prince Albert who condemned him as "that miserable scribbler," not to the secretary of war who, going down with the government, wrote the army that it should lynch him before he escaped the battle zone.

Ten years after Halberstam and Sheehan, two other young journalists would bring down an American president. Were they working outside the "legitimate framework of journalistic enterprise?" Or were Halberstam and Sheehan, Browne, Arnett, Charley Mohr, merely the pathfinders for a generation, the beginning of a long overdue pendulum swing? The press had been marching in lock-step with its government for a long while.

As to the United States government, aside from Conein's in-trigues, the cables show it wobbling all over the place. It was as if the policy were awaiting the arrival of Nolting's replacement.

A handsomely graying man with the chiseled features of a north-eastern blue blood and impeccable credentials from the American establishment, a Boston Brahmin bred into a historic family rivalry with the Irish upstarts of the Kennedy clan, Henry Cabot Lodge seemed the perfect political replacement for Nolting. Twice John Kennedy and Lodge had met in epic political contests, Kennedy winning both. First, in 1952, Kennedy dethroned him from a Massa-chusetts Senate seat held by his father before him. Then, in 1960, Kennedy beat him again when Lodge ran as Richard Nixon's vice-presidential running mate. With Kennedy's 1964 reelection cam-paign approaching, what better choice could the President make? Lodge remained unassailably Republican and eminently acceptable among the guardians of post–Second World War foreign policy. He gave Kennedy's shaky Vietnam policy a nicely bipartisan halo. If the halo lost it luster, the thorns could be shared too.

Lodge was also shrewd and tough. Maybe too shrewd and tough. Thich Duc Nghiep had him pegged immediately. "I don't think that Mr. Cabolodge"—he pronounced it like camouflage—"will be President Diem's cup of tea."

———

On arriving, Marguerite Higgins did what every visiting reporter did in the summer of 1963. She went to Xa Loi.

A banner draped across one wall of the courtyard caught her eye first: YOUTH OF VIETNAM FOLLOW RESOLUTELY IN THE FOOTSTEPS OF THICH QUANG DUC!

"Isn't it illegal to incite to suicide?" she asked her Vietnamese interpreter.

"Perhaps," he replied, his voice a shrug.

Next she met Thich Duc Nghiep, the Buddhist spokesman.

"Ah, Miss Higgins," he began in the herky-jerky, boola-boola fashion now familiar to the Saigon correspondents, "you are from New York. How is the play?"

"Play?" she asked innocently. "Did you have some particular play—drama—in mind?"

"No, no, Miss Higgins," he said, his hands busily drawing headlines in the air on a make-believe front page.

Duc Nghiep had been surrounded by Western newsmen for almost two months. But Higgins found this use of journalistic jargon remarkably sophisticated and a dead giveaway of the frail twenty-four-year-old monk's astonishing ability to manipulate the press.

Next the monk eyed the press pass hanging around her neck. WHITE HOUSE, it announced boldly. It was all the evidence needed by Duc Nghiep that Higgins was not only a spy but a superspy, and a most valuable one. The next day she received an urgent call at the Caravelle Hotel to return to Xa Loi for an audience with the new Buddhist leader, Thich Tri Quang.

Tri Quang was the forty-five-year-old bonze from Hue who had perplexed the U.S. consul with his enigmatic sky-is-blue replies. Since then, he had elbowed aside the older and more moderate Buddhist leaders in Saigon, escalating the movement's militancy. He also thought Higgins was a spy, and wanted her to carry a message to her boss.

"Thich Tri Quang rarely sees correspondents," Duc Nghiep said as he introduced Higgins to the bonze. "But since you represent the White House. . . ."

"I don't *represent* the White House," Higgins protested. "I am *accredited* to the White House."

"Precisely," Duc Nghiep smiled. Tri Quang nodded sagely.

Tri Quang then explained that the Buddhists were worried that Kennedy remained too close to Diem's repressions.

"It would be most unwise for President Kennedy to appear to be associated with Diem's actions," Tri Quang said. "There will be many more immolations. Not just one or two, but ten, twenty, maybe fifty. President Kennedy should think about these things. These events will blacken President Kennedy's reputation. . . ."

"Are you asking me to blackmail the President of the United States with this threat?" Higgins bristled.

"Not at all," the bonze said serenely.

Isolated in their pagodas, the conspiratorial Buddhists may have understood the role of the Cold Warrior journalist better than Higgins. After she returned to Washington, she passed on Tri Quang's message to Kennedy personally.

You didn't have to read between the lines to get Maggie Higgins's drift in the stories she sent home. The Buddhists became "riot-prone" with "monks rampaging through the streets," Xa Loi Pagoda "a center of political and wholly irreligious excitement" that strayed "far from offering the soothing harmonies of meditation and mysticism." The pagoda's "unrelenting mimeograph machines ground out the propaganda," and from its little back rooms the orders "went out to the suicide squads." What did the Buddhists want? she asked. "Diem's head," she answered, "and not on a silver platter but wrapped in an American flag." Tri Quang was demonized. "Machiavelli with incense," she wrote. "Deep, burning eyes stared out from a gigantic forehead . . . an air of massive intelligence, total self-possession, and brooding suspicion." As to the war, "the tragic irony of Vietnam today is that its world-wide image is being tarnished at a time when the war is going better than ever." She had made that decision before she left Washington.

On the advice of Robert Kennedy, she had been briefed in the Pentagon by Marine Major General Victor Krulak. At five foot five, Brute Krulak was the shortest general in the history of the marines, half the reason for his unusual nickname. The marines' leading counterinsurgency expert, he had become a favorite of the Kennedys. The relationship dated back to the Second World War, when a young navy lieutenant named Jack Kennedy used PT Boat 109 to rescue some of Krulak's men in the South Pacific.

Krulak had just returned from Vietnam, flush with the usual optimism. Progress was so clear, he wrote in his report to the Joint Chiefs, that "the shooting part of the war is moving to a climax" and the United States could start thinking about withdrawing some of its forces. Krulak made some other observations:

> . . . What is needed is a few venturesome newsmen who are willing to forego the comforts of the city and endure a little mud and discomfort. Those so inclined would be rewarded with a picture of resolution and progress which they would not quickly forget.

Briefing Higgins, Krulak made the same pitch. It was music to her ears.

349

Now, in Vietnam, she headed for the delta, happy to be rid of the incense of Xa Loi. She began thumping the Krulak line. The Saigon correspondents became "typewriter strategists" who were "seldom at the scenes of battle." For the rest of the summer it became the theme song of most of the old guard. These tyros wouldn't get their boots muddy, preferring to cover the shooting war from the bar of the Caravelle Hotel.

Young blood boiled. Even Higgins's old buddy, Keyes Beech, couldn't buy the line. "It was a goddamned lie," he said. The Buddhist crisis had indeed tied them to Saigon for much of the summer. Sheehan could still feel Tokyo's lash for straying at the wrong time. They grumbled that their new critic had spent three weeks in the country without being shot at in anger. The biggest story in the delta in the summer of 1963 was that you couldn't find a battle. She drove them to fits, and so did her gossipy tongue. They were tired and thin-skinned, and Maggie Higgins was irascible. They avoided her like the plague. But she planted little bomblets certain to find their way back to her targets.

One person who didn't duck Higgins was Charley Mohr. Mohr talked to everybody, one of the reasons he was such an extraordinary reporter. He charmed people, flattered them, diverted them with his humor. Sheehan's aide, Nguyen Ngoc Rao, loved him so much that he squealed excitedly each time he heard that Mohr was arriving: "Mister Charleymohr is coming! Mister Charleymohr is coming!" Even Madame Nhu fell under his charm. When one of his stories criticized her, she refused to believe he had done it. "It was the rewrite," she said. "I know it wasn't that nice Mr. Mohr."

One night in early August Mohr took Higgins to dinner at L'Amiral, a favored French restaurant behind the Caravelle that flew in fresh strawberries and artichokes from Dalat. Mohr came straight out about his own turnabout. "Anything—even a military junta— would be better than Diem," he told her. Higgins fired straight back: "Reporters here would like to see us lose the war to prove they're right," she said.

Higgins later denied using the words. But Mohr had no doubt. He quoted her in *Time*.

———

Meanwhile, the trouble in the streets escalated. More than one hundred Buddhist nuns were arrested for protesting in front of Nolting's residence. Police beat and arrested eighty in downtown Saigon. Pagodas were sealed off with barbed wire, and Nhu ordered the police to use further force. Still, the protests grew. Seven thousand crowded in and around Xa Loi to hear speeches urging new protests. Students joined in the street demonstrations, pitting the children of some of Saigon's most influential families against the Diem government. On July 30 crowds of sixty thousand staged protests in Saigon and four other cities. The police roundups intensified. University students and schoolchildren, sons and daughters of the bourgeoisie, began disappearing in the middle of the night.

Diem seemed lost. Chester Bowles met with him on his way to India, where he would become the new ambassador. His impression, he reported, was "of a man quite remote from reality."

Diem tried to make concessions but they came too late, and the Nhus undermined him at each turn. On August 3, Nhu threatened to crush Xa Loi Pagoda, and his wife told her paramilitary women that the Buddhists were guilty of treason and murder. On August 4, Pope Paul asked Diem not to ignore Buddhist rights. On August 5, another Buddhist burned himself to death. American servicemen, many of them billeted in apartments and hotels downtown, began cheering the demonstrators and showering garbage on the police.

The Buddhist leadership began fortifying Xa Loi. Duc Nghiep brought out half a dozen young monks to demonstrate the defense tactics. They lined up and fired their weapons—cans of bug spray. Other Buddhist weapons, Sheehan reported, included "grenades of salt and pepper wrapped in papers, pans of chili sauce and cans filled with lemon juice, red peppers and curry powder." The Buddhists would win by losing.

—

As July rolled ominously into August, the diplomatic and military arms of the American government headed for a ferocious showdown. All that held them together was their mutual belief that the war was still being won. "The military situation is steadily improving," Bowles wrote in the same assessment in which he concluded that Diem had lost touch. The military argued with

351

increasing passion, almost frenzy, as the political crisis grew, that the war was progressing *so* well it would be folly to tinker with a winning proposition. Harkins insisted that the war could be over by December.

But was it all a chimera?

To the correspondents, Horst Faas was the thermometer. Halberstam sometimes called him the best reporter in the group, the one who ventured farthest from the command and closest to the grunt. He distrusted the brass. They were the ones who got the little guy killed. "In civilian clothes all generals look small," he told Halberstam. Faas grew bored "sitting around waiting for Buddhists to burn themselves." So, through the summer, he was the only one going out regularly with the Vietnamese grunts.

It was easy to misunderstand Faas. All photographers elbow their way into position, and he was beefy, Germanic, and always searching for the bang-bang. He once went to battle wearing the slogan: "Do you want to live forever?" But Horst Faas did. Earlier in the summer he got in trouble with the Americans, who accused him of *leading* a Vietnamese Ranger unit. Tired and hungry, the Rangers had come upon a minefield and decided to work their way through it. Faas told them it was a foolish idea. Go around it, he said. Word went back that Faas had led them around it. He did not. He *followed* them.

Faas had not forgotten his run-in with Higgins in the Congo. Deep in the African bush, Higgins had played her oldest game, cozying up to the pilot of Faas's plane. Faas got bumped. Later, Higgins had the misfortune to find herself confined in a small Stanleyville elevator with the photographer. He grabbed her by the shoulders and shook her, roaring: "If you ever do this to me again, I will have you shot." Then he let her go, and added: "Or something." Higgins spiced up her next story with an account of an attack by a brutal German in the heart of darkest Africa.

Now, what Higgins was writing about the war, and what the brass was saying, didn't make any sense to him at all. When he came home to the villa, he told Halberstam how the war had changed in mere months. The Viet Cong had stepped up from company action to battalion action and then to the first regimental-force attack.

At dusk one day while Higgins took upbeat briefings in a delta command tent, Faas moved through high grass nearby with an ARVN platoon. Suddenly, it was hit by VC using automatic weapons. In minutes one third of the platoon lay dead in the ambush. He and the others struggled through swamps the rest of the night before finding a friendly outpost at dawn. It was impossible to convince Faas that the war was going well.

At about the same time, Mert Perry got word of a delta battle in which eleven helicopters were hit. In Saigon the next day, Neil Sheehan met the battle's American adviser. For the first time the guerrillas had a larger force than his 300-man battalion, the adviser told him. They also had more automatic weapons. The Viet Cong kept his men pinned down all day, breaking off as usual at night. If the Viet Cong had not followed their old habit, the adviser told Sheehan, they would have overrun his men.

Sheehan had another account. The last time he had been in the delta the outfit he was with had engaged in a brief skirmish that resulted in only a few bloodstains. The American adviser shrugged and called in a body count of four. Sheehan arrived back in Saigon just as the afternoon briefing began. Twenty-nine dead, forty-seven wounded, the briefer said. Sheehan stared at him until the man's eyes broke away. Then he let out an angry stage whisper—"Shit!" —and walked out of the room. Halberstam needed little convincing. Before the Buddhist crisis, he had reported the new ARVN habit of fighting sham battles and claiming victories. What could have changed, with Diem more worried than ever?

Entering their third month with the Buddhists, the reporters were exhausted and emotionally drained. Duc Nghiep ran on his own monkish regimen, rising at 4 A.M. to begin his calls, and he was full of more false alarms than a kid who liked fire trucks.

The stress was worst for Sheehan. Tokyo let up about Browne's photo exclusive, but other lacings continued without relief. In one brief period in July, Earnie Hoberecht sent a two-page letter henpecking him about "wasting" $9.36 and a three-page "Salesmanship Memo No. 3" explaining how to use the "pleasure motive" and the "desire-to-avoid-fear" motive to perform his other duties, selling and collecting. Hoberecht, however, had tried to give Sheehan some manpower. After bouncing Herndon back to Laos, he sent Sheehan an Australian who had an emotional breakdown and an American with whom he had a blazing personality conflict.

Sheehan was developing a tic, insomnia, and a hair-trigger response to slights from Tokyo.

In late July, Halberstam wrote Manny Freedman about receiving a visa extension through mid-October, adding: "I'm very tired (not a day off for two months) and frankly I long for the simple days of walking thru rice paddies." He also wanted back into the field because Maggie Higgins was traipsing around the country "taking dictation from Harkins," as he put it, and contradicting everything he reported.

Perry, Sheehan, and Halberstam made a deal. None of them could afford to abandon the Buddhist story. It was cresting. It could bring down Diem, and they would help it bring down Diem. They did not delude themselves about their goals. The Buddhist crisis had become the second half of their personal offensive. But now, seven months after Ap Bac, Harkins and his military still held on to the illusion that the war was being won. The reporters would have to disprove that all over again.

It was the kind of raw-boned advocacy that in 1963 shook cages. Decades later the debate would still rage in military seminars and government think tanks and at media roundtables examining the tactics of the first young correspondents in Saigon. Few asked, however, how well the interests of the American people were served by the tactics of a Marguerite Higgins, a Joe Alsop, a Richard Tregaskis.

But now, Perry, Sheehan, and Halberstam pooled their resources, covering for each other as they ducked out for a day here, a day there, to get the story in the delta. They had no doubt about what they'd find, and they found it.

—

Near the end of her visit, but not the end of her troublemaking, Higgins met with Madame Nhu at Gia Long. Midway through the interview she asked herself: How many hours have the President of the United States, the Secretary of State, and the American ambassador to Vietnam spent trying to silence this slip of a woman? Amid more talk about barbecues, Higgins concluded: Many hundreds, surely.

On that, Higgins was correct. The U.S. government, unable to muzzle the Vietnamese First Lady, now seemed driven to get her out of the way. Even as Higgins prepared for her interview, Undersecretary of State Ball cabled Nolting to talk with Diem once more and convince him: REMOVE MME NHU FROM SCENE, adding: WE HAVE IN MIND ACTION SIMILAR TO THAT TAKEN IN THE EARLY YEARS OF THE DIEM REGIME WHEN SHE SENT TO HONG KONG CONVENT. The next day President Kennedy was brought up to date: "The Department has instructed Nolting to go back to Diem and suggest to him that Madame Nhu . . . should be sent out of the country. In the meantime Madame Nhu has issued another blast, which is carried on the front page of the government newspaper, 'Times of Vietnam.' " Nolting had been put through these paces so many times with so little luck that he waited three days before answering. "Fact is," he finally cabled back, "Madame Nhu is out of control of everybody—her father, her mother, husband, and brother-in-law." That was quite a list. It included, in order, South Vietnam's ambassador to the United States, its emissary to the United Nations, the head of its secret police, and the country's president.

So, the incorrigible First Lady went right on talking. She even gave an interview to Halberstam, and in the doing left the impression that the more she disliked someone, the better story she gave him. The American Embassy, she began, had "threatened and blackmailed" her government to "shut me up." It wouldn't work. As for the annoying Buddhists, "I would beat the bonzes ten times more." Then she would "ignore them, so if they burn thirty women we shall go ahead and clap our hands. We cannot be responsible for their madness."

The Times editorial page went into shock, an editorial condemning her as "Lucretia Borgia Nhu."[2] The use of such inflammatory language outraged Madame Nhu. In a letter to the editor, she scolded the newspaper for its "gratuitously and unnecessarily insulting editorial . . . the tone of which amazes me." Didn't the great newspaper understand? The world had fallen under "a mad spell" and needed her "electroshock to resume its senses."

It was almost a relief when *Time* published an August 9 cover

2. Even *The Times* editorial board, however, bought into the line that the war progressed well despite the political crisis. The editorial cited "what seems definite progress in South Vietnam's struggle against the Viet Cong recently."

story on "The Queen Bee," fortified by eight hours of interviews between Madame Nhu and her favorite reporter. "I have told you things I have never told anyone else," the First Lady burbled, and the publisher's column of the newsmagazine was topped by a photograph of Charley Mohr, the raconteur, asking a question that brought Beautiful Spring to a hand-clapping giggle of delight. For Mohr, she even reduced the number of swats she would give the Buddhists from ten times more to a mere three.

The correspondents loved his original file. It was a massive piece —one hundred pages written and reported so well, Halberstam thought, it could have been published as a small, perceptive book. In New York it was honed down and rewritten—that was the only way *Time* did business—by a promising and talented young staffer named John Gregory Dunne. For *Time*, the article came as close to even-handed as the incurably biased newsmagazine could get. Even Madame Nhu seemed satisfied with the artful meshing of her outrageous behavior with plentiful examples of her power. "Power is wonderful," she once said, and the article played to the theme: "She rules the men who rule the nation." In a letter to *Time*, she wrote, "Used to being somehow mistreated by the American press, I can say that by comparison I find your behavior fair. . . ."

One of those who did not like the published story was Charley Mohr. By August, Mohr was also exhausted. With the full-court press of a cover story behind him, he had taken his family from Hong Kong to a holiday at an isolated resort in Mindanao in the southern Philippines. The magazine straggled in days late, and, by the time it did, Mohr had unwound just enough to blow his top.

All year Mohr had fought his win-one, lose-two battle with Otto Fuerbringer, the autocratic managing editor. He had begun his Madame Nhu file with a powerful sentence that didn't survive the rewrite: "Vietnam is a graveyard of lost hopes, destroyed vanity, glib promises, and good intentions." Now, in his isolation and exhaustion, it seemed the graveyard of his too. Mohr was furious, and he wrote Fuerbringer, that in itself being a mistake. The cover story, he wrote, had failed to "convey something which I believed; that she not only may cause the fall of the government but that she and the government *deserve* that fate." *Time*'s editors had shown, he continued, "a consistent pattern of contempt" for his reporting and the reporting of all the Saigon correspondents. Why did *Time*'s "pro-Diem editors" insist on calling the Saigon correspondents " 'anti-Diem' or 'vociferously anti-Diem' "? Mohr asked, adding, "I have come to the conclusion that an attempt is being made to discount or discredit American reporting from Vietnam. . . . *I am one of the 'reporters in Saigon' and Time is shelling its own troops.*"

The letter hit like a bombshell. "Intemperate," Mohr conceded later. "Terrible," said his protector, Richard Clurman, who stood between him and the furies of the Iron Chancellor. "Jesus Christ," said Fuerbringer, "you have to get Mohr out of there," and pushed Clurman to fire him.

Henry Luce's system of checks and balances prevailed, and Clurman staved off the threat. But now *Time*'s golden boy, the Lucian star whose salary he had quadrupled and praises he had sung to dinner audiences—"A reporter, and how!"—now Charley Mohr had still more in common with his buddies in Saigon. He was in deep trouble with the home office.

———

The pooled information from the war scene in the delta was dynamite. But Neil Sheehan never found time to write it for UPI. Mert Perry wrote a file for *Time*, but in the aftermath of the Charley Mohr episode his now-hostile New York editors killed it. So only David Halberstam made it into print with the article that burst the bubble about the progress of the war.

Nothing he wrote in Vietnam raised such a ruckus. Nothing brought down so much wrath. And nothing convinced him more fully that two years in Vietnam had produced little more than, as he put it, a "giant lying machine."

Halberstam ached to write the obvious: The ARVN had all but quit; the Viet Cong were winning the war. But that pushed the restrictive rules of his trade too hard, particularly when everyone else, including his own editorial page, was reporting that the war was going well; particularly when he, too, was taking a pounding from his editors. He had already pushed the editors well beyond their comfort level. Halberstam was becoming a celebrity, but he was no hero at that cluster of littered desks on the third floor of *The Times* where his copy was cleared each day. He had serious problems there, and Freedman had just warned him: Get off *"your soap box."* To push too hard now would mean no story at all. Halberstam was too smart for that. He was a politician. An angry one, perhaps. But a politician nevertheless.

So the front-page headline in the August 15 *Times* read: VIET- NAMESE REDS GAIN IN KEY AREA. He documented "ominous" gains by the guerrillas: They were moving unmolested in combat units as large as 1,000, several times larger than a year earlier; they were armed with the best American weapons, and modern Chinese and Soviet weapons as well; they boldly attacked ARVN regulars, whereas earlier they had mostly ambushed the less-well-trained civil guards. The rebels, who had so recently fought from and disappeared in the shadows, these troops written off so conde- scendingly as "little man in black pajamas," these little men now had the run of the delta and, as Halberstam quoted an American adviser, "They are almost cocky about it."

It was enough.

At the White House, President Kennedy angrily demanded an analysis from McNamara, then turned back to his morning meet- ing, a last talk with Ambassador-designate Henry Cabot Lodge. "I suppose these are the worst press relations to be found in the world today," the President lamented.

At the Pentagon, McNamara, in the way of the military maxim, started the President's request on its downhill roll.

It stopped first with General Krulak, who quickly assured Mc- Namara that Halberstam's story was already being dissected, "exposing its factual and statistical weaknesses." He continued:

> This is easy, but misses a key point. . . . [Halberstam] exhibits a lack of understanding of our entire Vietnam strategy. From the start, that strategy involved a purification process, north to south, driving the Viet Cong southward. . . .
>
> If Halberstam understood clearly this strategy, he might not have undertaken to write his disingenuous article.

So even if Halberstam was right, he was wrong. But who was being disingenuous here? One might assume that McNamara would need no reminder of a strategy that called for pushing the Viet Cong from the northern provinces into the rice-rich Mekong

Delta, where they fought at their best and could live forever off the land. But the U.S. military had struggled from the beginning to come up with a cohesive strategy. Roger Hilsman had looked at the overall plans at the beginning of 1963 and concluded in a memo for the White House: "Is there a plan? The answer is no. There are five or six plans, most of them competing. There is, consequently, great confusion." Harkins had held out during most of 1962 for his own brainchild, the "explosion" strategy. He found few takers, and by early 1963 both the name and the strategy had evolved into a National Campaign Plan with four vaguely defined objectives, such as "seek out and destroy Viet Cong strongholds" and "clear and hold areas dominated by the Viet Cong." It had gone into effect six weeks before Halberstam's story. Krulak's "purification" plan may have been buried somewhere in the fine print, but it surely hadn't worked. If evidence of that was needed, McNamara got it four days later when a strategic hamlet known as Ben Tuong was overrun by the Viet Cong and 137 of its 200 huts burned to the ground. Ben Tuong was the showplace hamlet to which the defense secretary had been escorted in his chinos and "Matterhorn boots" fifteen months earlier to see how the rural population would be protected. Ben Tuong was also north of Saigon, in the "purified" area.

McNamara's request landed next on Harkins's desk in Saigon, and even Halberstam heard about the thunder that roared out of the spartan MAC-V office near the Central Market: "I'll get that son of a bitch if it's the last thing I do!" Harkins then kicked the request down to his chief of operations, Stilwell the Bad.

Highly intelligent and ambitious men with different and conflicting paths to success, Stilwell and Halberstam were like two bulls in a cow pasture. The next morning the general and the offender brushed past each other in a hallway. Then Stilwell turned back and said icily, "Your story kept me up all night, Halberstam." His thin smile implied that the loss of sleep had been worth it. "I took it apart line by line and you got it dead wrong."

"General, you're a liar," Halberstam replied.

Stilwell's report, "An Appraisal of the Military Situation in the Mekong Delta Region," was fully declassified twenty years later, although he immediately entered a briefing room and gave other reporters the gist of it. The examination marked the beginning of perhaps the most elaborate scrutiny of a reporter's work the government had ever undertaken. It was a strange start, almost childlike. Where Halberstam said *A,* Stilwell responded *B.* The situation had deteriorated and turned ominous? Stilwell's response, in full: "Quote one—Delta military situation is better than last year but a formidable job remains." Not once did the general mention the "purification" strategy.[3]

Still, to the Pentagon it was boffo stuff. The Stilwell report said Halberstam was wrong, and that's all that was wanted. The military closed ranks around its numbers and its war, McNamara remained blinded by his own imperious certainties, and the occasional contrary view was ridiculed or suppressed.

George Allen, who had been analyzing Vietnam for the CIA since the early fifties, making him one of the handful of Americans with long and intimate knowledge of the place, had moved to the Defense Intelligence Agency in 1963. "For a while every time Halberstam did a story from the boonies, I was asked to do a report," Allen recalled. "I was impressed. It was good stuff and I said so." Allen was soon told that no more reports were needed.

But the government had just begun. Two weeks later, Kennedy asked McNamara for a line-by-line analysis of another Halberstam story. Where the first request had produced four single-spaced pages in response, this one produced sixteen. Next the President asked the CIA to analyze *every* story he had written since June.

The CIA knew its game. It concluded that Halberstam was accurate. But the agency played its politics carefully, as did all the multitudinous government hierarchies now in Vietnam. It gave a reply that would protect it against future analysis and current politics, concluding that Halberstam's facts were "by and large accurate" but his stories "invariably pessimistic" and "the conclusions which he draws from his facts, plus the emphasis of his reporting, tend to call his objectivity into question."

Then the agency added one remarkable display of deduction:

Article of 22 June 1963: "The general feeling is that the last six weeks have damaged the war effort irreparably."

---

3. Krulak kicked in again ten days later with another memo for McNamara: "It was easy to discredit the article, but it has not silenced—or influenced—Halberstam."

Comment: Although it may be said that events since that time have not been inconsistent with this statement, it may also be said as does Joe Alsop, that reporting of this sort has contributed directly to the current state of affairs existing in South Vietnam. President Diem is known by all to be in a highly emotional state. When asked by a trusted Vietnamese in mid-September what he considered his most difficult problem, President Diem cried out, "the press."

Rarely had a government agency conceded *that* much power to the press. The CIA had just made Halberstam responsible for the Buddhist crisis as well as Diem's crack-up.

Even dealing with people who did not want to see, the military could maintain its apparition only so long.

Later, in his book *To Move a Nation*, Roger Hilsman wrote that within months Washington would be "amazed" to see how bad the military situation had been at the time. The Viet Cong had not been pushed into the south but were lying low in the north and running rampant in the south. As many as one third of the battles the military counted as ARVN successes were the "sham affairs" Halberstam had reported even earlier.

Indeed, records show that within weeks the White House began getting a steady diet of reports contradicting the military optimism.

On September 8, Rufus Phillips, the American Mission's leading rural expert, went head-on against Krulak in a meeting with the President. The war in the delta was "emphatically not going well," he said, and the strategic hamlets in the region "are being chewed to pieces by the Viet Cong." On October 22, the Bureau of Intelligence and Research reported a "serious downturn" in the military situation in the delta dating back as early as July.

On October 23, Lodge reported "the Delta situation is serious; it gives cause for concern. . . ."

On December 6, the CIA acknowledged that the political crisis in Saigon had "tended to obscure a gradual intensification of Viet Cong guerrilla activity since mid-1963 [and] remains most critical in the Mekong Delta provinces. . . ."

On December 31, four and one-half months after Halberstam's story, William H. Sullivan wrote to his boss, W. Averell Harriman, after two recent trips to Vietnam:

There is a People's Republic of the Viet Cong existing within
the territorial limits of South Vietnam.... It occupies most
but not all of the territory known as the Delta Region of
South Vietnam beginning a few miles south of Saigon.

By that time the whole world had changed and the lies had
become prologue.

In the meantime, however, Halberstam, and his buddies, as well,
had become the targets of almost everyone. Not only were Nhu's
men lingering outside the door at 19 Ngo Duc Ke, but American
spooks hovered there too. From that moment on, Halberstam was
followed by American gumshoes, not always successfully, every
time he left Saigon. Rumors about hit lists proliferated. At home,
Hilsman wrote, "the attacks on Halberstam were particularly
vicious—suggesting every possible failing from being pro-
Communist to being pro-Fascist."

Halberstam showed an embassy friend a newspaper clipping
from home accusing him of being soft on Communism. "I think
you have to expect more of this kind of thing," the friend said and
shrugged. "I hope you don't have any left-wing ghosts in your
closet."

———

Marguerite Higgins left the day after Halberstam's story appeared,
armed with enough string, as they call it in her trade, for a six-part
series she would write at home for the *Herald Tribune.* He was glad
to be rid of her, but she would cause him far more trouble in
Washington than she had in Vietnam. Her stories moved *The New
York Times*'s "Maggie Higgins Hour" from Washington to Saigon
and Gerstenzang's obsessive naggings would drive Halberstam
into an exhausted frenzy of angry rebuttals until he finally threatened to quit on the spot.

The city Higgins left behind was ripping apart at the seams.
With the crisis now entering its fourth month, something had to
give. The anxiety had gone epidemic. The Buddhists had turned
almost giddy in anticipation of a martyrdom that would further
their cause, which clearly had become the ouster of the Diem government. Diem had gone silent, Madame Nhu had not, and Brother
Nhu had engulfed himself in drug-laced plots and intrigues so

complex that they were decipherable by no one. Diem's generals planned more strategy in bistros than war rooms. The Americans had hunkered down, one ambassador gone and the other not yet arrived. Anything could happen.

The rumor mill churned ceaselessly with word of coups, countercoups, middle-of-the-night arrests, assassinations, hit lists. There was no discounting all of it. Vietnamese were disappearing without a word.

Sheehan and Halberstam had received their first serious warning a few weeks earlier when Sheehan's man, Nguyen Ngoc Rao, was tipped off by the police. Rao was not the best of the small corps of Vietnamese legmen who worked for the Saigon correspondents. A visiting New York reporter once bribed him to steal the "blacks"— carbon copies—of Halberstam's and Sheehan's stories. But such was Saigon. Rao worked the police as well as any tough-talking cop-shop reporter in the States, and that made him worth a quirk or two. The police told Rao that they had the list in hand, but not the order to act on it. They even had specific instructions on how to do Sheehan and Halberstam—grenades through the glass window-wall at 19 Ngo Duc Ke, sapper-style to blame it on the Viet Cong. Maybe the palace is only trying to scare the Americans? Rao wondered. The police shrugged. After a summer of craziness, they were as skittish as everyone else.

A few nights later Sheehan visited the home of Pham Van Dong, the ARVN colonel who had steered him to Ap Bac and other stories. After a few minutes, Dong's guards came in to report that a suspicious taxi had rolled by the house several times with its lights out. The colonel took the threats seriously. He wouldn't let Sheehan leave. Finally, with both he and his driver armed, Dong put Sheehan on the floor of his staff car, drove aimlessly for a while, then made several loops through the public market before Sheehan leaped out and faded into the crowd.

Going back to his office/apartment was not comforting. The place was a shooting gallery. All that glass in front, no door out the back. The nickel-plated .38 he had bought was worthless except in the sweaty, foolish dreams he had of taking a few of them with him when he went. But the gun had become part of a necessary psychological ritual for him. Each night he would load the revolver and place it on his nightstand. Each morning he would immediately unload it and put it in the closet. Without the ritual, he couldn't sleep.

Halberstam was getting edgy too. Both of them were working exhaustingly long hours. By mid-August, the heat caused mirages of the mind, and the black leather jackets outside the window multiplied and multiplied again. The office became an oven and they sat across from each other bare-chested, writing endlessly, sweat rolling down to smudge their stories and turn them black with carbon and water. As the crisis heightened, Halberstam often pounded 3,000 or 4,000 words a day out of his Olivetti, and he produced so much so fast that the syntax often fractured and the sentences ran together in unintelligible streams. The government played tricks too. The PTT delayed their copy, lost it, scrambled it. Not once during Halberstam's stay in Vietnam did desk or correspondent attempt a New York–Saigon telephone call. Radiophoning New York was still so difficult that the correspondent and the desk did their communicating, or miscommunicating, in cable-ese. In New York the copy landed on the third-floor wedge of desks where, amid groans, the fractures would be splinted and the streams dammed. Terse cables went back to Saigon for clarifications and the temperamental, targeted, tired reporter would feel more temperamental, targeted, and tired. About that time Freedman, who was said to count in 23's, would spot the same 4,000 tangled words sent via Paris coming in at another 23 cents a word via Tokyo, Halberstam's insurance against the PTT. Good God! said New York, and the hostile cables flew again. Jesus Christ! responded Saigon, and the mood turned fouler. But not as foul as it would get.

On August 20, in a seedy bar chosen intentionally for its distance from the usual haunts of the Radio Catinat rumor mill, Halberstam and Sheehan met with an unusual source. Dang Duc Khoi had been Diem's assistant press officer since the beginning of the American involvement. He was also more, a Diem intelligence operative, an enterprising agent who worked whatever street available, a rogue and a scoundrel who thrived in the city's shadows. Saigon still had powerful criminal gangs, and Khoi favored gangster-owned bars, where he was a notorious womanizer. He was a good source.

Khoi had two startling bits of information for them. Brother Nhu, he said, planned to hit the pagodas full force as early as tonight, no later than tomorrow. The second tip landed closer to home. His gangster friends had been the latest to get a hit list from the palace. Khoi's name was on it, and they had warned him to disappear fast. The list contained two other names of interest: Halberstam and Sheehan. "They're going to *plastique* your office," he said, adding that he was taking the gangsters' advice.

Sheehan felt a sudden lurch of fear. Then he said the obvious, "We can't go anywhere, Khoi."

Halberstam and Sheehan began checking out Khoi's first tip. Khoi made his way down to the waterfront. By dawn he was gone, smuggled out in a load of fertilizer on a ship bound for Yokohama.

14

FLIGHT OF THE PIGEONS

The beat-up little blue-and-yellow Renault horned its way through the midnight crowds on the Rue Catinat, took the next to last turn before the river, and clattered up to the glass front at Number 19. Neil Sheehan dug for a thick wad of piaster notes. It had been a good night for the cabbie, not so good for Sheehan.

The UPI correspondent was dead certain now that Khoi's tip was on the money. Even some of the Buddhist wives of Diem's police had warned the bonzes that the raids were on. Sheehan and Halberstam had spent most of the evening touring the pagodas in the cramped Renault. At Xa Loi the great gate was closed, coils of barbed wire standing token guard, hardly a sound coming from within. The reporters had to awaken the early-rising monks. Yes, they knew the raid was coming, Duc Nghiep said serenely. Then he returned to bed. Visions of the strange young monk's aerosol-can defense and "Molotov" cocktails of curry powder with lemon juice ran through Sheehan's mind.

Shortly before midnight, with nothing more to do, the two correspondents decided to wait it out at home. Without a telephone or other resources, Halberstam would be completely isolated. Sheehan wouldn't. He had been beaten by Mal Browne's "human wave" too many times. Not only did he have Saigon 22–412, the phone he shared with Mert Perry, but the industrious Rao had scrounged a primitive police scanner that could monitor the deployment of the cops, often the troops too. Sheehan also had become something of an early day hacker. Terrified that communications would be cut during a coup d'état, he had discovered a way to get a telephone call out with the entire country shut down.

Now Sheehan looked around for the black leather jacket, found him, half-hidden in the shadows, and pushed open the Renault's battered door with a loud grinding of metal. He saw and heard Perry at the same time. "Now! Now!" Perry shouted. His huge body stretched, half-dressed, out his apartment window. "They're going in now!" Perry had returned moments earlier and begun undressing for bed when the call came that the police would go right after midnight.

Sheehan leaped back into the cab, shouting at the driver in the combination of pidgin Vietnamese and French he used when he became very excited. The cab raced back up the Catinat and around the massive twin basilicas of the Roman Catholic cathedral that dead-ended the street a few blocks from Halberstam's villa. Then it passed a floodlit police station. Two-and-one-half-ton trucks, traditional American troop carriers, formed up in the yard. Heavily armed police clambered into the backs of the canopied trucks. So did troops in battle gear. The cabdriver began protesting. Sheehan told him to go faster.

At the villa, Halberstam heard Sheehan's shouts and met him on the run. Back in the tiny cab, the two oversized Americans were all elbows and knees, and to the driver the trip became more like a hijack than a fare.

Rounding the corner, they suddenly found themselves alongside the troop caravan. Sheehan screamed at the terrified driver: *"Di di! Di di!"* Go! Go! *"Di di mao!"* Fast! Halberstam started to laugh. But they both knew what would happen if they fell behind the convoy. The police would swiftly close the street behind the last truck and they would be stranded blocks from Xa Loi. Sheehan, cursing, threatening, promising, all but steered the little cab in between the second and third trucks. They rode within yards of the pagoda gate, where the scene turned instantly to bedlam.

Assault squads poured into the streets. First the white-uniformed national police, known in Saigon without affection as the "white mice"; then the combat police, specially trained by the CIA for defense against sappers and urban terrorists. Last came the South Vietnamese Special Forces, some trying to disguise their identity beneath uniforms of the regular army, others forgetting the cover and wearing the berets and trim camouflage uniforms of the elite guard they were. They vaulted out of the trucks, machine guns held high. Officers began forming them up.

Sheehan and Halberstam watched briefly from the backseat of the cab. Even knowing this was coming, they were surprised. Several thousand men had been sent in to do a job several hundred could have done as easily. But the use of the elite units against the unarmed Buddhists dumbfounded them.

The Special Forces were easily identifiable, their officers trained at Fort Bragg in the image of President Kennedy's own select Green Berets. They had been groomed for the same roles—to fight using counterinsurgency tactics in small and deadly units, comfortable using the dark of the night and the silence of a knife to narrow the odds on the guerrillas' home turf. The correspondents had long been aware, and assumed the U.S. government had, too, that the South Vietnamese Special Forces rarely fought in the field. They had become a presidential guard, commanded by one of the most hated and feared men in Saigon, Lieutenant Colonel Le Quang Tung. Tung's terror tactics instilled such fear that the CIA considered him the third most powerful man in Vietnam. Still, using the elite guard against the Buddhists was analogous to using Green Berets to put down Negro protests at home. It was outrageous. To Halberstam, bringing in Tung smelled of one person—Ngo Dinh Nhu.

The taxi driver panicked. His rambunctious passengers had put him in a terrible mess. Troop convoys had converged on his location from three directions. Frantically, he jockeyed his car this way and that, trying to escape. The correspondents showered him with piasters and bailed out, Sheehan moving quickly to the left, Halberstam to the right. Buddies they were, but there was no point in sticking together now. Except safety, of course, which was no small consideration.

Sheehan watched for a few minutes before a familiar urgent gnawing came over him. He needed a telephone. Badly.

He dodged through the milling troops to the U.S. government office building next to Xa Loi, ran past a marine guard and double-timed up to the rooftop, where he had a panoramic view of the violence. The scene immediately reminded him of an old Second

World War movie, with the Gestapo rounding up French underground fighters after a sudden strike on Resistance headquarters.
But here, he reminded himself, the government was rounding up
its own people.

Below him, the din grew overwhelming. Inside the pagoda the
monks sounded a gong and began beating pots and pans to ward
off the attackers. But the white mice and the combat police flattened
the barbed wire and battered down the pagoda gate. The Special
Forces, machine guns at high port arms, formed up in V wedges
and charged.

The night exploded with staccato bursts from BARs, pistol shots,
tear-gas grenades, splintering doors, breaking glass, and hideous
screams. The trucks began to turn around and back up to the gate
one by one, the troops prodding bleeding Buddhists onto the
canvas-covered platforms. In the street Halberstam grew uneasy.
He was clearly in a place he was not supposed to be, seeing what
he was not supposed to see. Soldiers milled around him hostilely
and he felt like Gulliver about to be drawn down by angry Lillipu-
tians. He tried a ploy he had learned in the Congo, nonchalantly
bumming a cigarette from one of the suspicious soldiers, a role
reversal for a rich American. Taken aback, the trooper grinned
and offered both the smoke and a light. In the flare of the match
Halberstam confirmed what he thought: His new friend's shoulder
patch designated him as Special Forces.

Halberstam was less the poet and more the pragmatist than
Sheehan. Looking at the shoulder patch and watching the brutal
collection of the Buddhists, he saw the scene differently. In it, he
saw the crumbling of an American foreign policy.

About 400 monks and nuns were rounded up that night at Xa
Loi, and at least 1,000 more in simultaneous raids on other pagodas
throughout South Vietnam. The bloodiest attacks came in Hue,
where the crisis had begun three months earlier. At least 30 were
killed in the old imperial city.

A nationwide death toll became impossible to determine. Some
monks simply disappeared. A handful escaped. At Xa Loi two
made it over the pagoda wall and took refuge in the office building
from which Sheehan watched. Thich Tri Quang, leader of the mili-
tants and a prime target, sneaked out just before the raid and
eventually took refuge in the American Embassy. Tri Quang's asy-

lum caused a further ruffling of relations between the palace and the White House. By that time it didn't make much difference.

———

Mal Browne was tipped just minutes after Sheehan. Duc Nghiep called him from inside Xa Loi. "Mr. Browne, the police have come," he said. "They're shooting. Tell the American Embassy quickly." Then the phone went dead.

Browne arrived fifteen crucial minutes late, turned away by barbed wire and pistol-waving police. He soon found that he was shut out even more completely than that, as were all the correspondents. Except one.

So basic was the battle of minutes between the wire men that they went to extraordinary lengths to maintain unimpeded access to the crude communications system available to them. Cables could be sent only from the PTT building and were subject to technical and political delays that could turn vital minutes into hours—or worse. Telephone calls used the same primitive radio system—in a time without communications satellites or an undersea Pacific cable—*all* communications, including photographs, moved by radio telephone. They were subject to whims of the weather, of politics, of avarice. Like everything in Saigon, the system always worked better if oiled. The wire men delivered a steady stream of cosmetics and other doodads, small bribes from the PX, to the operators. With the supervisor, the cost went up. Sheehan was asked for a typewriter. As broke as he was, he had his priorities straight. He immediately bought a new typewriter from the PX, ruefully looking at a machine far better than the one he used himself, and delivered it to the supervisor. The next time he raced into the telephone building, a French businessman was arguing heatedly and, it appeared, endlessly, on the line to Paris. Suddenly, the businessman developed line problems. Atmospherics, the supervisor shrugged hopelessly. Sheehan's call went straight through.

From his perch in the U.S. government building, just before the phone lines went dead, Sheehan had called his office and dictated about 150 words—the first bulletin—to Don Becker, the Manila bureau chief in town briefly to help out. Becker sent Rao racing to the post office, where the Vietnamese aide found it surrounded by armed troops.

It was Sheehan's nightmare. Brother Nhu had shut down every-thing. Now no calls or cables would go through. By the time com-munications would reopen, full military censorship would be in effect—the only time in the long and tortured war ahead that the press would be overtly censored.

Earlier, Sheehan had briefed Becker—and left a long, compli-cated set of instructions in the office—about an emergency plan he had worked out months before with the help of Ivan Slavich. It would require ingenuity, persistence, a good deal of bluff—and a heavy dose of luck.

Slavich had led Sheehan through a communications maze, first showing him how to break into the Vietnamese military telephone system known as the Tiger Line; then get from the Vietnamese military operators to an American outfit called Strategic Army Communications, or STARCOM, which could route official callers to three destinations: Bangkok, Manila, or Okinawa. In Bangkok or Manila, the call could be connected to UPI bureaus. For Okinawa, Slavich had given him his wife's number.

Sheehan led Becker through the same maze, adding one final instruction: *For Christ's sake, sound official.*

Becker tried Manila first. Sorry, sir, lines out. He tried Okinawa. Lines out. Finally, in an exasperated general officer's voice, he said: "Get me Bangkok." For anyone from UPI, Bangkok was a despera-tion call. The Bangkok bureau was run by an unusually easygoing Thai stringer named Prasong Wittaya, and it was now well after midnight. The phone call got through, and a sleepy voice an-swered. "Hello, Wittaya," Becker began. "Mr. Wittaya not here," Wittaya answered and hung up.

By now, the STARCOM operator, a sergeant, had guessed that he wasn't dealing with General Harkins. He offered an idea. He had a plane coming in from Clark Field. If Becker would give him the message, he could radio it to the plane. The plane could radio it back to Clark Field. Clark could call UPI in Manila.

Sheehan's brief story was the only one to get out of Vietnam that night.

———

The midnight attacks ended the Buddhist rebellion more abruptly and ruthlessly than the Diem regime would ever deal with the Viet

Cong. By morning, virtually all of the country's Buddhist leaders were in jail or worse. Madame Nhu, who watched the assault on Xa Loi with her husband in a tank parked not far from David Halberstam, clapped her hands in joy. It was, she said, "the happiest day of my life." In Washington, her father, Tran Van Chuong, saw it differently. He quit in protest as Diem's ambassador to the United States. Her mother quit as ambassador to the United Nations. Even *Time*, in a move that would soon be ripe with irony, decided that Diem "may finally have shattered his own political usefulness."

Halberstam had been astute in spotting the handiwork of Ngo Dinh Nhu in the night's bloodletting. The raids had been a desperate act, designed to leave the incoming ambassador, Henry Cabot Lodge, with a done deal when he arrived two nights later. But Diem's brother had other plots up his sleeve as well. He now set about placing the blame on Diem's generals. Discrediting the generals had many attractions: It would muddy their own plans for a coup d'état and tarnish them in the eyes of the Americans who had clearly begun looking for new leaders to replace Diem. Nhu lay the groundwork artfully, and the generals fell easily into his trap. Just the day before he had maneuvered them into asking Diem to declare martial law to restore order during the Buddhist crisis. Hours after Diem agreed to the extraordinary military powers, the pagoda raids were launched without the generals' knowledge and without their troops. But that's not the way it looked. Nor is it the way the palace billed it, even when Brother Nhu's charade required hints that Diem had been reduced to a mere figurehead in a bloodless military coup. The American government fell into Nhu's trap as quickly as the generals.

William Trueheart, chargé d'affaires in the absence of an ambassador, cabled Washington that the "military now have a dominant role and although . . . they profess loyalty to [the] President, [the] latter's position would seem currently or potentially precarious with the generals appearing [to] have option of deposing him." The story, Trueheart acknowledged, could be a "self-seeking attempt to dissociate [Diem from the] Buddhist repression." But, he concluded, it has the "ring of truth to us."

General Harkins bought in without a blink, sending Maxwell

Taylor one of the most remarkable reports since Taylor had recommended Project Beef-Up twenty-one months earlier:

> .... As you know, our programs are completed. We have accomplished everything we set out to do after your visit in the fall of '61—all except ending the war, and that is not far off if things continue at present pace. . . .
>
> .... [T]he present situation might be a blessing in disguise. There exists for all practical purposes a military takeover with minimum violence. A few bones were bruised as the police and military took over the main Pagodas yesterday. Not that I'm for the military taking over—no indeed— but the state of affairs as they were, it was becoming evident things were getting out of control, and some measure of authority had to be established. That it was done without firing a shot and thru the nominal chain of command precluded a lot of bloodshed which would have been spilled [sic] if the rival factions tried to take over.

In fact, the American Mission, civilian and military, didn't have the foggiest notion what was going on and wouldn't figure it out for days. By 3 A.M., all the correspondents had converged on the old embassy building, not so much in search of news as communications facilities. For most this was the biggest story of their lives —and they had no way to get it home. Even the story Sheehan slipped out had no more than bare bones to it, a stark account without political detail or mention of the Special Forces. The embassy was a madhouse, its local phone lines cut by Nhu's operatives, its intelligence operations in disarray. One American official asked Halberstam plaintively, "Why didn't you tell us?" Astonished that all the resources of the American government had failed to pick up the same buzz as the reporters, he had no idea what to reply.

Trueheart, however, did agree to try to help the reporters. Breaking all previous rules, he offered to send out one brief story for each reporter on the embassy's protected communication system. It was one of the government's first, if ill-fated, attempts to help the press inform the American public since the mess in Vietnam had begun. About 4 A.M. Halberstam, Sheehan, and Rao arrived at the embassy with their stories. They had a second agenda and went directly to a small office where Mecklin was frantically working on a memo for Henry Cabot Lodge, who would arrive that evening.

The three men were exhausted and frightened. Khoi was on their mind. Assassination lists. Martial law. They knew a shooting curfew was coming. Isolated from their government in an increasingly hostile land, isolated now from their only tie to home, Saigon's romantic shadows quickly turned malevolent. Perhaps most worrisome: They were working on a story the American Embassy didn't understand but the palace surely did. For the palace, the full story of the raids could be fatal.

Halberstam had stayed downtown after the raids, a working binge naturally required that night, but feeling no safer in the villa anyway. Rao had been in the office, too, despite his wife's pleas to quit his job with the American reporters before it got him killed. Halberstam found him sprawled across the bed in the back room, tinkering with his police radio as it squawked a noisy babble of ominous news: Colonel Tung's men were using the confusion to make still more night arrests.

Sheehan was unusually jumpy. He had been working so hard, sleeping so little, that he had developed a slight stutter. His office was oppressively hot. His .38 no longer gave him solace. In the darkness the damnable glass wall became a one-way mirror: They could see in; he couldn't see out. He was jumping at his own shadow. He knew that they were playing mind games with him. They *loved* toying with people. They had their damned hit lists floating all over town. Madame Nhu's brother, Tran Van Khiem, had arrogantly drawn one up in front of Denis Warner, an Australian correspondent. He had flashed the names as he wrote them: Mecklin, Richardson, Conein, and then insinuated that he was starting on the newsmen. Warner called his bluff. He had asked Khiem if he knew anything about the U.S. Marines, whom Warner had covered in the Second World War. They were the fiercest fighters in the world, the Aussie said coolly, and he imagined they could clean out every Vietnamese soldier in Saigon in less than three hours. Khiem folded his list. But Warner, who considered Tran Van Khiem a thug and had described him in print as "the

Robespierre of Vietnam," took the threats seriously.[1] He warned his fellow correspondents to be careful, that they were targeted.

Sheehan, accustomed to an endless din, had never heard a night so quiet. In the aftermath of the raids the silence tightened around him like the apartment's claustrophobic walls. Sheehan worried that Brother Nhu had "gone bananas, just simply completely bananas." Charley Mohr thought they were all as crazy as hell. Khoi had no doubts. He had skipped out fast. Sheehan did not have a comfortable night at 19 Ngo Duc Ke. None of them did.

The two journalistic camps were at odds about how to handle the new risks with which they suddenly lived in the summer of 1963. They all found combat easier. Mal Browne's attitude was: *Don't let the sonsabitches see you sweat,* and he was stiff-necked about it. A few nights hence the police, during their spree of collecting dissidents, would pound on his apartment door at 2 A.M. in search of Le Lieu. He greeted them with his old German Schmeisser submachine gun and bluffed them into backing off. After that, Browne grew even stiffer. Don't let them intimidate you, he said, and he kept his crew in line on it. Peter Arnett went along with Browne. He would survive more than thirty years of combat reporting by running every necessary risk after taking every possible precaution. But now he wondered if everyone hadn't become so tired and emotionally vulnerable that all of them, including himself, hadn't gone a little balmy. His name showed up on one of the lists, but he settled for the psychological defense of a high-stakes poker player. We're so totally vulnerable, he told himself, if they wanted to kill us they would have done it by now, a shot in the back while in the field, a hit-and-run in Saigon's chaotic streets. Stanley Karnow, a few years older than the others and in town writing some damning articles about the Diem family for the *Saturday Evening Post,* was not so cavalier. "You can't write the story if you're dead," he said.

1. It was Khiem who, in 1986, was charged with murdering his—and Madame Nhu's—parents in their Washington home, then was committed to a mental institution in midtrial as too delusional to participate in his defense. Over the prosecutors' strong objections, he was released and deported to France in 1993 after a judge ruled he never would be competent to stand trial.

At 4 A.M. the three men—Halberstam, Sheehan, and Rao—slipped out of the office on Ngo Duc Ke. A few minutes later they cut around a corner away from the darkened riverfront and walked hurriedly into the old embassy building. They dropped off their stories and immediately sought out Mecklin. In effect, they asked him for asylum, not in the embassy, but in his house. A large villa, Mecklin's house did not have official diplomatic protection against intrusion but it had unspoken immunity. It also had twenty-four-hour-a-day guards. The exhausted reporters, near their breaking points, wanted a safe place to sleep during the new crisis.

Mecklin immediately said yes, although he felt a "hint of a dare" in the way they asked him. It was as if they were challenging him, he thought, "to choose sides or forever be damned." This posed deep problems. Mecklin would be sheltering, as he wrote later, "the two most controversial newsmen in town." He would hear plenty about it. He soon learned that both Secretary of State Dean Rusk and CIA Director John McCone complained that he was leaking secrets to the enemy while Halberstam and Sheehan stayed with him. How could they think a traitor could be so dumb, he marveled, as to invite the spies into his house? "It was an alarming glimpse of the degree to which the U.S. government had been poisoned at the very highest level by the feud," he concluded.

Sitting early that morning in an American Embassy with all its telephone lines cut, he thought Halberstam and Sheehan had good cause for fear. Mecklin had his ghosts too. One of his friends, a predecessor of Sheehan's, Gene Symonds of UPI, had been beaten to death by a mob in Singapore merely because he was a foreigner with a camera hanging around his neck. No one knew what was going on in Saigon now. He chuckled nevertheless about the ironies in what he called his "refugee problem." Just six weeks earlier Halberstam, Sheehan, and the other regulars had been in his office cursing him so angrily that one of his neighbors had come in to rescue *him*. And Mecklin himself was near the top of nearly every hit list the embassy had seen. Ngo Dinh Nhu had decided that he was a major CIA operative using the USIS as cover. The rumors that Mecklin would be killed eventually became so intense that Lodge offered to transfer him. He declined.

And so the beleaguered press attaché had houseguests for the next three weeks.

Saigon returned quickly to the timeless business of Asia, the same hopeless tangle of legs and machines in the traffic jams in its streets, the same cacophony of shrill barter over thousand-year eggs and fish so fresh they were still swimming.

On street corners, however, on the morning after the raids, soldiers stood with oversized American rifles. Jeeps mounted with .30 caliber machine guns cruised up the Rue Catinat, down Ngo Duc Ke and the Rue Pasteur. The city was placed on the anticipated 9 P.M. to 5 A.M. curfew—a shooting curfew, and no one disbelieved. The airport remained closed to all commercial traffic. The only American left with a working telephone was General Harkins, for priority military calls. South Vietnam was effectively closed to the outside world.

Harkins did not help open it. The general's men caught up with Sheehan's STARCOM sergeant, threatened him with court-martial, and shut him down tight. Browne and Sheehan both found a military passenger flight heading out to Manila and smuggled packets of stories aboard with friendly officers. But the fight with the reporters had moved into the theater of the absurd. The officers were discovered and also threatened with courts-martial. The packets came off the plane.[2] Briefly, transmitting through the Vietnamese censors became the only option, but the censors became a pointless joke. Their English poor, their judgment worse, everything of substance and much that wasn't was stricken. Sensitive to the religious issue, the censors cut the word "Catholic" every time they saw it. Editors at home began reading about the "Roman president of South Vietnam."

In Washington, the State Department didn't help, either. State watched the reporters' cables arrive and, shocked at Trueheart's poor sense of diplomatic decorum, quickly overruled his decision as "inadvisable." Dozens of stories stacked up in Foggy Bottom,

---

2. Sheehan found a second flight and succeeded in smuggling a story aboard. But it was headed for the place that, for UPI, had the curse of the Lotus Eaters on it—Bangkok. The serene Mr. Wittaya left the packet at the airport till the next day, canceling out what could have been Sheehan's second scoop.

unforwarded to the correspondents' news organizations. They were forwarded elsewhere. Across the top of Sheehan's article, a handwritten note to Kennedy's national security adviser, McGeorge Bundy, said: "These are *not* being delivered. State will give background to press. Mike is seeing that the info they contain gets to the President." The Saigon reporters were furious.[3] The background information given to the Washington press was wrong. Like the embassy, State bought in to Nhu's version and passed it on to the public.

Now began days of confusion and chaos that led to one of the most bizarre front pages in the history of *The New York Times*. Soon Halberstam, who, with Sheehan, was light years ahead on the story, found a way to smuggle it out of the country. When it arrived in New York, the U.S. government remained blinded by Nhu's mirrors. Faced with a choice between Washington and its angry young man, *The Times* couldn't make up its mind. In effect, the world's most influential newspaper told its readers to flip a coin (see page 379).

For the great gray lady the only saving grace was that its isolated Saigon correspondent had no way of knowing what had happened. Had he known, David Halberstam would have needed no communications system to be heard in New York.

Meanwhile, at the embassy on the morning after the pagoda raids, John Mecklin continued with the task that had kept him there all night: The rough draft of a report for the new ambassador.

"We are faced with a crisis of credibility such as seldom has happened before in a situation as critical as this," he told Henry Cabot Lodge. "You will hear indignant contrary views, but my observation is that not only the newsmen here but also a good many Americans in relatively senior official positions believe very nearly nothing that any official U.S. agency says about the situation in Vietnam."

Then he filled him in about the correspondents:

"Among the regulars, there is a mood that verges on hysteria.

---

3. None was as furious as Mal Browne. Browne did not discover till much later how Sheehan had succeeded in getting his story out. He fumed at Trueheart for days, thinking the embassy had let Sheehan's story through and had blocked his.

The New York Times.

NEW YORK, FRIDAY, AUGUST 23, 1963.

Two Versions of the Crisis in Vietnam: One Lays Plot to Nhu, Other to Army

Sources in Saigon Say Military Did Not Order Attacks—Washington's Reports Indicate Diem Yielded to Officers

The confused situation in South Vietnam was reflected yesterday in conflicting versions of the role played by the army high command in the Saigon regime's attacks this week against the Buddhists.

A dispatch from Saigon quoted reliable sources there as having said that the drive had been planned and executed in its initial stage without the knowledge of the army. But information received in Washington pictured South Vietnam's army commanders as having put pressure on President Ngo Dinh Diem to persuade him to act.

Plan Said to Be Nhu's

By DAVID HALBERSTAM

Special to The New York Times

SAIGON, South Vietnam. Aug. 22 — Highly reliable sources here said today that the decision to attack Buddhist pagodas and declare martial law in South Vietnam was planned and executed by Ngo Dinh Nhu, the President's brother, without the knowledge of the army.

These sources said that the Vietnamese Army had not seized power and that army commanders had been presented with a fait accompli.

Mr. Nhu is the chief adviser of President Ngo Dinh Diem. He is also head of the secret police, or special forces, which were said to have been his mili-

Kennedy Weighs Policy

By TAD SZULC

Special to The New York Times

WASHINGTON, Aug. 22—The United States Government believes that a group of Vietnamese Army commanders convinced President Ngo Dinh Diem that he should order a crackdown on the Buddhists and proclaim martial law.

High Administration sources said tonight that the situation in South Vietnam was vastly confused. They said this was probably only the opening chapter in a major power struggle.

The foremost factor emerging at this time from what the Government told of information flowing in from Saigon seemed to be the dominant position of the military.

379

They are exhausted after three months of an extraordinarily difficult story, emotionally engaged in the most violent four-letter terms, full of extravagant hopes that Lodge can square things away, and scared."

———

Charles Arnot was taking a terrible hazing. The ABC stringer stood on the runway apron, bulbous microphone in hand, cameraman facing him behind a tripod and a huge Auricon, soundman off to the side, cables snaking in all directions, kliegs bathing him in sweat as well as light and sending shimmers off the puddles left by the night's monsoon rain. Arnot, who had been in Saigon through most of the summer's Buddhist crisis, was trying to do one of those newfangled television routines, a stand-up. The catcalls from the print press rang out each time he began, ruining each effort.

"Henry Cabot Lodge, the new American ambassador to war-torn. . . ."

"Get professional, Arnot!"

"Henry Cabot Lodge, America's hope. . . ."

"Oh, shit, Arnot!"

About thirty-five newsmen milled around the awkwardly hulking television crews, the jeers good-natured, a release from the tension of the past forty-eight hours, a mild poke at this new substandard offshoot of serious journalism too. How could you take it seriously, this pesky new medium whose words and pictures disappeared immediately into the ether when yours were pounded as always into the historical permanence of lead, then given the proper gravity of ink on paper? To the print reporters, whose brethren in Washington were already scrambling to get on the tube, television was amateur night with a camera. While television was moving much faster than the isolated crew in Vietnam could see, it still struggled erratically to find a sense of itself. Arnot's cabled report on the pagoda raids had been a minor classic:

I HEARD MONKS SCREAM DUCKED BEHIND TREE ESCAPED HAIL GUNFIRE GRENADES TEARGAS BOMBS AS STEEL HELMETED PO-LICE FIXED BAYONETS ASSAULTED SAIGON'S MAIN BUDDHIST TEMPLE EARLY WEDNESDAY. PARADE AMBULANCES REMOVED

MANY DEAD WOUNDED IN BLOODY CLIMAX BUDDHIST PROTEST
WHICH DIEM SUDDENLY DECIDED SMASH MILITARILY. . . .

At the sound of engines descending through the night, the banter came to an abrupt halt, letting Arnot do his job. It was 9:30 P.M. The first thing Henry Cabot Lodge had done in Vietnam was break the curfew.

The correspondents had been bussed out to Tan Son Nhut, escorted by Diem's police, the roadway lined on both sides by soldiers, backs to the caravan, faces toward the people. Now the big plane, an old propeller-driven Lockheed Constellation—a Connie —taxied through the puddles, drawn to the only light at the empty airport, the kliegs of television, a new beacon. Times were changing. Henry Cabot Lodge would change a few things too.

Lodge emerged with blue eyes squinting, waving his trademark straw hat. At six foot three the man was all New England lank, no give to the frame, the hair clipped-back steel gray over the ears, the face more closed than the smile, the suit rumpled ever so slightly it might have been tailored with the soft wrinkles built in. The hat was also a prop, a patrician's playful ruse. His blood was as blue as his eyes. Already, a line about the ambassador-designate worked its way through the rounds of Americans in Saigon: "Our old mandarin can whip your old mandarin."

Lodge brushed quickly past Trueheart, Harkins, and the formal welcoming party. "Where," he asked, as if on cue, "are the gentlemen of the press?" He made no announcements and took no questions. But, in his first five minutes in Vietnam, the new man spoke only to the reporters. He told them that they were an indispensable part of the American democratic experiment, essential cogs in the system. He looked forward to working with them and helping them do their jobs. John Mecklin watched the faces and concluded that it was love at first sight.

Lodge had been given his cue. In telling him a week earlier that he was heading into the worst mess with reporters in all the world, President Kennedy instructed him: "I particularly want you to take personal charge of all press relations." Robert Manning, sent in after Arnett's beating in July, offered some thoughts. He said that "wounded ego" was part of the problem, especially among "correspondents who have a highly developed sense of importance." Give them "an 'in' feeling," he suggested; "invite them more often to, say, small dinners. . . ."

Lodge needed no prompting. He was a deft player of the game, and he let Mecklin know it immediately. There would be no leaks from the embassy, he told his press aide sternly. Except from the top. "The leak is the prerogative of the ambassador," he said. "It is one of my weapons for doing this job." Within days, he would schedule private dinners with David Halberstam, Neil Sheehan, and Mal Browne. They would be relaxed affairs, often lasting for hours. His wife, Emily, would add a homey touch. It would not be till afterward that the correspondents realized that the ambassador had said very little. Instead, he had asked them to fill him in, a flattering role reversal that they accepted with relish. In one such dinner the twenty-six-year-old Irish immigrant's son from Holyoke spent the evening unintentionally briefing the sixty-one-year-old Boston Brahmin. Afterward, when part of the magnetism had faded, Halberstam asked Neil Sheehan what he thought. Sheehan broke into a broad smile, deliberately enriching the brogue that life never quite drove out of him. "Ahhhh," he said, "he's what my Irish mother would call a crafty Yankee."

Lodge was crafty, all right. Smooth, too. He would give the reporters everything they wanted. Attention. Respect. Even occasional information. Then he would give them Diem, as well.

———

Finding the phone has made almost as many legends in journalism as finding the story. One of the most celebrated examples came just three months later in a motorcade in Dallas. Riding in a Secret Service car three cars behind the presidential limousine, Merriman Smith of UPI and Jack Bell of AP heard three shots ring out. Smith arm-wrestled the agents' car phone away from his rival, pinned Bell to the floorboards, dictated the first bulletin lead to his office, and then rolled over and smothered the phone with his body until the racing automobile reached Parkland Hospital. Bell, a distinguished reporter, never quite forgave Smith and never quite regained his reputation. Smith won the Pulitzer Prize.

Smith's 1963 Pulitzer carried with it a touch of unkind irony. Halberstam and Browne would share the award for international reporting for the year's work in Vietnam. Sheehan would be left out, one of the worst snubs in the history of the often-politicized prizes. The judges, having made their decision on Smith, would not give a second award to what they considered a second-rate and often sensational news agency.

Two of Sheehan's predecessors in Korea became minor legends for their ingenuity in getting the story home. In the opening days of the war, all communications collapsed beneath the blitzkrieg invasion by the North Koreans. The angst so consumed a United Press correspondent named Dick Applegate that other newsmen watched him in awe. He spun out his stories in so many directions, one of them *had* to get home. Once, he stuffed a story in a bottle and threw it in a river in the *hope* that there was a radio on the other side. Moments later, three bottles floated downriver toward him. "My god, men," he said quietly, "here come the rockets."

Applegate's colleague, Rutherford Poats, fell back on an age-old system, winging his story toward Tokyo by carrier pigeon. The bird made the 600-mile trip, 400 miles of it over the Sea of Japan, in eleven days. By that time the story was hopelessly outdated, but Poats's editors were so impressed that they put the story on the wire anyway.

AP's Mal Browne had the inventiveness of a scientist and the canniness of a born tinkerer. Stung by Sheehan's early success, Browne struck back quickly. Under the eyes of the censors at the PTT office, AP kept Horst Faas's pride and joy, a primitive photo-transmission machine. The contraption "scanned" photos mounted on a cylindrical drum and sent them home the same way every-thing went, by radio-telephone signal. For the next few days the scanner also picked up images of tiny gummed labels which Browne, his back to the machine and his smile directed at the censors, palmed onto the photos as the drum began turning. His postage-stamp "bulletins" broke several stories, including one about Diem's foreign minister, who shaved his head and quit in protest of the Buddhist repressions. The *New York Herald Tribune* found Browne's ingenuity more fascinating than the story and blew his cover by printing the photo, message label intact, on its front page.

Sheehan had some tricks left too. One was the UPI "code book." The old radio-telephone system was seriously vulnerable to snooping. Anyone could read anyone else's cable traffic. What radio-frequency hacking wouldn't do, a modest bribe at the PTT would. So both wire services kept crude codes for private messages about their business operations. At AP, dollars became "ironmen," at UPI, "brenna."[4] Meant for deals, not stories, the vocabulary was specialized and limited. On the second day, Sheehan and Ray Herndon, sprung from his Laotian exile just before the raids, spent hours condensing a complicated story to a 25-word message that would fool the censors but still make sense in Tokyo. It became a 600-word exclusive about the radical Buddhist leader, Thich Tri Quang, gaining political asylum in the American Embassy.

The holes in his system drove Ngo Dinh Nhu to fits, convincing him the correspondents had a secret transmitter. Unable to locate it, he became certain it was stashed in Mecklin's house with the rebel correspondents. Mecklin, Nhu now decided, was not an agent of the CIA but the chief of a much more deeply buried American secret service who ran his new houseguests as his top agents. Mecklin moved to the top of the assassination lists. So did Henry Cabot Lodge, who quickly proved he was not Diem's cup of tea. After several weeks of dealing with Nhu's loony antics, Lodge cabled Washington that he almost felt sorry for the erratic presidential brother. "He is wound up tight as a wire," Lodge reported. "He appears to be a lost soul, a haunted man who is caught in a vicious circle. The Furies are after him."

Meanwhile, the regime couldn't keep the airport closed forever. When it reopened on the third day, the floodgates opened with it. Now the correspondents could end-run the censors as simply as finding an agreeable outbound passenger—a tourist, a stewardess, a soldier on leave. The flight of the pigeons, they gleefully called their new routine. Flying in a new jet age, the Vietnam pigeons put Rutherford Poats's poor bird to shame. Hong Kong and Manila were only two and a half hours away, Bangkok and Singapore nearer.

Halberstam had been initiated into it in the Congo, when he and

---

4. His life being an endless struggle to stay afloat, Sheehan's cables were often semi-coded pleas: SEND JADE BRENNA SOONEST. Jade was code for 100.

a group of British correspondents were caught in a bloody ongoing battle for the central African town of Elisabethville. All cable communications were cut. At first, the pigeons were tourists trying to escape on rutted dirt roads. Eventually, the rookie from *The Times* got the job. He and the Fleet Streeters hired a Belgian bush pilot to fly Halberstam and all the stories to the nearby Northern Rhodesian railroad town of Ndola late each day.[5] The dusty little town had a telegraph office with penny-a-word cable rates left over from colonial days, and still called the empire rate.

In the mornings Halberstam covered the street fighting in Elisabethville. At three o'clock he pulled away to write. At four he ran to the old frontier hotel, the Leopold Deux, collected the other correspondents' stories, and made his way to the airport. After the 120-mile flight over the African badlands to Ndola, he dumped the stories on a surly telegraph operator and bunked down for the night at the only hotel in town—a run-down clapboard establishment next to the railroad tracks where the clattering night-run freights pounded at him like the machine guns during the day. At dawn he flew back to the real gunfire in Elisabethville, with the Belgian pilot growing more uneasy each day.

On the fourth day the airport was bombed—one bomb dropped by the single jet in the rebel Katanganese air force. It was the bomb that began the legend. Shrapnel! cried the Brits and *The Washington Post* too. A London tabloid correspondent wrote: "I wasn't hit, but David Halberstam of *The New York Times,* who was right next to me, was wounded, and my typewriter case was shattered." Later, a rival told Halberstam it was the fifth time the man's typewriter had been shattered since arriving in the Congo, a boon to his expense account. That same day, mortar fire destroyed the room of Cyril Ainsley of the *Daily Express.* Ainsley was absent, and a rival wrote that the mortar had struck his own room, telling the others he *had* to do it to fend off the inevitable rocket from his tabloid editor: WHY YOUR ROOM UNMORTARED?

Halberstam felt trapped in the pages of an Evelyn Waugh novel, where every young foreign correspondent worth his salt wanted to

5. Elisabethville is now Lumbumbashi. Northern Rhodesia has become Zambia. Ndola remains Ndola.

be trapped. Now, in Vietnam, the Saigon group found itself lodged between the same book covers. In ways they wouldn't see till much later, this moment became the high-water mark of a gilded age.

The story turned to sheer fun. Henry Cabot Lodge had been liberating, the opening of the airport more so. The adrenaline run of a good story coming to a head did the rest. Eighteen-hour days became nothing, twenty handled with a shrug and a yawn. They revved up like college kids on amphetamines, but the speed came from their own natural juices.

Halberstam wrote so many stories so fast that the sentences stumbled over each other once again. But he filed into a void with no return address. Normally, each day he would receive what *The Times* called a "frontings message." The brief cable told him whether his story had made page one, been shuffled into the inside pages, cut to a "short," or, god forbid, dealt to the purgatory of the "holdover bank." With the frontings message came the rockets, the criticisms and the kudos, the demands for clarifications and up-dates, the requests for Sunday stories and magazine pieces. Now, silence. The pigeons didn't make round-trips. Sheehan and Browne could read their stories coming back over the wire-service tickers at the embassy. Not Halberstam. Nor did anything addressed to *The New York Times* make it through the PTT office, where the blue pencils even censored the infallible words of the Pope asking Vietnamese Catholics to calm down. For a few days, it was a relief.

Sheehan, always wrestling with the instant deadlines of the wire game, loved the new deal. He wrote to the timing of the airline schedules, squeezing every last minute to polish up what he had so often sent out raw. One day he cut it so close he ran the story to the airport himself, arriving to see the boarding ramp pulling away from the plane. Package in hand, he vaulted the barrier in front of Diem's customs men, leaving them agog and dashed onto the field with both arms windmilling. The pilot cut two engines, the door reopened, the ramp rolled back, and Sheehan triple-stepped up the stairs toward a grinning stewardess. "U! P! I!" he shouted over the roar of the other engines, and his story made it out. Coming back into the terminal the customs men smiled and asked: "Did you make it?" God, how they hated the regime, he thought.

Even in his vacuum, Halberstam grew more famous and more controversial each day. *Esquire* magazine sent in a writer to profile

"Our Man in Saigon." It was long and flattering. SINCE SEPTEMBER, 1962, DAVID HALBERSTAM HAS BEEN IN THE MIDDLE OF THE MESS IN VIETNAM, WINNING ENEMIES AND INFLUENCING AMERICA, trumpeted one of the headlines. Halberstam was "a shoo-in" for the Pulitzer Prize, the writer, George J. W. Goodman,[6] predicted; word had it that Robert McNamara thought he was "about the brightest young reporter he'd ever met." It was a statement that, if he made it, McNamara quickly came to rue. No one would deflate Robert S. McNamara's image as a White Knight in Camelot as thoroughly as the young reporter from *The Times*.

The article was also insightful. "What has helped bring Halberstam to attention is not just his reporting," Goodman wrote, espying what was happening to all the young rebels with a cause: "It is the way the U.S. press in South Vietnam has become not only an observer, but a factor in the intramural squabbling that has gone along with the war." The correspondents were becoming the story, always a great danger in their craft, but a danger they had sought, advocates all.

Sheehan's little office, where they continued to work while overnighting at Mecklin's villa, became partly a bastion against the outside, partly a giddy gathering spot for the exhausted but exhilarated reporters. Goodman kept notes on a typical scene:

> 11:15 a.m. Halberstam, Sheehan, Keyes Beech of Chicago *Daily News*, are slouched on the city-room furniture. Ray Herndon, from UPI in Vientiane, Laos, walks in, announces, "I have a pigeon on the 1:15 to Singapore." Room comes to life.
>
> Sheehan, with new pigeon-deadline facing him, starts typing. Halberstam has dispatch all ready. Word goes down street, "Pigeon on 1:15 for Singapore . . ." Phone rings. Girl called Blue Lotus wants to talk to Sheehan. "Tell her I have a deadline, and to stop bothering me," Sheehan says.
>
> 2:30 p.m. Pigeon has flown, carrying copy from five correspondents. Lunch at Brodard's. Halberstam says, "Which of you is working for Colonel Tung [Nhu's top intelligence operative]?" Waiters giggle. Sheehan says, "I understand Minister [unnamed] is plotting a *coup d'état*. Better tell Colo-

6. Goodman later used the pen name Adam Smith.

nel Tung we're doing a story on that." Waiters look nervously at each other. "Are they really working for Colonel Tung?" I ask. Answer: "Of course." Newsboys push copies of *The Times of Vietnam*. . . . Sample headline: UPI LIES, LIES, LIES . . . "Me again," says Sheehan.

———

For a week the isolation was nearly total for Halberstam. Nothing from *The Times* made it through to Saigon, and the novelty of working in a vacuum quickly wore off. Halberstam would far rather pick a fight than get no human reaction at all. His ego required regular feedings. The silence became downright painful.

He gleaned some news from the wire tickers, some from the embassy. He knew Brother Nhu's con had kept the embassy confused for days. The place was dispirited, hanging on to a crumbling policy, changing ambassadors. The embassy had been in disarray before the raids. Nhu had done a superb job of keeping it that way. Not only were the embassy telephone lines cut, but so were the home lines. Even Saigon's multitudinous CIA agents were without phone links. After this embarrassment, the embassy's top people would carry walkie-talkies wherever they went. But, after the raids, they had trouble talking with each other, let alone unraveling Nhu's subterfuge.

So Halberstam knew that his reports directly contradicted the faulty information Washington received from Saigon, this time more pointedly than ever. He and Sheehan used the same pigeons, and Sheehan's stories were returning over the ticker. That meant that Halberstam's stories were getting home. But, at the penultimate moment—"a year's work has just paid off," he thought proudly—he had no idea what *The Times* was doing with them.

On the sixth day, a pigeon completed the first round-trip. Lee Griggs, the Tokyo correspondent for *Time* magazine, had left for Manila several days earlier with a stack of stories. Now he made the return trip carrying the first news from the outside. Lounging on Sheehan's tattered plastic sofa, Halberstam sprang eagerly to life. Reading the first message in his packet, however, he let out a furious yowl. It was a fronting:

YOUR STORY TWINNED WITH SZULC'S WASHINGTON SAYS GEN-
ERALS FORCE NHU TO SILENCE BUDDHISTS.

The twinning, as they called it in newspaper parlance, had
been a terrible affront to the newspaper's own man, virtually a
vote of no confidence. It had outraged the newspaper's staff in
New York as much as it now infuriated its isolated man in Saigon.
Griggs and Halberstam's buddies edged away from their hulking
friend as he tossed the cable angrily to the floor. Glancing at the
next message, a cable from his patron, James Reston, his mood
began to change:

KEEP GOING BECAUSE WE'RE ONLY GETTING PROPAGANDA THIS
END.

Quickly thumbing through the rest, he let out whoop after exultant whoop. The cables outlined a delayed chronology in which his
stories had overwhelmed the government. The final message, from
his often critical foreign desk, he read aloud:

STATE DEPARTMENT COMING AROUND TO YOUR VIEW WHAT
HAPPENED AND WHO DID IT AT PAGODAS STOP CHEERS AND
MORE CHEERS.

Sheehan's office erupted like a liberated fortress.
Mert Perry, whose editors at *Time* had been berating him for
failing to see the "big picture," pounded Halberstam on the back
and rumbled with laughter. "Washington finally got the *little* picture," he said.
Charley Mohr added to the accolades for both Halberstam and
Sheehan: "You guys are the first reporters I've ever known who
scooped the State Department by four days."
Not long afterward *Winners and Sinners,* an often self-critical
Times in-house publication, would confirm Mohr's view with its
own succinct compliment. In a small box under the headline "Coup
coup," it said simply: "*The New York Times* 1, State Department 0."
Halberstam leaned back and hoisted a Ba Moui Ba beer.

"Well, that's the end of the press controversy," he grinned at Mohr. "We've finally broken through. Now they'll understand."

About that, he could not have been more wrong.

———

Henry Cabot Lodge had landed with more than ambassadorial credentials. His grandfather, for whom he had been named, had been the golden Republican voice of American expansionism at the turn of the century, a close friend and ally of Teddy Roosevelt's. In the Spanish-American War, so they said, Teddy took Cuba and Cabot took the Philippines. The grandfather did his Rough Riding in the Senate, but he did it with the same élan and sense of historic mission as Roosevelt on San Juan Hill. The conquest of the Philippines carried the nineteenth-century war cry of Manifest Destiny, that self-assumed right of a brash young nation to push ever westward, beyond California, beyond the annexation of Hawaii, to the very shores of Asia. Now, in The American Century, a new Henry Cabot Lodge had come a step farther. He stood on the Asian continent itself, halfway around the world from his pedigreed roots in Massachusetts, both feet planted solidly in empire.

Lodge arrived with his mind made up. "You can't have the police knocking on the door at three o'clock in the morning, taking sixteen- and seventeen-year-old girls to camps . . . without laying the basis for assassination," he'd told Roger Hilsman as he left. Neil Sheehan, in that early one-on-one in which he had done all the talking, told Lodge that the ruling family was crazy, hated, and incapable of governing. As he was leaving, the reporter in him reemerged. "And what's your impression, Mr. Ambassador?" Sheehan asked. "About the same as yours," Lodge replied.

If his views needed reinforcement, Lodge soon received it. In the last days of August, the intrigues in Saigon became so byzantine they were impossible to unravel. But, when it came to intrigues, the machinations in Washington could not be outdone.

The correspondents had no idea how deeply the Buddhist crisis and their reporting had eroded the policy Homer Bigart had called "Sink or swim with Ngo Dinh Diem." The Pentagon stood pat, still believing General Harkins's assurances that its war was being won. The State Department, horrified by the effect that the imagery of burning monks and smashed pagodas had on America abroad, split wide open, and guerrilla warfare had begun.

Averell Harriman, the undersecretary of state for political affairs, led the anti-Diemists. At seventy-one, Harriman was aloof, tough, and smart. He had advised presidents since Franklin D. Roosevelt and, as Walter Isaacson and Evan Thomas later wrote in *The Wise Men*, he did it "more like a sovereign than a subject." He also had a deep and abiding distrust of the military. He thought Vietnam a mistake from the outset. When Maxwell Taylor, a Second World War commander of paratroops, first recommended Project Beef-Up, Harriman's reaction had been typical of the man. "You were wrong about wanting to send the 82nd Airborne into Rome and you've been wrong about everything since," he said. Harriman was shrewd if imperious. Once he moved on his intrigues, he chose as his lieutenants Michael Forrestal, one of his own young aides who had moved to the White House, and Hilsman, the onetime jungle fighter in Burma. Like good plotters anywhere, they moved on a Saturday.

On that hot summer day, August 24, 1963, two circumstances converged. The government finally concluded that it had been hoodwinked by Brother Nhu, and most of the top policy makers were out of town.

The President had gone home to Hyannisport, Robert McNamara to Wyoming to climb the Grand Tetons, Dean Rusk to Yankee Stadium to watch a ball game. CIA Director John McCone was on vacation, as was the President's adviser for national security affairs, McGeorge Bundy. Others were scattered about Washington on golf courses and following other weekend pursuits. Most of the city was preoccupied with Dr. Martin Luther King, Jr.'s March on Washington, his legions due to arrive in four days. It was far from universally presumed that they would arrive peacefully. The news from Saigon was also unsettling. POWER SHIFT TO NHU SEEN IN VIETNAM, read the page-one headline over Neil Sheehan's name in *The Washington Post*. On an inside page, Stanley Karnow wrote: "Even men close to Diem now speak calmly of a forthcoming assassination." It was a perfect day for, as Taylor called it later, "an end run."

Harriman and Hilsman wrote the piece of paper, a cable of new instructions for Lodge. From the White House, Forrestal sent Kennedy the overnight cables from Saigon and a memo telling him all agreed that Nhu had masterminded the pagoda events. "Averell and Roger," he wrote, "now agree we must move before the situation in Saigon freezes." Then he called Hyannisport and read Kennedy the draft cable. The President was cautious.

"Can't we wait till Monday when everybody is back?" he asked.

"Averell and Roger," Forrestal repeated, "really want to get this thing out right away."

Kennedy replied the way Harriman hoped. Then you go out and get everybody to sign on, Kennedy said in a half-challenge that bought time. Instead, it became a presidential imprimatur.

Over the next half-dozen hours deputy secretaries and aides de camp to the people who made war were hauled off golf courses and out of swank restaurants, signing on one by one, each easier to convince after another had signed. Of the Cabinet-level policy makers only Rusk approved it personally, and he did so, he said later, because he believed Kennedy had already made the decision.

At 9:36 P.M. the instructions went out as DEPTEL 243. So deeply did Department Telegram 243 have an impact on America's role in Vietnam, however, that it became known thereafter only as the Cable of August 24. It read, in part:

US GOVERNMENT CANNOT TOLERATE SITUATION IN WHICH POWER LIES IN NHU'S HANDS. DIEM MUST BE GIVEN CHANCE TO RID HIMSELF OF NHU AND HIS COTERIE AND REPLACE THEM WITH BEST MILITARY AND POLITICAL PERSONALITIES AVAILABLE.

IF, IN SPITE OF ALL YOUR EFFORTS, DIEM REMAINS OBDURATE AND REFUSES, THEN WE MUST FACE THE POSSIBILITY THAT DIEM HIMSELF CANNOT BE PRESERVED.

Asking Diem to banish his brother was like asking John Kennedy to dump Robert. Almost no one thought he would do it. Lodge knew he wouldn't. He cabled back immediately:

BELIEVE THAT CHANCE OF DIEM'S MEETING OUR DEMANDS ARE VIRTUALLY NIL. AT SAME TIME, BY MAKING THEM WE GIVE NHU

CHANCE TO FORESTALL OR BLOCK ACTION BY MILITARY. RISK, WE BELIEVE, NOT WORTH TAKING, WITH NHU IN CONTROL COMBAT FORCES SAIGON. THEREFORE, PROPOSE WE GO STRAIGHT TO GENERALS WITH OUR DEMANDS, WITHOUT INFORMING DIEM.

The State Department quickly agreed. The next morning, Henry Cabot Lodge went to Gia Long Palace and formally presented himself to Ngo Dinh Diem as the new ambassador from the United States. It was the first time they had met. In Washington, Kennedy returned to the White House to find McNamara, Rusk, and Taylor virtually parked at the Oval Office door, furious. McCone, still out of town, was also mad as hell. You've been bamboozled into ordering the overthrow of Diem, his top men told the President. Afterward, Kennedy told a friend: "My god! My government's coming apart."

That day's White House meeting on Vietnam became the most acrimonious yet. The President, in the way of all princes, opened the session by killing the messenger. He launched a ferocious attack on David Halberstam, venting bile that had been building for a week. Then came a long and angry debate. But even the losers in Harriman's coup agreed that it was too late. By then Lodge surely had given the word to the generals. The orders stood.

Nothing regarding Vietnam would ever be the same again.

———

That same Monday morning, Marguerite Higgins's series of stories began appearing in New York. Halberstam, without a full day's grace to savor his successes, was about to have a bad week. Sheehan too. They had become brothers, moving to the same rhythms as surely as if genetics had made the tie. Since the midnight ride in the tiny Renault, they had romped together on a week-long high. Now their story had crested, but it was far from over. And they were exhausted, nerve endings frayed, adrenaline run dry. "Working no-no sleep," Sheehan wrote to his editors atop one of his files. It should have been read as a warning.

Reporters are a thin-skinned lot, an odd trait among those who dish out so much. But no one became quite as notorious as Halberstam for failing to build the calluses he forced others to layer on thick. A few years later the magazine of New York's Overseas Press Club, *Dateline,* parodied him in a mock question-and-answer interview. A sample exchange:

Q: What about the correspondent himself? Should he have a tough hide? Do you, for instance, have a tough hide?

A: I think that question is a personal attack, and I'm offended. I take it as a reflection on myself and all the correspondents in Vietnam.

In Higgins he ran up against an antagonist who, among her other traits, was a shamelessly wicked gossip who never let particulars ambush her fun. She had Halberstam boiling before her stories made it to print.

The tale that did it involved a most unlikely conversation said to have taken place on the roof of the Caravelle Hotel. As she told it, Higgins had just returned from the field with a handful of photos of Viet Cong bodies. When she showed them to Halberstam, the ace young correspondent from *The New York Times* burst into tears, she gleefully told all of Washington that would listen. The story was preposterous. Even so, some believed it. One who did was Brute Krulak. The general took the story as proof that Halberstam was a sissy. Krulak, a good marine of such innovative mind that he designed the landing craft used in the island assaults of the Second World War, later conceded that his judgment had failed him badly on many counts in the summer of 1963. "We were all abysmally ignorant," he said of the many and disastrous mistakes. He made a lesser one—but one that caused the earth to quake nevertheless —by passing Higgins's gossipy tale on to a group of editors at *Time* magazine. The editors told Charley Mohr. Mohr told Halberstam.

Nothing small ever happened to David Halberstam. The event escalated. With Halberstam, *all* events escalated. Higgins's story and Krulak's repetition of it became "the penultimate assault on my manhood." These were times when real men went eyeball to eyeball with the Russians, the fate of the world at stake. Tough guys didn't cry.

A few weeks later, Krulak visited Vietnam. Halberstam was there to meet him. Not simply at the airport, but out on the tarmac. It became a scene few forgot, the twenty-nine-year-old, six-foot-three-inch reporter towering over the fifty-year-old, five-foot-five-inch marine general.

"My name is David Halberstam and I hear you've been telling people I was crying on the roof of the Caravelle Hotel," Halberstam began in a voice heard easily over the jet noise.

"Yes," Krulak replied. "I was quoting Maggie Higgins, as you probably know."

An eruption followed.

"I want to tell you that the story is a bunch of shit!!!" The words spilled out. "It is not true and no one ever showed me pictures like that and I did not break into tears and I just want you to fucking know it and don't *ever* put shit out like that again!"

"Well, it's not a GI Joe war, is it?" Krulak groped, surprised but unintimidated. "It's not a war with an Ernie Pyle, is it?"

Halberstam erupted again. The shouting continued for five minutes before they broke it off, two men of their times who had never seen each other before and would never see each other again. Higgins later denied telling the crying story, too, adding: "How should I know whether he's a coward? How does he know himself? He's never fought for anything." Thirty years later, however, Krulak still insisted she had told him the story.

No one could have set the dynamics in motion for the airport scene more adroitly than Marguerite Higgins. In her six-part series in the *New York Herald Tribune* she went after Halberstam with bigger guns than gossip. VIETNAM—FACT AND FICTION, the logo promised, and it didn't take a close reading to identify her choice as the fiction writer.

"Contrary to recent published reports that the situation in the rich Mekong River delta area has 'deteriorated,' " she wrote, "Gen. Paul Harkins insists that the opposite is true." Point by point in story after story she contradicted virtually everything Halberstam had reported, using Harkins and his self-deluding staff as her guide dogs. When Halberstam reported that the Viet Cong were building toward large-force mobile warfare, she found a Harkins aide to contradict him with the kind of arrogance that would come back to haunt so many men throughout the long war ahead:

What is mobility? Mobility means vehicles and aircraft. You have seen the way our Vietnamese units are armed—50 radios, 30 or 40 vehicles, rockets, mortars and airplanes. The Viet Cong have no vehicles and airplanes. How can they be mobile?

By 1963 the *Herald Tribune* neared the last rites, another sign of the end of an era. But there were still those who saw the *Trib* as New York's last great hope, a newspaper that had always kept the overweight *Times* on its toes, a thinking man's alternative to death by boredom in the endless gray columns of the other choice. Within months after her series, virtually all of Maggie Higgins's arguments came unglued. But many at her newspaper saw it sooner. The *Trib* had nourished the legend of the daring young girl correspondent; now it seemed stuck with a general's wife. Her Vietnam series, a paean to foolishness, was the last straw. "Marguerite Higgins will never pee outside Washington again," one of her editors is reported to have vowed. Later no one would claim the pithy line, although her foreign editor, Harry M. Rosenfeld, found it tempting. "If I thought I could get away with it, I'd grab it," Rosenfeld said. "She was wrong about everything she wrote, and we only had to wait a few months to find out." Also within a few months Higgins had taken her talents to *Newsday,* where she began writing a syndicated column.

Meanwhile, at Broadway and 43rd, Maggie Higgins's stories had done what she did best. They made waves. *The New York Times* crossed every "t," even the crooked ones. That was part of what made the newspaper great, part of what drove its greatest talents to the nearest bar.

The first packet of messages from home had contained virtually nothing but accolades. Even Nathaniel M. Gerstenzang, the night foreign editor with whom Halberstam had had that first dust-up in the Congo, sent kind words. Gerstenzang had no admirers among *The Times*'s foreign correspondents. Even his friends, who thought him highly intelligent, said he showed this trait only through the narrowest of scopes and, to boot, had one of the most disagreeable tempers in the world. But, briefly, Gerstenzang seemed to mellow. PLEASE TELL DAVE OUR ADMIRATION FOR TRE-MENDOUS JOB, he had cabled through a relay. HE WAY AHEAD OF OTHERS. Unfortunately, the pigeons then began delivering his missives on a daily basis:

INFORMATIVELY HIGGINS YESTERDAY REPORTED SITUATION IN
HINTERLANDS RE BUDDHISTS QUITE DIFFERENT. . . .

Followed by:

WHAT IS THERE TO MAGGIE HIGGINS STATEMENTS THAT IN
COUNTRYSIDE WAR ACTUALLY BEING FOUGHT. . . .

The daily barrage from the foreign desk reached a frazzled man.
To the first he replied:

ON THAT LITTLE GIRL I THINK IT SHOULD BE CLEAR WHICH SIDE
IS SLANTING STOP. . . .

And to the next:

MAGGIE COPY NOT TAKEN SERIOUSLY HERE AND PLEASE UN-
WORRY SINCE ENTIRE BUSINESS IS DELIBERATE PHONY STOP
LONGER MEMO ON THAT FOLLOWS. . . .

And then the longer memo:

HALBERSTAM TO GERSTENZANG INFORMATIVELY I AM SUR-
PRISED YOU BRING UP HIGGINS STORIES AT ALL SINCE THEY
STRIKE ME AS MOST DISREPUTABLE KIND OF REPORTING AND
THOROUGHLY DISCREDITED BY EVENTS STOP. . . . SHE SPENT
MOST OF HER TIME INTERVIEWING HEAD OF CIA BRACKET NOW
THOROUGHLY DISCREDITED UNBRACKET AND HARKINS WHO IS
A PARTICULARLY STUPID AND ILL-INFORMED MAN STOP. . . . WE
ARE ACCURATE AND SHE IS TOTALLY WRONG STOP. . . . WE ARE
NOT REPEAT NOT GOING TO ANSWER HER COPY OR GO BACK
OVER SAME GROUND FOR HER BENEFIT AS LONG AS I AM HERE
BEST REGARDS HALBERSTAM.

Then, by special pouch, came a letter from Gerstenzang:

SOME OF WHAT SHE HAS BEEN WRITING WOULD TEND TO BAL-
ANCE THE MATERIAL WE HAVE BEEN GETTING FROM SAIGON

RECENTLY. . . . I AM SURE THAT YOU WILL TAKE CARE OF THIS
ASPECT OF THE VIETNAMESE STORY AS SOON AS YOU CAN.

Smooth, the assistant foreign editor was not, although, by that
time, he had no intention of trying. Nor did the firebrand in Saigon.
The glass wall at 19 Ngo Duc Ke vibrated as if a soprano had just
hit high C. Back to New York went another cable:

GERSTENZANG IF YOU SEND ME ONE MORE CABLE REFERRING
TO THAT WOMANS COPY YOU WILL HAVE MY RESIGNATION
FORTHWITH BY RETURN CABLE AND I MEAN IT REPEAT MEAN IT
HALBERSTAM.

After a tense and brief cease-fire, Gerstenzang suggested a
"richly deserved" three- or four-week vacation in Hong Kong, an
idea quickly rebuffed. That same day Halberstam's exhausted
buddy received a cable from Tokyo requesting a Danish spin on
the story for a new client in Copenhagen. But that was UPI, and
Neil Sheehan had already had his blowout. Halberstam held out
four days after the return of the first pigeon before threatening to
quit. Sheehan waited only one.

The provocation was even less significant, involving a minor
story rewritten in Tokyo. But Sheehan was stretched so tight he
had no give left. He fired off cables to Earnie Hoberecht and two
editors as well, so angry he sent them straight through the censors,
letting them read every word:

PHONY AND WILDLY INACCURATE STORY MAKES UPI AND EVERY
REPORTER HERE LOOK LIKE IDIOTS STOP I CONSIDER WHOEVER
WROTE THAT STORY IN TOKYO AS INCOMPETENT AND DANGER-
OUS STOP IF THIS DOES NOT CEASE IMMEDIATELY AND [STORY
REWRITTEN] WITH BACKGROUND PUTTING IN CONTEXT THEN
MY RESIGNATION WILL FOLLOW BY URGENT CABLE STOP THIS
CABLE CENSORED STOP SHEEHAN.

Any reply by Hoberecht has been lost to the ages. But a "personal and private" letter found its way to Saigon from a buddy,
Bill Wright, who had worked with Sheehan during his brief night-
desk days in the old Mainichi Shimbun Building.

"Gads man!" Wright wrote. "Your protests and threats to resign came in here fast and furious today! The old KDD machine was literally smoking! I'm dashing this off so that it will get in your hands before you do anything drastic."

Wright, who later covered some nasty wars in Africa and Central America, then gave Sheehan a good-natured lecture on humility and equanimity. His star was soaring, Wright told him. "Don't, for God's (or Buddha's) sake, mar that by acquiring a reputation as a prima donna." Then he delivered the real gift and probably the best advice under the circumstances: "Enclosed is a box of genuine, LUBRICATED rubbers. GO OUT, MAN, AND GET YOURSELF LAID. YOU'LL FEEL MUCH BETTER!"

The hypertensive aftermath of the pagoda raids was soon lost in a swirl of rumors about CIA plots and a coup d'état that didn't happen. The pigeons were soon gone too. Censorship ended after three weeks, a lost cause never to be tried again in Vietnam.

But the many wars of the maverick correspondents had just begun. The intensity of their experience, the danger, the excitement, the brotherhood, the loneliness, the total commitment of time and energy, the total isolation from other cares, all this had armored them against slings from the outside, even those that came at them from their home court. So riveting was it all, as Halberstam had described it, that they had created their own reality in their own private universe, and the angers of a Nathaniel M. Gerstenzang or a John F. Kennedy became mere flailings in that far-off Land of the Big PX. Robert J. Manning, the former newsman and future editor of *Atlantic Monthly* whom Kennedy had sent to Saigon after the Arnett beating, phrased it less romantically: "They unquestionably are severely afflicted with 'localitis,' the disease which causes newsmen long assigned to the confines of one given situation to distort perspective by over-concentration on their own irritations, adventures and opinions."

No matter how their cocoon was described, the massed forces from the other world now came crashing through all their barriers.

"It looked like an armada," Halberstam said.

15

THE ARMADA

In launching her attack in the *Herald Tribune* Monday, August 26, Marguerite Higgins quickly picked up zealous allies, public and private. Thundering promptly to her support was another New York newspaper, the sensationalist right-wing *Journal American*. For a moment it looked like the beginning of a good old-fashioned newspaper war, with three New York dailies mixing it up to the roar of the newsboys. But, as quick as *The Times* might be to deluge its man with querulous cables, it would never stoop to a street fight with its lessers (which included everyone else in the business of churning out news). It surely would not mix it up with the Hearstian lowlifes at the *Journal American*.

Reading the *Journal American* was like stepping back in time. The newspaper was the direct descendant of William Randolph Hearst's *Journal*, the bombastic sheet that had given the world yellow journalism and turned a newspaper war into one with bullets. Sixty-five years earlier, Hearst and New York's other great tabloid general, Joseph Pulitzer of the *World*, cannonaded each other day after day in a circulation war of sensationalist headlines in which truth became not the casualty but the fatality. Then Hearst discovered Cuba. He found it before Teddy Roosevelt or Henry Cabot Lodge. He delivered it to them.

Hearst dispatched correspondents and artists, paying them then-staggering fees to stir up trouble between Spanish colonialists and Cuban peasants who self-evidently would prefer to become a large sugar plantation for their friendly northern neighbors. When his $3,000-a-month artist, Frederic Remington, complained that he could find no war to sketch, legend has it that Hearst wired back: YOU FURNISH THE PICTURES. I'LL FURNISH THE WAR.

The reply may be apocryphal. But no matter, Hearst furnished the war. In what his biographer, W. A. Swanberg, describes as the "most disgraceful example of journalistic falsehood ever seen," the publisher and his troops invented stories about Spanish crimes and atrocities, illustrated them with imaginary sketches of tortured maidens, and then hawked the "news" in as many as forty extra editions a day. Pulitzer matched Hearst dollar for dollar, fiction for fiction, extra for extra.

When the battleship *Maine* blew up in Havana harbor, an event most historians now consider an accident, the New York papers turned the sinking into an anti-Spanish battle cry that started men marching. The newspapers alone put 400 in the field. Circulations soared. Pulitzer's *World* sold 5 million copies in a single week. Hearst cheerfully advertised: "How do you like the *Journal*'s war?"

To John Mecklin, the Saigon correspondents had become as influential as those rambunctious legions of Pulitzer and Hearst. Always torn, he could never make up his mind as to whether that influence was good or bad. "In refusing to be intimidated, the Saigon press corps performed a distinct public service," he wrote afterward. He also wrote that their "unadorned reporting" had "wrecked a major American foreign policy."

The latter-day Hearstians had no doubts. In 1963 the *Journal American*, like most of the old Hearst papers, teetered on its last legs. It was a relic, still looking for outrageous headlines, wars to fight, battleships to sink. With a nudge from Maggie Higgins, Hearst's Washington columnist and national editor, Frank Conniff, set his sights on the biggest dreadnought around.

"Well, the good gray *New York Times* has decreed that the Diem government in Vietnam has got to go, so everybody take a firm stance and brace yourself for the emergence of an Asian Fidel Castro," Conniff began in the first of a drumbeat of columns. He attacked the Saigon correspondents as too young and too prejudiced, clearly lacking the abilities of "a competent reporter like Marguerite Higgins, whose byline carries authority." Halberstam became the new Herbert Matthews, the bogeyman of the right wing, helping *The Times* hand Kennedy a "political time bomb" in Vietnam "just as Cuba represented their loaded present to President Eisenhower." Then he attacked Halberstam with an old bugaboo:

> One thing we must say for Mr. David Halberstam, *The Times'* man in Saigon. He has resurrected from oblivion good old "reliable sources," an idiomatic usage that was, alack, fast disappearing from the reporter's arsenal. We stopped counting in Saturday's *Times* after 11 hits by good old "reliable sources" or his less sturdy brother, plain old "sources."

Identifying all sources is a journalistic ideal rarely met, and rarely ideal either. In her stories, Higgins named everyone. That meant quoting only those who were following the optimistic party line, lying to themselves or lying to her. Still, as loath as *The Times* might be to follow Hearst's Neanderthal line, Conniff's dig drew the reaction he hoped it would. Within forty-eight hours, amid the flood of Gerstenzang cables about Maggie Higgins, another missive from New York reached Halberstam: WOULD APPRECIATE YOUR INCLUDING IN ALL STORIES AT LEAST SOME INDICATION OF WHO SOURCES ARE . . . FEEL YOUR HABITUAL REFERENCES MERELY TO SOURCES IS INADEQUATE. Halberstam stewed and then rebutted: IF MY COLONEL USES NAME HE NO LONGER COLONEL. But a new grievance was added. In its assessments, even the CIA, with no apparent sense of irony, began reproaching him for his failure to name sources.

A very unhappy president also read Higgins on that pivotal Monday and needed no nudge to become a private ally. Ambushed first thing in the morning by his angry Cabinet officers, he was fuming by the time of the noon meeting on Vietnam. He looked around the room. All the players were there—Rusk, McNamara, and Taylor, still simmering because they had been outflanked over the weekend by the Cable of August 24; Harriman, Hilsman, and Forrestal, edgy about having done the flanking; Richard Helms, the CIA's deputy director for plans; Krulak and several others.

The President asked one quick housekeeping question: Given the cable approving a coup, had steps been taken to protect the 4,000 U.S. civilians now in Vietnam? Then he abruptly launched into a scathing attack on the man who once again had delivered him the news ahead of his own State Department. Even filtered through the diplomatic language of the meeting's minutes, Kennedy's anger was impossible to disguise:

> The President observed that Mr. Halberstam of *The New York Times* is actually running a political campaign; that he is wholly unobjective, reminiscent of Mr. Matthews in the Castro days. He stated that it was essential that we not permit Halberstam to influence our actions.

Moments later, according to the minutes, he added:

> ... when we move to eliminate this government, it should not be as a result of *New York Times* pressure.

Others at the meeting remembered the President's anger in stronger language: "Goddammit, I don't want you reading those stories in *The Times*. We're not going to let our policy be run by some twenty-eight-year-old kid."

Harriman and Hilsman, architects of the policy end run that made it look as if the administration was doing exactly that, tried to calm the President down.

But Kennedy was equally steamed at his own men and their weekend of palace intrigues. After hearing a review of the actions that led to the fateful cable, he exploded: "This shit has got to stop!" Later, Forrestal offered to resign. "You're not worth firing," Kennedy said. "You owe me something, so you stick around."

The meetings continued daily through the last week of August. Halberstam, on the front page virtually every day, became a fixation for Kennedy. By one count, the President made twelve separate attacks on him that week. Hilsman listened and thought ruefully: They had accused former President Eisenhower of reading the newspapers too little; now Kennedy is reading them too much. McGeorge Bundy tried to laugh the President out of it. Bundy had been dean at Harvard while Halberstam worked at *The Crimson*. Don't take college journalists too seriously, he advised. But Kennedy's venting inevitably seeped out of the White House and infected others. The criticisms became "most unpretty," Hilsman wrote later, and Halberstam, looking at it from the other side, recalled,

"We were the first people Kennedy didn't feed, the first to challenge him. He made it very personal."

At the Pentagon, Krulak continued with the crying story and the military began bandying about a new nickname for the correspondents: the Seven Dwarfs.

The attacks became so intense that Tom Wicker, the *Times* White House correspondent, ended a presidential trip in Palm Springs in a shouting match with Kennedy's longtime aide and appointments secretary, Kenneth O'Donnell. Wicker wrote his old friend about it:

> I guess you get echoes of all the furore. I had a ferocious argument with Ken O'Donnell, who says you are a schoolboy and that his CIA reports on you are that you lurk in your hotel and never talk to anybody. I told him he ought to be ashamed of himself (a) to have CIA reports on you, (b) to have a CIA that would make reports on you, and (c) to believe them if they did. Then I gave him a copy of your piece in *Times Talk* and told him to shove it up his arse.

In the White House pressroom the attacks became routine. Pierre Salinger, Kennedy's chubby, chummy press secretary, lost his good nature when it came to the correspondents in Saigon. He repeatedly grumbled that they were too green and were using sensationalized, irresponsible reporting to make a name for themselves. He hinted that they invented their sources. "That certainly came into our minds," Salinger said later. It was an especially pernicious charge, one that, if true, would be cause for firing by any of the news organizations for whom the correspondents worked.

The young Saigon group had too few defenders like Wicker in the cozy White House pressroom. Looking back from the distance of the white-hot media world of the late twentieth century, Kennedy's White House press corps seems to have come not from a different era but a different world. What modern presidential press secretary could permanently deflect a serious question with a joke? What modern president could end discussion about thousands of American soldiers with a one-word answer? In that environment, the Saigon correspondents became radicals, Halberstam a bomb thrower.

Halberstam was clearly no fan of the Washington press corps.

During his time in town, he came to look on it as a "semi-docile group doing its dance for Kennedy." Its performance while he was in Vietnam left him permanently embittered. When he finally came home, one White House reporter approached him and said, "I thought you'd be glad to hear that when your name came up at a dinner party last night I defended you." Halberstam said nothing. But this thought remained with him long afterward: "Well, fuck you, I don't need you to defend me. Just do your work."

Meanwhile, the onslaught caught the correspondents by surprise. They saw themselves as vindicated by events. Instead, the chorus of criticism escalated.

"What began as sniping turned into an orchestrated attack," Halberstam said. "It became a full-fledged war with more fronts than Vietnam. We were getting cannon fire from a different direction every day: the Pentagon regiment, the White House regiment, the embassy regiment, the press regiment, the right-wing regiment —and all of it feeding the regiments from our own offices."

———

It was a bad week for Kennedy to be preoccupied by anything, let alone Halberstam. In the White House meetings, he and his men were orchestrating the overthrow of an ostensibly friendly government, and suddenly the plans were coming together very quickly. For decades afterward the bright young men of the New Frontier would attempt to cleanse themselves of the dirtier parts of these beginnings that drew America deep into the moral morass of Vietnam. Rationalizations ran rampant: The Vietnamese generals did the planning, controlled the timing, determined the outcome. But the White House provided the clout. The CIA worked liaison, the administration promised the money, and, in Saigon, Lodge's private cables minced no words: WE ARE LAUNCHED ON A COURSE FROM WHICH THERE IS NO RESPECTABLE TURNING BACK: THE OVERTHROW OF THE DIEM GOVERNMENT. The U.S. government surely did not seek to have Diem and Nhu killed in the process, but CIA messages used no euphemisms for the possible, if not likely, outcome: GENERALS SAID THAT IF FIRST STEP OF THE COUP IS SUCCESSFUL, I.E., THE ASSASSINATION OF DIEM, THEY WOULD THEN SUPPORT COUP OPENLY.

Meanwhile, Saigon swirled with rumors. Plots overlapped black plots. Halberstam, Sheehan, and a *Saturday Evening Post* photographer, Burt Glinn, worked their way into the middle of one that called for more foolhardiness than it could reward in newsworthiness.

As the schemes multiplied in late August, the reporters concluded that only two groups were likely to act—the generals, who were talking to the U.S. government, and a group of junior officers, who were bolder but constantly outmaneuvered by their seniors. For reasons Halberstam never understood, the junior officers approached him and escorted him to a meeting in a darkened, claptrap building in Saigon's Chinese district of Cholon. Would he like to cover their coup from the inside? The plan was simple: Halberstam would be "kidnapped"—his not-too-convincing cover story if the coup failed—and then report the action from the rebel command post. Halberstam thought about it, found Sheehan and Glinn ready to join forces, and agreed. For days they carried military radios with an assigned band and their own call letters. No call ever came. The generals sidetracked the junior officers once again, using their usual gambit. They ordered their rivals' battalions out of Saigon, probably inadvertently saving the correspondents' lives.

Meanwhile, a flurry of activity at the end of August reflected the response to the Cable of August 24 and the expectation that the generals would act.

CIA station in Saigon to Langley, August 28:

SITUATION HERE HAS REACHED POINT OF NO RETURN. SAIGON IS ARMED CAMP. CURRENT INDICATIONS ARE THAT NGO FAMILY HAVE DUG IN FOR LAST DITCH BATTLE. . . . WE ALL UNDERSTAND THAT THE EFFORT MUST SUCCEED AND THAT WHATEVER NEEDS TO BE DONE ON OUR PART MUST BE DONE.

Lodge to Department of State, August 29:

THE CHANCE OF BRINGING OFF A GENERALS' COUP DEPENDS ON THEM TO SOME EXTENT; BUT IT DEPENDS AT LEAST AS MUCH ON US.

Kennedy to Lodge, August 29:

UNTIL THE VERY MOMENT OF THE GO SIGNAL FOR THE OPERA-
TION BY THE GENERALS, I MUST RESERVE A CONTINGENT RIGHT
TO CHANGE COURSE AND REVERSE PREVIOUS INSTRUCTIONS.

President Kennedy would eventually find that he would have a
very difficult time turning off what he had begun. But this time the
generals did it for him.

CIA station in Saigon to Langley, August 31:

THIS PARTICULAR COUP IS FINISHED.

The generals didn't trust the erratic Americans any more than
Diem and Nhu did. Diem and Nhu trusted them very little. They
had tracked all the week's events.

CIA PLANNED COUP D'ETAT, screamed the headline at the top of
the front page of the September 2 *Times of Vietnam*.

"Nonsense," responded the American Embassy.

"Something out of Ian Fleming," scoffed the State Department.

The American efforts had been justified, Lodge cabled home
secretly, "because the government of Vietnam has acted both as
liars and criminals."

With the open collapse of the move against Diem, the United
States "found itself at the end of August 1963 without a policy and
with most of its bridges burned," according to the Pentagon Papers.
But Henry Cabot Lodge was no Nolting. He had been in Saigon
scarcely a week and he had dug in. It appeared that Kennedy had
done so too.

On September 2, the President sat for an unusual television interview with Walter Cronkite. It was an historic moment for television, with CBS using the interview as the centerpiece in its first
half-hour evening news program. Gone forever were the days of
the fifteen-minute rip and reads; television was stepping into its
own world-changing future.[1] Kennedy accommodated by providing provocative news on his mess in Vietnam:

1. NBC went to a half-hour news program one week later. ABC waited
more than three years to make the move.

We are prepared to assist them, but I don't think the war can be won unless the people support the effort and, in my opinion, in the last two months, the government has gotten out of touch with the people. . . .

Could the Diem government regain the support it needed?

With changes in policy and perhaps with personnel I think it can. If it doesn't make those changes, I would think that the chances of winning it would not be very good.

It was the first time an American president had ventured so directly into the realm of television diplomacy. He had done so with remarkable bluntness, sending a message—*with changes in policy and perhaps with personnel*—that tightened the screws on an ally in a way that had rarely been done before.

Meanwhile, the screws on the Saigon correspondents also tightened. The next cannonade came from *Time* magazine, an attack so vitriolic it not only flayed the correspondents but rocked the huge and powerful Luce empire. Richard Clurman, *Time*'s chief of correspondents, was horrified. The press of 1963 was a far different creature from the one it would become. It had no ombudsmen or media critics, no shout TV or radio talkmeisters. "The press simply didn't write about itself in those days," Clurman looked back on it later. "And surely not the way we did it." In all the eccentric doings of Henry Luce's flashy newsmagazine, Clurman had never seen anything like this one. It was an attack designed to take no prisoners, not even—*certainly not*—its own man.

———

Charley Mohr had been cranky for a month. Since his shoot-out with Fuerbringer, nothing in the magazine resembled what he wrote. He had been blanked during the pagoda raids, blanked during the intrigues that followed. Now, in the second week of September, he sent off his strongest file yet. He bothered with none of the soft balancing edges that a smart man on the rise would put in a *Time* file that ran counter to New York's prevailing winds. And Mohr had been that, a smart man on the rise.

"The war in Vietnam is being lost," his file began and then

quoted angry American advisers: "One source said that American military reporting in the country 'has been wrong and false—lies, really. We are now paying the price.' "

He sent the dispatch to New York on a Friday and flew off into the wilds for a weekend with Ivan Slavich's helicopter pilots. It was Mohr's way of relaxing; he loved the *whump* of the helicopter blades, the weekend with the boys. Back on Monday, he found Mert Perry waving a handful of cables at him. "What the hell does this mean?" Perry asked, handing him one from Clurman.

Over the chief of correspondents' objections, *Time* had published a story in its Press section, which "you will find and I find unacceptable and that will cause a great deal of trouble," Clurman warned. Don't send any messages to Fuerbringer, he pleaded. The matter was so serious that Clurman asked Mohr to meet him halfway between Saigon and New York to talk about it. "Not at Wake Island," he added, unsuccessfully trying to add some lightness. A decade earlier Harry Truman had met Douglas MacArthur on the barren Pacific atoll shortly before firing him as commander of his armies in Korea. Clurman's idea of halfway was more civilized, more fitting with *Time*'s style. He chose Paris, where he took a suite at the Ritz.

"What does it mean?" Perry pushed.

Mohr frowned. It meant Otto Fuerbringer had upped the stakes. It also meant that *Time* had joined the armada. "It's another salvo in this private war of ours," he said. Perry's blackout in the columns of the magazine had been as total as his.

A handful of copies of *Time* arrived that afternoon from Hong Kong. The press story filled most of a page. Among the tired and beleaguered correspondents, it exploded like a Claymore mine:

> ... One of the more curious aspects of the South Vietnam story is that the press corps on the scene is helping to compound the confusion that it should be untangling for its readers at home.

For all the light they were shedding, the magazine continued, the correspondents' stories "might just as well have been printed in Vietnamese." Then *Time* got mean:

The newsmen have themselves become a part of South Vietnam's confusion, [their] reporting prone to distortions. . . .

In the camaraderie of the Hotel Caravelle's eighth-floor bar they pool their convictions, information, misinformation and grievances. But the balm of such companionship has not been conducive to independent thought . . .

Many of the correspondents seem reluctant to give splash treatment to anything that smacks of military victory. . . . When there is a defeat, the color is rich and flowing. . . .

Mal Browne, "just boiling with wrath," immediately cabled a threat to sue for libel (the magazine singled out AP). Halberstam shot off a letter to Clurman, charging that *Time* "missed the boat and frankly I think you missed it willfully." (The magazine gleefully zeroed in on the embarrassing "twinning" episode: "*The New York Times* threw up its hands helplessly, and beneath an editorial apology, printed two widely divergent accounts. . . .") Even Keyes Beech blew his top. He was sick of hearing "this bullshit" about the Caravelle bar. "It is a goddamned lie," the crusty ex-marine barked at Clurman a week later, "and so is the rest of that crap."

But *Time*'s assault was one more reminder, a most powerful one, of how totally alone the correspondents had become—and how flimsy their lifelines to home. Halberstam immediately covered his flank with one of his epic cables—a 1,200-word explanation to his managing editor, Turner Catledge. Neil Sheehan was preempted. From Tokyo, Hoberecht reminded him that he had been warned that his free-wheeling reporting would bring about something like this. It would be the last mild rebuke. Sheehan's life was about to become absolutely miserable.

While his buddies carried on about the press story, Mohr turned to the World section, where he had directed his latest report that the war was being lost. REPORT ON THE WAR, *Time* headlined its update. "The government soldiers are fighting better than ever," the story said.

"Shit," Mohr spat.

That night the group went drinking—Beech, Halberstam, Perry, Ray Herndon, Peter Arnett, Sheehan with his *citron pressé*, the lemon drink he nurtured during these sessions, all of them but Perry trying to talk Mohr out of quitting. Perry had already decided to quit too. They riveted on *Time*'s attack, the most bitter and nasty one so far. Mohr was furious about it too. But as he slugged down his scotch, his fixation turned to the World section. He knew how *Time* worked, how Fuerbringer worked. When Mohr arrived at the luxury of the Ritz, Clurman could promise almost anything, maybe even deliver up that old dream of Nairobi. Clurman could give him that. But he couldn't get Mohr's reporting into the magazine. Only Fuerbringer could do that. My God, it was a wacko system, he thought. He was riding an expense-account elephant to nowhere. The longer the gang drank and the more they tried to talk him out of quitting over the press piece, the more he drank and the more determined he became to quit over the total distortion of his reporting.

The next morning Mohr flew back to Hong Kong and talked with his wife, Norma. She backed him up. Suddenly, he laughed at an impish idea, one that only a decade amid *Time*'s opulence could have given him the audacity to do. Norma had had a tough time, much of it his fault. She deserved a trip to Paris. So Charley Mohr bought two first-class, expense-account air tickets, and they both flew west toward the Ritz, where he would quit.

To hell with the bastards, he thought; it's the *Time* way to do it.

———

In the wake of the stillborn coup, everything seemed to come unhinged.

First came the incident with the miraculous carp, a huge fish found swimming in a small pond near Da Nang. Local Buddhists became convinced that the fish was a reincarnated disciple of the Buddha. The district chief and his cronies, Diem followers, didn't like that idea, especially when pilgrimages to the pond grew larger and larger. They mined the pond. The fish swam on. They machine-gunned the pond. The fish swam on. They called in Colonel Tung's Special Forces, who grenaded the pond. The fish swam on into legend. Most of the world's newspapers found stories about the mystical carp irresistible. South Vietnamese Army helicopters began landing at the pond's shores, and ARVN troopers filled their canteens with its magical water.

In Washington, the policy makers floundered. At a White House meeting, Secretary of State Rusk voiced frustration that reports from that "snake pit," Saigon, might be causing all the trouble. Marguerite Higgins had ventured out into the countryside, he observed. He felt a strong need to hear the real voice of the Vietnamese people.

Edward R. Murrow, now running Kennedy's U.S. Information Agency, offered to ask the twenty-three Vietnamese working for him. The idea inspired. They could do a poll in Vietnam. Secretary of Defense Robert McNamara, the numbers glutton, volunteered to send General Krulak to do the job. We can have him back by Monday, McNamara said. This was Thursday. By now the State Department and the Defense Department were as suspicious of each other as Ngo Dinh Nhu and Henry Cabot Lodge. Rusk elbowed one of his Far Eastern experts, Joseph A. Mendenhall, onto the Defense Department plane to protect State from Krulak. Then he cabled Lodge:

IT HAS BEEN DECIDED TO MAKE AN INTENSIVE EFFORT TO OBTAIN AT FIRST HAND INFORMATION ON ATTITUDES . . . HELD BY WIDE SPECTRUM OF POPULACE. IT IS DESIRED TO DETERMINE TRENDS IN OPINION SINCE MAY 8 AND WHAT FEELINGS ARE NOW.

Rusk added that they wanted to "poll opinion in as short a time as possible," namely two days.

Krulak and Mendenhall were off the ground ninety minutes later, the general coincidentally headed for that unexpected airport greeting from David Halberstam as well. They returned Monday night. Briefing the President the next morning, Krulak was so certain of military victory, Mendenhall so certain the place was falling apart, Kennedy looked at them wryly and asked, "The two of you did visit the same country, didn't you?"

And, in Saigon, the coup that wasn't finally convinced the brothers that Madame Nhu needed a vacation. She began a trip around the world. President Kennedy observed that they had won half the battle. Now Diem had to persuade her to stop talking. So much for wishful thinking. She had not been consigned to a Hong Kong convent this time.

At her first international stopover, the semi-exiled First Lady accused an unnamed *New York Times* reporter, clearly Halberstam, and five other "traitors" of a plot against both Kennedy and Diem. The Dragon Lady's charges had begun to get fuzzy. But, wearing skintight blue silk adorned with jade, gold, and silver, with a demure black half-veil running diversionary tactics for the red sabers of her fingernails, she became an instant media sensation in the drab Yugoslavian city of Belgrade. Her words and photos flashed around the world: MRS. NGO DINH NHU LAYS A PLOT TO 6, INCLUDING TIMES REPORTER, the headline over the Belgrade story read in *The New York Times*.

Speaking in a rapid jumble of French and English, she laid it out: "There is a plot. There are only six persons in the plot and *The New York Times* is involved. Yes, we have some evidence."

Among the evidence Madame Nhu cited was *The Times*'s insistence on calling her husband the head of the secret police. "The police have never been secret," she said. Another was the newspaper's refusal to correct a mistake in one of her letters to the editor. When a reporter observed that the error had been corrected several days earlier, she shrugged. "Then that is one less evidence," she said. The story became what editors call a "one-day wonder," quickly disappearing. Madame Nhu's world tour, however, was heading for what she called the "cage of the lions"—the United States.

———

Next to Saigon came Joe Alsop. He arrived in a mood most foul, his swagger stick flailing. Even the fawning colonels from General Harkins's headquarters couldn't calm him down. Unsure who to rebuke for the mess he found, he cast blame everywhere.

The Kennedy administration had fallen into panic and chaos, so confused it had reduced itself to the "ridiculous spectacle" of "reacting like a bee-stung adolescent to the egomaniacal maunderings" of Madame Nhu.

The ruling family had simply gone nuts, Nhu having "lost touch with any kind of human or political reality beyond the bounds of his own tortured ego" and Diem "another man who has taken leave of reality." To the family, he gave his own ominous farewell: "So there will be some changes here."

But it was the correspondents who had done the real dirt, threatening to kick away Vietnam just as their foolish predecessors had abandoned China to the romantic image of "the great agrarian reformer," Mao Zedong. Now these new "high-minded" youths, these "twaddle-thinking" reporters had driven Diem "right around the bend." Diem had gone loony on him, no doubt about it, but the "egregious crusaders" of the press corps had driven the Vietnamese leader to it. "The constant pressure of the reportorial crusade," he wrote, had changed Diem from "a courageous, quite viable national leader into a man afflicted with galloping persecution mania, seeing plots around every corner." Alsop came in raging, as if determined to do *Time* one better.

The liberal in him would defend these misguided souls at the inevitable next round of subversive activities hearings, just as he had so haughtily promised six months earlier. But first he would lay out the case against them. This he proceeded to do in "Matter of Fact," the column that had become a parlor game for the powerful in Washington. "Matter of Fact" was not the kind of column cabdrivers read. It was the kind publishers clipped, and all the young crusaders soon had copies from home as if they might have missed Alsop on his angry passage through town.

Through all the fury of his visit, Alsop still saw the war being won. Joseph Alsop would always see the war being won. His proprietary interest ran so deep, back to his own romance with the Flying Tigers, back to the war years with Chiang Kai-shek in Chungking, and then to the great American fantasy of a China "lost," as if a fourth of the world's people, their lives and history barely grazed by a handful of missionaries and merchants, could be the West's, or America's, to lose at all.

But he would forfeit no more of his precious Asia! He would stop the slide at the first domino, South Vietnam. He had been here at the birthing of this odd half-country in the fifties. He had been here during Diem's re-election in April 1961 and smiled out of the front page of the *Times of Vietnam* with the other foreign personages after watching democracy at work, Diem having won 99 percent of the vote. He had been here with General Taylor, egging Kennedy on in "Matter of Fact," as the first plans for Project Beef-Up were hatched almost two years ago.

Alsop was very good at prodding the powerful. In 1971, when the Pentagon Papers provided the first peek at the great delusions of these years, eighty-four-year-old Arthur Krock, the doyen of *The*

New York Times's pundits, took aside the reporter who had delivered up the documents. Alsop was the one, Krock said; Alsop and Walt Rostow, the White House war-hawk. "They talked JFK into going to war," he told an older but wiser and newly controversial Neil Sheehan.

Alsop would stick with it till the bitter end, driving three administrations to fight on, waving the Pentagon's "captured documents" as proof that the Viet Cong were finally on the run. But the war would eventually bring him down, as it brought down everyone who touched it. The captured documents became a joke. Behind his back, they called him Joe All-Slop. The Georgetown parties continued, but McNamara, Bundy, and Taylor became faded knights at his table.

In 1963, Alsop still stood at the pinnacle. The private planes and escorts waited for him in Saigon, the inner sanctum opened to him in Washington, where Kennedy gave him extraordinary access to the workings of his government. His columns were appended to top-secret documents as if part of the government's own work product. In its assessments of the war, the Pentagon quoted him as authoritatively as its generals: *Joseph Alsop says; we agree.* So the rat-a-tat-tat of Alsop's September columns—he wrote half a dozen in two weeks—had unusual impact in Washington. They also fell like another sledgehammer on the now battered and bruised Saigon correspondents.

First, in a column headlined "The Crusaders," he tied them to his favorite theme: Some American reporters in China had "kept their heads despite the intoxicating crusading atmosphere of the wartime press hostel." But "the crusaders dominated and, one must add, sometimes warped the news." They regretted their foolishness later, he wrote, and then added an especially nasty poke: ".... except for two press hostel inhabitants, Izzie and Elsie Epstein, who revealed their role as Communist agents by retreating to Peking, where they still nauseatingly hold forth."

Up again came Cuba and the much-maligned Matthews. There was no one in Saigon quite like the man who had brought us Fidel Castro, Alsop wrote. But then, without naming names, he described someone who sounded quite like David Halberstam. The reporting scene in Saigon was typified by "one of the leading young crusaders" who had spent many weeks writing "passion-charged" political stories condemning the Diem regime from the safety of Saigon. Now, the young crusader finally was returning to the "fighting front," as Alsop described it.[2] "After all," Alsop wrote, quoting him anonymously, "there's another enemy to think about." The columnist all but huffed on the word "another," no more damning proof needed.

Kennedy loved the column, as did the Pentagon, which made copies as if it had been brought down the mountain by Moses. As he read Alsop's latest, the President was preparing to send McNamara and Taylor on yet another Saigon shuttle. Diem will probably complain about the press, he observed. Agree with him, he told McNamara. On the subject of the correspondents, Kennedy had gone beyond the pale, and he wouldn't find his way back.

In three weeks' time Halberstam had taken hits from Higgins, Conniff, *Time*—and his own people. But he blew all fuses over Alsop's attacks. Alsop was out to destroy him, he said to friends, the columnist's assault the "McCarthy-like charges of a bully and a coward."

Down deep, he was even more angry at *The Times* for failing to defend him. Halberstam's instinct was to *always* fight back, no matter how minor the insult. *The Times* had no such instinct. Others tried to get approval to respond. Robert Trumbull, a senior *Times* Asian correspondent, asked permission to sign a round-robin letter of protest to *Time* magazine. From Hong Kong, he cabled Halberstam the reply from Catledge:

EMPHATICALLY AGAINST NYKTIMES CORRESPONDENTS ENGAG-ING IN CONTROVERSIES WITH TIME. THEY RESPONSIBLE ONLY TO US AND WE HAVE FULL CONFIDENCE IN THEIR INTEGRITY. IF TIME IS RIGHT, WE SHOULD FACE IT SQUARELY AND TAKE CORRECTIVE ACTION. IF THEY ARE WRONG, WE SHOULD IGNORE IT.

Trumbull added a note that Joe Alsop was traveling through Hong Kong, "spreading his own propaganda" on his way home. "We ignore him, too," he wrote sarcastically.

2. If one word separated the old guard from the new, it was "front." There was no front in Vietnam, never would be. "You had to go back to the American Revolution to find a war like this," Keyes Beech finally decided. "Then we were the guerrillas."

Instead of a defense out of New York, the frontings and queries took on a nastier tone. ASSUME YOU KEEPING MATERIAL BALANCED, said one. EXACTLY WHAT IS HAPPENING THERE? asked another. Halberstam was in more trouble than anyone imagined. Not only were there rumors that he would be expelled by Diem, there were rumors that he would be recalled by *The Times*.

In Washington, no one took more guff for both Halberstam's reporting and his behavior than Reston. But the Washington bureau chief had a high regard for Halberstam and a low tolerance for Alsop's outbursts.[3] After the "crusaders" column, Reston uncharacteristically lost his good sense. He angrily telephoned the White House.

"Why don't you call Alsop off?" he challenged McGeorge Bundy.

"Don't you believe in freedom of the press?" Bundy tweaked him.

But, unlike the New York editors, Reston didn't withdraw into silence about *The Times*'s troublesome man in Saigon. A shrewd player of company as well as Washington politics, he often seemed to be lecturing the New York brass as well as the Washington politicians. "Part of the trouble comes from two different ways of looking at journalism," he told Halberstam's *Esquire* profiler, George J. W. Goodman, continuing:

When Harry Felt tells the boys, "Come on, get on the team," he is thinking of them as Americans in a foreign and complex situation where their country is involved, not as newspapermen. Dave and the rest of the boys are really carrying on an American tradition of journalism—the frontier editor with the gun in his middle drawer. H. L. Mencken said, "The only way to look at a politician is down." The more power they get, the closer you watch them.

A journalist does not belong to the embassy or to the

3. Later, after Sheehan had moved to *The Times*, Reston received a letter from Alsop that began: "Sheehan has plenty of competitors for the title of worst war correspondent in Saigon . . ." The letter went downhill from there. Reston needed no lectures, he rebutted, from someone "who seldom allowed the facts to interfere with his prejudices."

commander in chief of the theater. He has to report things as he sees them, and if he is getting out of line, it is up to his editor to get him back in. His function is to be the watchman on the wall, and by those standards Dave has come to the top of foreign correspondents this year.

The heat, coming from so many directions, also began to create an aura around Halberstam. Stanley Karnow cabled him:

DAVID. AFTER CRUDE TIME STORY THIS WEEK I'D BE SURPRISED IF YOU DIDN'T WIN PULITZER PRIZE.

Among the flood of book offers came a personal invitation from the grand old man of American letters, Alfred Knopf. Halberstam's book agent, Richard Connell, watched the hullabaloo with glee:

I assume you've seen the stuff in *Time* on yourself and the other reporters in Saigon. Doesn't it strike you that you're in a great position? Small and unpopular as that war is, you are the correspondent identified with it. You're in the same position as Shirer in Berlin, Reynolds in London, David Duncan in Korea, etc. You should come out of this a real star and with a little publicity and exploitation be in a position to just about choose your assignments for the rest of your life, i.e., enjoy life while everyone else frets, hates his job and/or wife.

Not yet thirty years old, Halberstam was about to become a media superstar, one of the last to do it without the instant-celebrity shimmer of television, one of the first in modern times to do it by intruding himself unabashedly into the events he observed. But first he had to outlast his story—and that was no sure thing.

———

By mid-September the only real war going on in Vietnam was the assault on the correspondents. Later, the participants in all roles in the drama would look back on the period between the failed coup in late August and the events of November 1–2 as "the interlude."

"It's so quiet here now that it's hard to imagine we had the best story in the world just a month ago," Nick Turner wrote his parents in New Zealand on September 21. Halberstam summed up the feeling of standstill: "So for the moment the Americans are, as one source said, 'sitting here giving a million and a half a day to a government we dislike and which we feel can't win the war.' "

Quiet, however, is a reporter's term for an absence of news. Quiet in any other sense, Saigon wasn't at all. The place crawled with Brother Nhu's not-so-secret police and buzzed with rumors, plots, schemes, intrigues, furtive generals, spooks of indeterminate loyalties, and new hit lists.

John Mecklin had a dream in which he discovered he had been "dealing for years with a government of madmen, where words were meaningless, where nothing that was supposed to have happened had really happened, yet there was no escape from continuing to deal with the madmen forever."

He had no escape from the Americans, either. Called to Washington for meetings—a welcome relief, he thought—Mecklin hitched a ride on General Krulak's return flight. In the windowless jet, the tension between Krulak (the Defense Department) and Mendenhall (the State Department) was so excruciating that Mecklin thought he had gone from funny farm to padded cell. The two men barely spoke. Mecklin made the mistake of carrying out some network television film. Krulak blew at him, furious that the offensive celluloid was aboard his plane. He rebuked Mecklin for smuggling and using his diplomatic status to violate South Vietnam's sovereignty, harassing him most of the way across the Pacific. Then the tough little marine general ordered the press officer to put the film off in Anchorage, adding that it might be a good idea if Mecklin stayed to guard it. "You can't believe this mess till you've seen it from the inside," Mecklin told a friend in Washington.

Harkins continued to believe that nothing was going wrong— except the press. "Thank goodness I do not get to read the newspapers until they are at least three days old," he cabled Maxwell Taylor, now the chairman of the Joint Chiefs of Staff. "If I got them as soon as you do, I would be afraid to go to work or I wouldn't know what to do. All is not black. No, far from it. . . . I remain as optimistic as ever."

Lulu Conein and General Don, who had been talking covertly since the Fourth of July, moved their meetings to the deep cover of a Saigon dentist's office.

Lodge, despite his relentless plotting against Diem—one aborted coup didn't deter him—found it "unbelievably idiotic" that the Vietnamese might plot against him. But he told Washington about precautions he was taking against his own assassination. Like the Australian Denis Warner, he threatened use of the U.S. Marines, although the ambassador's words had considerably more clout. He asked the palace, through a Vietnamese double agent, "whether GVN [Government of Vietnam] wishes to have such a horrible and crushing blow descend on them."

The *Times of Vietnam,* handed the biggest story of its life on the stillborn coup and then ignored by almost everyone, veered toward a public nervous breakdown. Gene Gregory made a habit of disappearing at odd times on long, mysterious business trips. He now disappeared, leaving his jumpy wife, Ann, to handle the crisis. NEW YORK TIMES LIES AGAIN: IS CAUGHT FLAT FOOTED, trumpeted one headline; SHE DIDN'T SQUAT FULL TIME AT XA LOI, read another, unflattering perhaps, but meant to praise Maggie Higgins. On the front page, ARVN troops smashed the Viet Cong's crack 514th Battalion day after day, only to have it return, phoenixlike, to be smashed again.

The Mat Vu's secret agents multiplied like mosquitoes. They had an odd habit of splashing a smear of red paint on their hubcaps, apparently so they could recognize each other, the telltale leather jackets and sunglasses not being enough. They sat outside most Americans' homes at night in taxis or astride their cyclos. Halberstam and Sheehan now saw leather jackets, sunglasses, and spinning red dabs everywhere they went.

As the interlude dragged on, Halberstam had the sinking feeling that he was running out of time. His visa would expire again October 15. THEY NOT LIKE ME HERE, he cabled New York. STRONG CHANCE I WILL BE EXCOMMUNICATED. Halberstam's editors pushed him to take a vacation and then hinted that he should combine it with home leave in New York. He was exhausted, clearly needed time off, and hadn't been home for more than two years. Sheehan and Mal Browne were getting the same kind of pressure. All their editors thought the exhaustion was making them erratic, and it was. "There was a lot of paranoia running through this group," Arnett said later. But a vacation sounded risky on a powder-keg story like this. Home leave sounded terminal.

Halberstam also had an agenda to complete. Quiet times didn't mean much to him. He didn't follow the news; he made it. When a Viet Cong bomb exploded in a movie theater playing Walt Disney's *The Lady and the Tramp* for 250 American women and children, Halberstam ran to the scene with Sheehan, then shrugged when it became clear that few were hurt. "Wire-service story," he said, and left.

Shortly afterward, Halberstam made news. In a story setting off new alarms in Washington, he wrote that the Strategic Hamlets program, Ngo Dinh Nhu's pet project and the cornerstone of the plan to protect the vast rural population, was nearing collapse in the delta. At best, an American adviser told Halberstam, the bamboo stockades had become places where "we baby-sit Viet Cong families." At worst, the adviser added, they were traps where soldiers "sit there waiting for the executioner." Many had been destroyed; most had never existed at all except in the scheming mind of Brother Nhu.

Actually, Halberstam missed the the full magnitude of the story by confining it to the southern regions he knew best. The hamlets were evaporating throughout the country. Just two weeks earlier, General Taylor had reported to the President on the success of the showpiece program. The numbers, given to the Americans by Nhu, validated by Harkins, repeated by McNamara, and passed on through Taylor to the President without a blink by any of the Americans, were remarkable: In eighteen months, 9,563,370 of South Vietnam's 12,500,000 peasants had been taken under the protection of the Diem government in 8,227 fortified hamlets. The numbers were not only remarkable, they were preposterous. Nhu's grandiose claim was a giant fraud, one very large Potemkin village. The Americans could not see the absurdity. They thrived on preposterous numbers.

No one was more surprised by Washington's angry reaction than Halberstam. "All you had to do was look," he said. Sheehan drove down Highway 4, the same route he had taken to visit John Paul Vann, and looked across the paddies at deserted ghost hamlets. Stanley Karnow, driving just outside Saigon, saw abandoned villages so torn up they might have been struck by a typhoon. Only the American government seemed unable to see.

Kennedy read *The Times* that morning and blew again, asking

McNamara to get to the bottom of it. To McNamara, numbers were the language of reason.[4] A week later he sent back the same figures and a sixteen-page analysis refuting Halberstam's story. He attached an Alsop column entitled "The War Can Be Won."

By now the Kennedy administration had fallen into such disarray over Vietnam, and the daily meetings had become so abrasive and contradictory, White House aides joked about it. One wrote a parody:

The Secretary of State opened the meeting, in the absence of the President, by urging that priority be given to the key question of the past thirteen hours: How did we get here, and Where do we go from here?

The Secretary of Defense . . . asked General Krulak to report on his latest sampling of opinion about the trainers of Vietnamese secret police at Fort Belvoir. . . .

Governor Harriman stated that he had disagreed for twenty years with General Krulak and disagreed today, reluctantly, more than ever; he was sorry to say that he felt General Krulak was a fool and had always thought so. . . .

(At this point the President entered the room.)

The President said that he hoped we were not allowing our policies to be influenced by immature twelve-year-old girls. . . .

Next time, he said, he hoped there would be a good map of Vietnam available.

In Saigon streets, the American military spooks from the CID and the regulars from the CIA elbowed the Mat Vu and other Vietnamese operatives for position to watch the newsmen. One evening Halberstam received a call from an old Harvard acquaintance who, in the euphemism that CIA recruits used at the time, had gone to work "for the government." The man was "passing through" from Tokyo and suggested dinner. Halberstam quickly

4. George Allen, the CIA and defense analyst, agreed. "Two and two always make four," he said of McNamara's numeric compulsion. "But first someone has to decide that two actually is two."

concluded that he had become his old college chum's new assignment.

The Mat Vu were more worrisome. The American agents were after the correspondents' sources. There was no telling what the Vietnamese were after. In September, Halberstam and Sheehan broke the embarrassing news that the CIA was continuing to finance Tung's Special Forces long after it became clear they had been diverted from the war effort into domestic police jobs like the pagoda raids. The stories were the first step toward drying up Tung's money, as the colonel readily recognized. That night Sheehan, working late and alone, received an anonymous telephone call: "You are in very big trouble."

By now, Sheehan was always edgy. Leaving the office, he saw nothing but red hubcaps until he rounded the corner at the Catinat. He headed for Mecklin's villa. But, with their host in Washington, their adopted home no longer seemed so secure. Outside the villa, he elbowed his way through Tung's men. Inside, he and Halberstam ran to the top floor and looked out over a neighborhood swarming with security men. Panicked, they set up an alarm system that came from the same B movie as their second-cab technique. They tied lamps together with shoestrings and suspended shaving-cream cans over mirrors, then set the contraptions on darkened stairs. Nothing happened. "Sure we were paranoid," Halberstam said. "But people *were* trying to get us. They had been scraping layers of skin off us for weeks. Our nerves were rubbed raw."

To Peter Arnett, a wave of medieval hysteria seemed to have swept over them. He was not left unaffected. As philosophical as he became about the death threats, he personalized the attacks on their reporting. The critics tripped a temper always poised at hair trigger. "There was no room for argument about what was happening on the ground in Vietnam," Arnett said. "We'd watched the Buddhists burn. We'd been with the soldiers, with the Vietnamese crossing those rotting bridges through the marshlands. So I was *sensitive* if a visitor questioned it, whether he was Joe Alsop or anyone else." Pushed, Arnett would haul critics out the door of the AP office and start slugging. Once, he took an entire group of visitors from his native New Zealand outside, quickly emptying the office as other correspondents rushed to stop the brawl.

As the interlude dragged on, most of the correspondents were scared, most were worried about being called home, and all were worried about being expelled. They took every possible precaution to avoid giving the regime an excuse, even abandoning Saigon's ubiquitous Hindu money changers and buying their piasters at Diem's banks at one third of their street value. Halberstam had another awkward problem.

———

Several months earlier, Nick Turner had come close to expulsion. To protect himself, he had reluctantly broken off with his Vietnamese girlfriend. Vietnam had been a land of anything goes. But it became a land of Madame Nhu's blue laws, a list of moral and sexual taboos so long you could be thrown out of the country for using the gift Neil Sheehan had been sent from Tokyo. "I can't afford to have a 'morals' scandal on my hands," Turner wrote friends, "and the only way to be sure is not to be seen looking at a woman."

Now Halberstam had to make a similar decision about Ricki. Sheehan, with Blue Lotus; Browne, with Le Lieu; Arnett, with Nina; Herndon, who had just met his future wife, Annie, all had similar problems. But none had become the prime target Halberstam had become. The others were also more smitten,[5] less ambitious—and their girlfriends considerably less encumbered. Ricki was still married. Halberstam delayed the decision till he neared the edge. Then Blue Lotus inadvertently made it easier for him. She wrote a letter and the *affaire de coeur* became, as Halberstam put it, "a bad French play."

Ricki and her husband, who enjoyed his own dalliances and rarely came home, had a marriage in the Parisian style. Calamities came not with the acts but with the need to confront them. The art was to avoid the confrontation. The letter, from Blue Lotus to Ricki, derailed the art, Blue Lotus's mistake being to write it, Ricki's to keep it, the husband's to read it. Reading it required action. Ricki's husband bought a pistol.

Scene change: The Halberstam-Faas villa. Ricki's husband barges in, expecting to find his wife and her lover in flagrant delight, a

———

5. All but Sheehan and Halberstam married their Vietnamese girlfriends.

crime of passion being the natural consequence. Instead—and this sort of thing had been the sad lament of both Blue Lotus and Ricki for some time—they are working. Ricki is translating, Halberstam writing. Suddenly, the outraged husband, his pistol not yet out of his back pocket, finds himself the subject of the outrage. Halberstam leaps up in a fury. *How dare you come in here and interrupt me while I'm working?!!* The offender is now chasing the offended around the huge front room, over the furniture, around the table. *How can I ever get any work done when people are always interrupting me?!!*

Finally, Halberstam realizes who he is chasing. In the French style, a face-saving is arranged. The letter about Dave and Ricki becomes a misunderstood letter about the journalist and his translator. Halberstam declares his intention to live out the new fiction. Ricki becomes heartbroken. She also becomes history.

———

Richard Clurman had already taken his suite at the Ritz by the time Charley Mohr, who had flown across the breadth of both Asia and Europe, landed in Paris on a morning flight.

Behind Clurman in New York a different kind of soap opera had begun the week before. Mohr had no doubt that, as usual, Clurman had been on the side of the angels during the battle in *Time*'s skyscraper warren above Manhattan. Indeed, the chief of correspondents had fought Otto Fuerbringer every inch of the way.

In a magazine that had created "group journalism," the attack on the Saigon correspondents had been distinctly singular. Fuerbringer had simply called in a writer and dictated it "with nothing but his own preconceptions to guide him," as Stanley Karnow described it later. Clurman was horrified. He knew it was a battle he could not win. Clurman once ruefully described the arrangement Luce had set up between him and Fuerbringer, who had total control over *Time*'s content: "I could hire almost anyone. I paid twice as much as anyone else. I would tell them that I had access to everything but a printing press. Of course, that's a pretty important thing not to have."

Not surprisingly, the two men despised each other. Clurman had tried everything to convince Fuerbringer to kill the piece. "It's just wrong, Otto," he argued. "It's a slander." This will backfire, he said; "it will cause the magazine no end of trouble." Nothing budged the Iron Chancellor. Clurman warned that it would cause Mohr to quit, a dangerous argument, he knew. That's what it is all about, the hallway gossips buzzed: This is Fuerbringer's way to fire Mohr. Force him to quit. "One thousand percent wrong," Fuerbringer said. And the press story stood.

Meanwhile, Mohr's file—*The war in Vietnam is being lost*—landed on the New York desk of John Gregory Dunne, the writer assigned to the World section. He took one look at the lead, groaned, and said, "Uh-oh."

Writing the Vietnam pieces had been like walking a minefield, he thought—trying to get some of Mohr, whom he had met and admired, into the magazine without tripping Fuerbringer's Pentagon-rigged Claymores. It had not been easy, and already he had set off some explosions in Saigon. "Get it right or don't write it," David Halberstam had hammered him in an angry letter after the Madame Nhu article a month earlier, leaving Dunne "damned annoyed." Still, he was not a Fuerbringer automaton and he wanted to keep some of Mohr's report in the magazine. But the war in Vietnam is being lost? In *Time*? As artful a writer as Dunne was, he couldn't make it work. Frustrated, he ducked out to have dinner with his fiancée, Joan Didion. He had a drink, then another. He thought briefly of avoiding the whole mess by calling in sick, then returned in the middle of the night to finish the job, working some of Mohr's pessimism into the story while tiptoeing, he thought, around Fuerbringer's land mines. He came in the next day, a Saturday, to find his story totally rewritten. He blew. By Tuesday, he was writing film reviews. Not long after that, he quit. If he were to write fiction, at which he was quite talented, he would do it for himself.

As soon as Mohr reached Paris, Clurman knew in his heart that he was fighting another battle he couldn't win. Mohr immediately announced that he was quitting. But Clurman was persistent. "Harry sent me over to keep you from resigning," he said, "and I'm going to do my job." They had lunch at the Ritz and argued through endless sumptuous courses. They went for a walk, out of the Place Vendôme, through the gardens of the Tuileries, past the gods and goddesses, arguing all the way. Clurman hired a hansom cab and they rode the rest of the afternoon, arguing. Finally, they realized that everyone outside had been staring into the cab. They both started laughing. "For Christ's sake," Mohr said, "they think we're having a lover's spat."

Mohr thought the whole thing was bizarre. He liked Clurman and Clurman liked him. "But it was crazy," he said later, "and it just got crazier." That night Clurman invited a dozen people to dinner. It made lunch look like a camping trip.

Afterward, Mohr quit again. Clurman ignored him. "Okay, Charley, what will it take?" he asked.

"Give me seventy lines for rebuttal," Mohr shrugged. In 1963, a column of type in *Time* was seventy lines long.

"That's impossible," Clurman replied. "No chance."

"Well, you asked."

"Well, it won't work."

Mohr shrugged again. "I didn't think it would work, either. I'm not saying it's plausible. You asked, and I'm saying that's what would prevent me from quitting."

"Wait a minute!" Clurman said suddenly. "It's not up to me to say no. It's Harry's magazine." He called Luce in New York. Come home immediately, Luce said, and Clurman caught the first plane.

In New York, Luce still wanted to save Mohr, one of his true favorites. "He's good good," he told Clurman. But he would not humiliate his managing editor. "I'm confused about Vietnam, not the war, but this press thing," Luce said. "When Kennedy is confused about Vietnam, he sends McNamara over. You're my McNamara." With Luce, that meant leave. Now. Clurman called Paris.

Mohr had just sat down to dinner with Norma when he heard the page. "Charley, Harry wants us to go back and do a second piece," Clurman said. Christ, Mohr thought, Clurman hadn't been on the ground more than a couple of hours.

"Dick, I quit," he protested. "This is unacceptable. You're just doing a report card on me."

"Meet me at Orly," Clurman replied.

The flight to Saigon was long and wet. Rather than argue, Mohr drank the first-class section dry. On the last leg, out of Bangkok, Clurman asked, "What are we going to tell the press?" Mohr fish-eyed him. "I have worked my way into the resignation mode," he said.

At Tan Son Nhut a surly Saigon press corps met the plane. "Mr.

Mohr has offered his resignation," Clurman answered the queries. "*Time* has not accepted it." Mohr stifled a chuckle. My God, he *sounds* like McNamara. "I quit," Mohr said.

For Clurman, who would make thirteen trips to Vietnam for Luce, this was the most perplexing. *Time*-style, he immediately took the largest suite at the Caravelle Hotel, which some of the correspondents found ironic. He hosted a lavish dinner, spending more in a night than Hoberecht spends in ten years, Ray Herndon thought.

The correspondents were furious. But most of them knew Clurman and, if they didn't all know what to make of him, they didn't dislike him. Most were awestruck by the way he spent Henry Luce's money, making jokes about it. Like Mohr, they knew Clurman wasn't the black hat. They showed him the way they worked, introduced him to their sources. Halberstam hauled out four months of his "blacks"—carbon copies of his stories—to prove his fairness. At dinner with Henry Cabot Lodge, the ambassador unabashedly called the group "brilliant," then raised Clurman's eyebrows by adding that "Halberstam might even be a genius." Now *that*, he said to himself, is a *major* policy change.

The longer Clurman stayed, the more he knew what he'd known before he left: Charley Mohr was right; *Time* was wrong. He flew back to Paris. En route, he sent Luce a message: The situation is hopeless, the war is lost, the story had been terrible, but he had no idea how to fix it now. "Our story was out of kilter in such deliberately irremediable ways," he cabled Luce, "that it is next to impossible right now to run a story in print setting matters straight." From Paris, Clurman called Luce. Come home immediately, the publisher said.

Now Clurman thought it was getting crazy. In New York, he and Luce sat down to write the story, using one of their highly paid writers for dictation. By the end of the day—a Saturday, the day the magazine "closed"—they had put together a somewhat meandering, back-and-forth story with one crucial sentence: "*Time* was wrong." Luce actually beamed at the result. "Well, that's a first," he said. And it was. Almost. Some time in the middle of the night, the three words disappeared. Without them, as one reporter said, *Time* now had two stories that "could have been written by Madame Nhu."

On Monday morning, Luce was furious. But Clurman watched him closely and thought there was a look of admiration at the very gall of the act of cutting the publisher's words. Fuerbringer never admitted he had done the deed. But later that day at dinner in Clurman's Manhattan apartment Luce quizzed his chief of correspondents.

"Dick, why does everyone tell me that Otto is such a son of a bitch?" he asked.

"I don't tell you that, Harry."

"No, you don't. But why does everybody else?"

"Because he is a son of a bitch, Harry," Clurman said.

The Iron Chancellor survived. Charley Mohr—"a reporter, and how!"—didn't. Nor did Perry, who, against Mohr's strong advice, quit with him.

The other correspondents kissed off the second story. But the tension ratcheted up another notch. If it could happen to Charley Mohr . . .

16

Teetering

Neil Sheehan could almost hear the tanks now, their treads clanking on the cobblestones, their gears wrenching angrily as the ungainly M-48s pivoted around narrow street corners they were not meant to negotiate.

With the all-night curfew removed, the dangers tolerable again, he had moved back into his downtown office-apartment. In his back-bedroom cranny, the nickel-plated .38 had returned to the night-stand, carefully loaded each night, carefully unloaded and stashed each morning. And once again he bolted awake from those awful sleeps—too sweaty, too fitful, far too short to be replenishing.

Then he would half-hear the sounds—the tanks, the troops, the noise of the M-113s, too, the APCs faster and lighter, wheeling through Saigon streets as if they were made for this job. Which, in a way, they were. Not worth a damn in the delta, an armored personnel carrier that couldn't climb the muddy bank of a canal. The anarchy of their track marks in the gray paddies of Ap Bac, a picture of disaster, was still etched in his mind. But in the streets they were lethal. They were made to order for overthrowing governments.

Such was Saigon, and so it had been since Diem had taken power nine years before. Someone once asked Roger Hilsman when the Americans heard the first rumor of a coup.

"1954," he answered, naming the year Diem came to power.

"1954?"

"1954 and every week afterward," he replied.

Now it would happen. Sheehan knew that. But not at night. It would start at the height of day, the siesta, when everyone's rhythms ebbed. He knew because those who would do it had told him, just as David Halberstam's sources had told him and, he assumed, Mal Browne's sources had told him.

The only questions left were when, and whether any of the original correspondents would be left to report it.

A month ago he had worried that it would be a grenade and, in his nightmares, he still saw one bouncing into the office, caroming in slow motion off the wall map below Harkins's trap, skittering this way and that like a little football they couldn't get before it got them. Or the regime would simply pull their visas. Madame Nhu had been threatening his since August. But now the real threat had shifted. Their adversarial reporting, attacked so aggressively by the old guard in September, had frightened their bosses as much as the palace. Despite its myths, American journalism was not a game for radicals. To be a radical on an American newspaper you had to *own* the newspaper. Journalism was a game for team players, an extension of the establishment. Always would be.

Charley Mohr had been the first casualty. Halberstam teetered on the edge. The scuttlebutt from the Rue Pasteur had AP pressuring Browne to take an untimely vacation and cool down.

Sheehan glanced at the mound of paper on the kitchen-table desk. More cables from Tokyo. Gripes about bookkeeping. Gripes about cable costs. Gripes about his gripes. Suddenly, Tokyo was picking him to pieces, trying to get him out too. *You're exhausted. Take a vacation. Get your head back together.* That was the new line everyone was getting. You're half-crazy from overwork. Take a vacation; get your perspective back. *And miss the coup d'état, you goddamn fools!* But Tokyo no longer believed him about that. Neil Sheehan was in more trouble than any of them.

For Halberstam, answers would always come easier. He found his truths quickly and flatly, the linear opposites of lies. Sheehan sought his in dimensions, looking at the ragged, uneven edges and trying to smooth them, the way nature slowly smooths a river rock. Thirty years later General Krulak would still despise Halberstam but would change his mind about Sheehan. Even Joe Alsop, who never changed his mind about anything, came in the end to like and admire this man who agonized his way tortuously toward his answers.

Halberstam liked to remember the free-wheeling side of Sheehan. They were buddies, and that kinship meant everything. "There was a zest to him that not everyone saw," he said. "People say I was loud. *We* were loud. We were boisterous. We liked each other. We had fun." And when Sheehan was rolling, he would laugh uproariously, joke in that uproarious Irish way, strut with Blue Lotus, do a mimic of Henry Cabot Lodge that would have fooled the ambassador's wife, Emily.

But when it came to the war, and it always came quickly back to that, he became possessed. Halberstam would see that later when his friend disappeared into his book. "They've remained close to the degree that Neil stays in touch with people, which is a phone call every four years or something," he said of Sheehan and another friend. Sheehan saw it in himself from the beginning. "What was amazing about my state of mind at the time was my immense concentration on what I was doing," he wrote in the diary of his first weeks in Vietnam. "I thought of no amusements or girls and my mind never wandered."

Now, after two years, his obsession brooked no nonsense. "Cut the horseshit," he abruptly stopped a droning interview with Roger Hilsman. He sent his visiting colleague, Don Becker, 400 miles up-country to prevent him from interviewing Harkins. Sheehan had heard enough from the general, no rounded edges possible on the man, and that meant the world had heard enough too. It was journalistic sacrilege. But it was Sheehan journalism. He fired back unflinchingly when Hoberecht criticized him. "Assumed you knew eye unfiled Harkins interview because unworthit," he replied, drawing on his best cable-ese:

NONE RESIDENT CORRESPONDENTS BOTHERING INTERVIEW HARKINS ANYMORE BECAUSE TEDIOUS MONOTONY HIS RE-MARKS STOP WE LEAVE HIM TO VISITING FIREMEN STOP THIS STORY UNLENDS ITSELF TO INTERVIEW TECHNIQUE STOP WHY YOU QUERYING ME HARKINS INTERVIEW STOP SHEEHAN

Sheehan's intensity worried Herndon. To the happy-go-lucky Texan, who was known to like a snooze past noon, it seemed as if

Sheehan *never* slept: "Up too late, up too early, he became a really hyper-tense guy. He was pleasant and we would laugh and joke. But as soon as the subject came to the war, he just drove himself. Halberstam would blow sky-high and then laugh, make a joke, even with the generals. But the war consumed Neil."

The degree to which it took him over, and he blocked out everything else, became remarkable. Halberstam talked about the total absorption of their experience, about creating their special universe. But Halberstam played the stock market while he was in Vietnam. Halberstam applied promptly for an overseas exemption for his income taxes. He shipped book outlines and pushed his agent on Hollywood deals. Halberstam wanted a stake in the real world when this was over.

Sheehan dropped everything like a man on the run with no intention of ever turning back. By late 1963 the outside world grew impatient, and all his delinquencies descended on him at the same and wrong time, as delinquencies do.

Suddenly he was in a mess with the Internal Revenue Service. Typically, he hadn't filed a tax return since 1960. Everyone thought it was funny except Sheehan and the IRS. He had just plain forgotten, he informed the tax people. "I apologize for being so late and hope it will not inconvenience you too much," he wrote them in October 1963 with the unworldly innocence of a man too long gone from the Land of the Big PX. Sheehan hadn't earned enough taxable income in the past three years to pay for the braid on Harkins's uniforms. But now he began a desperate search for lost records up and down the Pacific Rim—old chits from the army in Korea, stubs from Tokyo, anything he could find in the hash of the Saigon bureau's bookkeeping system. He was still working it out with the humorless revenuers six months later.

Then came the Pentagon, not with a McNamara investigation or a Krulak attack, but worse—a frontal assault from an irate bureaucracy. Sheehan had forgotten to get fingerprinted, allowing his credentials, his entrée to military aircraft and sundry other privileges handy to a war correspondent, to lapse. Not for a week or a month but for more than a year. The letters from the Defense Department to UPI became surly.

And then his bank. First National City of New York, exhausted by two years of those Michelin rubber-plantation checks, finally cut him off: "Dear Mr. Sheehan, It has been necessary for us to return unpaid a check issued by you against your Special Checking Account. In view of our previous notices to you, we must ask you to make arrangements to close your account."

Day-by-day living did not break through Sheehan's barriers. The UPI bureaucracy received the same nontreatment. He scrawled furious notes across the top of Tokyo's memos—**JESUS CHRIST! WHAT IN HELL IS GOING ON?!**—then never replied.

By the early sixties United Press International had begun a long downhill slide that would end decades later in a series of bankruptcies and bizarre rescue attempts by characters ranging from a Mexican high roller to the entrepreneurial televangelist Pat Robertson. Even in normal times, the youngest and most remote bureau chief was expected to sell news as well as write it, take photographs, arrange for Movietone newsreel and TV film, hire and fire stringers, hold costs down, and keep the books. But as the downhill slide started, the orders to SELL, COLLECT, DOWNHOLD became a gush.

"Ignore them, I say," Arthur J. Dommen, the Hong Kong bureau chief, advised him. That's what Sheehan did, more so than Dommen could ever have imagined.

On February 3, 1963, Sheehan received a letter—not the first—about his bureau's revolving expense account:

How much longer do you expect us to wait for your accounts? You have now been in Saigon going on ten months and we have yet to receive your first local accounting.

Eight months later, he received another:

Regarding your long overdue expenses, it has long ceased to be a laughing matter.

Sheehan hadn't filed a bureau office accounting since he'd arrived in May 1962. He simply didn't give a damn about expenses or photos or film or downholds. He had time for only one thing—the story. Now Tokyo had begun tinkering with that. "They started doing terrible things to him," Halberstam said. Under the heavy hand of his editors, his routine stories became as bland as Japanese rice. The tough ones simply disappeared.

Over the years Earnest Hoberecht had become the most rigid of old Asia hands. The first American correspondent to land in Japan, he stayed and gained fame, fortune, and a ration of power in an Americanized postwar Asia. He became one of the Far East's great postwar characters. By the early sixties he had also become afraid. UPI was having problems, and Hoberecht was not immune. He could lose that fame, that power; he could lose Tokyo. New York came down hard on him about his rabble-rouser in Saigon. So did the Saigon government, to whose propaganda agency Hoberecht was expected to *sell* UPI's services. Hoberecht was squeezed. Hard.

"I warned you that correspondents with special interests would be there, that people completely unfamiliar with Asia would be dashing in to write their own faulty interpretation," Hoberecht wrote Sheehan. He didn't *quite* say that Sheehan had become one of the bad guys. He simply shut him down. "You can't send out every story that is written," Hoberecht said later, and he didn't. He killed them.

In the crucial month of October, Sheehan's byline, which had been a fixture in *The Washington Post* in August and September, appeared only once in *The Post* and a cross section of major American newspapers.[1]

Shutting down Sheehan meant shutting down a significant part of the story in Saigon. Of all the correspondents, he had the best sources to be forewarned about a coup d'état. All had their strengths, Halberstam strong with the military, Browne entrenched deep in Vietnamese society. But Sheehan had those who played in the murk—Pham Van Dong, the shrewd Vietnamese colonel at Camp Le Van Duyet, the dusty old French cavalry post that also happened to be the headquarters of Saigon's most talkative and conniving generals; Lucien Conein, who gave him only fuzz but fuzz that sometimes took form around other bits and pieces of information, as well as other shadowy men, both Vietnamese and American, who spoke in riddles and enigmas. Many of the Americans had been introduced to him by Homer Bigart and used spar-

---

1. The newspapers, studied by University of North Carolina researchers, were *The New York Times*, *The Washington Post*, *Chicago Tribune*, *St. Louis Dispatch*, and *San Francisco Examiner*, which, except for *The Times*, had printed Sheehan regularly during August and September.

ingly since. He used them now. He interpreted them, wove them together, and, like any good reporter, he read the tea leaves. He noted when Lodge failed to stand for Diem at a ribbon cutting and knew that each little insult sent a message, that each message tightened the noose.

Brash youth also produced boldness. Now, in the morning light, with the fitful sleep sounds gone, the real sounds of Saigon squawking to life once again, Sheehan walked to his desk and brushed all the pesky cables from Tokyo on to a floor littered with weeks of earlier messages. He remembered what Bigart, the professor, had taught him: Ration your ammunition and then, when the end is near, use it all.

Sheehan started to work on a story even Hoberecht couldn't reject: that the United States was orchestrating the coup against its troublesome ally, that the crafty Yankee, Henry Cabot Lodge, was doing it.[2]

———

As September drifted slowly toward October, it wasn't certain that the fractious Kennedy administration could orchestrate anything. The in-house coup resulting in the Cable of August 24, followed by the Saigon generals' rapid move to the brink and back, had left the White House in bickering disarray, the worst of Kennedy's troubled presidency. The infighting over Vietnam policy—and, perhaps more important, Vietnam reality—had become ferocious. Kennedy fell back on an old standby—an inspection trip, this one headed by Robert McNamara and Maxwell Taylor and unusually long, with nine days allocated for visits and meetings in all parts of the country.

The decision to send the Pentagon's top two men drove the government's anti-Diem faction to fits. "These two men are opposed to our policy," Averell Harriman complained to a colleague, and, as Richard Reeves observed in *President Kennedy: Profile of Power*, by "our" policy Harriman did not mean the government's policy. He meant Averell Harriman's policy.

Harriman and his collaborators had less to fear than met the eye.

2. Sheehan labeled the story "analysis," giving him somewhat more latitude than he had in his daily reporting.

In Saigon they had an immovable ally. The coup against Diem had become "a rock rolling downhill," Henry Cabot Lodge said, and he wasn't about to step in front of it, or let anyone else try, either.

As the VIPs landed at Tan Son Nhut, the press and others in the official greeting party were given an unexpected Keystone Kops look at a government at war with itself. Lodge had decided to focus on McNamara, wisely writing off the chairman of the Joint Chiefs of Staff as an impossible convert. His first goal became to wean the civilian secretary away from General Harkins's unending optimism. At the airport, Lodge began the process literally. As McNamara bounded down the passenger ramp toward the welcoming committee, two of Lodge's muscular embassy men shifted like blocking backs in front of Harkins, physically preventing the general from greeting his boss. Even the photographers surged between Harkins and his man, reducing him to plaintive shouting: "Please, gentlemen, please let me greet the Secretary!"

From there the internecine battle patterned itself after the battle in the field—Harkins and his conventional forces controlled the day, Lodge and his guerrilla tactics the night.

The Vietnam to which Robert McNamara returned in the fall of 1963 was far different from the land he had visited sixteen months earlier. At the showplace hamlet he had toured in May 1962 the housing, the bunkers, and the makeshift plan for slit trenches were gone, as were the people. The radios he had placed throughout the countryside at a cost of $52 million had become the mainstay of a new Viet Cong communications network. He saw none of that.

Instead, Harkins ran McNamara and Taylor from one spit-and-polish unit to another for four solid days. This was Harkins's Vietnam—the one he complained no one ever went out to see, a handful of well-protected military command posts, an ARVN training camp, a secure Green Beret camp, a few showcase strategic hamlets built by forced labor and occupied by peasants who hated living in them (Harkins surely did not know these latter circumstances). They traveled from point to point in a virtual aerial flotilla —the general's private C-54 guarded by T-28 fighters and a swarm of Hueys.

Just as Homer Bigart and Charley Mohr had watched incredulously as McNamara fell for the slit-trench foolishness in 1962, others watched the new show in disbelief. At one stop, Harkins grandiosely displayed a huge cache of weapons captured from the Viet Cong. Mert Perry was sure that the number alone would alert McNamara that something had gone astray in the "secret" little war he had visited sixteen months earlier. To McNamara, they were a sure sign of success. "Chinese, I suppose," he said, fingering a 57-millimeter recoilless rifle. "American," an adviser corrected him delicately. Jesus, he just doesn't get it, Perry thought: *He* is outfitting the Viet Cong.

At another base, Mal Browne asked him about the war's new nickname. "I don't mind it being called McNamara's War," he replied briskly. "In fact, I'm proud to be associated with it."

At each stop an American briefer in razor-sharp khakis and yes-sir countenance glanced over McNamara's shoulder at the watchful faces of his commanding officer and the chairman of the Joint Chiefs of Staff, then rattled off the day's optimistic statistics. No problem for Harkins there. Smooth as silk.

But Lodge was shrewd. Each night he took the prize back, having arranged for McNamara to stay at the ambassador's residence. Lodge worked him relentlessly: The country was falling apart; the military had stopped fighting; Diem was a physical and emotional wreck, Nhu a dangerous man. A general in the army Reserve himself—he had fought Rommel in tank warfare in North Africa while holding his seat in the U.S. Senate—Lodge flat out told McNamara that he was being duped. "You don't know the army, Bob, if you think these people are going to tell you or say in front of Harkins what they really think unless it's what they think Harkins thinks. You just don't know your army."

The signs of disaster were everywhere. Near the end of the tour, McNamara and Taylor met with Vice President Nguyen Ngoc Tho, by then a quiet Diem opponent. Taylor brought up the strategic hamlets. "Why, General Taylor, don't you know?" Tho said. "There are not more than twenty to thirty properly defended hamlets in the whole country." They didn't believe him.

McNamara and Taylor had two other tasks in Saigon, one, the usual meeting with Diem, two hours of monologue by the Vietnamese leader, a much briefer lecture by McNamara, neither to any noticeable effect. The second task deviated from the normal protocol. It involved a game of tennis.

Robert Strange McNamara sat uncomfortably at the net, an odd sight, mopping the sweat from his brow, compulsively cleaning the fog off his rimless glasses, the tall tamarind trees at the Cercle Sportif offering no shade at center court. The two men on the grass, the sculpted American, Maxwell Taylor, and the unusually tall and suave Vietnamese, Major General Duong Van Minh, played a good game. There was nothing particularly unusual about the U.S. Chairman of the Joint Chiefs of Staff having a game with the military adviser to the president of South Vietnam. But Minh—Big Minh, as he was known—had not tendered any advice to Diem for years. He had a desk job.

None of them had come to the Cercle Sportif for the companionship. The Americans had come to get away from prying ears, to talk intrigue. The Vietnamese general had decided to talk only tennis. Later, in a quiet mahogany room, he still talked only tennis, a strange conversation for military men, counting the score in love, and an unwanted ending for the Americans—deuce.

Big Minh, a national hero, was possibly the most popular man in South Vietnam. He had also become the key to General Don's agonizingly slow manipulations against the palace, a deadly game. But Big Minh now said nothing of that, smiling at them instead through two broken front teeth, a mark of distinction given to him by Japanese torturers and one he kept the way Prussians had kept dueling scars.

Why should he confide in these men who talked too much and saw too little? The American government was divided, full of more plots than his. It leaked worse. Who would die with this leak? McNamara? Taylor? Minh would take their help, their money, their machines. More. But, until he was ready, he too would talk only to Lulu Conein, an American with some understanding of their needs and a full appreciation for the fine art of deceit.

Within a month, Big Minh would be the next leader of South Vietnam. His regime would last four months, and be brought down by the Americans just as the Americans would help him bring down Ngo Dinh Diem.

But Minh was right. McNamara was a man who could not see. So brilliant, so certain, so rational, such a prince of The American Can Do Century, he had become a computer ravenously consuming data until he had no memory left to compute. He listened to the numbers on the Viet Cong—30,000 in the field when he last visited, 30,000 killed since, 30,000 in the field now. Then he left-handed the numbers into his black notebook and moved on: How about pacification, ARVN battalion-combat hours, infiltration numbers?

The McNamara-Taylor report became a mass of contradictions and further self-deceptions. "The military campaign has made great progress and continues to progress," the report began, and Taylor went on to argue that the Viet Cong were losing so badly they would soon be reduced to mere "banditry." Perhaps Lodge budged McNamara an inch. Somewhat contradictorily, the report added: ". . . The Diem-Nhu government is becoming increasingly unpopular. There is no solid evidence of the possibility of a successful coup, but assassination of Diem or Nhu is always a possibility."

The report did little to extricate Kennedy from his dilemma. But he grasped at it in an attempt to pull his government back together. He directed what appeared to be a major policy change, a reversal of the Cable of August 24, in instructions to Saigon on October 5:

NO INITIATIVE SHOULD NOW BE TAKEN TO GIVE ANY ACTIVE COVERT ENCOURAGEMENT TO A COUP.

A cable from Saigon virtually passed it in the night. This one, also sent October 5, went from the CIA station in Saigon to CIA headquarters in Langley. It relayed a conversation between General Minh, who had been so silent at the Cercle Sportif, and Lucien Conein. Minh had told Conein that the military situation had turned hopeless and described a new plan to overthrow Diem. He asked for assurances:

GEN. MINH STATED THAT HE MUST KNOW AMERICAN GOVERN-MENT'S POSITION WITH RESPECT TO A CHANGE IN THE GOVERN-MENT OF VIETNAM WITHIN THE VERY NEAR FUTURE. . . . HE DOES NEED ASSURANCES THAT THE USG WILL NOT ATTEMPT TO THWART THIS PLAN.

Four days later, on October 9, the CIA responded, eyes only, in a cable to Lodge:

WE HAVE FOLLOWING ADDITIONAL THOUGHTS WHICH HAVE
BEEN DISCUSSED WITH PRESIDENT. WHILE WE DO NOT WISH
TO STIMULATE COUP, WE ALSO DO NOT WISH TO LEAVE IM-
PRESSION THAT U.S. WOULD THWART A CHANGE OF
GOVERNMENT. . . .

No greener light could be flashed. Kennedy's change of heart
had lasted four days and his government was back in the same
dither.

———

Lodge, having received his first unusual orders to scuttle Diem
only hours after his arrival in August, grew testily impatient with
the nervous twitterings in both Washington and Saigon. "The trouble is," he confided to Keyes Beech, "nobody around here has a
lust for power." Beech found Lodge worrisomely compulsive. So
did others. William Colby, director of the CIA's Far East operations,
and, later, head of the agency, thought him a dangerously "bucca-
neering" ambassador and a problem for the President. Kennedy
would soon agree, and, as the interlude dragged on, self-protective
"plausible denial" cables flew.

But Lodge soldiered on, often ruthlessly. He had made up his
mind, and he would follow the instructions of the Cable of August
24 no matter how much Washington fluttered. He would spend
much of his life afterward in an almost Nixonian effort to clean up
his Saigon act for history. It was a hard sell.

Meanwhile, the Vietnamese generals had good reason to move
slowly and carefully. They knew Washington remained divided
along lines especially perilous to them. The American military,
with whom they normally dealt, opposed their plans. The American civilians, whom they normally avoided, mostly supported
them. So, as McNamara and Taylor discovered at the Cercle Sportif,
the generals continued talking only through their trusted filter,
Lucien Conein.

That added to Washington's uneasiness. Conein was not fully
trusted by his own government. He was too much the loose wheel
for the blue-suited bureaucrats now a little bit pregnant with a very
messy plot. Over the years, Conein had burrowed so deeply into
the nether world all governments use but disavow that his truths

441

William Prochnau

had become hopelessly muddied. Neil Sheehan used great care in dealing with the bits and pieces provided by the man he called Three-Fingered Mordecai. Dealing with Conein, Sheehan thought, became like "peeling the layers off an onion" and, in the end, his best information even about Conein's doings came from the Vietnamese who kept their ears open at Le Van Duyet. Meanwhile, the Americans repeatedly tried to replace Conein with a more controllable agent. The efforts always came to naught. The generals would deal only with the man General Don called Lulu.

They had other problems. Diem and Nhu were not fools. They had developed an intricate defense against rebellion. Keeping their generals in check became its lynchpin. Their methods provided a telling insight into the paradox of Diem's failure to prosecute the war while successfully keeping his rivals at bay.

The three generals at the center of the major plot were Minh; Don, who continued to meet Conein in the Saigon dentist's office, and Don's brother-in-law, Le Van Kim. Trained by the French, they were among South Vietnam's best fighting generals, and, like Minh, some of the country's most popular figures. That made them all clear threats to the palace. Nhu handled Don and Kim as he had handled Minh, pulling them from the field and into fancy offices with no duties. They were knights without pawns, commanding not a single trooper.

Even with the shrewdest manipulation, the plotters needed one of the two loyalist generals who commanded the troops around Saigon. To the south was the preening, political palace favorite from the Ap Bac disaster, General Cao; to the north General Ton That Dinh, a thirty-eight-year-old former French paratrooper whose vanity, ego, and love of the fast life far outmatched his wisdom.

Loud and boastful, Dinh galavanted about town in a skintight tiger suit and a red jumper's beret always worn at a jaunty tilt. He went nowhere without his Cambodian bodyguard, a gorilla of a man who spoke neither Vietnamese nor French but whose elbows-out language was easily understood. Dinh owed the regime everything. A rice-bowl Catholic from Diem's hometown, he had moved rapidly past other young officers to the rank of brigadier. So lavishly had he been rewarded, and so certain were the brothers that

442

they had bought his trust, he was the only general told in advance about the pagoda raids. Afterward, Dinh bragged openly about the "victory" in which he had humbled the imperious Americans, defeated the arrogant Lodge before he'd arrived, and become "a great national hero" in the doing. A CIA analysis portrayed him as a "basic opportunist."

Dinh was a man whose flaws propelled him everywhere. With an unlikely and inadvertent push from the audacious young Texan Ray Herndon, he tumbled into the rebel camp like a character in a Shakespearian tragicomedy. David Halberstam had given Sheehan's backup man his ultimate accolade, and now Herndon red-assed Dinh from palace favorite into the center of the plot.

At a routine press conference, Dinh boasted as he always did about his heroics. Then he stepped into quicksand, attacking an unnamed but obvious "foreign power" plotting against his country. Herndon asked which foreign power the general was talking about. Dinh ducked. Herndon asked again. Dinh ducked again. By now, with no news to be had anyway, the Texan was having such fun that he couldn't stop. Surely a man of your importance, *a great national hero,* Herndon taunted him, knows the name of the foreign power plotting against your country. Dinh flushed and ducked again. Herndon could not bite his tongue: "Well, General, if you'd like to call Madame Nhu to find out, we'd all be delighted to wait."

The press, Vietnamese and American, burst into laughter. Dinh stalked out, humiliated, his Cambodian bodyguard elbowing a pathway straight to the officers' club and the scotch whisky. Unlike most Vietnamese, Dinh did not sip his intoxicants. He downed them. The plotting generals did not have long to wait. They caught Dinh in mid-afternoon and somewhere past mid-drunk. They commiserated about the offensive reporters, but it was the palace, as he should know, that had let him down. Dinh's ambitions knew few bounds. He had long yearned to become minister of the interior— head of the national police, a job Brother Nhu was of no mind to give him or any general. But the plotters prodded him. How could Nhu refuse a great national hero? Dinh made a trip to the palace.

Shortly afterward, the threesome became a foursome. Herndon's questions had been no more than simple impishness at a time when the lull had turned deadly dull. But a fourth general, with troops, changed everything. Neil Sheehan got a bonus too. The talkative new plotter also made his headquarters behind the louvered windows at Camp Le Van Duyet.

———

For the correspondents, other events also began building methodically toward a climax.

Since the pagoda raids, the regime had halted the Buddhist suicides by suppressing the bonzes and deploying "antisuicide squads"—soldiers with fire extinguishers—throughout downtown Saigon. On October 5, just before the crucial cables passed in the night, the tactics failed.

Tips to half a dozen correspondents came from a woman caller at about eleven-thirty in the morning: "Something may happen in the Central Market at noon." Anonymous telephone tips had become commonplace, and no one took the calls to mean another suicide. "A burning was very far from my mind, just outside my stream of consciousness," David Halberstam told his bosses afterward. But all gathered at the traffic circle outside the market and, shortly after noon, a blue cab skidded to a stop ten feet in front of Peter Arnett. A young monk stepped out alone, sank quickly into the lotus position, doused himself with gasoline, and lighted it. The flames burst so hot they forced Arnett to back away before taking the now-mandatory photographs.

The sixth public suicide, coming at a time of relative quiet, triggered a sequence of events and mini-dramas.

The regime responded with a new wave of repression and midnight arrests. The uneasy togetherness of the Kennedy administration had already begun to unhinge. Just the opposite now happened with the Saigon generals.

The beleaguered correspondents came in for new criticisms. Why, as human beings, did they not step in to stop the gruesome suicides? It was a legitimate question, one that was asked by observers as politically divergent as Madame Nhu and the *New York Herald Tribune*.

The October suicide happened so fast it is unlikely anyone could have prevented it, surely not Arnett. But he gave the critics a terrible answer: "As a human being I wanted to; as a reporter I couldn't." The more he said, the more he sank into the moral morass. If he had stepped in, Arnett said, the police would have hauled off the monk and killed him anyway. Furthermore, interceding would have thrust him directly into Vietnamese politics: "My role as a reporter would have been destroyed along with my credibility." It was a rationalization that would cause an editor to squirm. But, in the ethical isolation of journalism, the question had no answer. Malcolm Browne had dealt with it through artful avoidance: If you see an elephant on water skis, you take the picture. David Halberstam gave the fatalistic shrug of someone who, for once, saw no profound truths: "Watching a human being burn himself to death gives a man a helpless feeling and a reporter a rare confusion of personal emotion," he wrote. "Well, we covered it."

For the first time at a Buddhist suicide, one of the newsmen carried a television camera. Grant Wolfkill of NBC was held in special regard by the others. He had been taken captive in 1961 by Laotian guerrillas, the Pathet Lao, and released only recently. To the early correspondents, Wolfkill's experience represented their worst nightmare. He had been held eighteen months, moved constantly through the jungle and paraded through villages in a bamboo cage like a zoo animal. Wolfkill was tall, reed thin, and somewhat weakened from his ordeal. When the flames erupted, he brought his bulky 16-millimeter Bolex high and into full view. Everyone sensed the significance simultaneously. Wolfkill's camera would convert the potent image of Mal Browne's still photo into the incalculably more powerful new virtual reality of television. It was an escalation toward total war, a move into nukes. Brother Nhu's secret police charged out of the gathering crowd like a wolf pack.

Twenty feet away, Halberstam watched the showdown develop and, as always, stormed through the crowd hell-bent for action. That placed three newsmen in the center of the assault—Halberstam, Wolfkill, and John Sharkey, the NBC stringer-correspondent, all intent on protecting the film footage.

Five city blocks separated them from the relative safety of the Caravelle Hotel. But this time the police did not make their assault and back off. Instead, a bloody running battle ensued and, like halfbacks in a football game without referees, the newsmen juggled the camera back and forth in handoffs and laterals as one after the other went down. Two blocks from the hotel, Halberstam was the last to fall, beaten briefly unconscious. The Bolex skittered across the sidewalk, and Wolfkill, who had gone down earlier, tried to retrieve it, only to be felled again by gun butts. The police smashed Sharkey over the head with a sidewalk-café bar stool to end his last try.

The film didn't survive, but the battle foreshadowed the influence that television would eventually have in the big war coming. The incident also became the bloodiest and last of the showdowns between Brother Nhu's police and the correspondents.

Sharkey was the most seriously injured, the split in his head requiring six stitches. At an American hospital, doctors made their own political statement by elaborately wrapping his head in a huge white turban of bandages. He looked as if he had been hit by a tank. Lodge used the newsman and his outlandish headgear to pass a strong message to Diem and Nhu. "Here's John Sharkey of NBC who was beaten up by the police," he said as he introduced him to a group of visiting congressmen and television cameras rolled. Secretary of State Rusk strongly condemned the beating, further signaling America's retreat from Diem.

In the end, the beatings cost the palace more than it saved by capturing the film. They cast an air of fatal certainty over Saigon. The Diem regime seemed bent on a public suicide of its own.

———

Without film, NBC decided to use their reporter to make the story, flying him home, turban and all, for the pioneering "Today" show and other interviews. He arrived simultaneously with Madame Nhu, and the two met on an early edition of "Meet the Press." Threatened, the Vietnamese First Lady filibustered and ran out the clock, relegating Sharkey to a backdrop. But already a future filled with sound bites beckoned. Madame Nhu's histrionic monologues played poorly. By the time she reached the West Coast three weeks later, her ratings in that other American phenomenon, the public-opinion poll, had dropped to 8 percent.

In New York, Sharkey also got a firsthand sense of how slippery the home-field footing had become for the small corps of Saigon correspondents. After the television appearances, NBC set him up in an office for a series of newspaper interviews.

"*The New York Times* sent over a guy," Sharkey said later. "I can't remember his name, it was one of those incredibly Waspish names, three names, you know: Poolsbrooke Northcliffe So-and-So. He wasn't a reporter at all but worked in middle management. He came in with his yellow pad, closed the door, put the pad aside on the table, and said, 'Okay, now what about Halberstam?' He didn't give a shit about my story. He was concerned that Halberstam, as the government was saying, was too abrasive and writing the story nobody else was writing, making up his own little conflict, and so forth. This guy was just checking on him."

Sharkey was not part of the Halberstam-Sheehan axis, but the incident offended him greatly. He thought it was beneath *The Times*, and he responded angrily: "Your guy just works his ass off, and he knows the story. He can back up every word he writes."

But he concluded that Halberstam had deep problems indeed.

———

To the powerfully narrow men inside the walls at *The New York Times*, David Halberstam, still only twenty-nine, still with only three years at the newspaper, had become a problem. There are editors' papers and (far fewer) reporters' papers. No one had any doubt about where *The Times* of 1963 fit in that regard. "It was a highly structured newspaper and people had to conform to the rules and regulations," said Clifton Daniel, second in command in the newsroom and soon to become managing editor. He meant that the editors controlled, reining in mighty egos and mighty talents too. To a certain kind of bright young reporter it was as if *The Times* wanted to break them, the way a cowboy breaks broncos, sacrificing all that wild energy that had been so attractive in the first place for a ride with less turbulence, a saddled ride. Some fought it. A few quit. Others held on until the newspaper changed or the saddle no longer chafed. It was, after all, *The Times*. What else was there? But none reacted like Halberstam.

"He was a thorn in the side of everyone who wanted things to run smoothly," his friend Tom Wicker said later.

"The old school wasn't ready for him any more than it was ready for Vietnam," Harrison Salisbury said. "The old school was about to be razed."

But that was looking back. Neil Sheehan, who sat shirtless and sweating with Halberstam as the days ran out in 1963, had a different fix on it. Sheehan saw his buddy "fighting for his professional life."

The angry exchange of cables over Marguerite Higgins had brought his relations with the foreign desk, and particularly with Nathaniel Gerstenzang, to a low that could go no lower.

Poor relations with the night foreign editor amounted to something less than a professional crisis. "The battle of the titan and the midget," said one editor who worked the desk. But Gerstenzang was the main link to home. To a frazzled correspondent in the field, the abrupt jabs of his cable-ese arrived like the unrelenting water droplets of ancient Chinese torture. At the height of the Buddhist crisis Gerstenzang not only hammered Halberstam about Higgins, but the same compulsiveness that gave the world Achmed Sukarno produced a broken record of nonsense: Day after day he demanded that his exhausted correspondent track down the names of three obscure Saigon pagodas with little role in the story. The dialogue of the deaf had reached full unheard volume.

Word about the feuding moved quickly around the newsroom, and Halberstam received buck-up mail. One letter came from Greg MacGregor, the onetime Far East correspondent who had started off badly years earlier with Emanuel Freedman. Relegated by 1963 to the graveyard shift in New York, MacGregor wrote Halberstam:

> I know what it is like to be where you are and dealing with an often unsympathetic desk. At times they seem to be trying to knock you down, but just remember that the Freedman-Gerstenzang crowd have been living on only shrewdness for some time—between the lot of them they probably measure up to the mental powers of a retarded chimpanzee, without integrity, of course.

After more than two years, the system in New York was wearing out on Halberstam and Halberstam was wearing out on the system. He wrote more than ever, the reporting aggressive but the writing still long and often obtuse. On the desk there were no more stretches of forty-three nights with one editor and no more celebratory flings at the Blue Ribbon. An editor got Halberstam's copy for a week, no longer. Among the correspondents in Saigon the verb "gerst" had become as much a part of their language as "rocket" or "rollback," and equally dreaded. In New York, Gerstenzang, who also taught a copyediting class at Columbia University's Graduate School of Journalism, cut a stencil of one of Halberstam's most mangled efforts, changed the byline to "Hagstrom," and took copies to class for a workshop. It was not a private event. Five other *Times* copy editors taught simultaneously in the same room. Afterward, one of the students accused Gerstenzang of pulling his leg. "Nobody would write anything this bad for the newspaper," the student said. Those watching said they had never seen Nathaniel M. Gerstenzang smile so broadly.

At about that time, the newspaper's courtly and powerful managing editor, Turner Catledge, visited Nashville.

"We thought a lot of your man Halberstam while he was down here," a friend at the *Tennessean* said.

"Yes, he is a good reporter," Catledge responded. "Almost as good as he thinks he is."

Catledge was fed up and trying to decide what to do about it. He dealt with the internal problem directly, giving Halberstam a swift kick in the pants disguised in his Southern fashion as "a little fatherly advice." In a September letter he suggested that Halberstam worry less about questions from New York "that may seem senseless to you in Saigon" and more about "the things you write in Saigon [that] sometimes seem obscure here." He should stop thinking the messages came from "either a knave or a fool," Catledge warned, hinting that the missives were often directed to him from considerably higher personages than the signer. Toughen up your skin, cut down the cable tolls, and stop "wasting time, effort, money and adrenaline on quarrels," he instructed, adding "one final word" that, halfway around the world, sounded suspiciously like Southern sarcasm.

> We appreciate your advice on how long stories should be and how they should be played. However, we hope you understand that your advice cannot always be the sole determining factor.

The managing editor had more give in him, more tolerance of human quirks and flaws, than his fellow Southerner and anointed successor, Clifton Daniel. But he also believed in the strict formulary of an institution with codes and regulations strictly followed. He believed more: "A great newspaper is to some extent a political institution; to maintain its power it must use it sparingly." David Halberstam used nothing sparingly—not power, not words, not epithets. Halberstam did not merely rock boats. He made such waves he could sink them. Catledge knew how embarrassing it would be for *The Times* to recall its man in Saigon. It would be far easier if the South Vietnamese government would do it for him. But he was ready.

The New York Times of 1963 was not a risk taker. It was a newspaper attuned to the establishment and "by tradition opposed to crusading reporters," James Reston wrote. Its attorney boasted that, in the fifteen years he had represented her, the great gray lady had "never lost six cents in a libel suit," a fine record for a lawyer but one less worthy of boasts by the most important newspaper in the United States, perhaps the world. Vietnam and the adversarial journalism pioneered by Halberstam would begin the transformation of the newspaper into a better and still prouder institution. Over the next decade, Vietnam, as a story, would remain virtually the private preserve of *The Times*, turf staked out for it by the newspaper's brilliant brat and his Saigon buddies. But in the fall of 1963 no one knew better than Reston how nervous his protégé's "stormy talent," as he put it, had made the newspaper.

The Times did not always stand like a pillar behind its people. Herbert Matthews sat in not-so-splendid isolation seven floors above the newsroom in testament to that. Twice Reston had stepped in from Washington to protect Halberstam and save crucial stories—his exposé of the military debacle in the delta and the pagoda raids story that started Kennedy on his week of furies.

Reston was a godsend. But Halberstam did not take saves easily. He remained in deep trouble. He was playing against the clock and the clock was running.

As the awkward interlude in Vietnam stretched on and on, all the forces mounted to push David Halberstam away from his story before it ended. His visa was expiring again, his last monthly extension taking it to October 15. From Kuala Lumpur another *Times* correspondent arrived, ostensibly as his backup in case of expulsion. But, tired and paranoid, Halberstam saw the new man as insurance for *The Times* if it made the decision to yank him. Meanwhile, a rising new star, a young correspondent named Hedrick Smith, had been named as his permanent replacement, a routine rotation scheduled for late November. Halberstam had been stationed overseas, in war conditions and without a vacation trip home, for almost thirty months. Even he thought it was time for a change of scenery. But he didn't want to move too soon. The exhaustion made him erratic. His cables home alternated between begging for a vacation break and rebelling against the offers. Like the others, he was afraid to leave. As he felt the squeeze, his often-feisty cable language turned syrupy: VERY NICE INDEED TO BE WORKING FOR NYKTIMES. . . . DELIGHTED BY YOUR VERY GRACIOUS ATTITUDE. . . .

But, beneath the cover, he felt edgy, undermined, and insecure —"a little naked," he said. The outside world produced endless plaudits. "I would like nothing better than to see you in *Harper's* some day," Willie Morris, the wunderkind editor who had taken New York by storm, wrote in September. The inside world produced terse cables from Gerstenzang and swats from Catledge.

Long afterward Halberstam still vented his bitterness.

"There were a lot of high executives at *The Times* who really wanted to see my face rubbed in shit a little bit," he said. "They would not have been unhappy at all if I had been expelled. They don't like people to be expelled. They don't like to move furniture. But, at this point, I think they would have considered moving furniture the lesser of two evils."

It was also long afterward that one of the executives confirmed the mismatch of man and institution.

"There were many of us who thought he should be brought home on charges of insubordination and what all," said Clifton Daniel, who one year later became managing editor. "We couldn't do business on the basis that he wanted to work."

Halberstam had simply become too hot for *The Times,* a lightning rod for attention the paper didn't want. He had become part of the story he had been sent to cover, and that was not *The Times* way. Ironically, it would take the United States government to save him and, in the end, John F. Kennedy himself.

———

Mal Browne approached the end in trouble too.

Browne was different. Not as political, not as ostentatiously confrontational. "The wire-service guys were the grunts and the specials were the fighter pilots," said Leon Daniel, a UPI careerist who came in later. Browne had his own take on a wire-service reporter's role. "No newsman can afford to think about history," he told the photojournalist Susan D. Moeller. "He has to have something to put on the wire machine."

Still, Browne was every inch the radical. He was the first to say his countrymen were lying, the first to declare the American Embassy persona non grata—don't even bother to talk to them— an extraordinary bit of role reversal for any American correspondent of the era, let alone the man from the wire agency that fed Middle America its washed-of-passion, straight-as-a-string news. And he did it before the others had even arrived in Saigon. Homer Bigart admired him greatly. But why? puzzled Halberstam, who had settled on a different choice. "Because he's good," the grand old man replied.

If Neil Sheehan's UPI was founded by a news huckster and sometimes hyperventilated on sell-sell-sell, Mal Browne's AP was as intentionally bland as Grandma's mush. The Associated Press was a news cooperative owned by the newspapers who used it, and the newspapers who used it were owned by some of the most conservative men in America. On his trip home the previous spring Browne had sat wisely quiet through a lunch with Wes Gallagher, AP's general manager, and William F. Knowland, the reactionary publisher of the *Oakland Tribune*. Knowland had been the Republican majority leader of the U.S. Senate who gave Joe McCarthy free rein to chase Red shadows in the 1950s. He had also been a passionate supporter of Chiang Kai-shek, and he nattered all the way through lunch about the "overly liberal" reporting from the new Asian front, Vietnam.

Browne had somewhat more natural protection in the home office than the others. Gallagher had been a rebellious war correspondent himself, pushing so hard against the total controls of the Second World War that the army branded him a troublemaker and threatened to pull his credentials for the D-Day landing at

Normandy. But even Gallagher had trouble matching up Vietnam with the simpler yards-gained-yards-kept experience of his youth. A few months later, in early 1964, he visited the place. Browne took him into the delta where the Viet Cong had virtually taken over. He took him past the fraudulent ghost hamlets, past the old French mud forts now shot up and empty. Gallagher never doubted him again.

But that was later. In the fall of 1963, the assaults hurt Browne perhaps more than any of them. An attack by *Time* magazine damaged an Associated Press correspondent where it hurt most—among all those small-town, apple-pie clients spread across America's heartland. So, by October of 1963, Browne was taking a beating from his home office too: *Take a vacation; get your wind back, your perspective too. Now.*

In the second *Time* article on the Saigon press corps, meant to be a corrective to its earlier assault, the magazine reported that Browne had been ordered out of Saigon to "quiet down." He scoffed at the report as the further babblings of a discredited sheet. But he left for Tokyo in early October, and no one thought he had chosen to go. The heat was on.

Browne left town certain he would miss the final act in the drama he had walked into blindly on its first secretive day almost two years earlier. Hurriedly, he put together a code to bring him back at any sign of the coup d'état that now seemed inevitable. Once, during a shoot-out in front of his office, he had sent Le Lieu into the bathroom, where an extra wall of mortar would protect her. So now the signal for the big shoot-out would be:

LE LIEU IS IN THE JOHN.

Time, however, had done Browne a favor. It forced him out early.

———

A friendly American intelligence officer helped Halberstam out of his immediate problem with the South Vietnamese, tricking Gia Long into extending his visa from October 15 to November 15. But it would take a far more powerful boost than that to keep Halberstam in Saigon.

On October 22, 1963, President John F. Kennedy invited the new publisher of *The New York Times* to the White House for lunch.

Arthur O. (Punch) Sulzberger, thirty-seven years old, elevated suddenly and unprepared five months earlier after the unexpected death of fifty-year-old Orville Dryfoos, had not impressed the men of American power whom he had joined. They thought him a pushover, unequipped for the roughhousing of the bigs. They were wrong.

The meeting was Sulzberger's first with Kennedy. He asked Reston what to expect. Don't worry, his Washington man assured him. It's a social call. He will ask you about your children. Tell him a story or two, then ask about his.

A social call it was not. Kennedy started in immediately about Vietnam and *The Times*. "I was a young rookie, very nervous," Sulzberger recalled, "and he took me completely by surprise. He was relentless. I don't think he ever mentioned Halberstam by name. But he kept on about our coverage." The conversation made Sulzberger increasingly uncomfortable. Several minutes passed before he realized that the President was seriously asking him to remove Halberstam. "Clearly, if we had had any thought of making a change at that point," Sulzberger said, "we would have changed our mind."

In a conversation immediately afterward in the Washington Bureau offices Reston agreed. "Well, obviously we can't do what we were thinking of doing," he said. "We can't buckle in to that kind of stuff."

Precisely what *The Times* had been planning remains murky.

Sulzberger says he has no recollection of any plan to pull his controversial reporter. "Perhaps there was a routine transfer or a vacation scheduled," he said. "There would be no reason for me to know about that." But he is certain he would have known if someone of Halberstam's visibility was about to be moved for other reasons.

So what had the newspaper been thinking of doing?

Hedrick Smith was brought into the Sulzberger-Reston meeting a few minutes after the publisher returned from the White House. Smith did not have his visa for Vietnam at the time and was not planning to depart for at least another month. But he has a vivid recollection that Halberstam was leaving sooner—"within the next twenty-four to forty-eight hours"—until Kennedy blundered in.

"They thought he was getting tired," Smith said. "They were worried about his safety."

A year later, in his book, *The Making of a Quagmire*, Halberstam wrote:

> As a matter of fact, at that particular point I was supposed to go on a breather for a two-week rest, but to its everlasting credit *The Times* immediately canceled the holiday lest it appear to have acquiesed to this pressure.

Long after that, Halberstam insisted that he would not have left on vacation at that time even if ordered. Whatever, John F. Kennedy had unintentionally given Halberstam a lease on the story for the duration.

———

The only one without the luck of the Irish in those final days of October was the Irishman himself. Earnie Hoberecht not only killed Neil Sheehan's story implicating the Americans and Henry Cabot Lodge, but he blew his top. He called his brash young correspondent back to Tokyo. Come up here, take a rest, and clear your head of all this nonsense, he ordered. Pronto.

Sheehan could feel the bottom falling out. It was now the last week of October. Browne had been forced out but made it back safely, missing nothing. Halberstam had received a stay.[3] But Sheehan knew that he would have no such luck. He could feel it in his County Kerry bones. It was too late. The coup wouldn't wait for him. He fought like hell.

It was not easy to carry on an argument between Saigon and Tokyo about the timing of a coup d'état. First, he wrote a hand-carried letter. But, to Hoberecht, the Young Turks had finally gone over the edge, with his own man leading the way. They were "completely up their hands," he complained in a colloquialism that had more to do with the position of their heads vis-à-vis their

---

3. *The Times* did not tell its man about the Kennedy-Sulzberger incident. He heard about it later from Bernard Kalb, a former *Times* correspondent who had moved to CBS television.

backsides. Hoberecht wouldn't budge. Get up here, he cabled back. *Now.* Desperate, Sheehan chanced a telephone call. He was frantic, speaking in belabored code and then virtually straight out in the open: "This is the wrong time. It's boiling over down here. I know more than I can tell you on the phone." Hoberecht remained unmoved. "Come up here and take a rest, Neil," he said. "Or stay down there and wait for your last paycheck."

Faced with being fired, Sheehan flew to Tokyo—but not before setting up his own last-minute defenses. At the old cavalry post he talked with Pham Van Dong. Many plots were brewing in Saigon. But Dong was plugged in closer than ever to the most likely one. Now the fourth general, Dinh, used Camp Le Van Duyet as his headquarters, and he babbled like a woman. Dong promised to try to give Sheehan advance warning. They worked out a "go" signal: PLEASE BUY ME ONE BOTTLE OF WHISKY AT THE PX. Dong would deliver it to David Halberstam or Ray Herndon but no one else. They would pass it on in another coded signal, a cable to Tokyo: PLEASE BUY BLUE LOTUS TWO GEISHA DOLLS, KYOTO STYLE. If he were lucky, Sheehan would get the message in time to fly back. He didn't feel lucky.

"Earnie, I'm going to miss the coup," he despairingly told Hoberecht after he landed in Tokyo.

"Take your rest, Neil," Hoberecht repeated. "You're all going off your rockers with your coups and your plots. You, Halberstam, Browne, the bunch of you."

Sheehan laughed through his exasperation. Hoberecht clearly didn't believe a word he'd been writing. "Earnie!" he protested briefly. "The reporters are not plotting the overthrow of the regime! *Henry Cabot Lodge* is, *the U.S. government* is trying to get rid of these people!"

During his first day, Sheehan bounced around the office. To his colleagues he seemed the slightly becrazed kid from Saigon, warning executives and copyboys, veteran desk men and five-dollar-a-shift moonlighters: Be on the lookout for the geisha doll cable. *Call me anywhere, any time of the day or night,* he instructed, posting his hotel and room number in a dozen prominent places around the cluttered office.

Soon, the accountants caught up with him. They put him to work on the books, which he straightened out for the first time in eighteen months. Then he waited.

———

Hours after Sheehan arrived in Tokyo, Lucien Conein made another trip to the dentist. General Don had news. The plotters would act within a week—no later than November 2.

In Washington, the Kennedy government had never quite recovered its equilibrium after its own in-house coup. Since then, the White House had acted with near-neurotic zeal to provide cover for the obvious: It was now up to its ears in the overthrow of its ally of nine years, Ngo Dinh Diem.

From the beginning, McGeorge Bundy, Kennedy's national security adviser, became the chief White House operative. He had set out to keep the effort "totally secure and fully deniable," instructing Lodge to communicate in Saigon only orally and only with the CIA's acting chief of station, David Smith. That limited those in the know to three persons: Lodge, Smith, and Conein. Even Harkins was kept in the dark.[4] Bundy also fluctuated between mild concern and outright distress about Conein. "Is it possible to arrange a more secure system of contacts with General Don . . . perhaps through cutouts?" he queried Lodge earlier in October. A cutout is a go-between whose use would break, or "cut out," the direct link between the U.S. government and the plotters. But that was wishful thinking, and Lodge said so. Don wanted his old Second World War buddy, Lulu Conein, and that was that.

In effect, Bundy became the cutout for Kennedy, giving the President a slim measure of plausible denial. It was all smoke and mirrors. The messy trail of covert meetings led back to the Fourth of July, the cabled approval to August 24. The Americans wanted to have it both ways, control of the show and no responsibility for it.[5]

4. Ironically, some of the correspondents knew about the coup sooner than most of the upper echelon of the American government.
5. In an interview thirty years later Pierre Salinger still stuck by the line until excerpts from various cables were read to him.

After two months of White House complaints that the generals couldn't get their act together, the news from Conein gave Kennedy a severe case of cold feet. As with most presidential sneezes, it was catching.

An elaborate CIA presentation, with maps and color-coded Vietnamese troop positions, opened a nervous meeting of the White House Task Force on Vietnam late on the afternoon of October 29. The CIA's estimates showed the pro- and anti-Diem forces almost dead even at 9,800 each, with 18,000 uncommitted. In a coup attempt, in which the keys are secrecy, surprise, planning, private deals, opportunism, and quick shifts of allegiance, the numbers meant little. The numbers were also wrong. The generals' distrust of the Americans caused them to hide their most sensitive arrangements, including the absolutely crucial turn of General Dinh. Only days before, General Harkins, who had been shut out and didn't know better, had stunned General Don by telling him that U.S. policy opposed any coup. Conein had a lot of work done on his teeth later that day. Don calmed down. But he wouldn't show all his cards to anyone. The advance warning promised on the final plan was cut from two days to two hours.

The troop count spooked the White House further. The President's brother and alter ego, Attorney General Robert F. Kennedy, stepped quickly and surprisingly into the fray. Preoccupied with Martin Luther King, Jr.'s March on Washington during the week leading up to the intrigues of August 24, he now announced flatly that the coup was a rotten idea. Overthrowing Diem, he said, "would be putting the future of Vietnam and in fact all of Southeast Asia in the hands of one man not now known to us."

The statement rang like a stage cue for those who had been outmaneuvered in August. Maxwell Taylor quickly said that he agreed with the attorney general. John McCone quickly said that he agreed with Taylor. Averell Harriman desperately tried to stave off another counterrevolution. But the President was hooked by the opportunity to dodge. The numbers bothered him. He wanted the best of all worlds—a bloodless coup done with quickly, and no trace to his doorstep. To go into it with equal forces would be "silly," he said. He told Secretary of State Rusk to cable Saigon: "If Lodge agrees with this point of view, then we should instruct him to discourage a coup."

Normally, such words would be tantamount to a presidential command, albeit one very difficult to put into effect at that late date. But the White House had pulled the trigger on August 24. Stopping the bullet now required more wizardry than an American president possessed. Lodge did not even try to stop his "rock rolling downhill." On the issue of the coup he had become a fanatic and he found the eleventh-hour flailings foolish and irritating, sending Rusk a long, openly contentious cable and signing it, "Thanks for your sagacious instruction. Will carry out to best of my ability." Kennedy found the closing sarcastic, which it was.

"He sounds amused," his brother Bobby, said. "I told you he was going to be trouble."

"You know what's terrific about you?" the President flared. "You always remember when you're right."

In Saigon, the Diem regime blindly continued its suicidal ways. As the month ended, Beverly Deepe talked a shy sixteen-year-old Vietnamese high school girl into posing with Lodge in a routine street-scene photograph for *Newsweek*. The girl was immediately arrested and disappeared into the underground prison beneath the Saigon Zoo. Deepe was horrified. Terrible deeds were done in the political prison—electrical wires attached to women's nipples and other primitive tortures administered.

Later that evening, as he strolled up the Rue Catinat toward dinner, Ray Herndon was stopped by a fourteen-year-old boy. The youth handed him a folded piece of paper and quickly left. Puzzled, Herndon looked at the note. "Please buy me one bottle of whisky at the PX," it said.

A long time would pass before Herndon learned the boy's identity. He was Colonel Pham Van Dong's son and the conduit through whom Dong, confined to barracks as the generals poised for their final move, kept his promise to Sheehan. Herndon wasted no more time puzzling about any of this. Nor did the thought occur to him that he was privy to information that had not yet been given to the U.S. government. He went straight to the PTT office, where he sent an urgent cable to Tokyo:

PLEASE BUY BLUE LOTUS TWO GEISHA DOLLS, KYOTO STYLE.

17

THE END OF THE BEGINNING

Davi Halberstam rose early. There had been many false alarms in the past two months, many times when the generals, the colonels, and all the assorted plotters had feinted and drawn back. But this time Colonel Dong had gone dangerously out of his way to alert them. Halberstam knew who Dong had sent. His son, for God's sake. You don't ignore tips like that and thrive in Halberstam's business. And, for Halberstam, this *had* to be the day. He was running out of time, and he knew it. At the villa the Bep served him a hurried breakfast of fresh fruit and strong coffee. Then he ran out the door and hailed a cab to 19 Ngo Duc Ke. Mert Perry, scrambling to find work with anyone now that he had dumped *Time*, would be waiting. As would Ray Herndon, nervous as a cat.

By this time Halberstam had become a veteran of his trade—his persistent critics ignoring that he had been under fire in the unconventional little wars of his time as long as most of them had been at risk in their big wars. Too young? He was pushing thirty, a milestone that would soon leave him too old to be trusted by the generation of firebrands his war would ignite. Still, he remained the big, exuberant, irrepressible kid who had landed at the mouth of the Congo more than two years earlier—fresh, cocky, and dressed by Abercrombie & Fitch. He could not pass the lush grounds of the Cercle Sportif and make the turn into the rush of the Rue Catinat without drawing in his breath at the sheer good luck of his being there. He also remained the angry young man he always would be, a bull in America's china shop unable to pass Paul Harkins's villa without a muttered fuck-you. To the end, David Halberstam was incorrigible.

Only days earlier he had had another of those public confrontations that made his editors so uneasy. This one came with his perennial antagonist, General Richard Giles Stilwell, Stilwell the Bad. The two were some match. Both totally self-certain and ambitious, flagrantly bright, capable of outrageous and unembarrassed pomposity. They also hated each other. Everyone, reporter and soldier alike, could see the explosion coming. Stilwell stood briefing a group of leery correspondents about a mission from which they had been barred, making long and dubious claims about successes they had learned to doubt. Halberstam shifted impatiently from foot to foot. Finally, he could take it no longer. He interrupted, demanding to talk to Harkins and Lodge.

"I have no intention of bothering the general or the ambassador about this," Stilwell replied starchily.

The room fell silent. Then Halberstam replied with more starch than Stilwell could ever muster. "General Stilwell, we are not your corporals," he said. "We are *The New York Times*, United Press International, the Associated Press. You do not tell us what we can and cannot cover."

Across the room even General Robert York, who had plunged into the mud with Sheehan at Ap Bac, forced back laughter and flashed Halberstam a wink.

Now, on the fateful day of November 1, Halberstam hopped out of his cab, waved at the familiar crowd of the Mat Vu, undercover cops, and other assorted operatives, and walked through the glass doorway at number 19. Mert looked up with a casual grin. Rao was sprawled across the couch, listening to his police radio. Halberstam chuckled. What would Rao do after a coup d'état? He'd have no one left to talk to. All his sources were in Diem's secret police. They had occasionally wondered about him, his sources were so good. Could he be a double agent? A triple, working for them, Diem's police, and the Viet Cong? Halberstam shrugged a so-what. Nothing would ever be what it seemed in Saigon.[1]

---

1. Rao proved to be exactly what he claimed to be. Not all did. Of the Vietnamese aides, the reporters' favorite had been Pham Xuan An, Nick

He glanced at the morning's *Times of Vietnam,* shook his head at the usual attacks on the correspondents alongside Harkins's prediction that "victory is just months away," and tossed the paper onto the office's ever-growing mound of rubble. Yesterday's news. The *Times of Vietnam* would never publish again. Within twenty-four hours its offices would be burned to the ground, Ann Gregory seeking refuge at the U.S. Embassy.

At the kitchen-table desk Halberstam normally shared with Sheehan, Herndon sat glued to the old telephone, panic written on his face at the thought of going up alone against Mal Browne's legions. Halberstam reassured him. They had sent the cable. Sheehan would be back by early afternoon. In any case, this was no time to be making too many inquisitive phone calls. Why advertise what you already knew? They were the only correspondents in Saigon who knew that this was the day. Halberstam wanted to keep it that way.

There was more to that than Halberstam realized: They were also the only Americans in Saigon who were in the know.

———

The generals had spent the night orchestrating silent movements. Under cover of darkness, rebel forces quietly tightened a noose around Saigon. Loyalist forces found themselves dispatched to distant battles never to be fought. Generals Minh and Don had monitored the movements closely—for timing, for glitches, but mostly for double-crosses. Vietnam was the land of the double-cross, and many were about to get final, fatal lessons in the art.

The plan itself was simple.

Elite rapid-strike units of Vietnamese marines and airborne would make simultaneous attacks on communications facilities—the telegraph office, the city's two radio stations, the airport—and

---

Turner's assistant at Reuters. An went everywhere with the gang—with Sheehan on his first helicopter mission, to the disaster at Ap Bac, on raids deep into Camau. By the end of the war a dozen years later, he had become a full correspondent for *Time* magazine. But, back in those early days, the reporters had been wrong in their assumption that a hidden romance accounted for his periodic disappearances. Twelve years later, during the desperate evacuation of Saigon in 1975, An didn't take a helicopter out. He had been a spy for the Viet Cong all along.

other crucial targets such as the downtown naval barracks and police headquarters. Saigon was a remarkably compact city, many of the targets within easy walking distance of each other. With communications under their control, the rebels would then converge on Colonel Tung's Special Forces headquarters and the barracks of the super-loyalist presidential guard. Within hours, if all went well, they would encircle the ultimate target—Gia Long Palace. The key was General Dinh. The CIA hadn't counted his men in. The palace had gone a fatal step farther.

For almost nine years Diem and Nhu had outmaneuvered world-class schemers of all stripes. Now Brother Nhu had concocted a bizarre preemptive defense—a phony coup, code-named Bravo One, in which Dinh would storm the city and "drive" the brothers into hiding. With Saigon in chaos, the plotting generals would reveal themselves. Dinh would turn and smash them. "We shall trap the friends of the Americans in the dead shell of the capital city," Nhu boasted to his cronies. In the bloodbath the generals would be killed and anyone might be caught in the cross fire, Lodge and Conein being prime candidates, John Mecklin and a few of the pesky foreign newsmen attractive bonuses. Dinh, his giant ego still bruised, had turned.

The key to the generals' timing was the weekly luncheon meeting of the Vietnamese Joint General Staff at JGS headquarters near the airport. On this particular Friday, the generals had invited all the Vietnamese military hierarchy, including such Diem stalwarts as the chief of the presidential guard and Colonel Tung. Lured inside for lunch, the loyalists would find themselves captive, at the point of machine guns. The tanks would roll at 1:30.

Meanwhile, rumors fluttered everywhere. Only the night before, Lodge had sent home a cable naming ten separate groups plotting coups against the regime. It read like a rationale for the historians. When it came to scheming, Lodge dealt with friends and foes equally, keeping everyone off balance. By coincidence, Admiral Harry Felt was passing through Saigon. On the morning of November 1, he asked Lodge for an update on the coup. The ambassador wouldn't get the official go signal from the generals for several hours. Even so, he was deceptive in his answer. "There isn't a Vietnamese general with hair enough on his chest to make it go," Lodge replied. The American ambassador was more Vietnamese than the Vietnamese, Madame Nhu once said—and never in her life did she utter a compliment about Henry Cabot Lodge.

As the morning progressed, Admiral Felt attended one awkward meeting after another, the first at 9:15 with Harkins and General Don. Harkins remained completely in the dark. At one point he gestured toward a huge order-of-battle map and asked Don why two crack Vietnamese airborne battalions were unengaged. They were en route to battle, Don assured him. Felt looked askance. Harkins nodded, reassured. They were on their way to battle all right—in Saigon.

Forty-five minutes later Felt met with Diem at the palace. Felt rarely met with the chief of state. But Don had arranged the meeting, using the unsuspecting admiral to keep his target in town. Lodge also met with Diem, staying on for a private chat after Felt left for the airport at 11:30.

Diem suddenly looked a forlorn soul, small and lost, his body a dumpling and his face the pasty texture of one too. For once he seemed conciliatory, in no mood for two- and three-hour monologues. "Please tell President Kennedy I am a good and frank ally, that I would rather be frank and settle questions now than talk about them after we have lost everything," he said.

But the last meeting of the two mandarins was doomed. Lodge and Brother Nhu, two master intriguers, would have made a better pair that day. The American ambassador gave the Vietnamese leader no assurances, only a bizarrely ironic absolution from the rumors that Diem was trying to assassinate him. Lodge described his conversation in a cable to Washington later that afternoon:

> I said I could assure Diem that these rumors of [my] assassination had not in any way affected my feeling of admiration and personal friendship for him or for Vietnam. I had long admired his courage before coming to Vietnam and since getting to know him, I formed sentiments of friendship toward him. I was grateful to him for being so extremely nice to my wife and me.

Lodge left Gia Long at 11:45. By that time Vietnam was changed forever, the United States too.

———

On the top floor of Mainichi Shimbun Building in Tokyo the geisha dolls cable had arrived at 2:00 A.M. The night man, buried under the usual avalanche of work, spiked it along with the other incomings. By the time of the morning shift change, it lay beneath a long night of messages, more paper landing on top of it as each hour passed.

———

Mal Browne had sent his message to AP's Tokyo bureau several days earlier: LE LIEU IS IN THE JOHN. Since his return, Browne's code had taken on a slightly different meaning. He didn't have Sheehan's sources with their pinpoint timing. But his instincts told him that events were rapidly moving to a head. So many Vietnamese had been arrested after calling his office that he now answered the phone: "Associated Press. This call is being monitored by public officials. Go ahead, please." But his message to Tokyo didn't come after a tip and didn't predict a date. It was a gut call—a good one—for reinforcements. He got them. His "human wave" now had Herndon outnumbered by five to one. But Browne's two stalwarts were out of town. Peter Arnett was 600 miles away in Laos, routinely planning to fly back in mid-afternoon. Logistically, Horst Faas had strayed still farther, tromping through the marshy tangle of Vietnam's southern peninsula doing the jungle-rat duty he liked best.

The absence of Arnett and Faas cost Browne more than met the eye. It also shut down one of AP's crucial, and exclusive, early warning systems—a spy post fondly called the "Radio Station."

Having chosen a precarious life, Arnett and Faas compensated by combining their pleasure with its needs. In a coup attempt, they reasoned, a first target of any self-respecting rebel would be Radio Saigon. What better place to maintain a lookout than in the bordello across the street? It was a classy place, Arnett insisted, silk, not satin, many of the girls being the wives of Air Vietnam pilots just working for mad money. "I'll take the Radio Station," he would announce at the first hint of a coup. The rumors had come so fast and furiously in the past two months, many hours of lookout duty had been whiled away amid its silks, and the secret was kept from their rivals on Ngo Duc Ke as religiously as any covert operation of the Cold War. On November 1, however, the post went unmanned.

After ten weeks of chaos, and all the false alarms, a sort of jaded nonchalance ruled much of the city. Briefly, in mid-morning, the coup almost unraveled. A key to the plan involved neutralizing Diem's chief of naval operations at his headquarters in the downtown naval barracks on the Saigon River not far from the American Embassy and only blocks from the palace. November 1 was the chief's birthday, and friends visited him to offer greetings and invite him to join the coup. When he turned them down, they shot him. A brief skirmish ensued, and the generals, having powerful reasons to hold the coup until they had sprung their luncheon trap, scrambled to get the lid back on. They succeeded—to the everlasting embarrassment of one correspondent.

Minutes after the false start, James Robinson, NBC's Asia correspondent and the first man to routinely wear safari jackets on TV, was called back down the ramp from his plane to Hong Kong. "The coup! You can't leave, the coup is beginning!" cried his Vietnamese cameraman, who had watched the brief fight. "I've heard that one before," Robinson said and reboarded the plane. He later went into banking.

Robinson's bad guess was Peter Kalischer's opening. The caustic ex-marine and UPI man, who had moved into the new wonder world of television with CBS, acted purely on veteran's instinct. He and his cameraman awoke the morning of November 1 far to the south with a unit that had spent several days trying to rescue two captured Americans.

"Want to try one more day?" the American adviser asked.

"Some other time," Kalischer grunted. "It's pushin' anybody's luck to stay away from Saigon that long." His helicopter swooped back into Tan Son Nhut in the middle of the brief firefight to take the airport.

Kalischer's muscular swagger, implausible face, grating voice, and almost self-parodying Jungle Jim suit soon gave way to a blow-dry era of voice coaches and Dan Rather jackets.[2] But now it was

2. Rather, during his stint in Vietnam in 1966, made Robinson's safari jackets *de rigueur* for television—and a Saigon tailor, who made them overnight by the dozen, became rich beyond his dreams.

the gut feeling, that gnawing angst of a wire-service man, that carried television back to the story it would soon own.

Throughout the morning Halberstam, Herndon, and Perry nonchalantly conducted their routine rounds—reading the wireservice tickers at Mecklin's office, glancing through briefing transcripts, even checking in at Harkins's headquarters where no one had a glimmer.

Perry had been there longer than any of them now, even predating Browne, and he made the swings the others forgot. In late morning he drove out to the residential street the correspondents called Spook Row. There he found Lucien Conein on the terrace of his house, deep in animated conversation with several other CIA agents. Perry called out to him. "Gee, I can't talk to you now, Mert," Conein shouted back. "I've got to go." The mysterious man of so many names then hurried away, carrying a suitcase with him. Perry lost any lingering doubts. It was a few minutes past 11:30.

———

Inside his suitcase Lucien Conein had packed hand grenades, a pistol, a special CIA radio telephone, and 300,000 Vietnamese piasters—roughly $42,000—in escape money for the generals. Moments earlier he had received the two-hour notice and flashed the go code to the tight group with a need to know (no American military men included). When Perry drove up, Conein had been arranging for the dispatch of a twelve-man U.S. Special Forces A Team to protect his family if the coup failed. Then he hightailed it to the Vietnamese JGS headquarters near Tan Son Nhut airport.

Despite the U.S. government's elaborate efforts to distance itself later, Conein would stay inside rebel headquarters through the day and night, providing a play-by-play for the White House in a sequence of communications known as FLASH CRITICS—a designation reserved for messages considered "essential to national survival."

Lodge heard about the go-ahead at 11:45, when he returned from his meeting with Diem. He decided to take a late lunch on the embassy's roof. Saigon was a low-slung city, many of its downtown buildings only two or three stories tall. The old six-story embassy provided an ideal view of the city as battlefield. The pale pink walls of the ultimate target, the palace from which Lodge had just returned, stood only five blocks away across a sea of red tile roofs. Other natural targets—the naval barracks sat just behind it downriver—were spread about in easy view. The city's broader avenues, in which troops and armor would move, fanned out like spokes.

At about the same time Lodge got the word, David Halberstam and Ray Herndon stepped out of Sheehan's office two blocks away and hailed a cab for the airport and the last of Admiral Felt's awkward meetings. He had scheduled a noon press conference with generals Don and Harkins before returning to Hawaii. For Don, it made the timing tight.

Riding through town, Halberstam could feel it coming now. The sky was brilliantly blue and the midday sun punishing. Within minutes central Saigon would empty itself, a roar of motorbikes and cabs leading the daily exodus for the two-hour midday siesta. Shutters would descend over storefront windows. Street-corner hawkers would stash their wares. The city would become an open grid of tree-lined boulevards, all leading to the sprawling palace grounds of Gia Long. This was the time, he said to himself. This was the time it always happened.

At the airport, he watched Felt closely. The cocky little bugger is putting on one helluva show, he thought. It never occurred to Halberstam that Felt didn't know. General Don stood next to the admiral, chewing gum like a threshing machine and shifting anxiously from foot to foot. The moment Felt turned toward his boarding ramp, the nervous Vietnamese chief of staff brushed off General Harkins (who wouldn't be told until fifteen minutes after the coup had begun) and double-timed it to his waiting car, which sped away across the tarmac.

On their way back, Halberstam and Herndon diverted their cab past General Dinh's headquarters at Camp Le Van Duyet. Troops swarmed around the garrison, tanks kicking up billows of dust on the old cavalry parade ground as they jockeyed into position to be fueled.

It was 12:30. Herndon groaned. Where the hell was Sheehan? The first flight from Tokyo had arrived while they were at the airport. No Neil. He fought down an irrational urge to try an open telephone call. One look at Dinh's tanks told him that Tan Son Nhut would take few more incoming flights today. Maybe Sheehan had routed himself through Bangkok, or Manila, and would still make it. Maybe.

Meanwhile, Halberstam ordered the cab to take them to a tiny walk-up bistro near the Caravelle, the Aterbea. Herndon groaned again. Halberstam grinned. The tanks went into battle refueled; he went into battle refueled: the usual steak, double order of *pommes frites*, milk, two pieces of pie, two scoops of ice cream. Herndon shook his head. Sometimes the wire man's envy of the special bordered on murderous. Halberstam didn't have a deadline till tomorrow. Herndon had them every minute, today, tonight, and tomorrow. He had no appetite at all.

Perry soon joined them, and brought Charley Mohr's *Time* magazine replacement, Murray Gart, with him. (Mohr had retreated to a golden limbo in Hong Kong, hired by the *The New York Times* to begin January 1 and paid a munificent $9,000 by *Time*—as much as Hoberecht parted with in a year for both Sheehan and Herndon—to sit it out till then. Still, with that came the worst of agonies—a great story with no one to publish him.)

Halberstam had been so close to Mohr that he had trouble trusting Gart. Stubbornly, he sat through most of the lunch before finally blurting out the news.

"How good is your information?" Gart asked.

"As good as you ever get," Halberstam replied, a touch of aggravation in his voice.

He fished through his pocket for the bottle-of-whisky message. Gart was reading it when the café owner suddenly shouted at them: *Coups de fusil!* Shooting! The crackle of not-too-distant gunfire rattled through the café. They moved fast.

———

Sheehan saw no need to go into the office. His telephone number festooned the walls and he called in a half-dozen times a day, so often he knew he was driving everyone nuts.

He loved Tokyo, and even on his salary the postwar yen seemed to stretch forever. He liked Japanese art. He loved Kabuki. He took a traditional hotel with paper and bamboo inner walls, shoji screens, tatamis covering the floor, a futon, which he rolled up in the Japanese style each morning after he woke. And no heat. He immediately caught a flu.

Nothing was going to make this vacation pleasant. It wasn't a holiday. It was a banishment. He walked around the Ginza, worried, scared, killing time, calling in. He ran into a Japanese girlfriend from his earlier days, and the two of them took up briefly again. But he was miserable, morose, black-Irish company.

By Friday, November 1, he had loosened up some. He thought he would be loose of Hoberecht and back in Saigon by Monday. After lunch he and his friend went shopping, then looking for a movie or an afternoon Kabuki performance. He called in again. Nothing. Maybe he'd get through this after all.

———

Mal Browne got the jump. Tipped off by an embassy security agent, he raced to the riverfront in a new AP jeep and sped through the naval-barracks gate. A lone loyalist guard stopped him before he reached the buildings, pulled him from the jeep, and muscled him over a low wall. Seconds later, an explosion rocked the ground behind them. From the nearby embassy roof Lodge also watched the engagement begin. He saw a half-dozen ancient American-built fighter-bombers descend toward him in slow, rolling dives. It looked like an old Second World War movie. He said later that he found it exciting. On the ground Browne was less enthusiastic.

Halberstam and Herndon went immediately to the UPI office, where one of Sheehan's Vietnamese photographers, who had gone home for the siesta, had returned. The photographer told them excitedly that truckloads of marines had passed his house, the men shouting: "Come along, we are making the coup!" Halberstam ran back into the streets.

But the rebel forces had swept in so swiftly and decisively they not only overran their early targets in minutes but they overran the reporters too. It was the kind of precision the ARVN had rarely shown in the field.

The radio stations, the telegraph office, and the airport fell almost without fuss, cutting off communications to the outside world. Telephone lines were cut. Within the hour, the police and the navy surrendered, Browne retreating safely, and the headquarters of Colonel Tung's Special Forces was surrounded by marines, tanks, and M-113s. Tung, whose ruthless intelligence system had made him the scourge of Saigon, had made a crucial mistake. He had gone to lunch.

General Minh had made the announcement at precisely 1:30. Join us or die, he told the loyalists, and suddenly they were staring into machine guns and hearing doors click behind them. An hour later, only Tung held out. With a gun at his head, he telephoned his men and ordered them to surrender.

By then Browne had worked his way back to the office. The bureau at 158 Rue Pasteur sat so near Gia Long—just kitty-corner from the palace guard post—it actually fell within Diem's defense perimeter. Browne and his men had a ringside seat. But it was a precarious one, sitting in a direct line of fire to the palace. By mid-afternoon rebel troops began taking up positions above them in their building, drawing raking fire from the palace defenders. Browne had problems. He had to make his people safe. He also had to get a story out fast, with the PTT closed and the local phone lines cut.

Neil Sheehan's audacious feat the night of the pagoda raids had taught them all a lesson. Now everyone went straight to the Tiger Line, with their military sources set up well in advance. Even so, Browne's story didn't reach New York for almost four hours. Herndon's made it forty-two minutes later. It might as well have been a month.

But both wires lost the race. Peter Kalischer had learned his angst well during his United Press days in Korea. Barely off the helicopter at Tan Son Nhut, he bulldozed a few words out and CBS beat everyone. Even as the Young Turks reached the crest of their influence, their time was fading fast.

Meanwhile, Herndon's anxiety had turned to desperation. He knew he would have to do something extraordinary, and he knew it would be dangerous.

———

Inside the palace, Diem and Nhu began to lose faith that their elaborate plan for a countercoup would save them. The double-dealing leader of Bravo One, General Dinh, had spent the first hours of the coup avoiding their calls.

In mid-afternoon the generals called and put Colonel Tung on the line, again with a gun to his head. Tung told Diem that the Special Forces had surrendered. He was then taken outside and shot over a grave already dug. Moments later, Dinh finally accepted a call from the palace. The brothers were greeted by a burst of Vietnamese obscenities: "Dinh saved you mothers many times, but not now, you bastards. You shits are finished. It's all over."

Desperate, Diem began a round of calls to his most trusted military men outside Saigon. None would, or could, come to the phone. At 4:30 he called Henry Cabot Lodge. The conversation was tape-recorded:

DIEM: Some units have made a rebellion and I want to know: What is the attitude of the U.S.?

LODGE: I do not feel well enough informed to tell you. I have heard the shooting, but am not acquainted with all the facts. Also it is 4:30 A.M. in Washington and the U.S. government cannot possibly have a view.

DIEM: But you must have some general ideas. After all, I am a chief of state. I have tried to do my duty. I want to do now what duty and good sense require. I believe in duty above all.

LODGE: You have certainly done your duty. As I told you this morning, I admire your courage and your great contributions to your country. No one can take away from you the credit for all you have done. Now I am worried about your personal safety. I have a report that those in charge of the current activity offer you and your brother safe conduct out of the country if you resign. Had you heard this?

DIEM: No. (*And then after a pause:*) You have my telephone number.

LODGE: Yes. If I can do anything for your physical safety, please call me.

DIEM: I am trying to reestablish order.

The two men never spoke again. Lodge later told endlessly contradictory stories about his conversations with Diem on November 1, 1963—that he had guaranteed him safe passage out of the country, that he had told him he could stay on as titular head of state. Like other attempts he made to soften his role in the coup, none of Lodge's revisionist versions has the backing of contemporary records. "What would we have done with them if they had lived?" he asked Halberstam afterward. "Every Colonel Blimp in the world would have made use of them."

———

Lucien Conein's first FLASH CRITIC reached the Situation Room beneath the White House shortly after one in the morning. John Kennedy's aides did not awaken him till 3:00 A.M. He told them to come back at 6:00.

At 8:00, McGeorge Bundy chaired the morning staff meeting and reported that he and Forrestal had "spent a quiet night watching the cables from Vietnam." According to minutes of the meeting, "Bundy then commented that Diem was still holding out at the palace, adding that no one wanted to go in for the kill."

At 10:00, Kennedy came downstairs to meet with his senior advisers. No record of the meeting was kept, a rarity in a White House preoccupied with history. But the cables to Saigon that began emanating from it were preoccupied with decorum: control, distancing, denial, and public relations.

At 10:50, as the meeting continued, Kennedy left to attend Roman Catholic services at Holy Trinity Church. November 1 was All Saints' Day.

———

Meanwhile, Browne's two combat aces, Peter Arnett and Horst Faas, scrambled to get back.

That morning in Vientiane Arnett had routinely boarded an Air Vietnam flight to return to Saigon. The old propeller-driven plane made a brief stopover in Phnom Penh and then continued on. Nearing the Vietnamese border, twenty minutes from Saigon, it suddenly banked sharply and headed back into Cambodia.

Arnett had been in Southeast Asia for five years. He knew instantly what had happened, and he knew he couldn't miss it. He charged the cockpit door, pounding until the copilot opened up. Inside, the pilot was chattering with an air-traffic controller. The insurgents were threatening to shoot down any plane that tried to land at the closed airport. Arnett scoffed and played every trick in a hustler's bag, a journalist's, too, the con often being the same.

He begged. He inveigled. He played on the pilot's patriotism: *A Vietnamese plane has a right to land on Vietnamese soil.* He played on his fears: *Your family needs you! What will happen to them if you're not there?* "I have been in coups before," he intoned ominously. Finally, he provoked his own coup d'état, a passenger revolt. With everyone shouting at him, the pilot turned the plane once more, approaching Tan Son Nhut so low that he skimmed the trees at the end of the runway. Landing, Arnett stared into rows of tanks, all turrets turned toward them. But his bluff worked.

An hour later, at 3:30, he made the turn into the Rue Pasteur. Gunfire rattled all around him, and he advanced toward number 158 one tamarind at a time, hugging each before dashing for the cover of the next. As he ducked into the office, troops fired into the palace from the second-floor terrace of his apartment just above. A single defender remained at AP, an old wire-service pro named Ed White, whom Browne had brought in from Tokyo. "I'm holding down the fort," he said, puffing on his pipe. "I've said that plenty of times before, but for once it's true."

Browne had taken the others on a hasty retreat to a new headquarters on the roof of the Caravelle Hotel. Arnett retreated there, too, where they had a better view than Henry Cabot Lodge, and Johnnie Walker Red Label from the bar too. As daylight began to do its quick tropical fade, they watched snipers scampering over rooftops toward the palace. The fighting sagged into a lull. But the headwaiter in the Champs-Élysées Room promised that the tenth-floor restaurant would serve all night if the patrons would be patient. Some of the help had gone home.

Faas had more trouble. Deep in the southern swamps, he didn't hear the news till late in the afternoon—and then only in the form of reports of unusual radio traffic out of Tan Son Nhut. Like Arnett, he read the situation immediately. Faas was a man who chased action with a lust unexcelled, and the coup d'état was the hottest action of the war. He all but commandeered an airplane, taking Steve Stibbens, the hero-worshipping young *Stars and Stripes* reporter who followed him everywhere, along with him. They arrived over Saigon at dusk to find both sides nervous about aircraft with military markings. Tan Son Nhut radioed: no landings. Then the palace, which had taken attacks from rebel planes, reacted. The plane began taking fire.

"We can't land," the crew chief said. "Too much antiaircraft fire."

Gunfire had never deterred Faas before.

"Giff me a parachute," he demanded. "I vill jump."

Stibbens said he was going where Faas was going.

The crew chief stared at them, briefly at a loss for words. Then he told the pilot to get the hell out of there. Fast.

Thirty minutes later they landed at Vung Tau, the same seaside town to which Diem and Nhu had planned to exile themselves while Dinh pulled off the countercoup, Bravo One. By now it was dark and Saigon was seventy-five miles away, part of the drive through mangroves the Viet Cong had owned since the French were there. No one would make the drive. Faas tried to buy a jeep and again was rebuffed. Guttural sounds echoed in the night.

In Saigon, David Halberstam hailed a cab to take a look around. The cabbie grinned and drew a finger across his throat. *"Tong Thong fini,"* he said. President Diem is done for.

A strange calm had settled over the city. He made a quick pass by the barracks of the Presidential Guard, about a half-mile from the palace. The barracks had held out longest, although most of the super-loyalist guard had long since pulled back to the palace. A tank still fired an occasional round into the burning two-story wooden buildings. But troops were moving in unopposed, and other rebel tanks were backing away to redeploy for the final assault.

Still, with nightfall, even the gunfire around the surrounded palace had become more subdued. Nearby, a few people had returned to the streets, impassively going about whatever mysterious business they had to conduct on a night like this. A horde of children followed a single M-113 like very short infantrymen as it zigzagged purposelessly down a back street, firing wildly. After each burst, the children collected the spent brass casings, booty for trade in tomorrow's market. The demand for spent shell casings would be brisk.

On the Catinat, two very drunk Americans waved. "Tell them to knock off the noise!" one shouted. "They're bothering people." The street, one long block over from the palace, began to spring back to life. The tall Sikh doorman, in red uniform and turban, had moved back into business in front of the Caravelle. Iron grills came down off doorways. The girls began poking their heads out of the Florida Club and Uncle Sam's and the Honeymoon Lane.

How much we have changed this place in so short a time, Halberstam thought. Even the name. He and his group were among the dwindling few still holding out for the street's old French name that had so enticed Graham Greene.

Turning a corner into the street the Vietnamese called the Avenue of Flowers, Halberstam's cab came upon column after column of airborne troopers marching alongside perhaps twenty armored vehicles. With them, he saw a familiar Vietnamese photographer.

"Whose side?" he asked.

"Anti-Diemist."

Briefly, Halberstam watched, fascinated. The men marched briskly past him, proudly displaying the shoulder patches of the 7th ARVN Division. John Paul Vann's old division. More significant, they were the troops of General Cao, the strutting general at Ap Bac, no man more loyal to Diem, no man rewarded more lavishly for his loyalty. It was over.

———

In Tokyo, Neil Sheehan had taken his girlfriend home and gone alone to an early dinner at the Foreign Correspondents Club. It was a place where you could take a phone call at your table or go out to a booth. When the call came, he went to a booth. He knew this was the coup, and he knew he had missed it. The voice on the other end said, "Come back to the bureau right away. . . ." He dropped the phone before he heard another word, running back, too sick to hail a cab, and went straight to the ticker. It was an odd story, coming out of Seoul with reports of fighting in the streets of Saigon.

"Has ROX got anything?" he demanded of the desk man. "Herndon?"

The answer to both was no. But Sheehan knew. The South Korean embassy, using its own channels, had beaten the wires too.

"Holy Christ, Mother of God," he groaned, and moved to the message spike. He dug through almost to the bottom, then tore one off:

SHEEHAN. PLEASE BUY BLUE LOTUS TWO GEISHA DOLLS, KYOTO STYLE.

476

The feeling he had was one he would remember all his life. He was so sick he almost threw up.

"When did this come in?" His voice sagged.

No one knew. He called KDD, the Japanese cable office. It had arrived nineteen hours earlier. "Shit," he murmured. "Shit, shit, shit."

"But what does it mean?" the desk man asked.

Sheehan rolled his eyes around the room at the notes he had pasted on every wall, and erupted:

"It means a coup, you goddamned fool! It means the goddamned government is being overthrown in Saigon and I'm in fucking Tokyo!"

No one had ever heard a UPI office turn so silent.

———

A full moon illuminated Saigon as all the forces moved into position.

The generals placed most of their men and armor around the palace, as if preparing for a long siege. They had no such intention. Big Minh could barely control his fury at Diem's stubbornness, promising to flatten Gia Long if he didn't surrender.

Inside, the brothers' stubbornness had become a cover for their desperation. They had survived many times before with their Bravo Ones and their shrewd ability to know a man's price. They had made it through a situation almost as dire in 1960, when troops from the delta marched up to save them. That is why they had them there, why they had General Cao fighting phantom battles with no casualties. But no one was coming this time. In the end, they acted like brothers. Nhu, knowing he was the most despised, tried to convince Diem that they should split up. That way, Nhu might draw off most of the bile, saving Diem's neck. Out of the same fraternal sense, Diem would not go along, hoping that some residual respect for him might save Nhu. They stuck together.

At JGS headquarters, Conein continued to dispatch his reports to the embassy, which forwarded them to the White House as FLASH CRITICS.

Henry Cabot Lodge had long since left for his heavily guarded residence. A creature of rigid Yankee habit, he turned in for the night at the usual 9:30. Lodge had left John Mecklin profoundly discouraged. He had thought Fritz Nolting a kindly fool. Lodge, he concluded, was too shrewd by half.

On the embassy roof, Mecklin joined about forty people following the action in the darkness below. A convoy moved into the city across a bridge over the river. "I hope they're friendly," said a voice in the dark. "Who do you mean by 'friendly'?" asked another, and the crowd laughed. They started making bets. The Viet Cong would take over in eighteen months. There would be another coup in six months. Mecklin bet that American combat troops would be there in a year. He was off by four months.

The correspondents also moved into position.

At dusk, Ed White rejoined the AP team at the Caravelle after troops began stringing concertina wire around the office. Many of the stringers, other correspondents, and hangers-on came to the rooftop too. It made an odd scene. American music from the forties and fifties—dreamy Sinatra sounds, the crooning of Como and Crosby—wafted out over an old P.A., interrupted only by scratchy reminders about a military curfew. The Élysées delivered as promised, providing the necessary potables and other rations slowly but surely. Gia Long stood two hundred yards away, the ghostly moon glow of its walls crisscrossed by arching multi-colored tracer bullets.

Browne stood like a general directing his troops—Arnett to the U.S. military headquarters, White on rewrite, Roy Essoyan on color, where the hell is Faas? The phones came back up, and Browne worked them. It was an old wire-service maxim: Stay put, don't leave your communications. Adventures were for the specials. No one worked the phone better than Browne. At 10:00, running out of calls to make, he phoned the palace and asked for Ngo Dinh Nhu. A very long silence greeted him. Then the operator said: "Mr. Nhu cannot come to the telephone."

Down below, Ray Herndon turned frantic. He was getting his butt kicked good, and Sheehan would not arrive to help. He went to the rooftop, took one look at Mal's army, and beat a quick and ulcerous retreat. Memories of showing up at the first Buddhist suicide without his camera gnawed at his insides. "I was terrified," he said later. "By evening I knew how desperate my situation was and I knew I had to get something no one else had." This was no time for old maxims. The something, he decided, was the capture of Ngo Dinh Diem. Better to get killed trying, he thought, than face Hoberecht empty-handed again. Behind the old opera house he found a mean-looking outfit of rangers forming up. It was about midnight. He played a hunch, latched on, and stayed.

David Halberstam had little left to win or prove. He was about to go home forever controversial but the most famous young reporter of his time. While the others scrambled, he had the special's great luxury of spending the evening prowling about. He found some of the coup's leaders. The final assault on Gia Long would begin at 3:30 A.M., he learned. At 1:00 he did what no other correspondent in Saigon had the nerve to do. He returned to the office and took a nap. The noise would awaken him.

Herndon's wild hunch paid off. After two hours of siege, his rangers indeed moved on the palace. They marched down the broad avenue leading to the open market, turning right to join a column of tanks moving up Pasteur. As dawn approached, Herndon ducked behind the lead tank with a group of jittery troopers. Out of the darkness, Halberstam ducked in with them. The .50 calibers from the defenders clanged off the machine as it closed on the palace.

Down the street, another column turned into Pasteur from the other direction. Suddenly, a tank exploded in front of the AP office, the machine guns of the lingering palace guard picking off the crew members as they tried to escape.

Herndon's lead tank pivoted and began belching shells point-blank into the wall around the palace, carving a jagged hole. A tough little lieutenant ducked through. Then another ranger. Herndon went next, "that's how crazy I was."

He sprinted through the garden, triple-stepped up the stairs, and pushed through the great doors, ducking. Halberstam charged in a few strides behind. The place was empty. Herndon and the lieutenant raced up the next set of stairs to the living quarters, looked here, looked there. But the brothers were gone.

The rangers and the ARVN peasant boys, kids who still went into battle with live ducks hanging head down from their gun belts, shouted, caroused, and scooped up souvenirs. They grabbed at the gold tassels and took the drapes with them, shattered the china and scooped up the pieces. A great roar went up as they discovered Ngo Dinh Nhu's whisky. But they made no greater find than Madame Nhu's silk underwear, waving it over their heads like captured battle flags.

Halberstam stood in the great entrance hall as the little soldiers raced past him. He had been here only once before. Now, high above him, the ceiling fans that had circulated air sweet with jasmine had stopped dead. The rich silks hung in tatters from the walls. Even the kowtowing servants had disappeared somewhere into the night. The French had built Gia Long years before for the civilian governor of Cochinchina. The inheritor had not really been Diem. Surely not Nhu. If it had been anyone in this strange family, it had been Madame Nhu. She had given the place its colonialist afterlife, even choosing the language of the Court of Versailles over her own native tongue.

Moments earlier, charging low across the grounds and up the stairs, Halberstam had felt that special rush, that touch of Hemingway that all feel, even if some deny, during short bursts of combat. Now, the downside came over him, an emotional low so rare to his nature that he had trouble recognizing it. The palace depressed him. Even discounting the damage, it had a bygone look, a vestige of a time gone before the occupants knew it. Now the occupants were gone too. Madame Nhu would never be back. Neither would the brothers.

Halberstam forced the depression out quickly and continued around the room, kicking at the rubble. Near a far wall he uncovered an ornate Laotian sword. It was short and curved, most likely from Brother Nhu's collection. It was clearly Laotian, but, to Halberstam, it had a Gurkha look to it, and it reminded him not of the crazy family who had preoccupied him for so long but of the hellbent Indian general who had taken a liking to him in the Congo. "Come along, Garrison!" the general would mangle his name, and he knew he was in for one bad day in Africa. Halberstam unsheathed the sword, sheathed it again, slipped it under his arm, and walked back out onto the porch overlooking Gia Long's gardens. The sun was up, the beginning of another hot day in Saigon. He had a lot of writing to do.

———

Two hours later, Ngo Dinh Diem was dead, as was his brother. They had left the palace through a secret underground passageway early the previous evening, long before the final assault, and had spent the night trying to rally their forces from a hideout in Cholon. It was a hopeless task. They surrendered in front of a Chinese Catholic Church at 8:00 A.M. and were murdered moments later in the back of an M-113, which, as Diem had known all along, was far more deadly in the streets of Saigon than in the muck of the paddies.

The word first went out that the brothers had committed suicide. It was a story that wouldn't sell. By the time Charley Mohr stepped off the first plane from Hong Kong at the reopened airport late Saturday morning, the hawkers had already begun peddling photographs to the press. They showed the brothers beaten and shot, their hands bound behind them.

Cornelius Mahoney Sheehan bolted down the gangway of a noon plane from Tokyo, a flight he could have made the day before. He headed straight to 19 Ngo Duc Ke, waved off the looks from his buddies, and went to work on the story of how the brothers died.

Ray Herndon took AP's drubbing, then scored a clean sweep with the account of his night of derring-do. He scored another when a muscle-bound Cambodian pushed aside other reporters so that an ecstatic Vietnamese general in a red beret could bear-hug him. "You are the one who started it all!" General Ton That Dinh exulted to the mystified reporter. "You are the hero of the revolution!" He had no idea what Dinh was talking about until told where his press-conference taunts had led weeks before. Dinh then gave Herndon an exclusive, if vainglorious, account of the coup.

Horst Faas virtually hijacked a dawn flight from Vung Tau. At Tan Son Nhut he and Stibbens roared off in the black Falcon, skidding up to the AP office while the rebel tank still burned out front and soldiers still poured across the grounds into Gia Long. He recorded the day after in images of troops reveling in the palace and Americans dancing in the bars, liberated from Madame Nhu's blue laws. Most newspapers ran the dancers. They made Saigon seem so safe, and American, again.

Peter Arnett dragged two dead soldiers off his balcony in the morning and went night-clubbing with generals Don and Minh in the evening, toasting a new era, no way of imagining what it would mean to his life and so many others.

Peter Kalischer did an early-morning stand-up beneath Gia

Long's balustrade, then sped the film to Tan Son Nhut for the first flight to Japan. In Tokyo, a plane bound for Seattle was held on the runway. In Seattle, the cargo was slung aboard the run to New York. At LaGuardia Airport, a motorcycle met it for the final rush-hour sprint to midtown Manhattan. The film arrived at CBS twenty-four hours after it had left, so close to airtime that "they had to edit it with an ax." People marveled at the miracles technology had wrought—filmed news from the far side of the world flickering into American living rooms a mere day after it had happened.

In the debris at 158 Rue Pasteur, Malcolm Browne pinned a story by Keyes Beech to his newly pockmarked office wall. WHY THE U.S. DIDN'T BOUNCE DIEM, read the headline above a story written on the eve of the coup. Browne left it there for years, a yellowing symbol of the triumph of the Young Turks, prologue to a story none of them could yet see coming.

David Halberstam began a final frenzied rush that would guarantee him fame, fortune, and, with Browne, the Pulitzer Prize. His anatomy of a coup, published four days later, filled a full page of *The Times* with five thousand words on the intrigues of the Vietnamese generals and one paragraph on the role of the Americans. The skittish White House nevertheless ordered the CIA to put its minesweeper to the rabble-rouser's story. "A pretty impressive account," the agency reported back, finding only one error of fact. Halberstam had written that Diem had telephoned Lodge at 4:00 A.M. The call had been made at 4:30 P.M. As to errors of omission, the CIA made no observation of any kind.

In Washington, Marguerite Higgins called Roger Hilsman at two in the morning. "Congratulations, Roger," she said. "How does it feel to have blood on your hands?"

"Oh, come on now, Maggie," replied the author of the Cable of August 24. "Revolutions are rough. People get hurt."

Otherwise, the Kennedy people played the new game of plausible denial so totally that they sometimes deceived themselves. They had, indeed, neither sought nor ordered the deaths of Diem and Nhu. That was an act directed by the Vietnamese generals, although hardly an unpredictable one. But complicity? Responsibility? John Mecklin, who had been privy to neither the plans nor the cover stories while watching from the embassy roof, cut quickly through the nonsense. To argue that the United States was "not involved," he wrote, was "like claiming innocence for a night watchman at a bank who tells a known safecracker that he is going out for a beer."

For the correspondents it was a moment of great triumph. Rarely had such a small group of relatively young reporters attained such influence. Perhaps never had so few redefined the rules for the many who followed. They had exposed the government's lies and cast light on its ineptitude, two of the most fundamental functions of their craft. But it was a triumph to be tempered. It would take others to see and ask the most important questions of all. Could the United States win with *any* South Vietnamese government? *Should* the United States win? Did all those well-meaning, can-do, we've-got-the-answer Americans have any business at all in a far-off and alien land among a people in search of their own unique destiny?

The correspondents left those questions unasked. They were indeed men of their times, children of the Cold War all. They saw to their own horizon and no farther. "We missed the big one," Sheehan said later. "We surely did."

Over the next months South Vietnam disintegrated, politically and militarily. Eight inept governments rose and fell, many again pushed by the Americans. The ragtag guerrillas of the Viet Cong organized into an efficient army of regiments divided into 600-man battalions that roamed virtually at will. In one engagement, a VC main-force battalion wiped out a trapped ARVN battalion almost to the last man. CIA reports confirmed, and McNamara finally did, too, in December, that the military balance had begun to take a drastic turn for the worse in July, shortly before Halberstam had reported it.

The U.S. government's own secret history of the war, the Pentagon Papers, made this conclusion about the hole the United States had dug for itself, morally and otherwise:

Thus, the nine-year rule of Ngo Dinh Diem came to a sudden, bloody and permanent end, and U.S. policy in Vietnam plunged into the unknown, our complicity in the coup only heightening our responsibilities and our commitment in the struggling, leaderless land.

Whether John F. Kennedy realized how irreversibly he had stumbled into the swamp will never be known. He was assassinated three weeks later in Dallas. But, handed the FLASH CRITIC on November 2 reporting the deaths in the M-113, he turned ghostly pale. He stood up without a word to his assembled advisers, and walked from the room.

In Los Angeles, Madame Nhu, angry and despairing, had no doubt. Preparing to fly home when the word came, she had one final session with the press she so despised. "If really my family has been treacherously killed," she said, "it will be only the beginning, the beginning of the story."

18

ROLL CALL

David Halberstam left five weeks later. Before departing, he gave the Laotian sword to John Mecklin, it being clear that he had a more powerful weapon. The U.S. troop count stood at 16,000 advisers, with 145 killed. Halberstam returned to Vietnam once. By that time, in late 1967, the troop count stood at half a million, with 16,000 killed. The Johnson administration had begun a "progress" offensive of optimistic reports to calm public opinion, one high official predicting that the war could be won within six months. Six months later, during the Viet Cong's 1968 Tet Offensive, more than 200 Americans were killed each week. In the New York salons, on the campuses, and in the streets of the Movement, Halberstam became something of a mythic antiwar figure. He rode with the tide of it. But even this great mythmaker, when pressed, answered directly: "We didn't have hawks and doves when I was in Vietnam. The war was a given. We covered the war. The debate was about the deceptions and the lies. It was all lies and lies and lies."

In 1988, twenty-six years after he first traveled down Highway 4 to the Seminary, sixteen years after he began the Homeric journey of his book, Neil Sheehan finished *A Bright Shining Lie*. It was received with immediate critical acclaim and commercial success. He was awarded a long-overdue Pulitzer Prize, not the last of the group to earn one, merely the last of the group to get one. Since then he has made three more trips to Vietnam, one with his two daughters, who finally saw the distant place that consumed so

485

much of their father's life as they grew up. He has written a second small book about Vietnam, *After the War Was Over*, and in 1995 was at work on another opus, this one about the Cold War. The young Irish firebrand—"Ahh, so, another foolish Westerner come to lose reputation to Ho Chi Minh"—was graying and limping from one of life's random wounds. Neil Sheehan remained an intense man. But he had come back, seeing old friends, humor crackling, happy in his well-rounded family, a man liberated from a war that taught him how to subdue his own demons, the last prisoner of Vietnam free at last.

Malcolm Browne spent seven years in Vietnam. He also filled his life with other adventures and eccentricities. In 1965 he left AP and joined ABC television, then quit abruptly when assigned to cover a Miss Saigon beauty contest on a day of fierce fighting in the field. He joined *The Times*, quit *The Times*, rejoined *The Times*. He has been ever drawn to distant lands. Antarctica became a passion, he, almost a commuter. But that greatest love never faded. The land he first saw in 1961 forever captivated him. So did the woman. Browne and Huynh thi Le Lieu remain happily married. She works with political refugees in New York.

Charley Mohr was wounded in 1965, the first American correspondent blooded in the accelerating war. He later covered many wars. In 1989, on his sixtieth birthday, Mohr died at home of a heart attack. "A consummate correspondent," read the obituary in *The Times* of a reporter who had done everything. But it dwelled, as all recollections of Mohr would, on the Vietnam years: "He was one of a handful of correspondents including Neil Sheehan, David Halberstam, Peter Arnett, Malcolm Browne, Seymour M. Hersh, R. W. Apple, Jr., Homer Bigart, and Eugene L. Roberts, Jr., whose reporting challenged false official accounts and presaged the failure of American and South Vietnamese policies in the war." Of the nine reporters named, six, including Mohr, were there at the beginning.

Peter Arnett had no place to go, no ticket to punch, so he did it the hard way. He stayed to cover almost all the war and most of those that followed in a benighted time of endless human conflict. In the doing he made the long leap from the small whaling village on the downside of the world to the global village of the international Cable News Network—and became the most famous name and face of them all.

Horst Faas also stayed, going where others didn't, pushing ever deeper into the darknesses of a doomed war. He usually went alone. Eventually, others didn't want to go with him. He cut too close to the bone, too close to the soul. Some called him a war lover. But the only antiwar statement stronger than his published photos was that of his unpublished photos. Faas followed almost as many wars as Arnett, then became AP's photo editor in London. In honor of his fallen colleagues, Faas is assembling a book called *Requiem* displaying the best work of the photographers who died in Vietnam. There were many.

Homer Bigart steered clear of wars but could not avoid clerks. One night he was assigned to write about a riot. He wrote from the office, fending off editors as he took telephone calls from younger reporters in the streets. One called in terrified, rioters surrounding his phone booth and shaking it back and forth. "At least you are dealing with sane people," Bigart consoled him. Homer Bigart died in 1991 at age eighty-three.

Mert and Darlene Perry never did as well again. The very mention of their names brings a great smile, then a pensiveness, to every member of the group. After leaving *Time,* Mohr was immersed in offers. Not Perry. He bounced from second-rate job to second-rate job. In 1970, at age forty-one, unemployed, he died of a massive heart attack.

Ray Herndon stayed on, Annie actually elbowing some extra noodle money out of Asia Earnie to keep Sheehan's books straight. Herndon remained with UPI for more than a decade in Saigon, Paris, and Florida. But old Unipressers never die; they change jobs. In 1990, at the *Dallas Times-Herald,* he accomplished a red-ass newspaperman's dream: His reporting freed an innocent man from death row. In 1992 he became a projects editor for the *Los Angeles Times.* He and Annie remain happily married.

Peter Kalischer stayed with CBS, watching color arrive, satellites enter orbit, Minicams replace Auricons—and power shift in immense proportions. But he never lost his wire-service edge. In 1975, as in 1963, he beat everyone with the first bulletin about the fall of Saigon, this time to a different conqueror and ending a war that had become known as the first television war. Kalischer was forced into an early retirement in an economy wave in 1979. He died in 1991 at age seventy-six.

Pamela Sanders remained briefly in Vientiane as the war next door grew larger and the stringer jobs in Laos faded in and out. Then she got on with her vagabond life, marrying a career diplomat and, in addition to her novel, writing travel stories about distant, romantic lands. In 1994 she moved with her husband to Garmisch-Partenkirchen in the Bavarian Alps.

Asia Earnie Hoberecht fell by his own ax in 1966, a victim of budgetary and other wars in the constant turmoil at UPI. He remains one of the great legends of wire-service journalism. Well into his seventies, he also remains a salesman—of real estate in Watonga, Oklahoma.

Richard Clurman left *Time* in 1974, a year before the war's finish and twelve years after he told Henry Luce it would come to no good end. At seventy-one, he lives in Manhattan and writes well-regarded books on journalism. He still flies first-class, although the second seat now goes to his wife, Shirley.

François Sully returned to Vietnam in 1964. He survived an almost immediate attempt to expel him again but did not survive the war. Shortly before he was killed in 1971, he watched the body bags being carried away from yet another battle in yet another lost war and wrote that it reminded him of an old French war song: *"Chacun son tour . . . Aujourd'hui le tien, demain le mien"*—"to each his turn. Today yours, tomorrow mine." Sully left his life insurance —18 million piasters—to Vietnamese orphans.

Marguerite Higgins became one of the first media casualties. Flying home from her tenth trip to Vietnam in late 1965, her temperature rose to 105 degrees, a terrible foreboding of the last twist in that strange family haunt. On January 3, 1966, she died, as had her grandfather in the French colonial army seventy-five years earlier, of a rare tropical fever contracted in Vietnam. Higgins was forty-five. She was buried in Arlington National Cemetery.

Keyes Beech slogged on and on. During Saigon's final moments in 1975 he was sixty-one years old and found himself trapped in the hysterical crowd outside the walls of the American Embassy as the last helicopters prepared to leave. A desperate young Vietnamese man grabbed him and held on tight. "Adopt me and take me with you, and I'll let you go," he said. "Don't, and I won't let you go." Beech took one look at the youth's raw determination and said, "Oh, shit, I'll adopt you." A moment later, one of his fellow marines reached far down the wall and hoisted Beech to safety. The young Vietnamese didn't get out. Three years later the *Chicago Daily News* folded, a derelict of a time past. Beech worked briefly in Asia for the *Los Angeles Times*, then retired in 1983. He died in 1990 at age seventy-six.

Joseph Alsop wrote his last column on January 1, 1975, four months before the fall. It didn't mention Vietnam. He continued to hold court at dinner parties in his Georgetown home, a grand duke and grander character of the city of Washington, which had created and nourished him. Alsop died in 1989 at age seventy-six.

Dang Duc Khoi made it out on the fertilizer boat and wrote the bylined front-page story on the coup for the *New York Herald Tribune*. Duc Nghiep survived and took up studies at Columbia University in 1964. Beverly Deepe searched until she found the sixteen-year-old woman who was thrown into the prison beneath the zoo. She had been freed but wanted nothing more to do with Deepe. "Please don't come here anymore," she begged. "You bring me the unluckies."

Madame Nhu lingered in Los Angeles for several weeks after the coup, awaiting a call to return to save her country. She lives on the French Riviera and charges the press for interviews. The requests are few.

A Note

This book is about two unusual years at the beginning of a long war and a handful of news correspondents who lived them. Over the ensuing decade, this small group was followed by more than five thousand other reporters, some of them among the best that the storied history of war correspondents has produced. They deserve their own story, and I hope to read it.

—W.P.

ACKNOWLEDGMENTS

It has been a long time. To give acknowledgments without beginning with my family would make a mockery of all values. Persons whose lives span almost nine decades of time—from my mother to young Jesse and Melissa—have waited. My wife, Laura Parker, has done more than wait. She has been editor, researcher, interviewer, critic, and prodding muse as well as helpmate. Thank you, all of you.

Kris Dahl, at ICM, ranks in a class of one, my super-agent. I also thank Dorothea Herrey and Irene Webb.

Peter Osnos, my editor and publisher at Random House and Times Books, showed patience, confidence, and insight rare in these times. He has earned special thanks. Ruth Fecych, Victoria Mathews, and Nancy Inglis gave valuable editing help, Laura Taylor was always helpful; Paul Golob came and went too quickly but left much behind him. At Random House thanks also go to Robert Loomis, who both read the manuscript and gave helpful criticisms at a crucial moment.

Graydon Carter and George Hodgman at *Vanity Fair* looked at a half-finished manuscript, then committed to it with the kind of enthusiasm and support that would inspire any writer to finish his job. So did Robert Conte, Richard Waltzer, and Robert Cooper at Home Box Office. I don't believe Conte will ever fully understand how his telephone calls magically arrived at the time they were most needed. The Alicia Patterson Foundation provided financial support while I still groped. I am thankful to Margaret Engel, the executive director, all of the distinguished Patterson board, and those who helped me in seeking foundation funds: the late Howard Simons, William Greider, Lou Cannon, Benjamin C. Bradlee, and Richard L. Harwood, as well as Peter Osnos.

Many libraries assisted. The Library of Congress was invaluable, providing maps, obscure periodicals, obscure books, and, most of all, assistance in access to the Neil Sheehan papers. Nan T. Ernst, archivist in the library's Manuscript Division, deserves special mention for organizing Sheehan's papers. Dr. Harold Gottlieb and Charles Niles of the Mugar Memorial Library at Boston University were most helpful with the David Halberstam papers. The staff at the John F. Kennedy Presidential Library helped roust out papers I might never have found. The Lyndon B. Johnson Presidential Library was most useful. Among others were the Martin Luther King Public Library in Washington, the Seattle Public Library and, most especially, the extraordinarily helpful staff of the Coral Gables Public Library of Coral Gables, Florida, who were there when I felt at my most isolated and was not at all. The staff of the *Seattle Post-Intelligencer* library—most particularly, Lytton Smith—found nuggets. The University of Washington library had unexpected newspaper microfilm. Barbara Shapiro, the librarian for the Associated Press, assisted.

James Noonan of CBS provided valuable videotapes, as did Jack Langguth of the University of Southern California School of Journalism. Norma Mohr assisted me with the papers of her late husband, Charles Mohr. Betsy Wade made available many of Homer Bigart's letters, and Bigart's widow and literary executor, Else Bigart, provided permission for their use. Wade also read parts of the manuscript dealing with *The New York Times*'s foreign desk, correcting a number of errors. Any that remain are my fault, not hers; Wade assisted me while often disagreeing with my interpretation of the dispute between the desk and the correspondents. For that I thank her, and for being what all know her to be: gracious and professional. Richard M. and Shirley Clurman read the manuscript, each making helpful suggestions, and providing help that will never be forgotten. Stanley Karnow, Lee Lescaze, and R. W. (Johnny) Apple, Jr., also kindly read the manuscript and saved me from more than one humiliating error. Again, the corrections were theirs and appreciated; any remaining errors are mine. Deborah Susan Kalb unselfishly made her research, interviews, and unpublished Harvard University honors thesis available. Rebecca Parker was a superb researcher, Fred Gray a wizard who could get any recalcitrant computer, except the one that was fried by lightning, working again. Special thanks also to Cory Dean.

There are unexplainable entrances and exits in life. In the hope that the exits are not permanent but in recognition that the entrances produced unforseen good, thanks go to William Montalbano and Adi Shmueli.

Others who were helpful in various ways along the route include Anthony Marro, Ellen Brockman, and Kimberly Prochnau and Arne Whedbee.

Among those who provided bed, board, and friendship during work trips or very occasional moments of rest and recreation were Bruce and Shirley Parker and O. Casey Corr and Sally Tonkin. The writer who underestimates the value of friendships is not a writer. I became something of a recluse at times, but I could not have finished this book without my friends. It is clearly not possible to mention them all here, but among those who were always there were Corr and Tonkin; Dick and Shirley Clurman; George C. and Joan Wilson; Michael and Lisa Dobbs; Tom and Sue Fiedler; Johnny and Betsey Apple; Linda Gist; and Jeff, Stephanie, Brendan, Patrick, and Tegan Lane.

INTERVIEWS

In visiting this fairly recent moment in American history, one of the first dismaying discoveries is how little the press of the time wrote about itself. Even at a moment of such high drama, when to a rare degree the historical role of a handful of young reporters approached that of many government officials, the contemporary record is almost barren. Nor is the record replete with oral histories or the vast repositories of written records which help biographers and historians in rebuilding a moment of history. This made necessary a scouring for morsels across so broad a landscape that my index alone to documents, periodicals, and other written sources reached 54,000 words. In the end, however, the slim pickings made interviews the backbone of the book, and, in that, I was more than fortunate. I am greatly indebted to all in the following list, as well as to the very few who spoke but wished to remain anonymous. Some spoke to me briefly on the telephone, confirming, clarifying, or bringing into doubt a single incident. Others gave hours and days to my often repetitious and persistent questions. The principals were exceptionally generous. Neil Sheehan interrupted the ordeal of his own book for hours of taped interviews. He spoke to me, again for hours, while bedridden and in pain recuperating from restorative surgery to his injured leg. David Halberstam sat for the first interview in 1984, the last in 1995. In the intervening years we talked, by conservative estimate, at least one hundred times, most often briefly but on crucial occasions for hours or days. The datelines of the numerous taped telephone interviews with Peter Arnett, which continued for hours on all but one occasion, reads like the travelogue that became his life: Atlanta, Jerusalem, Baghdad. The latter lasted forty minutes, coming in the middle of the Gulf War. Nick Turner sent taped replies from New Zealand. Ray Herndon and his wife, Annie, allowed me to come back into their lives dozens of times for minute details and provided one of the greatest favors. They methodically inscribed my huge map of downtown Saigon with every 1962–63 point of interest—offices, homes, police stations, pagodas. Others—Malcolm Browne, Horst Faas, the late Homer Bigart, Charley Mohr, and Keyes Beech, and many more—were equally forthcoming. The late William C. Trueheart gave me insights into the workings and nonworkings of the U.S. Embassy in Saigon. Because this book went through two serious permutations, some gave their time to projects that must seem to them far from the final result. General William C. Westmoreland and his wife, Kitsy, took me into their home in Charleston for two days of interviews for a book that now ends before the general arrived in Vietnam. He should not consider his time wasted or his insights unhelpful. They contributed greatly, as did others who might not easily see their contributions in the lines of this book. The contributions are there, if not in the lines, between them, which often is as important.

Samuel Adams
George Allen
Joseph Alsop
R. W. Apple, Jr.
Peter Arnett
Don Becker
Keyes Beech
Yuko Beech
Homer Bigart
Bernie Birnbaum
Benjamin C. Bradlee
Peter Braestrup
Henry Brandon
Malcolm Browne
Wallace Carroll
Richard Clurman
George Crile
Clifton Daniel
Leon Daniel
John Gregory Dunne
Richard Dudman
Osborn Elliott
Horst Faas
Tom Fiedler
Ernest Furgurson
Harold Gal
Jeff Gralnick
David Halberstam
Jean Halberstam

Col. William M. Hammond, USA
Col. Gains Hawkins, USA (ret.)
David Henderson
Paul Hendrickson
Annie Herndon
Ray Herndon
Pham Boi Hoan
Earnest Hoberecht
William Jorden
Albert E. Kaff
Bernard Kalb
Deborah Kalb
Gloria Kalischer
Peter Kalischer
Stanley Karnow
Gen. John L. Klingenhagen, USA (ret.)
Lt. Gen. Victor Krulak, USMC (ret.)
Charles Kuralt
Kermit Lansner
Lee Lescaze
Cleve Mathews
James A. Michener
Charley Mohr
Norma Mohr
Peter Osnos
John H. Perry
William Pfaff
Eric Remner
James Reston
Harry M. Rosenfeld
Morley Safer
Pierre Salinger
Harrison Salisbury
Pamela Sanders
Richard Schapp
Jerrold Schecter
Daniel Schorr
John Sharkey
Catherine Sheehan
Maria Sheehan
Neil Sheehan
Susan Sheehan
Maj. Gen. Winant Sidle, USA (ret.)
Hedrick Smith
Jack Smith

INTERVIEWS

Col. Ivan Slavich, USA, (ret.)
Steve Stibbens
Arthur Ochs Sulzberger
David Tabacoff
William Trueheart
Nick Turner
Betsy Wade
Richard Wald
Mike Wallace
Bernard Weinraub
Gen. William C. Westmoreland, USA (ret.)
Mrs. William C. (Kitsy) Westmoreland
Tom Wicker
Col. J. Barrie Williams, USA (ret.)
George C. Wilson
Bill Wright
Barry Zorthian

DOCUMENTS AND SOURCES

The personal papers of David Halberstam and Neil Sheehan gave this book its flesh, and the willingness of these two men to allow me to browse freely in their pasts is a tribute to them and was a blessing to me. The Presidential Libraries of John F. Kennedy and Lyndon B. Johnson provided invaluable material ranging from contemporary documents to oral histories by the government participants. But no set of government documents proved as valuable as those provided by the Department of State in *Foreign Relations of the United States, 1961–1963: Vietnam. Volumes 1–4.* They were a treasure trove. Still, research is a foot soldier's march. The research for this book required a search through many millions of words reduced to several million words of notes. More often than not, the search was made through the microfilm libraries of periodicals and newspapers as well as books and official documents. The following is an attempt to provide an indication beyond the bibliography only of the major documents and written sources from which this book was drawn.

The New York Times, 1961–63, articles of Homer Bigart and David Halberstam.

The *Times of Vietnam,* Jan. 1961–Oct. 1963.

Maps: Vietnam, Cambodia, Laos, and the city of Saigon, Library of Congress maps collection.

Foreign Relations of the United States, 1961–63: Vietnam. Vol. 1–4.

U.S. Army Handbook for Vietnam, 1962.

Report on the War in Vietnam, General William C. Westmoreland and U.S. Grant Sharp, Government Printing Office, Washington, D.C., 1969.

Court transcript and various depositions taken for *Westmoreland* v. *CBS,* U.S. District Court, New York, 1984–85.

Chronological study of Robert McNamara's actions in Vietnam, 1963–68, compiled by Samuel Adams.

General resources of the John F. Kennedy Library (Boston, Mass.):
    White House central files
    National Security files
    Press files
    Oral Histories

Oral histories from the Lyndon B. Johnson Library (Austin, Tex.).

David Halberstam papers, Mugar Memorial Library, Boston University (Boston, Mass.):
    New York Times cables and letters, to and from the Congo (Zaire) and Saigon bureaus
    Expenses and Finances, the Congo and Saigon
    Personal correspondence and miscellany
    Musings, notes, and unpublished writing
    Miscellaneous documents regarding Congo and Vietnam experiences

Neil Sheehan papers, Library of Congress (Washington, D.C.):
    UPI stories from Saigon, unedited
    Personal log, or diary—April 1962–March 15, 1963
    UPI cables and letters, misc., to and from Saigon bureau
    General correspondence regarding Saigon bureau
    Earnest Hoberecht messages, to and from Saigon bureau
    Financial records
    Personal correspondence and miscellany

Adventures of the Saigon Press Corps, MACV Lists and Directives, vol. 1, compiled by Beverly Deepe Keever.

Records of the Association of Foreign Correspondents in Viet Nam, 1962–63, compiled by Beverly Deepe Keever.

Brief unfinished memoir of Charles Mohr.

Charles Mohr notes on interview with Diem and Nhu, 1963.

Personal correspondence of Homer Bigart, 1948–62.

Personal correspondence of Nick Turner, 1962–63.

Selected memos of Richard M. Clurman to Henry R. Luce, *Time* magazine, 1962–67.

Saints and Sinners (The New York Times).

Times Talk (The New York Times).

Associated Press Library.

Associated Press Asia *Log.*

Associated Press Tokyo *Log.*

Associated Press *Log.*

UPI Log.

Dateline (Overseas Press Club).

CNN transcripts.

CBS archives.

Congressional Record.

DOCUMENTS AND SOURCES

Magazines

America, American Heritage, Atlantic Monthly, Business Week, Broadcasting, Columbia Journalism Review, Commentary, Contemporary Review, Daedalus, Editor & Publisher, Encounter, Esquire, Foreign Affairs, Geo, Harper's Bazaar, Harpers, Interview, Life, Look, Marine Corps Gazette, MORE, The Nation, National Review, The New Leader, The New Republic, New Statesman, The New York Times Magazine, The New Yorker, Newsweek, Nieman Reports, Parade, Progressive, Publishers Weekly, Quill, Ramparts, The Reporter, Saturday Evening Post, Saturday Review, Time, U.S. News & World Report, Washington Monthly, Wilson Quarterly.

Newspapers

Boston Globe, Chicago Daily News, Honolulu Star-Bulletin, Miami Herald, Le Monde, The London Observer, New York Herald Tribune, New York Journal American, The New York Times, New York World-Telegram and Sun, Newsday, St. Louis Post-Dispatch, Seattle Post-Intelligencer, The Sunday Times (London), *Times of Vietnam, Torrington* (Connecticut) *Register,* Washington *Evening Star, The Washington Post, The State* (Columbia, S.C.), *Stars and Stripes.*

Videotapes

CBS News Special Report: Vietnam, "A War That Is Finished . . . ," CBS Television, April 30, 1975.

"Vietnam Reconsidered: Lessons from a War," a conference on the war and the media. School of Journalism, the University of Southern California, February 6–9, 1983.

"Vietnam—A Television History," vols. 1 and 2. Boston: WGBH Educational Foundation, 1985.

SOURCE NOTES

Elsewhere, I have provided the primary sources for this book—a bibliography, a list of interviews, and a compilation of personal collections, library sources, documents, and miscellany. To a limited degree, my own reporting experiences in Vietnam have contributed to the research. But I made my first relatively brief visit to Vietnam in 1965, two years after this book ends. By that time, 175,000 American troops were in the country, and it was a very different place.

While the interviews and the personal collections of the reporters have provided the brick and mortar, the writings of others obviously were essential to this book. The only significant contemporary account devoted to the battle between the correspondents and their various critics is Stanley Karnow's "The Newsman's War in Vietnam," *Nieman Reports*, December 1963. However, helpful accounts of the mood and flavor of the times came from George J. W. Goodman (Adam Smith) in "Our Man in Saigon," *Esquire*, January 1964, and Pamela Sanders in her novel *Miranda*. Overall, no single works were as helpful as John Mecklin's chronicle of his agonies as the chief government press spokesman, *Mission in Torment*, a rich source on the malady in Saigon, and Richard Reeves's *President Kennedy: Profile in Power*, an equally rich source on the malady in Washington. In addition to papers from the presidential libraries and the Pentagon Papers, useful books on the workings of the Kennedy government included William J. Rust's *Kennedy in Vietnam*; the efforts of Montague Kerns, Patricia W. Levering, and Ralph B. Levering in *The Kennedy Crises: The Press, the Presidency, and Foreign Policy*; and William Conrad Gibbons's *The U.S. Government and the Vietnam War: Executive and Legislative Roles and Relationships, Part II: 1961–1964*. However, as Reeves pointed out, the State Department's mid-1993 completion of the four volumes of *Foreign Relations of the United States, 1961–1963: Vietnam* made other compilations virtually obsolete.

By now, most of the early correspondents have added either autobiographies or serious histories to the array of writings on Vietnam. All these books were invaluable, and served a double purpose for me. As aforementioned, the pickings on the doings of the reporters themselves were slim indeed and required endless slogging through clippings, microfilm, documents, and minds most helpful but clouded by decades. Mecklin and Sanders helped greatly with keen eyes for a different kind of historical detail, one seen through nonfiction, the other through fiction. Richard Kluger's *The Paper: The Life and Death of the New York Herald Tribune* was valuable in looking at Homer Bigart, Marguerite Higgins, and the early Joseph Alsop as well as the texture of their craft. Several well-worn books proved helpful on the media institutions: Two books in particular on *The New York Times,* Gay Talese's *The Kingdom and the Power* and Harrison Salisbury's *Without Fear or Favor;* and two that looked at Time, Inc.: W. A. Swanberg's *Luce and His Empire* and David Halberstam's *The Powers That Be.* But most of what I sought about the correspondents and their story was buried far deeper in the morass of an information society not yet attuned to the double-click of a computer mouse.

Still, there are two interconnected stories here, one about a small group of pioneering reporters, the other about a country's descent into the sinkhole of an ill-starred war. The journalists may have left themselves unexamined but they provided far more than historians will credit them to the record of the American descent. To approach this subject without Neil Sheehan's *A Bright Shining Lie* or Halberstam's seminal *The Best and the Brightest* would be foolish indeed. Karnow's *Vietnam: A History* has become the bible. To do it without two others who, respectively, were a scholar and a writer first, but journalists as well, would be as reckless and as blind to history as the American government proved to be: In my work I kept Bernard Fall, the French scholar, perched on one shoulder, and Graham Greene, the British novelist, on the other. Simply to note the titles of Greene's journalism in *The New Republic,* as the French exited and the Americans entered in 1954 and 1955, tells the tale: April 5, 1954: "The War Will Be Decided by Men Who Never Waded Waist-Deep in Fields of Paddy"; April 12, 1954: "To Hope Till Hope Creates"; May 9, 1955: "Last Act in Indochina"; May 16, 1955: "Last Act in Indochina: II."

The chapter notes that follow are merely a guideline and by no means exhaustive.

1. A NICE LITTLE WAR IN A LAND OF TIGERS AND ELEPHANTS

Details of Mal Browne's arrival in Vietnam were taken from interviews with him, his two books, and an article in *Editor & Publisher,* September 15, 1962. Early descriptions of the war, the place, and the mood came from myriad sources including my own experiences, interviews with Browne, Homer Bigart, Peter Kalischer, William C. Trueheart, and others; the writings of Graham Greene, David Halberstam, Neil Sheehan, and Bernard Fall, among others; government records from the Kennedy Library and *Foreign Relations of the United States, 1961–1963: Vietnam. Volumes 1–4* (identified hereafter as State's history). Details of the November 11, 1961, National Security Council meeting, and the decision to begin Project Beef-Up, came from minutes located both in State's history and the Kennedy Library. Browne's background came from Browne, his books, a humorous biographical sketch he wrote for *The Times*, and from his colleagues. Observations about Kennedy and the press, as well as the conflict between his great personal appeal and a dangerous penchant for risk, came from personal observation of his presidency and the plethora of Kennedy books, the glowing and the not-so, the best and fairest of which was Reeves's *Profile*. I am grateful to Beverly Deepe Keever, as well as Browne, for providing information about the reporters on hand at the time. Sadly, of François Sully, some of the best material came, as it did with many of those who died, from his many obituaries in 1971. Karnow and Denis Warner in *The Last Confucian* provided the primary source material on the ruling family. Translations of the South Vietnamese press attacks on the U.S. government were located in the Kennedy Library. Details on the beginning of the defoliation program came from the Air Force history, *Operation Ranch Hand: The Air Force and Herbicides in Southeast Asia, 1961–1971*. The subsequent cables regarding attempts to plug leaks or maintain secrecy following the arrival of the first helicopters came from State's history. Trueheart's comments were made to me. The biographical information on Frederick Nolting and Paul D. Harkins came largely from the writings of Karnow, Halberstam, Sheehan, and Mecklin. Browne provided the material about his first missions and observations.

2. THE CHANGING OF THE GUARD

Interviews with Kalischer, John Sharkey, Jeff Gralnick, Jack Smith, and David Tabacoff helped me with the technical descriptions of infant television. Charles Kuralt told me of the ambush outside Saigon in 1961, James Noonan provided the transcript. Throughout, Michael J. Arlen's writings in *The New Yorker*, which he then expanded into his books, were crucial to understanding television and the war. James A. Michener wrote with wit and insight about what was not yet the "old guard" in his preface to Keyes Beech's 1954 *Tokyo and Points East*. Also helpful on the old guard was John Hohenberg's *Foreign Correspondence: The Great Reporters and Their Times*. Alsop's dinner parties are chronicled in too many places to be named, the turtle-soup story now hoary in Washington lore, his goadings of Maxwell Taylor recorded in his columns in *The Washington Post* in October 1961. As to Homer Bigart, every reporter worth his salt has a favorite tale. Among the best books were Kluger's *The Paper*, Hohenberg's *Foreign Correspondence*, and Beech's *Tokyo*. Hohenberg described the pivotal air missions at the beginning and end of the Second World War, and Bigart shared his thoughts with me about those defining moments and other events in his life shortly before his death. A helpful source was his anecdotal obituary in *The Times*, April 17, 1991, as were speeches at a joyous wake several months later in Halberstam's New York apartment. I am grateful for the help of his widow, Else Bigart, and the insights of his good friend Betsy Wade. The details of FARMGATE and the operations that led to the public lies by Nolting and President Kennedy in January 1962 were found in *Operation Ranch Hand*, as were the details of Jungle Jim, "Country 77," and the questions asked of FARMGATE volunteers. Kennedy's first trip to see the Green Berets in action at Fort Bragg (a man in a jet-pack landed at his feet) was described by Donald Duncan in *The New Legions*. The confrontation between the two reporters and Nolting in March was described in a cable to Washington (State's history). The failures of Cable 1006 were noted by both Mecklin and Pierre Salinger, Kennedy's press secretary, in an interview and his book *With Kennedy*. The text of the cable was among the documents in State's history. Mecklin dealt at length with the uproar resulting from barring reporters from the helicopters. Bigart's full account of the assault on Cai Ngai was found in the *Seattle Post-Intelligencer* of March 9, 1962. Many accounts have been written about the incessant plotting against Diem, Karnow's history among the best. The attempt to expel Bigart and Sully was described in detail by Mecklin and others. Neil Sheehan described his first weeks in Vietnam and his experiences with Bigart in interviews.

3. WHAT FOOLS WE MORTALS

Mecklin's *Torment* detailed the changes he found in Saigon in 1962 and the bitterness already existing toward the press. Nick Turner provided a description of the cricket chases in a May 26, 1963, letter to his parents in New Zealand. The primary sources on Henry Luce and the workings of *Time* were Swanberg, Halberstam's *The Powers That Be*, *The Ideas of Henry Luce*, edited by John K. Jessup, and interviews with Richard Clurman and the late Charles Mohr, as well as Halberstam and Karnow. On Mohr the sources somewhat overlap, but Halberstam's interview contributions became invaluable, as did an interview with Mohr's widow, Norma. Some details of Mohr's first week came from *Time*'s May 11, 1962, cover article on General Harkins. As with Bigart, everyone who knew Mert Perry had a story about him. I am indebted to Neil Sheehan for the account of Perry's two-word departure from UPI. Sheehan, Ray Herndon, and many other Unipressers assisted in the description of Asia Earnie Hoberecht. Nothing did the job as well as James A. Michener's rich profile in *Newsday*, February 23, 1957, and Hoberecht's own memoranda to Sheehan. The McNamara material comes from many sources, the most useful being my own experiences with him as a reporter in Washington in 1963 and at the Westmoreland-CBS libel trial in 1984, Paul Hendrickson's articles in *The Washington Post*, May 8–10, 1984, and Deborah Shapley's biography, *Promise and Power*. Mal Browne was the best source on how the Viet Cong used McNamara's own technology against him. Alsop's comment was made to me and a small group of reporters in 1963. I am indebted to Colonel J. Barrie Williams 'of Defense Intelligence and George Allen of the CIA for their help and openness while always protecting the code of their profession. The "Chinese hordes" quotation came from Phillip Knightley's *The First Casualty*, Rusk's cable from State's history. Of McNamara's visit to Ben Tuong, I am indebted to Norma Mohr, who found the unpublished account among Mohr's papers. Allen was present when McNamara ordered the radios. Recollections of the McNamara press conference came from the participants, particularly Sheehan and Mohr, and Shapley's biography.

4. OLD MAN, YOUNG MAN

William Pfaff's letter was found among the National Security Council White House files at the Kennedy Library. Kennedy's "no amount of American military assistance" statement came from the April 6, 1954, Congressional Record. I am grateful to Wade and Halberstam for Bigart's letters, to Sheehan for Bigart's parting comment at the airport. Description of the drive to the delta came dimly from my own recollections but vividly from Sheehan's, as well as from his book. The old PBS documentary was called "Fall of an Empire" and kept at the embassy as an object lesson rarely learned. Sheehan described his first meeting with Vann in one of our interviews. The primary source on John Paul Vann will always be Sheehan's book. Halberstam's *The Making of a Quagmire* and "The Ugliest American," which he wrote for the November 1964 *Esquire*, also contributed, as did interviews with Halberstam. Most references to Blue Lotus came from Sheehan's colleagues. The best source on Sheehan was Sheehan himself—he has a remarkable ability for candor and self-scrutiny, as well as a willingness to trust. His private log, or diary, written later and covering most of his first year in Vietnam ranges from the mundane to his deepest self-concerns. His wife, Susan, and his daughters, Maria and Catherine, were equally open and helpful. William Howard Russell's combat fatigue was noted by Knightley; Ernie Pyle's by Knightley and many others. Harrison Salisbury, in *Without Fear*, provided guideposts to Sheehan's roots and youth. But Sheehan remained the primary source for all, including, except for a few details from others, the story of his young triumph over alcoholism. Halberstam told the story of Sheehan's stage-whisper greeting on McNamara's second visit to Vietnam.

5. WE BAND OF BROTHERS

Sources for the interlude in Laos in the spring of 1962 included Arthur J. Dommen's *Conflict in Laos*, Jane Hamilton-Merritt's *Tragic Mountains*, Arnett's *Live*, Sanders's *Miranda*, Reeves's *Profile*, and several of the conventional contemporary histories of John Kennedy's presidency. But the memories of the correspondents who sat in Vientiane and waited were the best sources. The recollections of Herndon and Sanders, both on their first reporting adventures in a land that stretched reality, were almost photographic. Arnett knew the strange little country as well as any in Southeast Asia; Horst Faas would never forget it because boredom was a danger he could not tolerate. My biography of Arnett comes largely from his interviews; of Faas the same. Their colleagues added flavor to each. The romance between Sanders and Mohr was known to many, but the specifics were provided by Sanders in interviews. A mirror-image reflection exists in *Miranda*. The story of Le Lieu and her family, so complicated yet so common in factionalized Vietnam, was told by Browne. The text of his unanswered letter to Harkins came from Mecklin's *Torment*. Interviews with Browne, Arnett, and Faas provided detail for the arrival of the latter two. Browne's memorandum was described in his and Arnett's books, as well as their interviews. Madame Nhu's August outburst was described in the *Times of Vietnam* as well as Sheehan's unedited cables, and Sheehan's thoughts described in his log. The references to the Trung sisters and other legendary Vietnamese women came largely from Karnow's *Vietnam*. The account of Madame Nhu's childhood, marriage, and climb to power draws heavily on Warner's *Confucian*, Karnow's *Vietnam*, and various magazine profiles including "The Beautiful Battlers for Home and Motherland," in *The Asia Magazine*, September 1, 1963. Translations of Vietnamese newspaper attacks on Sully were found at the Kennedy Library. Mecklin wrote a helpful account. For the descriptions of French colonial days that Sully so loved to romanticize, I have drawn partly on the rich recollections of Howard Sochurek, a *Life* photographer who traveled with Sully on occasion, in Harry Maurer's book of oral history, *Strange Ground*; other recollections came from my own interviews. The Westmoreland tennis story was first told in Halberstam's *Brightest*. My thanks to Deepe for the minutes of the Vietnam Foreign Correspondents Association and the text of the protest messages over Sully's expulsion, and to Sheehan and others for recollections of the long night at the Caravelle.

6. HALBERSTAM'S WAR

For details of Sully's farewell party, the memories of each of the correspondents was tested to the hilt, and then tested again, because the arrival of David Halberstam made it such a symbolic event. For once, there was almost no agreement on details, so participants and readers alike must bow to plurality judgments. To Halberstam, the us-versus-them feeling, so familiar from his days in the South, was his strongest and most prophetic recollection. The history of *The New York Times* during the Red Scare of the fifties, as well as the Herbert Matthews affair, was culled mostly from Talese's *Power*, Turner Catledge's *My Life and The Times*, and Matthews's *A World in Revolution*. The nonstop crises of the Kennedy administration are central themes of the adulatory books of his aides, Ted Sorenson's *Kennedy* and Arthur M. Schlesinger, Jr.'s, *A Thousand Days;* the toll they took best seen in Reeves's *Profile*. The story of Halberstam's family, youth, college days, and early career came largely from him though interviews and his prolific writings. Among the writings: "The Shape of America," *Harper's Bazaar*, August 1972; "Starting Out to be a Famous Reporter," *Esquire*, November 1981; "Great Years at the *Crimson*," *Geo*, 1984. "Halberstam Recalls a Full Boyhood," in the June 30, 1973, *Torrington* [Connecticut] *Register*, also proved helpful. James Reston and Tom Wicker helped describe the workings of the *The Times*'s Washington bureau but the viewpoint is Halberstam's, as it should be. In writing about Halberstam's year in the Congo I drew most heavily on his interviews, two of his pieces in *Times Talk*—"It's Chaos for a Correspondent in the Congo," October–November 1961 and "Congo Boondocks: Land of Cannibals and Diamonds." Also useful was his article in the *The Times* of December 11, 1961: "Lunch in Katanga Spiced by Gunfire." But his letters, drawn from the collection at the Mugar Library, were among the best sources—long, rambling, and descriptive letters to a fading girlfriend, his boss Emanuel Freedman, his friend Russell Baker, and others describing living conditions, work, fun (or lack of it), adventures, etc. For details of Halberstam's efforts to gain a niche in the AP office in Saigon and the battle between Halberstam and Mal Browne for dominance in Saigon, I am grateful to all those who watched. They remained wonderfully vague to the end. Browne was the most forthcoming, and cared the least.

7. THE MAKING OF AN ANGRY MAN

Halberstam's first days in Saigon were described in his interviews, his articles in *The Times*, and *Quagmire*, with some descriptions and anecdotal entries coming from Sheehan's diary. Details on the problems of the F-111 warplane come from my own contemporary reporting and various newspaper articles, the best being Hugh Mulligan's Associated Press account June 30, 1968. Halberstam's first visit to the Seminary to meet Vann and his first mission with the ARVN came from interviews, *Quagmire*, and his article "The Ugliest American." Others, apparently unaware of Halberstam's presence nearby, have written about the battle he heard but did not witness. These include Hilsman, who made much of the battle's significance in *To Move a Nation*. State's history provided Taylor's unkind words about the Saigon press corps. Sources on Harkins are noted in text. Additionally, Karnow's *Vietnam*, Halberstam's *Brightest*, and Sheehan's *Lie* contributed. Details of the "Explosion Plan" and its quick death came from State's history. William C. Westmoreland's *A Soldier Reports* provided the description of Harkins and the refrain from Kipling. Admiral Harry Felt's "whispering campaign" cable was found among documents at the Kennedy Library. George Ball's warning and Kennedy's "crazier than hell" response was retold in Ball's *Memoirs*. Nolting wrote of the blight of Vietnam in his autobiography, *Tragedy*. Halberstam's explosive meeting with Nolting was described in Mecklin's *Torment* and Halberstam's interviews. I am indebted to a number of persons—Betsy Wade, Cleve Mathews, and others—for their assistance in describing the operation of *The Times*'s foreign desk. The operation of the fiefdoms has also been described elsewhere, as noted. The Kennedy Library produced records of the protests against the expulsion of James Robinson. The Zone D story was described by Mecklin in *Torment* and filled out by State's history and many interviews. The account of Halberstam's "angry man" letter to Nolting also came from *Torment* and a lengthy cabled report in State's history.

8. Rebels in the Field: The Colonels

Sources for Mecklin's flight over Dien Bien Phu included his own account in *Time*, April 19, 1954, a *Time* publisher's note, June 28, 1954, and Sochurek's interview in *Strange Ground*. Mecklin's experience with the death of Robert Capa comes largely from his account in *Life*, June 7, 1954. Westmoreland told me of his brutal rivalry with the marines and fleeting thoughts of quitting. Details of the rivalry between the air force and the army were first told to me by Neil Sheehan before publication of his book, then fleshed out by the book. When I arrived in Saigon in October 1965, among the first words of the major who briefed me were: "Now don't you be a Halberstam, don't be a Sheehan." Copies of the telegram to Raisig and the inscription for Ivan Slavich came from Halberstam's papers, as did most such items unless otherwise noted. All of the papers regarding Halberstam's reserve and draft status were among his collection at the Mugar Library. *Quagmire* described Halberstam's early Huey flight with Slavich. Both Sheehan and Slavich provided details about the army intelligence officer's visit and Sheehan's dive under the bed. Beverly Deepe remembered the flap over women on missions after Pam Sanders met Westmoreland deeper in the jungle than most generals went. Sanders related the afternoon at Vung Tau, which she also very slightly fictionalized in her book. I relied on the writings of Nolting, the reaction of Kennedy, and interviews with Trueheart and the correspondents for details on Majority Leader Mansfield's visit. Salinger described in an interview his approach to press relations in a simpler world. Cronkite's comment about endangering reporters was made in a 1973 *Playboy* interview. A copy of Mansfield's letter resides in the Kennedy Library, the President's response in Kenneth O'Donnell and David F. Powers's *"Johnny, We Hardly Knew Ye."* Vann's late-1962 preparations for battle came largely from Sheehan's *Lie* and Halberstam's *Quagmire* as well as interviews with Sheehan.

9. TURNING POINT

General Harkins's end-of-the-year meeting with the correspondents was described in a UPI story by Sheehan that apparently was killed in Tokyo. Writing about the battle of Ap Bac after Sheehan's exhaustive study of it in *A Bright Shining Lie* is an exercise in calculated redundancy, as more than one of my editors pointed out. But the battle is pivotal to the telling of the correspondents' story and I have bulled ahead. I had explored Ap Bac before Sheehan published, producing a workaday account of the battle and drawn reasonably accurate maps of the terrain and troop placements. The arrival of Sheehan with his book, however, was analogous to Moses coming down the mountain. While I salvaged snippets of my earlier endeavors, *A Bright Shining Lie* became my new guide. Flash-away sections of this chapter come from other sources. Halberstam's letter to Richard D. Burritt was found in his collection, references to The Shrink in Talese's *Power*. All of Neil Sheehan's "housekeeping" duties, his communications with Earnest Hoberecht, and his difficulties collecting from the *Times of Vietnam* are contained in his papers. His actions after the first tip came almost entirely from interviews. Nick Turner's additions to the story of the drives to Tan Hiep were helpful. I am indebted to Steve Stibbens, as well as Halberstam and Arnett, for details of their drive. Halberstam described the interview with Harkins both in *Quagmire* and in interviews. Sheehan's shelling by friendly fire was told dramatically in the rough draft of a cabled story to Tokyo, with handwritten notes about his emotions written in later. He also returned to his feelings about the event repeatedly in his log. I am indebted to Ellen J. Hammer's *A Death in November* for her account of Ngo Dinh Diem's birthday party the day of the battle. Felt's two antagonistic press conferences were first described in Karnow's December 1963 article for *Nieman Reports,* elaborated upon in *Quagmire* and elsewhere. Some confusion about the sequence of events and identification of reporters was clarified through many interviews. Hilsman wrote of his meeting with the correspondents and his report to Kennedy in *To Move a Nation,* but contradictory accounts were many.

10. WARNING SHOTS

John Hohenberg's *Foreign Correspondence: The Great Reporters and Their Times* was helpful in providing historical reference to earlier war correspondents, as was Phillip Knightley's *The First Casualty.* Kennedy made his plea for Cold War "self-censorship" in a speech to the nation's publishers, April 27, 1961. Theodore H. White's letter to Kennedy was found at the Kennedy Library; Susan D. Moeller discovered Larry Burrows's memo. Most of Madame Nhu's attacks on the press were printed in the *Times of Vietnam*, although the cable traffic in State's history shows how bothersome the U.S. government was finding her. The "Adviser Sheehan" headline ran in a Vietnamese-language newspaper and was reported by Halberstam in *Quagmire*. All the subsequent messages, including Mecklin's "astigmatic" reporters memo, were found in State's history. Mecklin's asides and his response to Denis Warner were reported in *Torment*. Many interviews, a September 23, 1963, article in *Newsweek*—"The Gregorys of Saigon"—and some material in State's history contributed to the section about the owners of the *Times of Vietnam*. Copies of some of Mohr's and Perry's original files ended up in Halberstam's records, which is where (with the exception of those given to me by Norma Mohr) I found them. In his book *Dangerous Company*, William Tuohy, who watched Mohr's actions at Hue in 1968, described the rescue attempt. On *Time*'s inner workings, Clurman was the best source, Karnow and Mohr also helpful. Karnow related the story of Otto Fuerbringer's observation about the Seventh Fleet and Laos. An article in the March 15, 1944, *Saturday Evening Post*—"The War to Get War News"—delivered some of the background on Richard Tregaskis. Halberstam related the story of their day in the field, first at a seminar at the University of Southern California and later in interviews. My thanks to Hohenberg, Morley Safer, and most of all Beech for the material that makes up Beech's mini-profile. Kluger's *Paper* was helpful on Alsop and most other sources are identified within the text. Halberstam described Alsop's speech to the correspondents; Karnow told of a similar one in Hong Kong. Tregaskis's attack on Sheehan was voiced about in Saigon, but the text is from his book, *Vietnam Diary*.

11. BATTLE STATIONS

Reeves captured the bleak mood in the White House after a year of difficulties. State's history filled in blanks on the shifting attitude toward Diem. The interrelationships of the correspondents in Vietnam came almost entirely from many hours of interviews. The disappearance of Colonel Daniel Boone Porter's end-of-tour report was noted in both Halberstam's *Quagmire* and Sheehan's *Lie*. John Paul Vann's sexual drive and the effect it had on his life and career was a central point in Sheehan's book. Halberstam's reactions to Vann's cynicism came from interviews. Reston made the second observation about Sheehan—"he literally cared so much"—in an interview. A. M. Rosenthal's greeting and first assignment to Sheehan were recorded in Salisbury's *Without Fear* and repeated to me by Sheehan. The story of the great ordeal of *A Bright Shining Lie* was told to me in many, many hours of interviews with Sheehan and his family. Most were done in 1988 for this project and an October 9, 1988, article in *The Washington Post Magazine*, just prior to publication of his book. Some details of the

Pentagon Papers episode came from Salisbury's *Without Fear;* some details about his auto accident from Susan Sheehan's "The Accident" in *The New Yorker,* September 25, 1978. Sheehan described the conversation with Ben Bradlee; the fuck-'em suit story I heard personally. As with the references in Chapter 8, the letters and communications about Halberstam's draft and reserve status came from his personal records. Attempts to determine whether his reserve unit was ever called to duty went for naught; all records from that era were destroyed in a fire at the U.S. Army Reserve Personnel Center in St. Louis, Missouri.

12. FIREFIGHT ON THE EIGHTFOLD NOBLE PATH

Mecklin's *Torment* and Pierre Salinger's *With Kennedy* provided detail of Mecklin's post-operative decision and his meeting with Kennedy. State's history contains the text of the new press policy, sent to Saigon May 21, 1963. I have used newspaper accounts, but Taylor Branch's *Parting The Waters* as the ultimate source, for details of civil-rights disturbances as they overlapped the Vietnamese Buddhist crisis in the summer of 1963. Bernard Fall's *Vietnam Witness,* Karnow's *Vietnam,* Hammer's *Death,* Halberstam's *Quagmire,* and Mecklin's *Torment* became primary sources on the Buddhist uprising in Hue and subsequent turmoil. Marguerite Higgins's *Our Vietnam Nightmare,* while biased and demonstrably wrong in many situations, still proved useful. State's history, Mecklin, and Reeves provided the words of the President and other public officials. Both Browne's books, *The New Face of War* and *Muddy Boots and Red Socks,* as well as interviews, provided the description of the burning suicide of the monk Thich Quang Duc; an oral history by Robert F. Kennedy yielded the President's stark reaction. Nolting's request to be relieved was revealed in State's history. Throughout the events of the summer, Sheehan's *Lie* proved most helpful. Regularly, here, the sources are self-evident or named in the text. Madame Nhu's outbursts were recorded faithfully in the *Times of Vietnam* and, usually, in the U.S. press, too. The CIA analysis of her strange relationship with her brother-in-law can be found in State's history. The messages from UPI came from Sheehan's collection in the Library of Congress. The best source on Conein was Karnow in interviews and his book. The correspondents soon realized how little embassy support they were receiving after Arnett's beating; Trueheart's cable, found in State's history, would have driven them to frenzy.

13. MAGGIE AND THE ROVER BOYS

Like Homer Bigart, everyone who came near Marguerite Higgins had a story about her. I'm indebted to Tom Wicker for recalling the "Maggie Higgins Hour" in *The Times* Washington bureau, to Richard Reeves for discovering that McGeorge Bundy called her "the firebug." As to the story of her life and work, the sources were many, not one of them neutral. Her only full biography, Antoinette May's *Witness to War*, was favorable, helpful, but regrettably flawed. The steam still rises from Kluger's *Paper* and Julia Edwards's *Women of the World: The Great Foreign Correspondents*, in which the chapter devoted to Higgins is called "The Outrageous Marguerite Higgins." In *Tokyo and Points East*, Keyes Beech devoted a chapter to her Korean exploits and, despite their arrangement, it was perhaps the most dispassionate. The article accompanying the starlet spread in *Life*, October 2, 1950, read like a story written to accompany a starlet spread. In the mix of all were recorded deeds that could not possibly have been done and words not possibly uttered, having concerned events after her death. I avoided the two novels said to be about her exploits in Berlin in an attempt to keep the waters no more than muddy. But I drew from all others—carefully, but not scrupulously. The last days of Nolting were best told by Mecklin, Nolting's autobiography, and interviews with Trueheart. Brother Nhu's assessment of the reporters was passed on in a report to the White House by Robert Manning. Knightley told of William Howard Russell's conflicts with the British government. Higgins's newspaper articles in July and August, and especially her book, *Nightmare*, best describe her movements in Vietnam. Her conversations are drawn from her book or interviews with those who talked with her. The accounts of the military deterioration, a picture opposite from that painted by Higgins, were described in Sheehan's *Lie*, Halberstam's *Quagmire*, but mostly from interviews with the correspondents. The beginnings of Charley Mohr's showdown with *Time* came largely from interviews with Clurman, Mohr, and Norma Mohr, as well as Halberstam's accounts in both *Quagmire* and *The Powers That Be*. Papers in both State's history and the Kennedy Library substantiate the U.S. government's remarkable reaction to Halberstam's August 15, 1963, article on military setbacks in the Mekong Delta; interviews with Halberstam and others filled in details. Accounts of the assassination threats abound in writings by Mecklin, Denis Warner, and others, including cables in State's history. The threat to blow up the office at 19 Ngo Duc Ke was related by Sheehan and Halberstam.

14. FLIGHT OF THE PIGEONS

Halberstam's *Quagmire* and Sheehan's acute memory provided detail for the depiction of their movements on the night of the pagoda raids. Sheehan and Don Becker also recalled, in detail, how they moved the only story out of Vietnam. I have used documents in State's history to show how completely the U.S. government was taken in by Ngo Dinh Nhu's ruse, although the August 23, 1963, front page of *The Times* offered enough evidence of its own. Other details came from Mecklin's *Torment*, Denis Warner in "Agony in Saigon: The Lady and the Cadaver" (*The Reporter*, October 10, 1963), and interviews with the correspondents. Stacks of the reporters' stories sent by the embassy but undelivered by the State Department reside in the Kennedy Library. My thanks to Don Becker for recalling the hazing, so typical of the times, that the print reporters gave ABC-TV's Charles Arnot the night of Lodge's arrival. Sheehan's book was most useful for details about Lodge's first days in Saigon. I relied on Michener's foreword for the story of Dick Applegate, Knightley's study for Rutherford Poats and his pigeon. All the Saigon correspondents had stories about their own "pigeons." Halberstam described the first return trip by Lee Griggs in *Quagmire* and interviews. Lodge would forever amend his story about the coup, but I relied on the most contemporary records: State's history and a 1965 oral history for the Kennedy Library in which he stated he knew before landing in Saigon that the pagoda raids were "the beginning of the end of the Diem regime." Bits and pieces about the fateful Cable of August 24 existed in many works as well as oral histories and documents at presidential libraries. They were pieced together best by Reeves in *Profile*, but, as he noted, he had the advantage of using State's history. I had that advantage, too, and it pulled together most of the loose ends. Halberstam and Krulak have remarkably similar memories of their airport showdown over the "crying" story. The exchange of cables between Halberstam and *The Times* are part of his collection at the Mugar Library. Sheehan's exchange with UPI is part of his collection at the Library of Congress.

15. The Armada

Marguerite Higgins's series of articles in the *Herald Tribune* was published August 26–31, 1963. The *Journal-American* published Conniff's attack August 26, although he wrote other articles attacking Halberstam and *The Times* throughout August and September. I relied heavily on W. A. Swanberg's two biographies, *Citizen Hearst* and *Pulitzer*, as well as Knightley's *Truth*, for anecdotal material on the rabble-rousing journalism in the Spanish-American War. Kennedy's angry reaction to the action of his own aides as well as to Halberstam came from many sources, the most comprehensive being, as usual, State's history. Hilsman, Taylor, and others wrote about it, McNamara skimmed it in *In Retrospect*. The actions of August 24 and the meeting of August 26 came up in dozens of oral histories. All cables, communications, and other dialogues among Kennedy administration officials from this point on came from State's history or papers in the Kennedy Library, unless otherwise noted. Charley Mohr's lead for the World section went unpublished in *Time* but has been published often since, perhaps for the first time in Halberstam's *Quagmire*. The story of Mohr's departure from *Time*, while written elsewhere, has been drawn almost entirely from interviews with Mohr, Norma Mohr, and Clurman and differs from other accounts in a number of minor respects. The Press and World section articles were published in the September 20, 1963, *Time*, which was postdated by about five days. Alsop's attack columns in *The Post* and other newspapers began September 23, although he wrote several other columns from Saigon prior to that. Bundy's retort to Reston comes from Kerns's *Kennedy Crises*. Mecklin's experiences with Krulak aboard the windowless jet were described in *Torment*. The parody of the Vietnam crisis meetings in the White House was first published in Schlesinger's *A Thousand Days*. The final act in Mohr's extended departure was described in interviews with Mohr, Norma Mohr, and Richard Clurman.

16. TEETERING

The opening section about Sheehan came from an amalgam of interviews with him and others, as well as materials in his papers at the Library of Congress. Hilsman's comments about coup rumors were made in an oral history for the Kennedy Library. The scene during McNamara's arrival at the airport was first described by Halberstam in *Quagmire*. The reporters keenly watched McNamara in the field; Lodge's conversation with him about being duped by the army was reported by Trueheart in an oral history for the Johnson Library. Vice President Tho's warning about the Strategic Hamlets program was reported back to the White House but disbelieved. The primary source for the tennis game with Big Minh was Maxwell Taylor's *Swords and Plowshares* but detail was pulled together from many sources. The unlikely story of the manner in which General Dinh joined the plotting generals was told to Sheehan after the coup by Colonel Dong and the plotters; a considerably more flattering confirmation was given by Dinh to Herndon. Arnett's comments on the burning suicide were made in his book, which also gave the best account of the running battle to save the television film. Halberstam, in a long private cable to *The Times,* and Sharkey, in an interview, added to the detail. Description of Halberstam's on-the-eve problems at *The Times* came from a compilation of interviews and records in his collection at Boston University. Browne's situation came from interviews with him and others. My thanks to Arthur O. (Punch) Sulzberger and Hedrick Smith for clarifying the oft-told story of Kennedy's attempt to have Halberstam recalled. Sheehan's records, an interview with Earnest Hoberecht, but mostly interviews with Sheehan put together the story of his ill-fated forced vacation. "He sounds amused"—the conversation about Lodge between Kennedy and his brother, Robert—came from a Robert F. Kennedy oral history at the Kennedy Library.

17. THE END OF THE BEGINNING

Of the contemporary accounts of the coup d'état, particularly the battle plan and movements of the insurgents, Stanley Karnow's "The Fall of the House of Ngo Dinh" in the December 21, 1963, *Saturday Evening Post* proved most useful. Also of help were Halberstam's account in *The Times*, November 6, 1963, Browne's article about the night fighting November 2, 1963, and Sheehan's after-battle account drawn largely from his source, Col. Pham Van Dong. Unfortunately, major parts of Sheehan's article were cut in Tokyo, although, as was their habit, he had shared his information with Halberstam and much of it made its way into *The Times*. Robert Shaplen's "Letter from Saigon" in *The New Yorker*, December 4, 1963, added some details. One of the best of the later accounts can be found in William J. Rust's *Kennedy in Vietnam*. The most detailed accounts of the correspondents' activities were found in Halberstam's *Quagmire* and Arnett's *Live From the Battlefield*. But even in these accounts, with the exception of Arnett's book, which was written in the far different world of media personalities in 1994, the reporters wrote little of themselves or their roles. Nor, despite the integral role they had played in America's first two fighting years in Vietnam, did anyone else—John Mecklin excepted. So, for the reporters' movements and actions, I relied almost entirely on interviews, cross-checked and sometimes filtered. The story of Pham Xuan An, the Viet Cong spy who became a *Time* correspondent, has been told and retold, never better than by Morley Safer in *Flashbacks*. Lodge's "hair on his chest" remark to Admiral Felt came from an interview with Felt for a September 10, 1980, article in *U.S. News & World Report*. Steve Stibbens provided the story about AP's spy post, "The Radio Station." General Dinh's epithet-filled telephone conversation with Diem and Nhu was reported by Karnow with, in the manner of the day, a precise number of dashes in place of the letters in each unprintable word. I took the liberty of filling in the dashes. Arnett and Faas told their own tales of their frantic returns to Saigon, although Stibbens added the in-character story about Faas's request to jump. Sheehan told the Tokyo story, still painful after thirty years. Herndon's story still causes him some wonder today. The final, anticlimactic moments in the palace were described by Herndon, Halberstam, and Faas, who walked in as if he hadn't missed a thing. Details of the deaths were pieced together over the next twenty-four hours, Marguerite Higgins's conversation with Hilsman reported by her in various places, including her book.

18. ROLL CALL

The final episodes are the result of reporting.

Bibliography

Alsop, Joseph W., with Adam Platt. *"I've Seen the Best of It": Memoirs*. New York: W. W. Norton & Co., 1992.

Arlen, Michael J. *The Camera Age*. New York: Farrar, Straus & Giroux, 1981.

———. *Living Room War*. New York: Viking Press, 1969.

———. *The View From Highway 1*, New York: Farrar, Straus & Giroux, 1976.

Arnett, Peter. *Live From the Battlefield*. New York: Simon & Schuster, 1994.

Aronson, James. *The Press and the Cold War*. New York: Bobbs-Merrill, 1970.

Baker, Carlos. *Ernest Hemingway: A Life Story*. New York: Charles Scribner's Sons, 1969.

Baker, Carlos, ed. *Ernest Hemingway: Selected Letters*. New York: Charles Scribner's Sons, 1981.

Ball, George. *The Past Has Another Pattern: Memoirs*. New York: W. W. Norton & Co., 1982.

Beech, Keyes. *Not Without the Americans*. New York: Doubleday, 1971.

———. *Tokyo and Points East*. New York: Doubleday, 1954.

Bowman, John S., ed. *The World Almanac of the Vietnam War*. New York: Pharos Books, 1985.

Braestrup, Peter. *Big Story: How the American Press and Television Reported and Interpreted the Crisis of Tet 1968*. Boulder, Col.: Westview Press, 1977.

Branch, Taylor. *Parting the Waters: America in the King Years, 1954–63*. New York, Simon & Schuster, 1988.

Bray, Howard. *The Pillars of the Post*. New York: W. W. Norton & Co., 1980.

Brodie, Fawn M. *Richard Nixon, the Shaping of His Character*. New York: W. W. Norton & Co., 1981.

Browne, Malcolm W. *Muddy Boots and Red Socks: A Reporter's Life*. New York: Times Books, 1993.

———. *The New Face of War*. New York: Bobbs-Merrill, 1965.

Buckingham, William A., Jr. *Operation Ranch Hand: The Air Force and Herbicides in Southeast Asia, 1961–1971*. Washington, D.C.: U.S. Government Printing Office, 1982.

Butler, David. *The Fall of Saigon*. New York: Simon & Schuster, 1985.

Capa, Robert. *Slightly Out of Focus*. New York: Henry Holt, 1947.

Catledge, Turner. *My Life and The Times*. New York: Harper & Row, 1971.

Clifford, Clark. *Counsel to the President, Clark Clifford: A Memoir*. New York: Random House, 1991.

Clurman, Richard M. *Beyond Malice: The Media's Years of Reckoning*. New Brunswick, N.J.: Transaction Books, 1988.

Cohen, Barbara. *The Vietnam Guidebook*. Teaneck, N.J.: Eurasia Press, 1990.

Colby, William E., and Peter Forbath. *Honorable Men: My Life in the CIA*. New York: Simon & Schuster, 1978.

Colby, William E. *Lost Victory*. Chicago: Contemporary Books, 1989.

Cooper, Chester L. *The Lost Crusade: Americans in Vietnam*. Cornwall, N.Y.: Cornwall Press, 1970.

Corson, William R. *The Betrayal*. New York: W. W. Norton & Co., 1968.

Dommen, Arthur J. *Conflict in Laos: The Politics of Neutralization*. New York: Praeger, 1971.

Duncan, Donald. *The New Legions*. New York: Pocket Books, 1967.

Edwards, Julia. *Women of the World: The Great Foreign Correspondents*. Boston: Houghton Mifflin, 1988.

Elliott, Osborn. *The World of Oz*. New York: Viking Press, 1980.

Elwood-Akers, Virginia. *Women War Correspondents in the Vietnam War, 1961–75*. Metuchen, N.J.: Scarecrow Press, 1988.

Emery, Edwin, and Michael Emery. *The Press and America*. Englewood Cliffs, N.J.: Prentice-Hall, 1978.

Epstein, Edward J. *Between Fact and Fiction*. New York: Vintage Books, 1975.

———. *News from Nowhere*. New York: Random House, 1973.

Esper, George, and the Associated Press. *The Eyewitness History of the Vietnam War, 1961–1975*. New York: Villard Books, 1983.

Fall, Bernard B. *Hell in a Very Small Place: The Siege of Dien Bien Phu*. Philadelphia: J. B. Lippincott & Company, 1967.

———. *Last Reflections on a War: Bernard B. Fall's Last Comments on Vietnam*. New York: Doubleday, 1967.

———. *Street Without Joy: Insurgency in Indochina, 1946–63*. Harrisburg, Pa.: The Stackpole Co., 1963.

———. *Two Vietnams: A Political and Military Analysis*, rev. ed. New York: Praeger, 1967.

———. *Viet-Nam Witness, 1953–66*. New York: Praeger, 1966.

Faulkner, F. D. "Bao Chi: The American News Media in Vietnam, 1960–1975." Ph.D. diss., University of Massachusetts, 1981.

Fenby, Jonathan. *The International News Services.* New York: Schocken Books, 1986.

FitzGerald, Frances. *A Fire in the Lake: The Vietnamese and the Americans in Vietnam.* Boston: Atlantic-Little, Brown, 1972.

Foreign Relations of the United States: Vietnam, 1961–1963, Vols. 1–4. Washington, D.C.: U.S. Government Printing Office, 1988–1991.

Furgurson, Ernest. *Westmoreland: The Inevitable General.* Boston: Little, Brown, 1968.

Galbraith, John Kenneth. *Ambassador's Journal.* Boston: Houghton Mifflin, 1969.

Geyer, Georgie Anne. *Buying the Night Flight: The Autobiography of a Woman Foreign Correspondent.* New York: Delacorte Press, 1983.

Gibbons, William Conrad. *The U.S. Government and the Vietnam War: Executive and Legislative Roles and Relationships, Part II: 1961–1964.* Princeton, N.J.: Princeton University Press, 1986.

Goulden, Joseph C. *Fit to Print: A. M. Rosenthal and The Times.* Secaucus, N.J.: Lyle Stuart, 1988.

Graff, Henry F. *The Tuesday Cabinet.* Englewood Cliffs, N.J.: Prentice-Hall, 1970.

Gramling, Oliver. *AP—The Story of News.* New York: J. J. Little, 1940.

Greene, Graham. *The Quiet American.* New York: Viking Press, 1956.

———. *Ways of Escape.* New York: Simon & Schuster, 1980.

Halberstam, David. *The Best and the Brightest.* New York: Random House, 1972.

———. *The Making of a Quagmire.* New York: Random House, 1964.

———. *One Very Hot Day.* Boston: Houghton Mifflin, 1968.

———. *The Powers That Be.* New York: Alfred A. Knopf, 1979.

Hamblin, Dora Jane. *That Was the Life.* New York: W. W. Norton & Co., 1977.

Hamilton-Merritt, Jane. *Tragic Mountains: The Hmong, the Americans and the Secret Wars for Laos, 1942–1992.* Bloomington, Ind.: Indiana University Press, 1993.

Hammer, Ellen J. *A Death in November: America in Vietnam, 1963.* New York: E. P. Dutton, 1987.

Hammond, William M. *The Military and the Media, 1962–68.* Washington: U.S. Army Center of Military History, 1988.

Higgins, Marguerite. *Our Vietnam Nightmare.* New York: Harper & Row, 1965.

———. *War in Korea.* New York: Doubleday, 1951.

Hilsman, Roger. *To Move a Nation.* New York: Doubleday, 1967.

Hohenberg, John. *Foreign Correspondence: The Great Reporters and Their Times.* New York: Columbia University Press, 1964.

Hoopes, Townsend. *The Limits of Intervention.* New York: McKay, 1970.

Humphrey, Hubert H. *The Education of a Public Man*. Garden City, N.Y.: Doubleday, 1976.

Isaacson, Walter, and Evan Thomas. *The Wise Men*. New York: Simon & Schuster, 1986.

Jessup, John K., ed. *The Ideas of Henry Luce*. New York: Atheneum, 1969.

Just, Ward. *In the City of Fear*. New York: Viking Press, 1982.

———. *To What End, Report from Vietnam*. Boston: Houghton Mifflin, 1968.

Kalb, Deborah Susan. "The Uncontrollable Element: American Reporters in South Vietnam, 1961–1963." Unpublished honors thesis, Harvard University, 1985.

Karnow, Stanley. *Vietnam: A History*. Rev. ed. New York: Viking Press, 1991.

Kearns, Doris. *Lyndon Johnson and the American Dream*. New York: Harper & Row, 1976.

Kelly, Tom. *The Imperial* Post. New York: Morrow, 1983.

Kerns, Montague, Patricia W. Levering, and Ralph B. Levering. *The Kennedy Crises: The Press, the Presidency, and Foreign Policy*. Chapel Hill, N.C.: University of North Carolina Press, 1983.

Kluger, Richard: *The Paper: The Life and Death of the New York Herald Tribune*. New York: Alfred A. Knopf, 1986.

Knightley, Phillip. *The First Casualty: From the Crimea to Vietnam: The War Correspondent as Hero, Propagandist, and Myth Maker*. New York: Harcourt Brace Jovanovich, 1975.

Lansdale, Edward Geary. *In the Midst of Wars: An American's Mission to Southeast Asia*. New York: Harper & Row, 1972.

Lederer, William J. *Our Own Worst Enemy*. New York: W. W. Norton & Co., 1968.

Lederer, William, and Eugene Burdick. *The Ugly American*. New York: W. W. Norton & Co., 1958

Levy, Leonard W. *Emergence of a Free Press*. New York: Oxford University Press, 1985.

Lodge, Henry Cabot. *As It Was: An Inside View of Politics and Power in the 50s and 60s*. New York: W. W. Norton & Co., 1976.

———. *The Storm Has Many Eyes: A Personal Narrative*. New York: W. W. Norton & Co., 1973.

Lubow, Arthur. *The Reporter Who Would Be King: A Biography of Richard Harding Davis*. New York: Charles Scribner's Sons, 1992.

MacDonald, J. Fred. *Television and the Red Menace*. New York: Praeger, 1985.

Manchester, William. *American Caesar: Douglas MacArthur, 1880–1964*. Boston: Little, Brown, 1978.

———. *The Glory and the Dream*. Boston: Little, Brown, 1974.

Mangold, Tom, and John Penycate. *The Tunnels of Cu Chi*. New York: Random House, 1985.

Marton, Kati: *The Polk Conspiracy: Murder and Cover-up in the Case of CBS*

News Correspondent George Polk. New York: Farrar, Straus & Giroux, 1990.

Matthews, Herbert L. *A World in Revolution.* New York: Charles Scribner's Sons, 1971.

Matthews, Joseph J. *Reporting the Wars.* Minneapolis: University of Minnesota Press, 1957.

Maurer, Harry, ed. *Strange Ground: An Oral History of Americans in Vietnam, 1945–1975.* New York: Henry Holt, 1989.

May, Antoinette. *Witness to War: A Biography of Marguerite Higgins.* New York: Penguin Books, 1985.

McCabe, Robert Karr. *Storm Over Asia.* New York: New American Library, 1967.

McNamara, John. *Extra! U.S. War Correspondents in Action.* Plainview, N.Y.: Books for Libraries Press, 1945.

McNamara, Robert S., with Brian VanDeMark, *In Retrospect: The Tragedy and Lessons of Vietnam.* New York: Times Books, 1995.

McPherson, Harry. *A Political Education.* Boston: Little, Brown, 1972.

Mecklin, John. *Mission in Torment: An Intimate Account of the U.S. Role in Vietnam.* New York: Doubleday, 1965.

Minor, Dale. *The Information War.* New York: Hawthorn Books, 1970.

Moeller, Susan D. *Shooting War: Photography and the American Experience of Combat.* New York: Basic Books, 1989.

Morris, Edward. *The Rise of Theodore Roosevelt.* New York: Coward, McCann, 1970.

Morris, Joe Alex. *Deadline Every Minute: The Story of the United Press.* Garden City, N.Y.: Doubleday, 1957.

Mueller, John E. *War, Presidents and Public Opinion.* New York: John Wiley & Sons, 1973.

Neal, Steve. *The Eisenhowers: Reluctant Dynasty.* New York: Doubleday, 1978.

Newman, John M. *JFK and Vietnam.* New York: Warner Books, 1992.

Nolting, Frederick. *From Trust to Tragedy.* New York: Praeger, 1988.

Oberdorfer, Don. *Tet!* New York: Doubleday, 1971.

O'Donnell, Kenneth, and David F. Powers. *"Johnny, We Hardly Knew Ye."* Boston: Little, Brown, 1970.

Page, Tim. *Tim Page's NAM.* New York: Alfred A. Knopf, 1983.

Pilger, John. *The Last Day: America's Final Hours in Vietnam.* New York: Random House, 1975.

Powers, Thomas. *The Man Who Kept the Secrets: Richard Helms and the CIA.* New York: Alfred A. Knopf, 1979.

Pratt, John Clark, ed. *Vietnam Voices.* New York: Viking Press, 1984.

Reeves, Richard. *President Kennedy: Profile of Power.* New York: Simon & Schuster, 1993.

Reston, James. *Deadline: A Memoir.* New York: Times Books, 1992.

Robertson, Nan. *The Girls in the Balcony.* New York: Random House, 1992.

Rust, William J. *Kennedy in Vietnam: American Vietnam Policy 1960–63*. New York: Charles Scribner's Sons, 1985.

Safer, Morley. *Flashbacks: On Returning to Vietnam*. New York: Random House, 1990.

Salinger, Pierre. *With Kennedy*. New York: Doubleday, 1966.

Salisbury, Harrison. *A Journey for Our Times*. New York: Harper & Row, 1983.

———. *Without Fear or Favor*. New York: Times Books, 1980.

Salisbury, Harrison E., ed. *Vietnam Reconsidered: Lessons From a War*. New York: Harper & Row, 1984.

Sanders, Pamela. *Miranda*. Boston: Little, Brown, 1978.

Scheer, Robert. *How the United States Got Involved in Vietnam*. Santa Monica, Calif.: Center for the Study of Democratic Institutions, 1965.

Schlesinger, Arthur M., Jr. *The Bitter Heritage: Vietnam and American Democracy 1941–1966*. Boston: Houghton Mifflin, 1967.

———. *A Thousand Days: John F. Kennedy in the White House*. Boston: Houghton Mifflin, 1965.

Schorr, Daniel. *Clearing the Air*. Boston: Houghton Mifflin, 1977.

Shaplen, Robert. *The Lost Revolution*. New York: Harper & Row, 1965.

———. *A Turning Wheel: Thirty Years of the Asian Revolution by a Correspondent for The New Yorker*. New York: Random House, 1979.

Shapley, Deborah. *Promise and Power: The Life and Times of Robert McNamara*. New York: Little, Brown, 1993.

Shawcross, William. *Sideshow: Kissinger, Nixon, and the Destruction of Cambodia*. New York: Simon & Schuster, 1978.

Sheehan, Neil. *A Bright Shining Lie: John Paul Vann and America in Vietnam*. New York: Random House, 1988.

Sheehan, Neil, et al. *The Pentagon Papers*. New York: Quadrangle Books, 1971.

Snyder, Louis L., ed. *A Treasury of Great Reporting*. New York: Simon & Schuster, 1949.

Sorenson, Theodore C. *Kennedy*. New York: Harper & Row, 1965.

Starr, Louis M. *Bohemian Brigade: Civil War Newsmen in Action*. New York: Alfred A. Knopf, 1954.

Stein, M. L. *Under Fire: The Story of American War Correspondents*. New York: Julian Messner, 1968.

Swanberg, W. A. *Citizen Hearst*. New York: Charles Scribner's Sons, 1961.

———. *Luce and His Empire*. New York: Charles Scribner's Sons, 1972.

———. *Pulitzer*. New York: E. P. Dutton and Co., 1967.

Talese, Gay. *The Kingdom and The Power*. New York: Anchor Books, 1978.

Taylor, Maxwell D. *Swords and Plowshares*. New York: W. W. Norton & Co., 1972.

———. *The Uncertain Trumpet*. New York: Harper, 1960.

Taylor, Telford: *Nuremberg and Vietnam: An American Tragedy*. Chicago: Quadrangle Books, 1970.

Tuohy, William. *Dangerous Company*. New York: Morrow, 1987.

Tregaskis, Richard. *Guadalcanal Diary*. New York: Random House, 1943.

———. *Vietnam Diary*. New York: Holt, Rinehart & Winston, 1963.

Tuchman, Barbara W. *The March of Folly: From Troy to Vietnam*. New York: Alfred A. Knopf, 1984.

———. *Stilwell and the American Experience in China, 1911–1945*. New York: Macmillan, 1972.

Turner, Kathleen J. *Lyndon Johnson's Dual War: Vietnam and the Press*. Chicago: University of Chicago Press, 1985.

Ungar, Sanford J. *The Papers and The Papers*. New York: E. P. Dutton and Co., 1972.

U.S. Army Area Handbook for Vietnam. Washington, D.C.: U.S. Government Printing Office, 1962.

Wade, Betsy, ed. *Forward Positions: The War Correspondence of Homer Bigart*. Fayetteville, Ark.: University of Arkansas Press, 1992.

Warner, Denis. *The Last Confucian*. New York: Macmillan, 1963.

Westmoreland, William C. *A Soldier Reports*. New York: Doubleday, 1976.

White, Theodore H. *The Making of the President 1960*. New York: Atheneum, 1961.

White, William, ed. *Byline: Ernest Hemingway*. New York: Charles Scribner's Sons, 1967.

Wicker, Tom. *On Press*, New York: Viking Press, 1978.

Wolfkill, Grant, with Jerry Rose. *Reported to Be Alive*. Boston: Houghton Mifflin, 1976.

INDEX